THE ROUTLEDGE HANDBOOK OF PHILOSOPHY OF ECONOMICS

The most fundamental questions of economics are often philosophical in nature, and philosophers have, since the very beginning of Western philosophy, asked many questions that current observers would identify as economic. *The Routledge Handbook of Philosophy of Economics* is an outstanding reference source for the key topics, problems, and debates at the intersection of philosophical and economic inquiry. It captures this field of countless exciting interconnections, affinities, and opportunities for cross-fertilization.

Comprising 35 chapters by a diverse team of contributors from all over the globe, the *Handbook* is divided into eight sections:

I. Rationality
II. Cooperation and Interaction
III. Methodology
IV. Values
V. Causality and Explanation
VI. Experimentation and Simulation
VII. Evidence
VIII. Policy

The volume is essential reading for students and researchers in economics and philosophy who are interested in exploring the interconnections between the two disciplines. It is also a valuable resource for those in related fields like political science, sociology, and the humanities.

Conrad Heilmann is Associate Professor of Philosophy at Erasmus School of Philosophy, Co-Director of the Erasmus Institute for Philosophy and Economics (EIPE), and Core Faculty of the Erasmus Initiative Dynamics of Inclusive Prosperity at Erasmus University Rotterdam, The Netherlands. He works on rational choice theory, fairness, finance, and other topics in the philosophy of economics.

Julian Reiss is Professor of Philosophy at Johannes Kepler University Linz, Austria, and Head of the Institute of Philosophy and Scientific Method. He is the author of *Causation, Evidence, and Inference* (Routledge, 2015), *Philosophy of Economics: A Contemporary Introduction* (Routledge, 2013), *Error in Economics: Towards a More Evidence-Based Methodology* (Routledge, 2008; Erasmus Philosophy International Research Prize), and more than 60 papers in leading philosophy and social science journals and edited collections.

ROUTLEDGE HANDBOOKS IN PHILOSOPHY

Routledge Handbooks in Philosophy are state of the art surveys of emerging, newly refreshed, and important fields in philosophy, providing accessible yet thorough assessments of key problems, themes, thinkers, and recent developments in research.

All chapters for each volume are specially commissioned, and written by leading scholars in the field. Carefully edited and organized, *Routledge Handbooks in Philosophy* provide indispensable reference tools for students and researchers seeking a comprehensive overview of new and exciting topics in philosophy. They are also valuable teaching resources as accompaniments to textbooks, anthologies, and research orientated publications.

Also available:

THE ROUTLEDGE HANDBOOK OF PHILOSOPHY OF EUROPE
Edited by Darian Meacham and Nicolas de Warren

THE ROUTLEDGE HANDBOOK OF SOCIAL AND POLITICAL PHILOSOPHY OF LANGUAGE
Edited by Justin Khoo and Rachel Katharine Sterken

THE ROUTLEDGE HANDBOOK OF POLITICAL EPISTEMOLOGY
Edited by Michael Hannon and Jeroen de Ridder

THE ROUTLEDGE HANDBOOK OF PHILOSOPHY AND IMPROVISATION IN THE ARTS
Edited by Alessandro Bertinetto and Marcello Ruta

THE ROUTLEDGE HANDBOOK OF IDEALISM AND IMMATERIALISM
Edited by Joshua Farris and Benedikt Paul Göcke

THE ROUTLEDGE HANDBOOK OF PHILOSOPHY OF ECONOMICS
Edited by Conrad Heilmann and Julian Reiss

For more information about this series, please visit: www.routledge.com/Routledge Handbooks-in-Philosophy/book-series/RHP

THE ROUTLEDGE HANDBOOK OF PHILOSOPHY OF ECONOMICS

Edited by
Conrad Heilmann and Julian Reiss

Routledge
Taylor & Francis Group
NEW YORK AND LONDON

First published 2022
by Routledge
605 Third Avenue, New York, NY 10158

and by Routledge
2 Park Square, Milton Park, Abingdon, Oxon, OX14 4RN

Routledge is an imprint of the Taylor & Francis Group, an informa business

Library of Congress Cataloging-in-Publication Data
A catalog record for this book has been requested

ISBN: 978-1-138-82420-1 (hbk)
ISBN: 978-1-032-13163-4 (pbk)
ISBN: 978-1-315-73979-3 (ebk)

DOI: 10.4324/9781315739793

Typeset in Bembo
by Apex CoVantage, LLC

CONTENTS

FIGURES

TABLES

NOTES ON CONTRIBUTORS

Antoinette Baujard is Professor of Economics at University Jean Monnet, France, and a member of the Groupe d'Analyse et de Théorie Economique (GATE) Lyon/Saint-Etienne at the Centre National de la Recherche Scientifique (CNRS). She is the co-editor (with R. Backhouse and T. Nishizawa) of *Welfare Theory, Public Action and Ethical Values: Revisiting the History of Welfare Economics* (Cambridge University Press, 2021).

Sebastiano Bavetta is Professor of Economics at the University of Palermo, Italy. He has published on political economy, the measurement of freedoms, and the perception of inequality. Besides academia, he has extensive political, consulting, and business experience.

Constanze Binder is Associate Professor of Philosophy at the Erasmus School of Philosophy and Co-Director of the Erasmus Institute for Philosophy and Economics (EIPE) at Erasmus University Rotterdam, The Netherlands. Her current research is situated within the philosophy of normative economics. Her latest book, *Freedom, Agency and Choice* (Springer, 2019), concerns the analysis of freedom and responsibility in welfare economics.

Hsiang-Ke Chao is Professor of Economics at National Tsing Hua University in Taiwan. He is the author of *Representation and Structure in Economics: The Methodology of Econometric Models of the Consumption Function* (Routledge, 2009) and co-editor of *Mechanism and Causality in Biology and Economics* (Springer, 2013) and *Philosophy of Science in Practice: Nancy Cartwright and the Nature of Scientific Reasoning* (Springer, 2017).

Christopher Clarke is a senior research associate at the Centre for Research in the Arts, Social Sciences, and Humanities (CRASSH), University of Cambridge, United Kingdom, and an assistant professor at Erasmus University Rotterdam, The Netherlands (EIPE, School of Philosophy). He works on the nature of causal explanation and causal inference, especially in political science and economics.

François Claveau holds the Canada Research Chair in Applied Epistemology and is an associate professor in the Department of Philosophy and Applied Ethics at Université de Sherbrooke, Canada. He has co-authored *Do Central Banks Serve the People?* (Polity, 2018) with Peter Dietsch and Clément Fontan and co-edited *Experts, sciences et sociétés* (Presses de l'Université de Montréal, 2018) with Julien Prud'homme.

Camilla Colombo is currently a postdoctoral fellow at the IMT School for Advanced Studies, Lucca, Italy. Her main areas of research are the cognitive and normative foundations of rational decision theory and applied ethics.

Boudewijn de Bruin is a professor at the University of Groningen, The Netherlands. He is the author of *Ethics and the Global Financial Crisis: Why Incompetence is Worse than Greed* (Cambridge University Press, 2015).

Peter Dietsch is a professor in the Department of Philosophy at the University of Victoria, British Columbia, Canada. His research focuses on questions of economic ethics. He is the author of *Catching Capital – The Ethics of Tax Competition* (Oxford University Press, 2015) and co-author, with François Claveau and Clément Fontan, of *Do Central Banks Serve the People?* (Polity, 2018).

Judith Favereau is Associate Professor of Philosophy of Economics and History of Economic Thought in the pluridisciplinary laboratory TRIANGLE at the University Lyon 2, France. She is affiliated with TINT – Centre for Philosophy of Social Science. Her research focuses on how development economics, experimental economics, and evidence-based policy interact together in order to fight poverty.

Benjamin Ferguson is Associate Professor of Philosophy and director of Philosophy, Politics, and Economics at the University of Warwick, United Kingdom.

James D. Grayot is a research associate at the Faculty of Philosophy, University of Groningen, The Netherlands, and visiting researcher at Vita-Salute San Raffaele University, Italy.

Till Grüne-Yanoff is Professor of Philosophy at the Royal Institute of Technology (KTH) in Stockholm, Sweden. He investigates the practice of modeling in science and engineering, develops formal models of preference consistency and preference change, and discusses the evaluation of evidence in policy decision-making. Till is editor of the journal *Economics & Philosophy*.

Francesco Guala is Professor of Political Economy in the Department of Philosophy of the University of Milan, Italy. He is the author of *The Methodology of Experimental Economics* (Cambridge University Press, 2005) and *Understanding Institutions* (Princeton University Press, 2016).

Daniel M. Hausman is Research Professor in the Center for Population-Level Bioethics at Rutgers University, USA, and the Herbert A. Simon Professor Emeritus at the University of Wisconsin–Madison, USA. He is a founding editor of the journal *Economics & Philosophy* and is the author of a half-dozen books and nearly 200 articles addressing issues at the boundaries of economics and philosophy. In 2009, he was elected to the American Academy of Arts and Sciences.

Conrad Heilmann is Associate Professor of Philosophy at Erasmus School of Philosophy, co-director of the Erasmus Institute for Philosophy and Economics (EIPE), and core faculty of the Erasmus Initiative Dynamics of Inclusive Prosperity at Erasmus University Rotterdam, The Netherlands. He works on rational choice theory, fairness, finance, and other topics in the philosophy of economics.

Tobias Henschen is a principal investigator of a research project on complexity in economics, which is funded by the German Research Foundation (DFG) and hosted by the Philosophy Department of the University of Cologne, Germany. He is currently writing a book on causality and objectivity in macroeconomics, which is under contract with Routledge.

Jennifer S. Jhun is Assistant Professor of Philosophy and a faculty fellow of the Center for the History of Political Economy at Duke University, USA.

Jurgis Karpus is a postdoctoral researcher at Ludwig Maximilian University (LMU) of Munich, Germany. In his work, he is primarily interested in the modes of reasoning by which we arrive at personal decisions when we socially interact with fellow humans and autonomous artificial agents.

Donal Khosrowi is a postdoctoral researcher at Leibniz University Hannover, Germany. His research interests and recent publications focus on causal inference in the social sciences (especially in economics and evidence-based policy), scientific representation, and values in science issues.

Jaakko Kuorikoski is Associate Professor of Practical Philosophy at the University of Helsinki, Finland. His main areas of specialization are the philosophy of economics and the philosophy of social sciences, and he has published widely on scientific explanation, modeling, simulation, and causality.

Guilhem Lecouteux is Associate Professor of Economics at Université Côte d'Azur, Nice, France. His research focuses on the challenges raised by behavioral economics for the foundations of normative economics and the role of behavioral sciences in the design and justification of public policies.

Aki Lehtinen is Talent Professor of Philosophy at Nankai University, Tianjin, China. He co-edited *Economics for Real* (Routledge, 2012). His most recent work is on confirmation in climate models, the philosophy of macroeconomics, generalization in modeling, and the philosophy of meta-analysis and simulated data.

Alexander Linsbichler is a lecturer in the Departments of Philosophy and Economics at the University of Vienna, Austria, a research fellow at the Center for the History of Political Economy at Duke University, USA, and a postdoctoral track fellow of the Austrian Academy of Sciences. He has published two books, including *Was Ludwig von Mises a Conventionalist? A New Analysis of the Epistemology of the Austrian School of Economics* (Palgrave, 2017).

Luis Mireles-Flores is a postdoctoral researcher at the Centre for Philosophy of Social Science (TINT), University of Helsinki, Finland. He is the founder and former editor of the *Erasmus Journal for Philosophy and Economics* (*EJPE*).

Ivan Moscati is Professor of Economics at the University of Insubria, Varese, Italy, and his research focuses on the history and methodology of decision theory. He is the author of *Measuring Utility* (Oxford University Press, 2018), and recent articles of his have been awarded best article awards by HES and ESHET, the two international societies for the history of economics.

Michiru Nagatsu is an associate professor at the Helsinki Institute of Sustainability Science and Practical Philosophy, University of Helsinki, Finland. He runs the Economics and Philosophy Lab and HELSUS Methodology Lab. His research uses a range of empirical approaches – including experimental philosophy, collaborations with scientists, interviews, integrated history, and philosophy of science – to study conceptual and methodological questions in the philosophy of science.

Robert Northcott is Reader in Philosophy at Birkbeck College, London, United Kingdom. He has published extensively on the philosophy of economics and is writing a book about the methodological position of nonlaboratory sciences generally.

William Peden is a teacher and researcher at the Erasmus Institute for Philosophy and Economics at Erasmus University Rotterdam, The Netherlands. He is researching the ideas of Jan Tinbergen and their connections to contemporary debates in the philosophy of economics.

Mantas Radzvilas is a postdoctoral research fellow in the Department of Biomedical Sciences and Public Health of the Marche Polytechnic University, Italy. His research interests are epistemic and evolutionary game theory, mechanism design theory, health-care economics, and the philosophy of economics.

Julian Reiss is Professor of Philosophy at Johannes Kepler University Linz, Austria (since October 2019), and Head of the Institute of Philosophy and Scientific Method. He is the author of *Causation, Evidence, and Inference* (Routledge, 2015), *Philosophy of Economics: A Contemporary Introduction* (Routledge, 2013), *Error in Economics: Towards a More Evidence-Based Methodology* (Routledge, 2008; Erasmus Philosophy International Research Prize), and over 60 papers in leading philosophy and social science journals and edited collections.

Mauro Rossi is Full Professor of Philosophy at the Université du Québec à Montréal, Canada. His main research interests are in value theory and prudential psychology. He is currently working (with Christine Tappolet) on a monograph on the relationship between well-being and psychological happiness, under contract with Oxford University Press.

Olivier Santerre is a master's candidate in computer science at Université de Montréal, Canada.

Aris Spanos is Professor of Economics at Virginia Tech, USA. He is the author of two textbooks in econometrics, *Statistical Foundations of Econometric Modelling* (Cambridge University Press, 1986) and *Probability Theory and Statistical Inference: Empirical Modeling with Observational Data* (Cambridge University Press, 2019), and co-editor of *Error and Inference: Recent Exchanges on Experimental Reasoning, Reliability, and the Objectivity and Rationality of Science* (Cambridge University Press, 2010) with D.G. Mayo. He has published more than 80 papers in refereed journals on economics, econometrics, statistics, and the philosophy of science.

Jan Sprenger is Professor of Logic and Philosophy of Science at the University of Turin, Italy. He specializes in research topics such as statistical inference, causality, probability, and scientific objectivity. His most recent major publication is the book *Bayesian Philosophy of Science* (Oxford University Press, 2019).

H. Orri Stefánsson is Associate Professor of Practical Philosophy at Stockholm University, Sweden, Pro Futura Scientia Fellow at the Swedish Collegium for Advanced Study, and advisor at the Institute for Futures Studies, Stockholm, Sweden. He works mostly on decision theory and related topics, with a current focus on decision-making under extreme uncertainty.

Alexandre Truc is a postdoctoral researcher at the Groupe de recherche en droit, économie et gestion (Gredeg-Nice) of the Centre National de la Recherche Scientifique (CNRS) and an associate researcher at the Centre interuniversitaire de recherche sur la science et la technologie (CIRST) at L'Université du Québec à Montréal (UQAM).

Melissa Vergara-Fernández is a postdoctoral researcher in the School of Philosophy of Erasmus University Rotterdam, The Netherlands. She works on the Values in Finance project, which is part of the university's Dynamics of Inclusive Prosperity initiative.

Philippe Verreault-Julien is a postdoctoral researcher at the Centre for Philosophy of Natural and Social Science, London School of Economics and Political Science, United Kingdom. His research primarily concerns the epistemology of scientific modeling, understanding, and explanation.

Alex Voorhoeve is a professor in the Department of Philosophy, Logic and Scientific Method at the London School of Economics and Political Science, United Kingdom, and Visiting Professor of Ethics and Economics at Erasmus University Rotterdam, The Netherlands. He has published widely on the theory and practice of distributive justice, especially as applied to health. He is author of *Conversations on Ethics* (Oxford University Press, 2009), a collection of dialogues with leading philosophers and economists, and co-author of *Making Fair Choices on the Path to Universal Health Coverage* (World Health Organization, 2014).

Kate Vredenburgh is an assistant professor in the Department of Philosophy, Logic and Scientific Method at the London School of Economics, United Kingdom.

Jack Vromen is Professor of Philosophy at Erasmus University Rotterdam, The Netherlands, director of Erasmus Institute for Philosophy and Economics (EIPE), and co-editor (with N. Emrah Aydinonat) of *The Journal of Economic Methodology*. His latest publications include *Neuroeconomics* (Routledge's *Critical Concepts in the Social Sciences* series, 2019), which he co-edited with Caterina Marchionni.

Mark D. White is the chair of the Department of Philosophy at the College of Staten Island/City University of New York (CUNY), USA, and a member of the doctoral faculty in economics at the Graduate Center of CUNY. He is the author or *Kantian Ethics and Economics* (2011) and the editor of *The Oxford Handbook of Ethics and Economics* (2019).

Stefan Wintein is Assistant Professor of Theoretical Philosophy at the Erasmus School of Philosophy (ESPhil) and member of the Erasmus Institute for Philosophy and Economics (EIPE), both at Erasmus University Rotterdam, The Netherlands. Together with Conrad Heilmann, he runs the Fairness Project.

ACKNOWLEDGEMENTS

We would like to express our sincere gratitude to Routledge's editors Andy Beck and Marc Stratton, as well as the student assistants Ruth Hinz and Vince Rijnberg.

1
INTRODUCTION

Conrad Heilmann and Julian Reiss

Economics' most fundamental questions are often philosophical in nature, and philosophers have, since the very beginning of Western philosophy, asked many questions that current observers would identify as economic. That beginning is sometimes given the date 585 BC, the year a solar eclipse occurred that the philosopher Thales of Miletus had predicted (Russell 1967). Thales showed that philosophy was not necessarily practically useless by applying his astronomical knowledge to forecast the harvest for the next autumn. He bought, at a very low price, all olive presses during the winter and resold them at a great profit when they were in high demand due to the good harvest. An economic forecast thus stands at the beginning of Western philosophy.

The interconnections between philosophy and economics are plentiful. At the heart of economic theory since the classical period (from the late 18th until the mid-19th centuries, from Adam Smith to John Stuart Mill) lies a theory of value, and value theory is a core concern in moral philosophy. Economists describe, explain, and evaluate a broad variety of social phenomena such as the rules and institutions of society, the inputs into production processes such as labor, capital, and the environment – as well as outcomes such as people's incomes and their distribution – and so do philosophers. Both economists and philosophers elaborate ideals, whether it is the perfect market or the perfectly just society, that analysts and policymakers can use as yardsticks and use to design interventions. Both economists and philosophers, therefore, have theoretical interests in description and analysis and normative interests in evaluation and the defense of goals and ideals.

Both economics and philosophy also know entrenched dichotomies. Every economist is familiar with dividing economics into a *positive* discipline, the descriptive and explanatory analysis of what there is or the "facts," and a *normative* discipline, the evaluative analysis of what ought to be or the "values." Philippe Mongin (1950–2020), who made groundbreaking contributions to the philosophy of economics, has explored the historical origins and conceptual contingencies of the distinction between positive and normative economics:

> *De tous les caractères qui mettent l'économie à part des autres sciences sociales, la distinction qu'elle fait passer entre ses recherches positives et normatives est l'un des plus singuliers qui soient.*[1]
>
> (Mongin 2018: 151)

Here, Mongin singles out the distinction between positive and normative economics as a distinct characteristic of economics, at least when compared to other social sciences. There are important similarities to a fundamental dichotomy in philosophy, however. In many European countries, the

DOI: 10.4324/9781315739793-1

distinction between *theoretical* and *practical* philosophy as different subdisciplines prevails – it is even used as an organizing principle of departments and learned societies. Theoretical philosophers think about subjects such as epistemology, the philosophy of science, logic, and metaphysics, and practical philosophers are concerned with aesthetics, ethics, and political philosophy – in short, questions of value. Immanuel Kant's slogan "*Alle Philosophie ist entweder theoretisch oder praktisch*,"[2] which has no doubt contributed to the pervasive popularity of the labels, also relates to similarly minded distinctions, such as Artistotle's distinction between moral and natural philosophy or Hume's between *is* and *ought*.

We do not wish to suggest a very strict or close parallel between positive economics and theoretical philosophy on the one hand and normative economics and practical philosophy on the other hand. We mention these distinctions to point to recent, and exciting, developments in the *philosophy of economics* that transcend both of these disciplinary distinctions in various ways. Indeed, when faced with the task of organizing the contributions to this *Handbook*, we deliberated at length about introducing broad supercategories such as "ethics" and "epistemology" or other labels that would point to the primary concerns of the authors of the chapters. We decided against that because we believe many contributions go beyond these dichotomies. For example, Antoinette Baujard's examination of the role values play in welfare economics or Kate Vredenburgh's survey of concepts of preference clearly have implications for both "positive" and "normative" economics, for both ethics and epistemology. Instead, we identified eight topical clusters – rationality, cooperation and interaction, methodology, values, causality and explanation, experimentation and simulation, evidence, and policy – and organized the chapters around these. The topical clusters showcase the joint thematic concerns of some chapters. The chapters themselves often contain methods from both practical and theoretical philosophy and/or have relevance for both positive and normative economics.

We submit the chapters of this *Handbook* in the belief that, two decades into the 21st century, the philosophy of economics could hardly be any more interesting. The sheer number and quality of contributions and contributors we see in conferences, journals, and book publications and the proliferation of first-rate study programs are all testimony to the simple fact that the philosophy of economics is now a field in its own right. Philosophers of economics are everywhere: the leading academic programs and institutes in the field have grown, and there are more of them too. Philosophy of economics has arrived.

It is important to acknowledge that neither the mainstream status nor the integrated nature of practical and theoretical concerns in the philosophy of economics came out of nowhere. Philosophy of economics is evolving in that manner because of excellent work in the different areas of research that make up the field. First, a generation of historians of economic thought, economists, and philosophers started to engage with methodological questions about economics in the second half of the 20th century. These efforts led to the establishment of a high-quality niche area of research often called "economic methodology" – with philosophers and economists engaging in cross-disciplinary research. At the turn of the millennium, researchers of economic methodology and philosophers of science interacted more and more. Currently, philosophy of economics has in part become a subfield of philosophy of science, being featured at key events and outlets in the philosophy of science. The *Oxford Handbook of Philosophy of Economics* is a high-profile culmination of this development (Kincaid and Ross 2009), as is a recent special issue of the *Journal of Economic Methodology* that examines the past, present, and future of "Economic Methodology and Philosophy of Economics" (Davis and Hands 2021). Both the twofold title and various contributions within it already point to the fact that, partly in isolation from economic methodology, various other research strands related to what we may nowadays subsume under the broad label "philosophy of economics" have gained momentum as well. The conceptual foundations of economic theory, especially individual, interactive, and social choice theory, matured into their own interdisciplinary research field. The *Oxford Handbook of Rational and Social Choice* showcases this fact (Anand, Pattanaik, and Puppe 2009). Value-related research, whether it be on ethical aspects of economics, formal ethics, or economically informed political philosophy, has gained in relevance. Work on topics within politics, philosophy, and economics (PPE) more generally began to thrive. The forthcoming *Routledge Handbook of Politics, Philosophy, and Economics* marks the latter trend. What we are witnessing now is that these research streams are coming together even more. The number of productive, often groundbreaking, interactions between methodologically related, value-oriented, and policy-related research is increasing. And we believe that this *Handbook* shows that research on the philosophy of economics is best when it combines these perspectives.

We also believe that we are witnessing a "philosophical turn" in the relationship between philosophy and economics: currently, the academic discipline of philosophy hosts the main study programs, scholars, journals, and conferences. This development is not without its shortcomings. Research at the intersection between two disciplines benefits from active and live engagement between both disciplines. That the interdisciplinary research field philosophy and economics is these days best described as a multifaceted *philosophy of* economics is an empirical fact that we assert, not a value we hold. Nor is it set in stone. One consequence of the current tilt to philosophy, though, is that getting a PhD in philosophy by specializing in the philosophy of economics is no longer the exception it was up until quite recently. In regard to younger generations and recent developments, our *Handbook* features, deliberately so, a broad range of scholarly generations. Philosophers of economics of the "first hour" have contributed, as have midcareer researchers and a number of rising stars in the field. While we are regretfully far from perfect in terms of representation of many salient demographic characteristics of authors, we do feel that the generational mix of authors in this *Handbook* is something about which we can be quite excited. In the remainder of this chapter, we will introduce the eight topical clusters of the book and provide a "sneak preview" of all 35 chapters.

We would like to use the opportunity here to thank all our authors for the hard work they put into writing their chapters, as well as their patience with us as editors. We think that the resulting volume presents what is among the best work in the field of philosophy of economics, and it demonstrates that the field is vibrant and concerned with questions that are both intellectually exciting and, much like Thales' astronomical explorations, of great practical use.

1. Eight Themes in the Philosophy of Economics

1.1 Rationality

One of the most famous definitions of economics characterizes it "as the science which studies human behavior as a relationship between ends and scarce means which have alternative uses" (Robbins 1932; Backhouse and Medema 2009). From there, it is a small step to consider as central the goal-directed, instrumental rationality of economic agents for the philosophical examination of the field as a whole. In philosophy, there is no shortage of approaches in which rationality takes a center stage, ranging from analyzing rationality as a fundamental capacity of individuals to reason and linking notions of intentionality to specific theories of instrumental rationality (Kolodny and Brunero 2020; Chang and Sylvan 2020). That is to say, rationality is regarded as a concern in both philosophy and economics, even when they are understood as separate disciplines. Naturally, questions of rationality have also been the subject of ongoing and evolving debate by scholars working at the intersection of philosophy and economics.

Methodologically speaking, rationality assumptions play a key role in expected utility theory, which has given economic theory and the whole of neoclassical economics their foundations, ever since von Neumann and Morgenstern (1944/1953) and Savage (1954/1972). A whole academic discipline that is invested in goal-oriented behavior can be built from the rational choices of a single agent that are only constrained by a handful of conditions that govern the structural consistency of their preferences and do not prescribe any particular taste or worldview, or so the "received view" of the rationality foundations of economics has it.

The examination of the manifold methodological and normative consequences of the received rationality foundations of economics and their linkage with various concepts from philosophical theories of rationality, as well as methodological and ethical concerns, have been staple concerns of the philosophy of economics. At the core of the examination are the components of expected utility theory. Expected utility theories characterize the choice dispositions of a rational agent by rational preferences that can be numerically represented by a pair of real-value utility and probability functions. With such a characterization in place, choices that rational agents face can be described, explained, predicted, evaluated, and influenced. Naturally, a research agenda of such ambition and scope triggers philosophical examination. We mention a few key currents in this vast array of research, many of which can be seen as separate fields in their own right.

- The basic structure of expected utility theory can be seen as an idealized variant of an attractive theory of instrumental rationality. As such, it is open to fundamental challenges (Jeffrey 1974; Sen 1977; Anderson 2001), as well as detailed ones: analysis of the axioms on preference in expected utility theory, in particular transitivity and completeness of preference relations, as candidates for rationality conditions has been a particular concern (e.g., Mandler 2005; Anand 2009; Bradley 2017).
- Circumstances of risk, where the utility and probability dimensions interact (Buchak 2017), and contexts of ambiguity and uncertainty, where they partly break down (Steele and Stefánsson forthcoming), have led to specialized literatures in both philosophy and economics.
- A rich literature on philosophical decision theory takes the foundational and conceptual concerns further, analyzing the precise epistemic motivation for the probability function (e.g., Joyce 1999; Greaves 2013) and the value dimension (e.g., Chang 2001; Paul 2014; Pettigrew 2019).
- Experimental and behavioral economists challenged and improved expected utility theories regarding risk, ambiguity, and uncertainty, as well as beyond: they investigated all kinds of static and dynamic behavior that depart from standard expected utility theory (for a historical account, see Heukelom 2014), and they also started a trend of policy intervention to improve the decision-making of individuals (Thaler and Sunstein 2008).
- The rise of behavioral economics (Angner 2019) also raises the question of the interrelations between economics and psychology (Grüne-Yanoff 2017) and, in particular, the conceptual content of concepts such as agency (Ross 2016) and preference (Gul and Pesendorfer 2008; Moscati 2021).

A classic resource in the philosophy of economics that analyzes some of the broader methodological and normative implications of the rationality foundations of economics is that of Hausman, McPherson, and Satz (2017). In this *Handbook*, two chapters provide a review of the very basic concepts of expected utility theory and its ingredients.

Ivan Moscati reviews the history of utility theory, taking the marginal revolution at the end of the 19th century as starting point and following it up to current behavioral economics. His chapter traces the main concepts at play, starting from diminishing marginal utility, through the ordinal and cardinal revolutions, to the emergence of expected utility theory as cornerstone of economic analysis, before turning to the experimental and behavioral challenges that have been transforming it ever since.

H. Orri Stefánsson tackles expected utility theory, explains its main elements, and reviews the empirical and conceptual criticism. He reviews both of the main variants of expected utility theory: first, he presents objective expected utility theory where the relevant probabilities are given, such as in von Neumann and Morgenstern's framework. Second, he turns to subjective expected utility theory, where probabilities are based on an individual's subjective degree of belief. In reviewing expected utility theories, Stefánsson puts the challenge that *risk* plays at the center of his analysis, critically discussing to what extent the assumptions that are necessary to capture the expected utility of risky acts are borne out by the empirical evidence.

Together, the chapters by Moscati and Stefánsson put in place the main elements of rational choice theory as used in the foundations of economic theory. Three more chapters on rationality examine recent debates in philosophy and economics that center around the concepts of preference and agency.

Guilhem Lecouteux critically assesses the argument advanced in behavioral welfare economics (BWE) that preference inconsistency and violations of rational choice theory are the result of errors and offers a direct justification for paternalistic regulations. He argues that (i) this position relies on a psychologically and philosophically problematic account of agency, (ii) the normative argument in favor of coherence is considerably weaker than it is usually considered, and (iii) BWE fails to justify why agents ought to be coherent by neoclassical standards.

Kate Vredenburgh examines the concept of a preference in economics. Her chapter focuses on two historically rooted views: mentalism, which takes preferences to be evaluative mental states, and behaviorism, which takes preferences to be mere summaries of patterns in behavior. The chapter adjudicates between these two views on the basis of two descriptive desiderata on the concept of a preference, namely, that it be able to play a role in scientific theories and models that predict and explain choice.

James Grayot examines the concept of agency in economics, classifying the many variants of the idea that individuals are sometimes better viewed as collections of subpersonal agents, each with its own interests or goals. Grayot's verdict is mixed. On the one hand, the modeling of persons as collections of agents has proved to be a useful heuristic for investigating aberrant choice behaviors, such as weakness of will, procrastination, addiction, and other decision anomalies that indicate internal or motivational conflict. On the other hand, the reasons and methods used to study subpersonal agents give rise to a frenzied and sometimes confusing picture about who or what economic agents are, if not whole persons.

1.2 Cooperation and Interaction

Individuals engage in actions of mutual benefit, pursue joint ventures, or codify shared goals. More generally, economic agents interact. On the one hand, economists analyze such interactions in the aggregate, that is, with general equilibrium models that characterize market outcomes. On the other hand, the rationality of individual behavior serves as a cornerstone of the analysis of cooperation and interaction in economics. The key methodology employed here is the use of game-theoretic models.

Game theory is a branch of applied mathematics that analyzes the interactions of *players* (humans, machines, computers, etc.) according to *rules* (order, knowledge, available choices), with *outcomes* (results of the game for any possible choice combination) formulated in *payoffs* (preference relations over outcomes that are assumed to satisfy the axioms of expected utility theory or material payoffs). Game theory has a large variety of variants (e.g., cooperative or non-cooperative, with complete or incomplete information) and types of models it uses [e.g., extensive form ("tree") or normal form ("matrix")]. Since von Neumann and Morgenstern (1944) first provided a systematic account of game theory, it has become a popular and influential tool in economics.

The application of game-theoretic models in economics raises a large number of methodological questions:

- How exactly can the mathematical models of game theory be used to capture real-world interactions, and which assumptions are necessary to do so (Grüne-Yanoff and Lehtinen 2012; Ross 2019)?

- What is the exact relation between models of individual rationality, notably assumptions about preference (Guala 2006)?
- What particular type of game theory is best suited for use in economics? For instance, what are the advantages and disadvantages of the Nash equilibrium refinement program when compared to epistemic game theory (de Bruin 2009)?
- How can game-theoretic models provide accounts of the emergence of cooperation, particularly norms and institutions (Bicchieri 1993, 2006; Binmore 2005)?

Many philosophers of economics take the (inherent limits of the) standard assumptions about individual rationality as their starting point when investigating matters of cooperation and social interaction. And so, traditionally, the study of game theory and its foundations has been the staple topic within the philosophy of economics. Two chapters in this section scrutinize game theory and its role in economics.

Jurgis Karpus and Mantas Radzvilas review what the standard and a number of nonstandard approaches to game theory say about what rational agents should do, what they should believe about others' actions and beliefs, and what they can expect to attain when they interact with other rational and not rational agents. They address these questions from the point of view of the standard approach, which is based on the postulate of best-response reasoning, and discuss how a number of alleged shortcomings of the standard approach have been proposed to be remedied by the theories of Pareto optimization, team reasoning, and virtual bargaining. They consider the case for dropping the fundamental but often problematic assumption of common belief in rationality. In the context of simultaneous- and sequential-move games, they discuss the theory of level-k reasoning, and they review recent developments in epistemic game theory.

Camilla Colombo and Francesco Guala examine coordination as a key challenge for research on the cognitive foundations of institutions. The standard approach until now has been to focus on mind-reading skills and to allow for bounded rationality. This approach, however, has empirical and theoretical shortcomings. Experimental data suggest that models of bounded rationality fail to explain convergence on focal points. And from a normative viewpoint, coordinating agents seem to have good reasons to flout strategic reasoning. This has led researchers to explore models of "belief-less reasoning" – such as team reasoning and solution thinking. If the justification for rule-following and institutional compliance cannot be found in standard or bounded rationality, reasoning modes that do not involve sophisticated mind reading may have both descriptive and normative pull.

Two further chapters in this section pursue different approaches, which are less reliant on specific game-theoretic insights, in order to examine the methodology and ethics of interaction.

Jack Vromen critically assesses assumptions in the social preference models of behavioral economics. His starting points are two seemingly puzzling facts. First, the irrationalities that are typically taken as central to human behavior by behavioral economists do not seem to play a role at all in the social preference models. Second, the latter are promoting prosocial behavior on the basis of social preferences and the former are not. Vromen's diagnosis is this: the "standard" perfect rationality-cum-self-interest model serves as the normative benchmark in behavioral economics, and it is also viewed as simple and elegant. Those who propose social preference models seem to prize covering a wider range of observed behaviors than the standard model over being psychologically more realistic.

Benjamin Ferguson surveys accounts of what exploitation is and addresses consumer responsibility in cases of exploitation. He outlines and critiques distributive and relational accounts of exploitation, as well as substantive and procedural accounts of transactional fairness. Next, he argues that, even though consumers are not directly responsible for exploitation, they can be complicit in the exploitation performed by others.

1.3 Methodology

The debate in economic methodology has shifted markedly over the past 30 or so years. In early 1990s, it was, to a large extent, engaged in discussions about the appropriateness of this or that "-ism" to characterize economics: realism, instrumentalism, positivism, operationalism, falsificationism, rhetoric (not an -ism but nevertheless a far-reaching methodological point of view), or pragmatism. Deirdre McCloskey once coined the apt term "big-M methodology" for work of this kind (McCloskey 1994: Ch. 19). As the label suggests, big-M methodology is concerned with the big "philosophical" questions about the nature and aims of economics as a science: do economists aim to provide truthful representations of the social world or merely predictively (or practically) successful models? Are economic theories falsifiable? If not, what does that tell us about the status of economics as a science? How are we to interpret statements that refer to unobservables such as preferences? What role does persuasion (as opposed to the search for truth) play in economics?

Let us mention a few "classics" in big-M methodology:

- Hutchison (1938) criticized economic theorizing on positivist grounds, arguing that the principles of economics are empirically empty because they are untestable and urging economists to focus on the development of empirical laws that are predictively successful.
- Operationalism is the view that concepts are defined by the measurement operations with which they are associated. Samuelson (1963, 1964) defended an operationalist view of preferences using the Weak Axiom of Revealed Preference (WARP).
- Friedman's paper from 1953 is rightly considered one of the most important texts in economic methodology in the 20th century, and it is certainly the most cited (see Claveau et al., Chapter 11). It defends the view that the proper test for economic theories is whether or not they make correct predictions in the intended domain of application, not by inspecting the "realisticness" of the assumptions from which they start. The paper is usually considered to be a classic statement of instrumentalism in economics (e.g., Boland 1979), but realist interpretations have been offered (Mäki 1992; Hoover 2009b).
- Though there are a number of Popperian or falsificationist methodologists in economics, Blaug's book *The Methodology of Economics or How Economists Explain* (Blaug 1992) has probably been the most influential in the field.
- McCloskey (1998) is, in a sense, the odd one out in this list as she is one of the most vocal critics of big-M methodology. Indeed, she rejects all of the preceding views as "modernist" and argues that we should instead pay attention to the way economists use language, numbers, graphs, and models to persuade each other. But the rhetoric of economics is, of course, just another large-scale, philosophical stance on how to interpret what economists do.

Today these kinds of questions have been all but superseded by what McCloskey calls "small-m methodology." Small-m methodological questions have to be addressed by any economist in their day-to-day work: How can we make causal inferences more reliable? Which of a number of concepts of causality is most appropriate for economics? What precise role do theoretical models play in economic reasoning? Can false models explain? Is p-hacking a problem and, if so, to what extent? What is the best strategy for econometric testing? What, if anything, can we learn from lab, field, and randomized experiments?

It is symptomatic of this shift in focus away from the big-M and toward small-m questions that the various -isms play hardly any role in this book. This is even true of the "Methodology" section, which combines a number of chapters of general interest. Only the chapters by Claveau et al. and Linsbichler briefly discuss realism, and both do so for reasons that have nothing to do with defending or criticizing a big-M methodology.

François Claveau, Alexandre Truc, Olivier Santerre, and Luis Mireles-Flores apply the tool of social network analysis to bibliometric data to investigate citation networks and to observe some historical trends in the field of philosophy of economics. "The field of philosophy of economics" is in fact a misnomer, because there are two separate bodies that have somewhat different research interests and form different citation networks. The first body of work is formed by the specialized associations, conferences, and journals such as the *Journal of Economic Methodology* and *Economics & Philosophy* and is therefore called the "Specialized Philosophy of Economics." Network analysis produces five topical clusters within this field, namely, moral philosophy, behavioral economics, big-M methodology, small-m methodology, and decision theory. The other body of work is formed by the *Journal of Economic Literature* classification code for "Economic Methodology": B4. Network analysis here forms six only partially overlapping clusters: institutional economics, critical realism, political economy, big-M methodology, small-m methodology, and history of economics. Interestingly, even within the clusters that share a label, there are considerable differences in substance. For instance, while "realist" is the most frequently found distinctive phrase in the big-M cluster of specialized philosophy of economics, this phrase does not appear in the top-10 list of the JEL big-M cluster; conversely, while "replication" is the most frequently found distinctive phrase in the small-m JEL cluster, it does not appear in the small-m cluster of specialized philosophy of economics.

Alexander Linsbichler's chapter provides an overview and discussion of the methodology of the Austrian School of economics (whose members include Carl Menger, Friedrich Wieser, Eugen Böhm-Bawerk, Ludwig Mises, Friedrich August Hayek, Fritz Machlup, Oskar Morgenstern, Gottfried Haberler, Israel Kirzner, Ludwig Lachmann, and Murray Rothbard). Linsbichler argues that despite the many members' diverse backgrounds, approaches, and interests, there is a remarkable convergence in their methodologies in a number of important respects. These commonalities are discussed in eight sections on action theory and interpretative understanding, subjectivism, methodological individualism, ontological individualism, apriorism, essentialism, formal methods, and economic semantics.

Hsiang-Ke Chao's chapter looks at philosophical issues regarding *scientific representation* in economics. Economists use a variety of tools (other than language) to represent economic phenomena: models, numbers (i.e., measurements), and diagrams. Chao argues that economists use these devices not for the goal of representation per se – that is, to supply us with a "mirror of the economy" – but rather as tools for reasoning and defending claims about the economy.

Melissa Vergara-Fernández and Boudewijn de Bruin take a closer look at finance, a subdiscipline of economics that tends to be sidelined by economic methodologists (with the important exception of Donald MacKenzie's influential study of the performativity of financial models; see MacKenzie 2008). Among other things, the authors discuss a central methodological problem for hypothesis testing in finance, the joint hypothesis problem, and identify it as an instance of the problem of underdetermination of theory by evidence. The second part of the chapter examines closely the Modigliani-Miller model and how modelers' value judgments can affect the construction and application of models. Values should, therefore, be part of model appraisal in economics.

1.4 Values

When philosophers speak of "value" (as in the aforementioned value theory), they refer very broadly to everything that is desirable – what is good or worth striving for. Things can be of either intrinsic value, that is, desirable for their own sake or instrumental value, that is, desirable as a means to an end that is worth striving for. Value judgments in that sense are judgments about the goodness (or badness) of things or actions or states of affairs or judgments about how things or actions or states of affairs ought to be.

A long tradition that goes back at least to the scientific revolution maintains that science proper should be free of value judgments. Scientists, this tradition maintains, analyze how the world is, not how it ought to be. While at least the social sciences may well examine phenomena such as religion or capitalism because some people find them desirable, the scientist suspends judgment on the matter (Weber 1904/1949).

The so-called "value-free ideal" (Reiss and Sprenger 2020) has been very influential in economics. The distinction between positive and normative economics is grounded in the very idea that positive economics examines economic phenomena as they are, not as they should be, and proceeds in a manner free of value judgments. Normative economics cannot quite be value free – it uses concepts such as Pareto *optimality*, second-*best* solution, and a consumer being *better off*, after all – but, at least according to some economists (Gul and Pesendorfer 2008: 8),

> [S]tandard economics has no therapeutic ambition; that is, it does not try to evaluate or improve the individual's objectives. Economics cannot distinguish between choices that maximize happiness, choices that reflect a sense of duty, or choices that are the response to some impulse. Moreover, standard economics takes no position on the question of which of those objectives the agent should pursue.

And yet, the value-free ideal has been under attack since the mid-20th century. The first two chapters in this section examine the feasibility of value freedom in economics. Antoinette Baujard addresses values in normative or welfare economics. Specifically, she takes up four theses concerning the role of value judgments in welfare economics: that ethical values are and should be out of the scope of welfare economics ("value neutrality"); that ethical values are acceptable if they are minimal and consensual ("value confinement"); that ethical values are acceptable if they are made explicit and formalized ("transparency"); and that no meaningful demarcation between factual and value judgments is possible ("entanglement"). Baujard then investigates their implications for the practice of welfare economics.

Julian Reiss turns to values in positive economics. According to a long-standing view, positive economics can and should be free from ethical, political, social, and cultural values. There are a number of reasons for thinking that the long-standing view is incorrect, among which Richard Rudner's argument from inductive risk, perhaps, has been the most influential (Rudner 1953). This chapter defends another version of the entanglement claim, namely, that the way *measurement procedures* are constructed and used in economics demonstrates that certain descriptive statements imply normative commitments. By using the measurement of consumer price inflation as its main case study, this chapter details the value judgments made both in the construction of the inflation index and in its use.

Serious reflection about economics therefore hinges on the values at play. Many philosophers of economics are invested in exploring the meaning of central evaluative concepts. Sometimes, this involves engaging in ethics with an eye on economics, and sometimes this involves engaging in economics with an eye on ethics. As John Broome observed in the opening of his 1999 collection *Ethics out of Economics*: "The traffic between ethics and economics travels in both directions."

Mark D. White offers an in-depth discussion of the relationship between economics and ethics. Specifically, he explores how exactly the relationship between economics and ethics has been playing out in recent research. White asks whether ethics is and should remain external to economics, or whether it should be considered to be an intrinsic and pervasive aspect of economics.

Plenty of values are important for economics, and two chapters analyze two key values: well-being and fairness. Both concepts play crucial roles in various subfields of philosophy and economics, notably investigations of distributive justice and welfare economics and political philosophy more generally (e.g., Adler 2012).

Mauro Rossi examines the nature of well-being and introduces and compares the main philosophical theories of well-being: mental state theories, preference satisfaction theories, objective list theories, and perfectionist theories.

Stefan Wintein and Conrad Heilmann review the so-called fair division theories in philosophy and economics that explore fairness as a distinct value concept. They focus on fair division theories in philosophy and economics that promote understanding fairness as a substantive, local, and objective concept. They also suggest that philosophical and economic theories in this area have much to offer to one another.

1.5 Causality and Explanation

According to Carl Menger, "understanding, predicting, and controlling economic phenomena" are the main aims of economics (Menger 1883/1986: 64). Learning the truth of causal claims is a good means to achieve all three. If, let us say, it is the case, as proponents of the quantity theory of money would have it, the growth rate of the money supply is the only source of inflation in the long run, we can use this knowledge to understand past inflations and hyper-inflations, to predict future inflations by observing the development of the money supply, and to control the inflation rate by controlling the money supply. So far, we maintain, there is little disagreement among methodologists.

There is little agreement, by contrast, on the question of how to understand causality itself. Philosophers tend to begin every discussion with a reference to David Hume's regularity account, according to which some event *C* causes another event *E* if and only if *C* and *E* are constantly conjoined and *E* follows *C* without any spatiotemporal gaps (see, for instance, Hoover 2008). But other than concurring that Hume's theory is deficient in one way or another (few causes are perfectly correlated with their effects; cause and effect may sometimes occur simultaneously, especially when the resolution of variables is relatively coarse as in macroeconomics; and causes may affect variables only after a considerable period of time has passed), there is no consensus about moving forward. Specifically in economics, the following accounts have contemporary relevance:

- *Mill's tendency account.* John Stuart Mill observed that, when understood as statements of regularities without exception, all causal claims are false (Mill 1874[1843]). The reason is that confounding factors can always interfere with the operation of the cause. At best, a cause *tends to* result in its effect, by which Mill means that (i) the cause *regularly* produces its effect in the absence of interferences and (ii) when interferences are present, the cause still *contributes systematically* to the outcome (Reiss 2008b).
- *The probabilistic account.* The probabilistic account builds on the idea that effects do not always follow their causes but are nevertheless correlated with them. Simple correlation is not causation, however, as two effects of a common cause will also be correlated. In philosophy of science, Patrick Suppes was one of the first to develop a systematic theory of causation that builds on the idea of "correlation after controlling for confounding factors" (Suppes 1970; Reiss 2016a). Very roughly, *C* causes *E* if and only if $P(E \mid C) > P(E)$ and there is no event *X* such that $P(E \mid C.X) = P(E \mid X)$. In economics, the closely related concept of Granger causality (Granger 1969) has been very influential.
- *The modularity account.* A connotation of causality that is quite different from correlation is that of "recipe for change": if *C* causes *E*, and we are able to manipulate *C*, then we can use the causal relationship to change *E*. In James Woodward's version of the theory, roughly, *C* causes *E* if and only if an ideal intervention on *C* changes *E* or its probability distribution (Woodward 2003). In economics, Kevin Hoover has presented a systematic development of this idea (Hoover 2001).

The two chapters on causality in this section provide in-depth discussions of probability and modularity theories in economics. Starting from Suppes' theory, Tobias Henschen goes through Granger causality, its generalization in vector autoregression (VAR), Arnold Zellner's account of causal laws, and the causal Bayes nets theory, which generalizes Suppes (1970). He examines specifically the ability of the various theories to help with the achievement of the aims of economics and argues, among other things, that Granger causality, while useful in the context of *prediction*, is not what is needed for *control* (i.e., policy).

Christopher Clarke takes up modularity theories. He argues that at least some of these theories fail when applied to simple supply and demand systems because the equilibrium constraint that is usually imposed results in ambiguity about what the direct causes of certain variables are. Worse, even when the ambiguity is resolved, the modularity theory answers a causal question that is not usually of interest to economists. Clarke then develops an alternative, called the ceteris paribus theory, which is loosely based on ideas put forward by the econometrician and Nobel Prize winner James Heckman.

Whether or not knowledge of causal relations helps with the economist's aim of understanding or explanation depends also on what one thinks a good scientific explanation is. Under the Hempel-Oppenheim covering-law model of explanation, for instance, a scientific explanation is a deductively valid argument that has a description of the phenomenon of interest as its conclusion and a "covering law" among its premises (Hempel and Oppenheim 1948). Whatever else one thinks a covering law is, if a cause does not necessitate its effect, the corresponding causal statement will not be able to play the role required by the model.

Apart from the question of whether and to what extent causal claims help one to realize the goal of explanation, there are numerous other explanation-related issues that are relevant to economics:

- Are there credible non-causal accounts of explanation? Specifically, how plausible are accounts of mathematical explanation (Lange 2013) and equilibrium explanation (Sober 1983), and what is their role in economics (Reiss 2008a; Hardt 2017)?
- How, if at all, does rational choice theory explain economic phenomena (Satz and Ferejohn 1994)? Specifically, what role do preferences play in economic explanations? If reasons are causes (Davidson 1963), are rational choice explanations a species of causal explanation (Lovett 2006) or rather one of explanation-as-unification (Fumagalli 2020; Vredenburgh 2020)?
- How, if at all, do economic models explain? Specifically, if successful explanation requires truth, is there a tension between the extensive use of idealizations in models and the desire to use them to explain economic phenomena (Reiss 2012)? If there is a tension, can it be resolved (Grüne-Yanoff 2013)?
- Do explanations have to refer exclusively to economic agents and the constraints under which they operate, or can social wholes explain (Hoover 2009a)?
- How do understanding and scientific explanation relate? Specifically, can we have understanding without explanation, and are there plausible examples of practices that yield understanding of economic phenomena without explaining them (Verreault-Julien 2017)?

Philippe Verreault-Julien's chapter takes us through these questions and provides a detailed discussion of the answers that have been proposed. He concludes that debates about explanation in economics are, at heart, debates about the proper aims of the discipline, that is, about what is desirable and what can be achieved. Verreault-Julien thus alludes to another way in which methodological issues are entangled with value judgments.

Jennifer S. Jhun examines the role of models in economic explanations in much greater detail. Using the Tealbook forecasts for the Federal Open Market Committee (FOMC) meetings as a case study, she argues that an integral part of model-based explanations are the narratives that accompany theoretical models. Moreover, the route from the "how possibly" account the model provides to a "how actually" explanation is far from algorithmic, as earlier work on economic models suggested (e.g., de-idealization by adding back omitted factors). Instead, the idealized model remains an integral part in a larger narrative practice, the aim of which is the construction of a coherent account of the causal structure at hand.

1.6 Experimentation and Simulation

In the 19th century, John Stuart Mill famously argued that economics is not an experimental science. The reason was simply that he did not see how the "method of difference" could work in economics. The method of difference compares two situations that are exactly identical except with respect to a single factor and, possibly, the phenomenon of interest. If the difference given by the factor's presence and absence makes a difference to the phenomenon of interest, the factor is among its causes; if not, the factor is not among its causes (Mill 1874[1843]). But with respect to the questions of interest to economists, we never find two situations that are similar enough. No two countries, say, differ only with respect to their trade policy so that we can examine empirically whether free trade has a positive or negative or no effect on economic growth. Similarly, we cannot experimentally free up trade, observe how the growth rate develops, and infer causality because too many other things will change with the policy change and in between the policy change and its possible effect.

Nor do we need to examine the economy empirically in order to establish principles inductively. Mill maintained that the fundamental principles of economics are already known. To learn a new, more specific principle, we simply apply the fundamental principle and add whatever we know about the specific situation as a constraint or an initial condition. We then deductively derive a prediction about what should happen in the specific situation, and we judge that the new principle is confirmed if the prediction is successful or that an inference has occurred otherwise (or a mistake was made in the derivation). Economics is, therefore, fundamentally a deductive science.

Skepticism about the worth of experiments in economics has survived well into the 20th century. As W. Allen Wallis and Milton Friedman write almost exactly 100 years after Mill (Wallis and Friedman 1942):

> It is questionable whether a subject in so artificial an experimental situation could know what choices he would make in an economic situation; not knowing, it is almost inevitable that he would, in entire good faith, systematize his answers in such a way as to produce plausible but spurious results.

Wallis and Friedman's reason for skepticism about experiments was different from Mill's. After the marginal revolution of the 1870s, the individual and individual behavior moved to the center of economists' attention. Unlike the aggregate phenomena on which classical economists such as Mill focused – such as the benefits of free trade, the distribution of income between the factors of production land, labor, and capital, and the causes of changes in the value of money – individuals can participate in experiments. However, as Wallis and Friedman argued, humans are responsive to the details of a situation, and when put in a situation as artificial as an economic experiment, his or her behavior will be different from behavior that obtains "naturally."

When Wallis and Friedman were writing, experimental economics was a fringe activity. Today it is a huge subdiscipline of economics, and it is one of the engines behind behavioral economics, itself a highly active new branch of economics. Economics has become an at least partially experimental science.

Today's experimental economists are not unaware of Mill's and Wallis and Friedman's concerns. Far from it. But they interpret these concerns not as principled obstacles to experimentation (dare we say, as a big-M problem?) but rather as a set of methodological challenges that needs to be addressed in the context of specific economic investigations. The methodological literature to address these challenges has consequently grown substantially over the past few decades.

As we have just seen, methodological issues are best addressed in the light of the purpose pursued by the activity under scrutiny. Alvin Roth has provided the following basic typology of reasons for which experiments are done (Roth 1995: 22):

- Speaking to theorists.
- Searching for facts.
- Whispering in the ears of princes.

"Speaking to theorists" refers to using experiments to test well-articulated theories. Experiments must therefore be designed such that they can be related to theories in unambiguous ways, which is not always easy [see, for instance, the problems of interpreting the "preference reversal" phenomenon in Steel (2008)]. "Searching for facts" includes experiments to study the effects of variables that are not predicted by any theory. These experiments often build on previous experiments and vary experimental conditions. Comparability with earlier experimental work is, therefore, important, and interpretability in the light of theory is at best secondary. Experiments of the first kind are fully compatible with Mill's deductivist stance. But, those of the second kind suggest a more inductivist approach where the collection of facts comes first and general principles may be established on the basis of these facts.

"Whispering in the ears of princes" concerns the use of economic experiments for policymaking. What is most important here is that the experiment yields results that enable reliable forecasts about how people behave outside of the experimental situation, specifically, in policy contexts. In other words, the Wallis and Friedman concerns have to be addressed successfully.

An alternative typology classifies experiments according to the system on which experimenters intervene, as well as the source of the intervention. Thus, one can distinguish the following:

- *Laboratory experiments.* Here "real people" (albeit usually highly selected people such as university students) are put in a tightly controlled and, hence, artificial situation manipulated by the experimenter.
- *Field experiments.* Here the intervention is directed by the experimenter but on individuals who remain in a barely controlled, natural situation.
- *Natural experiments.* Here the intervention also occurs naturally. These are nevertheless regarded as experiments because the structure of the situation is causally identical or at least very similar to a laboratory or field experiment.
- *Simulation experiments.* These are *in silico* experiments conducted by an experimenter, but on a computer. In agent-based simulations there are individual actors, but they have of course been programmed. Many other simulations solve dynamic mathematical equations.
- *Thought experiments.* The material of this type of experiment is the mind of the experimenter. They do exist in economics, but they play a comparatively small role (though see Reiss 2016b; Schabas 2018).

Michiru Nagatsu's chapter in this volume discusses laboratory experiments. Nagatsu examines closely the interrelation between the type or design of the experiment and its purpose, and he argues that experimenters often follow a "severe testing" approach to inductive reasoning, an approach that will be discussed in greater detail in Aris Spanos' chapter (see the next section). Nagatsu also looks at the methodological differences between experiments in economics and experiments in psychology and argues that the two fields should make better use of the benefits of mutual learning.

Judith Favereau's companion chapter addresses field experiments. Earlier it was stated that field experiments normally operate in a barely controlled, natural environment. Favereau argues that the rise of *randomized* field experiments in development economics has brought with it more rigid controls and manipulations, so that "the field vanishes" in these field experiments. While this move may make results more reliable in one sense, it also raises the Wallis-Friedman challenge. She concludes the chapter by developing some strategies for meeting the challenge.

Aki Lehtinen and Jaakko Kuorikoski's chapter turns to computer simulations. Unlike mathematical models, in whose solution an experienced economist can "see" why a certain result must hold, simulations are "epistemically opaque." Lehtinen and Kuorikoski ask what the implications of the epistemic opacity of simulations are for the achievement of the goals of economics (such as explanation and understanding), and they address this and other methodological questions in the context of Monte Carlo methods in econometrics, dynamic stochastic general equilibrium models, and agent-based macroeconomics.

Donal Khosrowi's chapter turns to evidence-based policy (EBP). He begins with an important distinction between "broad EBP" (roughly the demand that policy claims should be based on the best available evidence) and "narrow EBP" (roughly the demand that only randomized trials should be regarded as high-quality evidence) and argues that narrow EBP faces a number of specific methodological challenges. Among these challenges is the observation that the balancing of confounders between treatment and control groups obtains only in expectation, not for a particular instance, thus challenging the "gold standard" status of the method. Another challenge concerns the exportability of results from the test situation to a policy situation. A third challenge concerns the narrow limits of the kinds of questions that can be addressed using the method. The chapter ends with a number of suggestions for an improved understanding of what it means to base policy claims on the "best available evidence."

1.7 Evidence

The topic of evidence is at the same time a very old and a relatively recent one in economic methodology. Many of the influential debates, even in the big-M methodology of old, are at heart debates about the role of evidence. When Mill argues that economics is a deductive science, he is really saying something about how economists should and should not use evidence, namely, to confirm or disconfirm predictions derived from the fundamental principles and constraints and not as a base from which general principles are inductively established. Similarly, a core demand in Karl Popper's falsificationism is that scientists should seek possible evidence that conflicts with the theory under scrutiny, not just evidence that speaks in its favor (as the latter can always be found).

Yet, in recent times the biomedical and social sciences have witnessed the formation of movements that use the label "evidence-based X" (where X ranges over special sciences such as medicine, management science, and public policy), as though the demand to base claims on the best available evidence were something new. But what is new is not the grounding of claims on evidence but rather a certain understanding of what good evidence is. The focus is here on efficacy claims, for example, claims about whether a new drug produces better outcomes than existing alternatives or whether a policy reaches its intended goal. The idea then is that efficacy claims should always be underwritten with evidence produced by a randomized trial. Any other kind of evidence – from a nonrandomized intervention, a cohort study, a retrospective, observational study, models and simulations, expert judgment – is regarded as lower quality at best and discarded at worst.

This section collects chapters on evidence both in the more general, older sense and in the newer sense used in the evidence-based X movements.

Robert Northcott's chapter argues that, despite economics' recent empirical turn, the discipline is still excessively focused on theory development and, correspondingly, does not take empirical evidence seriously enough. Instead, economics should learn from other sciences, which develop their theories in closer concert with empirical application and refinement and do not hang on to some theoretical "orthodoxy" that has not been proven particularly efficient at generating empirical successes. He also argues that economics should take advantage of a much wider range of empirical methods (other than traditional econometrics and the various kinds of experiments), such as ethnographic observation, small-N causal inference (e.g., qualitative comparative analysis) and other qualitative methods (e.g., questionnaires and interviews), causal process tracing, causal inference from observational statistics, machine learning from big data, and historical studies.

Aris Spanos' chapter examines the way econometricians use statistical models to learn about economic phenomena of interest from evidence from a philosophy of science perspective. Specifically, he criticizes the "curve-fitting approach" of traditional econometrics, which all too often incorporates unverified assumptions about error terms and which has, in his view, produced a large number of unreliable results – despite its increased mathematical sophistication. He argues in favor of an alternative based on the concept of an "adequate statistical model."

William Peden and Jan Sprenger's chapter examines the issue of theory testing at a more general level. Using the debate between Jan Tinbergen and John Maynard Keynes as a prop, the chapter reviews the use of significance tests in economics from both a historical and a methodological perspective. The specific methodological concerns related to significance tests are the neglect of effect size as a quantity that is more relevant for economic policy than significance levels, publication bias, and the replication crisis in behavioral economics.

Daniel M. Hausman argues that health cannot literally be measured, but that it can be valued in a variety of ways. He questions whether health conditions should be valued by the extent to which they satisfy population preferences, as determined by surveys of representative samples.

1.8 Policy

Problems at the intersection of philosophy and economics – such as those surrounding rationality, cooperation, and analysis of theoretical concepts – are of interest to theorists in both disciplines. They can also be of practical importance, such as when the design and implementation of policies raise questions that need to be addressed by using both philosophical and economic methods.

Should tax competition be curbed? Should individuals be "nudged" or otherwise assisted in their decisions? How should policymakers approach contexts in which there is a lot of uncertainty? And on which grounds might markets be regulated? These are questions about policies, and they are questions about philosophy and economics.

Here, one of the most interesting recent developments in the philosophy of economics is analyzing issues of policy relevance, and tackling concrete problems of policymaking directly. This style of "applied" philosophy of economics is a marked departure from the more general hope that the philosophical reflections about economic concepts will be practically relevant in some way, such as by being taken up by economists. Frequently, philosophers of economics allude to Keynes' famous quotation of "some defunct economist" influencing policy in indirect ways in order to motivate the relevance of methodological reflections on economics, which are sometimes doubted, hard to trace, and therefore often taken to be a fundamental challenge to the field (e.g., Backhouse 2010; Vromen 2021). Indeed, it will be interesting to follow in what sense this style of philosophy of economics can provide a new kind of answer to an old question within the field.

Such applied and policy-focused contributions in the philosophy of economics do not rest only on the sophisticated analyses of methodological and conceptual questions that are examined in earlier sections of this *Handbook*. They also have an important political philosophy dimension. This link is most prevalent in the opening chapter to this section, in which Sebastiano Bavetta discusses contemporary political economy's frame of the liberal order to unveil its difficulty with the defense of such an order. He then suggests that the embodiment of individual perceptions, values, and beliefs in political economy's frame of the liberal order is instrumental to set in motion policies and institutional changes respectful of liberal institutions and supportive of the material and immaterial benefits secured by a liberal political order.

Two chapters in this section, by Constanze Binder and Alex Voorhoeve, respectively, pursue a conceptual approach to "applied" or policy-relevant philosophy of economics. Both contributions explore how certain positions in the analysis of concepts can be used to develop standards and guidelines for the development of policies.

Constanze Binder's chapter takes up the concept of freedom. Markets have been both defended and criticized by invoking freedom. For one, there are "all-out," general positions: for instance, defenses on the basis of freedom of choice or libertarian conceptions of freedom or criticism of markets by socialists. For another, there are also more limited, or nuanced, positions, such as those that analyze specific advantages and drawbacks and possible limitations of markets based on republican notions of freedom or on autonomy. The chapter by Binder reviews arguments for and against markets on the basis of such freedom conceptions and then proposes taxonomizing them. This, in turn, provides proposals for normative standards that can be used to assess policies that regulate markets.

Voorhoeve examines policies in "severely" uncertain situations, for example, in climate change and novel pandemics. In the context of so-called severe uncertainty, it is impossible to assign precise probabilities to relevant factors and outcomes. While there is a long history in both philosophy and economics of addressing the epistemic challenges of severe uncertainty – such as exploring theories of ambiguity and uncertainty aversion that use imprecise probabilities – such contexts also raise practical challenges. How should policymakers approach contexts in which they have to rely on less than perfect assessments? Voorhoeve outlines and defends what he calls an uncertainty-averse and egalitarian approach to policy evaluation. He demonstrates that egalitarian principles demand an especially careful treatment of the most vulnerable. He defends a theory of distributive justice that offers safeguards against individual and collective misfortune.

Two further chapters in this section, by Till Grüne-Yanoff and Peter Dietsch, respectively, pursue an approach to policy-relevant philosophy of economics that tackles a specific set of policies head-on. That is to say, they focus on a narrower set of possible policy interventions: Grüne-Yanoff analyzes policies that aim to regulate the behavior of individuals, and Dietsch looks at regulating tax competition.

Grüne-Yanoff offers an analysis of what he dubs "behavioral public policies." He begins with a point important for the analysis of such policies. He argues that, rather than presupposing as central a specific policy such as "nudging," it is key to appreciate the diversity of approaches in the family of behavioral public policies. The approaches to such policies can differ immensely: in terms of their goals, the mechanisms through which they operate, their effectiveness, and the contexts in which they perform best. Grüne-Yanoff divides behavioral policies into two kinds of causal mechanisms: nudges and boosts. Only when they appreciate these differences will policymakers stand a chance to evaluate the context-dependent performance of behavioral policies.

When jurisdictions design their tax code so as to aim to attract capital from outside, they partake in "tax competition." In his chapter, Peter Dietsch argues that tax competition should be regulated. Tax competition suffers from a trifecta of problems, or so Dietsch argues: it is undemocractic, exacerbates inequalities, and is inefficient. Regulation should aim to rectify these problems.

Notes

1 "Of all the characteristics that set economics apart from other social sciences, the distinction it makes between its positive and normative research is one of the most significant." (Translated by the authors)
2 "All philosophy is either theoretical or practical." (Translated by the authors)

Bibliography

Adler, M. 2012. *Well-Being and Fair Distribution*. Oxford, Oxford University Press.

Anand, P. 2009. "Rationality and Intransitive Preference." *The Oxford Handbook of Rational and Social Choice*. Oxford, Oxford University Press: 156–172.

Anand, P., Pattanaik, P. and Puppe, C. 2009. *The Oxford Handbook of Rational and Social Choice*. Oxford, Oxford University Press.

Anderson, E. 2001. "Unstrapping the Straitjacket of 'Preference'." *Economics & Philosophy* **17**: 21–38.

Angner, Erik 2019 "We're All Behavioral Economists Now." *Journal of Economic Methodology* **26**(3): 195–207.

Backhouse, R. 2010. "Methodology in Action." *Journal of Economic Methodology* **17**(1): 3–15.

Backhouse, R. and Medema, S. 2009. "Defining Economics: The Long Road to Acceptance of the Robbins Definition." *Economica* **76:** 805–820.

Bicchieri, C. 1993. *Rationality and Coordination*. Cambridge, Cambridge University Press.

Bicchieri, C. 2006. *The Grammar of Society: The Nature and Dynamics of Social Norms*. Cambridge, Cambridge University Press.

Binmore, K. 2005. *Natural Justice*. Oxford, Oxford University Press.

Blaug, Mark 1992. *The Methodology of Economics or How Economists Explain*. 2nd ed. Cambridge, Cambridge University Press.

Boland, Lawrence 1979. "A Critique of Friedman's Critics." *Journal of Economic Literature* **17**: 503–522.

Bradley, R. 2017. *Decision Theory with a Human Face*. Cambridge, Cambridge University Press.

Buchak, L. 2017. *Risk and Rationality*. Oxford, Oxford University Press.

Chang, Ruth. 2001. *Making Comparisons Count*. London, Routledge.

Chang, Ruth and Sylvan, Kurt 2020. *The Routledge Handbook of Practical Reason*. London, Routledge.

Davidson, Donald 1963. "Actions, Reasons, and Causes." *The Journal of Philosophy* **60**(23): 685–700.

Davis, J. and Hands, D. 2021. "Introduction: Economic Methodology and Philosophy of Economics Twenty Years Since the Millennium." *Journal of Economic Methodology* **28**(1): 1–2.

de Bruin, B. 2009. "Overmathematisation in Game Theory: Pitting the Nash Equilibrium Refinement Programme against the Epistemic Programme." *Studies in History and Philosophy of Science Part A* **40**(3): 290–300.

Friedman, Milton 1953. "The Methodology of Positive Economics." *Essays in Positive Economics*. Chicago, University of Chicago Press.

Fumagalli, Roberto 2020. "How Thin Rational Choice Theory Explains Choices." *Studies in History and Philosophy of Science* **83**: 63–74.

Granger, Clive 1969. "Investigating Causal Relations by Econometric Models and Cross-spectral Methods." *Econometrica* **37**(3): 424–438.

Greaves, H. 2013. "Epistemic Decision Theory." *Mind* **122**(488): 915–952.

Grüne-Yanoff, T. 2013. "Genuineness Resolved: A Reply to Reiss' Purported Paradox." *Journal of Economic Methodology* **20**(3): 255–261.

Grüne-Yanoff, T. 2017. "Reflections on the 2017 Nobel Memorial Prize Awarded to Richard Thaler." *Erasmus Journal for Philosophy and Economics* **10**(2): 61–75.

Grüne-Yanoff, T. and Lehtinen, A. 2012. "Philosophy of Game Theory." *Philosophy of Economics. Handbook of the Philosophy of Science*. U. Mäki, Ed. Oxford, North-Holland: 531–576.

Guala, F. 2006. "Has Game Theory Been Refuted?" *Journal of Philosophy* **103**(5): 239–263.

Gul, Faruk and Pesendorfer, Wolfgang 2008. "The Case for Mindless Economics." *The Foundations of Positive and Normative Economics: A Handbook*. A. Caplin and A. Schotter, Eds. New York, Oxford University Press: 3–39.

Hardt, Lukasz 2017. *Economics Without Laws: Towards a New Philosophy of Economics*. Basingstoke, Palgrave Macmillan.

Hausman, D., McPherson, M. and Satz, D. 2017. *Economic Analysis, Moral Philosophy, and Public Policy*. 3rd ed. Cambridge, Cambridge University Press.

Hempel, Carl and Oppenheim, Paul 1948. "Studies in the Logic of Explanation." *Philosophy of Science* **15**: 135–175.

Heukelom, F. 2014. *Behavioural Economics: A History*. Cambridge, Cambridge University Press.

Hoover, Kevin 2001. *Causality in Macroeconomics*. Cambridge, Cambridge University Press.

Hoover, Kevin 2008. "Causality in Economics and Econometrics." *The New Palgrave Dictionary of Economics*. Steven N. Durlauf and Lawrence E. Blume, Eds. Basingstoke, Palgrave Macmillan.

Hoover, Kevin 2009a. "Microfoundations and the Ontology of Macroeconomics." *The Oxford Handbook of Philosophy of Economics*. Harold Kincaid and Don Ross, Eds. New York, Oxford University Press: 386–409.

Hoover, Kevin 2009b. "Milton Friedman's Stance: The Methodology of Causal Realism." *The Methodology of Positive Economics*. Uskali Mäki, Ed. Cambridge, Cambridge University Press: 303–320.

Hutchison, Terence 1938. *Significance and Basic Postulates of Economic Theory*. London, Palgrave Macmillan.

Jeffrey, R. C. 1974. "Preference among Preferences." *The Journal of Philosophy* **71**(13): 377–391.

Joyce, J. 1999. *The Foundations of Causal Decision Theory*. Cambridge, Cambridge University Press.

Kincaid, H. and Ross, D. 2009. *The Oxford Handbook of Philosophy of Economics*. Oxford, Oxford University Press.

Kolodny, Niko and Brunero, John 2020. "Instrumental Rationality." *The Stanford Encyclopedia of Philosophy* (Spring 2020 Edition). Edward N. Zalta, Ed. URL = <https://plato.stanford.edu/archives/spr2020/entries/rationality-instrumental/>.

Lange, Mark 2013. "What Makes a Scientific Explanation Distinctively Mathematical?" *British Journal for Philosophy of Science* **64**(3): 485–511.

Lovett, Frank 2006. "Rational Choice Theory and Explanation." *Rationality and Society* **18**(2): 237–272.

MacKenzie, Donald 2008. *An Engine, Not a Camera: How Financial Models Shape Markets*. Cambridge (MA), The MIT Press.

Mäki, Uskali 1992. "Friedman and Realism." *Research in the History of Economic Thought and Methodology* **10**: 171–195.

Mandler, M. 2005. "Incomplete Preferences and Rational Intransitivity of Choice." *Games and Economic Behavior* **50**(2): 255–277.

McCloskey, Deirdre 1998. *The Rhetoric of Economics*. 2nd ed. Madison (WN), University of Wisconsin Press.

McCloskey, Donald 1994. *Knowledge and Persuasion in Economics*. Cambridge, Cambridge University Press.

Menger, Carl 1883/1986. *Investigations into the Method of the Social Sciences with Special Reference to Economics*. New York (NY), New York University Press.

Mill, John Stuart 1874[1843]. *A System of Logic*. New York (NY), Harper.

Mongin, P. 2018. "Les origines de la distinction entre positif et normatif en économie." *Revue philosophique de Louvain* **116**: 151–186.

Moscati, I. 2021. "On the Recent Philosophy of Decision Theory." *Journal of Economic Methodology* **28**(1): 98–106.

Paul, L. A. 2014. *Transformative Experience*. Oxford, Oxford University Press.

Pettigrew, R. 2019. *Choosing for Changing Selves*. Oxford, Oxford University Press.

Reiss, Julian 2008a. "Explanation." *The New Palgrave Dictionary of Economics*. Steven N. Durlauf and Lawrence E. Blume, Eds. Basingstoke, New Palgrave.

Reiss, Julian 2008b. "Social Capacities." *Nancy Cartwright's Philosophy of Science*. Stephan Hartmann and Luc Bovens, Eds. London, Routledge: 265–288.

Reiss, Julian 2012. "The Explanation Paradox." *Journal of Economic Methodology* **19**(1): 43–62.

Reiss, Julian 2016a. "Suppes' Probabilistic Theory of Causality and Causal Inference in Economics." *Journal of Economic Methodology* **23**(3): 289–304.

Reiss, Julian 2016b. "Thought Experiments in Economics and the Role of Coherent Explanations." *Studia Metodologiczne* **36**: 113–130.

Reiss, Julian and Sprenger, Jan 2020. "Scientific Objectivity." *Stanford Encyclopedia of Philosophy*. Edward Zalta, Ed. Stanford (CA), CSLI.

Robbins, L. 1932. *An Essay on the Nature and Significance of Economics Science*. London: Macmillan.

Ross, D. 2016. *Philosophy of Economics*. Dordrecht, Springer.

Ross, D. 2019. "Game Theory." *The Stanford Encyclopedia of Philosophy* (Winter 2019 Edition). Edward N. Zalta, Ed. URL = <https://plato.stanford.edu/archives/win2019/entries/game-theory/>.

Roth, Alvin 1995. "Introduction to Experimental Economics." *Handbook of Experimental Economics*. John Kagel and Alvin Roth, Eds. Princeton, Princeton University Press: 3–110.

Rudner, Richard 1953. "The Scientist Qua Scientist Makes Value Judgments." *Philosophy of Science* **20**(1): 1–6.

Russell, Bertrand 1967. *The Autobiography of Bertrand Russell*, Vol. 1. London, George Allen and Unwin.

Samuelson, Paul 1963. "Discussion." *American Economic Review* **53**(2): 231–236.

Samuelson, Paul 1964. "Theory and Realism: A Reply." *American Economic Review* **54**(5): 736–739.

Satz, Debra and Ferejohn, John 1994. "Rational Choice and Social Theory." *Journal of Philosophy* **91**(2): 71–84.

Savage, L. 1954/1972. *The Foundations of Statistics*. Dover Publication.

Schabas, Margaret 2018. "Thought Experiments in Economics." *Routledge Handbook of Thought Experiments*. Michael Stuart, Yiftach Fehige, and James Robert Brown, Eds. New York (NY), Routledge: 171–182.

Sen, A. K. 1977. *Rational fools: A Critique of the Behavioral Foundations of Economic Theory*. Philosophy & Public Affairs: 317–344.

Sober, Elliott 1983. "Equilibrium Explanation." *Philosophical Studies* **43**: 201–210.

Steel, Daniel 2008. *Across the Boundaries: Extrapolation in Biology and Social Science*. Oxford, Oxford University Press.

Steele, K. and Stefansson, H. O. forthcoming. *Beyond Uncertainty: Reasoning with Unknown Possibilities*. Cambridge University Press.

Suppes, Patrick 1970. *A Probabilistic Theory of Causality*. Amsterdam, North-Holland.

Thaler, R. H. and Sunstein, C. R. 2008. *Nudge: Improving Decisions about Health, Wealth and Happiness*. Penguin Books.

Verreault-Julien, Philippe 2017. "Non-Causal Understanding with Economic Models: The Case of General Equilibrium." *Journal of Economic Methodology* **24**(3): 297–317.

Von Neumann, J. and Morgenstern, O. 1944/1953. *Theory of Games and Economic Behavior*. Princeton, Princeton University Press.

Vredenburgh, Kate 2020. "A Unificationist Defence of Revealed Preferences." *Economics and Philosophy* **36**(1): 149–169.

Vromen, J. 2021. "What Are We Up to?" *Journal of Economic Methodology* **28**(1): 23–31.

Wallis, W. Allen and Milton Friedman 1942. "The Empirical Derivation of Indifference Functions." *Studies in Mathematical Economics and Econometrics in memory of Henry Schultz*. O. Lange, F. McIntyre, and T. O. Yntema, Eds. Chicago, University of Chicago Press.

Weber, Max 1904/1949. " 'Objectivity' in Social Science and Social Policy." *The Methodology of the Social Sciences*. Edward Shils and Henry Finch, Eds. New York (NY), Free Press: 49–112.

Woodward, James 2003. *Making Things Happen*. Oxford, Oxford University Press.

PART I

Rationality

2

HISTORY OF UTILITY THEORY

Ivan Moscati

1. Introduction: From Labor to Utility

The notion of utility began playing the central role in economic theory that it has maintained until today in the early 1870s, when it was used to explain the exchange value of commodities. This is the ratio at which one commodity exchanges with other commodities or, in modern terms, its relative price. Before 1870, exchange value was generally explained by using the so-called labor theory of value, which was advocated among others by Adam Smith (1776/1976), David Ricardo (1821/1951), John Stuart Mill (1848/1871), and Karl Marx (1867/1990). This theory states that the exchange ratio between two commodities is proportional to the quantity of labor directly used to produce the commodity (the so-called direct labor) plus the quantity of labor necessary to produce the capital employed in the production of the commodity (the so-called indirect labor). However, as some of its proponents acknowledged, the theory has a number of problems. For instance, if two commodities contain different proportions of direct and indirect labor, their exchange ratio depends not only on the quantity of labor necessary to produce them but also on the profit rate prevailing in the economy. Moreover, the exchange value of several commodities, and notably of corn, depends not only on the quantity of labor necessary to produce them but also on their demand.

In the early 1870s, William Stanley Jevons in England, Carl Menger in Austria, and Léon Walras, a Frenchman based at the University of Lausanne in Switzerland, independently put forward a different explanation of exchange value. Jevons (1871), Menger (1871/1981), and Walras (1874/1954) argued that the exchange value of a commodity depends on the utility that it has for the individuals in the economy and more precisely on the *marginal* utility of the commodity. This is the additional utility associated with an individual's consumption of an additional unit of the commodity.

2. The Marginal Revolution and Early Utility Theories, 1870–1900

Jevons, Menger, and Walras assumed that the marginal utility of each commodity diminishes as an individual consumes a larger quantity of it and that individuals attempt to maximize the utility they obtain from commodities. On the basis of these assumptions, they were able to construct a theory of value that, unlike labor theory, holds for all commodities, independent of their type and nature and

DOI: 10.4324/9781315739793-3

independent of whether they are consumption goods or productive factors. Furthermore, building on the utility theory of value, Jevons, Menger, and Walras were able to construct comprehensive theories of exchange, price, and markets.

More precisely, Jevons (1871) represented utility as a mathematical function and modeled economic behavior as aimed at utility maximization. Moreover, he showed that when utility-maximizing agents exchange commodities, the exchange ratio between any two commodities is equal to the ratio of the marginal utilities of the commodities. Menger (1871/1981) illustrated how the value of each production factor depends on the marginal utility of the consumption goods produced by using that factor. With his general equilibrium theory, Walras (1874/1954) offered a model to analyze how commodity prices are determined in a system of interrelated competitive markets.

During the last quarter of the nineteenth century, the utility-based approach to economic analysis was refined and extended by a second generation of marginalists. In particular, in England, Francis Ysidro Edgeworth (1881) perfected Jevons' theory of exchange, and in doing this he introduced an analytical tool that later became popular in economics, namely, indifference curves. Alfred Marshall (1890) investigated in detail how the demand for commodities derives from the individual's maximization of utility, developed the supply-and-demand model that quickly became ubiquitous in economics, and expounded this model to analyze the working of competitive markets. Moreover, Marshall introduced the notion of consumers' surplus to evaluate the efficiency of the economic allocation of goods. In Austria, Eugen von Böhm-Bawerk (1889/1891) showed how marginal-utility theory can explain the exchange ratio not only between commodities available at the same time but also between commodities available at different points in time.

Although by around 1900 most economists accepted utility theory, it was not lacking in critics. Since its emergence in the 1870s, two main criticisms have been raised against the utility-based approach to economic analysis.

First, critics pointed out the apparent unmeasurability of utility and contended that such unmeasurability undermines the utility-based theory of value. If utility cannot be measured, they argued, explanations of exchange value based on marginal utility, such as, "The exchange ratio between two commodities is 2:1 *because* the ratio of their marginal utilities is 2:1," are flawed. In turn, if the utility-based explanation of exchange value is flawed, so are the theories of price and markets built upon it (see, e.g., Cairnes 1872/1981; Levasseur 1874/1987).

Notably, the early utility theorists and their critics shared the same understanding of measurement, an understanding that today we would call the "unit-based" or "ratio-based" view of measurement. According to this view, the property of an object (e.g., the length of a table) is measured by comparing it with some other object that displays the same property and is taken as a unit (e.g., a meter-long ruler) and then assessing the numerical ratio between the unit and the object to be measured (if the ratio is 3:1, the table of our example is 3 m long). When applied to the measurement of utility, this conception of measurement connects the measurability or unmeasurability of utility with the possibility or impossibility of identifying a unit of utility that could be used to assess utility ratios.

The second main criticism against utility theory was that it portrayed human beings in a misleading way, that is, as purely selfish subjects who pay no heed to others and are focused only on their material well-being at the expense of any social, ethical, or religious motivations. As one critic put it, utility theory would deal "with imaginary men – 'economic men' . . . conceived as simply 'money-making animals'" (Ingram 1888; similar criticisms were raised by von Schmoller 1883 and Veblen 1898).

The early utility theorists offered a variety of possible solutions to the problem of the unmeasurability of utility. For instance, Jevons speculated that a unit to measure utility, although not available at that time, may become so in some near future. Walras argued that, although no unit of utility exists, by assuming the existence of such a unit, that is, by treating utility as if it were measurable, we can derive satisfactory laws of demand, supply, and exchange. Edgeworth suggested that utility can be measured on the basis of psychological introspection by taking the just-perceivable increment of the sensation of pleasure as a measurement unit. Marshall took the individual's willingness to pay for a commodity as an indirect measure of utility, with money as the measurement unit. Böhm-Bawerk claimed that individuals can assess utility ratios directly, that is, assessing by introspection how many times a utility is greater than another.

It is fair to say that none of the proposed solutions to the problem of the apparent unmeasurability of utility was perceived as compelling, not only by critics of utility theory but also by utility theorists themselves. Thus, around 1900 the problem was still an open one.

Concerning the criticism that economics deals with selfish and unrealistic "economic men," early utility theorists addressed it by broadening the notion of utility so as to capture all possible motivations to human action. While Jevons and Menger gave a relatively narrow definition of utility – Jevons identified it with low-level pleasures and Menger with the capacity of satisfying physiological needs – Walras, and even more explicitly, Marshall, and the American economist Irving Fisher (1892) gave a broader definition of utility. Basically, Marshall and Fisher identified utility with whatever satisfies a desire, any desire: selfish or altruistic, material or spiritual, moral or immoral, healthy or unhealthy. Accordingly, economic men who maximize utility need not be selfish "money-making animals"; they could well be, for example, altruistic individuals who attempt to maximize the well-being of others.

The strategy of broadening the notion of utility to avoid the criticism that it is too narrow was effective, but it came at a cost. The economic notion of utility had a weaker link to its original intuitive psychological content and was in danger of becoming a black box containing all possible motives for human action.

3. The Ordinal Revolution Between Preferences and Choices, 1900–1950

Many of the problems associated with the unmeasurability of utility were solved by the so-called ordinal revolution, which was initiated around 1900 by Vilfredo Pareto, an Italian economist who in 1893 had succeeded Walras at the University of Lausanne. The ordinal revolution basically consisted of the gradual construction of a theory of demand and equilibrium that is independent of the assumption that utility is measurable. Pareto and subsequent "revolutionaries" pursued the goal of superseding measurable utility along two distinct lines that, using more modern terminology, can be called the preference-based approach and the choice-based approach. In effect, Pareto and other eminent ordinalists, such as John Hicks and Paul Samuelson, explored both lines of research.

In the *Manual of Political Economy*, Pareto (1906/1909/2014) adopted the preference-based approach. Here, the primary concept is that of preference: individuals have well-behaved preferences between combinations of goods and are able to rank combinations according to their preferences. Like Marshall and Fisher, Pareto adopted a broad definition of preferences. For him, preferences can express any type of taste: selfish, altruistic, or even masochistic, healthy or unhealthy, material or spiritual (see Vredenburgh, Chapter 5, and Vromen, Chapter 9).

In the *Manual*, utility is just an ordinal numerical index that represents the individual's preference ranking between combinations of goods by assigning higher numbers to more preferred combinations. In mathematical terms, the ordinal nature of utility is expressed by the fact that the utility function is unique up to increasing transformations, that is, if the utility function $U(x)$ represents the individual's preference ranking, any other utility function $U^*(x) = F[U(x)]$, where F is any increasing function, also represents the individual's preference ranking.

In other writings, Pareto (1900/2008, 1911/1955) advocated a choice-based approach in which the primary element is the individuals' indifference curves. Pareto conceived of an indifference curve as something that could be elicited experimentally by observing the individual's choices, that is, without any reference to psychological introspection. However, he never attempted to actually perform an experiment to identify the indifference curves of a real individual.

Pareto's analysis was highly innovative but, as observed by many authors from the 1930s on, defective with respect to both the preference-based and the choice-based lines of attack. In particular, Pareto frequently referred to notions that are not invariant to increasing transformations of the utility index and are therefore inconsistent with the ordinal approach to utility. The most important of these notions is the one at the core of early utility theories, namely, that of diminishing marginal utility.[1]

Up until the early 1930s, Pareto's idea of restating demand and equilibrium analysis independent of measurable utility found many supporters who, however, did not address the issues that Pareto had left open. Things changed abruptly in the mid-1930s, when a new generation of economists solved most of Pareto's unanswered problems. The second important phase of the ordinal revolution was initiated in 1934 by an article jointly co-authored by John Hicks and Roy Allen, then two young economists based at the London School of Economics (LSE).

Hicks and Allen (1934) followed the choice-based approach and attempted to construct demand theory without introducing utility indices. As for Pareto, the cornerstone of Hicks and Allen's analysis was the indifference curve, and more precisely the marginal rate of substitution (MRS), which corresponds to the slope of the indifference curve. Hicks and Allen defined the MRS between commodities x and y as the quantity of commodity y that just compensates the individual for the loss of a marginal unit of x. This is a definition in terms of commodity quantities and is independent of utility. Based on the MRS so defined, and the assumption that indifference curves are convex, Hicks and Allen were able to determine the relationships between the demand for goods, their prices, and consumer income in terms of elasticity and to decompose the effect of a price change on demand into what in current microeconomics are called the substitution effect and the income effect. Hicks and Allen's 1934 article quickly became the new reference point for utility and demand theorists.

Around 1935, Allen and others rediscovered a paper published by Russian economist and statistician Eugen Slutsky and completely neglected for almost 20 years. In this paper, Slutsky (1915/1952) anticipated many of the results later obtained by Hicks and Allen. Unlike the two LSE economists, however, Slutsky expressed his theory in terms of a utility function and its derivatives. In 1936 Allen called attention to Slutsky's paper and showed that the results contained in it are in fact independent of measurability assumptions on the utility function and therefore also hold in a purely ordinal framework (Allen 1936).

Allen's article paved the way for the establishment of preference-based, ordinal utility theory as the mainstream approach to demand analysis. Although for a while Allen insisted on the utility-free approach, after 1936 Hicks set forth his analysis in terms of ordinal utility indices. Most notably, in *Value and Capital* Hicks (1939) fine-tuned the ordinal approach to utility theory. He then represented Slutsky's results in a systematic and mathematically clear way and demonstrated, more thoroughly than Allen had done, that these results were ordinal in nature. Hicks also showed that the results he and Allen had obtained in 1934 using the marginal rate of substitution could be obtained through ordinal utility indices in a theoretically rigorous and much simpler way.

The third and final stretch of the ordinal revolution began in 1938 with an article published by American economist Paul Samuelson when he was a doctoral student at Harvard University. Just like Pareto and Hicks, Samuelson explored both the preference-based approach to demand and equilibrium analysis and the choice-based approach. Here I will focus on Samuelson's contributions to the latter.

In his "A Note on the Pure Theory of Consumer's Behaviour," Samuelson (1938a) criticized the choice-based analysis put forward by Hicks and Allen (1934) because it relied on the assumption that indifference curves are convex. For Samuelson (1938a: 61), however, this assumption depends on dubious introspective considerations: "Just as we do not claim to know by introspection the behaviour of utility, many will argue we cannot know the behavior of . . . indifference directions." As an alternative to Hicks and Allen's convex indifference curve approach, Samuelson put forward his own version of the choice-based approach, which built on a single assumption about the coherence of consumer behavior. This assumption states that if an individual buys consumption bundle x in a situation when she could also have afforded consumption bundle y, in any other situation when both x and y are affordable the individual cannot buy y and discard x. Later on, Samuelson's version of the choice-based approach was called "revealed preference theory," and his assumption was called the Weak Axiom of Revealed Preference. In particular, in his 1938 paper Samuelson proved that almost all of the restrictions on the demand functions that derive from the constrained maximization of an ordinal utility function can also be obtained by starting from the Weak Axiom.

Between 1938 and 1948, Samuelson explored some important implications of preference-based, ordinal utility analysis and did not further develop his own version of the choice-based approach to consumer demand. Notably, in *Foundations of Economic Analysis* (1947), Samuelson presented the theory of consumer behavior following an ordinal utility approach substantially equivalent to that used by Hicks in *Value and Capital* (1939). *Foundations* quickly became a reference book for postwar students of economics of no less importance than Hicks's *Value and Capital*. The two books provided a systematized version of the ordinal utility approach to consumer and demand theory that has remained canonical up to this day.

In 1948, Samuelson published an article that built a bridge between the choice-based and the preference-based approaches to demand theory. He showed that, in the case of only two goods, the observation of a sufficient number of a consumer's choices satisfying the Weak Axiom makes it possible to elicit the consumer's indifference curves (Samuelson 1948). In 1950, an article by the Dutch-American economist Hendrik Houthakker and a prompt follow-up by Samuelson transformed the bridge between the two approaches into a revolving door. Houthakker (1950) introduced a coherence assumption on consumer behavior that was stronger than Samuelson's Weak Axiom – the so-called Strong Axiom of Revealed Preference – and proved that if the choices of a consumer satisfy the Strong Axiom, these choices can be interpreted as the result of the constrained maximization of the consumer's well-behaved ordinal preferences. Samuelson (1950a) completed Houthakker's contribution by showing that the reverse is also true, that is, if a consumer maximizes her well-behaved ordinal preferences under the budget constraint, those choices satisfy the Strong Axiom. Houthakker's and Samuelson's articles showed that the choice-based approach and the preference-based approach to demand theory are substantially equivalent, and in this sense they brought to a conclusion the ordinal revolution initiated by Pareto in 1900.

4. Entering Cardinal Utility, 1900–1940

A lesser known part of the research on utility theory during the ordinal revolution concerns the progressive definition and stabilization of the current notion of cardinal utility as utility unique up to linear increasing transformations. In mathematical terms, a utility function $U(x)$ is called cardinal if it is unique up to a subset of the increasing transformations, namely, the linear increasing transformations. That is, if the utility function $U(x)$ represents the individual's preferences, any other utility function $U^*(x)$ obtained by multiplying $U(x)$ by a positive number α and then adding any number β, that is, a transformation $U^*(x) = \alpha U(x) + \beta$, with $\alpha > 0$, also represents the individual's preferences.

Cardinal utility is stronger than ordinal utility and weaker than the notion of unit-based measurable utility envisaged by the early utility theorists.[2] In particular, cardinal utility allows for rankings that are ruled out by ordinal utility, namely, the rankings of utility differences and marginal utilities. Accordingly, in a cardinal-utility framework it is possible to recover the notion of diminishing marginal utility used by the early utility theorists and dismissed by ordinalists. Cardinal utility nonetheless remains weaker than unit-based measurable utility, and in particular it does not allow for the assessment of utility ratios, that is, for judgments of the type, "The utility of x is six times greater than the utility of y."

The notion of cardinal utility was the eventual outcome of a long-lasting discussion regarding the possibility that individuals are not only able to rank combinations of goods but also capable of ranking transitions from one combination to another. The discussion was inaugurated by Pareto in the *Manual* (1906/1909/2014), continued through the 1920s, and accelerated after the publication of Hicks and Allen's 1934 article. In particular, the Polish-American economist Oskar Lange (1934) claimed that the capacity of individuals to rank transitions implies that the utility function representing their preferences is unique up to linear increasing transformations. Henry Phelps Brown (1934) of Oxford University showed that Lange's claim was unwarranted. The Austrian mathematician and economist Franz Alt (1936/1971) specified what assumptions should be added to the assumption that individuals are capable of ranking transitions in order to obtain a utility function unique up to linear increasing transformations. Finally, Samuelson (1938b) coupled the expression "cardinal utility," which had been previously used with other meanings, with utility unique up to positive linear transformations. Until the mid-1940s, however, cardinal utility remained peripheral in utility analysis.

5. The Rise and Stabilization of Expected Utility Theory, 1945–1955

In the decade following the end of World War II, the area of most intense research in utility theory was associated with the rise of expected utility theory as the dominant economic model of decision-making under risk (see also Stefánsson, Chapter 3).

Before 1945, early utility theorists and ordinalists had used utility theory mainly to explain decisions concerning riskless alternatives, such as decisions between consumption bundles available with certainty. Economists did have a theory for analyzing decision-making under risk, namely, the expected utility hypothesis advanced by Daniel Bernoulli (1738/1954) in the eighteenth century. According to this hypothesis, individuals prefer the risky prospect, for example, a lottery or a gamble, with the highest expected utility. The latter is given by the average of the utilities $u(x)$ of the possible outcomes of the prospect, each weighted by the probability that the outcome will occur. Thus, for example, the expected utility of a lottery yielding either outcome x_1 with probability p or outcome x_2 with probability $(1-p)$ is given by $u(x_1) \times p + u(x_2) \times (1-p)$.

In the nineteenth century, the expected utility hypothesis was adopted by some leading marginalists, such as Jevons and Marshall, but in the 1920s and 1930s it came under sustained criticism from various quarters. Among other things, critics argued that individuals evaluate risky alternatives by looking at the mean, the variance, and possibly other elements of the distribution of the uncertain outcomes rather than only the expected utility of the outcomes. By the late 1930s and early 1940s, the fortunes of expected utility theory were so low that in the two major economic treatises written in this period – Hicks's *Value and Capital* and Samuelson's *Foundations* – the theory is not even mentioned.

The fortunes of expected utility theory (EUT) began to recover in 1944, when Hungarian-American polymath John von Neumann and Austrian-American economist Oskar Morgenstern published their *Theory of Games and Economic Behavior* (1944/1953). In this book, von Neumann and Morgenstern made several seminal contributions to economic theory, and in particular they put forward an axiomatic version of EUT. They showed that if the preferences of the decision-maker between risky prospects satisfy certain axioms, then she will prefer the prospect with the highest expected utility. Expected utility is calculated by using a cardinal utility function – later called the von Neumann–Morgenstern utility function – whose existence is warranted by the axioms.

Beginning in the late 1940s and until the mid-1950s, the exact assumptions underlying EUT, the normative plausibility of these assumptions and henceforth of EUT, the descriptive power of the theory, and the nature of the von Neumann–Morgenstern cardinal utility function became the subject of intense debate in which all major utility theorists of the period took part. Among them were Milton Friedman, Leonard J. Savage, Jacob Marschak, Paul Samuelson, Kenneth Arrow, William Baumol, Robert Strotz, Armen Alchian, and Daniel Ellsberg in the United States and Maurice Allais, Edmond Malinvaud, Dennis Robertson, George Shackle, and Ragnar Frisch in Europe.

The outcomes of this debate can be summarized as follows. Marschak, Samuelson, Savage, and others made clear that von Neumann and Morgenstern's axiomatization of EUT contained an implicit but central assumption that Samuelson christened the "Independence Axiom" (Marschak 1948, 1950; Samuelson 1950b; Friedman and Savage 1952; Malinvaud 1952). Samuelson, Savage, Marschak, and other economists eventually came to see the Independence Axiom as a requisite for rational behavior in conditions of risk and, thus, as normatively compelling. Accordingly, they accepted EUT as a normative theory of rational behavior under risk, although they remained skeptical about its descriptive power (Marschak 1951/1974; Samuelson 1952; Savage 1954). Friedman, Strotz, Alchian, and others, instead, accepted EUT because they considered it a simple and descriptively valid theory (Friedman and Savage 1948; Friedman 1953; Strotz 1953; Alchian 1953).

At any rate, for one reason or another, by the early 1950s the majority of economists came to accept EUT. In that period and at least until the early 1960s, the main antagonist of EUT remained Allais, who rejected EUT on both the normative and the descriptive levels (Allais 1953). Part of Allais's argument against EUT was based on a choice situation, which later became known as the "Allais paradox," in which the majority of subjects made choices that violated EUT but were justifiable on plausible normative grounds.

Concerning the nature of the von Neumann–Morgenstern cardinal utility function $u(x)$, Friedman, Savage, Baumol, and Ellsberg eventually made it clear that it is not equivalent to the utility function $U(x)$ used by earlier utility theorists to analyze choices between riskless alternatives. More precisely, although the function $u(x)$ featured in the expected utility formula $u(x_1) \times p + u(x_2) \times (1-p)$ and the riskless utility function $U(x)$ orders alternatives in the same way, they need not be linear transformations of each other (Baumol 1951; Friedman and Savage 1952; Ellsberg 1954; Savage 1954; Baumol 1958). Accordingly, certain properties of the von Neumann–Morgenstern utility function $u(x)$, such as its concavity, cannot be interpreted as if they express concepts associated with the traditional utility function $U(x)$, such as diminishing marginal utility.

The fundamental reason why the two functions are not equivalent is that the von Neumann–Morgenstern function $u(x)$ is elicited from the individuals' preferences between risky prospects and therefore conflates all possible factors that may influence these preferences. That is, the von Neumann–Morgenstern function $u(x)$ reflects not only the utility of the outcomes, which is captured by the traditional utility function $U(x)$, but also the individual's attitude toward risk, the way she may subjectively distort the objective probabilities of the outcomes, the pleasure or displeasure she may associate with the very act of gambling, and possibly other factors that affect her preferences between risky prospects.

The debate on the nature of the von Neumann–Morgenstern utility function $u(x)$ had an important side effect: it led Friedman, Savage, Strotz, Alchian, and Ellsberg to elaborate a conception of utility measurement that definitely liberated it from any association with units and ratios (Friedman and Savage 1952; Strotz 1953; Alchian 1953; Ellsberg 1954; Savage 1954; Friedman 1955). According to this novel view of measurement, to measure utility requires the assignment of numbers to objects – be they riskless commodity bundles, lotteries, or the uncertain outcomes of lotteries – by following a definite set of operations. These numbers are called utility numbers or, more briefly, utilities. The way of assigning numbers to objects is largely arbitrary and conventional. The essential restriction is that the assigned utility numbers should allow the economist to predict the choice behavior of individuals. In particular, the numbers that the von Neumann–Morgenstern utility function $u(x)$ assigns to the outcomes of risky prospects are valid insofar as they allow the economist to predict which risky prospect the individual will choose.

Within the conventionalist and prediction-oriented view of utility measurement advocated by Friedman and others, the contrast between ordinal and cardinal utility fades away. From this perspective, in fact, it is no longer the case that utility is intrinsically cardinal or intrinsically (just) ordinal. Rather, ordinal and cardinal utility indicate two equally legitimate ways of assigning numbers to the objects of choice. Accordingly, in areas of economic analysis where ordinal utility suffices to obtain valuable results, such as demand analysis and general equilibrium theory, only ordinal utility is needed. In other areas of economic analysis, such as the theory of choice under uncertainty, where manageable models and valuable results need cardinal utility, it can be legitimately adopted.

The view of utility measurement advocated by Friedman and others quickly became standard among mainstream utility theorists (see Chao, Chapter 13). Its success goes far toward explaining the flourishing of models of individual behavior based on cardinal utility (see, e.g., Luce 1956; Debreu 1958; Koopmans 1960) and the peaceful cohabitation of cardinal and ordinal utility within utility analysis that began in the mid-1950s and has continued to the present day.

6. Utility Theory Goes Experimental, 1950–1980

As mentioned in Section 3, Pareto imagined an experiment to empirically identify indifference curves, but he never attempted to actually perform it. In the early 1930s, the American psychologist Louis Leon Thurstone conducted a laboratory experiment to elicit the indifference curves of a real individual (Thurstone 1931). However, most commentators of the 1930s and early 1940s judged the assumptions underlying Thurstone's experiment to be highly problematic and therefore remained skeptical about its significance.

It was only in the 1950s that experimental methods began playing a significant role in utility theory, when a number of researchers based in the United States attempted to test the descriptive validity of EUT in controlled laboratory settings. The trajectory of the experimental research on EUT during the period 1950–1985 may be characterized as "from confidence to skepticism."

Friedrich Mosteller and Philip Nogee (1951), Donald Davidson, Patrick Suppes, and Sidney Siegel (1957), and the other experimenters of the 1950s were confident about EUT and designed their experiments so as to neutralize some psychological factors that could jeopardize the validity of the theory. Accordingly, they tended to conclude that their experimental findings supported the descriptive validity of EUT.

The experimenters of the early 1960s, such as Gordon Becker, Morris DeGroot, and Jacob Marschak (1964), also interpreted their experimental findings as validating EUT: the theory was not

100 percent correct, but it still appeared to be an acceptable descriptive theory of decision-making under risk. Also in terms of comparative goodness of fit, EUT seemed to perform better than alternative decision models such as the maximin model, according to which individuals prefer the risky prospect with the highest minimum payoff.

Beginning in the mid-1960s, the validity of EUT was increasingly called into question. In 1961, Ellsberg had envisaged another choice situation in which, just as in the Allais paradox, the majority of subjects make choices that violate EUT, but this can be justified on plausible normative grounds (Ellsberg 1961). Until the mid-1960s, however, the Allais and Ellsberg paradoxes had a negligible impact on decision theory. One reason for this lack of impact was that, until that moment, the two paradoxes remained thought experiments without any laboratory confirmation.

Beginning in the mid-1960s, actual laboratory experiments confirmed the frequency of the choice patterns imagined by Allais and Ellsberg, while the psychological phenomena that could explain these patterns began to be investigated in a systematic way (see, e.g., Becker and Brownson 1964; Fellner 1965; Morrison 1967; MacCrimmon 1968). Between the late 1960s and the early 1970s, other decision patterns violating EUT were highlighted by a group of young psychologists based at the University of Michigan: Sarah Lichtenstein, Paul Slovic, and Amos Tversky (Slovic and Lichtenstein 1968; Tversky 1969; Lichtenstein and Slovic 1971). Beginning in the mid-1970s, a number of alternative theories to EUT, such as Jagdish Handa's certainty equivalence model (1977), Karmarkar's subjectively weighted utility model (1978), and Daniel Kahneman and Amos Tversky's prospect theory (1979), were put forward to explain such decision patterns. The new decision theories, in turn, suggested further decision patterns that violate EUT and led to new experiments to test these possible violations. This research was the beginning of what later came to be called behavioral economics (see Lecouteux, Chapter 4).

7. Utility Within Behavioral Economics, 1980–Present

The blossoming of alternative theories to EUT that began in the mid-1970s has continued to the present (see also Lecouteux, Chapter 4). Some notable non-EUT models that have been advanced in the last 40 years are the rank-dependent utility theory (Quiggin 1982; Yaari 1987), Choquet expected utility theory (Schmeidler 1989), maxmin expected utility theory (Gilboa and Schmeidler 1989), cumulative prospect theory (Tversky and Kahneman 1992), and the smooth model of ambiguity aversion (Klibanoff, Marinacci, and Mukerji 2005). Without entering into the specific features of these theories (see Gilboa 2009 for a comprehensive review) here, three general comments on the post-1980 research on the theory of decision-making under uncertainty are in order.

First, today EUT still remains the primary model in numerous areas of economics dealing with risky decisions, such as finance, the theory of asymmetric information, and game theory. EUT's resilience seems very much due to its simplicity and adaptability, as well as to the fact that none of the alternative theories has yet achieved among economists the level of consensus that EUT once enjoyed.

Second, the large majority of non-EUT models are still based on the utility notion, or some slightly modified version of it, and on the idea that individuals choose the alternative corresponding to the maximum utility. For instance, in the rank-dependent model, the utility of a lottery yielding either outcome x_1 with probability p or outcome x_2 with probability $(1-p)$ is given by $u(x_1)\times w(p)+u(x_2)\times[1-w(p)]$, where the function $w(p)$ is a weighting function that captures the subjective distortions of objective probability p. The theory states that, if the preferences of the decision-maker between risky prospects satisfy certain axioms, then she will prefer the prospect with the maximum rank-dependent utility $u(x_1)\times w(p)+u(x_2)\times[1-w(p)]$.

Third, non-EUT models typically attempt to unpack the diverse factors that influence the individual's preferences between risky prospects and that, in EUT, are all conflated into the von

Neumann–Morgenstern utility function $u(x)$. For instance, as we have seen, the rank-dependent model explicitly separates the utility of outcomes from the subjective distortion of the objective probabilities. The problem with the unpacking of the von Neumann–Morgenstern utility function and, more generally, with the opening of the black box that the utility notion has become since Marshall, Fisher, and Pareto is that there are many different ways of doing the unpacking. That is, different non-EUT models focus on different factors that may influence the individual's preferences between risky prospects, such as loss aversion, ambiguity aversion, the existence of a reference point for utility, or the subjective distortion of objective probabilities, which, in turn, can be modeled in different ways. It is fair to say that there is still considerable debate about exactly what these influencing factors are and about whether and how their respective impact varies over different choice situations. This ongoing debate is one of the reasons why no single theory of decision-making under uncertainty has yet replaced EUT as the new paradigm in economics.

The characteristics of the post-1980 research in the theory of decision-making under uncertainty are similar to those recognizable in other areas of behavioral research about decision-making. For instance, in the theory of intertemporal choice, the standard model was the so-called discounted-utility (DU) model introduced by Samuelson (1937) and axiomatized by Tjalling Koopmans (1960). According to this model, in facing alternative streams of monetary payments from the present time $t = 0$ until a future time $t = T$, the individual behaves so as to maximize the discounted sum of the future utilities of the payments, that is, so as to maximize the function $\sum_{t=0}^{T} \delta^t U(x_t)$, whereby δ is a subjective discount factor that is constant over time and captures how much the individual evaluates future utility. The higher δ, the more the individual evaluates future utility and is therefore willing to defer present consumption in favor of future consumption.

Beginning in the 1980s, Richard Thaler (1981), George Loewenstein (1987), and other behavioral economists began to call attention to frequently observed decision patterns that violate the DU model and to advance a variety of alternative models of intertemporal choice that could account for those violations (see Frederick, Loewenstein, and O'Donoghue 2002 and Cohen et al. 2020 for reviews of this literature). As in the case of non-EUT models, non-DU models are still based on the utility notion and the idea that individuals maximize utility. Moreover, non-DU models also attempt to unpack the diverse factors that may influence the individual's intertemporal decisions and that in the DU model are all conflated in the utility function $u(x)$ and the discount factor δ. Finally, different non-DU models point to different factors that may influence intertemporal preferences, such as the changing of the discount factor δ over time, or the utility individuals derive from the anticipation of future consumption. However, there is as yet no consensus about what these factors are or about whether their respective impact varies over different choice situations.

8. Conclusions

The notion of utility took center stage in economic analysis with the marginal revolution of the 1870s. As reviewed in this chapter, over the last 150 years that notion has survived a number of transformations in economics, such as the ordinal revolution or the rise of behavioral economics.

The resilience of the utility notion seems in part due to its flexibility. As we have seen, between 1870 and 1900 the utility notion lost its initial, narrow identification with the notions of pleasure or need to become an all-encompassing concept capable of capturing any possible motivation to human action. This broad notion of utility dominated economics until at least the 1980s, when a need to unpack and tell apart the diverse psychological factors that influence human behavior reemerged in the discipline (see Grayot, Chapter 6). At any rate, through all the transformations it has undergone, the notion of utility remains a cornerstone of much economic theory, and economists still explain prices, individual behavior, market equilibria, and other relevant economic phenomena by referring to it.

Acknowledgments

Some portions of this chapter draw on Moscati (2018). Other reconstructions of the history of utility theory or part of it can be found in Stigler (1950), Howey (1960), Chipman (1976), Fishburn (1989), Mandler (1999), Giocoli (2003), Hands (2006), Heukelom (2014), and Mongin (2019).

Related Chapters

Chao, Chapter 13 "Representation"
Grayot, Chapter 6 "Economic Agency and the Subpersonal Turn in Economics"
Stefánsson, Chapter 3 "The Economics and Philosophy of Risk"
Lecouteux, Chapter 4 "Behavioral Welfare Economics and Consumer Sovereignty"
Vredenburgh, this volume, Chapter 5 "The Economic Concept of a Preference"
Vromen, Chapter 9 "*As If* Social Preference Models"

Notes

1 To see why, consider the following numerical example. An individual prefers three apples to two apples and prefers two apples to one apple. The utility index $U(x)$ representing these preferences should then satisfy the following property: $U(3) > U(2) > U(1)$. For instance, it could be that $U(3) = 6$, $U(2) = 5$, and $U(1) = 3$. In this case, the marginal utility (MU) of the apples is diminishing: $MU(1) = 3 - 0 = 3$, $MU(2) = 5 - 3 = 2$, and $MU(3) = 6 - 5 = 1$. But $U(x)$ is unique up to any monotonic increasing transformation, so that, for instance, $U^* = U^4$ also represents the individual's preferences regarding apples: $U^*(1) = 81$, $U^*(2) = 625$, and $U^*(3) = 1{,}296$, and in fact $U^*(3) > U^*(2) > U^*(1)$. However, the marginal utility of the apples is now increasing: $MU^*(1) = 81 - 0 = 81$, $MU^*(2) = 625 - 81 = 544$, and $MU^*(3) = 1{,}296 - 625 = 671$.

2 Unit-based measurable utility is unique only up to a subset of the linear increasing transformations, namely, the proportional transformations: another utility function $U^*(x)$ obtained by multiplying $U(x)$ by a positive number α, that is, a transformation $U^*(x) = \alpha U(x)$, with $\alpha > 0$, also represents the individual's preferences.

Bibliography

Alchian, A. (1953) "The Meaning of Utility Measurement," *American Economic Review* 43: 26–50.
Allais, M. (1953) "Le comportement de l'homme rationnel devant le risque: Critique des postulats et axiomes de l'école americaine," *Econometrica* 21: 503–546.
Allen, R.G.D. (1936) "Professor Slutsky's Theory of Consumer's Choice," *Review of Economic Studies* 3: 120–129.
Alt, F. (1936/1971) "On the Measurability of Utility," in J.S. Chipman and others (eds.) *Preferences, Utility, and Demand*, 424–431, New York: Harcourt Brace Jovanovich.
Baumol, W.J. (1951) "The Neumann – Morgenstern Utility Index – An Ordinalist View," *Journal of Political Economy* 59: 61–66.
Baumol, W.J. (1958) "The Cardinal Utility Which Is Ordinal," *Economic Journal* 68: 665–672.
Becker, G.M., DeGroot, M.H. and J. Marschak (1964) "Measuring Utility by a Single Response Sequential Method," *Behavioral Science* 9: 226–232.
Becker, S.W., and Brownson, F.O. (1964) "What Price Ambiguity? Or the Role of Ambiguity in Decision-Making," *Journal of Political Economy* 72: 62–73.

Bernoulli, D. (1738/1954) "Exposition of a New Theory on the Measurement of Risk," *Econometrica* 22: 23–36.
Böhm-Bawerk, E. von (1889/1891) *Capital and Interest: The Positive Theory of Capital*, Vol. 1, London: Macmillan.
Cairnes, J.E. (1872/1981) "New Theories in Political Economy," in R.D.C. Black (ed.) *Papers and Correspondence of William Stanley Jevons*, Vols. 7, 146–152, London: Macmillan.
Chipman, J.S. (1976) "The Paretian Heritage," *Revue Européenne des Sciences Sociales* 14: 65–173.
Cohen, J., Ericson, K.M., Laibson, D. and White, J.M. (2020) "Measuring Time Preferences," *Journal of Economic Literature* 58: 299–347.
Davidson, D., Suppes, P. and Siegel, S. (1957) *Decision Making: An Experimental Approach*, Stanford: Stanford University Press.
Debreu, G. (1958) "Stochastic Choice and Cardinal Utility," *Econometrica* 26: 440–444.
Edgeworth, F.Y. (1881) *Mathematical Psychics*, London: Kegan Paul.
Ellsberg, D. (1954) "Classic and Current Notions of 'Measurable Utility'," *Economic Journal* 64: 528–556.
Ellsberg, D. (1961) "Risk, Ambiguity, and the Savage Axioms," *Quarterly Journal of Economics* 75: 643–669.
Fellner, W. (1965) *Probability and Profit*, Homewood: Irwin.
Fishburn, P.C. (1989) "Retrospective on the Utility Theory of von Neumann and Morgenstern," *Journal of Risk and Uncertainty* 2: 127–158.
Fisher, I. (1892) *Mathematical Investigations in the Theory of Value and Prices*, New Haven: Yale University Press.
Frederick, S., Loewenstein, G. and O'Donoghue, T. (2002) "Time Discounting and Time Preference: A Critical Review," *Journal of Economic Literature* 40: 351–401.
Friedman, M. (1953) "Choice, Chance, and the Personal Distribution of Income," *Journal of Political Economy* 61: 277–290.
Friedman, M. (1955) "What All Is Utility?" *Economic Journal* 65: 405–409.
Friedman, M. and Savage, L.J. (1948) "The Utility Analysis of Choices Involving Risk," *Journal of Political Economy* 56: 279–304.
Friedman, M. and Savage, L.J. (1952) "The Expected-Utility Hypothesis and the Measurability of Utility," *Journal of Political Economy* 60: 463–474.
Gilboa, I. (2009) *Theory of Decision under Uncertainty*, Cambridge: Cambridge University Press.
Gilboa, I. and Schmeidler, D. (1989) "Maxmin Expected Utility with Non-Unique Prior," *Journal of Mathematical Economics* 18: 141–153.
Giocoli, N. (2003) *Modeling Rational Agents*, Cheltenham: Elgar.
Handa, J. (1977) "Risk, Probabilities, and a New Theory of Cardinal Utility," *Journal of Political Economy* 85: 97–122.
Hands, D.W. (2006) "Integrability, Rationalizability, and Path-Dependency in the History of Demand Theory," *History of Political Economy* 38: 153–185.
Heukelom, F. (2014) *Behavioral Economics: A History*, New York: Cambridge University Press.
Hicks, J.R. (1939) *Value and Capital*, Oxford: Clarendon Press.
Hicks, J.R. and Allen, R.G.D. (1934) "A Reconsideration of the Theory of Value," *Economica* 1: 52–76, 196–219.
Houthakker, H.S. (1950) "Revealed Preference and the Utility Function," *Economica* 17: 159–174.
Howey, R.S. (1960) *The Rise of the Marginal Utility School, 1870–1889*, Lawrence: University of Kansas Press.
Ingram, J.K. (1888) *A History of Political Economy*, Edinburgh: Black.
Jevons, W.S. (1871) *The Theory of Political Economy*, London: Macmillan.
Kahneman, D. and Tversky, A. (1979) "Prospect Theory: An Analysis of Decision under Risk," *Econometrica* 47: 263–292.
Karmarkar, U.S. (1978) "Subjectively Weighted Utility: A Descriptive Extension of the Expected Utility Model," *Organizational Behavior and Human Performance* 21: 61–72.
Klibanoff, P., Marinacci, M. and Mukerji, S. (2005) "A Smooth Model of Decision Making under Ambiguity," *Econometrica* 73: 1849–1892.
Koopmans, T.C. (1960) "Stationary Ordinal Utility and Impatience," *Econometrica* 28: 287–309.
Lange, O. (1934) "The Determinateness of the Utility Function," *Review of Economic Studies* 1: 218–225.
Levasseur, P.E. (1874/1987) "Compte – Rendus des séances et travaux de l'Académie des sciences morales et politiques," in A. Walras and L. Walras (eds.) *Oeuvres économiques complètes: L. Walras, Mélanges d'économie politique et sociale*, Vol. 7, 529–532, Paris: Economica.
Lichtenstein, S. and Slovic, P. (1971) "Reversals of Preference between Bids and Choices in Gambling Decisions," *Journal of Experimental Psychology* 89: 46–55.
Loewenstein, G. (1987) "Anticipation and the Valuation of Delayed Consumption," *Economic Journal* 97: 666–684.
Luce, R.D. (1956) "Semiorders and a Theory of Utility Discrimination," *Econometrica* 24: 178–191.

MacCrimmon, K.R. (1968) "Descriptive and Normative Implications of the Decision-Theory Postulates," in K. Borch and J. Mossin (eds.) *Risk and Uncertainty*, 3–32, London: Macmillan.
Malinvaud, E. (1952) "Note on Von Neumann – Morgenstern's Strong Independence Axiom," *Econometrica* 20: 679.
Mandler, M. (1999) *Dilemmas in Economic Theory*, New York: Oxford University Press.
Marschak, J. (1948) "Measurable Utility and the Theory of Assets," Cowles Commission for Research in Economics, Economics Discussion Paper 226.
Marschak, J. (1950) "Rational Behavior, Uncertain Prospects, and Measurable Utility," *Econometrica* 18: 111–141.
Marschak, J. (1951/1974) "Why 'Should' Statisticians and Businessmen Maximize Moral Expectation?" in J. Marschak (ed.) *Economic Information, Decision, and Prediction: Selected Essays*, Vol. 1, 40–58, Dordrecht: Reidel.
Marshall, A. (1890) *Principles of Economics*, London: Macmillan.
Marx, K. (1867/1990) *Capital: A Critique of Political Economy*, Vol. 1, London: Penguin.
Menger, C. (1871/1981) *Principles of Economics*, New York: New York University Press.
Mill, J.S. (1848/1871) *Principles of Political Economy*, 7th ed., London: Longmans, Green.
Mongin, P. (2019) "The Allais Paradox: What It Became, What It Really Was, What It Now Suggests to Us," *Economics and Philosophy* 35: 423–459.
Morrison, D.G. (1967) "On the Consistency of Preferences in Allais' Paradox," *Behavioral Science* 12: 373–383.
Moscati, I. (2018) *Measuring Utility: From the Marginal Revolution to Behavioral Economics*, New York: Oxford University Press.
Mosteller, F. and Nogee, P. (1951) "An Experimental Measurement of Utility," *Journal of Political Economy* 59: 371–404.
Pareto, V. (1900/2008) "Summary of Some Chapters of a New Treatise on Pure Economics by Professor Pareto," *Giornale degli Economisti* 67: 453–504.
Pareto, V. (1906/1909/2014) *Manual of Political Economy: A Critical and Variorum Edition*, A. Montesano and others (eds.), New York: Oxford University Press.
Pareto, V. (1911/1955) "Mathematical Economics," *International Economic Papers* 5: 58–102.
Phelps Brown, E.H. (1934) "Notes on the Determinateness of the Utility Function, I," *Review of Economic Studies* 2: 66–69.
Quiggin, J. (1982) "A Theory of Anticipated Utility," *Journal of Economic Behavior and Organization* 3: 323–343.
Ricardo, D. (1821/1951) *On the Principles of Political Economy and Taxation*, Cambridge: Cambridge University Press.
Samuelson, P.A. (1937) "A Note on Measurement of Utility," *Review of Economic Studies* 4: 155–161.
Samuelson, P.A. (1938a) "A Note on the Pure Theory of Consumer's Behaviour," *Economica* 5: 61–71, 353–354.
Samuelson, P.A. (1938b) "The Numerical Representation of Ordered Classifications and the Concept of Utility," *Review of Economic Studies* 6: 65–70.
Samuelson, P.A. (1947) *Foundations of Economic Analysis*, Cambridge, MA: Harvard University Press.
Samuelson, P.A. (1948) "Consumption Theory in Terms of Revealed Preference," *Economica* 15: 243–253.
Samuelson, P.A. (1950a) "The Problem of Integrability in Utility Theory," *Economica* 17: 355–385.
Samuelson, P.A. (1950b) "Probability and the Attempts to Measure Utility," *Economic Review* 1: 167–173.
Samuelson, P.A. (1952) "Probability, Utility, and the Independence Axiom," *Econometrica* 20: 670–678.
Savage, L.J. (1954) *The Foundations of Statistics*, New York: Wiley.
Schmeidler, D. (1989) "Subjective Probability and Expected Utility without Additivity," *Econometrica* 57: 571–587.
Slovic, P. and Lichtenstein, S. (1968) "The Relative Importance of Probabilities and Payoffs in Risk Taking," *Journal of Experimental Psychology* 78: 1–18.
Slutsky, E. (1915/1952) "On the Theory of the Budget of the Consumer," in G.J. Stigler and K.E. Boulding (eds.) *Readings in Price Theory*, 27–56, Homewood: Irwin.
Smith, A. (1776/1976) *An Inquiry into the Nature and Causes of the Wealth of Nations*, Oxford: Oxford University Press.
Stigler, G.J. (1950) "The Development of Utility Theory," *Journal of Political Economy* 58: 307–327, 373–396.
Strotz, R.H. (1953) "Cardinal Utility," *American Economic Review, Papers and Proceedings* 43: 384–397.
Thaler, R. (1981) "Some Empirical Evidence on Dynamic Inconsistency," *Economics Letters* 8: 201–207.
Thurstone, L.L. (1931) "The Indifference Function," *Journal of Social Psychology* 2: 139–167.
Tversky, A. (1969) "Intransitivity of Preferences," *Psychological Review* 76: 31–48.
Tversky, A. and Kahneman, D. (1992) "Advances in Prospect Theory: Cumulative Representation of Uncertainty," *Journal of Risk and Uncertainty* 5: 297–323.
Veblen, T. (1898) "Why Is Economics Not an Evolutionary Science?" *Quarterly Journal of Economics* 12: 373–397.

Von Neumann, J. and Morgenstern, O. (1944/1953) *Theory of Games and Economic Behavior*, Princeton: Princeton University Press.

Von Schmoller, G. (1883) "Zur Methodologie der Staats und Sozialwissenschaften," *Jahrbuch für Gesetzgebung, Verwaltung und Volkswirtschaft im deutschen Reich* 8: 974–994.

Walras, L. (1874/1954) *Elements of Pure Economics*, London: Allen and Unwin.

Yaari, M.E. (1987) "The Dual Theory of Choice under Risk," *Econometrica* 55: 95–115.

3

THE ECONOMICS AND PHILOSOPHY OF RISK

H. Orri Stefánsson

1. Introduction

Decisions often have to be made without knowing for sure which outcome will result from one's choice. When deciding between taking the train or driving to work, for instance, one may be unsure about several factors that could determine the outcome of these choices, such as whether the train will be on time and whether an accident will cause congestion on the road. Similarly, important economic decisions, such as choosing between pension plans, have to be made with imperfect knowledge of crucial factors, for instance, how long one will live and the actual returns of the different pension plans. A common way to put this is that decisions such as these are not made in situations of *certainty*.

Decisions that are not made in situations of certainty differ widely in terms of how much or little the decisionmaker knows. The extent of a decisionmaker's knowledge, in a particular situation, can be usefully characterized with reference to the elements of the decisionmaker's *decisionproblem*. A decisionproblem, as I shall be using the term, consists of two or more *options*, a set of *outcomes* that each of these options could result in, and a set of *states of the world* (or simply states) that determines which outcome results from each option. In the preceding transport decisionproblem, for instance, the options include driving and taking the train, the states include facts about how well the trains run and how much traffic there is on the road, and the outcomes include arriving on time and arriving late.

If the decisionmaker is fortunate enough to know which state obtains, then her decision is made in a situation of certainty. When she does not know which state obtains, we can nevertheless draw important distinctions depending on how much the decisionmaker does know about the states of the world. Sometimes, for instance, a decisionmaker knows – or at least "deems suitable to act as if" she knew (Luce and Raiffa 1989/1957: 277) – the *probabilities* of the different states of the world. A game of roulette would typically be treated as a situation where the gambler knows the probabilities of the relevant states and, by implication, the probabilities of the possible outcomes of choosing each option. For instance, a player of European roulette knows that there is a probability of 1/37 that the ball ends up in the pocket numbered 5 (state); hence, she knows that if she chooses to bet on number 5 (option), then there is a 1/37 probability that she will win (outcome). Following Knight (1921), economic theorists typically use the term "risk" for such choices, and they say that the roulette gambler is making a decision *under risk*.

DOI: 10.4324/9781315739793-4

In contrast, when betting on a soccer match, one does not know all the relevant probabilities. The outcome of the match may, for instance, depend on whether the hotheaded midfielder of the home team gets a red card, whether the star striker of the away team gets injured, and so on. But the probability that the midfielder gets a red card is hard to know. We might know that so far she has received a red card in 10% of all games she has played, but we do not know whether her mood on the day in question will be better or worse than normal. And it might be even less plausible to say that we can know the probability with which the star striker gets injured on the day in question. We might, however, know all the states of the world that could determine which of the (say, three) outcomes (home team wins, away team wins, draw) obtains. In that case, economic theorists, again following Knight (1921), would use the term "uncertainty"; and they would say that the bettor is making a decision *under uncertainty* (but not under risk).

In some decisionproblems, a decisionmaker's lack of knowledge is more severe than in either of the two preceding examples. In particular, sometimes a decisionmaker might not even know all of the states of the world that could determine the outcome of her decision, and/or she might not be aware of all the possible outcomes that could result from her decision. When we evaluate the option of implementing solar geoengineering as a response to the climate crisis, for instance, there are plausibly important states of the world and potential outcomes that we have not yet considered. More generally, when considering new technologies and radical policies, we may suspect – for example, on the basis of past experience of similar decisions – that there are important contingencies that we cannot yet articulate. In addition, one might often not even know about all the available options; for instance, presumably there are some options for responding to the climate crisis that nobody has yet considered. Decisions where an agent lacks knowledge of some of the possible states, outcomes, or options are said to be made in a situation of "unawareness" [for recent reviews of this literature, see, for example, Schipper (2015) and Steele and Stefánsson (2021)].

This chapter will be almost exclusively concerned with how economic theorists (in particular, socalled "neoclassical" or "orthodox" economic theorists) treat risk as previously defined. I shall start, in the next section, by outlining the theory that neoclassical economists use to predict, explain, and guide choices in situations of risk. In Section 3, I discuss some of the main challenges, both empirical and philosophical, to this orthodox treatment of risk. In Section 4, I briefly discuss how neoclassical economists tend to approach decisionmaking under uncertainty and an important challenge faced by this approach. Section 5 concludes the chapter.

2. Risk in Economic Theory

Recall that a decision under risk is one where the relevant decisionmaker knows, or acts as if she knows, the probabilities with which the available options deliver the possible outcomes. This is often described as decisionmaking with *objective* probabilities. But that terminology may be misleading. For instance, if we assume that the behavior of roulette wheels is deterministic, the most commonsensical account of objective probabilities[1] is arguably that the ball has a probability of 0 of ending up in any pocket except one, namely, the one that it will actually end up in, for which the probability is 1.

Nevertheless, to bet on a roulette wheel is an archetypical example of decisionmaking under risk in economic theory, where the decisionmaker is modeled as acting on the basis of knowledge of a nontrivial probability distribution, where "nontrivial" means that more than one outcome is assigned a positive probability. Hence, I shall use the term "known probabilities" rather than "objective probabilities" when describing decisionmaking under risk.

Now, my preferred terminology might be misleading too, because some might not find it appropriate to describe the roulette gambler as "knowing" the probabilities of the various outcomes. For instance, the epistemic skeptic might complain that, given my terminology, nobody ever makes decisions under risk, while the determinist could argue that, because one can only know that which is true, decisions under risk only involve trivial probabilities. So, the reader should keep in mind that when I speak of known probabilities, what I really mean is that the decisionmaker finds it suitable to act as if she knows the relevant probabilities (Luce & Raiffa 1989/1957, Ibid.).

It is also worth noting that a decisionmaker may quite reasonably find it suitable to act as if she knows the relevant probabilities even when these are in fact not knowable. For instance, suppose that a patient is considering undergoing a surgery and learns that one million patients "like her," in the physiologically relevant sense, have undergone the surgery and that it has been successful in 99% of these cases. Or, suppose instead that a person is considering investing in government bonds and finds that all experts agree that there is at least a 90% chance that the bonds will yield a return of at least 5%. In these cases, the *true* probabilities in question may not be knowable – for instance, perhaps the true probability with which a particular patient will have a successful surgery cannot be known. Nevertheless, it would seem reasonable for these decisionmakers to act *as if they know* the relevant probabilities: in the first case, that there is a 99% chance that the surgery will be a success, and in the second case, that there is at least a 90% chance that the bonds will yield a return of at least 5%. So, I will treat examples like these as decisionmaking under risk.

The orthodox (neoclassical) approach in economics when it comes to explaining, predicting, and guiding decisionmaking under risk is a theory that is often called *objective* expected utility theory. "Objective" here refers to the probabilities assumed by the theory, rather than the utility. In what follows, I shall simply call the theory in question "expected utility theory," but later I shall consider *subjective* expected utility theory (where the probabilities are subjective).

Informally, expected utility theory says that the value of a risky option equals the option's *expectation* of utility, where "utility" is a measure of the desirability of the option's potential outcomes, and the expectation is calculated by multiplying each outcome's utility by its probability and then adding up all of these probabilityweighted utilities. To state this more precisely, we need to introduce some formal definitions and notation.

2.1 The vNM Theory

Let L_i be a "lottery" from the set **L** of lotteries and O_k the outcome, or "prize," of lottery L_i that arises with probability p_{ik} (where, of course, $\Sigma_j p_{ij} = 1$). It is important to stress that the term "lottery" is a technical one; informally, it can be any risky option, that is, an option that could result in different outcomes, for which the decisionmaker of interest knows (or acts as if she knows) the probabilities. The representation result that I discuss next requires the set **L** of lotteries to be rather extensive: it is closed under "probability mixture," which means that if $L_i, L_j \in \mathbf{L}$, then compound lotteries that have L_i and L_j as possible outcomes are also in **L**. The expected utility of L_i is defined as

vNM expected utility equation. $EU(L_i) = \Sigma_k u(O_k) \cdot p_{ik}$

According to expected utility theory, a rational preference between lotteries corresponds to the lottery's expected utilities, in the sense that one lottery is preferred over another just in case the one offers a higher expectation of utility than the other. When this relationship between preference and expected utility holds, we say that the preference can be *represented as maximizing expected utility*. (Why only "represented as"? Because the utility is simply a way of numerically describing the preference; no claim is made about utility corresponding to anything that the agent recognizes. We shall get back to this issue soon.)

To state more formally the aforementioned relationship between rational preference and expected utility, we need some additional notation. Let $\precsim$ denote a *weak* preference relation. So $A \precsim B$ means that the agent we are interested in considers option B to be at least as preferable as option A. From the weak preference relation, we can define the *strict* preference relation, $\prec$, as follows: $A \prec B =_{\text{def}}$

$A \precsim B$ and $\neg(B \precsim A)$, where $\neg X$ means "it is not the case that X." So, $A \prec B$ means that the agent prefers B to A. Finally, indifference, $\sim$, is defined as $A \sim B =_{\text{def}} A \precsim B$ and $B \precsim A$. This means that the agent we are interested in considers A and B to be equally preferable.

Economists and decision theorists generally take there to be a close conceptual connection between preference and choice. Least controversially, a rational person who prefers B to A has a tendency to choose B over A, if given the option. More controversially, some economists have wanted to *define* preference (or "revealed preference"; Samuelson 1938, 1948) in terms of choice; to prefer B over A *means* having a tendency to choose B over A. How closely to tie preference to choice is an issue that we will have reason to revisit.

We say that there is an expected utility function that represents the agent's preference $\precsim$ between lotteries in **L** just in case there is a utility function u and a probability function p such that for any $L_i, L_j \in \mathbf{L}$:

$$L_i \precsim L_j \Leftrightarrow EU(L_i) = \sum_k u(O_k) \cdot p_{ik} \leq EU(L_j) = \sum_k u(O_k) \cdot p_{jk}$$

Economists are, at least by tradition, skeptical of claims about people's attitudes that cannot, in principle at least, be reframed as claims about choice behavior.[2] Fortunately, claims about preferences can, at least in theory, be reframed as claims about (hypothetical) choice behavior, assuming that people generally (or at least rationally) choose what they prefer. Hence, it is no wonder that economists were impressed when von Neumann and Morgenstern (vNM) demonstrated that claims about utilities – for instance, the claim that a person maximizes expected utility – can be reformulated as claims about a person's preferences between lotteries.[3] In particular, vNM proved that if a person's preferences between lotteries satisfy a number of constraints, or *axioms*, then she can be represented as maximizing expected utility.

The following notation will be used to introduce the vNM axioms[4] of preference: $\{pA, (1-p)B\}$ denotes a lottery that results in either A, with probability p, or B, with probability $1-p$. $p \in [0, 1]$ means that p takes a value between 0 and 1 (inclusive) whereas $p \in (0, 1)$ means that p takes a value strictly between 0 and 1 (so, excluding 0 and 1). Note that the set **L** of lotteries contains "trivial" lotteries – that is, lotteries with only trivial probabilities – in addition to nontrivial ones. Because the "expected" utility of a trivial lottery equals, by the expected utility equation, the utility of the only outcome that it might result in, it follows, from a theorem we are about to state, that because these axioms hold for any lottery, they also hold for any outcome. The set of all possible outcomes is denoted **O**.

Axiom 1 (Completeness). For any $L_i, L_j \in \mathbf{L}$, either $L_i \precsim L_j$ or $L_j \precsim L_i$

Axiom 2 (Transitivity). For any $L_i, L_j, L_k \in \mathbf{L}$, if $L_i \precsim L_j$ and $L_j \precsim L_k$ then $L_i \precsim L_k$

Axiom 3 (Continuity). For any $L_i, L_j, L_k \in \mathbf{L}$, if $L_i \prec L_j \prec L_k$ then there is a $p \in (0, 1)$ such that

$$\{pL_i, (1-p)L_k\} \sim L_j$$

Axiom 4 (Independence). For any $L_i, L_j \in \mathbf{L}$, if $L_i \precsim L_j$ then for any $L_k \in \mathbf{L}$, and any $p \in [0, 1]$:

$$\{pL_i, (1-p)L_k\} \precsim \{pL_j, (1-p)L_k\}$$

Axiom 5 (Reduction of compound lotteries). For any $L_i, L_j \in \mathbf{L}$, if for any $O_k \in \mathbf{O}$, $p_{ik} = p_{jk}$, then $L_i \sim L_j$

The Completeness axiom says that an agent can compare, in terms of the weak preference relation, all pairs of options (i.e., lotteries) in **L** and, by implication, all outcomes in **O**. Whether or not completeness is a plausible rationality constraint depends, for instance, on what sort of options are under consideration and how we interpret preferences over these options. If **O** includes all kinds of outcomes – for example, curing cancer and eradicating poverty – then completeness is not immediately compelling. If, on the other hand, all options in the set are quite similar to each other, say, all options are pension plans, then completeness is more compelling.

The plausibility of completeness also depends on how closely we tie the interpretation of preference to *actual* choices, that is, choices that a person is actually faced with. As Gilboa (2009) notes, after having defined completeness as a property of a weak preference relation,

> If we take a descriptive interpretation, completeness is almost a matter of definition: the choice that we observe is defined to be the preferred one. Taking a normative interpretation, the completeness axiom is quite compelling. It suggests that a certain choice has to be made.
>
> (pp. 51–52)

Here Gilboa is clearly thinking of preference in relation to decisions that the agent actually faces. As previously mentioned, however, the domain of, for instance, the preference relation in the vNM theory is far from containing only decisions that a person will actually face. Due to this, Aumann (1962) claimed that

> Of all the axioms of utility theory, the completeness axiom is perhaps the most questionable. Like others of the axioms, it is inaccurate as a description of real life; but unlike them, we find it hard to accept even from the normative viewpoint. Does "rationality" demand that an individual make definite preference comparisons between *all* possible lotteries. . . ? For example, certain decisions that our individual is asked to make might involve highly hypothetical stations, which he will never face in real life; he might feel that he cannot reach an "honest" decision in such cases.
>
> (p. 446)

Few people would, however, question the plausibility of transitivity as a requirement of rationality.[5] Informally, transitivity says that if one option is at least as preferable as another option, which is at least as preferable as a third option, then the first option is at least as preferable as the third option. To see why preference must be transitive for it to be possible to represent it numerically, it suffices to notice that if the first option is assigned at least as high a number as the second option, which is assigned at least as high a number as the third option, then, necessarily, the first option is assigned at least as high a number as the third option.

There is a straightforward defense of transitivity that hinges on the sure losses that may befall anyone who violates the axiom (Davidson et al. 1955). This is the socalled *money pump* argument. It is based on the assumption that if a person finds one option at least as preferable as another, then she should be happy to trade the one for the other. Suppose she violates transitivity; for her, $L_i \precsim L_j$, $L_j \precsim L_k$, but $L_k \prec L_i$.[6] Moreover, suppose she presently has L_i. Then she should be willing to trade L_i for L_j. The same goes for L_j and L_k: she should be willing to trade L_j for L_k. She strictly prefers L_i to L_k, so she should be willing to trade in L_k plus some sum £*x* for L_i. But now she is in the same situation as where she started, having L_i but neither L_j nor L_k, except that she has lost £*x*! This process could be repeated, so the argument goes, thus turning the person into a "money pump."

Continuity implies that no outcome is so bad that an individual should not be willing to take some gamble that might result in her ending up with that outcome, but might otherwise result in her ending up with a marginal improvement on her status quo, provided the chances of the better outcome are good enough. Intuitively, continuity guarantees that an agent's evaluations of lotteries are appropriately sensitive to the probabilities of the lotteries' outcomes.

Some people find the Continuity axiom too strong. Is there any probability p such that a person would be willing to accept a gamble that has that probability of her losing her life and probability $(1 - p)$ of her winning £10 (Luce & Raiffa 1989/1957, 27)? Many people think there is not. However, the very same people would presumably cross the street to pick up a £10 bill they had dropped. But that is just taking a gamble that has a very small probability that they will be killed by a car but a much higher probability that they will gain £10.

Reduction of compound lotteries is an often forgotten axiom of expected utility theory. Perhaps the reason for this is that it seems, on the face of it, so compelling. Informally, the axiom simply ensures that two lotteries that confer the exact same probabilities on the possible outcomes are assigned the same value. For instance, a lottery that delivers £5,000 if a fair coin comes up heads three times in a row (but otherwise delivers £0) is assigned the same value as a lottery that delivers £5,000 if a yellow ball is randomly drawn from an urn containing seven white balls and one yellow ball (but otherwise delivers £0). And that may seem very plausible. However, note that the axiom implies that it does not matter whether the probability of an outcome is the result of the probability of a sequence of events (e.g., the coin coming up heads three times in a row) or a single event (e.g., a yellow ball being drawn). Some have complained that this rules out assigning any (dis)value to gambling as such, an issue to which we shall return in Section 3.3.

Independence implies that when two alternatives have the same probability for some particular outcome, our evaluation of the two alternatives should be independent of our opinion of that particular outcome. Intuitively, this means that preferences between lotteries should be governed only by the features of the lotteries that differ; the commonalities between the lotteries should be ignored. A preference ordering must satisfy some version of the Independence axiom for it to be possible to represent it as maximizing what is called an *additively separable* function: for instance, a function according to which the value (i.e., expected utility) of an option is a (probability-weighted) *sum* of the values of the option's possible outcomes.

To see this, suppose L_i and L_j are two alternatives, or lotteries, such that L_i will either result in outcome A, which has probability p, or result in outcome C, which has probability q, and L_j will either result in outcome B, which has probability p, or result in outcome C, which has probability q. Then $EU(L_i) \leq EU(L_j)$ just in case $pu(A) + qu(C) \leq pu(B) + qu(C)$. And the latter, of course, holds when, and only when, $pu(A) \leq pu(B)$. So an expected utility representation implies that when two alternatives have the same probability of some particular outcome, our evaluation of the two alternatives should be independent of what we think of that particular outcome, which is exactly what independence requires. Independence has, however, been extensively criticized. We shall look at that criticism in more detail in Section 3.1. For now, we will focus on the representation theorem to which von Neumann and Morgenstern's (2007/1944) axioms give rise:[7]

Theorem (von Neumann–Morgenstern). *Let* **O** *be a finite set of outcomes,* **L** *a set of corresponding lotteries that is closed under probability mixture, and* $\precsim$ *a weak preference relation on* **L**. *Then* $\precsim$ *satisfies axioms 1–4 if and only if there exists a function u, from* **O** *into the set of real numbers, that is unique up to positive linear transformation*[8] *and relative to which* $\precsim$ *can be represented as maximizing expected utility.*

One important implication of the preceding theorem is that, in principle at least, talk about a person's "utilities" can now be translated into talk about the person's preferences and, thus, her tendency to choose. Moreover, the result shows that the assumption that a rational person acts so as to maximize expected utility can be stated as an assumption about the person's choice tendencies. In light of the behaviorist inclination that has dominated neoclassical economics (recall endnote 2), it is no wonder that economists embraced vNM's result.

For instance, note that vNM's theorem establishes that it is meaningful to ask about how the difference in utility between, say, two outcomes compares to the difference in utility between some other two outcomes. For instance, suppose we know that some agent prefers apples (*A*) to bananas (*B*), which she prefers to citrus fruit (*C*). We might be interested in knowing how the difference according to her – that is, the difference in utility – between *A* and *B* compares to the difference between *B* and *C*. And vNM's result seems to ensure that we can indeed meaningfully ask such questions.

The way to answer the preceding question, according to vNM's theory, is to construct a lottery between *A* and *C* and find out what probability the lottery has to confer on *A* for the agent to be indifferent between, on the one hand, this lottery and on the other hand getting *B* for sure. The higher this probability, the greater the difference in utility between *B* and *C* compared to the difference between *A* and *B*. Intuitively, the higher this indifference probability, the fewer risks the person is willing to take in her pursuit of *A* rather than *B* when the risk can also result in *C*. This in turn suggests that she does not deem *A* *much* better than *B* compared to how much worse she considers *C* than *B*. For instance, if the person requires this probability to be 0.75, then that implies, by vNM's theory, that *B* is three-quarters of the way up a utility interval that has *A* on the top and *C* on the bottom.

So, it would seem that vNM's result ensures that we can ask how the strength of a person's preference between one pair of *risk-free* outcomes compares to the strength of her preference between another pair of *risk-free* outcomes; the way to answer this question is to look at the person's preferences between *risky* lotteries. However, this inference from attitudes to risky lotteries to attitudes to riskfree outcomes has been a topic of hot debate, which will be reviewed in Section 3.

2.2 Risk Aversion

A noticeable feature of the expected utility equation, which has given rise to much discussion and debate, is that it assumes *risk neutrality with respect to utility*. If L_i is a *nontrivial* lottery whose expected utility is x, and L_j is a *trivial* lottery whose expected utility is also x, then an agent whose preferences maximize expected utility – that is, an agent whose preferences satisfy axioms 1–5 – is indifferent between L_i and L_j. In other words, such a person is indifferent between any lottery whose expected utility is x and a *sure outcome* whose utility is x.

In contrast, the expected utility formula does not assume risk neutrality with respect to the outcomes to which utilities are attached. Suppose for instance that **O** is a set of possible wealth levels. Then the expected utility equation is consistent with the agent of interest being either risk averse or risk seeking with respect to wealth levels and, in fact, consistent with the agent being risk averse when it comes to levels of wealth within some ranges while being risk seeking when it comes to levels of wealth within other ranges. This is fortunate, because universal risk neutrality would be neither empirically nor normatively plausible.

Let's take an example to illustrate the claims in the previous paragraph. Suppose that some person is offered a 50–50 gamble between winning £5,000 and losing £5,000. This lottery, or gamble, is what is called "actuarially fair": its expected monetary payoff is 0. Now, let's say that the person in question has a pregamble wealth of w. If the person is risk *neutral* with respect to monetary amounts in the range from w − £5,000 to w + £5,000, then she is indifferent between accepting and rejecting this 50–50 gamble. However, if the person is risk *averse* when it comes to monetary amounts in this range, then she will turn down the gamble (and would continue to do so even if the potential gain were slightly increased). In contrast, if she is risk *seeking*, then she will accept the gamble (and would continue to do so even if the potential gain were slightly decreased). Let us, however, focus on risk aversion. To make sense of a person turning down the 50–50 gamble between winning £5,000 and losing £5,000, within the vNM framework, we assume that the person has a utility function over quantities of money that is *concave* over the relevant interval, which means that its graph has the shape depicted in Figure 3.1. Informally, this means that, within this range, an additional pound

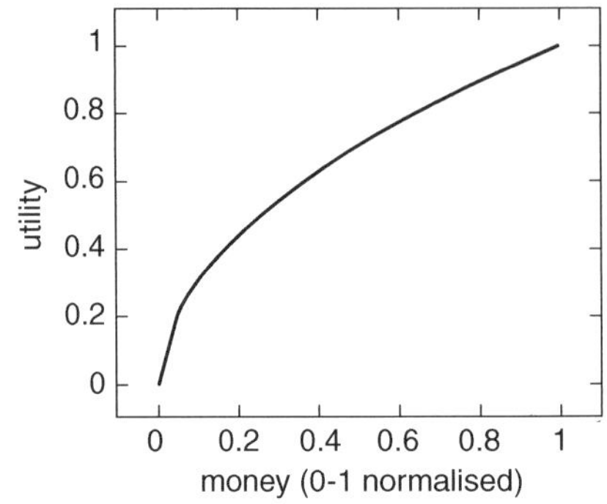

Figure 3.1 Diminishing marginal utility

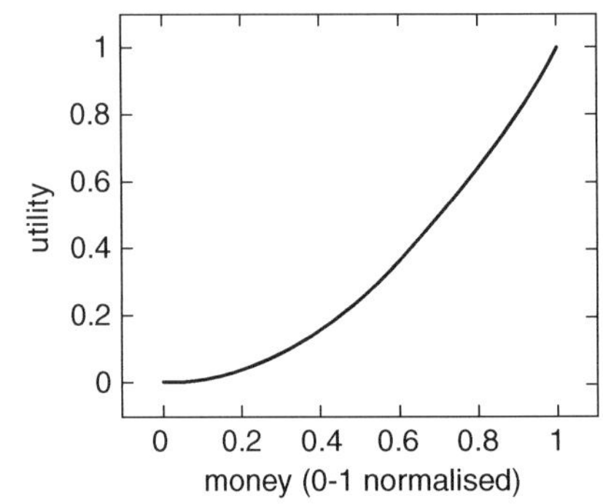

Figure 3.2 Increasing marginal utility

results in a smaller increase in utility as we move up within this range. Even less formally, this means that a pound is worth less (in utility) the more pounds the person already has, or, as it is often put, pounds have *diminishing marginal utility* (within this range). And that surely seems like a common psychological phenomenon. Whether it explains risk aversion is, however, an issue to which we shall return in the next section.

So, the von Neumann and Morgenstern (2007/1944) framework seems to be able to account for risk aversion, and it can account for risk-seeking behavior too; for a risk- seeking person, the utility function is convex rather than concave, as in the graph in Figure 3.2. Informally, this means that, for amounts within the relevant range, a pound is worth more (in utility), the more pounds the person already has.

Finally, the framework can account for agents who display risk-seeking behavior when it comes to monetary amounts within some ranges, while displaying risk-averse behavior when it comes to amounts within other ranges. Consider, for instance, the fact that many people gamble in the casino – which seems to suggest risk-seeking behavior – while at the same time insuring their house – which seems to suggest risk-averse behavior. In a seminal application of expected utility theory, Friedman and Savage (1948) attempted to account for such behavior by a utility function that has a convex shape when relatively small sums of money are involved (representing risk-seeking behavior in the casino), while having a concave shape when larger sums of money are involved (representing risk-averse behavior in insurance markets). A utility function with such a shape is depicted in the graph in Figure 3.3.

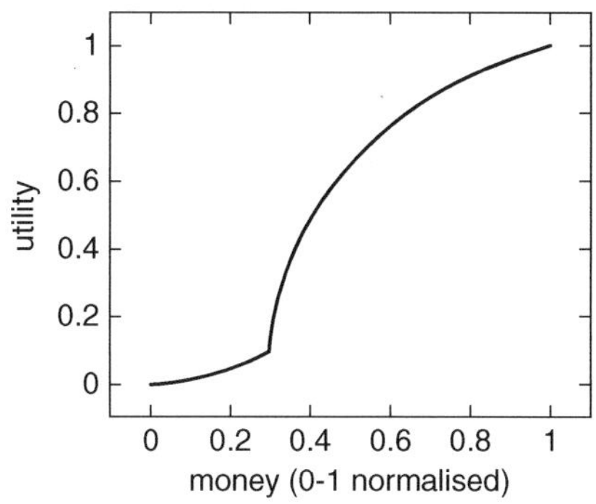

Figure 3.3 Decreasing and increasing marginal utility

So, the framework that orthodox (neoclassical) economists use to explain, predict, and recommend choices under risk may seem flexible enough to, formally at least, represent people's differing attitudes to risk. However, in the next section we encounter some arguments purporting to show that the framework is not as flexible as its proponents have claimed.

3. Critiques of the Orthodox Treatment of Risk

Expected utility theory as, for instance, developed by von Neumann and Morgenstern (2007/1944) has come under heavy criticism over the past decades. Some of this criticism is empirical, in that it uses experiments and other data to argue that people often do not act as the theory predicts. Other criticism is normative, where the complaint is that even perfectly rational people need not always act as the theory prescribes. Finally, some of the criticism is more conceptual, in that the complaint concerns attitudes or concepts that seem important for decisionmaking but that the theory completely ignores.

3.1 Allais' Challenge

Independence is perhaps the vNM axiom that has been most critically discussed. Although the axiom seems compelling – in particular from a normative point of view – when considered in the abstract, there are famous examples where many people find that they, even on reflection, violate the axiom. A particularly wellknown such example is the socalled *Allais paradox*, which the French economist Allais (1953) first introduced. The paradox turns on comparing people's preferences over two pairs of lotteries similar to those given in Table 3.1. The lotteries are described in terms of the prizes (outcomes) that are associated with particular numbered tickets, where one ticket will be drawn randomly (for instance, L_1 results in a prize of £2,500 if one of the tickets numbered 2–34 is drawn).

In this situation, many people strictly prefer L_2 over L_1, but they also prefer L_3 over L_4, a pair of preferences that I shall refer to as *Allais' preferences*.[9] Moreover, some scholars argue that this is a rationally permissible combination of preferences. A common way to rationalize the preferences is that, in the first choice situation, the risk of ending up with nothing after choosing L_1, when one could have had £2,400 for sure by choosing L_2, outweighs the chance that L_1 offers a better prize (£2,500). In the second choice situation, however, the minimum one stands to gain is £0 no matter which choice one makes. Therefore, one might reason that the slight extra risk of £0 that L_3 carries over L_4 is worth taking due to L_3's chance of the better prize.

While the preceding reasoning may seem compelling, Allais' preferences conflict with the Independence axiom.[10] Note that in the second choice scenario, option L_3 is a lottery that with

Table 3.1 Allais' paradox

	1	2–34
L_1	£0	£2,500
L_2	£2,400	£2,400

	1	2–34	35–100
L_3	£0	£2,500	£0
L_4	£2,400	£2,400	£0

probability 0.34 results in lottery L_1 but that otherwise results in £0, whereas option L_4 is a lottery that with probability 0.34 results in lottery L_2 but that otherwise results in £0. So, by the Independence axiom, if one prefers L_2 to L_1, then one should prefer L_4 to L_3. And because Allais' preferences violate the Independence axiom, it cannot be represented as maximizing expected utility.

There is no doubt that many people do, in fact, have preferences such as Allais'. Hence, some socalled *behavioral* economists have constructed decision theories that are meant to capture this type of preference without being normative, that is, without the theories being (necessarily) intended as either guides or criteria for rational decisions. Examples of such theories include *prospect theory* (Kahneman & Tversky 1979; Tversky & Kahneman 1992), *regret theory* (Loomes & Sugden 1982; Bell 1982), and *rank dependent utility theory* (Quiggin 1982). Because my focus here is on the orthodox (i.e., neoclassical) economic account of risk, I shall not discuss these behavioral theories in detail. An overview of descriptive decision theories can be found in Chandler (2017), while Angner (2012) is a more general introduction to behavioral economics.

Responses vary greatly when it comes to what *normative* lesson to draw from Allais' paradox. Leonard Savage, one of the founders of expected utility theory for subjective probabilities (Savage 1972/1954), famously failed the Allais test – that is, "failed" in the light of his own theory – but reported that, having realized his mistake, he reasoned himself into agreement with the theory and thus away from Allais' preferences (Savage 1972/1954, 101–103; for a discussion of Savage's reasoning, see Dietrich et al. 2020).

Others have argued that if it is, in fact, rationally permissible to take into account, when evaluating L_1, the regret or disappointment that one predicts one will experience if one gets £0 when one could have chosen £2,400 for sure, then that should somehow be accounted for in the description of L_1 (see, e.g., Weirich 1986; Broome 1991b). In particular, one should, according to this view, redescribe the £0 outcome of L_1 as something like "£0 + disappointment." But that makes the preference in question consistent with the Independence axiom, because L_3 is then no longer a lottery between £0 and L_1. Hence, the *paradox* might seem to have been resolved. Table 3.2 provides an illustration, where δ stands for whatever negative feeling that one predicts one will experience if one ends up with £0 when one could have chosen £2,400 for sure.

Finally, some have argued that Allais' preferences are indeed rationally permissible *and* are better captured by some *normative* alternative to (vNM's) expected utility theory. This view is particularly popular among philosophers and has, for instance, recently been defended by Buchak (2013) and by Stefánsson and Bradley (2019). Among economists, the dominant view still seems to be that, although we may have to depart from expected utility theory for descriptive purposes, that is, when explaining or predicting choices, expected utility theory is still unchallenged as a normative theory (see also Lecouteux, Chapter 4, and Baujard, Chapter 15).

Table 3.2 Allais' paradox re-described

	1	2–34
L_1	£0 + δ	£2,500
L_2	£2,400	£2,400

	1	2–34	35–100
L_3	£0	£2,500	£0
L_4	£2,400	£2,400	£0

3.2 *Rabin's Challenge*

Another wellknown criticism of the descriptive accuracy of expected utility theory is based on Rabin's (2000b) socalled *calibration results*, the fundamental insight behind which is that expected utility theory cannot plausibly explain many people's aversion to risk when small sums of money are at stake. In short, the problem is that, once a utility function has been calibrated to capture risk aversion with respect to small stakes, it will be so concave as to imply what Rabin thinks is "absurdly severe" risk aversion when more is at stake (Rabin 2000a).

A similar point had been made many decades earlier by Samuelson (1963), who pointed out that that an expected utility maximizer who turns down a 50–50 gamble between wining $200 and losing $100, and would do so if he were $19,800 richer or $9,900 poorer, must also (to maintain consistency) turn down a bundle consisting of 100 such independent gambles. But the bundle would seem quite hard to turn down: it has a monetary expectation of $5,000 and only has a 1/2,300 chance of resulting in the bettor losing money. "A good lawyer could have you declared legally insane for turning down this gamble," Rabin (2000a, 206) remarks.

Rabin in effect extended Samuelson's observation to a general calibration theorem, into which different smallscale gambles can be plugged to see which largescale gambles an expected utility maximizer must reject, if she rejects the inputted small-scale gambles. And the implications indeed do seem absurd. The theorem for instance establishes that an expected utility maximizer who always (i.e., irrespective of her pregamble wealth) turns down a 50–50 gamble between winning $105 and losing $100 will (if consistent) turn down a single 50–50 gamble between losing $2,000 and winning any amount whatsoever – including an infinite amount!

Now, the preceding result assumes that the decisionmaker turns down some particular gamble irrespective of her wealth. But Rabin's result in fact has implications even for risk-averse expected utility maximizers about whom we only know that they would turn down a particular gamble when their wealth is in some particular range. For instance, the theorem implies that a risk-averse expected utility maximizer who, when her pregamble wealth is up to $300,000, turns down a 50–50 gamble between losing $100 and winning $125 would, when her wealth is no more than $290,000, turn down a 50–50 gamble between losing $20,000 and winning $540,000,000,000,000,000,000!

Although Rabin's results may be surprising, the logic behind the result is relatively straightforward. Recall that, within expected utility theory, the form of the utility function is the only thing that can be varied to account for different attitudes to risk. In particular, risk aversion is equated with a concave utility function or diminishing marginal utility. And, as (Rabin 2000b, 1282) nicely illustrates,

> if you reject a 50–50 lose $10/gain $11 gamble because of diminishing marginal utility, it must be that you value the eleventh dollar above your current wealth by *at most* (10/11) as much as you valued the tenth-to-last-dollar of your current wealth. Iterating this observation,

> if you have the same aversion to the lose \$10/gain \$11 bet if you were \$21 wealthier, you value the thirty-second dollar above your current wealth by at most (10/11) × (10/11) ≈ (5/6) as much as your tenth-to-last dollar. You will value your two-hundred-twentieth dollar by at most (3/20) as much as your last dollar, and your eight-hundred-eightieth dollar by at most (1/2,000) of your last dollar. This is an absurd rate for the value of money to deteriorate – and the theorem shows the rate of deterioration implied by expected-utility theory is actually quicker than this.

A natural response to Rabin's results – and, in fact, the response Rabin himself suggested (Rabin 2000b, 1288–1289) – is that, at least when it comes to explaining people's aversion to risk when little is at stake, expected utility theory should be replaced by some theory that incorporates what is called *loss aversion*. The most important features of such theories are, first, that they incorporate some *status quo* and define utility in terms of changes in wealth relative to this status quo, rather than in terms of absolute wealth. Moreover, such theories postulate that people are more concerned by losses than with gains relative to this status quo; informally, the disutility of losing \$100 is greater than the utility of gaining \$100, relative to any status quo. Such loss aversion is one of the key ingredients of prospect theory (Kahneman & Tversky 1979), which, as previously mentioned, will not be discussed in any detail in this chapter.

3.3 Phenomenological Challenges

Another common complaint against the vNM approach is that it mischaracterizes attitudes to risk. Such attitudes, the complaint goes, need to be more clearly distinguished from attitudes to riskfree outcomes than the vNM approach allows. Recall that this approach *equates* different attitudes to risk with different forms of the utility function over quantities of risk-free outcomes; for instance, risk aversion with respect to money is equated with diminishing marginal utility of money. A problem with this equation, according to the critics, is that attitudes to risk per se simply seem to be a different type of psychological attitude than attitudes to quantities of riskfree outcomes. But, as vNM themselves pointed out, "concepts like 'specific utility of gambling' [i.e., what I called attitudes to risk per se] cannot be formulated free of contradiction" within their framework (von Neumann & Morgenstern 2007/1944, 28).

Critics of expected utility theory argue that, contrary to what the aforementioned equation implies, it is conceptually possible that two individuals evaluate the possible outcomes of a bet in the same way (and agree about their probabilities) but nevertheless differ in whether they accept the bet, for instance, due to different gambling temperaments (Watkins 1977; Hansson 1988; Buchak 2013; Stefánsson & Bradley 2019). For instance, imagine that two people both insist that they evaluate money linearly, which means that the difference (in utility) between, say, winning £50 and "winning" £0 is exactly as great as the difference between winning £100 and winning £50. Nevertheless, one of them is eager to accept, while the other turns down, a 50–50 gamble between winning £100 and losing £100. And the explanation they give is simply that they have different attitudes to taking risks; one of them enjoys gambling, while the other detests it.

A standard response that economists have made, historically at least, when confronted with criticism like the preceding is to suggest a *formalistic* interpretation of expected utility, according to which the role of expected utility theory is not to capture what actually goes on in people's minds, when making a decision, but simply to mathematically *represent* and *predict* choices (see, e.g., Friedman & Savage 1948; Harsanyi 1977). If that is the aim, then as long as we can represent, say, a risk-averse decisionmaker *as if* she were maximizing the expectation of some concave utility function, then it does not matter that we are conflating two conceptually distinct psychological attitudes. In other words, as long as, say, diminishing marginal utility is behaviorally indistinct from aversion to risk per se, it does not matter whether or not these are psychologically distinct.

The formalistic interpretation has been criticized by several philosophers of economics.[11] One complaint is that we often do want to be able to explain, rather than simply describe, behavior in terms of the maximization of a utility function. In other words, we want to be able to say that a person chose an alternative *because* it was the alternative with the highest expected utility according to her. Moreover, when using decision theory for decisionmaking purposes (such as in policy analysis), we need to assume that the utilities upon which we base the recommendations exist prior to (and independently of) the choices that the theory recommends. That is, if we want to be able to recommend a risky option because it is the one that maximizes expected utility, then we must understand "utility" as something that is independent of the decisionmaker's choices – and conceptually distinct from the representation of her preferences – between risky options.

However, a proponent of the vNM theory might respond that the theory is only meant to apply to persons and situations where attitudes to risk per se have no influence on the person's preferences. Even with that limitation, the theory is very powerful; for instance, it allows us to derive a precise utility function over quantities of goods from the person's preferences between lotteries. In fact, Binmore (2009) points out that it is only *because* a vNM utility function cannot account for attitudes to risk per se that such a function can plausibly explain the agent's choice in situations where risk is lacking:

> It is often taken for granted that gambling can be explained [within an expected utility framework] as rational behavior on the part of a risk-loving agent. The mistake is easily made, because to speak of "attitude to risk" is a positive invitation to regard the shape of [a person's vNM function] as embodying the thrill that she derives from the act of gambling. But if we fall into this error, we have no answer to the critics who ask why [vNM functions] should be thought to have any relevance to how [the person] chooses in riskless situations.
>
> (p. 54)

Moreover, Binmore identifies reduction of compound lotteries as the reason why the vNM framework is not equipped to represent agents who are not neutral to risk per se.

> [Reduction of Compound Lotteries] takes for granted that [a person] is entirely *neutral* about the actual act of gambling. She doesn't bet because she enjoys betting – she bets only when she judges that the odds are in her favor. If she liked or disliked the act of gambling itself, we would have no reason to assume that she is indifferent between a compound lottery and a simple lottery in which the prizes are available with the same probabilities.
>
> (Ibid., original emphasis)

In other words, proponents of the vNM framework face a dilemma. They can accept that their framework cannot account for any potential thrill or anxiety that an agent derives from the act of gambling, that is, the framework cannot account for attitudes to risk per se. Or they can accept that the utility functions that the framework allows the modeler to derive cannot be used to explain or predict how the modeled agent chooses in a riskless situation. So, either the framework cannot account for attitudes to risk per se, or it is of little relevance to choice without risk.

4. Uncertainty

So far the focus has been on decisionmaking under risk, that is, situations where the agent knows – or, at least, deems suitable to act as if she knows – the relevant probabilities. Betting on roulette is a paradigm example. In contrast, when betting on a soccer match, one does not, as previously mentioned, know all the relevant probabilities, nor would one typically find it suitable or reasonable to act as if one knows these probabilities. In the latter case, economic theorists say that the bettor is making a decision *under uncertainty*.

Leonard Savage's (1972/1954) decision theory is without a doubt the bestknown normative theory of choice under uncertainty, in particular within neoclassical economics. Savage formulated a set of preference axioms that guarantees the existence of a pair of probability and utility functions, relative to which the preferences can be represented as maximizing expected utility. The theory is often called *subjective* expected utility theory, as the probability function is assumed to be subjective (in contrast to the previously discussed expected utility theory with "objective" or known probabilities). Because the focus of this chapter is decisionmaking under risk, I shall only present Savage's theory very briefly here; a somewhat more detailed account can be found in Steele and Stefánsson (2015).

The primitives in Savage's theory are outcomes (or "consequences" as Savage called them) and states of the world, the former being whatever is of ultimate value to the agent, while the latter are features of the world that the agent cannot control and about which she is typically uncertain. Sets of states are called *events*. The options over which the agent has preferences in Savage's theory are a rich set of *acts*, which formally are functions from the set of outcomes to the set of states of the world. So, an agent can choose between acts, and the outcome of an act is determined by what is the true (or the actual) state of the world.

The following notation will be used to state Savage's representation result: f, g, etc. are various acts, that is, functions from the set **S** of states of the world to the set **O** of outcomes, with **F** being the set of these functions. $f(s_i)$ denotes the outcome of f when state $s_i \in \mathbf{S}$ is actual. The subjective expected utility of f according to Savage's theory, denoted $U(f)$, is given by

Savage's expected utility equation. $U(f) = \sum_i u(f(s_i)) \cdot P(s_i)$

The result Savage proved can be stated as follows.[12]

Theorem (Savage). *Let $\preceq$ be a weak preference relation on* **F**. *If $\preceq$ satisfies Savage's axioms, then the following hold:*

- *The agent's uncertainty with respect to the states in* **S** *can be represented by a* unique *(and finitely additive) probability function, P.*
- *The strength of her desire for the sure outcomes in* **O** *can be represented by a utility function, u, that is unique up to positive linear transformation.*
- *The pair (P, u) gives rise to an expected utility function, U, that represents her preferences for the alternatives in* **F**, *i.e., for any $f, g \in \mathbf{F}$:*

$$f \preceq g \Leftrightarrow U(f) \leq U(g)$$

I will not present all of Savage's axioms. Instead, I focus on what is arguably the cornerstone of Savage's subjective expected utility theory and which corresponds to von Neumann and Morgenstern's Independence axiom.

To state the axiom in question, we say that act f "agrees with" act g in event E if, for any state in event E, f and g yield the same outcome.

Axiom 6 (Sure Thing Principle). *If f, g and f', g' are such that*

- *f agrees with g and f' agrees with g' in event $\neg E$,*
- *f agrees with f' and g agrees with g' in event E,*

- *and* $f \preceq g$,

then $f' \preceq g'$.

The idea behind the Sure Thing Principle (STP) is essentially the same as that behind independence: because we should be able to evaluate each outcome independently of other possible outcomes, we can safely ignore states of the world where two acts that we are comparing result in the same outcome. And, for that reason, the Allais paradox – or at least some variant of it without known probabilities – is often seen as a challenge to the STP. If we put the principle in tabular form, this may be more apparent. The setup involves four acts with the following form.

	E	$\neg E$
f	X	Z
g	Y	Z
f'	X	W
g'	Y	W

The intuition behind the STP is that if g is weakly preferred to f, then that must be because the consequence Y is considered to be at least as desirable as X, which by the same reasoning implies that g' is weakly preferred to f'.

One of the most discussed challenges to Savage's theory – in fact, a challenge to both STP and Savage's definition of comparative belief – is based on a choice situation devised by Daniel Ellsberg (1961). The choice situation gives rise to what is often called the *Ellsberg paradox* because, when confronted with the choices he presented, most people exhibit a pair of preferences – "Ellsberg's preferences" – that seem intuitively rational but nevertheless conflict with Savage's theory.

Imagine an urn containing 90 balls, 30 of which are red and the remaining 60 are a mix of black and yellow balls in a proportion that is unknown to the decisionmaker. A ball will be randomly drawn from the urn, but first the decisionmaker is offered two choices each between a pair of bets. The four bets are presented in Table 3.3. First, she is offered a choice between bet f, which results in a prize of \$100 if a red ball is drawn (but nothing otherwise), and bet g, which pays out \$100 if a black ball is drawn (but nothing otherwise). Many people, it turns out, choose f over g. Next, the decisionmaker is offered a choice between f', which results in a prize of \$100 in the event that a red or yellow ball is drawn (but nothing otherwise), and g', which pays out \$100 if a black or yellow ball is drawn (but nothing otherwise). This time many people prefer g' over f'. In fact, many people prefer both f over g and g' over f', in accordance with Ellsberg's preferences.

The intuitive justification for this pair of preferences is that when offered the choice between f and g, people prefer the former because they *know* that they then have a 1/3 chance of receiving \$100, whereas the chance that the second bet will result in them winning \$100 can be anywhere from 0

Table 3.3 Ellsberg's bets

	Red	Black	Yellow
f	\$100	\$0	\$0
g	\$0	\$100	\$0
f'	\$100	\$0	\$100
g'	\$0	\$100	\$100

to 2/3. The same type of reasoning would lead to a choice of g' over f': bet g' is known to have a 2/3 chance of delivering the \$100, whereas f' offers a chance of anywhere between 1/3 and 1/1.

However, it is not too difficult to see that there is no single probability function over the relevant events relative to which Ellsberg's preferences can be represented as maximizing expected utility (if we assume that Table 3.3 correctly represents the decisionproblem). The problem is that if a person prefers \$100 to \$0, then, by Savage's utility representation, the first preference, $g \prec f$, reveals that the person takes it to be more probable that a red ball will be drawn than that a black ball will be drawn, but the second preference, $f' \prec g'$, reveals that the person takes it to be more probable that a black or yellow ball will be drawn than that a red or yellow ball will be drawn. But there is no probability function such that a red ball is more probable than a black ball, yet a black or yellow ball is more probable than a red or yellow ball. Hence, there is no probability function relative to which a person with Ellsberg's preferences can be represented as maximizing expected utility, as defined by Savage.

It is also easy to verify that Ellsberg's preferences are inconsistent with Savage's Sure Thing Principle. The principle states that because f and g yield the same outcome in the event that a yellow ball is drawn, we can ignore this event when choosing between f and g. The same holds when choosing between f' and g'. But when we ignore this event in both choices, f becomes identical to f' and g becomes identical to g'. Therefore, a preference for f over g is, according to the STP, only consistent with a preference for f' over g'. So Ellsberg's preferences (f over g and g' over f') are inconsistent with the STP.

Perhaps the most common rationalization of Ellsberg's preferences, at least within economics, is to suggest that people are using a *maximin expectation* rule,[13] which tells them to choose an alternative whose worst possible expectation is better than (or at least as good as) the worst possible expectation of any other alternative [Gilboa and Schmeidler (1989) axiomatized this rule and, to some extent, popularized it within economics].

Recall that, in the first of Ellsberg's choice situations, the monetary expectation of betting on red is known to be \$33.33 (because one knows that 30 balls out of 90 are red). However, the monetary expectation of betting on black could be anywhere between \$0 and \$66.67. So it might make sense for a person who is *averse to uncertainty* (or averse to *ambiguity*, as it is often called) to bet on red, which is precisely what the maximin expectation rule prescribes. Analogous reasoning would lead to a bet on black or yellow (bet g') in the second of Ellsberg's choice situations. So, the maximin expectation rule prescribes choices in accordance with Ellsberg's preferences.

An alternative rationalization of Ellsberg's preferences, which was recently proposed by the philosopher Richard Bradley (2016) but has not been as influential in economics, is that people with Ellsberg's preferences take quantities of chances to have decreasing marginal utility, such that, for instance, the difference in utility between no chance of \$100 and a 1/3 chance of \$100 is greater than the difference in utility between a 2/3 chance of \$100 and the certainty of \$100.

The question of how (and, in fact, whether) to rationalize Ellsberg's preferences – and, more generally, how to think of rational decisions under uncertainty – is a matter of active debate that will not be settled here.

5. Concluding Remarks

Neoclassical economists use expected utility theory to explain, predict, and guide choices in situations of risk and the similar theory of subjective expected utility theory to explain, predict, and guide choices in situations of uncertainty. The main aim of this chapter has been to, first, describe these theories and, second, to discuss some of the challenges that these theories face. Because a considerable part of the chapter has been devoted to the challenges, I would like to end with two remarks in expected utility theory's favor, remarks that support both the objective (vNM) and the subjective (Savage) versions of the theory.

First, when it comes to descriptive purposes, some economists have forcefully argued that we do not yet have a good reason for giving up on expected utility theory. The reason is that, although we have found that in some experimental settings, different descriptive theories have better predictive success than expected utility theory, there is no single descriptive theory that performs better than expected utility theory across these different experimental settings. Hence, some economists suggest that we should favor simplicity over complexity and stick with expected utility theory (e.g. Binmore 2009, 58–59).

Second, a forceful argument for the normative plausibility of expected utility theory comes from considerations that are similar to the money pump argument that we have already encountered when discussing the Transitivity axiom. For instance, a money pump–like "dynamic consistency" argument can be made in favor of both the Independence axiom and the Sure Thing Principle – the axioms of, respectively, objective and subjective expected utility theory that have received the most criticism. In particular, it can be shown that a decisionmaker who violates either independence or the Sure Thing Principle would do better, by her own assessment, if she satisfied the axiom (for a recent overview, see Gustafsson forthcoming). In fact, expected utility theory as a whole can be derived from what may seem to be nothing but dynamic consistency constraints (Hammond 1987, 1988). So, while some think that examples such as the paradoxes of Allais and Ellsberg undermine the normative standing of expected utility theory, we still have compelling dynamic and practical arguments in favor of the theory.[14]

Related Chapters

Baujard, A., Chapter 15 "Values in Welfare Economics"
Lecouteux, G., Chapter 4 "Behavioral Welfare Economics and Consumer Sovereignty"

Notes

1 However, for a sophisticated account of objective probabilities that does not entail this, see Hoefer (2007) and Frigg and Hoefer (2010).

2 Robbins (1932), Samuelson (1938, 1948), and Friedman (1953) are some influential economists in this behaviorist tradition; for an overview, see Angner and Loewenstein (2012), particularly Section 2.2.

3 Ramsey (1990/1926) had actually already suggested a stronger result, that is, one that simultaneously derives a probability function and a utility function from the agent's preference [a project later continued by, for example, Savage (1972/1954) and Jeffrey (1990/1965)]. Nevertheless, this result of Ramsey's was never nearly as influential in economics as vNM's, perhaps partly because Ramsey neither gave a full proof of his result nor provided much detail about how it would go, but probably also partly because Ramsey's construction assumes certain psychological facts about agents (in particular, which prospects are considered "ethically neutral," that is, of neither negative nor positive value) that are prior to the expected utility representation (for a discussion, see Bradley 2001).

4 The axioms I present are not exactly the ones vNM presented. In fact, my choice of axioms is determined mainly by pedagogical reasons.

5 But of course, for almost any claim, one can find a philosopher arguing against it. Notable philosophers who question the claim that transitivity is a requirement of rationality include Temkin (1987, 1996, 2012) and Rachels (1998).

6 Here I am assuming completeness. After all, if completeness is not assumed, then one might violate transitivity by weakly preferring L_j to L_i and weakly preferring L_k to L_j, while having no preference when it comes to L_i vs. L_k.

7 Kreps (1988) and Peterson (2009) each provide accessible but different illustrations of how the theorem can be proven.

8 That u is unique up to a positive linear transformation means that, for the purposes of the representation, u is considered to be equivalent to all and only those functions u' that satisfy $u' = a + ub$ for some number a and positive number b.

9 Kahneman and Tversky's article (1979) contains an influential empirical study of Allais' preferences.
10 Thus the "paradox": many people think that independence is a requirement of rationality, but nevertheless also think that Allais' preferences are rationally permissible.
11 See, for instance, Broome (1991a), List and Dietrich (2016), Reiss (2013), Bradley (2017), and Okasha (2016).
12 I assume that the set **O** is finite, but Savage proved a similar result for an infinite **O**.
13 This is a variant of the maximin decision rule, which tells the individual to choose an alternative whose worst possible outcome is better than (or at least as good as) the worst possible outcome from any other alternative.
14 Financial support from Riksbankens Jubileumsfond (through a Pro Futura Scientia XIII fellowship) is gratefully acknowledged.

Bibliography

Allais, M. (1953), 'Le comportement de l'homme rationnel devant le risque: Critique des postulats et axiomes de l'école Américaine', *Econometrica* **21**(4), 503–546.
Angner, E. (2012), *A Course in Behavioral Economics*, Palgrave Macmillan.
Angner, E. & Loewenstein, G. (2012), 'Behavioral economics', *in* U. Mäki, ed., *Philosophy of Economics*, North-Holland, pp. 641–689.
Aumann, R. J. (1962), 'Utility theory without the completeness axiom', *Econometrica* **30**(3), 445–462.
Bell, D. E. (1982), 'Regret in decision making under uncertainty', *Operations Research* **30**(5), 961–981.
Binmore, K. (2009), *Rational Decisions*, Princeton University Press.
Bradley, R. (2001), 'Ramsey and the measurement of belief', *in* D. Corfield & J. Williamson, eds., *Foundations of Bayesianism*, Springer.
Bradley, R. (2016), 'Ellsberg's paradox and the value of chances', *Economics and Philosophy* **32**(2), 231–248.
Bradley, R. (2017), *Decision Theory With a Human Face*, Oxford University Press.
Broome, J. (1991a), 'Utility', *Economics and Philosophy* **7**(1), 1–12.
Broome, J. (1991b), *Weighing Goods*, Basil Blackwell.
Buchak, L. (2013), *Risk and Rationality*, Oxford University Press.
Chandler, J. (2017), 'Descriptive Decision Theory', *in* E. N. Zalta, ed., *The Stanford Encyclopedia of Philosophy*, Winter 2017 edn, Metaphysics Research Lab, Stanford University.
Davidson, D., McKinsey, J. C. C. & Suppes, P. (1955), 'Outlines of a formal theory of value, I', *Philosophy of Science* **22**(2), 140–160.
Dietrich, F., Staras, A. & Sugden, R. (2020), 'Savage's response to Allais as Broomean reasoning', *Journal of Economic Methodology*, 1–22.
Ellsberg, D. (1961), 'Risk, ambiguity, and the Savage axioms', *Quarterly Journal of Economics* **75**(4), 643–669.
Friedman, M. (1953), 'The methodology of positive economics', *in Essays in Positive Economics*, University of Chicago Press, pp. 3–43.
Friedman, M. & Savage, L. J. (1948), 'The utility analysis of choices involving risk', *Journal of Political Economy* **56**(4), 279–304. URL: www.jstor.org/stable/1826045
Frigg, R. & Hoefer, C. (2010), 'Determinism and chance from a Humean perspective', *in* Dennis Dieks et al., eds., *The Present Situation in the Philosophy of Science*, Springer, pp. 351–271.
Gilboa, I. (2009), *Theory of Decision under Uncertainty*, Cambridge University Press.
Gilboa, I. & Schmeidler, D. (1989), 'Maxmin expected utility with nonunique prior', *Journal of Mathematical Economics* **18**(2), 141–153.
Gustafsson, J. E. (forthcoming), *MoneyPump Arguments*, Cambridge University Press.
Hammond, P. (1987), 'Consequentialism and the Independence axiom', *in* B. Munier, ed., *Risk, Decision and Rationality*, Springer.
Hammond, P. (1988), 'Consequentialist foundations for expected utility theory', *Theory and Decision* **25**(1), 25–78.
Hansson, B. (1988), 'Risk aversion as a problem of conjoint measurement', *in* P. Gärdenfors & N.E. Sahlin, eds., *Decision, Probability, and Utility*, Cambridge University Press.
Harsanyi, J. C. (1977), 'On the rationale of the Bayesian approach: Comments on Professor Watkins's paper', *in* R. Butts & J. Hintikka, eds., *Foundational Problems in the Special Sciences*, D. Reidel Publishing.
Hoefer, C. (2007), 'The third way on objective probability: A sceptic's guide to objective chance', *Mind* **116**(463), 449–496.
Jeffrey, R. (1990/1965), *The Logic of Decision*, The University of Chicago Press.
Kahneman, D. & Tversky, A. (1979), 'Prospect theory: An analysis of decision under risk', *Econometrica* **47**(2), 263–292.

Knight, F. H. (1921), *Risk, Uncertainty and Profit*, Houghton Mifflin Company.

Kreps, D. (1988), *Notes on the Theory of Choice*, Avalon Publishing.

List, C. & Dietrich, F. (2016), 'Mentalism versus behaviourism in economics: A philosophyofscience perspective', *Economics and Philosophy* **32**(2), 249–281.

Loomes, G. & Sugden, R. (1982), 'Regret theory: An alternative theory of rational choice under risk', *The Economic Journal* **92**, 805–824.

Luce, R. D. & Raiffa, H. (1989/1957), *Games and Decisions: Introduction and Critical Survey*, Dover Publications.

Okasha, S. (2016), 'On the interpretation of decision theory', *Economics and Philosophy* **32**(3), 409–433.

Peterson, M. (2009), *An Introduction to Decision Theory*, Cambridge University Press.

Quiggin, J. (1982), 'A theory of anticipated utility', *Journal of Economic Behavior & Organization* **3**(4), 323–343.

Rabin, M. (2000a), 'Diminishing marginal utility of wealth cannot explain risk aversion', *in* D. Kahneman & A. Tversky, eds., *Choices, Values and Frames*, Cambridge University Press.

Rabin, M. (2000b), 'Risk aversion and expected utility theory: A calibration theorem', *Econometrica* **68**(5), 1281–1292.

Rachels, S. (1998), 'Counterexamples to the transitivity of better than', *Australasian Journal of Philosophy* **76**(1), 71–83.

Ramsey, F. P. (1990/1926), 'Truth and probability', *in* D. H. Mellor, ed., *Philosophical Papers*, Cambridge University Press.

Reiss, J. (2013), *Philosophy of Economics: A Contemporary Introduction*, Routledge.

Robbins, L. (1932), *An Essay on the Nature and Significance of Economic Science*, Macmillan & Co.

Samuelson, P. A. (1938), 'A note on the pure theory of consumer's behavior', *Economica* **5**, 61–71.

Samuelson, P. A. (1948), 'Consumption theory in terms of revealed preference', *Economica* **15**, 243–253.

Samuelson, P. A. (1963), 'Risk and uncertainty: A fallacy of large numbers', *Scientia* **98**, 108–113.

Savage, L. (1972/1954), *The Foundations of Statistics*, Dover Publication.

Schipper, B. C. (2015), 'Awareness', *in* H. van Ditmarsch, J. Y. Halpern, W. van der Hoek, & B. Kooi, eds., *Handbook of Epistemic Logic*, College Publications, pp. 77–146.

Steele, K. & Stefánsson, H. O. (2015), 'Decision theory', *in* E. Zalta, ed., *Stanford Encyclopedia of Philosophy*, Metaphysics Research Lab, Stanford University, https://plato.stanford.edu/entries/decision-theory/.

Steele, K. & Stefánsson, H. O. (2021), *Beyond Uncertainty: Reasoning with Unknown Possibilities*, Cambridge University Press.

Stefánsson, H. O. & Bradley, R. (2019), 'What is risk aversion?' *British Journal for the Philosophy of Science* **70**(1), 77–102.

Temkin, L. (1987), 'Intransitivity and the mere addition paradox', *Philosophy and Public Affairs* **16**(2), 138–187.

Temkin, L. (1996), 'A continuum argument for intransitivity', *Philosophy and Public Affairs* **25**(3), 175–210.

Temkin, L. (2012), *Rethinking the Good: Moral Ideals and the Nature of Practical Reasoning*, Oxford University Press.

Tversky, A. & Kahneman, D. (1992), 'Advances in prospect theory: Cumulative representation of uncertainty', *Journal of Risk and Uncertainty* **5**(4), 297–323.

von Neumann, J. & Morgenstern, O. (2007/1944), *Theory of Games and Economic Behavior*, Princeton University Press.

Watkins, J. (1977), 'Towards a unified decision theory: A nonBayesian approach', *in* R. Butts & J. Hintikka, eds., *Foundational Problems in the Special Sciences*, D. Reidel Publishing Company.

Weirich, P. (1986), 'Expected utility and risk', *British Journal for the Philosophy of Science* **37**(4), 419–442.

4

BEHAVIORAL WELFARE ECONOMICS AND CONSUMER SOVEREIGNTY

Guilhem Lecouteux

> *[T]he only purpose for which power can be rightfully exercised over any member of a civilised community, against his will, is to prevent harm to others. His own good, either physical or moral, is not a sufficient warrant. He cannot rightfully be compelled to do or forbear because it will better for him to do so, because it will make him happier, because, in the opinion of others, to do so would be wise, or even right. . . . The only part of the conduct of any one, for which he is amenable to society, is that which concerns others. In the part which merely concerns himself, his independence is, of right, absolute. Over himself, over his own body and mind, the individual is sovereign.*
>
> *It is, perhaps, hardly necessary to say that this doctrine is meant to apply only to human beings in the maturity of their faculties. . . . Those who are still in a state to require being taken care of by others, must be protected against their own actions as well as against external injury.*
>
> (John Stuart Mill 1859/2003: 80–81)

1. Behavioral Economics' Challenge to Consumer Sovereignty

Consumer sovereignty constitutes a central principle in the mainstream tradition of welfare economics.[1] When assessing what is good for society, the theorist[2] (she) takes individual "welfare" as an input, that is, her assessment of what makes an individual (he) better off. Even though finding an appropriate way to aggregate measures of individual welfare into a social welfare function has been – and still is – a core challenge of theoretical welfare economics, the traditionally accepted way to measure individual welfare is to use the satisfaction of individual preferences. If an individual prefers an alternative x to y (and, therefore, would choose x if asked to choose between x and y), then this individual's welfare is deemed to be higher when he obtains x.[3] By taking preference satisfaction as the normative criterion, theorists do not form any judgment about the agents' preferences and leave them the freedom to choose as they wish. Individual choices are taken as indicators of the agents' economic welfare, which can be used as inputs in normative analysis. This led to a consensus that normative economics is about *social interactions* (e.g. whether markets constitute a good mechanism to allocate resources) and should consider the individuals' preferences as their protected sphere of liberty.

The development of behavioral economics, however, challenged this consensus. The accumulation of experimental findings that human subjects put in lab conditions are prone to preference reversals and inconsistencies indeed led a growing number of economists to question the relationship between individual choice and welfare. The standard narrative among behavioral economists is that

DOI: 10.4324/9781315739793-5

real individuals choose "poorly" (e.g. Sunstein 2020: 39) and, therefore, that leaving them make their own choices could be harmful for them. In the words of Camerer *et al.* (2003), who – simultaneously with Sunstein and Thaler's (2003) proposal for "libertarian paternalism" – explicitly argue that behavioral economics gives a direct justification for "asymmetric paternalism,"

> In a sense, behavioral economics extends the paternalistically protected category of "idiots" to include most people, at predictable times. The challenge is figuring out what sorts of "idiotic" behaviors are likely to arise routinely and how to prevent them, while imposing minimal restrictions on those who behave rationally.
>
> (Camerer *et al.* 2003: 1218)

Camerer *et al.* draw a distinction between two types of individuals: the "idiots" and "those who behave rationally."[4] While rational agents should be free to choose as they prefer, most real individuals should be protected against their own actions – echoing Mill's harm principle; it is as if behavioral economics revealed that most individuals are akin to children because their behavior in the lab indicates that they are not "in the maturity of their faculties." Our higher expertise, as theorists, then legitimizes calls for paternalistic regulations in the agents' own interest. The aim of *behavioral welfare economics* (BWE) consists, then, of looking for strategies to recover a normatively satisfactory notion of "economic welfare" from the possibly incoherent choices of the agents.[5]

Contrary to the principle of consumer sovereignty – which treats consumer preferences as a given and not subject to the theorist's scrutiny and judgment – most of the literature on BWE considers that incoherent preferences are the symptom of a deficient psychology and, therefore, that they should not be integrated in welfare analysis. While a significant emphasis in this literature is put on the need to respect the true preferences of the agent – Sunstein (2014) calls it a "means paternalism," whose aim is to help the individuals to achieve their own ends, *as judged by themselves* – behavioral welfare economists are endowed with the duty of helping non-rational agents to obtain what they "truly" want. The preferences of an individual are worth respecting *only if he is "rational" in the neoclassical sense.*[6] Far from a principle of "consumer sovereignty," BWE implicitly advances a principle of "sovereignty of the neoclassical consumer."

The aim of this chapter is to question the widespread position among behavioral economists that incoherent preferences *do* pose a normative problem and that preference inconsistency gives a straightforward justification for paternalistic regulations. I start by presenting in more detail how BWE analyzes such incoherent preferences, and I highlight the problematic account of agency it presupposes, which is based on the model of the *inner rational agent* (Section 2). I then question the claim that revealing incoherent preferences is normatively problematic (Section 3), and I argue that – if we accept that people ought to reveal coherent preferences – it is far from clear why people ought to be coherent by neoclassical standards (Section 4). I conclude by stressing that the BWE critique of consumer sovereignty is probably misplaced and that a shift in the analysis from cognitive biases to the general processes of preference formation could offer a much more forceful argument in favor of regulation – which would, however, be of a very different nature than the nudge agenda (Section 5).

2. Behavioral Welfare Economics and the Inner Rational Agent

2.1 Interpreting Deviations From Rational Choice

Neoclassical welfare economics assumes that agents are "rational" in the sense that (i) their preferences are complete and integrated[7] and (ii) they act in an instrumentally rational way to satisfy those preferences. Those two assumptions can be interpreted either literally or as a formal representation of the agent's behavior. According to the former interpretation, the agent has stable "tastes" and "objectives" and has the cognitive ability to make the best choice in any given choice situation. According to the latter, however, the agent behaves *as if* (i) and (ii) were true, and her preferences are directly defined by her actual choices [see Guala (2019) and Vredenburgh (Chapter 5) on the distinction between mentalistic and behavioristic interpretations of preferences].

Behavioral economics' challenge to welfare economics is that human subjects – when put in lab conditions – often behave very differently from the predictions of rational choice theory (see, e.g., Kahneman 2011 and Camerer 2011 for references). This suggests that at least (i) or (ii) must be rejected as an empirical statement. If we reject (i), we cannot represent the agent's preferences by a utility function anymore, leaving us with no obvious way to measure – and, more fundamentally, define – the subjective welfare of the agent. This raises the daunting philosophical question of which normative criterion to use in the absence of a welfare metric. If we reject (ii) while maintaining (i), however, the agent has well-ordered preferences that can be represented by a utility function. However, he fails to maximize it because of a lack of instrumental rationality: the agent's subjective welfare is well defined (whose maximization could offer an appealing normative criterion), although his choices now only give an *indirect* source of information (e.g. Köszegi & Rabin 2007).

In the early days of behavioral economics, Simon (1955) endorsed the first interpretation and rejected the notion of individual utility functions, while still emphasizing the existence of a form of rationality – which was, however, procedural rather than substantial. The new behavioral economics that emerged with the "heuristics and biases" program of Kahneman and Tversky (see Sent 2004) – and which later became mainstream and shaped the development of BWE – predominantly endorsed the second interpretation of behavioral findings [i.e. keep (i) while rejecting (ii)]. Most of the contributions to the literature in BWE treat deviations from rational choice as *errors* – caused by the defective psychology of the individual – and aim to reconstruct the underlying "true" preferences of the agent, which he would have revealed if freed from reasoning imperfections and biases.

2.2 The Inner Rational Agent

Together with Gerardo Infante and Robert Sugden, I have argued that this literature treats human agency as if a person were made up of a neoclassically rational agent – an *inner rational agent* – "trapped" within an error-prone psychological shell, which distorts how the inner agent interacts with the real world (Infante *et al.* 2016a, 2016b). Our critique is not that behavioral economists think that this is a *realistic* description of the person but rather that they consider that an actual person, if freed from reasoning imperfections, would reveal neoclassical preferences. It is assumed that the person has some latent capacity to generate complete and integrated preferences, though his many psychological biases are likely to *interfere* with this latent capacity. There is, however, no psychological explanation for such latent preferences (Sugden 2015) and no clear theoretical foundation for assuming that the overall integrated preferences of an agent with context-dependent preferences would be neoclassical (Krause & Steedman 1986; Lecouteux & Mitrouchev 2021). Indeed, while behavioral economists found countless theories in cognitive psychology to explain how people *deviate* from norms of rational choice, rational choice itself remains unexplained. Consider, for instance, time preferences: it is commonly considered in BWE that time inconsistency is normatively problematic and that it is the result of a deviation (by, for example, a present bias) from the "correct" way of discounting future outcomes – exponential discounting. I will argue in section 4.2, however, that the various explanations that we could endorse to justify why discounting one's future utility is not irrational would imply behaviors compatible with hyperbolic rather than exponential discounting. If we accept that people can deviate from time neutrality (which I suggest would be the only acceptable preferences if time-inconsistent preferences are rejected), then we must *postulate* that exponential discounting is the right discounting model.

Another issue with postulating the existence of true preferences is its contradiction with the "as judged by themselves" clause. Indeed, any deviation from the prediction of rational choice theory is explained as a violation of assumption (ii) (that agents are instrumentally rational) and not of assumption (i) (that we have complete and integrated preferences). It is not clear, however, why we could not imagine that persons are instrumentally rational, even though their preferences are nonstandard and generate apparently incoherent choices. If one's preferences are a matter of personal tastes, then there is little reason to expect those subjective tastes to conform to the neoclassical axioms. Take loss aversion as an illustration (see Harrison & Ross 2017 for a similar argument). Two mechanisms could explain the typical pattern of risk preferences associated with loss aversion. First, the individual can genuinely experience a higher cognitive cost when facing losses – "utility loss aversion," captured by the parameter λ in Tversky and Kahneman (1992). Second, he can exhibit different probability weighting functions in the gain and loss domains – "probabilistic loss aversion" (Schmidt & Zank 2008).[8] In regard to utility loss aversion, there is no straightforward reason to maintain that we can ignore the aspects of the agent's psychology that generate a relative sensitivity to losses versus gains. In regard to probabilistic loss aversion, the interpretation of the weighting function as a form of perceptual error and a case of wrong belief about probabilities could justify regulations designed to limit the agent's ignorance (which would be acceptable even by liberal standards). However, if we understand the weighting function as a matter of *sensitivity* to changes in probability while knowing the right probability (Fox *et al.* 2015: 54–55), then it is far from clear that we can ignore the aspects of the agent's psychology that lead to such weighting.

To summarize thus far, BWE interprets incoherent preferences as the deviations from underlying coherent preferences. The existence of such true preferences (either actual or counterfactual), however, lacks any psychological explanation, and nothing guarantees that the preferences that are supposed to represent what the individual prefers, by his own light, ought to conform to the traditional axioms of rational choice theory. I will now argue that the normative argument against preference inconsistency is considerably weaker than is usually recognized.

3. What Is the Problem (If Any) With Incoherent Preferences?

The common justification of behavioral paternalism is that incoherent preferences are likely to generate preference reversals and may be a source of later regret. The individual would have been better off if a benevolent planner had helped him to make the right decisions earlier; given our higher expertise, we theorists are legitimized to identify the cases in which the individuals are likely to make mistakes. I see four objections to this line of argument.

First, in a situation of preference reversal, nothing guarantees that the regrets expressed by my later self are the symptom of a mistake made by my earlier self and that improving the situation of my earlier self, *as judged by the later self*, would have been welfare enhancing for the earlier self. The possibility that my preferences or identity may change over time, as well as that we cannot a priori rely on the sole judgment of a later self and ignore the judgment of an earlier one, implies that regrets cannot systematically offer a justification for paternalistic interventions.[9]

Second, despite casual claims that incoherent preferences expose the individual to money pumps, that is, to exploitation by malevolent third parties, the empirical evidence that incoherent preferences lead to welfare losses – or that individuals would not be able to adjust their behavior over time to avoid such losses – is seriously lacking [see the systematic review of the literature by Arkes *et al.* (2016)]. Cubitt and Sugden (2001) also suggest that money-pump arguments are theoretically flawed, because a precise definition of a money pump highlights that an invulnerability to money pumps does *not* require one to exhibit coherent preferences by neoclassical standards. We could, therefore, have individuals who are invulnerable to money pumps, while exhibiting nonstandard preferences.

Third, the empirical evidence that individuals make incoherent choices is based on choices realized in the controlled environment of a lab experiment. Now, in most real-life settings, the uncertainty faced by decision-makers is much more radical (people are rarely asked in their daily lives to choose between different prospects with known probabilities). Being "irrational" in the lab therefore gives little evidence that the agent is not rational outside the lab. Vernon Smith formulated this concern as follows (from an unpublished letter to Harsanyi 1989):[10]

> Another issue that has long bothered me in interpreting "violations" of vNM utility is the following: decision makers are accustomed to making decision in environments in which there is uncertainty about how many states there are, an uncertainty as to the description of every possible state. We bring subjects into the laboratory where we put them in environments in which we can guarantee what the alternative states are, and that the set is exhaustive. To what extent do people make "mistakes" in the latter environment because there [*sic*] intuition is programmed for the former? . . . For example, people tend to overweight the likelihood (sample) relative to their priors in well-defined Bayesian "learning" experiments. Well, this makes sense intuitively if the sample is a major source of learning about how rich is the set of states! Its like you had just drawn a green ball from an urn thought to contain only black and red balls.

If we want to express normative judgments about how people behave in real life, we need a realistic model of the individual's cognition, because the "computations of a model of cognition need to be tractable in the real world in which people live, not only in the small world of an experiment with only a few cues" (Gigerenzer *et al.* 2008: 236). Optimization models and Bayesian updating are very relevant in the small world of a controlled lab experiment – and experimental subjects frequently deviate from their theoretical predictions – though they are inadequate in fundamentally uncertain large worlds,[11] for which simple heuristics might be normatively more relevant (Gigerenzer & Sturm 2012: 262–264).

Last but not least, we should also question how "obvious" the general normative argument is against inconsistency. A likely bias is that theorists – the actual persons thinking about those questions – also tend to excessively value the importance of consistency. Nozick (1981: 407) suggests, for instance, that "philosophers are people with very strong motivations to avoid inconsistency," mostly because they are a self-selected group of people – by their origins and training – who value consistency highly. This is probably even truer of behavioral economists, who – because of their training in economics and their use of mathematical models and Bayesian techniques – have been taught for years that inconsistency was highly problematic and that experimental economics discovered anomalies and deviations from the norm of rational choice. There is, however, no straightforward ethical argument (apart from an explicit endorsement of some form of epistocracy) in favor of entrusting a group of people with PhDs in economics or philosophy, who are sociologically very far from being representative of the general population, with the task of defining what kind of lives people in general could normatively desire. As Sugden (2006: 50) puts it,

> When political philosophy is written from the stance of the moral observer, the reality of these risks is too easily overlooked. In proposing his own conception of what is valuable, an author has to provide a reasoned defence of his position. In doing this, it is easy to slip into assuming that anyone who understands these reasons will find them convincing. Without noticing, we can make the transition from the belief that we are right to the belief that we will come out on the winning side of a reasoned discussion about what is right. So, we are inclined to think, we have nothing to fear from allowing evaluative issues to be resolved in

> a properly conducted democratic process. Indeed it is surprisingly easy to go further, and to imagine that the process has already been carried out, and everyone *has* agreed with us.
> (Sugden 2006: 50, original emphasis)

Even though our own training and background as theorists – and then our own convictions as citizens about what constitutes a good life – might let us consider that consistency is of utmost importance, respect for the "as judged by themselves" clause should also mean respect for the rights of other people to act irrationally.

4. What Are Coherent Preferences?

Suppose now, for the sake of the argument, that incoherent preferences do pose a normative problem. The question that directly follows is which criterion of "coherence" should be used to define what is the "right" behavior. If we look at the literature in behavioral economics, the typical deviations documented by lab experiments are deviations with respect to (i) social preferences, (ii) time preferences, and (iii) risk preferences. Welfare-relevant preferences are supposed to be self-interested, time preferences consistent with *exponential discounting* and risk preferences consistent with *subjective expected utility theory*. To be coherent by neoclassical standards means to respect the conditions listed here. My aim in this section is to highlight that different norms of consistency may accommodate deviations from neoclassical standards. This means that we could very well be coherent with respect to a certain standard, while still exhibiting what a neoclassical theorist would consider as an inconsistency.

4.1 Social Preferences

Regarding social preferences, I will not discuss here the problems that may arise from double counting utilities in welfare measures and whether we should exclusively consider our own counterfactual self-interested welfare, purified from concerns regarding others (as suggested by, e.g., Hausman 2012). We can, however, keep the focus on questions of choice consistency by noting that neoclassical consistency requires agents to act systematically on the same preferences. This means that if I am apparently prosocial with an anonymous partner in a lab experiment (e.g., I give a significant share of my endowment in a dictator game), then it is also assumed that I will continue to be prosocial in the rest of the experiment and possibly outside the lab too.

It would, however, be perfectly sensible to imagine that I could be prosocial in certain environments, with certain partners, and under specific circumstances, while being selfish in many other cases. If we model sociality with an intention-based rather than outcome-based model, subjects could apparently "switch" between selfish and prosocial preferences, depending on the circumstances. This would be considered a case of preference inconsistency by neoclassical standards, but not necessarily within the framework of, for example, psychological games (Geanakoplos *et al.* 1989; Battigalli & Dufwenberg 2009; see Battigalli *et al.* 2019 for an overview) or team reasoning (Sugden 1993; Bacharach 2006; see Lecouteux 2018 for an overview). The question that arises here is whether we can legitimately ignore prosocial *intentions* in normative analysis; if not, then we should refer to a standard of consistency that accommodates such intentions, which is not true of BWE.[12]

4.2 Time Preferences

Now consider time preferences. Exponential discounting means that the individual uses a constant discount rate over time, which guarantees that his choices are time consistent. Now, an interesting question would be to know whether neoclassical rationality requires a specific value for this discount rate. When considering the agent over time, if we assume that "all parts of one's future are also parts of oneself; that there is a single, enduring, irreducible entity to whom all future utility can be ascribed" (Frederick 2003: 90) – which seems to be the case in neoclassical analyses of time preferences, with the assignment of an *undated* utility function to the agent – then there is no decisive argument for discounting future utilities. Temporal neutrality, with an equal weighting of all time periods, is, for instance, explicitly endorsed by O'Donoghue and Rabin (1999).

I have argued elsewhere that if we accept the argument that time-inconsistent choices reveal a mistake, then people *ought to be time neutral* (Lecouteux 2015). This is a rather strong normative claim, and there are many reasons why people could legitimately discount future outcomes. It is worthy to note, however, that if we consider the various reasons that could justify – from a normative perspective – discounting the future, it seems that the agent should *not* use a constant discount rate.

A first reason for discounting one's future utilities is the uncertainty of the future and that agents have a noisy estimation of their future utilities (because of a limited ability to foresee future experiences). Even if we consider unbiased noise, Gabaix and Laibson (2017) show that the resulting behavior is consistent with hyperbolic rather than exponential discounting. Another related motive that could justify discounting the future is the possibility of dying (or, at least, of not being able to collect outcomes in the future). However, this probability will not be constant over time, which will justify the use of a nonconstant discount rate. A third motive for discounting one's future utilities would be that one's preferences and identity are likely to evolve over time, as in Parfit's (1984) complex view of identity. This, however, also generates behavior consistent with hyperbolic rather than exponential discounting (Lecouteux 2015). Last, we can consider the opportunity cost of time in terms of financial savings. We should, however, again use a constant discount rate only if interest rates were themselves constant over time (which is obviously not the case).

4.3 Risk Preferences

Finally, consider risk preferences (Stefánsson, Chapter 3). When evaluating a prospect with known probabilities, an agent whose choices are consistent with expected utility maximization behaves as if he has a linear valuation of probabilities and a strictly increasing – but not necessarily linear – valuation of outcomes. The first problem is that it would be perfectly sensible to define conditions for coherent preferences with a nonlinear valuation of probabilities, such as in rank-dependent utility [see Wakker (2010) for a detailed discussion and an axiomatization] or the closely related, risk-weighted expected utility of Buchak (2013). These models can indeed be axiomatized while only slightly relaxing the conditions under which expected utility holds – the critical condition being unrestricted trade-off consistency, and there are good normative arguments in favor of weaker versions such as rank trade-off consistency or comonotonic trade-off consistency.

A second problem is the distinctive treatment of probabilities and outcomes in subjective expected utility theory. Indeed, for the same reason that increasing one's income by a fixed amount has a different marginal impact whether one is a beggar or a millionaire (captured by the degree of concavity or convexity of one's utility function), an increase in the probability of occurrence of the best outcome by 1 percentage point will have a different marginal impact on one's preferences, depending on the initial level of the probability (the impact will be significant if the initial probability is 0% or 99%, though it is likely to be negligible for, e.g., 40%). Descriptively, we tend to perceive both outcomes and probabilities nonlinearly. Normatively, however, there is no obvious reason why we ought to treat probabilities linearly *and not outcomes*. This leads to an inconsistency in neoclassical rationality: if we allow for a nonlinear perception of outcomes – and therefore allow for deviations from risk neutrality – then the agent's preferences contain a Dutch book (de Finetti 1931; see also

Wakker 2010: Chap. 1).[13] This means that if the possibility of being exploited by a third party is the symptom of preference inconsistency, then neoclassical rationality should require risk neutrality.

Even though we accept the view that our preferences ought to be coherent, the position that we ought to be coherent by neoclassical standards is rather weak. If we leave social preferences aside, it seems that a strict understanding of what it means to be coherent should imply time neutrality (any motive that could justify discounting the future would indeed also justify hyperbolic discounting) as well as risk neutrality (because it is the only risk attitude protecting us from a Dutch book). There are, however, other standards of consistency that seem normatively acceptable, though they will generate behaviors inconsistent with neoclassical standards. Before pointing out people's deviations, BWE should first justify why we ought to be (i) self-interested, (ii) time consistent, and (iii) expected utility maximizers.

5. Concluding Remarks: Changing BWE's Lens

I have argued in this chapter that, contrary to the conventional wisdom of BWE, the fact that subjects put in the lab violate the standards of (neoclassical) rational choice should *not* be interpreted as a mistake on the agent's behalf. Such evidence, therefore, does not offer a straightforward argument in favor of paternalistic regulations. BWE's argument indeed relies on the validity of the model of the inner rational agent, it probably overestimates the normative appeal of consistency, and it fails to properly justify why the "correct" way of behaving should be consistent with neoclassical standards.

I would like to conclude this chapter by emphasizing that my argument is not against paternalism per se, but rather against the *justification* for paternalism advanced in BWE. While I do not consider incoherent preferences to be fundamentally problematic, BWE highlights one important point that could justify regulations: the fact that people's preferences could be manipulated by third parties for their own personal, commercial, or political interests (unlike the benevolent nudgers and choice architects central to BWE). The normative problem does not lie in the preferences but in the process of preference formation. This point echoes Galbraith's (1938) early critique of the consumer sovereignty principle, which similarly rejected the idea of a difference between rational and irrational preferences put forward by Kahn (1935). According to Chirat (2020), Galbraith rather emphasized the *endogeneity* of preferences and that "the formation of preferences does not lie in the inner rational individual but in a cultural scheme and social interactions" (Chirat 2020: 267). If individual preferences are the product of a social system, it is problematic to use them as the fundamental building block of welfare analysis. BWE should probably acknowledge both the individual and the social determinants of our preferences and behaviors, rather than merely blaming the defective psychology of individual agents taken in isolation. An endorsement of the view that our preferences are fundamentally *shaped* by the social environment and the supply side of the market[14] would probably justify more ambitious social policies than nudges, whose aim is to correct *ex post* anomalies in our behaviors rather than to tackle *ex ante* the causes of such anomalies.

Related Chapters

Baujard, Chapter 15 "Values in Welfare Economics"
Stefánsson, Chapter 3 "The Economics and Philosophy of Risk"
Vromen, Chapter 9 "*As If* Social Preference Models"

Notes

1 Hutt (1940: 66) defines the principle of consumer sovereignty as "the controlling power exercised by free individuals, in choosing between ends, over the custodians of the community's resources, when the

resources by which those ends can be served as scarce." See Desmarais-Tremblay (2020) for a historical discussion.

2 I will use the generic term "theorist" to refer to the actual economist, philosopher, or outside observer who intends to model a choice problem and to derive a normative judgment about it. I will occasionally use the pronoun "we" to refer to theorists in general (I imagine that most readers could indeed find themselves in this position).

3 I will not discuss, in this chapter, the relationship between welfare and preference satisfaction and, in particular, whether "welfare" should be interpreted substantively – preferences being either constitutive or providing evidence about welfare – or formally – in which case welfare is defined by the satisfaction of preferences [see Lecouteux (forthcoming) on these questions in the context of BWE].

4 The distinction is common in this literature with, for instance, the opposition between "Humans" and "Econs" for Sunstein and Thaler or between Mr. Spock and Homer Simpson – such dual-self models are routinely used to contrast the "rational" and "psychological" parts of human agency.

5 See Baujard, Chapter 15, for an analysis of values in welfare economics.

6 The "proper" definition of rational, and what it means to be "rational in the neoclassical sense," will be discussed later.

7 By *integrated* (see Sugden 2018), I mean non-stochastic, context-independent, and internally consistent – consistency being defined by axioms such as transitivity or the sure thing principle. Completeness and integration typically imply the formal conditions that allow a utility representation of preferences.

8 For didactic purposes, it is usually simpler to present loss aversion in terms of utility loss aversion – the introduction of probability loss aversion indeed requires first explicating the notions of gain and loss ranks. It should, however, be noted that experimental tests of cumulative prospect theory suggest that the adequate explanation is in terms of probability weighting. Harrison and Swarthout (2016) indeed review the experimental tests of cumulative prospect theory and find that, in the few properly calibrated experiments, λ tends to be close to 1.

9 I have developed this argument in more detail in regard to retirement savings and time-inconsistent preferences in Lecouteux (2015).

10 I am very grateful to Dorian Jullien for sending me a scan of this letter during his stay at Duke University, USA.

11 I discuss in detail this distinction in terms of small and large worlds (in Savage's sense) in Lecouteux (2021).

12 On prosocial preferences, see also Vromen, Chapter 9.

13 The intuition is the following. Consider two complementary prospects such that P_E pays 1 if and only if E happens, and $P_{\bar{E}}$ pays 1 if and only if E does not happen. If we are (say) risk averse, we will value both prospects at less than their expected value. Someone who buys P_E and later $P_{\bar{E}}$ from us would therefore spend less than 1. However, the same individual would then be able to sell us the two prospects bundled together at a price of 1 (because $P_E \cup P_{\bar{E}}$ pays 1 for sure). We would then end up with a sure loss.

14 In the context of addictive behaviors, Ross (2020) argues that becoming un-addicted is mostly a question of improving one's heuristics (and, therefore, a matter of individual decisions), while addiction is the outcome of socially engineered addictive environments. An adequate policy against addiction should therefore not only help individuals to quit (thanks to, e.g., boosts) but also address the fact that the business model of some industries is precisely to foster addiction, such as the cigarette industry or social networking sites.

Bibliography

Arkes, H.R., Gigerenzer, G., and Hertwig, R. (2016) "How Bad is Incoherence?" *Decision* 3(1): 20.

Bacharach, M. (2006) *Beyond Individual Choice: Teams and Frames in Game Theory*, Princeton, NJ: Princeton University Press.

Battigalli, P., Corrao, R., and Dufwenberg, M. (2019) "Incorporating Belief-Dependent Motivation in Games," *Journal of Economic Behavior & Organization* 167: 185–218.

Battigalli, P., and Dufwenberg, M. (2009) "Dynamic Psychological Games," *Journal of Economic Theory* 144(1): 1–35.

Buchak, L.M. (2013) *Risk and Rationality*, Oxford: Oxford University Press.

Camerer, C.F. (2011) *Behavioral Game Theory: Experiments in Strategic Interaction*, Princeton, NJ: Princeton University Press.

Camerer, C.F., Issacharoff, S., Loewenstein, G., O'Donoghue, T., and Rabin, M. (2003) "Regulation for Conservatives: Behavioral Economics and the Case for 'Asymmetric Paternalism'," *University of Pennsylvania Law Review* 151(3): 1211–1254.

Chirat, A. (2020) "A Reappraisal of Galbraith's Challenge to Consumer Sovereignty: Preferences, Welfare and the Non-Neutrality Thesis," *The European Journal of the History of Economic Thought* 27(2): 248–275.

Cubitt, R.P., and Sugden, R. (2001) "On Money Pumps," *Games and Economic Behavior* 37(1): 121–160.

De Finetti, B. (1931) "Sul Significato Soggettivo Della Probabilita," *Fundamenta Mathematicae* 17(1): 298–329.

Desmarais-Tremblay, M. (2020) "WH Hutt and the Conceptualization of Consumers' Sovereignty," Oxford Economic Papers 72(4), 1050-1071..

Fox, C.R., Erner, C., and Walters, D.J. (2015) "Decision Under Risk: From the Field to the Laboratory and Back," in G. Keren and G. Wu (eds.), *The Wiley Blackwell Handbook of Judgment and Decision Making*, Chichester, West Sussex: Wiley-Blackwell: 43–88.

Frederick, S. (2003) "Time Preference and Personal Identity," in G. Loewenstein, D. Read, and R. Baumeister (eds.), *Time and Decision: Economic and Psychological Perspectives on Intertemporal Choice*, New York, NY: Russell Sage Foundation: 89–113.

Gabaix, X., and Laibson, D. (2017) *Myopia and Discounting* (No. w23254), National Bureau of Economic Research.

Galbraith, J.K. (1938) "Rational and Irrational Consumer Preference," *The Economic Journal* 48(190): 336–342.

Geanakoplos, J., Pearce, D., and Stacchetti, E. (1989) "Psychological Games and Sequential Rationality," *Games and Economic Behavior* 1(1): 60–79.

Gigerenzer, G., Hoffrage, U., and Goldstein, D.G. (2008) "Fast and Frugal Heuristics are Plausible Models of Cognition: Reply to Dougherty, Franco-Watkins, and Thomas," *Psychological Review* 115(1): 230–239.

Gigerenzer, G., and Sturm, T. (2012) "How (Far) Can Rationality be Naturalized?" *Synthese* 187(1): 243–268.

Guala, F. (2019) "Preferences: Neither Behavioural nor Mental," *Economics & Philosophy* 35(3): 383–401.

Harrison, G.W., and Ross, D. (2017) "The Empirical Adequacy of Cumulative Prospect Theory and its Implications for Normative Assessment," *Journal of Economic Methodology* 24(2): 150–165.

Harrison, G.W., and Swarthout, T. (2016) *Cumulative Prospect Theory in the Laboratory: A Reconsideration*, Experimental Economics Center Working Paper Series.

Hausman, D.M. (2012) *Preference, Value, Choice, and Welfare*, Cambridge, MA: Cambridge University Press.

Hutt, W.H. (1940) "The Concept of Consumers' Sovereignty," *The Economic Journal* 50(197): 66–77.

Infante, G., Lecouteux, G., and Sugden, R. (2016a) "Preference Purification and the Inner Rational Agent: A Critique of the Conventional Wisdom of Behavioural Welfare Economics," *Journal of Economic Methodology* 23(1): 1–25.

Infante, G., Lecouteux, G., and Sugden, R. (2016b) "'On the Econ Within': A Reply to Daniel Hausman," *Journal of Economic Methodology* 23(1): 33–37.

Kahn, R.F. (1935) "Some Notes on Ideal Output," *The Economic Journal* 45(177): 1–35.

Kahneman, D. (2011) *Thinking, Fast and Slow*, New York, NY: Farrar, Straus and Giroux.

Köszegi, B., and Rabin, M. (2007) "Mistakes in Choice-Based Welfare Analysis," *American Economic Review* 97(2): 477–481.

Krause, U., and Steedman, I. (1986) "Goethe's Faust, Arrow's Possibility Theorem and the Individual Decision Taker," in Elster, J. (ed.), *The Multiple Self*, Cambridge: Cambridge University Press: 197–231.

Lecouteux, G. (2015) "In Search of Lost Nudges," *Review of Philosophy and Psychology* 6(3): 397–408.

Lecouteux, G. (2018) "What Does 'We' Want? Team Reasoning, Game Theory, and Unselfish Behaviours," *Revue d'économie politique* 128(3): 311–332.

Lecouteux, G. (2021) "Welfare Economics in Large Worlds: Welfare and Public Policies in an Uncertain Environment," in H. Kincaid and D. Ross (eds), *Elgar Modern Guide to the Philosophy of Economics:* 208-233.

Lecouteux, G., and Mitrouchev, I. (2021) *The 'View from Manywhere': Normative Economics with Context-Dependent Preferences*, GREDEG Working Paper 2021-19.

Mill, J.S. (1859/2003) "On Liberty," reprinted in D. Bromwich and G. Kateb (eds.), *On Liberty*, New Haven, CT: Yale University Press.

Nozick, R. (1981) *Philosophical Explanations*, Harvard: Harvard University Press.

O'Donoghue, T., and Rabin, M. (1999) "Doing it Now or Later," *American Economic Review* 89(1): 103–124.

Parfit, D. (1984) *Reasons and Persons*, Oxford: Oxford University Press.

Ross, D. (2020) "Addiction is Socially Engineered Exploitation of Natural Biological Vulnerability," *Behavioural Brain Research* 386: 112598.

Schmidt, U., and Zank, H. (2008) "Risk Aversion in Cumulative Prospect Theory," *Management Science* 54(1): 208–216.

Sent, E.M. (2004) "Behavioral Economics: How Psychology Made its (Limited) Way Back into Economics," *History of Political Economy* 36(4): 735–760.

Simon, H.A. (1955) "A Behavioral Model of Rational Choice," *The Quarterly Journal of Economics* 69(1): 99–118.

Smith, V. (1989) "Letter to John Harsanyi, October 12, 1989," in Vernon Smith Papers, Correspondence, Box number 14, 1989 June-Dec (Folder 2 of 3); at David M. Rubenstein Rare Book and Manuscript Library, Duke University.

Sugden, R. (1993) "Thinking as a Team: Towards an Explanation of Nonselfish Behavior," *Social Philosophy and Policy* 10(1): 69–89.

Sugden, R. (2006) "What We Desire, What We Have Reason to Desire, Whatever We Might Desire: Mill and Sen on the Value of Opportunity," *Utilitas* 18(1): 33–51.

Sugden, R. (2015) "Looking for a Psychology for the Inner Rational Agent," *Social Theory and Practice* 41(4): 579–598.

Sugden, R. (2018) *The Community of Advantage: A Behavioural Economist's Defence of the Market*, Oxford: Oxford University Press.

Sunstein, C.R. (2014) *Why Nudge? The Politics of Libertarian Paternalism*, New Haven/London: Yale University Press.

Sunstein, C.R. (2020) *Behavioral Science and Public Policy*, Cambridge: Cambridge University Press.

Sunstein, C.R., and Thaler, R.H. (2003) "Libertarian Paternalism is not an Oxymoron," *The University of Chicago Law Review* 70(4): 1159–1202.

Tversky, A., and Kahneman, D. (1992) "Advances in Prospect Theory: Cumulative Representation of Uncertainty," *Journal of Risk and Uncertainty* 5(4): 297–323.

Wakker, P.P. (2010) *Prospect Theory: For Risk and Ambiguity*, Cambridge: Cambridge University Press.

5

THE ECONOMIC CONCEPT OF A PREFERENCE

Kate Vredenburgh

1. Introduction

Preferences are normatively and descriptively central to economics. The view of markets as being led by an invisible hand that coordinates the (self-interested) free actions of butchers, brewers, and bakers to produce more valuable outcomes – from the perspective of efficiency and also perhaps egalitarian social relations[1] – than individuals acting alone has been deeply entrenched in economics from Smith onward. Preferences are also core to two principles of neoclassical economics – optimization and equilibrium – as well as to economics' chief normative standard for judging institutions, policies, and outcomes – Pareto efficiency.

And yet, economists also seem to care very little about preferences. Exogenous preferences are often conveniently assumed to allow for a tractable solution to what Hayek calls "the economic problem," or the best way to allocate a given set of means.[2] Furthermore, it is often claimed that economics is ultimately concerned with discovering relationships between macrovariables, rather than understanding individual decision-making.

This tension is reflected in a deep disagreement over the correct interpretation of the concept of a preference. The so-called marginalists[3] of the late nineteenth century, such as Jevons, Walras, and Edgeworth, grounded their marginal revolution in psychological conceptions of utility inspired by Benthamite social theory's hedonic calculus of pleasure and pain. Moved by measurement and other concerns that cast doubt on the scientific integrity of a psychological concept of utility, later economists such as Pareto, Hicks, and Allen moved to focus on the ranking of choice alone, rather than the mental states that produce that ranking.[4] However, they did not completely succeed in excising the psychological from choice modeling, and psychology has again gained prominence in economics through certain successes of behavioral economics.[5]

This chapter addresses itself to the puzzling, seeming co-existence of psychological and nonpsychological interpretations of "preference" in economics.[6] Because of the enormity and importance of the question of the correct concept of preference in economics, as well as the richness of the work addressing it, a chapter on this topic will always be hopelessly incomplete without narrowing its focus. Accordingly, I will set aside normative arguments about the concept of a preference and focus on descriptive applications of preference-based choice frameworks.[7]

After introducing the methodology of the article (Section 2) and some background about preferences in economics (Section 3), in Sections 4 and 5 I will discuss two prominent interpretations: mentalism and behaviorism. Section 6 discusses arguments for and against each view. Section 7

DOI: 10.4324/9781315739793-6

discusses two views that attempt to move the debate beyond the mentalism and behaviorism divide. Section 8 concludes by suggesting another path forward, namely, a focus on the background scientific commitments driving the debate.

Finally, before we jump in, I want to address a certain kind of skepticism about the usefulness of philosophical argumentation about the concept of a preference for scientific practice. One might consider the arguments about the concept of a preference to be mere metaphysical speculation that does not impact economic practice. However, without clarity on what type of features of the world preferences represent, there will be downstream unclarity about which types of evidence should be used to build and test models.[8] And so, conceptual clarity is important for good scientific practice.

2. Methodology

There are at least two different strategies one might take to adjudicate the debate over the correct concept of a preference for economics. The first strategy is, so to speak, more external to economics and starts either with ontology or with epistemology. Starting with ontology, one might ask what preferences are in light of one's preferred methodology for ontological theorizing. Starting with epistemology, one might develop a theory of instrumental rationality and ask what mental states figure in rational means-ends reasoning.

A second strategy takes a philosophy of science approach to adjudicating the debate, starting with scientific theories and practice and asking what "preference" should be in order to make sense thereof.[9] This latter strategy is the one I will pursue here. In particular, I will treat "preference" as a theoretical term. Theoretical terms are introduced into a scientific theory for some particular scientific purpose that cannot be accomplished by previously well-understood terms. One of the central questions around theoretical terms is how they become intelligible to users of the theory. What I will refer to as the standard account treats them as either implicitly or explicitly defined by the theory in which they are embedded, in terms of primitives or already well-defined terms.[10]

With that methodological framing in place, we will move to background on preferences.

3. Preferences

The study of microeconomics is often introduced to students through the parable of Robinson Crusoe: abandoned on a desert island, he acts as both producer and consumer and must decide how to split his time optimally between harvesting coconuts and leisure. A standard microeconomics graduate textbook skips the narrative niceties and begins with models of individual rational choice, which is the basis of consumer demand. Microeconomics since Alfred Marshall, as well as sometimes macroeconomics, standardly models productive agents such as firms as profit maximizers and consuming agents such as individuals or households as utility maximizers.

Axiomatized choice theories[11] – formal choice models that can be divided up into decision theory, game theory, and social choice theory – are the heart of such standard microeconomic and macroeconomic analyses. Accordingly, much of the philosophical and economic debate around the concept of a preference has focused on axiomatized choice theories. This chapter follows that trend, in part because axiomatized theories of individual choice are methodologically diverse and, thus, raise a number of issues pertinent to the present discussion.[12]

Axiomatized choice theories start from the idea that agents choose on the basis of their preferences and information, and in light of constraints that determine which options are available. This idea of choosing on the basis of preferences is then formalized. These formalizations often start with a non-empty set of mutually exclusive objects of choice (x, y, z . . .). A binary relation, the so-called weak preference relation, is then defined over the set, where "x is weakly preferred to y" can be informally glossed as "x is at least as good as y." The weak preference relation is assumed to be both *complete* – for every two options x and y, the agent weakly prefers either x to y, y to x, or both (meaning she is indifferent between the two) – and *transitive* – if the agent weakly prefers x to y and y to z, then she weakly prefers x to z. Within the framework at issue, a representation theorem is proven that shows that agents can be represented as expected utility maximizers within the formal framework if and only if certain axioms hold.[13]

The binary preference relation is a formal object in a theory, one that needs to be interpreted. Because we are treating preference as a theoretical term, its interpretation is constrained by the postulates of the theory in which it is embedded. Two additional postulates are central to economic theorizing about choice. Axiomatized choice theories often posit the following connection between preference and choice: the individual chooses those options that are at least as good as the other feasible options in that choice context.[14] The second postulate is *stability*, or the assumption that an agent's preference for x over y does not change across contexts.[15]

Thus, whatever entity "preference" refers to, it should at least satisfy the postulates of being comparative, stable, transitive, complete, and linked to an optimal choice. With that background in place, we will move on to the discussion of mentalist and behaviorist interpretations of preference.

4. Preferences as Mental

Mentalist interpretations of the concept of preference have the most august pedigree in economics. Mentalist views, unsurprisingly, take preferences to be a mental state. Different mentalist views posit different types of mental states, usually conative states, as the referent of "preference". This section discusses three categories of such views: desire-based views, total comparative evaluation views, and functionalist views.

The close link between preferences and choice may lead one to posit that preferences should be interpreted as a type of comparative desire, as both desires and preferences exhibit the same conceptual or causal connection between having the mental state with some state of affairs as its content and acting to bring about that state of affairs.[16] Different views may adopt a wider sense of desire as choice-worthiness or a narrower sense of desire as pleasure.[17] As mentioned in the introduction, the latter view has a long history in economics: Jevons, for example, influenced by Bentham, posited a hierarchy of pleasure and pains.[18] Recent research in neuroeconomics and behavioral economics has revived the interpretation of preference as a hedonic state, aiming to measure the "true" utility, understood as a measurable psychophysical magnitude, that stands behind so-called decision utility, a mathematical representation of preference.[19]

The interpretation of preference as referring to desires, however, can make the assumption of stable preferences puzzling. For many of us, the desire for coffee over tea is not stable; it may be closer to a whim, or it may be highly dependent on the environment and other facts about my physical and mental states, especially which properties of the coffee or tea I am attending to at the moment of choice.

One response to this problem has been to move to an interpretation of preference upon which all of the relevant factors that might, when attended to selectively across contexts, undermine stability are already taken into account in one's preference ranking. This second type of mentalist view takes preferences to be total comparative judgments of relative desirability (Bradley 2017) or total subjective comparative evaluations (Hausman 2011), that is, mental states whose rankings reflect all of the agent's relevant reasons. I will focus on Hausman (2011) as an example. For Hausman, to rank coffee over tea is to consider all the dimensions along which one might compare coffee and tea and come up with a ranking in light of how coffee fares against tea, taking into account all relevant considerations. Because preferences are by definition complete and transitive, Hausman argues that agents' rankings must already incorporate all of the subjective evaluative considerations that determine choice.[20] And, while preferences need not be stable, they are more likely to be, because agents have not arbitrarily selected a subset of some dimensions along which to compare options (Hausman 2011: 35).

While Hausman's account addresses the issue with stability faced by desire-based accounts, it does so at the cost of an implausible account of the cognitive demandingness of preferences – implausible both as a reconstruction of the economic view of preferences and in light of cognitive science.[21]

A third type of view, the functionalist views, adopts Hausman's move to abstract the content of preferences but does not commit to a particular type of content or story about preference formation.[22] Functionalism takes a mental state to be individuated by the causal relations in which it stands to other states, as well as the causal relations between the inputs and outputs of the state.[23] The mental state preference, then, is picked out or defined in terms of its functional role, such as the motivational role that it plays in producing a choice in response to certain sensory inputs (say, the perception of feasible options), as well as the causal relations that it typically stands in with other mental states such as belief.

5. Preferences as Behavioral

The second family of interpretations we will consider is behavioral interpretations, which usually find their home in so-called revealed preference approaches in microeconomics.[24] Paul Samuelson's (1938) "A Note on the Pure Theory of Consumer's Behavior" originated the revealed preference program in microeconomics, although a behavioral interpretation of preference has its roots in earlier work by Pareto, Hicks, Allen, and others who black-boxed psychology to focus on choice ranking. Samuelson showed analytically that the theory of consumer behavior can be modeled by demand functions – the amount of each good that will be purchased given a set of prices and the agent's income – and consistency constraints on those demand functions. The key consistency constraint on choices proposed by Samuelson is the so-called the Weak Axiom of Revealed Preference (WARP), which states that if a consumer purchases bundle B at price p when bundle C is available, then if C is chosen at price q, B is not available. The consumer's actions are taken to "reveal" a preference for B over C, where revelation is merely a matter of engaging in a certain pattern of consistent behavior.[25]

Revealed preference approaches sometimes refer to an inference procedure to identify psychological preferences from choice behavior. However, the target interpretation here is one upon which revealed preferences merely summarize information about choice behavior. They do not represent the desires, intentions, or other psychological underpinnings of that behavior. So, to ascribe a revealed preference to Abel for coffee over tea is to say that he chooses or would choose coffee instead of tea in contexts where both are feasible options.

The example brings out one major choice point in fleshing out the behaviorist interpretation of preference, namely, whether the preference relation represents actual or counterfactual behavior.[26] *Actualist* interpretations take revealed preferences to be mere summaries of patterns in an agent's actual choice behavior across similar contexts. So, for example, if Barry always actually chooses coffee over tea, then Barry's choice behavior can be summarized by revealed preference for coffee over tea. *Qua* object in the world, revealed preferences are just patterns of actual choices.

So-called *hypothetical* interpretations take revealed preferences to summarize what agents would choose in a context. A representational object such as the revealed preference relation can be unpacked as a series of counterfactuals of the form, "in context K, this agent chooses option x; in context L, this agent chooses option y."[27] *Qua* object in the world, hypothetical revealed preferences are behavioral dispositions, attributable to agents, to make certain choices in a variety of actual and counterfactual circumstances. To attribute a revealed preference to Zeynep for coffee over tea, for example, is to attribute a behavioral disposition to Zeynep to choose coffee over tea in contexts where she has a choice between both.

The actualist interpretation of revealed preferences is more in keeping with some of the original empiricist motivations for the view.[28] However, it sits uneasily with much of economic practice and policy advising, where economists use counterfactual information about choices to infer what would happen (for example, on the basis of an exogenous shock), even if that event never does happen. Accordingly, this chapter focuses on the hypothetical revealed preferences (henceforth, the "hypothetical" qualifier will be dropped).

6. Behaviorism vs Mentalism

There is a long history of arguments for and against behavioral or mental interpretations of the concept of preference, and there is not nearly enough space to do justice to the range of motivations for and objections to both views. This section focuses on two big questions: are preferences causes? And, do they explain?

6.1 Causation

Causation is central to descriptive, predictive, and explanatory projects in economics.[29] All else being equal, an interpretation of preference upon which preferences can be part of the causal structure of economic systems is superior to one on which they cannot. Mentalist interpretations of preference seem to have an obvious advantage here. Pre-theoretically, mental preferences are quite obviously a cause of individual choice. However, the same does not hold of behaviorist interpretations. How can an agent's past – or, even more absurdly, counterfactual – choices of coffee over tea cause her to choose coffee when faced with tea today?

While the inability of revealed preferences to play the role of a cause may seem obvious, it is worth spelling out. One of the most serious causal objections to behaviorism focuses on the role of belief in producing choice.[30] The first premise of the objection states that, because different beliefs can produce the same choice, economists must also model beliefs in order to impute the correct preferences to an agent. It is often supported by a pair of contrasting cases like the following:

1. Cemal prefers to see the new romantic comedy over the new war film. But, he believes that the new romantic comedy is not playing in any theaters close to him. So, he goes to see the new war film.
2. Cemal prefers to see the new war film over the new romantic comedy. He believes that both are playing in at least one theater close to him. So, he goes to see the new war film.

Assuming that one does not want to sacrifice the intuition that Cemal has different preferences in the two cases, the theorist must model Cemal's beliefs about which films are playing.[31] The second premise asserts that beliefs are psychological states that cause choice. The third premise states that only psychological states can causally combine with psychological states to cause choice. So, preferences must be psychological, in order to cause choice behavior.

This argument has been taken to be devastating for behaviorist views. Most proponents of behaviorism accept the conclusion that revealed preference explanations cannot be causal explanations.[32] They then argue that frameworks that use a behavioral interpretation of preference have other advantages that outweigh their inability to provide causal explanations. For example, some behaviorists are skeptical that a single concept of preference could both play a role in a general theory of decision-making and play a role in causal explanations, due to the wide heterogeneity of the causal mechanisms that generate individual and aggregate choices.[33] Because axiomatic choice theories are a central part of the microfoundations of economics, they ought to be general and, thus, are excluded from causally explaining choices.

However, the argument is not as devastating as it first appears. There is room for the behaviorist to challenge all three premises. The challenges to the first and second premises admit that some information about the options must play a role in modeling, but they deny that doing so requires representing an agent's beliefs, understood as a psychological state. The challenge to the third premise, by contrast, focuses on issues around causal structure.

Let's start with the first premise, that economic models must represent beliefs. One might admit that to handle cases like the preceding Cemal case requires some mentalism, but only of a limited sort, namely, mentalism about the options.[34] The problem raised by the description of the options in the Cemal case is that the options are not consistent with the agent's beliefs, nor are they described in such a way as to pick out features that matter for the agent's choice.[35] Cemal is better modeled as preferring to see a war film over no film, because seeing the romantic comedy is not compatible with his beliefs, that is, feasible. Because describing options in this way is desirable for choice modeling generally, we have a principled response to supposedly devastating cases like the Cemal case.

The second premise, that beliefs are psychological states that cause choice, seems to be beyond dispute. However, some economic models arguably represent nonpsychological concepts of belief. In some models, belief is better understood as common information in the system, which could be considered either a property of the environment or a nonpsychological property of the agents.[36] This property of the environment or the agent would then trigger revealed preferences, that is, belief-dependent behavioral dispositions. This move is, of course, an idealization in the case of human agents, as agents always have both public and private information, as Hayek made much of.[37] But, this idealization is apt in stable environments with repeated interactions around homogeneous goods and information about their common value, or in environments where agents can learn the optimal strategy.[38]

Finally, the behaviorist may push back against the third premise, that only psychological states can combine with belief – understood psychologically – to cause choice. Here, there is a common strategy with the argument against premise two: appeal to economic models that, under a certain interpretation, discount the premise. Agent-based models are promising evidence against the claim that only psychological preferences can combine with psychological beliefs to cause choice. They offer evidence that revealed preferences can be causes at two levels: first, of individual choices and, second, of aggregate patterns.

For example, Schelling's (1971) Spatial Proximity model aims to understand one potential mechanism for housing segregation, namely, individual preferences. The surprising result of Schelling's model is that segregation is compatible with a variety of individual preferences, including a very small discriminatory preference and a preference for being in the minority. The model shows this result by first setting up two populations of agents who occupy spaces on a board (i.e., dwellings). Each agent has a behavioral disposition to move if a certain percentage or more of her neighbors belong to a different group (call this her tolerance threshold).[39]

The Spatial Proximity model is best known for the case where each group's tolerance threshold is the same and the groups are of roughly equal size. In that case, the model has two equilibrium states: when $F < 1/3$, a random pattern emerges; when $F > 1/3$, a segregated pattern emerges. The model is robust to changes in various elements of the model. Thus, Schelling's simple model allows us to ask and answer counterfactual questions about individual behavior and aggregate results thereof, indicating that it isolates a potential causal mechanism.[40] We can explain agents' choices to move in terms of their tolerance threshold and the composition of their neighborhood. Different parameters of the model can also be adjusted in order to answer counterfactual questions about the conditions under which segregated equilibria are produced. This ability to answer such counterfactual questions suggests that Schelling's model represents possible causal mechanisms by which revealed preferences cause both individual choices to move and patterns of segregation.[41]

Before we move on, it is worth noting that the initial setup of the causal challenge to behaviorism was weaker support for a mentalist interpretation than it may have appeared to be. If we grant that a pre-theoretical interpretation of preference picks out something that can play a causal role in individual decision-making, it is only weak evidence that mental preferences – as defined by axiomatized choice theories – cause choice. And indeed, there is a preponderance of empirical evidence that individuals do not choose as axiomatized choice theories represent them as choosing.[42] To give just one example: social and moral norms and expectations sometimes determine behavior through psychological mechanisms that are very different from the optimization imputed by axiomatized choice frameworks.[43]

6.2 Explanation

Revealed preferences are also taken to be at a serious explanatory disadvantage. The explanation of Denish's choice of coffee over tea in terms of her behavioral disposition to choose coffee over tea, says the critic, does, at least, inform us that she does so regularly, but it leaves us not much more enlightened as to why she chooses coffee over tea. For that, we require an explanation of her behavior in terms of her mental states, such as her beliefs and desires.[44]

Again, it behooves us to dig more deeply into this complaint in order to reveal the explanatory advantages and disadvantages of mentalism and behaviorism. Rather than rely on a particular account of explanation, I will focus on three commonly agreed upon properties of good explanations: nontriviality, empirical testability, and generality.

The objection that revealed preference explanations are trivial has a long history, going back at least to J.S. Cairne's (1872) criticisms of marginalists such as Jevons, through to Sen (1982). The triviality of purported revealed preference explanations is easily seen by example. Suppose, for the sake of simplicity, a theorist predicts which drink Edwina will choose from a list of oolong tea and a cappuccino. She might do so using a revealed preference relation over those choices, constructed from past observations of choices between those options. The explanation would run as follows: "Edwina will choose oolong tea because she is disposed to choose oolong tea over a cappuccino."

But, while such examples make claims of triviality compelling, more work needs to be done to articulate what the revealed preference theorist is being charged with. One way of understanding the triviality charge is as positing a vicious circularity. This circularity is straightforward on an actualist interpretation of the revealed preference relation. The revealed preference relation summarizes a long conjunction of choice events, and the choice to be explained is one conjunct. The choice to be explained then partly explains itself.[45] Some hypothetical accounts of revealed preferences may escape this charge of circularity. If the theorist were to interpret hypothetical revealed preferences as a behavioral disposition, for example, the representation of this disposition may not contain the choice to be explained.

A second way of cashing out the triviality worry is the concern that the revealed preference relation is puzzlingly close to a tautology, for an empirical science. "Fei Fei chose coffee over tea because she tends to choose coffee over tea" leaves us only slightly more enlightened as to why Fei Fei chose coffee over tea than an explanation of why Gary is an unmarried man in terms of his bachelorhood. Of course, a preference relation summarizes a good deal of information about regularities in individual behavior. Furthermore, it is not trivial to figure out the logical consequences of ascribing a particular preference to individuals when modeling an individual decision-problem or a system with interacting agents. Consider the conceptual exploration of potential mechanisms of segregation enabled by Schelling's Spatial Proximity model. The threshold at which segregated equilibria are produced is, for example, not obvious and arguably strikes us as an explanatory insight.

If the complaint about revealed preference explanations is not a complaint about their conceptual triviality, perhaps it is best understood as an empirical complaint. There is a strong version of the complaint that argues that revealed preference models have no testable implications, as the modeler can always rationalize a set of observed choices as the result of preference maximization. However, the revealed preferences in explanations are not entirely empty of empirical content, due to consistency constraints imposed on preferences.[46] Furthermore, many modeling applications of axiomatized choice theories make additional assumptions about individual preferences that add empirical content, such as the common assumption that people prefer to consume more rather than less.[47]

So, a better way to understand the complaint is as arguing that the content of a revealed preference explanation is severely underdetermined, due to the flexibility of the theory and its reliance on choice data.[48] If an individual seems to display inconsistent behavior, she can be reinterpreted as having changed her preferences, or the choice context may be reinterpreted as containing different options. Note, however, that this charge of empirical underdetermination also applies to standard axiomatic choice frameworks with a mental interpretation of preference.[49] The issue here, as Dietrich and List (2016a) argue, is the evidence base, and it is, in principle, available to the behaviorist and mentalist alike to expand the evidence base for their models beyond choice data without changing the concept of preference. Thus, neither the circularity nor the empirical underdetermination problem are strong arguments for mentalism over behaviorism.

The flexibility of behavioral preferences previously alluded to has also, interestingly, been claimed as grounding one of the interpretation's chief advantages over mentalism: contributing to a more general framework for understanding economic phenomena.[50] Why might that be? One of the foundations of standard economic analysis is optimization under constraints, both individually and for interacting agents. Frameworks built on optimization are usually taken to be fruitful for modeling the behavior of a wide variety of systems, and that is because the same small set of distinctly economic variables usually determines the outcomes of interest – namely, aggregate level variables – in a wide variety of systems.[51] Among the relevant economic variables, individual psychology, as well as variations therein, is taken to be of negligible causal influence.[52] Finally, the mathematical tractability of axiomatized choice frameworks – enabled by assumptions about preferences such as completeness, transitivity, monotonicity, etc. – allows economists to easily incorporate auxiliary assumptions and the values of key economic variables that do important explanatory work.[53] So, axiomatized choice theories with revealed preferences can model a more diverse set of phenomena within a single framework and are thus more unifying and preferable, *ceteris parabis*.[54]

Of course, this generality comes at the cost of a continuity or unification with psychology, another sort of desirable unification. Proponents of unification with psychology, cognitive science, or neuroscience will push this sort of generality, taking it to be beneficial not only in itself but also for economics because "ceteris paribus, the more realistic our assumptions about economic actors, the better our economics" (Rabin 2002: 658). Here we have a final explanatory argument for mentalism: because mentalist interpretations of preference are more psychologically realistic, and more realistic explanations are superior, they are to be preferred.[55]

Gul and Pesendorfer, two prominent defenders of behaviorism, take issue with Rabin's claim. They can be read as arguing that models that are more psychologically realistic are generally more realistic. And that is because they are skeptical about a general realism across psychology and economics, because (1) neither discipline has – or perhaps could have – formulated a general theory of human nature that can be used to explain phenomena of interest to both disciplines, and so (2) each discipline uses abstractions suited to the phenomena it studies. Their position here can be explained by a strong metaphysical thesis or a weaker metaphysical thesis plus an epistemic thesis. A weaker version of the metaphysical thesis posits causal and structural complexity in social systems, which, in combination with cognitive and technological limitations, prevents theorists from detecting general, compact patterns that predict and explain such systems (the epistemic thesis). A stronger version of the metaphysical thesis posits ontological emergence, where not all of the properties or laws of higher level systems reduce to lower level properties or laws.

We began with two views about the correct concept of preference in economics and, after a series of arguments, have ended up with a potential disagreement over emergence. The next section discusses two proposals for the interpretation of preference that offer alternatives to mentalism and behaviorism, perhaps allowing us to escape the morass of behaviorism vs mentalism without tackling such fundamental questions.

7. Beyond the Behaviorism and Mentalism Divide?

Two recent contributions to the debate over the concept of a preference aim to push the debate beyond the historically entrenched mentalism and behaviorism divide. They take two different approaches to doing so. Guala (2019) seeks a unified concept of preference that inherits the strengths of both the mentalist and the behaviorist views and escapes devastating problems with each. Angner (2018), by contrast, argues against a unified concept of preference across economic theories on the basis of its status as a theoretical term.

Guala (2019) aims to formulate an interpretation of preference that can account for the wide range of types of agents to which axiomatized choice frameworks are applied, from human agents to hermit crabs to firms.[56] He argues that preferences are psychologically and nonpsychologically realizable, belief-dependent dispositions to choose some option A in circumstances C. Important to the dispositionalist account is that there is an underlying causal base B that, in circumstances C, causes the agent to choose A. The disposition brackets the causal base, explaining the occurrence of choice A in terms of the disposition and circumstances C. This higher level of description is useful for the economist's purposes because dispositions are *multiply realizable* by underlying causal bases of different physical kinds.[57]

However, the fact that different types of physical systems are describable by the same mathematics does not yet establish that they share a common physical structure, in virtue of which preference refers to a single kind. Guala is alive to this potential worry and analogizes preference with the concept of a force in physics, where the entities that are the object of study of different branches of physics receive the same "abstract interpretation" (Guala 2019: 384).

It is important in Newtonian mechanics, however, that different forces add up to a net force, giving the theorist reason to posit a single kind. There is no such theoretical push, however, in the case of preference. The widespread use of preferences to model different types of systems in economics is more analogous to modeling different types of systems as a spring. Doing so can be predictively useful to model systems where an elastic solid body is deformed – from the compression of a spring in one's ballpoint pen to the bending of a tall building in strong wind. However, it would be a mistake to interpret acoustics, seismology, and molecular mechanics as studying systems with the same ontology. Rather, the description of a system as a spring, or as containing agents that have rational preferences, ascribes a common feature to the dynamics of these systems – that choices exhibit a certain kind of consistency, for example – without positing a similar ontology or otherwise similar causal structure.

That Guala runs into this problem is not surprising because of a long-standing disagreement about whether dispositions causally explain.[58] Here, Guala seems to run into an explanatory dilemma. If one takes the spring analogy seriously, Guala's proposal shares a purported disadvantage with behavioral interpretations, namely, that the very abstract concept of a preference does not show suitable causal unity among its micro-realizers, even if it is an epistemically useful concept for summarizing dynamic or other properties of causally very different systems. To avoid this charge, however, and reject the spring analogy requires tying the interpretation of preference more closely to the causal structure of certain systems. However, that move strips the belief-dependent dispositional interpretation of its lauded generality.

Perhaps Guala's attempt fails to identify a unified concept of preference in economics because there is not such a unified concept. Drawing on work by Nagel (1961), Angner (2018) argues that the philosophical debate is misguided, insofar as it seeks an explicit definition of preference. Because preference is a theoretical term, it is implicitly defined by the postulates of the theory in which the term is embedded.[59] Indeed, Angner (2018: 676) proposes a radical context relativity of the meaning of preference: it is defined entirely by the postulates of the theory in which it is embedded.

This way of cashing out the standard view of theoretical terms is found in work by Nagel, Lewis (1983), and others, but it is also a radical view of their meaning, one that is incongruent with broader theories of meaning for natural language and empirical scientific practice.[60] Even within the standard view of theoretical terms, it is implausible that their meaning is entirely stipulative. One might – as Lewis later did – take there to be a naturalness constraint on reference, where some entities are better candidates for reference than others by virtue of being more natural.[61]

One might also posit other constraints particular to the social sciences. One such constraint comes from a common desideratum for concepts in the social sciences, namely, that they are continuous with those of folk psychology.[62] In the case of choice modeling, philosophers such as Hausman (2011) maintain that interpretations of choice-theoretic models ought to be continuous with folk psychological notions of the causes of behavior. Acceptance of both of these constraints may favor a mentalist referent of preference rather than a behaviorist one.

However, neither this additional constraint nor a naturalness constraint on theoretical terms immediately pushes us back to a unified concept. Indeed, one can maintain Angner's insight that the work done by the concept of preference, and thereby its meaning, is likely different across theories and in their application to different types of markets without adopting a radical pluralism.[63] It may be that economics needs multiple concepts of preference that serve different theoretical purposes, some of which may be grounded in folk psychology.[64]

8. Conclusion

Unfortunately, neither Guala's (2019) nor Angner's (2018) view seems to be able to break the gridlock between behaviorism and mentalism. And, indeed, both raise questions similar to those of the behaviorist and mentalist views: do dispositions explain? What is the appropriate level of abstraction to model preferences? Are there constraints on the reference of "preference" beyond those determined by the theoretical context?

Sections 5 and 6 explored how deeply the debate over the correct concept of preference is driven by background methodological, epistemic, and metaphysical divides. This is not surprising – if philosophers of science and economists were concerned merely as to what concept of preference economists currently use, they would exclusively use methodologies such as examining the postulates of theories and surveying economists. However, the question at issue is what the correct concept of preference is for economic theorizing, a question that is informed but not settled by economic practice or by practicing economists' opinions about their own practice. As such, the debate is driven by a larger background disagreement, such as disagreements over explanation, emergence, unification in the sciences, abstraction, and idealization.

The fact that the debate over the correct concept of preference is the site of such trenchant disagreement about big picture questions about science has also sometimes muddied the argumentative waters. For example, much of the disagreement between behavioral economists and defenders of neoclassical economics about the status and content of key postulates in which preferences feature is often taken to speak to the question of whether preference refers to behaviors or mental states. However, those arguments are better reconstructed as targeting the empirical status of the postulates featuring preferences, rather than the concept itself.[65] For additional clarity, and to make progress moving forward, more focus should be directed to these background disagreements.[66]

Related Chapters

Grayot, Chapter 6 "Economic Agency and the Subpersonal Turn in Economics"
Lecouteux, Chapter 4 "Behavioral Welfare Economics and Consumer Sovereignty"
Moscati, Chapter 2 "History of Utility Theory"

Notes

1 See Anderson (2017) for an intellectual history of free market ideology.
2 As Hayek, that master observer of human life, says,

> What is the problem we wish to solve when we try to construct a rational economic order? On familiar assumptions, the answer is simple enough. *If* we possess all the relevant preferences, and *if* we command complete knowledge of available means, the problem which remains is purely one of logic. That is, the answer to the question of what is the best use of the available means is implicit in our assumptions.
>
> (Hayek 1948: 77)

He was, of course, skeptical of the assumptions that generate such an easy – in the sense of analytical, although not in the sense of trivial – solution.
3 So named because they explained the exchange value of a commodity in terms of its marginal utility, rather than its labor value.
4 Lewin (1996) and Moscati (2018). For example, Hicks (1956: 6, quoted from Sen 1982: 56) claimed that "econometric theory of demand does study human beings, but only as entities having certain patterns of market behavior; it makes no claim, no pretense, to be able to see inside their head."
5 See also Moscati, Chapter 2 Grayot, Chapter 6, and Lecouteux, Chapter 4.
6 Lewin (1996) calls this "Sen's paradox."
7 This division is, of course, artificial, given that the frameworks I will discuss are frameworks representing *rational* choice.
8 Dietrich and List (2016a: Section 3.2) and Gul and Pesendorfer (2008: Chapter 1) take one of the central stakes of the debate between neoclassical behaviorists and behavioral economists or mentalists to be which evidence should be used to build and test models and theories.
9 Dietrich and List (2016a), Guala (2019), and Angner (2018) take a philosophy of science approach to this debate.
10 This characterization of the standard view follows Strevens (2012).
11 Term borrowed from Herfeld (2018a).
12 See Hands (2012, 2013) and Herfeld (2018a).
13 Rational choice theory, for example, can be formulated by taking choice, preference, or utility as basic; the three formulations are equivalent under certain coherence assumptions. The formulations in terms of choice and preference are most relevant for this chapter. However, as many decision theorists and most economists standardly treat "utility" as reducible to preference (Oshaka 2016), I will sometimes discuss utility when it is plausibly being interpreted as a mathematical representation of preference.
14 Kreps (2013: 3).
15 Hausman (2011: 16).
16 According to Dietrich and List (2013: 104), decision theory is "thoroughly Human," representing agents as choosing so as to maximize their desires in light of their beliefs.
17 Schroeder (2015: 3.3).
18 Moscati (2018: Chapter 2: 2.1.1).
19 One might either target "true utility" at the psychological level via so-called experienced utility, a hedonic state that causally influences choice, or at the neurological level via so-called neural utility, the computation of subjective value by specific neural areas (Fugamalli 2019). For a critical discussion of this research program, see Fugamalli (2019).
20 Hausman (2011: Chapter 4.1).
21 Angner (2018: 667–668), Binmore (2008: 13).
22 See Dietrich and List (2016a: 268) for an example of the former and List and Pettit (2011) for an example of the latter.
23 Block (1978: 262).

24 I will use "behaviorism," "revealed preferences," and "behavioral interpretation" to refer to the interpretation of preferences as mere behavior. As Clarke (2016) argues, a behaviorist interpretation of preference is separable from other theoretical commitments of traditional twentieth century behaviorism, such as the commitment that mental states do not exist. Indeed, Binmore (2008) and other modern behaviorists acknowledge that mental states cause individual behavior and that choice data are generated from latent psychological variables.

25 Further theoretical work was done by Little (1949) and Houthakker (1950). Afriat (1967) then extended this theoretical work to the empirical study of consumer choice through the Generalized Axiom of Revealed Preference [see also Kreps (2013: Chapter 4) for discussion].

26 Hausman (2011: 24–25).

27 See, for comparison, Block (1978: 263) on behaviorism about the mind, on which behaviorism is spelled out in terms of a series of input-output relations.

28 Hausman (2011) identifies Samuelson (1938) and Little (1949) as holding the actualist view, in light of their empiricist commitments, and Binmore (1994) as holding the hypothetical view.

29 One of the main aims of econometrics over the last three decades has been to estimate causal effects across a wide variety of economic outcomes in different populations, which has become particularly important for the evaluation of policies. Given the increasing experimental – and, particularly, causal – focus in economics, it is a serious cost to an interpretation of "preference" if preferences cannot play the role of causes.

30 Hausman (2011), Rosenberg (1993), and Guala (2019).

31 Some economists, such as Gul and Pesendorfer (2008), are willing to bite the bullet here regarding whether economic methodology can or ought to distinguish between the cases.

32 See Binmore (2008: 1.9) on what he calls the Causal Utility Fallacy.

33 See Binmore (2008) and Ross (2014b: 251–252).

34 Thoma (2021).

35 Thoma (2021).

36 Guala (2019: 396–397) uses the example of a hiring process where the information in job applications influences the hiring decision without that information being identical to any individual or sum of psychological states. Thus, the relevant beliefs, he contends, are not best understood psychologically.

37 Hayek (1948: Chapter 4).

38 It is often maintained that ongoing markets are just such institutional environments that embed past information and channel behavior without agents having to grasp the rules whereby the system works in its entirety [see Hayek (1948: Chapter 4), Ross (2005, 2014a), and Satz and Ferejohn (1994)]. Furthermore, many markets are designed to reduce private information about the uncertain characteristics of the good (as contrasted with private information about individual tastes), thus avoiding problems raised by asymmetric information [see Milgrom (1979a, 1979b) and Wilson (1977) for results that, in first-price auctions with enough participants, the price aggregates information about common value]. See also Ross (2014a) for a discussion of the importance of learning.

39 The Spatial Proximity model is a theoretical model used to explore possible mechanisms [see Sugden (2000), Aydinonat (2007), and Weisberg (2013: 7.1.1)]. However, because the aim of the argument is to motivate the claim that preferences can be causes, a theoretical model is sufficient for current dialectical purposes.

40 Here I am using an overly simple heuristic for causation, namely, that the outcome would not have occurred (or would have been different) if the cause had not occurred (or been different). This heuristic provides some – but certainly not decisive – reason to think a potential causal mechanism has been identified.

41 Note that one could deny that axiomatized choice theories explain individual choices but argue that aggregate phenomena are causally explained by the interactions of agents who are well described by axiomatized choice theories [see Herfeld (2018b) and Ross (2014b)].

42 Otherwise, they would have to be capable of "feats of superhuman calculation," as Binmore says (2008: 1.9). See Camerer, Loewenstein, and Rabin (2004) and Thaler (1994) for evidence from behavioral economics.

43 Pettit (1995), Cudd (2014), Sen (1982: Essay 4). Sen (1982: 94–99), for example, argues that while commitment may not significantly determine behavior in consumer markets, it is an important motivator in areas of life such as public goods and production. Furthermore, he argues that commitment cannot be accommodated by standard axiomatized choice frameworks. For work that integrates norm-motivated behavior into nonstandard formal choice models, see Bossert and Suzumura (2009), Bhattacharyya, Pattanaik, and Xu (2011), and Dietrich and List (2016b).

44 Steele (2014).

45 See Vredenburgh (2020) for a conditional defense of revealed preference approaches against the circularity charge.

46 See Sen (1982: 90) discussing comments in Samuelson (1955), as well as Camerer, Loewenstein, and Prelec (2005: 10).
47 This is formally represented as the assumption that preferences are monotone or strictly monotone (Kreps 2013: 2.1).
48 See Hodgson (2012), Dietrich and List (2016a), and Sen (1982).
49 See Dietrich and List (2016b) and Hodgson (2012).
50 By "generality" here, I mean what Weisberg (2013: 6.2.5) calls "p-generality" or the number of possible target systems to which a model applies. Generality, of course, is not the only desideratum on explanations. Otherwise, scientists could achieve spurious generality – by, say, replacing a generalization with the disjunction of it and another generalization – for a more general explanation. Thus, the literature on scientific explanation usually proposes an additional criterion for a good explanation, targeting an empirical similarity among the phenomena as a desideratum on explanations (Strevens 2008; Weslake 2010).
51 This assumption is more plausible for markets, which are usually structured by similar institutions, property rights, other legal regulations, and monetary structures. See Ross (2014a).
52 For arguments that the focus on explaining aggregate variables privileges explanations that abstract away from the individual psychology that produces the decision, see Dowding (2002), Ross (2005), and Guala (2019). There is much more to be said on this point, but here are a few things. In support of the general claim that variation in individual psychology does not influence standard results in microeconomics, one might appeal to attempts to found microeconomics on models without classically rational agents, such as Becker (1962) and Gode and Sunder (1993) [see Ross (2014b: Chapter 5) for a discussion]. Of course, in some markets, individual psychology is causally significant as work in behavioral finance, for example, has shown. Finally, the point that individual psychology is of negligible importance should not be confused with another point economists sometimes make when pushed on descriptive and normative questions about preferences, namely, that economic models do not represent individuals' preferences when the models are properly interpreted, despite appearances [Ross (2014a) reads Samuelson (1955) in this way]. However, just because economists aim to explain stable patterns rather than individual behavior does not support the more radical claim that those stable patterns are neither explained nor constituted in part by an appeal to facts about individual preferences. Such an argument would presuppose either instrumentalism – economic models merely aim to capture the data – or a strong metaphysical or epistemic emergence – individual behavior is not relevant to modeling aggregate phenomena. On the issue of emergence, see Herfeld (2018b).
53 Interestingly, some critics take the fact that much of the explanatory work is done by these auxiliary assumptions to be a mark against axiomatized choice theories (Hodgson 2012). This complaint either assumes that a component of a successful explanation should be explanatory on its own or relies on the ability to separate the explanatory contributions of different components of an explanation.
54 See Mäki (1990, 2001) and Ross (2005) for work on unification in economics.
55 A number of behavioral economists and philosophers, such as Thaler (2000), Angner and Loewenstein (2012), and Hausman (2011), have also argued that the falsity of assumptions about human behavior in axiomatized choice-theoretic models makes for bad economics.
56 See also Satz and Ferejohn (1994). Elwood and Appel (2009), for example, attribute preferences to hermit crabs in order to explain when they leave different qualities of shells in response to electric shocks.
57 See, for example, Fodor (1974: 105–107), who argues that not every natural kinds or properties of the special sciences are more basic physical kinds or properties. That is because entities with different underlying physical structures can realize the same state. As Block (1978: 264–265) notes in response to a point by Kim (1972), that physical objects have *some* physical properties in common, the argument must be that there is no *nontrivial* physical kind or property that is common between these realizers.
58 Molière's satire of a group of physicians who explain opium's sleep-inducing power by reference to its "dormitive virtue" is often wheeled out to cast doubt on the explanatory power of dispositions. Lewis (1986) takes dispositions to be explanatory, but that may hinge on a somewhat particular feature of his account of causal explanation.
59 An example implicit definition view is one according to which theoretical terms are taken to be implicitly defined by correspondence rules, that is, sentences that contain theoretical and nontheoretical terms and that thereby link theoretical terms to a number of nontheoretical terms in such a way as to generate an interpretation of those theoretical terms (Carnap 1939).
60 On the former, see Hawthorne (1994); on the latter, see Strevens (2012), although Strevens makes this point as part of an argument for a nonstandard account of the meaning of theoretical terms.
61 See Hawthorne (1994).
62 A general version of this thought – most famously articulated by Weber (1978/1922) – is that human motivation, one of the building blocks of the social sciences, is introspectively accessible to the scientist, whereas

the building blocks of the natural sciences are not introspectively available. However, controlled experiments to discover robust generalizations are (more) available in the natural sciences, unlike the social sciences.
63 Ross (2014a) and Herfeld (2018a) stress the latter point.
64 See Sen (1982: Chapter 4, especially 4.7) for what I take to be an example of this view.
65 Guala (2019: 388).
66 This strategy is taken by Dietrich and List (2016a) and by Moscati (2018).

Bibliography

Afriat, S. N. (1967) "The Construction of Utility Functions from Expenditure Data," *International Economic Review 8*: 67–77.

Anderson, E. (2017) *Private Government: How Employers Rule our Lives (and Why We Don't Talk About It)*, Princeton: Princeton University Press.

Angner, E. (2018) "What Preferences Really Are," *Philosophy of Science 84(4)*: 660–681.

Angner, E. and Loewenstein, G. (2012) "Behavioral Economics," in U. Mäki (ed.) *Handbook of the Philosophy of Science: Philosophy of Economics*, Amsterdam: Elsevier: 641–690.

Aydinonat, N.E. (2007) "Models, Conjectures and Exploration: An Analysis of Schelling's Checkerboard Model of Residential Segregation," *Journal of Economic Methodology 14(4)*: 429–454.

Becker, G. (1962) "Irrational Behavior and Economic Theory," *Journal of Political Economy 70*: 1–13.

Bhattacharyya, A., Pattanaik, P.K. and Xu, Y. (2011) "Choice, Internal Consistency and Rationality," *Economics and Philosophy 27(2)*: 123–149.

Binmore, K. (1994) *Game Theory and the Social Contract*, Cambridge, MA: MIT University Press.

Binmore, K. (2008) *Rational Decisions*, Princeton: Princeton University Press.

Block, N. (1978) "Troubles with Functionalism," in C.W. Savage (ed.) *Minnesota Studies in the Philosophy of Science Vol. IX*, Minneapolis: University of Minnesota Press: 261–325.

Bossert, W. and Suzumura, K. (2009) "External Norms and Rationality of Choice," *Economics and Philosophy 25*: 139–152.

Bradley, R. (2017) *Decision Theory with a Human Face*, Cambridge: Cambridge University Press.

Cairnes, J.E. (1872) "New Theories in Political Economy," *Fortnightly Review 17*: 71–76. Reprinted in Peart, S. (ed.) (2003) *W.S. Jevons: Critical Responses*, vol. 3, Abingdon: Taylor and Francis.

Camerer, C., Loewenstein, G. and Prelec, D. (2005) "Neuroeconomics: How Neuroscience Can Inform Economics," *Journal of Economic Literature 43(1)*: 9–64.

Camerer, C., Loewenstein, G. and Rabin, M. (eds.) (2004) *Advances in Behavioral Economics*, Princeton: Princeton University Press.

Carnap, R. (1939) *Foundations of Logic and Mathematics, International Encyclopedia*, vol. I, no. 3, Chicago: University of Chicago Press.

Clarke, C. (2016) "Preferences and the Positivist Methodology in Economics," *Philosophy of Science 83*: 192–212.

Cudd, A. (2014) "Commitment as Motivation: Amartya Sen's Theory of Agency and the Explanation of Behavior," *Economics and Philosophy 30(1)*: 35–56.

Dietrich, F. and List, C. (2013) "A Reason-Based Theory of Rational Choice," *Noûs 47(1)*: 104–134.

Dietrich, F. and List, C. (2016a) "Mentalism vs Behaviorism in Economics: A Philosophy-of-Science Perspective," *Economics and Philosophy 32(2)*: 249–281.

Dietrich, F. and List, C. (2016b) "Reason-Based Choice and Context-Dependence: An Explanatory Framework," *Economics and Philosophy 32(2)*: 175–229.

Dowding, K. (2002) "Revealed Preference and External Reference," *Rationality and Society 14*: 259–284.

Elwood, R. and Appel, M. (2009) "Pain Experience in Hermit Crabs?" *Animal Behavior 77*: 1243–1246.

Fodor, J. (1974) "The Special Sciences (or: The Disunity of Science as a Working Hypothesis)," *Synthese 28(2)*: 97–115.

Fugamalli, R. (2019) "(F)utility Exposed," *Philosophy of Science 86(5)*: 955–966.

Gode, D. and Sunder, S. (1993) "Allocative Efficiency of Markets with Zero-Intelligence Traders: Markets as a Partial Substitute for Individual Rationality," *Journal of Political Economy 101*: 119–137.

Guala, F. (2019) "Preferences: Neither Behavioral nor Mental," *Economics and Philosophy 35(3)*: 383–401.

Gul, F. and Pesendorfer, W. (2008) "The Case for Mindless Economics," in A. Caplan and A. Schotter (eds.) *The Foundation of Positive and Normative Economics*, New York: Oxford University Press: 3–39.

Hands, D.W. (2012) "Realism, Commonsensibles, and Economics: The Case of Contemporary Revealed Preference Theory," in A. Lehtinen, J. Kuorikoski, and P. Ylikoski (eds.) *Economics for Real: Uskali Mäki and the Place of Truth in Economics*, Part II, Chapter 7, Abingdon: Routledge.

Hands, D.W. (2013) "Foundations of Contemporary Revealed Preference Theory," *Erkenntnis* 78: 1081–1108.
Hausman, D. (2011) *Preference, Value, Choice, and Welfare*, Cambridge, UK: Cambridge University Press.
Hawthorne, J. O'Leary. (1994) "A Corrective to the Ramsey-Lewis Account of Theoretical Terms," *Analysis 54(2)*: 105–110.
Hayek, F. von. (1948) "The Use of Knowledge in Society," in *Individualism and Economic Order*, Chicago: University of Chicago Press, Chapter 4.
Herfeld, C. (2018a) "The Diversity of Rational Choice Theory: A Review Note," *Topoi 39*: 329–347.
Herfeld, C. (2018b) "Explaining Patterns, not Details: Reevaluating Rational Choice Models in Light of Their Explananda," *Journal of Economic Methodology 25(2)*: 179–209.
Hicks, J.R. (1956) *A Revision of Demand Theory*, Oxford: Oxford University Press.
Hodgson, G. (2012) "On the Limits of Rational Choice Theory," *Economic Thought 1(1)*: 94–108.
Houthakker, H. (1950) "Revealed Preference and the Utility Function," *Economica 17*: 159–174.
Kim, J. (1972) "Phenomenal Properties, Psychophysical Laws, and the Identity Theory," *The Monist 56(2)*: 177–192.
Kreps, D. (2013) *Microeconomic Foundations I*, Princeton: Princeton University Press.
Lewin, S. (1996) "Economics and Psychology: Lessons for Our Own Day from the Early Twentieth Century," *Journal of Economic Literature 34*: 1293–1323.
Lewis, D. (1983) "How to Define Theoretical Terms," in *Philosophical Papers: Volume I*, Oxford: Oxford University Press, 78–96.
Lewis, D. (1986) "Causal Explanation," in D. Lewis (ed.), *Philosophical Papers Vol. II*, Oxford: Oxford University Press, 214–240.
List, C. and Pettit, P. (2011) *Group Agency*, Oxford: Oxford University Press.
Little, I.M.D. (1949) "A Reformulation of the Theory of Consumer's Behaviour," *Oxford Economic Papers 1(1)*: 90–99.
Mäki, U. (1990) "Scientific Realism and Austrian Explanation," *Review of Political Economy 2*: 310–344.
Mäki, U. (2001) "Explanatory Unification: Double and Doubtful," *Philosophy of the Social Sciences 31(4)*: 488–506.
Milgrom, P. (1979a) *The Structure of Information in Competitive Bidding*, New York: Garland Publishing Company.
Milgrom, P. (1979b) "A Convergence Theorem for Competitive Bidding with Differential Information," *Econometrica 47*: 679–688.
Moscati, I. (2018) *Measuring Utility: From the Marginal Revolution to Behavioral Economics*, Oxford: Oxford University Press.
Nagel, E. (1961) *The Structure of Science: Problems in the Logic of Scientific Explanation*, London: Routledge and Kegan Paul.
Oshaka, S. (2016) "On the Interpretation of Decision Theory," *Economics and Philosophy 32*: 409–433.
Pettit, P. (1995) "The Virtual Reality of Homo Economicus," *The Monist 78(3)*: 308–329.
Rabin, M. (2002) "A Perspective on Psychology and Economics," *European Economic Review* 46: 657–685.
Rosenberg, A. (1993) *Economics: Mathematical Politics or Science of Diminishing Returns?* Chicago: University of Chicago Press.
Ross, D. (2005) *Economic Theory and Cognitive Science: Microexplanation*, Cambridge: MIT University Press.
Ross, D. (2014a) "Psychological Versus Economic Models of Bounded Rationality," *Journal of Economic Methodology 21(4)*: 411–427.
Ross, D. (2014b) *Philosophy of Economics*, London: Palgrave Macmillan.
Samuelson, P. (1938) "A Note on the Pure Theory of Consumer's Behaviour," *Economica 5*: 61–71.
Samuelson, P. (1955) *The Foundation of Economics*, Cambridge: Harvard University Press.
Satz, D. and Ferejohn, J. (1994) "Rational Choice and Social Theory," *Journal of Philosophy 91*: 71–87.
Schelling, T.C. (1971) "Dynamic Models of Segregation," *Journal of Mathematical Sociology 1*: 143–186.
Schroeder, T. (2015) "Desire," in E.N. Zalta (ed.) *The Stanford Encyclopedia of Philosophy* (Summer 2017 Edition), URL = <https://plato.stanford.edu/archives/sum2017/entries/desire/>.
Sen, A. (1982) *Choice, Welfare, and Measurement*, Cambridge, MA: The MIT Press, Chapter 4: "Rational Fools: A Critique of the Behaviorist Foundations of Economic Theory."
Steele, K. (2014) "Choice Models," in N. Cartwright and E. Montuschi (eds.) *Philosophy of Social Science: A New Introduction*, Oxford: Oxford University Press, 185–207.
Strevens, M. (2008) *Depth*, Harvard: Harvard University Press.
Strevens, M. (2012) "Theoretical Terms Without Analytic Truths," *Philosophical Studies 160(1)*:167–190.
Sugden, R. (2000) "Credible Worlds: The Status of Theoretical Models in Economics," *Journal of Economic Methodology 7(1)*: 1–31
Thaler, R. (1994) *The Winner's Curse: Paradoxes and Anomalies of Economic Life*, Princeton: Princeton University Press.

Thaler, R. (2000) "From Homo Economicus to Homo Sapiens," *Journal of Economic Perspectives 14(1)*: 133–141.
Thoma, J. (2021) "In Defense of Revealed Preference Theory," *Economics and Philosophy 37(2)*: 163–187.
Vredenburgh, K. (2020) "A Unificationist Defense of Revealed Preference," *Economics and Philosophy 36(1)*: 149–169.
Weber, M. (1922/1978) "The Nature of Social Action," in *Wirtschaft und Gesellschaft*. Reprinted in W.G. Runciman (ed.), *Max Weber: Selections in Translation*. Cambridge: Cambridge University Press, 7–32.
Weisberg, M. (2013) *Simulation and Similarity: Using Models to Understand the World*, Oxford: Oxford University Press.
Weslake, B. (2010) "Explanatory Depth," *Philosophy of Science 77(2)*: 273–294.
Wilson, R. (1977) "A Bidding Model of Perfect Competition," *Review of Economics Studies 4*: 511–518.

6

ECONOMIC AGENCY AND THE SUBPERSONAL TURN IN ECONOMICS

James D. Grayot

1. Introduction

A recurring theme in the history of economic thought is the idea that individuals are sometimes better thought of as collections of *subpersonal* agents, each with its own interests or goals. The modeling of persons as collections of agents has proved to be a useful heuristic for investigating aberrant choice behaviors, such as weakness of will, procrastination, addiction, and other decision anomalies that indicate internal or motivational conflict. Yet, the concepts and methods used to study subpersonal agents give rise to a frenzied and sometimes confusing picture about who or what economic agents are, if not individual persons.

In this way, the subpersonal turn in behavioral economics and neuroeconomics marks an important break with mainstream theorizing about economic agency. According to the mainstream view, (a) agents have well-defined preferences and make decisions so as to realize those preferences; (b) preferences accurately reflect an agent's information about their options; and (c) agents update their beliefs about their options in light of changing information. While philosophers and methodologists may quibble about the finer points of each condition, the consensus is that the economic agent is a human person, albeit an idealized one (Rubinstein 2006; cf. Ross 2005, 2012).[1]

But if persons are collections of subpersonal agents, closer inspection of the concepts "subpersonal" and "agent" is warranted. The aim of this chapter is to explore how the concept of the economic agent has changed following the subpersonal turn in economics. I will focus on answering three questions. First, what makes up the subpersonal domain, and how does it relate to the economic study of decision-making? Second, what are the units of subpersonal economic analysis? Third, at what level of subpersonal processing might these units or entities be found?

In Section 2, I introduce three ways of understanding the subpersonal domain, and in Sections 3 and 4, I survey attempts by behavioral economists and neuroeconomists to develop an economics of the subpersonal. Both sections characterize a different conception of subpersonal agency. In Section 5, I consider the philosophical implications of these conceptions for future economic research.

2. Parsing the Domain of the Subpersonal

The realm of the subpersonal ranges over diverse metaphysical and psychological terrain. In one sense, we might call an event *subpersonal* if it is not directly accessible to conscious thought. Though

DOI: 10.4324/9781315739793-7

we have reasonably clear access to our own thoughts (most of the time), we do not have direct access to our brains and their physiological properties – which is to say, we do not have access to the processes that subvene and support conscious thought. For this reason, neural-physiological processes are paradigmatic of subpersonal events because they are effectively quarantined from *personal-level* events, like beliefs, intentions, and other mental states that we can access by introspection. This is the standard sense in which philosophers and cognitive scientists understand the subpersonal (Dennett 1987, 1991; Hornsby 2000).

There are, however, other senses in which we might deem an event subpersonal. For example, basic urges and subconscious motivations often play an important part in how we reason and make decisions. Strong emotions and visceral reactions like anger, hunger, and sexual arousal are good examples of this second sense because they can be highly influential on our thoughts without our being aware of it (Loewenstein 1996, 2000; Metcalfe & Mischel 1999). These subpersonal events may start out as inaccessible to introspection (and in some cases remain inaccessible), but they are different from the standard sense of subpersonal in that they need not, and perhaps cannot, be expressed solely in neural-physiological terms. This is either because they are functionally irreducible to neural-physiological processes and mechanisms or because casting them in terms of a neural-physiological explanation is epistemically undesirable.[2]

Another sense in which we might call an event subpersonal is if it pertains to or covers only a very limited frame of a person's time horizon. For instance, we might describe persons who allow their current impulses to dictate their future affairs as "myopic" because these actions seem to be isolated from their global plans. In this third sense, the subpersonal may also include time slices of a person's biography that are bracketed or deviate from other personal-level goals or interests (Frederick, Loewenstein, & O'Donoghue 2002; Heilmann 2010).

My point in elaborating these senses is not to impose strict constraints on how the domain of the subpersonal is to be partitioned and understood; it is just to illustrate that one can parse the subpersonal in various ways relative to different philosophical purposes.

In the next two sections, I present a potted survey of two ways in which economists have attempted to parse the domain of the subpersonal. As we will see, the methods and models involved cut across the three senses presented above and raise interesting questions about how we should think about the economic agent in contemporary economic research. Table 6.1 loosely categorizes how these accounts of agency will be surveyed. I will use the term *neural agent* to denote cases in which models ascribe utilities or value functions to neural-physiological processes or mechanisms, whereas I will use the term *virtual agent* to refer to all other cases of ascriptions of utilities or value functions to subpersonal events that do not correspond to strictly neural-physiological processes or mechanisms.[3]

Table 6.1 Parsing the domain of the subpersonal

	Virtual agents		*Neural agents*	
Type of analysis	Picoeconomics	Multiple-agent models	Behavioral economics in the scanner (BES)	Economics of neural activity (ENA)
Units of analysis	Short-term, medium-term, and long-term interests	Temporal selves/ dual cognitive processes	Brain regions/neural systems	Individual neurons/ groups of neurons
Level of analysis	Molar level	Spans molar and molecular levels	Spans molar and molecular levels	Molecular level

3. Virtual Agents

3.1 Early Behavioral Economics and Picoeconomics

While early choice models in economics were generally not interested in explaining the psychological aspects of decision-making (cf. Samuelson 1937), modeling innovations by Strotz (1955), Phelps and Pollak (1968), and later Schelling (1980, 1984) showed how intrapersonal and intertemporal dynamics could lead to preference changes. The idea behind these models is that an individual's latent preferences could be modeled as competing interests, which are distinguished by unique value functions. As a precursor to modern *multiple-self* models, these models demonstrated how myopic and weak-willed behaviors could be manifested and then rationalized as a trade-off between short-term and long-term interests. These interests were thus treated as independent agents. However, it was not until the 1980s and early 1990s that decision researchers began to make explicit connections between economic and psychological approaches to modeling intrapersonal and intertemporal bargaining among *virtual* agents. These connections span what are now generally regarded as separate but overlapping research programs in behavioral economics, picoeconomics, and instrumental decision theory.[4]

Thaler and Shefrin (1981; cf. Shefrin & Thaler 1988) were among the first to develop the idea of a motivationally divided self into a psychologically intuitive model for behavioral economics. Their *dual-self* model interpreted intertemporal choice as an intrapersonal conflict between the interests of a long-run "planner" self and a short-run "doer" self. Though this was based on prevailing psychological theories of mental accounting of the time (see Kahneman & Tversky 1979; Thaler 1985), Elster (1987) and Loewenstein (1996, 2000) extended this idea by positing that motivational conflict between short-term and long-term selves could be attributed to "hot" and "cold" emotional states (see also, Metcalfe & Mischel 1999). These attempts to model motivational conflict in terms of virtually present agents precipitated later attempts by behavioral economists to interpret selves as discrete cognitive processes.

Psychological research on weakness of will, procrastination, and addiction has provided further elaboration on the structure of subpersonal economic agency and its effects on intertemporal choice. Among other contributions, Ainslie's *picoeconomics* (1992, 2001; see also Rachlin 2000; Green & Myerson 2004) has provided a novel way to understand paradigmatically irrational choice phenomena as the result of hyperbolic discounting. Similar to early planner-doer models in economics, which posited that an individual's forward-looking and prudent self imposes constraints on the consumption habits of their myopic self, Ainslie's characterization of motivational conflict envisions short-term, medium-term, and long-term *interests* engaged in bargaining games, where each seeks to strengthen its own prospects by leveraging support from other interests. To maintain behavioral stability (i.e., achieve equilibrium among competing interests) and to avoid entering into dangerous consumption patterns (i.e., ceding control to short-term interests), a person's long-term interests may try to constrain their short-term interests or may adopt strategies that make short-term interests ineffective. However, unlike planner-doer models in behavioral economics, Ainslie's conception of the person as a community supposes a dynamically more complex picture of the subpersonal domain, with interests continuously emerging and presenting new (virtual) opportunities to engage in games with other interests. While some long-term interests may be prudent from the perspective of the individual who is wary of their short-term urges, there is no "planner" per se to which we would ascribe rational authority.

3.2 Modern Behavioral Economics and Dual-Process Theory

Interestingly, behavioral economists working within the dual-self framework have generally eschewed picoeconomic interpretations of intrapersonal and intertemporal conflict; instead, they have pursued modeling approaches that place greater emphasis on the cognitive processing of decisions. In this way, the subpersonal agents that selves were intended to formally represent have been slowly and systematically updated to cohere with changing trends in cognitive psychology (see Angner & Loewenstein 2012). In fact, one sees separate research trajectories within behavioral economics utilizing the rhetoric of *dual-process theory*.

One trajectory corresponds to individual decision-making in the heuristics and biases tradition. In social and cognitive psychology, dual-process models of reasoning and judgment have helped to illuminate why and how framing effects and other quirks of human reasoning give rise to choice phenomena that seem to systematically deviate from expected utility theory (Tversky & Kahneman 1973, 1974; cf. Kahneman, Slovic, & Tversky 1982). The framework of dual-process theory provides an account of how the differential activation of separate cognitive processing types (one fast, automatic, and reactive; the other slow, controlled, and deliberative) can support complex mental operations – such as implicit and explicit learning, rule-following and deductive inference, and counterfactual reasoning – while also being prone to judgmental biases and reasoning errors (Evans 2006, 2008; Evans & Stanovich 2013).

Though behavioral economic models in the heuristics and biases tradition are not in the habit of positing virtual agents (understood as transient selves or interests), the modeling of decisions as the outcome of separate cognitive processing types indicates that economists do believe that persons are, in some (possibly literal) sense, divided. Many behavioral economists have thus come to adopt a simpler and more generic form of dual-process theory which casts decision-making as the outcome of the interaction of distinct *systems*, namely, System 1 and System 2 (Kahneman & Frederick 2002, 2005; Kahneman 2003, 2011; cf. Strack & Deutsch 2004; Alós-Ferrer & Strack 2014). Most interpretations of the dual-system view treat System 2 as an inner rational agent, one which monitors System 1 and intervenes to prevent it from making biased judgments that result in suboptimal decisions. It is often suggested that, were it not for the error-prone processing of System 1, persons would adhere to the norms of rationality prescribed by logic and probability theory and would more closely resemble *Homo economicus* agents of neoclassical economics (Kahneman 2011; cf. Infante, Lecouteux, & Sugden 2016).

3.3 Multiple-Agent Models in Behavioral Economics

The idea that individual decision-making is governed by distinct systems that correspond to separate cognitive processing types carries over into another research trajectory in behavioral economics. Grayot (2019) describes how attempts by behavioral economists to integrate the mathematics of dual-self models with contemporary dual-process frameworks from cognitive psychology have given rise to a new style of "multiple-agent" model. Multiple-agent models retain the use of virtual agents to flesh out the cognitive dynamics from which motivational conflict arises; they do this by investigating how controlled and automatic processes, respectively, influence choice behaviors over different time spans. In some instances, the internal dynamic between intertemporal selves serves to establish the conditions under which an individual is able to exhibit self-control (construed as a sequential game between selves); in other instances, the conflict between the motivations to consume now or later is modeled as a trade-off by deliberative and affective systems (or some other variation of the dual-process framework), the outcome of which depends upon how much energy it takes for one system to exert control over the other. Examples of this kind of decision modeling can be found in Bénabou and Tirole (2002), Bernheim and Rangel (2004), Benhabib and Bisin (2005), Loewenstein and O'Donoghue (2005), Fudenberg and Levine (2006), among others.

While multiple-agent models clearly traffic in virtual agents, that is, they posit intrapersonal and intertemporal selves that range over short-lived subpersonal events, it can be difficult to ascertain what, exactly, the units and targets of economic analysis are in such models. This is because, by recruiting the psychological concepts of dual-process theory to substantiate the behavior of temporal selves, an individual's transient interests (which are formally modeled as temporal selves) as well as their cognitive systems (which are taken to dictate their selves' competing interests) become candidates for the ascription of utilities or value functions. This means that both interests and cognitive systems may take the role of the subpersonal agent. I will return to this issue below.

4. Neural Agents

4.1 Two Styles of Neuroeconomics

In opposition to behavioral economic models that posit virtual agents and then proceed to hunt for candidate entities for the ascription of utilities and value functions, neuroeconomic models aim to understand how neurobiological mechanisms literally represent and compute value in human brains (Montague & Berns 2002; Glimcher 2003; Camerer, Loewenstein, & Prelec 2005; Bernheim 2009). However, much like behavioral economics, the neuroeconomics landscape is quite diverse, and it is often difficult to determine the common goals, methods, and explanatory ambitions of disparate neuroeconomic models (Konovalov & Krajbich 2019). For this reason, when it comes to understanding what distinguishes neural agents from virtual agents, we also need to distinguish between different approaches to neuroeconomic modeling. To simplify things, I adopt the view presented in Ross (2008) and further elaborated in Harrison and Ross (2010) and Vromen (2011), which presents two styles of neuroeconomics.

One style, called "behavioral economics in the scanner" (BES), tries to infer how individuals form their preferences by tracking decision-making processes in the brain. As the name suggests, the methodology of BES involves running laboratory experiments on persons while studying their brains and then drawing inferences about which regions or structures of the brain are involved in the processing of different choice tasks. Importantly, this method of inference depends on correlating observations of increased activation in particular brain areas with different features of the decision-making process. Examples of BES can be found in Sanfey et al. (2003), McClure et al. (2004), Camerer, Loewenstein, and Prelec (2004, 2005), Hsu et al. (2005), Sanfey et al. (2006), Knutson et al. (2007), McClure et al. (2007), and Brocas and Carrillo (2008, 2014).

The other style, alternatively called "neurocellular economics" (Harrison & Ross 2010) and "economics of neural activity" (ENA; Vromen 2011), uses econometric methods to model critical neurobiological functions in the brain at the moment decisions are made; it is not intended (at least not originally[5]) to explain where individuals' preferences come from. ENA is centered on the research program started by Glimcher (2003; see also Platt & Glimcher 1999) that proposes to use expected utility theory to study neural activity – that is, it takes expected utility theory to be the null hypothesis and explores the degree to which neural populations optimize in accordance with it. ENA posits that the brain encodes and integrates all dimensions of a prospect into a single measure of subjective value. According to Kable and Glimcher (2007, 2009), the computation of value can be expressed in terms of a two-stage algorithm: all decisions are funneled through an initial valuation stage in which special neurons encode an *offer* value. To say that value is encoded means that the firing rates of neural cells covary linearly with changes in the subjective value of rewards. Next, different neurons encode a *chosen* value, which enables the brain to compare the offer values of each option and select the one with the highest chosen value. Once an option is selected, a separate mechanism prompts a motor response to execute the decision. Kable and Glimcher are explicit that offer value signals are the literal value representations that decision theorists posit as utilities. This encoding takes place in the brain in the striatum-dopamine circuit and projects through the frontal cortex (specifically, the orbitofrontal cortex and the ventromedial prefrontal cortex).

According to Vromen (2011), however, BES and ENA should not been treated as competing methodologies; rather, they should be understood as investigating different stages of the same decision-making process. BES is concerned with "upstream" neural processes, where cognitive *and* affective processing of prospects takes place; ENA is concerned with "downstream" neural processes, which occur just before motor circuits are activated and decisions executed. This is an important consideration for understanding what constitutes a neural agent since each style picks out different candidate entities for the ascription of agency.

4.2 Two Interpretations of Neural Agents

For proponents of BES, perhaps the most important neuroeconomic insight is that human behavior results from the interaction of multiple, specialized neural systems – though this is typically cast in dualistic terms. Here are just a few examples: for Sanfey et al. (2003), interaction takes place between the anterior insula (emotional system) and the dorsolateral prefrontal cortex (cognitive system); for Camerer, Loewenstein, and Prelec (2005) it is between the amygdala/nucleus accumbens (automatic processing) and the anterior cingulate/prefrontal cortex (executive control); for McClure et al. (2004) and McClure et al. (2007) it is between the limbic system/paralimbic cortex (midbrain dopamine center) and the lateral prefrontal cortex/posterior parietal cortex (deliberative system); for Brocas and Carrillo (2008, 2014) it is between the ventral striatum/amygdala (impulsive system) and the ventromedial and dorsolateral prefrontal cortex/anterior cingulate (reflective system). For proponents of BES, the interactions between domain-specific systems justify the application of economic principles of optimization to the brain: given that the brain has limited energy resources, different system interactions may be seen as matter of resource allocation.

By contrast, Kable and Glimcher (2007, 2009) suggest that reward and information systems are not as discrete and well partitioned as proponents of BES often make them out to be. Because the processes involved in decision-making are so highly distributed throughout the brain, it is perhaps better to think of the brain as a complex but ultimately unitary system (Rustichini 2008; Vromen 2011). This has the following repercussions for how one might interpret neural agency: Whether one is permitted to call a neural system a neural agent will depend upon whether the behavior of the system in question can be modeled *independently* of the behavior of the individual person (that is, without attributing to neural systems intentional qualities we would typically attribute to whole persons, such as preferences). Because it remains a debated issue what comprises or delineates dual systems at the neural-physiological level (Grayot 2020), one is likely to run into challenges that mirror those of behavioral economic approaches to subpersonal agency here, namely, that it is unclear whether one ought to think of transient selves as agents (which represent motivationally divergent interests) or whether one ought to think of neural systems as agents (which represent contrasting modes of information processing in the brain). Reflecting on this issue, one may get the impression that BES seeks to reduce transient selves *to* neural systems. This would then justify our interpretation of neural systems *as* neural agents. But, as I will explain further, this view incurs important ontological problems.

5. Observations and Implications

The partitioning of individuals into virtual agents and neural agents has enabled decision researchers to better understand why persons typically fail to behave like *Homo economicus* agents, and also why aberrant choice behaviors and decision anomalies seem to be relatively common in humans. However, because virtual agents and neural agents can be correlated with different subpersonal events – many of which seem to overlap – more needs to be said about the diverse characteristics of both virtual and neural agents. But first, two caveats.

First, contrary to appearances, not all behavioral economists and not all neuroeconomists posit subpersonal agents for the same purposes: some purposes are empirical, for example, to predict or explain decision anomalies in the lab or in the field; whereas other purposes are prescriptive, for example, to identify guidelines for making good decisions; and others still are purely theoretical, for example, to investigate the counterfactual conditions under which decision anomalies could arise. Second, what counts as a suitable candidate for the ascription of subpersonal agency will depend upon (a) what kind of choice phenomenon one wishes to model and (b) how far one is willing to deviate from the mainstream view of economic agency. With this in mind, we may begin by clarifying a potential source of misunderstanding about some core differences between virtual agents and neural agents.

5.1 Molar Versus Molecular Perspectives About the Subpersonal

After reading the preceding description, one may be tempted to think that, as a general rule, when behavioral economists posit and ascribe utilities or value functions to subpersonal entities, these should always be interpreted as virtual agents, whereas when neuroeconomists do the same, these should always be construed as neural agents. In other words, one may be tempted to think that the virtual-neural distinction simply describes how behavioral economists and neuroeconomists approach subpersonal analyses of choice behavior.

It is true that, at a certain level of generality, there are two types of subpersonal economic analysis going on here, and these styles do correspond superficially to the sorts of phenomena that behavioral economists and neuroeconomists are typically interested in modeling. But, beyond this apparent connection, what distinguishes virtual agents from neural agents is a far more contingent and nuanced matter. It is perhaps helpful here to introduce a related but separate distinction. According to Ross (2006), one may cleave the domain of the subpersonal by taking either a *molar* or a *molecular* perspective. The molecular-level perspective pertains to the first subpersonal sense described in Section 2: its target of analysis is the brain and its physiological properties; personal-level properties like beliefs, desires, and intentions are not included here. By contrast, the molar-level perspective pertains (roughly) to my second and third subpersonal senses: its targets of analysis are events that are functionally irreducible to neurophysiological events – this includes personal-level properties that range over specific but often limited time spans. For this reason, Ross states that molar-level descriptions "situate behavioral systems in environmental contexts," whereas molecular-level descriptions are "computational and cognitivist in character" (Ross 2012: 718).

Ross regards Ainslie's picoeconomics (1992, 2001) as an exemplary molar-level approach to subpersonal economic analysis. This is because the subpersonal entities posited by Ainslie (communities of agents) may encode short-term, medium-term, or even long-term interests. Any attempt to interpret or reduce these interests to the neurophysiological, i.e., molecular, level would fail to capture what interests encode for Ainslie – namely, manifest behavior embedded in a personal-level context. By comparison, Ross regards Glimcher's economics of neural activity (i.e., "neurocellular economics" (2003); see also Kable & Glimcher 2007, 2009)) as an exemplary molecular-level approach to subpersonal economic analysis. As indicated in Section 4, the target of analysis for ENA is the brain, in particular the neural algorithms operating primarily in the frontal cortex. The behavioral profile of these neurons is determined by evolution, not by personal-level interests, and thus each group of neurons maximizes value according to its biological function. As such, ENA *does not* conflate neural agents with virtual agents and, therefore, draws no direct inferences about the effects of neural processing on individual choice behavior.

Though the molar-molecular distinction is helpful for clarifying why one might think there are just two styles of subpersonal economics, namely, those that traffic unambiguously in virtual agents (picoeconomics) and those that traffic unambiguously in neural agents (ENA), this organizing principle runs into difficulties when it comes to making sense of economic models that seem to traffic in both virtual agents and neural agents simultaneously or models that fail to disclose what type of agent is being posited to begin with. This, unfortunately, is the case for many behavioral economic models, both those fitting the description of multiple-agent models and BES models.

Ross (2012) recognizes that many behavioral economic models (including those in BES) betray an ontological ambiguity regarding the relationship between persons and subpersonal units. In an attempt to clarify this ambiguity, he considers four ways this relationship might be reconstructed:

1. Either (a) persons can be modeled (synchronically) as multiple subagents with conflicting utility functions, or (b) persons are modeled (synchronically) as multiple subagents with different time preferences.
2. Persons can be modeled (diachronically) as multiple subagents, each of which controls the whole person's behavior for a limited time horizon; each subagent possesses a different utility function, but later agents' utilities depend on investments by earlier agents.
3. Persons retain (to a degree) their agential autonomy, but their choice behaviors can be interpreted as the outcome of molecular processes.

If we buy into this schema, then we are left with two options for interpreting the ontology of models that straddle the molar-molecular divide, namely, 1b and 3.[6] Further reflection indicates that 1b leads to a form of methodological reduction, in which molar-level phenomena (e.g., impulsive consumption or procrastination) are replaced by molecular analyses and explanations. For example, the time-discounting model of McClure et al. (2007) ascribes time preferences directly to neural systems in the brain, namely, the mesolimbic dopamine system, as opposed to the whole person. While not all neuroeconomic models aspire to the same sort of reduction, the majority of BES models exhibit something like what is described in 1b, and this raises questions about what the targets of subpersonal economic models are supposed to be for BES. Thus, option 3 remains. Ross is somewhat cryptic about which sorts of models might occupy this ontological position – though it seems clear that at least some of the multiple-agent models discussed in Section 3 might manifest this kind of quasi-reductionistic ontology.

5.2 A Partial Diagnosis of Ontological Ambiguity

Both multiple-agent models and BES waver in how they conceive the economic agent. This is not difficult to see. The questions we need to clarify are: what is the source of this ontological ambiguity, and why does it matter?

Let's start with the premise that economic theory applies to an entity or modular process to the extent that this target implements choices that vary systematically under changes in incentives. This implies that choices and incentives can be jointly specified under axioms that at least respect stochastic dominance. If we presume this to be a minimal condition for economic agency, then we can potentially assign preferences to all sorts of entities – not just persons but also to neurons, nonhuman animals, and even evolutionary strategies (Ross 2005; cf. Grayot 2017). The ontological problem that multiple-agent models and BES similarly face is that it is unclear *who* or *what* implements choice according to the preceding premise. And the reason for this might have something to do with how *prospect theory* has been filtered through dual-process and dual-system models in behavioral economics.

Recall that, according to prospect theory (Kahneman & Tversky 1979), decision-making involves a two-step procedure in which an initial editing stage codes, orders, and adjusts outcomes of a given choice, and a secondary evaluation stage computes the expected value of those "edited" outcomes. Prospect theory postulates that for every choice, there is a reference point that establishes how the agent will edit and evaluate outcomes – the reference point is what sets the framing of a particular choice – and it is what allows prospect theory to assert that persons are generally risk averse, especially with regard to losses. The issue of ontological ambiguity looms large here because in order for prospect theory to be a thoroughly *economic* theory, it needs to suppose that these decision-making procedures respect stochastic dominance. Cumulative prospect theory (Tversky & Kahneman 1992) provides the necessary restrictions to achieve this, but, in doing so, it takes the perspective of the personal-level agent because it is by appeal to the person's reference point that we make sense of this restriction.[7] But no one supposes that the whole person deliberately runs the computations assumed by cumulative prospect theory! So, these decision procedures must be computed subpersonally.

If prospect theory and its various theoretical extensions in behavioral economics and BES[8] are intended to describe and possibly explain how subpersonal decision-making processes relate to personal-level choice behaviors, they do so at the risk of obscuring their target of analysis – which is to say, they are ambiguous about who or what their model is really about. This is for one of two possible reasons.

First, for those who are committed to dual-process theory, there is no consensus as to whether the sorts of decision procedures characterized by cumulative prospect theory are attributable to System 1, System 2, or some interaction between the two. As explained in Grayot (2020), this is due to the fact that dual-process theory is not a mechanistic theory – the story of the functional interactions of System 1 and System 2 is often question-begging or incomplete. To put this into perspective, in multiple-agent models it is left unspecified whether System 2 – being the reflective/deliberative system – is meant to be an extension of the personal-level agent who thinks and deliberates about their choices, or whether it is meant to be a separate subpersonal agent whose actions serve as a preliminary step for deliberation. If it is the former, then further conceptual work is needed to clarify how the System 1 – System 2 distinction relates to or maps onto the personal-subpersonal distinction. If it is the latter, then further empirical work is needed to motivate why we should think of System 2 as a rational system to begin with.[9] This brings me to the second point.

Attempts by some practitioners of BES to flesh out the inner workings of System 1 and System 2 in mechanistic terms do not resolve the preceding ontological dilemma. Here's why. It is commonplace for BES models to appeal to executive control and conflict monitoring functions of the prefrontal cortex to justify taking a two-system view of economic decision-making. When people resist temptation or exert effort to keep their impulses in check, it can be characterized in terms of an override procedure carried out by the central executive. But, in such cases, it would be misleading to think that the central executive (or whatever neural mechanism one takes to be responsible for blocking automatic and emotional processing) literally computes one's prospects in line with cumulative prospect theory. In fact, it would be misleading to think that anything in the brain computes this. A *person* could compute this, but this is typically *not* what people do when they make decisions, which is why prospect theory was originally taken to indicate that decision-making is largely governed by subpersonal processes – the kind that are not accessible to introspection.

To summarize the problem, the trajectory of behavioral economic theorizing linking prospect theory, cumulative prospect theory, and dual-process theory, which has both directly and indirectly influenced multiple-agent models and BES models, demands that the economic agent be both a personal-level entity, that is, a human person, and a rough assortment of subpersonal processes that sometimes, but not always, correspond with discrete neural mechanisms. But because neither the person nor any discrete mechanism is believed to carry out the requisite computations, there is no stable entity to which we can ascribe subpersonal agency.

6. Conclusion

We can draw a few general conclusions from this chapter's survey. First, rather than thinking that there are just two styles of subpersonal economic analysis – one corresponding to molar-level analysis involving virtual agents and another corresponding to molecular-level analysis involving neural agents – we instead have four types of subpersonal economic analysis involving different sorts of virtual and neural agents (see Table 6.1 in Section 2).

Second, whereas picoeconomics and ENA are relatively unambiguous regarding the ontology of the virtual and neural agents they posit, the same cannot be said for the majority of multiple-agent models and BES models. Though BES models characteristically appeal to neural mechanisms and processes, their aim is to account for personal-level choice behaviors; this obscures the ontology of the economic agent. Multiple-agent models exacerbate this ambiguity by conflating virtual agents, that is, transient selves, with cognitive processes that are governed by, but do not reduce to, various neural systems in the brain. Hence, for both BES models and multiple-agent models, it is an open question as to the units and levels at which the models are expected to explain (if indeed they do explain). Though this may sound like just a philosopher's gripe, the question of ontology is important *if* we expect subpersonal economic analysis to do more than merely speculate about what is happening "under the hood."

Finally, the taxonomy I have provided here is helpful, not just because it showcases important ontological distinctions one can draw with respect to the four types of subpersonal economic analysis, but also because it allows one to track how insights from psychology and neuroscience have been incorporated into economic thought in interesting and perhaps unexpected ways.

Acknowledgments

I am very grateful to Conrad Heilmann and Don Ross for feedback and advice while writing this chapter. I would also like to thank Philippe Verreault-Julien, Zoi Terzopoulou, and Enrico Petracca for helpful comments along the way.

Related Chapter

Lecouteux, Chapter 4 "Behavioral Welfare Economics and Consumer Sovereignty"

Notes

1 This statement requires a bit of unpacking. What I am calling the "mainstream view" is typically associated with the *neoclassical* interpretation of the economic agent. However, this association is possibly misleading. For instance, Ross argues that there is no reason to suppose that the neoclassical economic agent is human – an economic agent is just "a reference point for ascription of a utility function," and "utility functions are constructed from preference functions or represent preference relations" (2012: 696). See Davis (2012) for a related interpretation.

2 See, for example, Ross and Spurrett (2004) and Weiskopf (2011) for defenses of nonreductive functional explanations in the cognitive and behavioral sciences.

3 My understanding of *virtual agent* and *neural agent* is based on their usage by Ross (2005, 2012).

4 For the sake of space, I have left out of this survey instrumental decision theoretic approaches to intrapersonal and intertemporal choice. For recent analyses, see Bermúdez's (2018) collection.

5 See Vromen (2011) for commentary on and analysis of Glimcher's perspective with regard to the project of ENA.

6 Following the discussion about molar- and molecular-level analysis, Ross (2012) contends that 1a is representative of ENA insofar as one does not attempt to draw inferences about individual behavior from neural computations of value, whereas 2 is clearly representative of picoeconomics.

7 See Ross (2014: 206–222) for a more thorough discussion of this point.

8 Here I am supposing that the models I refer to as multiple-agent models as well as those I have labeled as BES are generally committed to or built upon cumulative prospect theory.

9 In Grayot (2020: 124–128), I discuss several reasons why economists should not think of System 2 as a rational system and, thus, should not equate it with an inner rational agent.

Bibliography

Ainslie, G. (1992). *Picoeconomics: The Strategic Interaction of Successive Motivational States within the Person*. Cambridge, UK: Cambridge University Press.

Ainslie, G. (2001). *Breakdown of Will*. Cambridge, UK: Cambridge University Press.

Alós-Ferrer, C., & Strack, F. (2014). From dual processes to multiple selves: Implications for economic behavior. *Journal of Economic Psychology*, 41, 1–11.

Angner, E., & Loewenstein, G. (2012). Behavioral economics. In Uskali Mäki (Ed.), *Handbook of the Philosophy of Science: Philosophy of Economics* (pp. 641–690). Amsterdam: Elsevier.

Bénabou, R., & Tirole, J. (2002). Self-confidence and personal motivation. *The Quarterly Journal of Economics*, 117(3), 871–915.

Benhabib, J., & Bisin, A. (2005). Modeling internal commitment mechanisms and self-control: A neuroeconomics approach to consumption – saving decisions. *Games and Economic Behavior*, 52(2), 460–492.

Bermúdez, J. L. (Ed.). (2018). *Self-Control, Decision Theory, and Rationality: New Essays*. Cambridge, UK: Cambridge University Press.

Bernheim, B. D. (2009). The psychology and neurobiology of judgment and decision making: What's in it for economists? In P. W. Glimcher, C. F. Camerer, E. Fehr, & R. A. Poldrack (Eds.), *Neuroeconomics: Decision Making and the Brain* (pp. 113–125). New York, NY: Academic Press.

Bernheim, B. D., & Rangel, A. (2004). Addiction and cue-triggered decision processes. *The American Economic Review*, 94(5), 1558–1590.

Brocas, I., & Carrillo, J. D. (2008). The brain as a hierarchical organization. *The American Economic Review*, 98(4), 1312–1346.

Brocas, I., & Carrillo, J. D. (2014). Dual-process theories of decision-making: A selective survey. *Journal of Economic Psychology*, 41, 45–54.

Camerer, C., Loewenstein, G., & Prelec, D. (2005). Neuroeconomics: How neuroscience can inform economics. *Journal of Economic Literature*, 43(1), 9–64.

Camerer, C. F., Loewenstein, G., & Prelec, D. (2004). Neuroeconomics: Why economics needs brains. *Scandinavian Journal of Economics*, 106(3), 555–579.

Camerer, C., Loewenstein, G., & Rabin, M. (Eds.). (2011). *Advances in Behavioral Economics*. Princeton, NJ: Princeton University Press.

Davis, J. B. (2012). The homo economicus conception of the individual: An ontological approach. *Philosophy of Economics. Handbook of the Philosophy of Science*, 13, 459–482.

Debreu, G. (1959). *Theory of Value: An Axiomatic Analysis of Economic Equilibrium* (No. 17). New Haven, CT: Yale University Press.

Dennett, D. C. (1987). *The Intentional Stance*. Cambridge, MA: MIT Press.

Dennett, D. C. (1991). *Consciousness Explained*. New York: Little Brown & Co

Elster, J. (Ed.). (1987). *The Multiple Self*. Cambridge, UK: Cambridge University Press.

Evans, J. S. B. T. (2006). Dual system theories of cognition: Some issues. *Proceedings of the 28th Annual Meeting of the Cognitive Science Society*, 202–207.

Evans, J. S. B. T. (2008). Dual-processing accounts of reasoning, judgment, and social cognition. *Annual Review of Psychology*, 59, 255–278.

Evans, J. S. B. T., & Stanovich, K. E. (2013). Dual-process theories of higher cognition advancing the debate. *Perspectives on Psychological Science*, 8(3), 223–241.

Frederick, S., Loewenstein, G., & O'Donoghue, T. (2002). Time discounting and time preference: A critical review. *Journal of Economic Literature*, 40(2), 351–401.

Fudenberg, D., & Levine, D. K. (2006). A dual-self model of impulse control. *The American Economic Review*, 96(5), 1449–1476.

Glimcher, P. (2003). *Decisions, Uncertainty, and the Brain*. Cambridge, MA: MIT Press

Grayot, J. D. (2017). The quasi-economic agency of human selves. *Œconomia. History, Methodology, Philosophy*, 7–4, 481–511.

Grayot, J. D. (2019). From selves to systems: On the intrapersonal and intraneural dynamics of decision making. *Journal of Economic Methodology*, 26(3), 208–227.

Grayot, J. D. (2020). Dual process theories in behavioral economics and neuroeconomics: A critical review. *Review of Philosophy and Psychology*, 11(1), 105–136.
Green, L., & Myerson, J. (2004). A discounting framework for choice with delayed and probabilistic rewards. *Psychological bulletin*, 130(5), 769.
Harrison, G., & Ross, D. (2010). The methodologies of neuroeconomics. *Journal of Economic Methodology*, 17(2), 185–196.
Heilmann, C. (2010). Rationality and time: A multiple-self model of personal identity over time for decision and game theory. *London School of Economics and Political Science (United Kingdom).*
Hornsby, J. (2000). Personal and sub-personal; A defense of Dennett's early distinction. *Philosophical Explorations*, 3(1), 6–24.
Hsu, M., Bhatt, M., Adolphs, R., Tranel, D., & Camerer, C. F. (2005). Neural systems responding to degrees of uncertainty in human decision-making. *Science*, 310(5754), 1680–1683.
Infante, G., Lecouteux, G., & Sugden, R. (2016). Preference purification and the inner rational agent: A critique of the conventional wisdom of behavioural welfare economics. *Journal of Economic Methodology*, 23(1), 1–25.
Kable, J. W., & Glimcher, P. W. (2007). The neural correlates of subjective value during intertemporal choice. *Nature Neuroscience*, 10(12), 1625–1633.
Kable, J. W., & Glimcher, P. W. (2009). The neurobiology of decision: Consensus and controversy. *Neuron*, 63(6), 733–745.
Kahneman, D. (2003). Maps of bounded rationality: Psychology for behavioral economics. *The American Economic Review*, 93(5), 1449–1475.
Kahneman, D. (2011). *Thinking, Fast and Slow*. New York, NY: Farrar, Straus and Giroux.
Kahneman, D., & Frederick, S. (2002). Representativeness revisited: Attribute substitution in intuitive judgment. In D. Kahneman & T. Gilovich (Eds.), *Heuristics and Biases: The Psychology of Intuitive Judgment* (pp. 49–81). Cambridge, UK: Cambridge University Press.
Kahneman, D., & Frederick, S. (2005). A model of heuristic judgment. In K. Holyoak & R. Morrison (Eds.), *The Cambridge Handbook of Thinking and Reasoning* (pp. 267–293). Cambridge: Cambridge University Press.
Kahneman, D., Slovic, P., & Tversky, A. (Eds.). (1982). *Judgment Under Uuncertainty: Heuristics and Biases*. Cambridge: Cambridge University Press.
Kahneman, D., & Tversky, A. (1979). Prospect theory: An analysis of decision under risk. *Econometrica*, 47(2), 263–292.
Knutson, B., Rick, S., Wimmer, G. E., Prelec, D., & Loewenstein, G. (2007). Neural predictors of purchases. *Neuron*, 53(1), 147–156.
Konovalov, A., & Krajbich, I. (2019). Over a decade of neuroeconomics: What have we learned? *Organizational Research Methods*, 22(1), 148–173.
Loewenstein, G. (1996). Out of control: Visceral influences on behavior. *Organizational Behavior and Human Decision Processes*, 65(3), 272–292.
Loewenstein, G. (2000). Emotions in economic theory and economic behavior. *The American Economic Review*, 90(2), 426–432.
Loewenstein, G., & O'Donoghue, T. (2004). *Animal spirits: Affective and deliberative processes in economic behavior.* Available at SSRN 539843.
McClure, S. M., Ericson, K. M., Laibson, D. I., Loewenstein, G., & Cohen, J. D. (2007). Time discounting for primary rewards. *Journal of Neuroscience*, 27(21), 5796–5804.
McClure, S. M., Laibson, D., Loewenstein, G., & Cohen, J. (2004). Separate neural systems value immediate and delayed monetary rewards. *Science*, 306, 503–507.
Metcalfe, J., & Mischel, W. (1999). A hot/cool-system analysis of delay of gratification: Dynamics of willpower. *Psychological Review*, 106(1), 3.
Montague, P. R., & Berns, G. (2002). Neural economics and the biological substrates of valuation. *Neuron*, 36, 265–284.
Phelps, E. S., & Pollak, R. A. (1968). On second-best national saving and game-equilibrium growth. *The Review of Economic Studies*, 35(2), 185–199.
Platt, M., & Glimcher, P. (1999). Neural correlates of decision variables in parietal cortex. *Nature*, 400, 233–238.
Rachlin, H. (2000). *The Science of Self-Control*. Cambridge, MA: Harvard University Press.
Ross, D. (2005). *Economic Theory and Cognitive Science: Microexplanation*. Cambridge, MA: MIT Press.
Ross, D. (2006), The economics of the sub-personal: Two research programs. In B. Montero & M. White (Eds.), *Economics and the Mind* (pp. 41–57). London: Routledge.
Ross, D. (2008). Two styles of neuroeconomics. *Economics & Philosophy*, 24(3), 473–483.

Ross, D. (2012). The economic agent: Not human, but important. In U. Mäki (Ed.), *Philosophy of Economics* (pp. 691–735). Amsterdam: Elsevier.

Ross, D. (2014). *Philosophy of Economics*. London, UK: Palgrave Macmillan.

Ross, D., & Spurrett, D. (2004). What to say to a skeptical metaphysician: A defense manual for cognitive and behavioral scientists. *Behavioral and Brain Sciences*, 27(5), 603–627.

Rubinstein, A. (2006). *Lecture Notes in Microeconomic Theory*. Princeton, NJ: Princeton University.

Rustichini, A. (2008). Dual or unitary system? Two alternative models of decision making. *Cognitive, Affective, & Behavioral Neuroscience*, 8(4), 355–362.

Samuelson, P. A. (1937). A note on measurement of utility. *The Review of Economic Studies*, 4(2), 155–161.

Sanfey, A. G., Loewenstein, G., Cohen, J. D., & McClure, S. M. (2006). Neuroeconomics: Integrating the disparate approaches of neuroscience and economics. *Trends in Cognitive Science*, 10(3), 108–116.

Sanfey, A. G., Rilling, J. K., Aronson, J. A., Nystrom, L. E., & Cohen, J. D. (2003). The neural basis of economic decision-making in the ultimatum game. *Science*, 300 (5626), 1755–1758.

Schelling, T. (1980). The intimate contest for self-command. *Public Interest*, 60: 94–118.

Schelling, T. (1984). Self-command in practice, in policy, and in a theory of rational choice. *American Economic Review*, 74: 1–11.

Shefrin, H. M., & Thaler, R. H. (1988). The behavioral life-cycle hypothesis. *Economic Inquiry*, 26(4), 609–643.

Strack, F., & Deutsch, R. (2004). Reflective and impulsive determinants of social behavior. *Personality and Social Psychology Review*, 8(3), 220–247.

Strotz, R. H. (1955). Myopia and inconsistency in dynamic utility maximization. *The Review of Economic Studies*, 23(3), 165–180.

Thaler, R. H. (1985). Mental accounting and consumer choice. *Marketing Science*, 4(3), 199–214.

Thaler, R. H., & Shefrin, H. M. (1981). An economic theory of self-control. *The Journal of Political Economy*, 89(2), 392–406.

Tversky, A., & Kahneman, D. (1973). Availability: A heuristic for judging frequency and probability. *Cognitive Psychology*, 5(2), 207–232.

Tversky, A., & Kahneman, D. (1974). Judgment under uncertainty: Heuristics and biases. *Science*, 185(4157), 1124–1131.

Tversky, A., & Kahneman, D. (1992). Advances in prospect theory: Cumulative representation of uncertainty. *Journal of Risk and Uncertainty*, 5(4), 297–323.

Vromen, J. (2011). Neuroeconomics: Two camps gradually converging: What can economics gain from it? *International Review of Economics*, 58(3), 267–285.

Weiskopf, D. A. (2011). Models and mechanisms in psychological explanation. *Synthese*, 183(3), 313.

PART II

Cooperation and Interaction

7

GAME THEORY AND RATIONAL REASONING

Jurgis Karpus and Mantas Radzvilas

1. Introduction

Game theory studies interactive decision situations – games – in which several agents make choices that jointly determine the outcome that obtains. More simply, "[a] game is being played whenever people have anything to do with each other" (Binmore 2007, 3).

Because most economic activities involve at least two parties (e.g., a buyer and a seller), game theory naturally plays an important role in economics. For one, economists use it to explain and predict the behavior of economic agents (e.g., consumers, firms). Methodologically, the theory establishes rules of rational behavior, which, assuming economic agents to be rational, enable it to predict what happens in the market.[1]

The fact that game theory postulates what *rational* decision-makers do means that it carries a normative component as well. As is the case with any theory that suggests what people should do (and game theory does, if we assume that people should be rational), this normative component is of particular interest to philosophers. When should people consult game theory in deciding what to do and is the theory's account of rationality correct are questions that philosophers scrutinize a lot.[2]

While, in principle, the normative and the descriptive branches of game theory can be developed and studied independently, in practice they are intricately intertwined (Aumann 1985; Selten 1988). On the one hand, normative game theory may not care if people's choices in real markets are not rational. On the other hand, if game-theoretic postulates of rational choice prescribe the best courses of action for the attainment of people's personal goals, we may expect people to adjust their choices over time by learning from their past mistakes, so that those choices become aligned with what the theory prescribes.

Empirical studies have repeatedly shown that in many games people's choice behavior appears to deviate from what the theory predicts (Colman 1999; Camerer 2003). Philosophers and economists debate the reasons underlying these deviations, and the responses offered range from explanations that allude to people's irrationality or inexperience to refinements of rational choice theory so as to represent more complex and diverse motivations of decision-makers than the standard game theory allows.

In this chapter, we will review a snippet of these ongoing debates. In particular, we will focus on how rational decision-makers are theorized to reason. We will consider what the standard approach and a number of nonstandard approaches to game theory say about what rational agents (i) should do, (ii) should believe about others' actions and beliefs, and (iii) can expect to attain when they

DOI: 10.4324/9781315739793-9

interact with other rational and not rational agents. In Section 2, we will address these questions from the point of view of the standard approach, which is based on the postulate of best-response reasoning. In Sections 3 and 4, we will discuss how a number of alleged shortcomings of the standard approach have been proposed to be remedied by the theories of Pareto optimization, team reasoning, and virtual bargaining. In Sections 5 and 6, we will consider the case for dropping the fundamental but often problematic assumption of common belief in rationality. In the context of simultaneous-move games, we will discuss the theory of level-k reasoning (Section 5), and in the context of sequential-move games, we will review recent developments in epistemic game theory (Section 6). With Section 7, we will conclude and offer a few perspectives for the future.

2. Best-Response Reasoning

Standard game theory is built on the assumption of best-response reasoning: rational decision-makers make choices so as to best satisfy their personal preferences over the possible outcomes of a game, given their beliefs about what other players do. Importantly, when all players choose rationally and their beliefs about others' choices are accurate (true), no player has an incentive to unilaterally change her choice. When this holds, players are in a Nash equilibrium (Nash 1951).

Consider the famous prisoner's dilemma game. Two players, simultaneously and independently from one another, choose one of two options: *cooperate* or *defect*. The game is shown in Figure 7.1a, where one player chooses between the options identified by rows and the other chooses between those identified by columns. The numbers in each cell are payoffs to the row player and the column player, respectively. Mutual cooperation is better for both players than mutual defection. However, each player has an incentive to defect when the other cooperates. [For the original story behind the game, see, for example, Peterson (2015).]

If payoffs accurately represent players' preferences over the four outcomes of the game, rational best-response reasoners will defect no matter what they believe about the other player's choice: irrespective of what the other does, defection yields a higher payoff. Hence, if players believe each other to be rational, they will expect each other to defect. Consequently, they will expect to end up at the outcome where they both get payoff 1. If they do not believe the other to be rational, they may expect payoff 3. Indeed, mutual defection constitutes the only Nash equilibrium in this game – it is the only combination of choices from which no player has an incentive to unilaterally deviate.

Consider also the Hi-Lo game of Figure 7.1b. Here two players choose either a *high* or a *low* prize. If both choose the *high* prize (for short, "choose *high*"), each gets payoff 2. If both choose *low*, each gets payoff 1. If they mis-coordinate, both get 0.

The mutual choice of *high* and the mutual choice of *low* constitute two Nash equilibria in this game (there is a third equilibrium in which players randomize between the two options, but we will not consider that here). Consequently, what rational players do depends on what they believe their co-player will do: the goal here is to match the other player's choice. But, unlike in the prisoner's dilemma, their beliefs about each other's choice cannot be determined simply by engaging in best-response reasoning. Because best-response reasoning yields a conditional recommendation about what to do, and because both players reason alike, there is no way for them to predict what the other will do. As a result, rational players cannot rule out the possibility of ending up at an outcome in which they both get 0 (they might mis-coordinate their actions). In other words, any combination of players' choices in this game is rationalizable in terms of best-response reasoning. Simply put, a choice is rationalizable if it is a best response to a belief about the other's choice. It is rationalizable under the assumption of common belief in rationality, if one's belief about the other's choice is also rationalizable [i.e., the other, being rational, could make that choice, given her own belief about the one (Bernheim 1984; Pearce 1984)]. Thus, best-response reasoning does not guarantee that rational players will end up in a Nash equilibrium. The concept of the Nash equilibrium is simply too

	cooperate	defect
cooperate	2 2	3 0
defect	0 3	1 1

(a)

	high	low
high	2 2	0 0
low	0 0	1 1

(b)

Figure 7.1 (a) The Prisoner's Dilemma game and (b) the Hi-Lo game

restrictive to characterize all rationally permissible behaviors in games, unless we make strong (often unjustified) assumptions concerning players' private beliefs about each other.

3. Pareto Optimization

The prisoner's dilemma example shows that the only rational solution of a game can be socially suboptimal: mutual defection is worse for both players than mutual cooperation in this game. The fact that rational decision-makers themselves predict this outcome and knowingly play their individual parts in its realization triggered a debate about whether this constitutes a paradox of rationality. Gauthier (2013, 2015) is a convinced advocate of the view that this is so. His argument is as follows.

If the only rational choice in this game is to defect, cooperation can be rational only if the game is altered in some way. The prisoner's dilemma can be transformed into a game in which mutual cooperation is rational by making defection costly, such that both players no longer prefer the outcome in which they defect when their co-player cooperates to the outcome in which they both cooperate. One way to achieve this is to hire an arbiter who punishes defectors. If the cost of rationalizing cooperation does not exceed the potential benefits to be gained thereby, rational players would be willing to pay a fee to transform their game in this way. But the fact that rational players are ready to incur a cost in order to attain an outcome that is available to them at no cost to begin with is paradoxical. Why pay for something that is available for free?

Consequently, Gauthier argues that the core principle of rational reasoning in games is Pareto optimization, which rules out the attainment of socially suboptimal outcomes. (An outcome of a game is not Pareto optimal if another outcome yields a higher payoff to some player without making any other player in the game worse off.) Because the outcome associated with mutual defection is not Pareto optimal, a rational solution of the prisoner's dilemma game requires at least one player to cooperate. The firmly established empirical fact that roughly half of people cooperate in the one-shot version of this game (Colman 1999; Camerer 2003) suggests that many may indeed share Gauthier's intuition that cooperation in this game is not outright irrational.

An ardent defender of the opposite side in the debate is Binmore (2015). His argument draws on the close connection between rational players' choices, their preferences over outcomes, and payoffs that present those preferences in games. According to Binmore, if the payoff structure of the prisoner's dilemma game accurately represents the interacting players' preferences over outcomes – preferences that encapsulate everything that the players deem to be motivationally relevant to make their choices – cooperation simply does not make sense.

To see why, we first need to clarify this interpretation of preference. A preference is a comparative relation over the objects of choice that induces a preferential ranking of those objects in terms of their choice-worthiness. These evaluative rankings are subjective, and they may be partial or total (Hausman 2012). A partial ranking indicates the objects' choice-worthiness in terms of a particular criterion, for example, the extent of pleasure a decision-maker expects to derive from acquiring those objects. A total ranking indicates the objects' choice-worthiness overall. In order to make sense of someone's choices from both the normative and the descriptive points of view, we are interested in preference as the latter. Consider Alice, who prefers Cape Town to New York in terms of beauty, but New York to Cape Town in terms of buzz.[3] It is insufficient for us to know her two partial rankings of the two cities if our goal is to explain, predict, or evaluate Alice's decision about where to live. Instead, we need to know her evaluative ranking of the two cities overall. Given this interpretation of preference, a rational decision-maker always chooses what she personally prefers the most. This is because her preference subsumes all motivationally relevant considerations that ultimately determine her choice (see also Ross 2019).

Returning to the Prisoner's Dilemma, consider the case when the column player cooperates. The fact that the row player's payoff is greater when she defects means that she prefers defection to cooperation overall. This is the row player's all-things-considered, comparative, evaluative judgment about what is best for her when the other party cooperates, and if we assume that she acts rationally, this judgment is revealed by her choice when she defects. The same holds for when the column player defects. As such, cooperation can never be rational because it goes against the row player's preference no matter what the column player does. If she cooperates, either she is irrational or her preferences over outcomes are different from those suggested by the payoff structure of the Prisoner's Dilemma game.

The argument is convincing, yet it rests on two substantial claims. The first is that payoffs associated with the possible outcomes of a game *can* capture all motivationally relevant factors that ultimately determine a player's choice. The second is that we ought to adopt a purely behavioristic interpretation of preference – the view that a rational player's preference is always revealed by her actual choice.

Gauthier admits that more has to be said for his theory to be convincing (2013). However, the hunch that something may be amiss with the two claims that underlie Binmore's argument has appeared in other contexts. For the concern that payoff representations of players' preferences over outcomes may not be able to capture *all* motivationally relevant factors that the players care about when they make choices in games, see Falk et al. (2003), McCabe et al. (2003), and Guala (2006). For a more general criticism of the behavioristic interpretation of preference in economics, see Dietrich and List (2016) and Vredenburgh, Chapter 5.

4. Team Reasoning and Virtual Bargaining

While Gauthier uses the Prisoner's Dilemma to argue that the core principle underlying the standard conception of rational reasoning in games is mistaken, the Hi-Lo game has been used to argue (e.g., by Bacharach 2006) that the standard conception is incomplete because it is not restrictive enough. Best-response reasoning yields a conditional recommendation of what to do and thus fails to resolve the seemingly trivial decision-problem that a player faces in this game. Mutual choice of *low*, which constitutes one Nash equilibrium, intuitively does not strike one as being rational. While the choice of *low* is the best that one can do when the other player chooses *low*, the puzzling question is why would a rational player believe another rational player to choose *low* in the first place? Best-response reasoning is silent about why *high* seems to be the obvious choice for rational players in this game.

The problem is not limited to games with multiple Nash equilibria. Consider the game shown in Figure 7.2.[4] Mutual choice of *middle* constitutes the only Nash equilibrium in this game, but it is not the only combination of players' choices that is rationalizable in terms of best-response reasoning. For example, it is rational for the row player to choose *up* if she believes that the column player will choose *left*. The column player could rationally do that, believing that the row player will choose *down*, and so on in the cycle *right* → *down* → *left* → *up*. Consequently, any combination of players'

	left	middle	right
up	0 3	2 0	3 0
middle	0 2	4 4	0 2
down	3 0	2 0	0 3

Figure 7.2 Anything goes?

choices in this game is rationalizable in terms of best-response reasoning. Yet, *middle* seems as obvious a choice here as *high* is in the Hi-Lo game.

Putting this broader notion of best-response rationalizability aside, we will return to the Hi-Lo game. The question of how rational agents manage to successfully coordinate their actions in the face of multiple Nash equilibria has sparked what can be called the Nash equilibrium refinement program (de Bruin 2009). The goal of the program is to narrow down equilibria to those that have some conceptually and mathematically attractive properties: for example, risk dominance (some equilibria may be less risky to pursue than others), payoff dominance (one equilibrium may be preferred by all players over another; Harsanyi and Selten 1988), and trembling hand robustness (some equilibria may be safer in light of possible mistakes by other players; Selten 1975). Importantly, the refinement program retains the standard conception of rational reasoning but suggests additional criteria that rational agents *may* consider when selecting among the available equilibria in games. Missing, however, are explanations of how and when *may* turns into *will* or *should*, and *why* rational agents would adopt one but not another of these criteria when deciding what to do.

Another strand of literature considers why some Nash equilibria are more salient than others, irrespective of their mathematical properties. Salience in many of these works, however, has little to do with the rationality of agents (see the next chapter in this volume). While it is possible, for example, to explain the choice *high* with reference to social customs (choosing *high* may be a matter of following a social convention) or even bounded rationality (*high* is the uniquely best choice if the other player chooses randomly), the need to appeal to extra-rational considerations to explain it seems unsatisfactory. This intuition prompted the development of the theory of team reasoning, which posits that people sometimes switch from best-response reasoning to reasoning as part of a team – a group of individuals who strive for the attainment of a common goal (Sugden 1993; Bacharach 2006; Colman and Gold 2018; see also Colombo and Guala, Chapter 8).

A best-response reasoner asks, "what should *I* do to best promote *my* interests?" She first forms a belief about what others in a game will do and then makes a choice in light of that belief. A team reasoner asks, "what should *we* – the players in this game – do to best promote *our* interests?" She first identifies the best outcome for the group and then plays her individual part to realize that outcome.

Because mutual choice of *high* is unambiguously best for both players in the Hi-Lo game, *high* is the uniquely best choice for players who team reason. Thus, team reasoning resolves the Nash equilibrium selection problem in the Hi-Lo game. The theory can also account for instances of non-best-response play. The Prisoner's Dilemma game is a prime example: if mutual cooperation is associated with the best outcome for the pair, players who team reason may in fact cooperate. Whether that is rational, however, depends on whether a convincing response can be offered to Binmore's argument in the previous section (see also Browne 2018; Gold and Colman 2020).

Apart from the need to clarify its position from the normative point of view, two key questions for this theory are the following: (i) when do people reason as part of a team, and (ii) what do people do when they team reason (Karpus and Gold 2017)? Regarding both, the theory has been developed in a number of directions. Bacharach (2006) argued that the mode of reasoning with which an agent solves a game is a matter of that agent's psychological makeup and may lie outside of her conscious control. For Sugden (2015), a player may consciously choose to endorse team reasoning when this can lead to the attainment of a mutually beneficial outcome, and when she has sufficient assurance that others in a game team reason too. Elsewhere (Karpus and Radzvilas 2018), we suggested that decision-makers may switch from best-response reasoning to reasoning as part of a team when the former fails to resolve a decision-problem at hand. For a similar idea see also the next chapter in this volume.

With regard to what team reasoners do, it has been theorized that they seek Pareto-efficient outcomes (Bacharach 1999, 2006), maximize the team's aggregate payoff (Bacharach 2006; Colman et al. 2008, 2014; Smerilli 2012), seek mutually advantageous outcomes (Sugden 2011, 2015), or strive to maximize the extent of mutual advantage associated with the possible outcomes of a game (Karpus and Radzvilas 2018). While predictions of these models vary somewhat in specific games, empirical tests of the theory have produced supporting, albeit sometimes mixed, results (Colman et al. 2008, 2014; Bardsley et al. 2010; Bardsley and Ule 2017; Faillo et al. 2017; Isoni et al. 2019).

In some respects, the theory of virtual bargaining is similar to the theory of team reasoning (Misyak and Chater 2014; Misyak et al. 2014). It posits that when decision-makers deliberate about what to do in games, they reason in terms of a virtual bargaining process. A virtual bargainer asks, "if we – the players in this game – *were to bargain* over the possible outcomes, which outcome would we settle on in an agreement?" She first identifies a set of feasible agreements, where a feasible agreement is an outcome such that no player can unilaterally deviate from it to gain a personal advantage at the expense of someone else.[5] She then strikes a tacit (virtual) bargain with other players to settle on one outcome from the identified set and plays her individual part to realize that outcome.

While the theory does not specify how players reach a virtual bargain, Misyak and Chater (2014) suggest utilizing Nash's (1950) axiomatic approach to solving explicit bargaining decision-problems as a viable example. Proposing a few compelling axioms the outcome of a bargaining process needs to satisfy, Nash showed that people would settle on the outcome that maximizes the product of their payoff gains relative to a nonagreement baseline. Operationalized this way, virtual bargaining easily resolves the Nash equilibrium selection problem in the Hi-Lo game: mutual choice of *high* constitutes a feasible agreement that uniquely maximizes the product of players' payoff gains measured from any other outcome in this game.

A key outstanding question for the theory of virtual bargaining is that of how this mode of reasoning can be generalized to apply across a wide set of games. Because the existing approaches to solving explicit bargaining decision-problems (Nash 1950; Kalai and Smorodinsky 1975; Kalai 1977) rely on the existence of a nonagreement baseline – a unique outcome that obtains if players fail to reach agreement – the theory needs to provide a general account (if such account is possible) of what this baseline is when players bargain tacitly to solve decision-problems that, in and of themselves, are not explicit bargaining decision-problems to begin with.

While precise operationalizations of both theories are still being developed and reinterpreted, there is a broader question looming too: are these theories descriptive or normative accounts about how people reason or should reason in games? If normative, do they offer an alternative rationalization of choices without claiming that best-response reasoning is irrational, or do they contend for the status of describing the only rationally permissible mode of reasoning in games? If, on the other hand, these are merely descriptive accounts, they have not really resolved the crux of the puzzle that was presented to the standard theory with the Hi-Lo example: why, in the absence of extra-rational considerations, does it seem obvious that rational agents should choose *high* in this game?

5. Best-Response Reasoning Without Common Belief in Rationality

In some games (e.g., the Prisoner's Dilemma), it is easy for players to predict the Nash equilibrium outcome when they best-response reason. In others, the Nash equilibrium prediction relies heavily on the assumption of common belief in rationality. Namely, that all players believe that all players are rational, all players believe that all players believe that all players are rational, and so on. A case in hand is the Guessing game, in which each of a large number of players, simultaneously and independently from one another, chooses a (real) number from the closed interval [0, 100]. Whoever's chosen number is closest to two-thirds of the average of all chosen numbers wins (in the case of a tie, winners share the prize).

In the only Nash equilibrium in this game, each player picks 0. To see this, consider any other distribution of chosen numbers and focus on the player who picked the highest number. Clearly, two-thirds of the average is lower than that number. So, given everyone's choices, this player could do better by lowering her chosen number.

Nagel (1995) conducted experiments with three variants of this game. Contrary to the Nash equilibrium prediction, hardly anyone chose 0. The distribution of chosen numbers had a large spread and two peaks: one close to the number 25 and the other near 35. The winning number was close to the first peak.

This reveals two things. First, anyone who plays according to the Nash equilibrium prediction does not win. Second, if we drop the assumption of common belief in rationality, virtually all choices are rationalizable (e.g., any number lower than 100 is rational if one believes that everyone else chooses 100).

What should rational agents do in this game? Clearly, if they care about winning, they should abandon the assumption of common belief in rationality. Instead, they should try to predict what other, not fully rational, players will do and best-respond to that.

The cognitive hierarchy theory (Camerer et al. 2004) models this form of reasoning. It posits that players in games are of different cognitive levels. Level-0 players do not reason at all and choose randomly. Others use best-response reasoning but differ in what they believe about everyone else. Level-1 players believe that other players are level 0, level-2 players believe that others are level 1 or lower (level 0), and so on. Importantly, people's beliefs about others are false most of the time (a level-k player's belief about others is true only if she is the only level-k player and there are no players of cognitive levels k + 1 or higher).

In the Guessing game, level-0 players pick numbers randomly. The average of their chosen numbers is 50. Level-1 players believe that others are level 0 and choose 2/3 × 50 = 33 1/3. Level-2 players believe that others are level 0 or level 1. Suppose 40% are level 0 and 60% are level 1. The average of their chosen numbers is 0.4 × 50 + 0.6 × 33 1/3 = 40. Thus, level-2 players may choose 2/3 × 40 = 26 2/3. The level-1 and level-2 players' choices fit Nagel's empirical findings almost spot-on.

The cognitive hierarchy theory (and other models of level-k reasoning; Nagel 1995; Crawford et al. 2008) is clearly a descriptive theory about how people reason. Alongside the theory of team reasoning, it has lately been used to account for many people's choices in game theory experiments (Nagel 1995; Crawford et al. 2008; Bardsley et al. 2010; Colman et al. 2014; Faillo et al. 2017; Isoni et al. 2019). Nevertheless, while descriptively the theory yields accurate predictions in many scenarios, there is a question of how well it generalizes across a wide variety of games.

The theory offers a convincing explanation for why people deviate from the Nash equilibrium prediction in games that offer little scope for mutually advantageous play and require players to undergo many iterations in their beliefs about each other's choices when deciding what to do. It is, however, less convincing as an explanation of such deviations (or of successful coordination of players' actions) in the rather simple Prisoner's Dilemma and Hi-Lo games. For example, in order to account for the fact that roughly one-half of people cooperate in the one-shot Prisoner's Dilemma, the theory needs to suggest that nearly everyone begins their play without employing any form of strategic reasoning at all. Explanations offered by the theories of team reasoning and virtual bargaining in these games seem more intuitive (see also the next chapter in this volume).

6. Rational Reasoning in Sequential Games

Thus far, we have focused on games in which players make choices simultaneously without knowing what other players choose. In sequential games, players take turns making choices through time. A sequence of choices made by a player is determined by that player's strategy – a choice plan that specifies the player's choice for every possible gameplay situation in which that player may have to make one. The outcome of a sequential game is determined by a game-ending combination of sequences of players' choices.

Consider the four-stage Centipede game shown in Figure 7.3 (similar to a game first studied by Rosenthal 1981). Two players – A and B – take turns in deciding whether to continue the game (*C* for A and *c* for B) or stop (*S* for A and *s* for B). By choosing to continue, a player delegates the next choice to the opponent. Squares represent decision nodes – gameplay situations where a player has to make a choice. Choices at decision nodes marked with "PA" and "PB" are made by A and B, respectively. Number pairs are payoffs: the left number is the payoff for A, and the right number is the payoff for B.

Both players prefer the game to end later rather than earlier. However, at any stage, each player prefers to stop the game rather than allow her opponent to do so in the stage that follows. A's (B's) strategy specifies her choices at decision nodes PA-1 and PA-2 (PB-1 and PB-2). Thus, A's possible strategies are *CC*, *CS*, *SC*, and *SS*; B's are *cc*, *cs*, *sc*, and *ss*.

In perfect-information games, players know all past choices of their opponents. In imperfect-information games, some of their opponents' past choices may be unknown. Both perfect- and imperfect-information sequential games are dynamic games: as a game progresses, players obtain or infer information about their opponents' past choices and use it to revise their beliefs about their opponents' beliefs and strategies. In light of the revised beliefs, they may modify their own strategies to keep them optimal (i.e., maximizing their expected payoff).

Game theorists have offered a number of Nash equilibrium refinements for this purpose. These refinements, for example, the subgame-perfect Nash equilibrium in perfect-information games

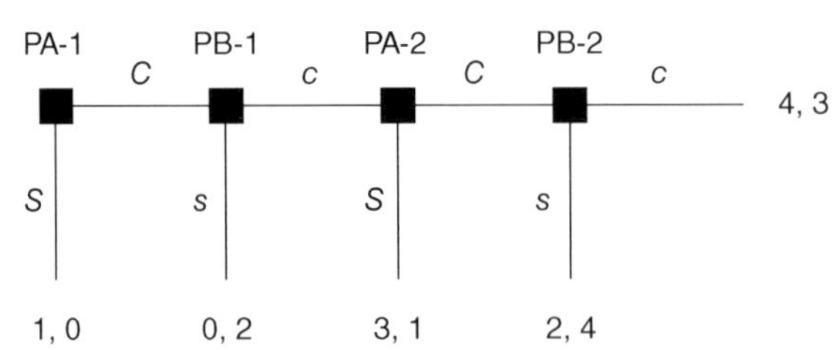

Figure 7.3 The four-stage Centipede game

(Selten 1965), not only require each player's strategy to maximize her final payoff in light of the actual constraints imposed by other players' strategies, but also impose additional restrictions on a player's chosen strategy by requiring its prescribed choices to be optimal at *every* possible gameplay situation in which the player may find herself throughout the game.

In imperfect-information games, equilibrium refinements, for example, the sequential equilibrium (Kreps and Wilson 1982) or the perfect Bayesian equilibrium (Fudenberg and Tirole 1991), impose restrictions on players' strategies on the basis of beliefs they are rationally permitted to form about their opponents' choices. For that, game-theoretic analysis has to be augmented with a model of players' probabilistic beliefs about their opponents' past and future choices, combined with rules by which players are rationally required to revise these beliefs as a game progresses. Both perfect Bayesian equilibrium and sequential equilibrium require players to revise their beliefs according to Bayes' rule, and each player's equilibrium strategy must be sequentially rational: it must assign a sequence of choices that is optimal at every gameplay situation in light of beliefs that the player is rationally permitted to hold at those stages of the game (Myerson 1991; Rubinstein and Osborne 1994).

The epistemic conditions under which players converge on an equilibrium in sequential games are highly restrictive. Arguably, the most problematic is the correct belief condition: each player must believe that her opponents hold correct beliefs about her own first-order beliefs – beliefs about her opponents' strategies (Perea 2012, 2017). This condition imposes unrealistic constraints on players' beliefs in sequential games, especially those where players have imperfect information about their opponents' past choices or face uncertainty about some other strategically relevant feature of a game. In such situations of uncertainty, it seems reasonable to expect players to initially consider multiple hypotheses about their opponents' strategies and beliefs, and later rule out hypotheses that are not compatible with the observed choices of their opponents.

In recent years, epistemic game theorists have developed formal concepts for more refined analyses of players' reasoning in dynamic games. In their models, the conditional belief system is augmented with a type space to represent not only each player's beliefs about their opponents' strategies but also their beliefs about opponents' epistemic types that encode the opponents' first-order and higher beliefs (Battigalli and Siniscalchi 1999, 2002, Perea 2015). Each player's uncertainty about an opponent's beliefs can be represented with a probability distribution over the opponent's epistemic types that assigns positive probability to more than one type. Because different types may use different optimal strategies, the player may initially assign positive probability to her opponent's multiple strategy-type combinations and later revise her beliefs about the opponent's type and strategy once new information about the opponent's choices becomes available.

Epistemic game theory studies players' beliefs about their opponents' strategies and types under the assumption of common belief in rationality. This epistemic assumption naturally gives rise to the rationalizability concept for dynamic games: each player engages in a reasoning procedure that eliminates opponents' strategy-type combinations that the player deems impossible under common belief in rationality – that is, incompatible with the player's belief that her opponents are rational (i.e., always use optimal strategies) and express common belief in rationality. Over the years, epistemic game theorists have developed a number of suboptimal-strategy elimination and strategy-set restriction algorithms for dynamic games (Perea 2012).

Epistemic analysis of perfect-information sequential games has revealed a complex and potentially problematic relation between common belief in rationality and backward induction – a procedure that is commonly used to determine the rational solutions of such games. When applied to the Centipede game, the procedure first determines B's optimal choice at PB-2, which is *s*. This information is then used to determine A's optimal choice at PA-2, which is *S*. The process continues until the procedure determines players' optimal choices at every remaining decision node of the game – *s* at PB-1 and *S* at PA-1. Thus, backward induction suggests that the game should end at PA-1 with

A choosing *S*. This process of reasoning was widely considered to be justified by common belief in rationality: A, believing that B is rational and expresses common belief in rationality, should expect B to predict that (i) A will stop the game at PA-2 in response to A's expectation that B will stop it at PB-2 and, therefore, (ii) opt for the strategy to stop the game at PB-1. In response to this prediction, A's optimal strategy must stop the game at PA-1.

Backward induction is problematic because it ignores the possibility of strategic "surprise" choices, which may motivate players to change their initial beliefs about their opponents (Pettit and Sugden 1989; Ben-Porath 1997). A surprise choice of an opponent may prompt a player to abandon the initial common belief in rationality and, consequently, revise her beliefs about that opponent's strategy. As a result, the player may rationally adopt a different strategy than the one prescribed by the backward induction procedure.

In the Centipede game, A's choice to stop the game at PA-1 is optimal if she expects B to maintain a belief in A's rationality at PB-1 and choose *s*. However, A can make a surprise choice at PA-1 and choose *C*. After observing A's choice *C*, B may consider a number of hypotheses explaining why A made this choice, for example:

1. A is not rational and chooses randomly: *C* with probability 0.5 and *S* with probability 0.5.
2. A is rational and believes that B is rational. However, A expects B to adopt hypothesis 1 after B has seen A choose *C* at PA-1.

If B adopts hypothesis 2, then choice *s* is optimal at PB-1, because B would expect A, being rational, to choose *S* at PA-2. Thus, if A believes that B will adopt hypothesis 2, A has no incentive to make the surprise choice, and the backward induction prescription of choice *S* at PA-1 remains optimal. If, however, B adopts hypothesis 1, then choice *c* is optimal at PB-1 because it yields an expected payoff of 2.5, which is higher than the payoff of 2 associated with choice *s*. Thus, if A believes that B will adopt hypothesis 1, then A expects her surprise choice *C* at PA-1 to yield a higher expected payoff than choice *S*, and therefore A chooses *C* at PA-1.

Epistemic game theorists have noted that common belief in rationality can be analyzed not only as a forward-looking concept that imposes restrictions on players' beliefs about their opponents' future choices but also as a concept that requires players to form beliefs about their opponents' future choices by taking into account the opponents' past choices. Common belief in future rationality – an epistemic concept that, in different technical and conceptual formulations as well as in different degrees of generality, has been discussed by Asheim (2002), Quesada (2002, 2003), Clausing (2003, 2004), Asheim and Perea (2005), Feinberg (2005), Perea (2010, 2014), Baltag et al. (2009), and Bach and Heilmann (2011) – requires each player to believe that her opponents will make optimal choices in every present or future gameplay situation, irrespective of their past choices in a game. In the Centipede game, B, expressing common belief in future rationality, could believe that A's surprise choice of *C* at PA-1 was irrational, yet would believe that A will definitely follow an optimal strategy going forward and choose *S* at PA-2.

Common strong belief in rationality, introduced and studied by Battigalli (1997) and Battigalli and Siniscalchi (1999, 2002), requires each player to interpret all past choices of her opponent as parts of some optimal strategy in every situation where such an interpretation is possible. Thus, each player who expresses common strong belief in rationality cannot interpret her opponent's past surprise choice as irrational if there is some hierarchy of that opponent's first-order and higher beliefs that makes that choice a part of an optimal strategy.

Both refinements preserve some form of common belief in rationality in dynamic games. The debate continues, however, as to whether there are certain gameplay situations in which no version of common belief in rationality should be upheld.

7. Conclusion

The standard game theory's assumptions of best-response reasoning and common belief in rationality have both been criticized on multiple fronts. Some criticisms call for a reassessment of what counts as rational and irrational in games, and, with that, alternative models of reasoning have been proposed. Because these alternative models hinge on the ways in which the normative and the descriptive branches of game theory are intertwined, they reinvigorate some pertinent questions. To what extent should our intuitions about what count as rational and empirical findings drawn from game theory experiments inform the theory of rational choice? Can and should theoretical developments that emerge from such insights complement the standard account of rational reasoning or go a step further to supplant it? These are, in some respects, philosophical questions, and further interaction between economists and philosophers to answer them will no doubt be fruitful.

Other criticisms point to the excessively stringent epistemic conditions that have to be met for the standard game-theoretic solution concepts to materialize in real-life decision-making. In this regard, modeling of the dynamic belief formation of rational agents has become the focus of the expanding field of epistemic game theory. To the best of our knowledge, however, nothing has yet been developed at the intersection of the emerging alternative accounts of rational reasoning and the dynamic belief formation processes studied by this field. Future research in this area, we believe, will help to strengthen or undermine the normative appeal of the theories of team reasoning and virtual bargaining (but see the next chapter in this volume for a different approach).

It is difficult to empirically assess the competing theories about reasoning, because in many games their predictions overlap. Testing, thus, has to go beyond mere observations of people's choices in experiments. Behavioral game theory is slowly moving in this direction, for example, in developing methods to elicit people's beliefs in addition to their choices (Croson 2000; Blanco et al. 2010; Schlag et al. 2015; Rubinstein and Salant 2016). While there is not yet an established standard on how best to do this, it will certainly help disentangle the various competing hypotheses about how people reason in games.

Acknowledgments

Both authors contributed equally to developing and writing this paper. Jurgis Karpus was supported by LMUexcellent, funded by the Federal Ministry of Education and Research (BMBF) and the Free State of Bavaria, Germany, under the Excellence Strategy of the Federal Government and the Länder.

Related Chapters

Colombo and Guala, Chapter 8 "Institutions, Rationality, and Coordination"
Vredenburgh, Chapter 5 "The Economic Concept of a Preference"

Notes

1 This is not the sole purpose of game theory in economics. Economists also use it, for example, to design incentive structures for interacting agents in order to attain desired policy objectives. Two prominent branches of applied game theory in this regard are mechanism design and auction theory.
2 Philosophers' interest in game theory is not limited to the definition of rational choice. For an overview, see Grüne-Yanoff and Lehtinen (2012). For a philosophically informed discussion of the fundamental concepts of game theory, see also Rubinstein (1991).
3 We borrowed this from a similar example used by Reiss (2013, p. 32).

4 We adapted this from a similar example used by Bernheim (1984, p. 1012) and thank Carl-David Reese for bringing Bernheim's game to our attention.
5 For this reason, mutual cooperation in the Prisoner's Dilemma game is not a feasible agreement. As such, this marks a key difference between the theory of virtual bargaining and the theory of team reasoning.

Bibliography

Asheim, G. B. (2002) On the epistemic foundation for backward induction. *Mathematical Social Sciences* 44: 121–144.

Asheim, G. B. and Perea, A. (2005) Sequential and quasi-perfect rationalizability in extensive games. *Games and Economic Behavior* 53: 15–42.

Aumann, R. J. (1985) What is game theory trying to accomplish? In K. Arrow and S. Honkapohja (eds.) *Frontiers of Economics*, Basil Blackwell.

Bach, C. W. and Heilmann, C. (2011) Agent connectedness and backward induction. *International Game Theory Review* 13: 195–208.

Bacharach, M. (1999) Interactive team reasoning: A contribution to the theory of co-operation. *Research in Economics* 53: 117-147.

Bacharach, M. (2006) *Beyond Individual Choice*. N. Gold and R. Sugden (eds.)., Princeton University Press.

Baltag, A., Smets, S. and Zvesper, J. A. (2009) Keep "hoping" for rationality: A solution to the backward induction paradox. *Synthese* 169: 301–333.

Bardsley, N., Mehta, J., Starmer, C. and Sugden, R. (2010) Explaining focal points: Cognitive hierarchy theory versus team reasoning. *The Economic Journal* 120: 40-79.

Bardsley, N. and Ule, A. (2017) Focal points revisited: Team reasoning, the principle of insufficient reason and cognitive hierarchy theory. *Journal of Economic Behavior and Organization* 133: 74-86.

Battigalli, P. (1997) On rationalizability in extensive games. *Journal of Economic Theory* 74: 40-61.

Battigalli, P. and Siniscalchi, M. (1999) Interactive beliefs, epistemic independence and strong rationalizability. *Research in Economics* 53: 247-273.

Battigalli, P. and Siniscalchi, M. (2002) Strong belief and forward induction reasoning. *Journal of Economic Theory* 106: 356-391.

Ben-Porath, E. (1997) Nash equilibrium and backwards induction in perfect-information games. *Review of Economic Studies* 64: 23-46.

Bernheim, B. D. (1984) Rationalizable strategic behavior. *Econometrica* 52: 1007–1028.

Binmore, K. (2007) *Playing for Real*, Oxford University Press.

Binmore, K. (2015) Why all the fuss? The many aspects of the Prisoner's Dilemma. In M. Peterson (ed.) *The Prisoner's Dilemma*, Cambridge University Press.

Blanco, M., Engelmann, D., Koch, A. K. and Normann, H.-T. (2010) Belief elicitation in experiments: Is there a hedging problem? *Experimental Economics* 13: 412-438.

Browne, K. (2018) Why should we team reason? *Economics and Philosophy* 34: 185-198.

Camerer, C. F. (2003) *Behavioral Game Theory*, Princeton University Press.

Camerer, C. F., Ho, T.-H. and Chong, J.-K. (2004) A cognitive hierarchy model of games. *The Quarterly Journal of Economics* 119: 861–898.

Clausing, T. (2003) Doxastic conditions for backward induction. *Theory and Decision* 54: 315–336.

Clausing, T. (2004) Belief revision in games of perfect information. *Economics and Philosophy* 20: 89–115.

Colman, A. M. (1999) *Game Theory and Its Applications in the Social & Biological Sciences*, Routledge.

Colman, A. M. and Gold, N. (2018) Team reasoning: Solving the puzzle of coordination. *Psychonomic Bulletin & Review* 25: 1770-1783.

Colman, A. M., Pulford, B. D. and Lawrence, C. L. (2014) Explaining strategic cooperation: Cognitive hierarchy theory, strong Stackelberg reasoning, and team reasoning. *Decision* 1: 35-58.

Colman, A. M., Pulford, B. D. and Rose, J. (2008) Collective rationality in interactive decisions: Evidence for team reasoning. *Acta Psychologica* 128: 387-397.

Crawford, V. P., Gneezy, U. and Rottenstreich, Y. (2008) The power of focal points is limited: Even minute payoff asymmetry may yield large coordination failures. *The American Economic Review* 98: 1443-1458.

Croson, R. T. A. (2000) Thinking like a game theorist: Factors affecting the frequency of equilibrium play. *Journal of Economic Behavior and Organization* 41: 299-314.

de Bruin, B. (2009) Overmathematisation in game theory: Pitting the Nash equilibrium refinement programme against the epistemic programme. *Studies in History and Philosophy of Science* 40: 290-300.

Dietrich, F. and List, C. (2016) Mentalism versus behaviourism in economics: A philosophy-of-science perspective. *Economics and Philosophy* 32: 249-281.

Faillo, M., Smerilli, A. and Sugden, R. (2017) Bounded best-response and collective-optimality reasoning in coordination games. *Journal of Economic Behavior and Organization* 140: 317-335.

Falk, A. Fehr, E. and Fischbacher, U. (2003) On the nature of fair behavior. *Economic Inquiry* 41: 20-26.

Feinberg, Y. (2005) Subjective reasoning-dynamic games. *Games and Economic Behavior* 52: 54–93.

Fudenberg, D. and Tirole, J. (1991) Perfect Bayesian equilibrium and sequential equilibrium. *Journal of Economic Theory* 53: 236-260.

Gauthier, D. (2013) Twenty-five on. *Ethics* 123: 601-624.

Gauthier, D. (2015) How I learned to stop worrying and love the Prisoner's Dilemma. In M. Peterson (ed.) *The Prisoner's Dilemma*, Cambridge University Press.

Gold, N. and Colman, A. M. (2020) Team reasoning and the rational choice of payoff-dominant outcomes in games. *Topoi* 39: 305-316.

Grüne-Yanoff, T. and Lehtinen, A. (2012) Philosophy of game theory. In U. Mäki (ed.) *Handbook of the Philosophy of Economics*, Elsevier.

Guala, F. (2006) Has game theory been refuted? *The Journal of Philosophy* 103: 239-263.

Harsanyi, J. C. and Selten, R. (1988) *A General Theory of Equilibrium Selection in Games*, MIT Press.

Hausman, D. (2012) *Preference, Value, Choice, and Welfare*, Cambridge University Press.

Isoni, A., Poulsen, A., Sugden, R. and Tsutsui, K. (2019) Focal points and payoff information in tacit bargaining. *Games and Economic Behavior* 114: 193-214.

Kalai, E. (1977) Proportional solutions to bargaining situations: Interpersonal utility comparisons. *Econometrica* 45: 1623-1630.

Kalai, E. and Smorodinsky, M. (1975) Other solutions to Nash's bargaining problem. *Econometrica* 43: 513-518.

Karpus, J. and Gold, N. (2017) Team reasoning: Theory and evidence. In J. Kiverstein (ed.) *The Routledge Handbook of Philosophy of the Social Mind*, Routledge.

Karpus, J. and Radzvilas, M. (2018) Team reasoning and a measure of mutual advantage in games. *Economics and Philosophy* 34: 1-30.

Kreps, D. M. and Wilson, R. (1982) Sequential equilibria. *Econometrica* 50: 863-894.

McCabe, K. A., Rigdon, M. L. and Smith, V. L. (2003) Positive reciprocity and intentions in trust games. *Journal of Economic Behavior & Organization* 52: 267-275.

Misyak, J. and Chater, N. (2014) Virtual bargaining: A theory of social decision-making. *Philosophical Transactions of the Royal Society B* 369: 20130487.

Misyak, J., Melkonyan, T., Zeitoun, H. and Chater, N. (2014) Unwritten rules: Virtual bargaining underpins social interaction, culture, and society. *Trends in Cognitive Sciences* 18: 512-519.

Myerson, R. M. (1991) *Game Theory: Analysis of Conflict*, Harvard University Press.

Nagel, R. (1995) Unravelling in Guessing games: An experimental study. *The American Economic Review* 85: 1313–1326.

Nash, J. (1950) The bargaining problem. *Econometrica* 18: 155–162.

Nash, J. (1951) Non-cooperative games. *Annals of Mathematics* 54: 286–295.

Pearce, D. G. (1984) Rationalizable strategic behavior and the problem of perfection. *Econometrica* 52: 1029–1050.

Perea, A. (2010) Backward induction versus forward induction reasoning. *Games* 1: 1-21.

Perea, A. (2012) *Epistemic Game Theory: Reasoning and Choice*, Cambridge University Press.

Perea, A. (2014) Belief in the opponent's future rationality. *Games and Economic Behavior* 83: 231-254.

Perea, A. (2015) Finite reasoning procedures for dynamic games. In S. Ghosh and R. Verbrugge (eds.) *Models of Strategic Reasoning*, LNCS 8972, Springer.

Perea, A. (2017) Forward induction reasoning and correct beliefs. *Journal of Economic Theory* 169: 489-516.

Peterson, M. (2015) Introduction. In M. Peterson (ed.) *The Prisoner's Dilemma*, Cambridge University Press.

Pettit, P. and Sugden, R. (1989) The backward induction paradox. *Journal of Philosophy* 86: 169-182.

Quesada, A. (2002) Belief system foundations of backward induction. *Theory and Decision* 53: 393–403.

Quesada, A. (2003) From common knowledge of rationality to backward induction. *International Game Theory Review* 5: 127–137.

Reiss, J. (2013) *Philosophy of Economics: A Contemporary Introduction*, Routledge.

Rosenthal, R. (1981) Games of perfect information, predatory pricing and the chain-store paradox. *Journal of Economic Theory* 25: 92-100.

Ross, D. (2019) Game theory. In Edward N. Zalta (ed.) *The Stanford Encyclopedia of Philosophy* (Winter 2019 Edition), https://plato.stanford.edu/archives/win2019/entries/game-theory/.

Rubinstein, A. (1991) Comments on the interpretation of game theory. *Econometrica* 59: 909-924.

Rubinstein, A. and Osborne, M. J. (1994) *A Course in Game Theory*, MIT Press.

Rubinstein, A. and Salant, Y. (2016) "Isn't everyone like me?" On the presence of self-similarity in strategic interactions. *Judgment and Decision Making* 11: 168-173.

Schlag, K. H., Tremewan, J. and van der Weele, J. J. (2015) A penny for your thoughts: A survey of methods for eliciting beliefs. *Experimental Economics* 18: 457–490.

Selten, R. (1965) Spieltheoretische Behandlung eines Oligopolmodells mit Nachfrageträgheit. *Zeitschrift für die gesamte Staatswissenschaft* 121: 301–324, 667–689.

Selten, R. (1975) A reexamination of the perfectness concept for equilibrium points in extensive games. *International Journal of Game Theory* 4: 25–55.

Selten, R. (1988) *Models of Strategic Rationality*, Springer.

Smerilli, A. (2012) We-thinking and vacillation between frames: Filling a gap in Bacharach's theory. *Theory and Decision* 73: 539–560.

Sugden, R. (1993) Thinking as a team: Towards an explanation of nonselfish behavior. *Social Philosophy and Policy* 10: 69–89.

Sugden, R. (2011) Mutual advantage, conventions and team reasoning. *International Review of Economics* 58: 9–20.

Sugden, R. (2015) Team reasoning and intentional cooperation for mutual benefit. *Journal of Social Ontology* 1: 143–166.

8
INSTITUTIONS, RATIONALITY, AND COORDINATION

Camilla Colombo and Francesco Guala

1. Introduction

There is general agreement among social scientists that institutions have an enormous impact on human well-being. Some economists have even tried to quantify it: according to Darren Acemoglu and James Robinson, for example, institutions account for three-quarters of the difference in the growth of European colonies between the 17th and the 19th centuries (Acemoglu et al. 2001; Acemoglu and Robinson 2012). In another influential study, Rodrik et al. (2004), using a sample of 140 countries, find that institutions trump every other plausible variable, including geography and trade, and account for most of the difference in growth between countries across time.[1] Hidden behind these empirical studies, however, lie some unresolved conceptual issues. What *are* institutions, to begin with, and how do they promote human flourishing and well-being?

Economists used to focus on the study of *one* specific kind of institution, namely, the market. But over the last few decades, they have come to accept that the market is hardly a single thing and that the way markets function depends to a large extent on the existence of other institutions, such as legal and moral codes (e.g. Friedman 2008; Granovetter 2005). Economic models tend to hide these dependencies. The traditional economic approach consisted of analyzing the behavior of rational agents who try to satisfy their preferences in a market-like setting, within the limits imposed by budget constraints. The existence of background institutions such as money, contract relations, judiciary systems, and taxation used to be taken for granted. Although economists have often assumed that institutions emerge from interactions among rational agents, until recently the study of these processes was rarely undertaken, and even now we only have a partial understanding of the relationship between institutions and individual behavior. One reason to take institutions seriously, then, is to understand whether standard economics, driven by methodological individualism, is a viable project, and how far it can go.

Another reason to take institutions seriously transcends economics and concerns human sociality in general. Although many other animal species live in groups, only *Homo sapiens* creates institutions. This capacity seems to be related to our exceptional cooperative skills and adaptability: we constantly develop new ways of working together, adapting our schemes of cooperation to new environments, new technologies, and our changing aspirations and goals. Institutions thus may hold the key to solve the puzzle of human uniqueness: what is the secret of our success? Which traits make us different and special in the animal kingdom?[2]

DOI: 10.4324/9781315739793-10

One seemingly obvious explanation is that we are much smarter than other animals. Thanks to our powerful cognitive apparatus, we are able to create sophisticated theoretical representations of the environment, to predict future events, to transmit information efficiently, and to make effective decisions in light of the available information. As Karl Popper once put it, our theorizing gives us the opportunity to eliminate bad ideas before natural selection eliminates us. This seemingly obvious explanation faces some difficulties, however. Many years of research on the psychology of decision-making have shown that people's beliefs and choices deviate significantly and systematically from those expected by rational agents (Stefánsson, Chapter 3; Lecouteux, Chapter 4; Vromen, Chapter 9). They deviate, moreover, for good reasons: rational decision-making in some situations is too complex for limited creatures like us, and in other situations, as we shall see, it even hampers coordination and cooperation.

For these reasons, since the 1970s an influential research program has tried to explain the emergence and function of institutions in terms of *bounded rationality*.[3] The guiding principle of bounded rationality theory is that cognitive resources are scarce. People have to make do with imperfect information and with limited time to identify the optimal course of action. Institutions in such cases provide "cognitive scaffoldings" that facilitate decision-making. The scaffoldings, out of metaphor, take the form of rules that – by prescribing how to perform certain tasks – allow a more efficient use of limited cognitive resources (e.g. Hart 1990; Denzau & North 1994; Clark 1997). However, notice the tension here: on the one hand, the creation of institutions seems to be possible by virtue of our unique cognitive skills. On the other hand, institutions are needed because our cognitive skills are limited. We have institutions because we are smart, but we need institutions because we are not that smart.

In this chapter, we will explore these two ideas: the fact that *Homo sapiens* seems to be endowed with unique cognitive abilities, and the fact that these abilities alone appear to fall short in explaining human sociality. We will do it by focusing on a key issue that lies at the core of rational choice theory: the problem of coordination. People coordinate in a huge number of situations to pursue goals that they would not be able to attain individually, and institutions help them to do it efficiently. Yet, the theory of rational choice is unable to explain how this process takes place. The problem has been recognized since at least the 1950s, and yet it has been relatively neglected compared to widely discussed puzzles such as the prisoner's dilemma or public goods games, which are the topics of literally thousands of articles and books. Paradoxically, most philosophers and economists have now come to accept that problems of cooperation are solved by changing the structure of incentives, so as to turn them into coordination games.[4] But this strategy obviously can hardly be called a "solution" if we lack an account of how coordination works.

We begin by explaining the relationship between institutions and problems of coordination in Section 2, where we also discuss the function of rules. Section 3 focuses on the formation of beliefs that are necessary for coordination according to standard game theory, and Section 4 shows how the problem may be solved by introducing a "whiff" of bounded rationality. Having discussed the pros and cons of this solution, in Section 5 we present an alternative approach based on the hypothesis of "belief-less reasoning," which departs more radically from the standard game-theoretic framework. In Section 6, we conclude with a few remarks on open issues and future research.

2. Institutions as Rules

What is an institution? Giving a definition is far from easy.[5] When we talk about institutions, we usually have in mind paradigmatic examples such as armies, parliaments, churches, firms, or stock markets. The challenge is to explain what these seemingly disparate things have in common. The most popular approach in the social sciences has been to conceptualize institutions as *systems of rules*.[6] In an influential contemporary statement, the economic historian Douglass

North claims that institutions "are a guide to human interaction" that help us to do things such as "greet friends on the street, drive an automobile, buy oranges, borrow money, form a business, bury our dead" (1990: 3–4). Help is required primarily to cope with ignorance and uncertainty:

> The uncertainties arise from incomplete information with respect to the behavior of other individuals in the process of human interaction. The computational limitations of the individual are determined by the capacity of the mind to process, organize, and utilize information. From this capacity taken in conjunction with the uncertainties involved in deciphering the environment, rules and procedures evolve to simplify the process. The consequent institutional framework, by structuring human interaction, limits the choice set of the actors.
>
> (North 1990: 25)

North's proposal is based on the idea that following a rule is cognitively less expensive than finding the optimal solution for every single problem that we face, on a case-by-case basis. A rule-follower dispenses with the work of surveying the possible actions, predicting their effects, evaluating them, and choosing the best one. She just follows a directive that, more often than not, leads to a satisfactory solution.[7] This simple account seems to presuppose that rules by themselves can somehow influence behavior. But is it so? There are good reasons to doubt it.

A rule takes the form of an imperative statement, such as "do X" or "if X, do Y."[8] When a driver disembarks from the ferry at Dover, for instance, she immediately sees several signs that say, "Drive on the left." This is useful, for if she is a newcomer, she may not know about the local practice or she may need a reminder. And yet, drivers – both locals and newcomers – ultimately drive on the left *because of the practice*, not because of the rule. They do so because they expect everyone to drive on the left and, given this expectation, it is in their interest to do the same.

This suggests that institutions cannot be *just* rules. (In the legislation of any country, there are plenty of rules that people do not follow, after all.)[9] Institutions are best characterized as *rules that people are motivated to follow*. Since the motivation is provided by other people, an understanding of institutions requires an understanding of interactive behavior.

Economics has developed a powerful apparatus to represent problems of interactive choice by using the formalism of game theory (see also Chapter 7 by Karpus and Radzvilas). In game-theoretic models, each individual or "player" is supposed to choose from a menu of actions or strategies, the outcomes of which depend on the decisions of *all* of the individuals who are involved. Players' interests are represented in succinct form by means of preference rankings or utility functions over the outcomes (see also Chapter 5). Sometimes the configuration of individual preferences is such that several mutually beneficial patterns of behavior are available. In the simple case of traffic, there are at least two plausible patterns: driving on the left and driving on the right.

These two patterns correspond to the pair of strategies (L, L) and (R, R) in the matrix in Figure 8.1. Each pair is an *equilibrium in pure strategies* of a game of pure coordination.[10] The payoffs reflect the fact that each player is indifferent between the two equilibria, and each equilibrium is preferable to any out-of-equilibrium outcome (R, L) or (L, R). Two factors then motivate British drivers: their preference for coordination and the expectation that the other drivers will drive on the left.

Notice that the strategies may be identified by rules (such as "Drive on the left" or "Drive on the right"). From an *internal* point of view then – the perspective of an agent who has to make a decision – institutional rules provide guidance by indicating a coordinative strategy among the many available ones. From an *external* point of view instead – the perspective of an observer – an institution describes a possible equilibrium of the game. An institution like driving on the left thus is best

	L	R
L	1, 1	0, 0
R	0, 0	1, 1

Figure 8.1 The driving game

defined as a *rule in equilibrium*: an imperative prescribing a set of actions that is in each individual's interest to follow, assuming that the others are going to do the same. We shall call this view the *rules-in-equilibrium* theory of social institutions.[11]

3. Rationality and Beliefs

The account of institutions as rules in equilibrium leaves one crucial question unanswered: even if the rule says that we must drive on the left in Britain, and even if everyone has been following the rule up until now, what makes us believe that they will do the same the next time around? Where do our expectations of conformity come from? More generally, what is the relationship between rules, expectations, and actions?

From a game-theoretic perspective, the key issue is that verbal statements do not change people's incentives. So, if the structure of a coordination game is not modified, the problem of equilibrium selection remains unresolved, regardless of the content of the rule (Aumann 1990; Basu 2018). Intuitively, of course, we all feel that we have good reasons to follow a rule like drive on the left. But this intuition is very difficult to justify: rational deliberation in such cases does not seem to help. Remember that, in normal circumstances, the reason or motive to drive on the left is constituted by the expectation that the other drivers will do the same. Now, I can form such an expectation only if I believe that the other drivers expect *me* to drive on the left. But my choice is precisely what is at stake; so how can they form *their* expectations, if I have not decided what to do yet? Circular reasoning leads to a regress: there seems to be no way to justify the beliefs that are necessary for rational rule-following or to generate the expectations (motives) that can make an institution work.

The standard way to get out of this conundrum, which is widely accepted by contemporary game theorists, is to invoke the notion of *salience*, introduced by Thomas Schelling (1960) in his pathbreaking work on tacit bargaining. Salience is the property of an outcome or a set of strategies to "catch the eye" or "stand out from the crowd" for reasons that may have little to do with strategic reasoning. Salience may be based on pure perception, culture, or a mix of these factors. Precedence, for example, immediately highlights one particular equilibrium – the one corresponding to the behavioral pattern that has been observed in the relevant community over a certain period of time. Among the possible solutions, for example, the tradition of driving on the left makes the LL equilibrium of the traffic game salient in Britain.[12]

In spite of its intuitive appeal, salience is a notoriously difficult notion to pin down and especially to formally incorporate in the theory of rational choice. The account of coordination by salience that is most popular among game theorists, originally sketched by David Lewis (1969), relaxes the assumption of full rationality and introduces elements of limited cognition. Salience, according to Lewis, breaks the circle of reasoning about others' beliefs by providing a "bottom line": a nonstrategic, predictable behavior upon which the expectations and choices of all the individuals can be based.

> Precedent is merely the source of one important kind of salience: conspicuous uniqueness of an equilibrium because we reached it last time. We may tend to repeat the action that succeeded before if we have no strong reason to do otherwise. Whether or not any of us really has this tendency, we may somewhat expect each other to have it, or expect each other to expect each other to have it, and so on – that is, we may each have first and higher-order expectations that the others will do their parts of the old coordination equilibrium, unless they have reason to act otherwise.
>
> (Lewis 1969: 36–37)

"Brute propensity" plays a key role in Lewis' account: the tendency to repeat a successful action, lacking a strong reason to do otherwise Such a propensity clearly cannot be the consequence of a rational process of deliberation. Lewis does not say exactly what sort of mechanism may lay behind it (a purely biological one perhaps) because, he suggests, it may not even matter: an *imagined* or *supposed* propensity will do just as well ("whether or not any of us really has this tendency").

Behavioral economists have formally developed this idea in the theory of so-called "level-k reasoning" (Nagel 1995; Stahl & Wilson 1995; Camerer et al. 2004). The "levels" refer to players' capacity for *meta-representation*, that is, the capacity to form beliefs about beliefs. A level-1 player, for example, is only able to form beliefs about the behavior of others (e.g. a belief that Jill will choose L). A level-2 player is able to form beliefs about first-order beliefs (e.g. a belief that Jack believes that Jill will choose L), and so forth. A naïve individual, with a brute propensity to choose a given option, is a level-0 player, and at the opposite end of the spectrum, a fully rational agent with unlimited cognitive capacities should be able to form beliefs of any level of complexity. But realistically, in a population of real human beings, we should only find players who can engage in limited meta-representation, at various levels of complexity.

Lewis' point in the paragraph quoted previously is that coordination does not even require naïve (level-0) players to exist. It is sufficient that some players (a group of level-1 reasoners, for example) behave *as if* they were facing a group of level-0 players or, alternatively, that some level-2 players behave as if they were facing a population of level-1 reasoners (which in turn presupposes a tacit belief in the existence of level-0 players).[13] The mechanism is simple: the existence (or believed existence) of naïve players increases the probability of successful coordination on the salient option. In the case of traffic in the United Kingdom, for instance, it tilts the balance of probability just enough to make driving on the left rational. The only necessary assumption is that someone in the population is *not* endowed with unlimited capacities of meta-representation.

4. Problems with Level-k Reasoning

So far, we have argued that the circularity involved in the game-theoretic explanation of coordination can be solved by introducing the idea that people are not perfectly rational reasoners, but suffer from cognitive shortcomings, and that cognitive abilities come in degrees in a population of individuals. Level-k theory is a specific model that captures and formalizes this intuition. Level-k explanations, however, preserve a key idea of game theory, namely, that players are strategic reasoners who choose their best response to the expected actions of the other players. The only departure from full rationality concerns meta-representation (or mind reading), that is, the capacity to form beliefs about beliefs. The idea is that people lack this *competence* to some degree: they are unable to climb the ladder of meta-representation beyond a certain level. (A level-2 player for example can only reach level 1 while trying to represent the mental state of another individual.) This interpretation connects the theory of salience with the idea of bounded rationality, and perhaps for this reason it is popular among contemporary economists.

In this section, we show that level-k theory may itself suffer from some shortcomings and may not be the most adequate explanation for the emergence of coordination. Specifically, this interpretation seems to be inconsistent with behavioral evidence. Later, in Section 5, we will argue that meta-representation might not be required in order to achieve and sustain coordination. Rather, the solution of coordination tasks might appeal to a different mode of reasoning with respect to the game-theoretic approach, which is still at the core of level-k theory. We will call this model "beliefless reasoning."

As discussed at the end of Section 3, level-k theory is based on the assumption of the existence different groups of players, with different cognitive skills. Crawford et al. (2013) survey the results of a large number of experiments with adult subjects engaged in strategic games and attempt to identify the levels of cognitive sophistication that are displayed across the population. Most experiments employing the level-k framework classify about 50% of the subjects as level-1, 30–40% as level-2, and less than 10% as level-3 reasoners. However, the data indicate that these distributions are unstable – different levels must be postulated in order to explain the data from different experiments. This variability suggests that either the level-k model is underspecified or the same individuals use different forms of reasoning depending on the strategic problem they are facing. They do not lack the *competence* of meta-representation, in other words: they rather *exercise* it differently in different contexts.

Evidence in favor of this interpretation comes from a remarkable experiment designed by Judith Mehta et al. (1994). Recall that, according to level-k theory, cognitively sophisticated players should anticipate the choices of naïve players, that is, they should converge on what the latter perceive as primarily salient (the option that "stands out from the crowd" or "first comes to mind"). Mehta and colleagues found instead that primarily salient options are not always focal points for coordination. In their experiment, for example, when asked to name a year (any year) in a nonstrategic context, most people mention the year of their birth. This primarily salient option, however, is not chosen when the goal is to coordinate, that is, to choose the same year chosen by another player: in such a situation, people tend to name the *current* year. Similarly, the primarily salient number (7) is not the focal point (1) when people are asked to choose a real number. The primarily salient color (blue) is different from the focal point (red) when asked to choose a color, and so on and so forth.

This behavior is consistent with various remarks made by Schelling in *The Strategy of Conflict* (1960). Schelling says that salience is *intentionally* used by players to coordinate:

> What is necessary [for the players] is to coordinate predictions, to read the same message in the common situation, to identify the one course of action that their expectations of one another can converge on. They must "mutually recognize" some unique signal that coordinates their expectations of each other.
>
> (Schelling 1960: 54)

As noticed by Sugden and Zamarròn (2006), expressions such as "finding the key" or the "clue" or solving the "riddle" recur frequently in *The Strategy of Conflict*, not just metaphorically or for illustrative purposes. Far from acting mechanically, and burdened by their cognitive limitations, coordinating players are portrayed by Schelling as goal-driven, intentional agents who try to find the solution of a difficult puzzle. Such an approach goes against the spirit and rationale of level-k theory, where coordination relies upon naïve players who do not even consider the interactive nature of the problem.

Notice also that, as a theory of strategic reasoning, level-k theory is supposed to apply to *all* games, including games of pure competition. But in *The Strategy of Conflict*, Schelling argues that "the intellectual processes of choosing a strategy in pure conflict and choosing a strategy of coordination are of wholly different sorts" (1960: 96). In coordination games, in fact, people have *good reasons* for being nonstrategic. Thoughts about others' beliefs (and beliefs about beliefs), even if done competently and systematically, do not lead anywhere in a cooperative setting, while looking for a plausible (salient) solution does. The question is, can this simple intuition be turned into a theory of rational coordination?

5. Belief-less Reasoning

In this section, we review two attempts to articulate more precisely the processes of nonstrategic reasoning that may lead to coordination. We shall also highlight the common features of these approaches, in particular concerning the role played by belief attribution.

According to team reasoning, proposed by Michael Bacharach, Natalie Gold, and Robert Sugden,[14] problems of coordination are solved by means of a "transformation in the unit of agency." Arguably, in fact, the creation of collective identities is an important function of institutions (think of political parties, football teams, or firms): identity manipulation may induce individual agents to conceive of the coordination game as a *collective problem* for the group, rather than a problem to be solved individually. Transformation of the unit of agency has the effect of turning the strategic problem into a parametric decision (a decision for a single player), as in the following inferential scheme (TR):

1. The team's goal is to maximize its payoff.
2. *S* is the obvious way to achieve this goal.
3. *S* implies that I choose s_1 and you choose s_2.
4. I will choose s_1 and you will choose s_2.

We have used the letter *S* in this schema to refer to a salient solution of a coordination game. Salience may be grounded on purely cognitive mechanisms, cultural factors, or mere precedence as explained by Schelling and Lewis. The individual strategies that constitute *S* are labeled s_1 and s_2. Notice that the TR scheme does not include beliefs among its premises. On the contrary, the scheme can be used to *derive* expectations about players' behavior, as in the conclusion of the argument (step 4), and possibly also expectations about their beliefs, assuming that the other players reason in the same way. The key point is that the premises 1–3 only include information about the preferences of the team, the most obvious way to satisfy such preferences, and the actions or strategies that are to be implemented by each individual player in order to satisfy them.

Like level-k theory, TR also presupposes that there is a nonlogical way to identify the "obvious" (i.e. salient) solution. But unlike level-k theory, it does not postulate an *unreflective* disposition to choose the salient option or a brute tendency to repeat a behavior that has been successful in the past. Quite the contrary: once the salient solution has been identified, the conclusion of TR (and, hence, the action to be chosen) follows from a process of instrumental reasoning. It is, more precisely, a form of instrumental *belief-less* reasoning: the players do not predict the action of the other individual by first representing her preferences and beliefs. Rather, they focus on the available options, looking for features that make one profile of strategies focal.

Following Adam Morton (2003), we may say that the players are "solution thinkers," who are looking for the key to solve a problem of coordination. The process of strategic reasoning then is turned on its head: instead of trying to predict the action of the other player from an identification of her preferences and beliefs, each individual tries to find the best or most obvious way to coordinate and *then* attributes an appropriate set of beliefs to the other player. Here is Morton's summary description of this reasoning process:

> One first thinks of an outcome which one can imagine the other person or persons both would want to achieve and would believe that one would try to achieve. One then thinks out a sequence of actions by all concerned that will lead to it. Lastly, one performs the actions that fall to one's account from this sequence . . . and expects the other(s) to do their corresponding actions.
>
> (Morton 2003: 120)

Notice that Morton's account does not mention any transformation of agency, suggesting that the reasoning behind solution thinking may be formulated in purely individualistic terms. From the point of view of an individual player, the inference may be reconstructed as follows (ST) (Guala 2018, 2020):

1. My goal is to maximize my payoff, and your goal is to maximize your payoff.
2. *S* is the obvious way to achieve these two goals.
3. *S* implies that I choose s_1 and you choose s_2.
4. I will choose s_1 and you will choose s_2.

The most striking similarity between team reasoning and solution thinking is that they are both forms of belief-less reasoning. As Sugden points out, "it is because players who think as a team do not need to form expectations about one another's actions that they can solve coordination problems" (1993: 87). The two theories, however, circumvent the problem of circularity of (higher order) beliefs in different ways. In team reasoning, the beliefs of the other player are ignored because there is no other player to begin with. Each player does her part in a collective action, assuming that the other team members are doing the same. Solution thinking, in contrast, is an individualistic mode of reasoning, which does not require a transformation of the unit of agency. Each player ignores the beliefs of the others, because meta-representation is *not* the key for solving the problem of coordination.

6. Summing Up and Looking Ahead

To understand coordination is a key challenge for economists, psychologists, and philosophers interested in the cognitive foundations of institutions. The standard approach until now has been to emphasize, on the one hand, the distinctive skills that allow humans to "read the minds" of their co-specifics and, on the other hand, to search for cognitive limitations that may simplify mind reading and solve the problem of circularity in belief attribution. This approach, which is consistent with the idea of bounded rationality, has inspired the development of sophisticated theoretic models and is currently very popular among behavioral scientists.

The bounded rationality narrative, however, suffers from empirical and theoretical shortcomings. We have seen that experimental data do not support the theory. And the theory, moreover, has curious normative implications: it suggests that we should adopt a mistaken mode of reasoning in order to solve a task that rationality cannot solve! This is peculiar because, as Schelling pointed out, an intelligent player should be entitled to search for a different solution, if standard strategic reasoning fails. A set of interesting questions thus arises once alternative theories of decision – such as team reasoning or solution thinking – are taken seriously. If the process of coordinating is not rational, at least in the standard strategic sense, what kinds of justification and legitimacy are left for rule-following and institutional compliance? Are institutions grounded on inherently irrational thinking? These questions open up the wider debate about the definition of the concept of rationality, a topic too large and complex to be adequately addressed here. We can merely conclude by offering some preliminary remarks, which hopefully will stimulate more discussion on this topic.

First of all, let us notice that a group of team reasoners or solution thinkers (that is, belief-less reasoners) would do better in coordination tasks than a group of standard strategic thinkers. But practical success does not necessarily imply rationality – several nonrational heuristics may lead to the solution of decision-problems with which perfectly optimizing agents would struggle. A stronger consideration in favor of belief-less reasoning is that its main rival – perfect strategic rationality – is hopeless. We do not dispense with strategic reasoning just because it is too cumbersome or cognitively demanding, but because it suffers from a fundamental logical flaw, that is, circular reasoning and infinite regress. In such circumstances, an alternative theory that is able to lead to coordination seems to enjoy a rather strong normative appeal.

If the standard game-theoretic approach falls short, what could be more rational (not merely efficient) than using a more effective mode of reasoning? More specifically, once individuals realize that mind reading leads to circularity, should they perhaps ignore higher order beliefs and abandon strategic thinking? To answer these questions would require a deep revision of the notion of rationality – an ongoing project in the philosophy of economics that, we think, will be enriched by the inclusion of belief-less reasoning in the toolbox of choice theory.[15]

Related Chapters

Karpus and Radzvilas, Chapter 7 "Game Theory and Rational Reasoning"
Lecouteux, Chapter 4 "Behavioral Welfare Economics and Consumer Sovereignty"
Stefánsson, Chapter 3 "The Economics and Philosophy of Risk"
Vredenburgh, Chapter 5 "The Economic Concept of a Preference"
Vromen, Chapter 9 "*As If* Social Preference Models"
Nagatsu, Chapter 24 "Experimentation in Economics"

Acknowledgements

Research for this chapter was funded by the Department of Philosophy "Piero Martinetti" of the University of Milan under the Project "Departments of Excellence 2018-2022" awarded by the Ministry of Education, University and Research (MIUR).

Notes

1 For a dissenting view, see Glaeser et al. (2004).
2 Compare, e.g., Tomasello (2009) and Seabright (2010).
3 See, e.g., Simon (1997) and Gigerenzer and Selten (2002).
4 Incentives may be changed by centralized systems of punishment (Baldassarri & Grossmann 2011; Andreoni & Gee 2012), by turning one-shot interactions into indefinitely repeated games (Binmore 2005), by decentralized punishment backed up by social preferences (Fehr & Fischbacher 2002; Bowles & Gintis 2013), or by social norms (Elster 1989; Bicchieri 2006), to name a few prominent proposals. The literature is too vast to be reviewed here, but see, for example, Peterson (2015) for a recent volume on cooperation dilemmas.
5 And perhaps not even necessary for some purposes; see Hodgson (2019).
6 See, e.g., Weber (1910), Parsons (1935), North (1990), Hodgson (1988), and Mantzavinos (2001).
7 See also Heiner (1983, 1990).
8 Philosophers call such statements "regulative rules" in order to distinguish them from "constitutive rules." The distinction is at the core of the influential theory of institutions developed by Searle (1995). Since there

are good reasons to believe that constitutive rules are reducible to regulative ones, however (Hindriks 2009; Guala & Hindriks 2015; Hindriks & Guala 2015), we will always refer to rules in the regulative sense in this chapter.

9 Basu (2018) calls it "the problem of ink on paper," in the sense that it is somewhat mysterious how people's behavior may be changed by merely writing a rule or stating it verbally.

10 There are other possible patterns that involve randomized behavior (i.e. driving on the right or left with a certain probability), but for the sake of simplicity we will ignore these "mixed strategies." In the matrices, we follow the usual convention of representing players' strategies on rows and columns and their preferences with real numbers (the first one for the row player and the second for the column player). Although we use 2 × 2 games for ease of presentation, the moral of the story can be generalized to interactive situations with more players and more strategies.

11 Versions of this theory have been proposed by Aoki (2011), Greif and Kingston (2011), Guala and Hindriks (2015), Hindriks and Guala (2015), and Guala (2016).

12 In *The Strategy of Conflict*, Schelling remarked that "precedence seems to exercise an influence that greatly exceeds its logical importance or legal force," and "there is . . . a strong attraction to the status quo ante" (1960: 67–68). This insight led directly to the development of David Lewis' (1969) influential theory of convention.

13 The empirical evidence is consistent with the hypothesis that most people reason at levels 1, 2, and 3, while practically no one seems completely naïve or seems to engage in reasoning at level 4 or above (see Crawford et al. 2013).

14 Sugden (1993, 2000, 2003, 2015), Bacharach (1999, 2006), Gold and Sugden (2007), and Gold and Colman (2018).

15 Some steps in this direction have been taken by Sugden (1993, 2000, 2003), Bacharach (2006), Gold and Sugden (2007), Hurley (1989), Karpus and Radzvilas (2018), and Colombo and Guala (2020), among others.

Bibliography

Acemoglu, D., Johnson, S. and Robinson, J. A. (2001) "The Colonial Origins of Comparative Development: An Empirical Investigation," *American Economic Review* 9: 1369–1401.

Acemoglu, D., and Robinson, J. A. (2012) *Why Nations Fail: The Origins of Power, Prosperity, and Poverty*, New York: Crown Books.

Andreoni, J., and Gee, L. K. (2012) "Gun for Hire: Delegated Enforcement and Peer Punishment in Public Goods Provision," *Journal of Public Economics* 96: 1036–1046.

Aoki, M. (2011) "Institutions as Cognitive Media Between Strategic Interactions and Individual Beliefs," *Journal of Economic Behavior and Organization* 79: 20–34.

Aumann, R. J. (1990) "Nash Equilibria are Not Self-enforcing," in J. J. Gabszewicz, J. F. Richard, and L. A. Wolsey (eds.) *Economic Decision Making: Games Econometrics and Optimization: Contributions in Honour of Jacques H. Drèze*, Amsterdam: Business and Economics: 201–206.

Bacharach, M. (1999) "Interactive Team Reasoning: A Contribution to the Theory of Co-operation," *Research in economics* 5: 117–147.

Bacharach, M. (2006) *Beyond Individual Choice: Teams and Frames in Game Theory*, Princeton, NJ: Princeton University Press.

Baldassarri, D., and Grossman, G. (2011) "Centralized Sanctioning and Legitimate Authority Promote Cooperation in Humans," *Proceedings of the National Academy of Sciences* 108: 11023–11027.

Basu, K. (2018) *The Republic of Beliefs*, Princeton, NJ: Princeton University Press.

Bicchieri, C. (2006) *The Grammar of Society: The Nature and Dynamics of Social Norms*, Cambridge: Cambridge University Press.

Binmore, K. (2005) *Natural Justice*, Oxford: Oxford University Press.

Bowles, S., and Gintis, H. (2013) *A Cooperative Species: Human Reciprocity and its Evolution*, Princeton, NJ: Princeton University Press.

Camerer, C. F., Ho, T. H., and Chong, J. K. (2004) "A Cognitive Hierarchy Model of Games," *Quarterly Journal of Economics* 119: 861–898.

Clark, A. (1997) "Economic Reason: The Interplay of Individual Learning and External Structure," in J. Drobak and J. Nye (eds.) *The Frontiers of the New Institutional Economics*, San Diego: Academic Press.

Colombo, C., and Guala, F. (2021) *Rational Coordination Without Beliefs*, Erkenntnis, forthcoming.

Crawford, V. P., Costa-Gomes, M. A., and Iriberri, N. (2013) "Structural Models of Nonequilibrium Strategic Thinking: Theory, Evidence, and Applications," *Journal of Economic Literature* 51: 5–62.

Denzau, A. T., and North, D. C. (1994) "Shared Mental Models: Ideologies and Institutions," *Kyklos* 47: 3–31.
Elster, J. (1989) *The Cement of Society: A Survey of Social Order*, Cambridge: Cambridge University Press.
Fehr, E., and Fischbacher, U. (2002) "Why Social Preferences Matter – the Impact of Non-selfish Motives on Competition, Cooperation and Incentives," *The Economic Journal* 112: C1–C33.
Friedman, D. (2008) *Morals and Markets: An Evolutionary Account of the Modern World*, New York, NY: Macmillan.
Gigerenzer, G. and R. Selten (eds.) (2002) *Bounded Rationality: The Adaptive Toolbox*, Cambridge, MA: MIT Press.
Glaeser, E. L., La Porta, R., Lopez-de-Silanes, F. and Shleifer, A. (2004) "Do Institutions Cause Growth?" *Journal of Economic Growth* 9: 271–303.
Gold, N. and Colman, A. (2018) "Team Reasoning and the Rational Choice of Payoff-Dominant Outcomes in Games," *Topoi* 39: 305–316.
Gold, N., and Sugden, R. (2007) "Collective Intentions and Team Agency," *Journal of Philosophy* 104: 109–137.
Granovetter, M. (2005) "The Impact of Social Structure on Economic Outcomes," *Journal of Economic Perspectives* 19: 33–50.
Greif, A. and Kingston, C. (2011) "Institutions: Rules or Equilibria?" in N. Schofield and G. Caballero (eds.) *Political Economy of Institutions, Democracy and Voting*, Berlin: Springer: 13–43.
Guala, F. (2016) *Understanding Institutions*, Princeton, NJ: Princeton University Press.
Guala, F. (2018) "Coordination, Team Reasoning, and Solution Thinking," *Revue D'économie Politique* 128: 355–372.
Guala, F. (2020) " Solving the Hi-lo Paradox: Equilibria, Beliefs, and Coordination" in A. Fiebich (ed.) *Minimal Cooperation and Shared Agency*, Berlin: Springer: 149–168.
Guala, F. and Hindriks, F. (2015) "A Unified Social Ontology," *Philosophical Quarterly* 65: 177–201.
Hart, O. (1990) "Is 'Bounded Rationality' an Important Element of a Theory of Institutions?" *Journal of Institutional and Theoretical Economics* 146: 696–702.
Heiner, R. A. (1983) "The Origin of Predictable Behavior," *American Economic Review* 73: 560–595.
Heiner, R. A. (1990) "Imperfect Choice and the Origin of Institutional Rules," *Journal of Institutional and Theoretical Economics* 146: 720–726.
Hindriks, F. (2009) "Constitutive Rules, Language, and Ontology," *Erkenntnis* 71: 253–275.
Hindriks, F. and Guala, F. (2015) "Institutions, Rules, and Equilibria: A Unified Theory," *Journal of Institutional Economics* 11: 459–480.
Hodgson, G. M. (1988) *Economics and Institutions*, Cambridge: Polity Press.
Hodgson, G. M. (2019) "Taxonomic Definitions in Social Science, with Firms, Markets and Institutions as Case Studies," *Journal of Institutional Economics* 15: 207–233.
Hurley, S. (1989) *Natural Reasons*, Oxford: Oxford University Press.
Karpus, J., and Radzvilas, M. (2018) "Team Reasoning and a Measure of Mutual Advantage in Games," *Economics & Philosophy* 34: 1–30.
Lewis, D.K. (1969) *Convention: A Philosophical Study*, Oxford: Basil Blackwell.
Mantzavinos, C. (2001) *Individuals, Institutions, and Markets*, Cambridge: Cambridge University Press.
Mehta, J., Starmer, C., and Sugden, R. (1994) "The Nature of Salience: An Experimental Investigation of Pure Coordination Games," *American Economic Review* 84: 658–673.
Morton, A. (2003) *The Importance of Being Understood: Folk Psychology as Ethics*, London/New York: Routledge.
Nagel, R. (1995) "Unraveling in Guessing Games: An Experimental Study," *American Economic Review* 85: 1313–1326.
North, D. (1990) *Institutions, Institutional Change and Economic Performance*, Cambridge: Cambridge University Press.
Parsons, T. (1935) "The Place of Ultimate Values in Sociological Theory," *International Journal of Ethics* 45: 282–316.
Peterson, M. (Ed.). (2015) *The Prisoner's Dilemma*, Cambridge: Cambridge University Press.
Rodrik, D., Subramanian, A., and Trebbi, F. (2004) "Institutions Rule: The Primacy of Institutions over Geography and Integration in Economic Development," *Journal of Economic Growth* 9: 131–165.
Schelling, T. C. (1960) *The Strategy of Conflict*, Cambridge, MA: Harvard University Press.
Seabright, P. (2010) *The Company of Strangers*, Princeton, NJ: Princeton University Press.
Searle, J. (1995) *The Construction of Social Reality*, London: Penguin.
Simon, H. A. (1997) *Models of Bounded Rationality: Empirically Grounded Economic Reason* (Vol. 3), Cambridge, MA: MIT press.
Stahl, D. O., and Wilson, P. W. (1995) "On Players' Models of Other Players: Theory and Experimental Evidence," *Games and Economic Behavior* 10: 218–254.
Sugden, R. (1993) "Thinking as a Team: Toward an Explanation of Nonselfish Behavior," *Social Philosophy and Policy* 10: 69–89.

Sugden, R. (2000) "Team Preferences," *Economics & Philosophy* 16: 174–204.
Sugden, R. (2003) "The Logic of Team Reasoning," *Philosophical Explorations* 6: 165–181.
Sugden, R. (2015) "Team Reasoning and Intentional Cooperation for Mutual Benefit," *Journal of Social Ontology* 1: 143–166.
Sugden, R., and Zamarrón, I. E. (2006) "Finding the Key: The Riddle of Focal Points," *Journal of Economic Psychology* 27: 609–621.
Tomasello, M. (2009) *Why We Cooperate*, Cambridge, MA: MIT Press.
Weber, M. (1910) "Diskussionsrede zu dem Vortrag von A. Ploetz über Die Begriffe Rasse und Gesellschaft," in *Gesammelte Aufsätze zur Soziologie und Sozialpolitik*, Tübingen: Mohr: 456–462.

9

AS IF SOCIAL PREFERENCE MODELS

Jack Vromen

1. Introduction

Behavioral economics is probably best known for its detection of a host of choice anomalies: behaviors that systematically deviate from predictions of standard economic models assuming perfect (or full) rationality. Behavioral economists argue that these anomalies result from cognitive biases. They have identified quite a few such biases (cf. Ariely 2008; Lecouteux, Chapter 4). Cognitive biases are believed to impair agents' decision-making, and this might prevent them from satisfying their preferences to the fullest possible degree. Nonintrusive policy measures such as nudges (Thaler and Sunstein 2008) have been proposed to help agents better satisfy their preferences (see also Grüne-Yanoff, Chapter 35).

Behavioral economists have also engaged in developing social preference models. Social preference models seem to convey a completely different message. In these models, the standard assumption of perfect rationality is often retained: agents with social preferences are assumed to be rational utility maximizers. What makes these models different from standard models is not that they accommodate cognitive biases, but that they include social preferences next to self-interested preferences in agents' utility functions. Moreover, it is assumed that social preferences lead to prosocial behavior, which is costly for the agent. Nevertheless, the presumption here is not that the behaviors of agents with social preferences can be improved by policy interventions. On the contrary, the idea is that prosocial behavior should not be corrected. If anything, it should be encouraged and promoted.

Thus, behavioral economics seems to host two research areas that are quite distinct in two ways. What is vehemently denied in the one area, that real humans of flesh and blood exhibit perfectly rational behavior, is simply assumed in the other. And what is taken as a legitimate reason for ameliorative policy measures in the one area, that people fail to optimally serve their own interests, seems to elicit the opposite policy response in the other area. This chapter aims to shed light on these prima facie remarkable discrepancies within behavioral economics. Each of these discrepancies poses a puzzle. The first puzzle is why social preference model proponents believe that costly prosocial behavior should be promoted, while other behavioral economists hold that behaviors that are costly for the agent should be corrected. The second puzzle is why proponents of social preference models assume that agents behave fully rationally, while the whole point of the "heuristics and biases" part of behavioral economics is to show that agents often are not fully rational. I will first have a closer look at two social preference models that have been particularly influential in behavioral economics:

DOI: 10.4324/9781315739793-11

fairness (inequality-aversion) models (Fehr and Schmidt 1999; Bolton and Ockenfels 2000) and social image models (Bénabou and Tirole 2006).

2. Two Exemplary Social Preference Models

Economists have been talking about social preferences in several ways. In the social welfare function literature, for example, a social welfare function represents the social preferences that someone, such as a citizen or a policymaker, has with respect to social states (Weymark 2016). There is no presumption that these social preferences are reflected in actual behavior; social preferences might only indicate how a person thinks or feels about various social states. Social preference models in behavioral economics presume not only that at least some people have social preferences but also that they act on them. Indeed, the overall claim of these models is that we cannot explain a bewildering variety of behavioral evidence unless we assume that people have social preferences and act on them.

Many such social preference models have been developed by behavioral economists. The sorts of social preferences hypothesized in them vary considerably. For example, we have models in which people are assumed to be altruistic (in either its pure or impure form; cf. Andreoni 1989), to be concerned with efficiency (or social welfare; Charness and Rabin 2002), and to care about reciprocity (so-called reciprocity-oriented social preferences; cf. Rabin 1993; Dufwenberg and Kirchsteiger 2004). Here, I will focus on two "outcome-oriented" social preference models that have been particularly influential in behavioral economics (DellaVigna 2018): fairness (inequality-aversion) models (Fehr and Schmidt 1999; Bolton and Ockenfels 2000) and social image models (Bénabou and Tirole 2006).[1]

Both Fehr and Schmidt (1999) and Bolton and Ockenfels (2000) aim to develop a "motivation model" that is simple, yet general enough to be consistent with the often seemingly conflicting behavioral evidence gathered in the various experiments conducted with different games.[2] In some games, such as market games, subjects in experiments often seem to act as if they are all completely selfish, whereas in other games, such as the ultimatum game (UG) and the dictator game (DG), their behavior seems to be led by fairness concerns. The "motivation models" that Fehr and Schmidt (1999) and Bolton and Ockenfels (2000) have developed aim to identify the motives driving the subjects' behaviors in these experiments. Both models posit that subjects care about not only their own pecuniary payoffs but also their relative payoffs.[3] It is this latter concern that is taken to be their social preference. As Fehr and Schmidt (1999) put it: subjects are inequity averse not only in that they dislike disadvantageous inequity (i.e., they dislike receiving less than others) but also in that they dislike advantageous inequity (i.e., they also dislike receiving more than others).

Fehr and Schmidt (1999) and Bolton and Ockenfels (2000) argue that the robust ("stylized") facts in the UG and DG especially violate the predictions of the standard self-interest model. In the UG, proposers generously offer to respondents some 40–60% of the total amount to be divided (which respondents often accept, so that the division is as proposed), and respondents typically refuse to accept low offers (roughly less than 20%, so that both proposers and respondents get nothing). In the DG, in which recipients must accept the offer made by the dictator, dictators offer considerably less than what proposers offer in the UG, but they still offer roughly some 20%. As can be quickly recognized, proposers in the UG need not be led by equity concerns. They might be led solely by selfish considerations, for if they expect responders to reject low ("unfair") offers, it is in their own self-interest to make higher offers (offers they expect respondents to accept). But the fact that responders do, in fact, turn down low offers cannot be so easily explained by self-interest. After all, they would gain positive rather than zero payoffs for themselves if they accepted low offers. Furthermore, the fact that proposers do offer a substantive amount (even though it is much less than what they offer in the UG) in the DG suggests that they too are not completely selfish. According to Fehr and Schmidt (1999) and Bolton and Ockenfels (2000), these violations of the standard model show the need for a social preference model (SPM).

Bénabou and Tirole (2006) seem to be driven by the same aim as Fehr and Schmidt (1999) and Bolton and Ockenfels (2000): to develop a simple, parsimonious motivational model that is consistent with all of the observed robust facts. Bénabou and Tirole (2006) have developed a slightly more complex, less parsimonious model because they believe that simple and parsimonious models such as the one developed by Fehr and Schmidt (1999) are unable to explain the new facts that have been observed. A particularly telling example is provided by Dana et al. (2006, 2007). They show that if people can choose to remain ignorant about what part of others' payoffs depends on their own decisions, they tend to offer considerably less to others than when they are keenly aware of that. The same holds if they (think they) can conceal from others what part of the others' payoffs depends on their own decisions. This implies that people may care more about maintaining a social and self-image of being fair ("appearing to themselves and others that they are fair") than about fairness ("being fair"). Examples like this prompted Bénabou and Tirole (2006) to posit *social and self-image* as a motive in addition to "greed" (to obtain the highest possible pecuniary payoffs for themselves) and "intrinsic motivation" (to contribute voluntarily to the social good). With this amended social preference model, they can explain why the introduction of extrinsic incentives (such as paying people to do the right thing) can crowd out prosocial behavior: people might be discouraged from doing the right thing, because they might anticipate that others would suspect that they are doing the right thing just for the money (and not because they are fair or intrinsically motivated to do the right thing; see also Bavetta, Chapter 32, and Wintein and Heilmann, Chapter 19).

On the basis of the foregoing brief discussion of a few exemplary social preference models, we can say that three common features of these social preference models stand out. First, their proponents[4] aim to develop general models that are consistent with all available data across different games, while being as simple and as parsimonious as possible. Let's call this the "*good models*" desideratum. Second, they want their models to be explanatory and track causal determinants of behavior in actual decision-making processes. They do not seem to be satisfied with *as if* models that succeed in being consistent with the available choice data, but make behavioral assumptions that do not accurately represent key components in actual decision-making processes. Instead of the *as if* models that some nonbehavioral economists are satisfied with, they want to develop "because" models that succeed in identifying such causal components. Let's call this the "*psychological realism*" desideratum. Third, they believe that both of the preceding desiderata can be satisfied by inserting just one social preference (or at most two) as a separate argument in the utility function. Each of these social preferences is believed to correspond with real motives underlying behavior. As they retain the assumption that people are perfectly rational utility maximizers, they apparently also believe that the behaviors explained by their social preference models are (at least approximately) perfectly rational.

Let us first have a closer look at prosocial behavior, the sort of behavior that has prompted behavioral economists to develop social preference models. What exactly is prosocial behavior, and what is it that makes prosocial behavior so precious to SPM proponents?

3. The "Standard Self-Interested" Model as the Normative Benchmark

Sometimes behavioral economists simply portray "prosocial behavior" as nice behavior that should be promoted as much as possible and in which only people who care about the interests of others (that is, who have social preferences) engage (Capraro et al. 2019). We are told neither why prosocial behavior should be promoted as much as possible nor why only people acting on their social preferences would be engaged in it. This rather simplistic portrayal needs considerable qualification. To see this, consider again our previous brief discussion of inequity aversion and social image. In Fehr and Schmidt's (1999) model, the disadvantageous part of inequity aversion need not reflect a concern for the interests of others, or some impartial concern for fairness, but rather a concern for one's own relative standing. What people primarily led by disadvantageous inequity aversion dislike is not that others do not receive enough, but rather that they themselves do not receive enough compared to others. If anything, they envy others for having more than they have themselves. Similarly, in Bénabou and Tirole's (2006) model, the concern for social image does not seem to reflect a concern for the interests of others, but rather a concern for one's own interests.[5] People primarily led by this concern are not necessarily nice or kind to others; they only want to appear to others as nice and kind people. They will care about the interests of others only if they believe that it is instrumental to boosting their own social image. If they can afford not to be kind and nice to others without damaging their social image, they will do that. In short, people led by social preferences need not care about the interests of others.

What this suggests is that "social preferences" do not necessarily identify particular non-self-serving motives. Sometimes social preferences are contrasted with antisocial or "malevolent" preferences (such as envy, spite, and sadism) aimed at harming people (Harsanyi 1982). But, as we just saw, envy might also be the motive underlying disadvantageous inequity aversion in Fehr and Schmidt's (1999) conception of fairness. Thus, the same "nasty" motive might underlie both social and antisocial preferences.

Social preference models are usually contrasted with "standard" self-interested models. But this too might be a bit confusing. As many economists have recognized, one's engagement in prosocial behavior might be called self-interested in the sense that doing so best satisfies the agent's preferences, that it yields maximum utility to the agent, or that the highest psychic satisfaction might be gained from it for the agent (Andreoni 1989). Thus, a person who ultimately only cares about her own psychic satisfaction, and who sympathizes with another person, might help that other person for instrumental reasons. SPM proponents do not deny that prosocially behaving people, acting on their social preferences, can be psychologically selfish in this sense (de Quervain et al. 2004). But, they maintain that social preferences are non-self-interested in another sense: they are not aimed at obtaining the highest possible material payoffs for themselves. In other words, "self-interest" is supposed to refer to one's own material (mostly monetary or pecuniary) payoffs.

Correspondingly, "prosocial behavior" can be said to refer to a particular material payoff profile: it is costly (−) to the agent and beneficial (+) to others (Bénabou and Tirole 2006), where costs and benefits are measured in terms of material payoffs. The intended contrast here is with antisocial behavior, which has a different (−/−) material payoff profile: antisocial behavior is costly not only to the agent but also to others.[6] People behaving antisocially incur personal costs in harming other people. Thus, if people engage in antisocial punishment (Herrmann et al. 2008), that is, if they incur personal costs by punishing cooperators (or contributors to public goods), they thereby diminish both their own material payoffs and those of the cooperators they punish.

Antisocial punishment is sometimes contrasted with altruistic punishment (Fehr and Gächter 2002; Fehr et al. 2002). Altruistic punishment is seen as the negative part of the social preference of strong reciprocity. In altruistic punishment, it is not cooperators but defectors (or noncontributors) who are punished. But here it seems we encounter yet another problem: altruistic punishment does not seem to fit the particular material payoff profile of prosocial behavior. Just as with antisocial punishment, the material payoff profile seems to be −/− rather than −/+. The only difference between altruistic and antisocial punishment seems to be that the targets ("the others") of the punishments differ. What is it about altruistic punishment that enchants proponents? One might be inclined to argue that it is not nice (or just, or right, etc.) to punish cooperators, while it is nice (or just, or right, etc.) to punish defectors. But unless one is prepared to argue that more cooperation is always good (and more defection is always bad), this needs further justification.

Insofar as proponents of strong reciprocity provide a (sketch of a) justification for why more cooperation is desirable in public goods games, it is that it contributes to *social* welfare. Fehr and

Gächter (2000) showed that if agents are given the opportunity to incur personal costs to punish defectors, the average rate of contributions to public goods does not decline over time (as is usual in games without this opportunity) but is maintained at its initially high level. This helps to keep the total provision of public goods close to an optimal provision, something from which all benefit.

The normative benchmark implicitly invoked here is the standard one, based mainly on the Pareto principle (Angner 2015). When we apply the principle, the criterion of whether people are better off in one situation compared to another is whether they receive higher material payoffs. Apparently, behavioral economists see no need to tweak this benchmark. One might think that SPM proponents believe that (the satisfaction of) social preferences should somehow be included in the understanding of what it is that can make people better off. If people genuinely care about satisfying their social preferences, as the SPM proponents clearly assume, their well-being seems to be enhanced by satisfying *all* of their preferences, including the social ones, even if that means that they forego material payoffs by doing so. But such a belief is not reflected in the normative benchmark that they (mostly implicitly) invoke. Their normative benchmark suits the standard self-interest model in that the well-being of individuals is measured in terms of the degrees to which they satisfy their self-interested preferences (as they understand these). In other words, they assume that the very model that they reject on "positive grounds" provides the proper normative benchmark for their own social welfare evaluations.[7]

Thus, the reason why behavioral economists believe that prosocial behavior should be promoted as much as possible is because it contributes to the social (or common) good. The immediate effect of the payoffs for those punished is negative, but the eventual effect for the group, population, or society as a whole is supposed to be positive.[8] That is why the behavior is called prosocial and even altruistic (Kitcher 2010). Is the behavior costly to the agent (or punisher)? Proponents of strong reciprocity go to great lengths to argue that it is and that the behavior of strong reciprocators cannot be rationalized by self-interest models. They acknowledge that the behavior of "weak" reciprocators, who supposedly only reward cooperation by cooperating themselves and punish defection by defecting themselves (but who do not incur further personal costs on top of that), can be rationalized by self-interest models (cf. the so-called Folk Theorems in repeated game theory). But they adamantly deny that the same can be done with strong reciprocity (see, e.g., Gintis et al. 2005).

What makes this denial questionable, however, is that they engage in evolutionary explanations of how strong reciprocity could have evolved (Bowles and Gintis 2011). And strong reciprocity is not the only social preference for which social preference model proponents have sought an evolutionary explanation. Many SPM proponents have engaged in attempts to show how social preferences (such as a concern for relative status; cf. Bolton and Ockenfels 2000) could have evolved, presumably to strengthen their case that social preferences do actually exist (are "for real"). They seem to accept the standard premise required to give an acceptable evolutionary explanation: individuals with social preferences must have outperformed individuals with different preferences in terms of the material payoffs gained over their lifetime. With respect to reciprocity in particular, the basic idea is that initial costs incurred by rewarding cooperators for cooperating (thereby foregoing the extra payoffs that could be obtained by defecting) are recouped later in life by the benefits they gain from increased rates of cooperation. These evolutionary explanations do not and cannot establish that what people with reproductively successful preferences (or behavioral types) are ultimately after is their own material payoff. This conclusion would confuse evolutionary explanations with proximate ones. But what they can establish is that the self-interest model is consistent with particular sorts of prosocial behavior. If a standard evolutionary explanation can be given for a social preference, the sort of prosocial behavior associated with the social preference can be rationalized by assuming that people behave *as if* they were maximizing their own material payoffs.[9]

This section resolved the first puzzle mentioned at the beginning: why do SPM proponents believe that prosocial behavior should be promoted, even though prosocial behavior is costly to the agent by definition? The answer is that prosocial behavior is believed to be conducive to social welfare, where social welfare is understood in terms of the standard self-interest model. What is more, the reach of the standard self-interest model might extend further than SPM proponents seem to be willing to concede. We saw that the attempts of proponents to give evolutionary explanations for social preferences suggest that prosocial behaviors can be rationalized by *as if* self-interest models after all.

4. Why Would We Assume That Prosocial Behavior Is Perfectly Rational?

In this section, I turn to the second puzzle: why do SPM proponents assume that people behave fully rationally, while the whole point of the heuristics and biases type of behavioral economist is to show that and explain why people often fail to behave fully rationally? I will discuss in particular whether SPM proponents have good reasons to believe that, in the sorts of games and situations for which they have developed their models, people do in fact behave rationally, that is, whether their social preference models meet the second "psychological realism" desideratum in this regard. Put more straightforwardly, what evidence do SPM proponents have for believing that deviations from the standard self-interest model are due to preferences and motives other than self-interested ones and not (or not also) due to cognitive biases (or other sources of less than fully rational behavior)?

The short answer is not much. And they know it, or at least they should know it by now. Fehr and Schmidt (1999) and Bolton and Ockenfels (2000) suggest that because the sorts of games that their models are meant to cover are simple, there is no reason to assume that people's behaviors reflect rationality failures (see also Fehr and Schmidt 2006). Apparently, they believe that the simpler the games (or, more generally, the strategic choice situations people are in), the less likely it is that observed deviations from the standard self-interest model are due to rationality failures. And indeed there are games that are considerably more complex than, for example, the UG and DG, for which we might expect biased and false beliefs and reasoning errors and the like to occur more often than in simple games. But evidence has been mounting that the behaviors of agents are also affected by biased beliefs in so-called simple games. One such biased belief that recently attracted much attention is the so-called consensus effect. The consensus effect occurs when people believe that the perceptions and thoughts of others are similar to their own.[10] As these beliefs are about what others believe, they are called second-order beliefs. Normally, when there are different types of people in the population with different perceptions, thoughts, and beliefs, these second-order beliefs are plainly false. Yet, they seem to greatly affect what people do in, for example, sequential prisoner's dilemmas, trust games, and DGs.

Consider the DG again. As we saw earlier, findings in the DG – that dictators offer a nonnegligible amount of money to recipients (even though recipients must accept any offer) – have also been seen as evidence for the causal efficacy of fairness considerations. It later turned out that the choices of dictators are quite sensitive to what they think others expect from them.[11] Charness and Dufwenberg (2006) propose a guilt-aversion model to capture this. They posit that people might feel guilty if their behavior falls short of others' expectations. Ellingsen et al. (2010) devised experiments to control for the impact of the consensus effect. Their hypothesis is that dictators might base their decision not on what others *actually* expect from them, but rather on what they *believe* others expect from them, and that this second-order belief might reflect the dictator's own expectations (if they were in the position of the recipient) rather than the actual expectations others have. This hypothesis is borne out by the findings in their experiments. Ellingsen et al. find almost zero correlation between the recipient's actual expectation and the dictator's allocation, and they conclude that the guilt-aversion hypothesis lacks empirical support.

One reason why SPM proponents did not seriously consider the possibility of cognitive biases in the behaviors they studied might have been that they linked this possibility to the learning models (e.g., Roth and Erev 1995; see Fehr and Schmidt 1999; Bolton and Ockenfels 2000) that were developed to account for the observed deviations from the standard self-interest model. Those learning models tended to emphasize that the deviations might be only temporary and likely to be eliminated in due time in learning processes. SPM proponents wanted to oppose these learning models. They wanted to show not only that what might be behind the deviations are motives other than self-interested ones but also that this means that the deviations might not be transient: prosocial behaviors are "here to stay" (Fehr and Henrich 2003). This interpretation of their results is not implausible, but this of course falls short of establishing that the deviations are *only* due to other motives and not also due to cognitive biases. Conversely, the discovery of cognitive biases in the production of the deviations also does not establish that all people are purely self-interested. Once we allow for the possibility of cognitive biases, however, many new combinations of motives and beliefs open up that jointly could possibly have produced the behaviors to be explained. The complicates the identification of the true motives underlying the behaviors even further.[12]

In sum, the SPM proponents have marshalled almost no evidence to support their assumption that agents behave fully rationally. If anything, the available evidence suggests that cognitive biases also abound in the behaviors they study. SPM proponents might still think they have good reason to assume full rationality though. That is what I will turn to now.

5. *As If* Social Preference Models

With their social preference models, behavioral economists think that they meet both the good model desideratum and the psychological realism desideratum. In the previous section, I showed that their assumption that agents behave fully rationally does not meet the psychological realism desideratum. In this section, I argue that the assumption does meet the good model desideratum – at least, if we accept the criteria that they think the desideratum implies. Indeed, retention of the assumption of full rationality seems to be driven primarily by their desire to develop what they consider to be good economic models. It thus seems that SPM proponents value meeting the good model desideratum more highly than meeting the psychological realism desideratum. This calls into question whether their social preference models can claim to be the because models that they say they aspire to, rather than the *as if* models that they officially dismiss.

What behavioral economists call the standard self-interest model is often seen (also by its proponents) as an *as if* model. Thus understood, this model posits that people behave as if they were all purely self-interested and as if they were perfectly rationally pursuing their own interests. Another way of putting this is to say that the model's claim is that the actual behaviors of people can be rationalized by making two basic assumptions: that all people are purely self-interested and that they are perfectly rational. What the model does not claim is that people behave in the ways they do *because* their only motive is to serve their own interests and *because* they succeed in actually making the optimizing calculations and deliberations as stipulated in the model (e.g., see Fumagalli 2019). With this *as if* self-interest model, we could say its proponents had a *simple*, parsimonious model that they believed was *general* enough to be *empirically consistent* with the extant data across different behavioral domains. Thus, they held that their model exhibited the theoretical virtues of simplicity (parsimony), generality, and empirical consistency that they believe good economic models should exhibit (Fehr and Schmidt 1999; Gabaix and Laibson 2008).

It seems that the SPM proponents share this view of what theoretical virtues good economic models should exhibit[13] and disagree only about the degree to which the self-interest model exhibits these virtues. What they call into question are the generality and empirical consistency of the standard self-interest model. As we have seen, they claim in particular that the standard self-interest model cannot account for the prosocial behaviors observed in various games and contexts. Social preference model proponents do not question that the standard self-interest model is simple and parsimonious.

On the contrary, they consider the standard self-interest model to be the simplest model possible. They are looking for models that are general enough to fit all available behavioral data with as few deviations from the two assumptions of the self-interest model as possible, because the incorporation of other motives, limitations, and failures of rationality all come at the expense of simplicity. And that is also why they pride themselves in constructing slightly more complex models than the standard self-interest model, with just one or two social preferences inserted in the utility function, and leaving the perfect rationality assumption intact.

As we have seen previously, however, this attitude might be considerably less helpful in meeting the psychological realism desideratum. To be more precise, the impression created by the social preference models (when taken literally as an attempt to identify real causal factors in the decision-making process) that the same limited set of motives combined with perfectly rational decision-making are the main drivers of all of the behaviors observed across different games and contexts might be largely illusory.[14] Recent evidence suggests that people might have different motives in different games and contexts, for example, and might base their decisions on biased beliefs (Blanco et al. 2011). It is possible that social preference model proponents initially thought they had good reasons to believe otherwise. But it seems more likely that their concern for meeting the good model desideratum weighed more heavily for them than their concern for meeting the psychological realism desideratum.[15]

This would explain why social preference model proponents cling to the full rationality assumption of the self-interest model, even though they did not engage in a serious examination of whether the perfect rationality assumption is really warranted. Even more tellingly, I think, is that this would also explain the way in which social preferences are treated in games for which the predictions of the standard self-interest model turn out to hold pretty well. Part of the bewildering variety of evidence that Fehr and Schmidt (1999) want to account for is the "seemingly" self-interested behavior in market games. In contrast to cooperation and bargaining games, in which very unequal divisions of payoffs are only rarely observed, unequal divisions of payoffs (which are in line with the predictions of the standard self-interest model) are frequently observed in market games. Yet, Fehr and Schmidt (1999) argue that this does not imply that people are actually only motivated by material self-interest and that fairness considerations are absent among market participants. They show that these findings, which are consistent with the standard self-interest model, are also consistent with their inequity-aversion model.

Does this show that market participants are at least partly motivated by a concern for fairness (understood as inequity aversion)? Clearly not. Their model, the stylized facts, and their reasoning do not warrant such a positive answer. It only warrants the negative conclusion that the observations do not exclude the possibility that market participants are also partly led by fairness considerations. Fehr and Schmidt show that, even in a mixed population of self-interested and fairness-minded individuals, very unequal divisions of payoffs might nevertheless materialize. The main reason for this is that in a competitive market, no participant can enforce more equitable outcomes. As they themselves observe, this holds irrespective of how many participants are fairness driven. Thus, they in fact show that what kind of motives market participants have is explanatorily irrelevant.[16]

Fehr and Schmidt make no serious attempt to show that, in competitive markets, a sizable number of the participants are at least partly fairness driven. Presumably, they simply assume that it is unlikely that people who are at least partly fairness driven in some types of games and contexts are not at all so driven in other types of games and contexts. But recent studies of the patterns of individual behavior suggest exactly the opposite: it is likely that people who have one sort of motive in some types of games have other sorts of motives in other types of games (Blanco et al. 2011). Suppose empirical research were to point out that what many observers intuitively sense is true (see also, e.g., Falk and Szech 2013): in competitive markets people tend to be more motivated by (or perhaps feel more free to act on the basis of) material self-interest than in other contexts. Then, if we aim for psychological realism, the simplest self-interest model would fit competitive markets better than social preference models, whereas in other contexts the slightly more complex social preference models would be superior to self-interest models.

In sum, social preference model proponents primarily seem to be driven by the desire to satisfy the first, good model desideratum. They aim to develop the simplest possible model, which to them means the model with the fewest possible deviations from the standard self-interest-cum-perfect rationality model that is general enough to be empirically consistent with all of the available behavioral data across different games and contexts.[17] They might believe that the models they developed also meet the "psychological realism" desideratum. But, appearances notwithstanding, they do not show that the social preferences and associated motives are the main drivers of the observed behaviors or that the social preferences and associated motives produce the behaviors in a rational way. In this regard, their social preference models resemble the standard *as if* models that they want to get rid of more than their official rhetoric suggests (Berg and Gigerenzer 2010; Blanco et al. 2011; Grüne-Yanoff 2017).[18]

6. Conclusion

Let us get back to the two puzzling discrepancies within behavioral economics that we started out with. First, the reason why social preference model proponents believe that prosocial behavior should be promoted, even though the behavior is costly to the agent by definition, has been clarified. Insofar as these proponents give an explicit justification of this normative stand, it is based on standard social welfare considerations: more prosocial behavior eventually leads to increased material payoffs for all. The normative benchmark invoked here is one in which material self-interest stands for individual well-being. Apparently, then, the plea of the proponents to insert social preferences into the utility function as extra arguments in addition to material self-interest is not considered by them to be a good reason to modify this standard normative benchmark. Second, the fact that most social preference models retain the assumption of perfect rationality (while proponents of the biases and heuristics tradition in behavioral economics emphatically oppose this assumption) should be taken with a grain of salt. It need not reflect a conviction of the SPM proponents that, in the games and contexts in which social preferences supposedly affect behaviors, people actually do behave in a perfectly rational way. Rather, it reflects their belief that there is no need to change (or relax) the perfect rationality assumption. They argue that a change in the postulated preferences suffices to have a general model that is consistent with the wide variety of behavioral data, but to change (or relax) the perfect rationality assumption is an unnecessary move that would compromise the simplicity of the model.

All of this shows clearly that, despite all of the behavioral economists' misgivings about the standard self-interest-cum-perfect rationality model, this model provides the ideal reference model for behavioral economists in several respects. The model not only provides the (mostly implicit) normative benchmark for their social welfare assessments but also exhibits the theoretical virtues they think all good economic models should have, in particular simplicity (or parsimony), generality, and empirical consistency. Social preference model proponents believe that their models outperform the standard self-interest-cum-perfect rationality model with respect to generality and empirical consistency. But with respect to simplicity, they believe that the simple model cannot be beaten. Indeed, they implicitly define the simplicity in their own models in comparison to the twin assumptions of pure self-interest and perfect rationality: ceteris paribus, they prefer the model with the fewest deviations from the two assumptions. In a sense, then, one could argue that the recognition that the standard self-interest-cum-perfect rationality model is treated as the ideal reference model by behavioral economists provides the key to resolving both puzzles.

Acknowledgments

The chapter greatly benefited from comments made by N. Emrah Aydinonat, Roberto Fumagalli, and Conrad Heilmann. All remaining errors are the author's.

Related Chapters

Bavetta, Chapter 32 "Freedoms, Political Economy, and Liberalism"
Grüne-Yanoff, Chapter 35 "Behavioral Public Policy: One Name, Many Types. A Mechanistic Perspective"
Lecouteux, Chapter 4 "Behavioral Welfare Economics and Consumer Sovereignty"
Wintein and Heilmann, Chapter 19 "Fairness and Fair Division"

Notes

1 Andreoni and Bernheim (2009) develop a model similar to that of Bénabou and Tirole (2006).
2 See Levitt and List (2007) for an influential critique of the reliance on findings in lab experiments and Binmore and Shaked (2010) for a mostly methodological incisive critique of Fehr and Schmidt (1999). See also Fehr and Schmidt's (2010) reply to Binmore and Shaked (2010).
3 They do not assume that all people care equally about their relative payoffs. They leave room for heterogeneity in this respect.
4 To avoid clumsy and lengthy formulations, I will henceforth call proponents of social preference models simply SPM proponents.
5 Something similar can be argued with respect to the concern for self-image. People led by this concern are not necessarily furthering the interests of others. They only do that if it is instrumental to their self-image. Assuming that furthering the interests of others is costly for themselves, they do not further the interests of others if that is not harmful to how they see themselves.
6 Note that this differs from how Woodward (2008) defines prosocial behavior: behavior that is costly to the agent (leaving open the possibility that it is also costly to others).
7 A discussion of whether the standard normative benchmark can be maintained when the existence of non-self-interested concerns is granted has to wait for another occasion.
8 If the threat of being punished by altruistic punishers is credible to would-be defectors, this could deter them from actually defecting. In this way, altruistic punishers need not actually punish all that much.
9 Additional assumptions to be made here are that the self-interested people should sufficiently value future payoffs and are farsighted. For further discussion of evolutionary ("ultimate") and proximate explanations of strong reciprocity, see Vromen (2012, 2017). An interesting outstanding issue is whether evolutionary explanations can also be given for antisocial preferences and behaviors.
10 Mullen et al. (1985) describe the false consensus effect as an egocentric bias that occurs when people estimate consensus for their own behaviors (that is, they believe that their behavior is relatively common and appropriate). Engelmann and Strobel (2012) argue that the effect should be seen as an information processing deficiency similar to the availability heuristic (Tversky and Kahneman 1973) – it can be overcome.
11 In social norms models (Bicchieri 2006), the importance of mutual expectations is stressed. Space limits prevent me from going into the interesting issue of how social preference models and social norms models relate to each other.
12 This identification problem is discussed further in Manski (2002). It seems that the solution proposed by Manski (to independently obtain information about subjects' preferences and expectations beyond the experimental data that social preference modelers rely on) has gained some currency among behavioral economists investigating social preferences (Miettinen et al. 2019; van Leeuwen et al. 2019). In fact, I believe that the problem of correctly identifying the true motives and beliefs is aggravated even further by the fact that the behavioral opportunities (or constraints) often vary widely between different games and contexts.
13 Gabaix and Laibson (2008) identify seven key properties of economic models. Next to the three highlighted here (parsimony, generalizability, and empirical consistency), they distinguish tractability, conceptual insightfulness, falsifiability, and predictive precision. It seems that with their conceptual insightfulness property, they roughly want to capture what I call psychological realism.

14 One could also argue that the models are not really explanatory (in the sense of causal explanation): instead of identifying real causal drivers of the behaviors to be explained, they merely describe patterns in these behaviors.

15

> In this paper we ask whether this conflicting evidence can be explained by a single simple model. Our answer to this question is affirmative if one is willing to assume that, in addition to purely self-interested people, there are a fraction of people who are also motivated by fairness considerations. No other deviations from the standard economic approach are necessary to account for the evidence. In particular, we do not relax the rationality assumption.
>
> (Fehr and Schmidt 1999, pp. 818–819)

16 One could also argue here that if it is something like competitive pressure rather than particular motives that is really driving the observed behaviors, then what should be modeled is how competitive pressure results in behavior (rather than "irrelevant motives").

17 See also Sent (2004) and Heukelom (2014). Fehr and Schmidt (2006) concede that psychological game theory, with its emphasis on the (meta)beliefs of agents, might be more realistic about the actual deliberations made by agents. But they shy away from it because of its greater complexity.

18 One could also argue that this is why social preference models are models in economics, rather than in psychology (Ross 2014; Katsikopoulos 2014).

Bibliography

Andreoni, J. (1989) "Giving with Impure Altruism: Applications to Charity and Ricardian Equivalence," *Journal of Political Economy 97*(6): 1447–1458. https://doi.org/10.1086/261662

Andreoni, J., and Bernheim, B. D. (2009) "Social Image and the 50–50 Norm: A Theoretical and Experimental Analysis of Audience Effects," *Econometrica* 77(5): 1607–1636. https://doi.org/10.3982/ECTA7384

Angner, E. (2015) "Well-being and economics," in G. Fletcher (ed.) *The Routledge Handbook of Philosophy of Well-Being* (pp. 492-503) Routledge. https://www.routledgehandbooks.com/doi/10.4324/9781315682266.ch40

Ariely, D. (2008) *Predictably Irrational: The Hidden Forces That Shape Our Decisions* (1st ed.), Harper.

Bénabou, R., and Tirole, J. (2006) "Incentives and Prosocial Behavior," *American Economic Review 96*(5): 1652–1678. https://doi.org/10.1257/aer.96.5.1652

Berg, N., and Gigerenzer, G. (2010) "As-If Behavioral Economics: Neoclassical Economics in Disguise?" *SSRN Electronic Journal*. https://doi.org/10.2139/ssrn.1677168

Bicchieri, C. (2006) *The Grammar of Society: The Nature and Dynamics of Social Norms*, Cambridge University Press.

Binmore, K., and Shaked, A. (2010) "Experimental Economics: Where Next?" *Journal of Economic Behavior & Organization 73*(1): 87–100. https://doi.org/10.1016/j.jebo.2008.10.019

Blanco, M., Engelmann, D., and Normann, H.T. (2011) "A Within-Subject Analysis of Other-Regarding Preferences," *Games and Economic Behavior* 72(2): 321–338. https://doi.org/10.1016/j.geb.2010.09.008

Bolton, G. E., and Ockenfels, A. (2000) "ERC: A Theory of Equity, Reciprocity, and Competition," *American Economic Review 90*(1): 166–193. https://doi.org/10.1257/aer.90.1.166

Bowles, S., and Gintis, H. (2011) *A Cooperative Species: Human Reciprocity and Its Evolution*, Princeton University Press.

Capraro, V., Jagfeld, G., Klein, R., Mul, M., and de Pol, I. van. (2019) "Increasing Altruistic and Cooperative Behaviour with Simple Moral Nudges," *Scientific Reports 9*(1): 11880. https://doi.org/10.1038/s41598-019-48094-4

Charness, G., and Dufwenberg, M. (2006) "Promises and Partnership," *Econometrica 74*(6): 1579–1601. https://doi.org/10.1111/j.1468-0262.2006.00719.x

Charness, G., and Rabin, M. (2002) "Understanding Social Preferences with Simple Tests," *The Quarterly Journal of Economics 117*(3): 817–869. https://doi.org/10.1162/003355302760193904

Dana, J., Cain, D. M., and Dawes, R. M. (2006) "What You Don't Know Won't Hurt Me: Costly (But Quiet) Exit in Dictator Games," *Organizational Behavior and Human Decision Processes 100*(2): 193–201. https://doi.org/10.1016/j.obhdp.2005.10.001

Dana, J., Weber, R. A., and Kuang, J. X. (2007) "Exploiting Moral Wiggle Room: Experiments Demonstrating an Illusory Preference for Fairness," *Economic Theory 33*(1): 67–80. https://doi.org/10.1007/s00199-006-0153-z

DellaVigna, S. (2018) "Structural Behavioral Economics," in *Handbook of Behavioral Economics: Applications and Foundations 1* (Vol. 1, pp. 613–723), Elsevier. https://doi.org/10.1016/bs.hesbe.2018.07.005

de Quervain, D. J.-F., et al. (2004) "The Neural Basis of Altruistic Punishment," *Science 305*(5688): 1254–1258. https://doi.org/10.1126/science.1100735

Dufwenberg, M., and Kirchsteiger, G. (2004) "A Theory of Sequential Reciprocity," *Games and Economic Behavior 47*(2): 268–298. https://doi.org/10.1016/j.geb.2003.06.003

Ellingsen, T., Johannesson, M., Tjøtta, S., and Torsvik, G. (2010) "Testing Guilt Aversion," *Games and Economic Behavior 68*(1): 95–107. https://doi.org/10.1016/j.geb.2009.04.021

Engelmann, D., and Strobel, M. (2012) "Deconstruction and Reconstruction of an Anomaly," *Games and Economic Behavior 76*(2): 678–689. https://doi.org/10.1016/j.geb.2012.07.009

Falk, A., and Szech, N. (2013) "Morals and Markets," *Science* 340: 707–711. DOI: 10.1126/science.1231566

Fehr, E., Fischbacher, U., and Gächter, S. (2002) "Strong Reciprocity, Human Cooperation, and the Enforcement of Social Norms," *Human Nature 13*(1): 1–25. https://doi.org/10.1007/s12110-002-1012-7

Fehr, E., and Gächter, S. (2000) "Cooperation and Punishment in Public Goods Experiments," *American Economic Review 90*(4): 980–994. https://doi.org/10.1257/aer.90.4.980

Fehr, E., and Gächter, S. (2002) "Altruistic Punishment in Humans," *Nature 415*(6868): 137–140. https://doi.org/10.1038/415137a

Fehr, E., and Henrich, J. (2003) "Is Strong Reciprocity a Maladaptation? On the Evolutionary Foundations of Human Altruism," in P. Hammerstein (ed.) *Dahlem Workshop Report. Genetic and Cultural Evolution of Cooperation* (pp. 55–82), MIT Press.

Fehr, E., and Schmidt, K. M. (1999) "A Theory of Fairness, Competition, and Cooperation," *The Quarterly Journal of Economics 114*(3): 817–868. https://doi.org/10.1162/003355399556151

Fehr, E., and Schmidt, K. M. (2006) "Chapter 8 The Economics of Fairness, Reciprocity and Altruism – Experimental Evidence and New Theories," in *Handbook of the Economics of Giving, Altruism and Reciprocity* (Vol. 1, pp. 615–691), Elsevier. https://doi.org/10.1016/S1574-0714(06)01008-6

Fehr, E., and Schmidt, K. M. (2010) "On Inequity Aversion: A Reply to Binmore and Shaked," *Journal of Economic Behavior & Organization 73*(1): 101–108. https://doi.org/10.1016/j.jebo.2009.12.001

Fumagalli, R. (2019) "(F)utility Exposed," *Philosophy of Science* 86(5): 955–966.

Gabaix, X., and Laibson, D. (2008) "The Seven Properties of Good Models," in A. Caplin and A. Schotter (eds.) *The Foundations of Positive and Normative Economics*, Oxford University Press.

Gintis, H., Bowles, S., Boyd, R., and Fehr, E. (ed.) (2005) *Moral Sentiments and Material Interests: The Foundations of Cooperation in Economic Life*, MIT Press.

Grüne-Yanoff, T. (2017) "Reflections on the 2017 Nobel Memorial Prize Awarded to Richard Thaler," *Erasmus Journal for Philosophy and Economics*, Volume 10, Issue 2, Fall 2017, pp. 61-75. https://doi.org/ 10.23941/ejpe.v10i2.307

Harsanyi, J. (1982) "Morality and the Theory of Rational Behaviour," in A. Sen and B. Williams (eds.) *Utilitarianism and Beyond* (1st ed., pp. 39–62), Cambridge University Press. https://doi.org/10.1017/CBO9780511611964.004

Herrmann, B., Thoni, C., and Gachter, S. (2008) "Antisocial Punishment Across Societies," *Science 319*(5868): 1362–1367. https://doi.org/10.1126/science.1153808

Heukelom, F. (2014) *Behavioral Economics: A History*, New York, NY: Cambridge University Press

Katsikopoulos, K. V. (2014) "Bounded Rationality: The Two Cultures," *Journal of Economic Methodology 21*(4): 361–374. https://doi.org/10.1080/1350178X.2014.965908

Kitcher, P. (2010) "Varieties of Altruism," *Economics and Philosophy 26*(2): 121–148. https://doi.org/10.1017/S0266267110000167

Levitt, S. D., and List, J. A. (2007) "What Do Laboratory Experiments Measuring Social Preferences Reveal About the Real World?" *Journal of Economic Perspectives 21*(2): 153–174. https://doi.org/10.1257/jep.21.2.153

Manski, C. F. (2002) "Identification of Decision Rules in Experiments on Simple Games of Proposal and Response," *European Economic Review 46*(4–5): 880–891. https://doi.org/10.1016/S0014-2921(01)00222-7

Miettinen, T., Kosfeld, M., Fehr, E., and Weibull, J. W. (2019) *Revealed Preferences in a Sequential Prisoners' Dilemma: A Horse-Race between Six Utility Functions*, CESifo Working Paper Series No. 6358. https://papers.ssrn.com/sol3/papers.cfm?abstract_id=2939010

Mullen, B., Atkins, J. L., Champion, D. S., Edwards, C., Hardy, D., Story, J. E., and Vanderklok, M. (1985) "The False Consensus Effect: A Meta-Analysis of 115 Hypothesis Tests," *Journal of Experimental Social Psychology 21*(3): 262–283. https://doi.org/10.1016/0022-1031(85)90020-4

Rabin, M. (1993) "Incorporating Fairness into Game Theory and Economics," *The American Economic Review 83*(5): 1281–1302.

Ross, D. (2014) "Psychological Versus Economic Models of Bounded Rationality," *Journal of Economic Methodology 21*(4): 411–427. https://doi.org/10.1080/1350178X.2014.965910

Roth, A. E., and Erev, I. (1995) "Learning in Extensive-Form Games: Experimental Data and Simple Dynamic Models in the Intermediate Term," *Games and Economic Behavior 8*(1): 164–212. https://doi.org/10.1016/S0899-8256(05)80020-X

Sent, E.-M. (2004) "Behavioral economics: how psychology made its (limited) way back to economics," *History of Political Economy 36*(4): 735-760. DOI: 10.1215/00182702-36-4-735

Thaler, R. H., and Sunstein, C. R. (2008) *Nudge: Improving Decisions about Health, Wealth and Happiness*, Penguin Books.

Tversky, A., and Kahneman, D. (1973) "Availability: A Heuristic for Judging Frequency and Probability," *Cognitive Psychology 5*(2): 207–232. https://doi.org/10.1016/0010-0285(73)90033-9

van Leeuwen, B., Alger, I., and Weibull, J. W. (2019) *Estimating Social Preferences and Kantian Morality in Strategic Interactions*, TSE Working Paper 19–1056. www.tse-fr.eu/sites/default/files/TSE/documents/doc/wp/2019/wp_tse_1056.pdf

Vromen, J. (2012) "Human Cooperation and Reciprocity," in K. Binmore and S. Okasha (eds.) *Evolution and Rationality* (pp. 158–184), Cambridge University Press. https://doi.org/10.1017/CBO9780511792601.009

Vromen, J. (2017) "Ultimate and Proximate Explanations of Strong Reciprocity," *History and Philosophy of the Life Sciences 39*(3): 25. https://doi.org/10.1007/s40656-017-0151-4

Weymark, J. (2016) "Social Welfare Functions," in M. D. Adler and M. Fleurbaey (eds.) *The Oxford Handbook of Well-Being and Public Policy* (Vol. 1), Oxford University Press. https://doi.org/10.1093/oxfordhb/9780199325818.013.5

Woodward, J. (2008) "Social Preferences in Experimental Economics," *Philosophy of Science 75*(5): 646–657. https://doi.org/10.1086/594511

10
EXPLOITATION AND CONSUMPTION

Benjamin Ferguson

1. Introduction

On September 11, 2012, a fire engulfed a garment factory in Karachi, Pakistan, killing over 250 of the 600 workers who were inside.[1] Despite the factory receiving a certificate from Social Accountability International, which purportedly demonstrated that it met international safety standards, many of the workers were trapped by grills placed over the factory's windows (Walsh and Greenhouse 2012). These workers worked more than 60 hours per week and earned the minimum wage of $83 per month.

In the aftermath, there were many questions about who was responsible for the tragedy. The factory owners were initially arrested, but in their defense they pointed to an Italian firm that inspected the factory and awarded the certificates on behalf of Social Accountability International. However, the Italian firm did not carry out the inspections itself, but instead subcontracted with another firm. At the time of the fire, the factory was producing jeans for KiK, the largest discount textile retailer in Germany. Eventually, in November 2018, KiK was sued in Germany with the plaintiffs seeking both financial compensation and an admission of responsibility for the deaths (Deutsche Welle 2018). However, the company's CEO argued that the fire "was not a violation of the company's duty of care" and that withdrawing production from Pakistan was not an option, because such an action "wouldn't help the people in those countries at all" (Deutsche Welle 2018).

This case raises interesting questions about the poor working conditions in sectors like the garment industry. The mistreatment of such workers is often labeled exploitation, yet it is hard to pinpoint just who – if anyone – is responsible for this exploitation. Although the German lawsuit sought to place the ultimate responsibility with KiK, the company's name, which stands for *Kunde ist König* (the customer is king) suggests another option: perhaps *consumers*, and their desire for low prices and fast fashion, are ultimately responsible for the wrongs of exploitation.

Before we can assess questions about responsibility, we first need a better understanding of what exploitation *is*. So, in Section 2 I will examine existing accounts of what exploitation is before returning to questions about the roles and responsibilities of consumers in Section 3. Section 4 concludes.

2. What Is Exploitation?

Nearly all accounts of exploitation accept the following working definition: *to exploit someone is to take unfair advantage of them*. However, there is considerable disagreement about what, precisely,

DOI: 10.4324/9781315739793-12

this means. The most prominent accounts of exploitation are *distributive accounts*. These approaches claim that A exploits B (and, so, takes unfair advantage of her) when he receives more and B less than either would have received in a fair transaction. Distributive accounts place a strong emphasis on the "unfairness" component of the working definition. Alternative accounts argue that exploitation is not a matter of maldistribution but, rather, has to do with the quality of the interaction that occurs between the exploiter and the exploited. These *relational accounts* place a greater emphasis on the "advantage taking" component. In this section I will outline both approaches, beginning with distributive accounts.

2.1 Distributive Accounts

According to distributive accounts, a transaction is an exploitation if and only if it is distributively unfair. Distributive unfairness obtains if and only if something that can be distributed – a *distribuendum* – is distributed in a way that violates a particular fairness criterion. Distributive accounts appeal to two different kinds of transactional fairness, *substantive* and *procedural* (see also Wintein and Heilmann, Chapter 19).

2.1.1 Substantive Accounts of Unfairness

Substantive accounts claim a transaction is unfair if and only if the allocations it generates depart from input-insensitive fairness criteria. That is, whether the allocations are fair does not depend on background circumstances such as contributions, entitlements, or historical injustices. Thus, substantive accounts employ what Nozick calls a patterned principle of distributive justice (Nozick 1974: 156). Substantive accounts include those that claim a fair price is determined by the cost (Reiff 2013) of labor embodied (Marx 1867) in production, that it is equivalent to a worker's marginal contribution to production (Pigou 1920; Robinson 1933) and to a wage that meets the transactors' basic needs (Sample 2003), that it involves *equal* gain, and that the fair price is determined by various rational solutions to bargaining problems (Ferguson and Ostmann 2018). Much has been said about the various merits and problems that each of these approaches faces on its own (Zwoinski and Wertheimer 2016; Ferguson and Steiner 2018). However, I want to focus here on a problem that arises for *all* substantive accounts of transactional fairness.

Such accounts are responsibility *insensitive*. Because they are insensitive to the past actions of agents, they cannot easily incorporate these actions (and their consequences) into their verdicts about what makes transactions fair. They cannot, for example, distinguish between a case in which B's vulnerability to A is the result of B's own choices and a case in which it is the result of prior injustice. This feature of substantive accounts creates a moral hazard and allows for free riding Ferguson (2016). Moral hazards occur when someone has an incentive to *increase* their exposure to risk because the cost of those risks will be borne by someone else. If B knows that A must offer her particular terms in a transaction that are fixed by a substantive fairness criterion, she has an incentive to take risks she would not otherwise take because the consequences of those risks turning out badly will be borne by A. This is true regardless of how the substantive fairness criterion is specified.

For example, suppose B is a wealthy business owner, who is contemplating whether to buy a risky investment. She knows that if the gamble goes well, she will make a lot of money, but if it does not, the loss would put her at a disadvantage when she bargains with her suppliers. In order to avoid this bad outcome, B would not ordinarily take the risk. However, if the price that her suppliers (A, in this example) can charge is fixed by a substantive fairness criterion, then if the bad outcome does occur, B will not have to bear the consequences (at least those that stem from his reduced bargaining power). Her suppliers, however, will be disadvantaged by the substantive criterion because it constrains their ability to capitalize on the consequences of B's choices. Moral hazards are, intuitively, unfair because they create situations in which others bear the costs of one's own actions. Because substantive distributive accounts allow for moral hazards, they are not very compelling accounts of transactional fairness.

2.1.2 Procedural Distributive Accounts

Procedural distributive accounts, on the other hand, *are* responsibility sensitive, and thus they offer a more plausible alternative because they are input *sensitive*. They claim that a transaction is unfair when the distributions it generates are the result of procedural flaws in the transaction process, such as historic injustice. While defenders of procedural and substantive accounts can agree that a 70/30 division of transactional gains between A and B is *unequal*, unlike a substantive egalitarian account, a procedural account would only describe the transaction as unfair – and thus exploitative – if this allocation was the result of a procedural flaw, for example, of B having been the victim of prior injustice. Prominent procedural accounts include Alan Wertheimer's (1996) claim that a fair transaction is the price that would obtain in a hypothetical competitive market[2] and Hillel Steiner's (1984, 1987) claim that A exploits B when A gets more and B gets less than either would have received because of a prior rights violation. Like the various substantive accounts, the merits of each of these procedural accounts have been hotly debated (Zwoinski and Wertheimer 2016; Ferguson and Steiner 2018). But once again, there is a problem common to all of them. Each of these accounts allows the fair price to be off the *contract curve*.

In order to understand what this means and why it is a problem, consider a typical transaction. Suppose B wants a snack, and A is selling apples. Each transactor will have a certain price that they are not willing to go above or below. These points are what economists call the transactors' reservation prices. For example, if B is willing to pay as much as \$1 but no more, this is her reservation price, and if A will accept as little as \$0.25 but no less, this is his. Any transaction that occurs *between* these points is a mutually beneficial transaction that both parties prefer over not transacting. The line defined by all of the points between these two reservation prices is the contract curve, that is, the set of all mutually beneficial transactions.

If an unfair transaction is morally impermissible and the fair price is off the contract curve, then no mutually beneficial transaction can be morally permissible (Ferguson and Ostmann 2018). Perversely, this means that even though A and B prefer transacting at any point on the curve over not transacting, none of these transactions is morally allowed. Thus, fairness criteria that allow the fair price to lie off the contract curve also allow for situations in which rational and morally motivated agents will refrain from engaging in mutually beneficial transactions, an outcome that is worse for everyone.

Now, unlike the problem for substantive accounts of transactional fairness, which was brought about by a feature that is *essential* to substantive accounts, the contract curve problem is not caused by the fact that Wertheimer's or Steiner's accounts are procedural. Rather, it arises because the distribuendum that each of these accounts employs is not constrained to the contract curve. This problem can be solved either by using "gain" (the surplus the transactors receive above their reservation prices) as the distribuendum or by normalizing alternative distribuenda to the contract curve.

The contract curve problem and the moral hazard problem suggest two desiderata for an account of transactional fairness: a plausible account should (i) be responsibility sensitive so that it avoids free riding and moral hazard problems and (ii) employ distribuenda that are constrained by the contract curve. One approach that satisfies both desiderata is to say that a transaction is fair when the distribution of gains that it generates is the result of just endowments of bargaining power (Ferguson and Ostmann 2018; Risse and Wollner 2019). This approach is procedural and sensitive to agents' historical actions, so it can avoid the moral hazard problem. It also uses gains as the distribuendum and so avoids the contract curve problem. Because it can avoid the main objections to existing accounts of fair transactions, this bargaining-based account seems to be on the right track as an account of fair transactions. But does it also provide a compelling account of exploitation?

2.1.3 Pervasive Exploitation

Suppose that A has a fruit stand, and B wanders up, exchanges pleasantries with A, buys an apple for $0.50, and goes on her way. Nothing *seems* especially unfair about the price, and it is certainly not a paradigmatic case of exploitation. Yet, for all we know, one of these transactors has just exploited the other. If prior injustice has altered either party's bargaining power in a way that skews the price she is willing to accept, then the transaction is unfair. And, according to distributive accounts, if it is unfair, then it is exploitative. This same insight can be applied to *any* transaction. This account of exploitation makes it pervasive and leaves us unable to distinguish exploitative transactions from nonexploitative ones (Ferguson 2020).

One response is to say that the problem is the result of a flawed account of a fair transaction. While we should not dismiss this possibility out of hand, it is hard to see how an account could avoid both the moral hazard objection and the contract curve problem, while also avoiding pervasiveness. This is because the pervasiveness is primarily the result of the appeal to historic injustice: because we do not know precisely how historical injustices have affected bargaining power, we cannot always identify unfair transactions. Yet, without the historical sensitivity that procedural accounts bring to the table, we cannot solve the moral hazard problem. An alternative response to the pervasiveness issue is to reject the fundamental claim of distributive accounts: that exploitation is tantamount to an unfair transaction. This is the approach that relational accounts take.

2.2 Relational Accounts

The pervasiveness problem suggests that there is more to exploitation than mere unfairness. As Jonathan Wolff puts it, distributive accounts fail to account for that "one nagging doubt . . . that, somehow, there just seems to be more to exploitation than unequal exchange" (1999: 107). Wolff goes on to suggest that exploitation involves a failure to treat others as ends in themselves, and he suggests that what this means is cashed out in different ways by different ethical traditions. Unfortunately, each of the ways that Wolff interprets these traditions results in an analysis that, ultimately, still appeals to fairness. For example, Wolff claims that,

> taking a Kantian interpretation of what it is to be an end in itself leads us to a "fairness" norm. Kantian exploitation . . . is to use another person's vulnerable circumstances to obtain their actual compliance with a situation that violates norms of fairness.
>
> (Wolff 1999: 114)

So, while Wolff may be right that exploitation seems to involve something more, he does not explain what this something more might be. Two approaches that *do* offer analyses that go beyond unfairness are Nicholas Vrousalis's (2013, 2016, 2018) domination-based approach and a hybrid account that appeals to exploiters' intentions (Ferguson and Steiner 2018; Ferguson 2020).

2.2.1 Domination

According to Vrousalis, A economically exploits B when "A and B are embedded in a systematic relationship in which A instrumentalizes B's economic vulnerability to appropriate (the fruits of) B's labor" (2013: 138). In addition, exploitation requires asymmetric vulnerability, so that "only when

A instrumentalizes B's vulnerability to enrich herself, *such that A subordinates B*, does A exploit B" (Vrousalis 2016: 530). And A behaves in this way when she uses her power over B in a disrespectful way, that is, when she uses her power in a way that cannot be "advanced as putative justifications for action in the context of embarrassment-free dialogue among interested parties" (Vrousalis 2013: 139–140).

Vrousalis's account captures the idea that exploitation is the dividend of servitude; to exploit others is to use one's power to extract gain from them. Importantly, Vrousalis also claims that not only is an unfair transaction insufficient for exploitation but it is also unnecessary. His argument (2013: 149, n. 54) takes the following form:

P1 Fairness is responsibility-constrained equality.
P2 Exploitation can arise from *any* material inequality.
C Therefore, unfairness is not necessary for exploitation.

The argument is valid, and Vrousalis simply takes P1 as a given definition. Of course, as we saw in the discussion of distributive accounts, not all approaches to fairness accept P1; substantive accounts of transactional fairness are *not* responsibility sensitive. However, we also saw that excluding responsibility sensitivity leads to the moral hazard problem. So, let us grant Vrousalis P1. In this case, P2 is the crucial premise. Vrousalis supports P2 with the following case:

> **Rescuer.** A finds B in a pit. A can get B out at little cost or difficulty. A offers to get B out, but only if B agrees to pay a million euros or to sign a sweatshop contract with A. B signs the contract.
>
> (Vrousalis 2013: 148)

Vrousalis claims that P2 is exploitation regardless of whether B is responsible for her plight. If the rescuer case is exploitation, then, it seems, we must grant P2 and, thus, the conclusion that unfairness is unnecessary for exploitation.

I suspect many will agree that the rescuer case is prima facie exploitation. However, I *also* suspect they form this intuition on the basis of their belief that it is *unfair* for A to charge B $1 million for a rescue. But, if this is the reason they think the rescuer example is exploitation, then the case does not support the conclusion that unfairness is unnecessary for exploitation. Rather, it serves as an argument against P1. And if P1 is false, then Vrousalis's argument also fails.

Not only is the argument against unfairness unsuccessful, but the removal of unfairness from an account of exploitation creates problematic false-positive cases. As Richard Arneson argues, there are many cases where people "use [others'] vulnerabilities to secure advantages for themselves – but in which there is no unfair division of advantages from the interaction and so nothing that qualifies as morally objectionable exploitation" (Arneson 2016: 10). As an example, he offers a case in which a person living in an isolated community has access to only one qualified surgeon who can perform a lifesaving surgery. Though the person would be willing to give everything he owns in exchange for the surgery, the surgeon's actual price "is modest, better than fair. This is business as usual for the surgeon. She makes her living by striking bargains like this with people in [such] conditions." Arneson argues that, "One can seek advantage for oneself without seeking unfair advantage for oneself" (Arneson 2016: 10).

Even if Vrousalis's attempt to provide an account of exploitation that does not depend on an appeal to unfairness fails, his insight that exploitation involves a flaw in how we relate to others, such as domination, seems to be correct. One alternative that retains an appeal to unfairness, but also makes room for these relational flaws, is an account that appeals to exploiters' *mental states*.

2.2.2 Awareness

According to the awareness account, A exploits B just in case A gains unfairly from B, and either A believes that the gains he receives in the transaction wrong B or A is culpably unaware that the gains he receives in the transaction wrong B. (Ferguson 2020: 10). The awareness account is a hybrid account that combines elements of distributive and relational accounts.

Like the distributive accounts (and unlike Vrousalis's account), the awareness account makes unfairness a necessary condition for exploitation. The fairness component of the awareness account should satisfy the two desiderata for a fair transaction discussed previously. That is, it should be both responsibility sensitive and constrained by the contract curve. And, as we saw, one account of a fair transaction that satisfies both of these desiderata is a bargaining-based account, according to which a transaction is fair when the distribution of gains reflects just endowments of bargaining power on the parts of the transactors.

The awareness account also includes an additional condition that limits the scope of distributive accounts, thereby addressing the pervasiveness problem. The account requires not only that the transaction must be unfair to be exploitative but also that A believes his gains wrong B or ought to have believed this. This condition allows us to draw a distinction between ordinary, everyday transactions and exploitations: exploitations are those transactions where the exploiter is *aware* or negligently unaware that his interaction with the exploited is morally problematic, but yet he does nothing to constrain his advantage over her. Unfortunately, the awareness account faces an objection as well. It implies that at least some instances of slavery might not have been exploitation. Although many slave owners likely believed their treatment of slaves wronged these persons, especially as emancipation movements gained steam, it is possible that at some point at least some slave owners did not believe they wronged their slaves because they accepted false theories about "natural" racial hierarchies. It may even be that, given the climate in which they operated, some slave owners were not negligent in holding these beliefs. If slave owners exploited slaves *regardless* of whether they believed they wronged their slaves (or were negligent in failing to hold this belief), then the awareness account cannot be correct.

In this section I have outlined a number of accounts of what exploitation is. The most prominent approaches, distributive accounts, claim that exploitation is tantamount to an unfair transaction. The problem with this claim is that the most plausible theories of fair transactions suggest that unfair transactions are widespread and, indeed, more widespread than the ordinary notion of exploitation. Relational accounts, on the other hand, focus on the quality of the interaction that occurs between exploiter and exploited. The domination approach makes unfairness unnecessary for exploitation. However, not only is the argument against unfairness unsuccessful, but without the inclusion of an unfairness condition the domination account seems to identify many perfectly reasonable transactions as exploitations. Finally, the awareness account offers a hybrid approach that combines distributive and interactive elements. However, it too faces a problem because it seems to imply that some instances of slavery were not exploitations.

Accounts of "what exploitation is" encounter a tension between the intuition that certain kinds of extreme unfairness must be exploitation, regardless of whether the unfairness involved contains interactive flaws, and the intuition that other forms of unfairness are not sufficient on their own to warrant the label of exploitation. Until this tension can be resolved, we will not have a comprehensive account of what exploitation is.

3. What Are Consumers' Responsibilities?

I began with a discussion of the tragic deaths of garment workers in Karachi, Pakistan, and I asked whether consumers might ultimately be responsible for certain instances of exploitation. Even if it is difficult to say precisely what exploitation is or whether it is wrong, if fair transactions are morally better than unfair ones, then consumers should be concerned whenever their actions undermine fairness. In this final section, I focus first on whether consumers can really be held responsible for unfair wages and, second, on the practical steps consumers can take to address exploitation.

3.1 Complicity and Competitive Markets

There are two common arguments against the idea that consumers bear any responsibility for the conditions and pay of those who work in garment industry sweatshops (and similarly problematic industries). The first and most direct is that because it is firms, not consumers, that directly transact with workers, consumers cannot be exploiters. The second is that market competition prevents consumers from making a meaningful difference in the lives of these workers.

3.1.1 Complicity

As the details of the Karachi case make clear, there is often a long chain of suppliers between factory workers and consumers. Usually, consumers buy from retailers, who contract with production companies, who contract with factories, who pay workers. If exploitation is a property of individual transactions, then, because the only transaction consumers engage in is with retailers, if consumers exploit anyone, it seems they must exploit *retailers*. (A similar argument entails that if workers are exploited by anyone, they are exploited by the factory owners.) There is good reason to think that exploitation *is* a property of transactions,[3] and so this argument is likely sound. However, even if consumers' behavior is not exploitation in a strict sense, there is no reason to think they are "off the hook" morally speaking.

A may technically refrain from murder if he hires C to kill B, and he may similarly avoid theft if he hires C to steal from B, but in both cases he is a *complicit* accessory to these crimes. Similarly, if firms pay workers less because customers demand cheap clothing, this demand (and consumption behavior) makes consumers *complicit* in a chain of flawed transactions that ends in the exploitation of workers (Wieland and van Oeveren 2019). Indeed, as Ferguson and Ostmann (2018: 311) point out, even if firms do not pass their unfair gains on to consumers but instead "retain the full [unfair gain] their ability to extract this benefit from workers depends on and occurs because of consumer purchases." So, in short, while consumers do not directly exploit workers, they can nevertheless be held responsible for their complicity in the exploitation of workers by others.

3.1.2 Market Competition

The second objection to the claim that consumers bear some responsibility for the workers' plight is based on the idea that consumers do not have any reasonable options for acting differently because they are constrained by market competition. Now, the claim that individuals are responsible only if they could have done otherwise (known as the *principle of alternate possibilities*) is much debated (Frankfurt 1969; Otsuka 1998). But for the moment, let us assume it is true. Is it really correct that consumers cannot do otherwise? After all, we surely have many alternatives when it comes to selecting clothing. There are two arguments for thinking consumers cannot do otherwise, at least not in a meaningful sense.

The first is that, in perfectly competitive markets, an increase in wages leads to an increase in the amount of labor supplied (because higher wages are more attractive to workers) and a decrease in the amount of labor demanded by firms (because paying higher wages is less attractive to employers). And so, as a consequence, fewer people are employed, but they are employed at higher wages. Suppose that consumers can choose between two scenarios. In scenario A, they buy from a firm that pays 1,000 workers $2 per day; in scenario B, the firm raises wages and pays 500 workers $4 per day, but lays off 500 workers. It is unclear that the move from A to B leads to a meaningfully better state of affairs. So, while consumers may indeed have *options*, for example, buying from firms that operate under scenario A or buying from those that opt for scenario B, it is not clear that the choices available to consumers can meaningfully avoid harming workers.

The second argument is that in competitive markets all individuals are price takers: that is, as individuals they have no power to affect market prices. Suppose, for example, that a person decides to boycott KiK in response to the Karachi fire. In a competitive market, their refusal to purchase clothing from KiK will not be sufficient to induce the firm to change its prices. Their individual action will have a negligible effect on the market. Of course, they might respond that that is not how boycotts work; the idea is not that one person *alone* will influence KiK's behavior. Rather, boycotts are *political* movements that are intended to inspire a *collective* group of consumers to change their behavior. If enough consumers boycott a firm then, they may collectively have enough power to induce firms to alter their prices. However, it turns out that, in practice, boycotts are rarely successful. As Ferguson and Ostmann (2018: 309) point out,

> Numerous studies have found that the market effects of boycotts are negligible . . . and even those generally perceived to have successfully impacted their target's financial position, such as boycotts of apartheid South Africa, had little visible effect on the financial markets.

Furthermore,

> the risks of a[n unsuccessful] boycott are also substantial. While the boycott is ongoing, consumer demand for sweatshop products is reduced . . . if unsuccessful, these negative effects will not be offset by greater gains [in the form of fairer wages].
>
> (Ferguson and Ostmann 2018: 309)

So, in sum, consumers' "distance" from exploited workers in the supply chain may exonerate them from exploitation, but it does not insulate them from the more important objection that they are complicit in workers' exploitation. On the other hand, consumers may be excused if the constraints of market competition mean they have no options that could meaningfully improve workers' lives.

3.2 What Should Consumers Do?

Typical responses to problems raised by sweatshops can be classified as either "dismissive" or "instinctive." The instinctive response argues that, because sweatshops provide poor working conditions and unfair pay, they are wrong. In order to avoid complicity with these conditions, consumers should simply buy goods produced elsewhere, by workers who are paid fair or living wages. The instinctive response focuses primarily on sweatshops' unfairness rather than the welfare they provide. In contrast, the dismissive response points out that, "sweatshop labor often represents the best option available for desperately poor workers to improve their lives and the lives of their family" (Powell and Zwolinski 2011: 449). Because sweatshops offer real improvements in worker welfare compared to these workers' next best alternatives, advocates of the dismissive option suggest that the best thing consumers can do is to continue to support sweatshop labor. The dismissive response focuses primarily on welfare rather than unfairness.

These responses correspond to different intuitions about exploitation's wrongfulness. Defenders of the instinctive response think that it is better not to transact than to transact unfairly. Defenders of the dismissive response think that at least some welfare gain is better than none, even if the total gains in the transaction are unfairly distributed. However, there is a third option that Florian Ostmann and I (Ferguson and Ostmann 2018) call the compensatory option, in which *consumers* transfer the difference between the price workers actually receive and the fair price directly to the workers. The compensatory option dominates both the dismissive and the instinctive alternatives because it is at least as fair as nontransaction, but provides greater welfare. Furthermore, we point out that when workers' high production volume and low cost of living are taken into account, the amount of this compensation is likely to be a very small proportion of a garment's purchase price. Of course, the compensatory option faces implementation hurdles. The identification of exploited workers and the transfer of funds pose unique challenges to this approach. Nevertheless, if these practical issues can be overcome, we think the compensatory option is the best way for consumers to avoid complicity in exploitation and to improve the lives of those who make the products we wear and consume. The possibility of this alternative shows that, contrary to the market-based arguments presented earlier, consumers *can* be held responsible for exploitation, because there is at least one available alternative – direct compensation – that mitigates unfair pay.

4. Conclusion

I began with a discussion of a practical case: the fire that claimed the lives of hundreds of garment workers in Karachi, Pakistan. The natural response to such tragedies is to condemn the exploitative practices of firms in sectors like the garment industry. However, in the two sections that followed, I noted that not only is there no consensus on just what exploitation is it is also sometimes difficult to explain how consumers could be held responsible for it. I noted that individual consumers are unlikely to be able to influence firms via boycotts, but they could provide direct monetary transfers to workers that would mitigate the unfair wages these workers receive.

Acknowledgments

I thank Sameer Bajaj and the editors of this volume for helpful comments and suggestions.

Related Chapter

Wintein and Heilmann, Chapter 19 "Fairness and Fair Division"

Notes

1 The death toll is disputed: some records show 262 deaths, others 289 or 310.

2 Previously, I (Ferguson 2018) categorized market-based accounts as substantive, because they do not *explicitly* appeal to power, injustice, or other considerations that might undermine the procedural legitimacy of a transaction. I now think this categorization is incorrect. Market-based accounts incorporate these features indirectly, because the prior actions of individuals will affect supply and demand and thus market prices.

3 Although there are theories of exploitation that are compatible with the claim that it is not transaction-based (Veneziani 2007), these accounts also generally allow for the definition of the predicates "is exploited" and "is exploiter," but not for the relation "A exploits B."

Bibliography

Arneson, R. (2016) Exploitation, Domination, Competitive Markets, and Unfair Division, *The Southern Journal of Philosophy*, 54(51): 9–30.

Deutsche Welle. (2018, Nov. 29) *German Clothing Discounter KiK on Trial for Pakistan Factory Fire*, <https://p.dw.com/p/396uk>.

Ferguson, B. (2016) Exploitation and Disadvantage, *Economics & Philosophy*, 32(3): 485–509.

Ferguson, B. (2018) Exploitation, in *Oxford Research Encyclopedia of Politics*. Ed. William Thompson, New York: Oxford University Press.

Ferguson, B. (2020) Are We All Exploiters?, *Philosophy and Phenomenological Research*, 13, forthcoming.

Ferguson, B. and Ostmann, F. (2018) Sweatshops and Consumer Choices, *Economics and Philosophy*, 34(3): 295–315.

Ferguson, B. and Steiner, H. (2018) Exploitation, in *The Oxford Handbook of Distributive Justice*. Ed. S. Olsaretti, Oxford: Oxford University Press: 533–555.

Frankfurt, H. (1969) Alternate Possibilities and Moral Responsibility, *Journal of Philosophy*, 66(23): 829–839.

Marx, K. (1867/, 1906–1909) *Capital: A Critique of Political Economy*. Volumes 1–3, Chicago: C.H. Kerr and Company.

Nozick, R. (1974) *Anarchy, State, and Utopia*, Oxford: Blackwell.

Otsuka, M. (1998) Incompatibilism and the Avoidability of Blame, *Ethics*, 108(4): 685–701.

Pigou, A. (1920) *The Economics of Welfare*, London: Macmillan.

Powell, B. and Zwolinski, M. (2011) The Ethical and Economic Case Against Sweatshop Labor: A Critical Assessment, *Journal of Business Ethics*, 107(4): 449–472.

Reiff, M. (2013) *Exploitation and Economic Justice in the Liberal Capitalist State*, Oxford: Oxford University Press.

Risse, M. and Wollner, G. (2019) *On Trade Justice: A Philosophical Plea for a New Global Deal*, Oxford: Oxford University Press.

Robinson, J. (1933) *The Economics of Imperfect Competition*, London: Macmillan.

Sample, R. (2003) *Exploitation: What It Is and Why It's Wrong*, Boulder, CO: Rowman and Littlefield.

Steiner, H. (1984) A Liberal Theory of Exploitation, *Ethics*, 94(2): 225–241

Steiner, H. (1987) Exploitation: A Liberal Theory Amended, Defended and Extended, in *Modern Theories of Exploitation*. Ed. A. Reeve, London: Sage: 132–148.

Veneziani, R. (2007) Exploitation and Time, *Journal of Economic Theory*, 132(1): 189–207.

Vrousalis, N. (2013) Exploitation, Vulnerability, and Social Domination, *Philosophy and Public Affairs*, 41: 131–157.

Vrousalis, N. (2016) Exploitation as Domination: A Response to Arneson, *Southern Journal of Philosophy*, 54: 527–538.

Vrousalis, N. (2018) Exploitation: A Primer, *Philosophy Compass*, 13(2).

Walsh, D. and Greenhouse, S. (2012, Dec. 7), Certified Safe, a Factory in Karachi Still Quickly Burned, *New York Times*, p. A1.

Wertheimer, A. (1996) *Exploitation*, Princeton: Princeton University Press.

Wieland, J. and van Oeveren, R. (2019) Participation and Superfluity, *Journal of Moral Philosophy*, 1–25, forthcoming.

Wolff, J. (1999) Marx and Exploitation, *The Journal of Ethics*, 3(2): 105–120.

Zwoinski, M. and Wertheimer, A. (2016, Fall) Exploitation, in *The Stanford Encyclopaedia of Philosophy*, Ed. Edward N. Zalta, <https://plato.stanford.edu/archives/fall2016/entries/exploitation/>.

PART III

Methodology

11
PHILOSOPHY OF ECONOMICS?
Three Decades of Bibliometric History

François Claveau, Alexandre Truc, Olivier Santerre, and Luis Mireles-Flores*

1. Introduction

What is philosophy of economics? An intuitive approach to this question would be to define the two terms – philosophy and economics – and then find ways the two could intersect. We do not adopt this strategy. Ours is inspired by the sociology of science, which has firmly established that any scientific subcategory – and, indeed, science itself (Gieryn, 1983) – is the outcome of social processes of inclusion and exclusion (Whitley, 2000; Abbott, 2001). Hence, instead of trying to capture what corresponds to some a priori definition of "philosophy of economics," we propose to take a serious look at what has been socially characterized as such.

A first social property of our object is its dual labels: many scholars switch almost seamlessly between "philosophy of economics" and "economic methodology." Although philosophy and methodology are hardly synonyms, the two labels are roughly interchangeable when it comes to linguistic practices. The interchangeability is only rough, because the distinction is itself grounds for boundary work – for instance, Mäki (2012, p. xv) suggests that the choice of label depends "on the primary disciplinary context of the activity."

Once this ambivalence is accepted, two ways are open to identify the philosophy of economics. First, it is an established research field. It is structured like all scientific fields: with learned societies (most prominently, the International Network for Economic Method or INEM), institutes, specialized journals, anthologies, and handbooks. For the rest of the chapter, we will refer to this field as "Specialized Philosophy of Economics." Second, the JEL classification system has one code for "Economic Methodology" (code B4 since 1991), which allows us to identify another philosophy of economics. The JEL system is "a standard method of classifying scholarly literature in the field of economics."[1] It has been developed and updated through a series of negotiations (for a detailed history of these social processes, see Cherrier, 2017). In what follows, we will refer to the body of work identified by the relevant JEL code with the phrase "JEL Economic Methodology." More precisely, we will exclude from JEL Economic Methodology the work that falls into Specialized Philosophy of Economics. By this procedure, we can compare two mutually exclusive philosophies of economics: one representing a specific scientific field and the other a collection of work tagged with a specific code in a standard classification system, but not directly associated with the established field.

Our goal in this chapter is to map the content of these two philosophies of economics. All maps are perspectival – they do not show all there is about a location – but any good map informs us about some relevant structural features of the location. Our map – using bibliometric data and network

DOI: 10.4324/9781315739793-14

analysis – is meant to show some of the most popular subject matter of the two philosophies of economics and to indicate changes in their popularity over the last 30 years. Because subject matter can be individuated in various ways, other detection techniques might find subjects that do not exactly correspond to ours.[2] Yet, our results do capture important structural features of the two philosophies of economics, as well as key differences between the two.

In Section 2, we present our data, and in Section 3, we present our method. Results and discussions about the two philosophies of economics are contained in Section 4. The discussions are where we relate our findings to claims found in the existing literature on the content and evolution of philosophy of economics. To keep each section short, we have pushed additional material to a Technical Appendix.[3] It includes a detailed presentation of our procedure, the R code used to generate our results, and additional tables and figures.

2. Data

It is well established that the systematic study of citation patterns gives a valuable perspective on the cognitive structure of science (Cole et al., 1978; Boyack et al., 2005). This type of work has been applied to a variety of fields, including economics (e.g., Claveau and Gingras, 2016; Angrist et al., 2020) and philosophy (Noichl, 2019). We thus suggest using citation data originating from the two philosophies of economics under study to uncover the evolution of their contents since the 1990s.

The first corpus represents the Specialized Philosophy of Economics – a field that started taking shape in the late 1970s. Among the influential philosophers of economics, the consensus is that there are two main field journals: *Economics and Philosophy* (*E&P*) and the *Journal of Economic Methodology* (*JEM*).[4] We have retrieved, from Elsevier's Scopus database,[5] all articles and reviews published in these two journals from 1990 to 2019 inclusively (30 years). Because *JEM* did not start publishing until 1994, we only have data from *E&P* for the first four years. The 1,007 documents – 475 from *E&P* and 532 from *JEM* – have, in total, 33,760 references. Some data cleanup routines have been necessary for these references, especially to improve the detection of cited books (which are plenty in the field).

The second corpus – i.e., JEL Economic Methodology – couples EconLit[6] with Web of Science.[7] EconLit allows us to retrieve documents tagged with the relevant JEL codes. In Web of Science, we then find a subset of these documents, a procedure that gives us, most importantly, the full references of these documents.

The JEL classification system has been quite stable since 1991 (Cherrier, 2017). In its hierarchical structure, it includes the code "B4 Economic Methodology," situated below "B History of Economic Thought, Methodology, and Heterodox Approaches" and above "B40 General," "B41 Economic Methodology," and "B49 Other." In the prior classification system, Economic Methodology was code 00360.

EconLit indexes "the most sought-after economics publications."[8] A noteworthy but little known feature of EconLit is that professional classifiers select the final codes for each document (Cherrier, 2017, p. 569), although authors typically suggest codes and journals themselves can use these author-provided codes. Consequently, the documents that we retrieve as Economic Methodology in EconLit are those that have been judged to be such by a standardized procedure of the American Economic Association.

Two characteristics of the EconLit database required choices on our part. First, EconLit includes many types of documents – for example, books and PhD theses – but we take only the content of academic journals. Second, it includes journals outside the standard frontier of economics but deemed to be of interest to economists. For instance, it indexes the *American Political Science Review*. Because it is interesting to study the profile of articles in non-economics journals that are tagged as "Economic Methodology," we include articles irrespective of the disciplinary association of their journal.

Web of Science has a more selective coverage of journals than EconLit.[9] We nevertheless find 167 journals in Web of Science that have at least one article tagged as Economic Methodology in EconLit. Two further restrictions are applied to the corpus. First, we remove articles published in *E&P* and *JEM* to make our two corpora mutually exclusive. Second, we drop the three articles from 2019, because this small number is attributable to indexing delays in both EconLit and Web of Science. We are thus left with 1,362 documents in 165 journals from 1990 to 2018, giving a total of 63,267 references. The journals producing the most papers in this corpus are *Cambridge Journal of Economics* (13.1%), *Journal of Economic Issues* (6.7%), and *History of Political Economy* (6.5%). Using a classification of journals from the US National Science Foundation, we find that 77.5% of the articles in this corpus are published in a journal from economics; thus, a sizable number of articles come from journals having a less solid relationship with economics.

Figure 11.1 indicates the number of articles over the studied period in the two corpora. Publications per year are trending upward in both corpora, although the temporal distribution for JEL Economic Methodology is closer to a U-shape, with 2000–2009 being a decade with a comparatively lower output. An inspection of the documents most frequently cited by the corpora already signals that they are not mirror images of each other. Some references are almost equally popular in the two corpora – for example, Friedman (1953) is first in Specialized Philosophy of Economics and second in JEL Economic Methodology. However, other sources have contrasting popularity. For instance, Hausman (1992) is the second most popular reference in Specialized Philosophy of Economics but 27th in JEL Economic Methodology, while the most popular reference in this corpus, Lawson (1997), is 11th in the other corpus.[10] We need a more systematic method to investigate these similarities and differences.

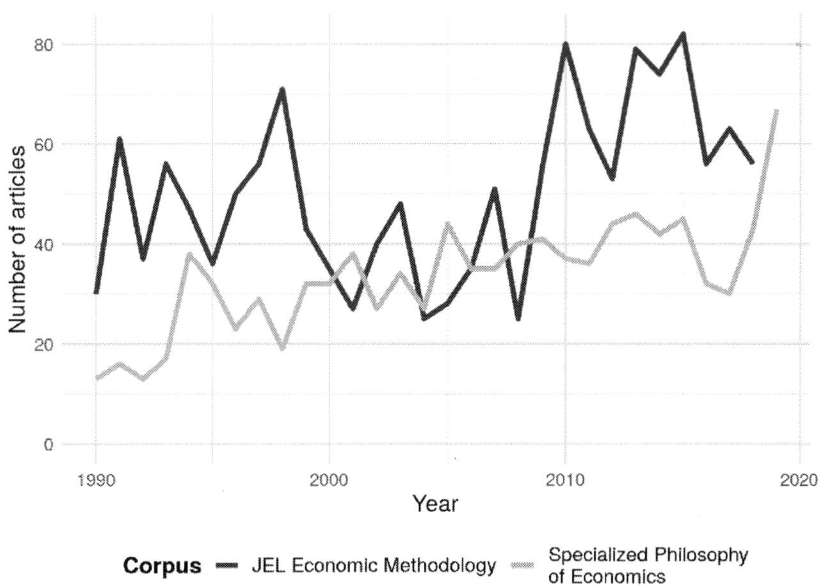

Figure 11.1 Number of articles in the two corpora

3. Method

References in scientific documents can be interpreted as constituting social networks. In this chapter, we focus on the similarity between citing documents. According to bibliographic coupling (Kessler, 1963), two documents are similar to the extent that they share entries in their respective bibliographies. Our normalized measure of this similarity takes into account the length of both bibliographies. If two papers have fully identical bibliographies, the weight of the edge connecting them is 1, while it is zero if their bibliographies have no reference in common.

We construct two bibliographic coupling networks – one for each corpus. The nodes of each network are thus documents that are published between 1990 and the late 2010s. On each network, we apply the Louvain community detection algorithm (Blondel et al., 2008), which creates a partition of nodes – that is, of citing documents – by trying to maximize a measure called "modularity" (Newman and Girvan, 2004). A partition is highly modular to the extent that weighted edges inside each cluster tend to be higher than the average weighted edge. In other words, the algorithm identifies clusters of articles having more similar bibliographies among themselves than with articles in other clusters.

Community detection algorithms are heuristic devices to identify salient structural components in networks. The clusters detected should not be reified for three reasons. First, our algorithm has a stochastic component, which implies that results might vary slightly each time the algorithm is used. Second, the algorithm looks at a specific, fixed "resolution." There are most certainly meaningful subclusters or macroclusters that could be identified by an algorithm at a different resolution. Finally, and most importantly, our method is only one simple way to detect clusters in a network with an important temporal component. In the construction of our network and in the community detection, we treat the system as static – that is, the year of publication of the citing document is not taken into account. Only after the detection do we map the share of each cluster through time (see our Figures 11.3 and 11.5). This method has the great advantage of simplicity, but numerous other options exist that include the temporal dimension more upstream in the method (see Rossetti and Cazabet, 2018, for a survey of options). We implemented the simple method as a first pass and found the results sufficiently telling for the purpose of this chapter.

Once the clusters are detected, we use two sources of information to identify what they are mostly about. First, we extract the most frequent references per cluster over the whole period and for each decade (see Tables 11.1 and 11.2). Second, we extract keywords from the title of the citing documents (the nodes) in each cluster. The identification of keywords is based on the standard term frequency-inverse document frequency (tf – idf). This measure takes into account the number of times each phrase appears in the cluster (tf), as well as how unique the phrase is to this cluster relative to the cluster as a whole (idf).

Finally, we name each cluster. This step is where our insider knowledge as philosophers of economics plays a prominent role: on the basis of the most frequent references and the keywords for each cluster, it was relatively straightforward for us to manually attribute labels and, thus, go from a set of documents with a variety of properties to an object called, for example, "Big M" or "Critical Realism." These labels are mostly mnemonic devices, and readers are free to rename the clusters at will.

4. Results and Discussions

We present our results for the two philosophies of economics in separate subsections. However, the second discussion – the one following the results about JEL Economic Methodology – uses the other philosophy of economics as an explicit contrast.

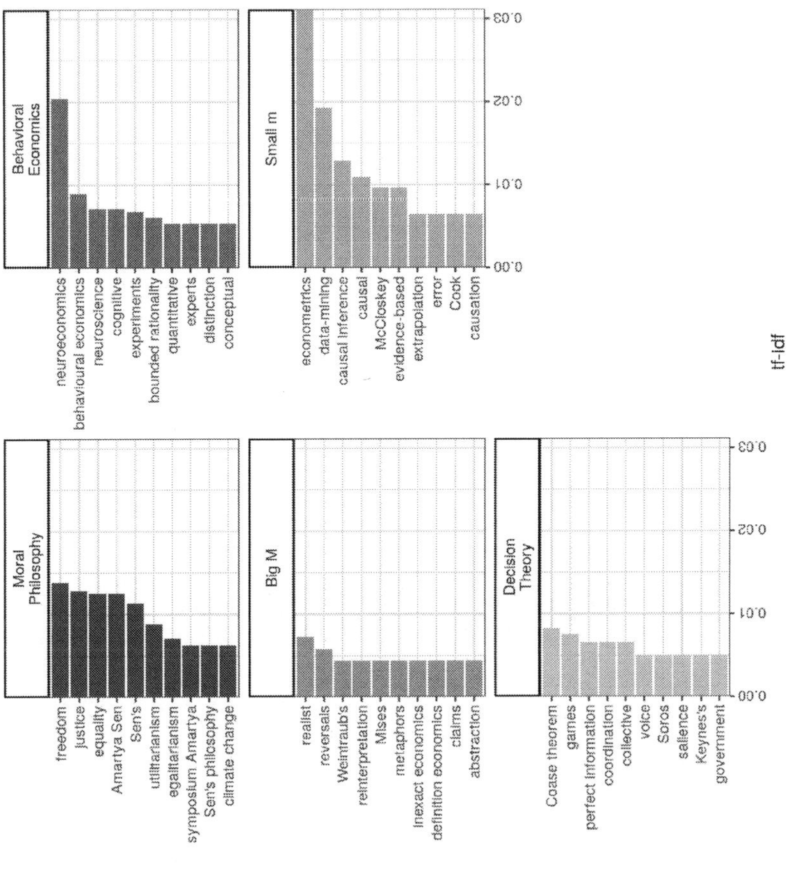

Figure 11.2 Clusters detected in the corpus of Specialized Philosophy of Economics: Top 10 most distinctive phrases (tf-idf) per cluster in the title of articles

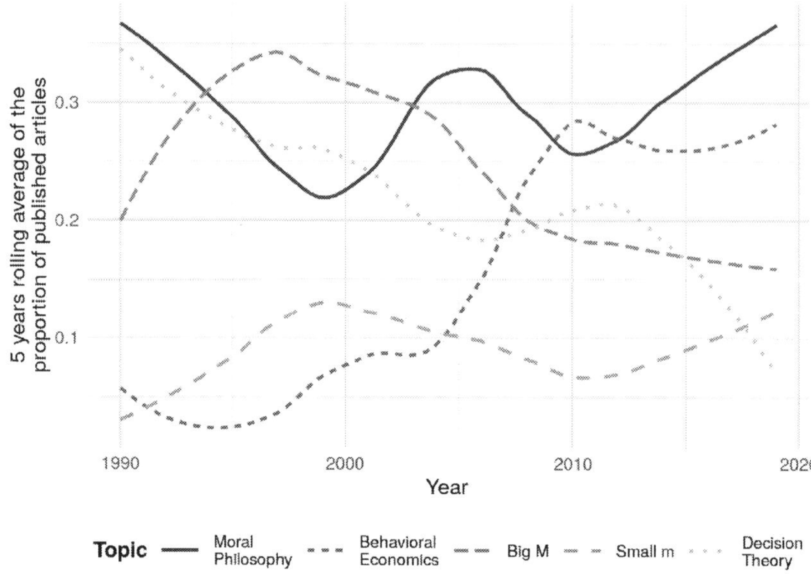

Figure 11.3 Clusters detected in the corpus of Specialized Philosophy of Economics: Article share of clusters over time (smoothed using local polynomial regression)

Table 11.1 Most-cited documents per cluster in the corpus of Specialized Philosophy of Economics*

Cluster	*Full period*	*1990–1999*	*2000–2009*	*2010–2019*
Moral Philosophy	Rawls 1971 Nozick 1974 Parfit 1984 Sen 1970 Broome 1991	Rawls 1971 Parfit 1984 Nozick 1974 Harsanyi 1955 Broome 1991	Rawls 1971 Broome 1991 Nozick 1974 Scanlon 1998 Arrow 1951	Rawls 1971 Sen 1999 Sen 1970 Broome 2004 Harsanyi 1955
Behavioral Economics	Kahneman 1979 Savage 1954 Camerer 2005 Gul 2008 Ross 2005	Kahneman 1979 Friedman 1953 Keynes 1971 Allais 1953 Becker 1993	Kahneman 1979 Savage 1954 Ellsberg 1961 Smith 1982 Allais 1953	Savage 1954 Kahneman 1979 Camerer 2005 Gul 2008 Kahneman 2011
Big M	Hausman 1992 Friedman 1953 McCloskey 1985 Blaug 1962 Robbins 1935	Hausman 1992 McCloskey 1985 Blaug 1962 Friedman 1953 Rosenberg 1993	Hausman 1992 Friedman 1953 Hands 2001 Hutchison 1938 Blaug 1962	Hausman 1992 Friedman 1953 Reiss 2012 Robbins 1935 Hands 2001
Small m	Haavelmo 1944 Hoover 2001 McCloskey 1985 Pearl 2001 Spirtes 2000	McCloskey 1985 Mirowski 1989 Cooley 1985 Engle 1987 Gilbert 1986	Haavelmo 1944 Hoover 2000 Hendry 1995 Hoover 2001 Kuhn 1962	Deaton 2010 Haavelmo 1944 Pearl 2001 Spirtes 2000 Hoover 2001

Cluster	*Full period*	*1990–1999*	*2000–2009*	*2010–2019*
Decision Theory	Keynes 1936 Luce 1957 Pearce 1984 Aumann 1976 Lewis 1969	Keynes 1936 Binmore 1987 Selten 1975 Aumann 1976 Bernheim 1984	Hollis 1998 Keynes 1921 Keynes 1936 Lewis 1969 Bernheim 1984	Soros 2013 Bacharach 2006 Keynes 1936 Mackenzie 2008 Schelling 1960

*Only first authors are included.

Table 11.2 Most-cited documents per cluster in the corpus of JEL Economic Methodology

Cluster	*Full period*	*1990–1999*	*2000–2009*	*2010–2018*
Institutional Economics	Nelson, 1982 North, 1990 Robbins, 1935 Marshall, 1920 Smith, 1776	Nelson, 1982 Williamson, 1985 Veblen, 1919 Marshall, 1920 Williamson, 1975	Nelson, 1982 North, 1990 Hayek, 1948 Robbins, 1935 Marshall, 1920	Robbins, 1935 North, 1990 Smith, 1776 Marshall, 1920 Nelson, 1982
Critical Realism	Lawson, 1997 Lawson, 2003 Bhaskar, 1978 Bhaskar, 1989 Fleetwood, 1999	Lawson, 1997 Bhaskar, 1978 Bhaskar, 1989 Lawson, 1994 Bhaskar, 1986	Lawson, 1997 Lawson, 2003 Bhaskar, 1978 Bhaskar, 1989 Fleetwood, 1999	Lawson, 1997 Lawson, 2003 Lawson, 2012 Lawson, 2006 Bhaskar, 1978
Political Economy	Searle, 1995 Marx, 1970 Marx, 1973 Wendt, 1999 George, 2005	Marx, 1970 Marx, 1973 Ollman, 1993 Hegel, 1969 Cohen, 1978	Searle, 1995 Searle, 1983 Searle, 1969 Searle, 1990 Tuomela, 1995	Searle, 1995 George, 2005 Searle, 2010 Wendt, 1999 King, 1994
Big M	Friedman, 1953 Kuhn, 1970 McCloskey, 1998 Blaug, 1992 Popper, 1968	Friedman, 1953 Kuhn, 1970 McCloskey, 1998 Blaug, 1992 Popper, 1968	Friedman, 1953 Kuhn, 1970 Popper, 1968 Caldwell, 1982 McCloskey, 1998	Friedman, 1953 Kuhn, 1970 McCloskey, 1998 Popper, 1968 Keynes, 1936
Small m	Leamer, 1983 Keynes, 1936 Lucas, 1981 Sraffa, 1960 Leamer, 1978	Stokey, 1989 Davidson, 1982 Arrow, 1971 Keynes, 1936 Leamer, 1978	Keynes, 1936 Leamer, 1983 Sraffa, 1960 Arrow, 1971 Schwartz, 1986	Leamer, 1983 Keynes, 1936 Lucas, 1976 Sims, 1980 Lucas, 1981
History of Economics	Schumpeter, 1954 Marshall, 1920 Smith, 1776 Schumpeter, 1934 Schumpeter, 1950	Schumpeter, 1954 Hayek, 1948 Marshall, 1920 Smith, 1776 Becker, 1976	Schumpeter, 1954 Blaug, 1985 Blaug, 1980 Mill, 1848 Hayek, 1967	Schumpeter, 1954 Keynes, 1936 Smith, 1776 Schumpeter, 1934 Marshall, 1920

4.1 Specialized Philosophy of Economics

4.1.1 Results

When applied to the Specialized Philosophy of Economics, the method described in Section 3 detects five clusters. Using our knowledge of the field, we named these clusters by interpreting the phrases with the highest tf – idf scores (Figure 11.2) and the documents cited most often in each cluster (Table 11.1):

Moral Philosophy (*n* = 277): This cluster on moral and political philosophy includes more articles overall than any other in the Specialized Philosophy of Economics. Rawls (1971) is its main reference, and its keywords are unmistakably associated with the literature on liberal egalitarianism.

Behavioral Economics (*n* = 173): This cluster regroups articles about philosophical issues concerning behavioral economics, neuroeconomics, and experimental economics (Lecouteux, Chapter 4; Grayot, Chapter 6; Nagatsu, Chapter 24). Kahneman and Tversky (1979) is the most-cited document in this cluster. There are also many references to seminal papers in microeconomics, like Allais (1953) or Savage (1954).

Big M (*n* = 215): Articles in this cluster are typically about general concerns such as realism, abstraction, explanation (Verreault-Julien, Chapter 22), and the scientific nature of economics.[11] This cluster extensively cites scholars that are close to the INEM, such as McCloskey (1985), Blaug (1992), Hausman (1992), Hands (2001), and Reiss (2012). These references are mixed with seminal methodological contributions by economists such as Robbins (1935) and Friedman (1953).

Small m (*n* = 91): Methodological issues discussed in this cluster relate to causal inference, econometrics, statistical significance, evidence, and prediction. It is the smallest cluster overall. Like the Big M cluster, some of its most-cited documents are from scholars close to the INEM, such as McCloskey (1985)[12] and Hoover (2001). Its other highly cited documents are contributions to techniques of statistical and causal inference (e.g., Haavelmo, 1944; Pearl, 2000; Deaton, 2010).

Decision Theory (*n* = 193): This cluster focuses on philosophical issues related to decision theory (including game theory). One initially surprising property is that Keynes's *General Theory* (1936) is the most-cited document in this cluster. Looking more closely, we find that most articles citing this foundational book in macroeconomics do not focus on Keynes's macroeconomics, but rather on its underlying theory of human behavior.[13] The other highly cited documents are mostly classics in game theory, such as Luce and Raiffa (1957), Aumann (1976), and Pearce (1984). Finally, another initially surprising property is the presence of (George) Soros in the cluster's keywords and as one of the most cited authors in the last decade. This property is explained by the 2013 publication of a special issue about Soros's theory of human reflexivity in the *Journal of Economic Methodology*, with 13 comments replying to Soros's lead article.

After having briefly described each cluster, we can note various changes over the period (see Figure 11.3). First, two clusters have become more peripheral to the specialty since the 1990s: Big M and Decision Theory. After its peak of popularity in the mid-1990s at approximately 34% of all publications, Big M has steadily declined to represent around 16% of publications in Specialized Philosophy of Economics at the end of the period. The declining presence of Decision Theory from 35% to around 7% is even more dramatic. Second, Behavioral Economics stands out as a more recently popular cluster: its share of yearly publications climbed quickly from 2005 to 2010 and has stayed relatively high since then. Finally, two clusters exhibit no uniform trend: Moral Philosophy and Small m. The share of the first cluster fluctuates significantly but remains high overall, averaging 29% for the period. In contrast, Small m has fluctuated around a lower average share at just below 10%.

4.1.2 Discussion

The clusters detected in the Specialized Philosophy of Economics map onto standard characterizations of the field. In the *Stanford Encyclopedia of Philosophy*, Hausman begins the entry "Philosophy of Economics" with the following division:[14]

> "Philosophy of Economics" consists of inquiries concerning (a) rational choice, (b) the appraisal of economic outcomes, institutions and processes, and (c) the ontology of economic phenomena and the possibilities of acquiring knowledge of them. Although these inquiries overlap in many ways, it is useful to divide philosophy of economics in this way into three subject matters which can be regarded respectively as branches of action theory, ethics (or normative social and political philosophy), and philosophy of science.
>
> (Hausman, 2008)

Before the rise in importance of the Behavioral Economics cluster around 2005, the mapping between Hausman's typology and our automated detection was simple: Decision Theory was the cluster highly related to action theory, Moral Philosophy was the cluster associated with ethics, and the other two clusters – Big M and Small m – can be interpreted as containing topics related to philosophy of science.

The recent prominence of Behavioral Economics shows how the branches can overlap. We even venture to say that the captivation of philosophers of economics for research in behavioral economics (with neighboring neuroeconomics and experimental economics) can partly be explained by the fact that the three branches can all find something useful in it: action theorists find some material on (ir)rationality in this research, ethicists react to its policy ramifications (e.g., the literature on nudges), and philosophers of science are fond of its claims to renew empirical methods in economics (e.g., with experiments) and to reject the alleged instrumentalism of the modeling culture in economics.

Regarding the evolution of Big M, our results mesh relatively well with the story told by Hands:

> [T]he vast majority of the methodological literature of the last decade . . . is not based on grand universalistic philosophy of science; it is applied philosophical inquiry aimed at the practical methodological issues of practitioners within specific subfields and sensitive to the issues, challenges, and constraints they face.
>
> (Hands, 2015, p. 76)

We indeed find a significant decline in Big M since the late 1990s. What Big M is has also changed: its three most distinctive keywords for the last decade are "stylized facts," "world models," and "explanation paradox" (the title of Reiss, 2012), which strongly suggest that the epistemic status of models is what primarily occupies recent scholars in this cluster.

To some extent, our results also corroborate Hands's point that the attention has turned toward "practical methodological issues," although the issues that are addressed by the contemporary philosophy of economics appear to be primarily associated with behavioral economics. In parallel, the share of articles in the Small m cluster has remained stable. Echoing historical claims about the rise of a pluralistic mainstream in economics (Colander et al., 2004; Davis, 2006), Hands (2015, p. 72) suggests that methodological attention has turned not only toward "neuroeconomics, experimental economics, behavioral economics" but also toward "evolutionary economics; and the associated new tools such as computational economics, agent-based modeling, and various new empirical techniques." We do not see such a turn in the cluster of Specialized Philosophy of Economics.

All in all, our results about recent "methodological" work in the Specialized Philosophy of Economics corroborate the presence of the three trends put forth in a recent survey by Luis Mireles-Flores:

> (a) the philosophical analysis of economic modelling and economic explanation; (b) the epistemology of causal inference, evidence diversity and evidence-based policy and (c) the investigation of the methodological underpinnings and public policy implications of behavioural economics.
>
> (Mireles-Flores, 2018, p. 93)

Outside strictly methodological work, the decreasing share of Decision Theory in the Specialized Philosophy of Economics is a notable characteristic of our results that appears to have escaped the attention of commentators. Is it that philosophical aspects of decision and game theories are no longer being studied as often? Evidence points in another direction: this type of work has moved elsewhere – that is, to journals other than the two included in our corpus. Using the Web of Science, we have tracked citations of Luce and Raiffa (1957), Aumann (1976), and Pearce (1984), the three publications that are most cited in the Decision Theory cluster and are unambiguously classics for decision and game theories.[15] We note first that annual citations of these documents have been roughly steady since the 1990s (a combined 90–100 citations per year). Second, we find evidence that reflexive or philosophical work citing these sources is becoming more common. Indeed, only 4% of citations of these sources in the 1990s came from journals classified as philosophy or science studies. This share was 10% in the 2010s. The philosophy journal *Synthese* has been the third most frequent originator of citations of these classics in the 2010s.[16] In short, the philosophical study of decision and game theories is alive and well, but it has become peripheral to the core journals of Specialized Philosophy of Economics.

4.2 JEL Economic Methodology

4.2.1 Results

Six clusters are detected when applying the method described in Section 3 to our second corpus of articles. We follow the same procedure to name these clusters (i.e., with Figure 11.4 and Table 11.2), retaining the label for some clusters when the parallels are obvious:

Institutional Economics (n = 500): The most distinctive keyword for this cluster gives away its identity as "institutional economics" (Rutherford, 1994). The cluster leans toward evolutionary economics (Nelson and Winter, 1982), "old" institutional economics (e.g., Veblen, 1919; Keynes, 1936), and the pre-1945 history of economics (Smith, 1776; Marshall, 1890; Robbins, 1935). Yet, it also relates to "new" institutional economics – for example, with citations of Williamson (1985) and North (1990). The publication venues of its articles are diverse, with the *Journal of Economic Issues* (associated with the *Association for Evolutionary Economics*) coming first with 9%.[17]

Critical Realism (n = 243): Like the cluster Institutional Economics, the most distinctive keyword for this cluster is the name of a school of thought. The second keyword – "Post Keynesian" – also has an extremely high tf – idf, indicating that our algorithm detects post-Keynesian economics as being tightly knitted with Critical Realism when it comes to methodology. This cluster can be characterized as highly concentrated in two ways. First, almost all of the top references are to either Roy Bhaskar (considered the founder of critical realism) or Tony Lawson (its most famous proponent in economics). Second, 42% of its articles are published in the *Cambridge Journal of Economics*, by far the strongest association between a journal and a cluster in this corpus.

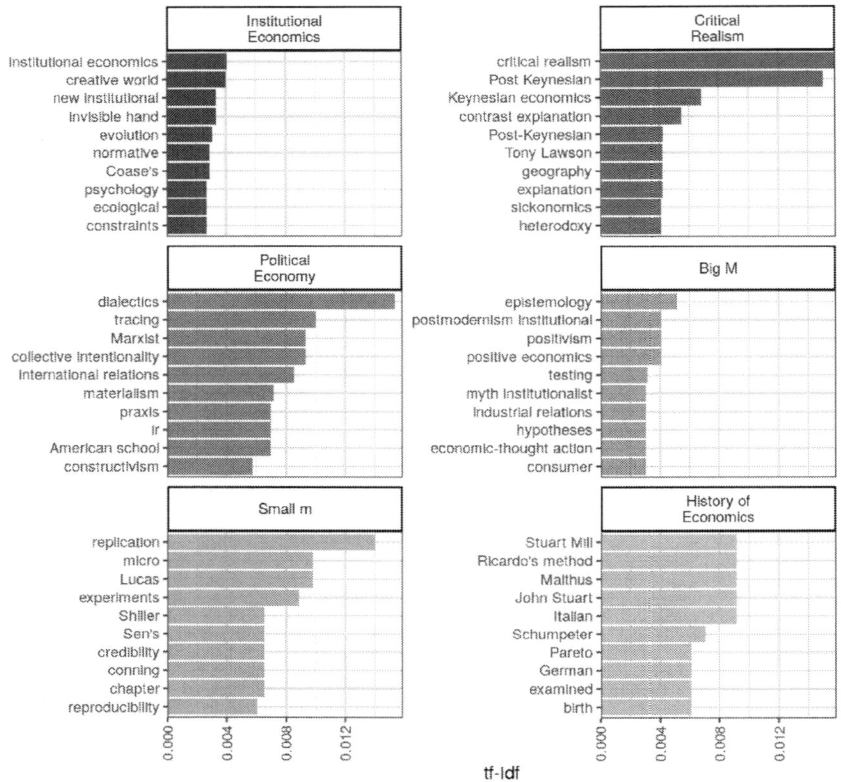

Figure 11.4 Clusters detected in the corpus based on the JEL code Economic Methodology: Top 10 most distinctive phrases (tf-idf) per cluster in the title of articles

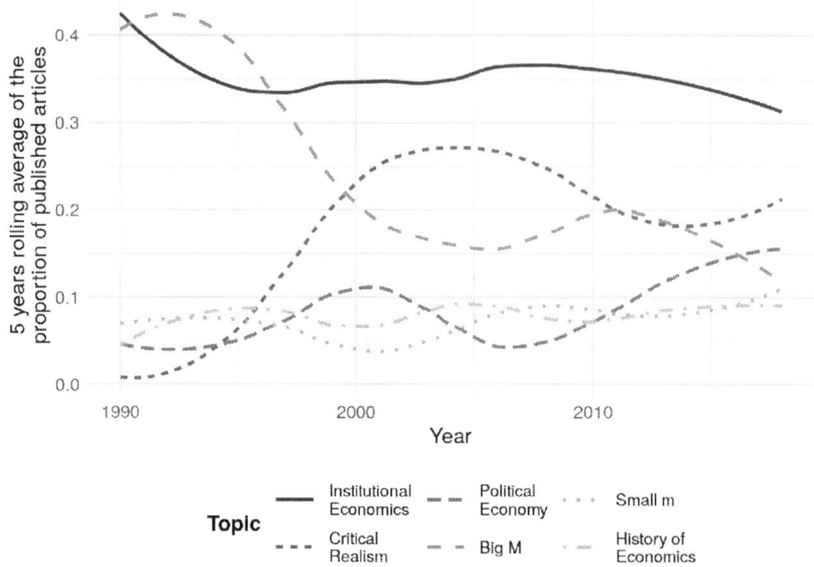

Figure 11.5 Clusters detected in the corpus based on the JEL code `Economic Methodology': Article share of clusters over time (smoothed using local polynomial regression)

Political Economy (*n* = 130): This cluster has a strong Marxian flavor, with keywords such as "dialectics" and abundant references to Marx. It also has some associations with social ontology, with keywords such as "collective intentionality" and references to Searle. Finally, it also discusses social scientific methods that are not used extensively in economics, such as case studies – there are many references to a textbook on this method (George and Bennett, 2007). Although the cluster might be said to be heterogeneous, it is held together by being mostly about methodological discussions on the study of the economy but lying outside the borders of economics. Indeed, 60% of the articles in this cluster are published in journals that are not in economics according to the NSF classification – for example, 22% are in the journal *Science and Society*.

Big M (*n* = 329): This cluster has similarities with the cluster that we label identically in the other corpus: it asks the big questions about the status of economics as a science. More specifically, central sources for this cluster are Friedman (1953), some classical sources in the philosophy of science (Popper, 1934; Kuhn, 1962), Blaug (1980) as an interpreter of these sources for economics, and McCloskey (1998) as a critic of the use of these sources.

Small m (*n* = 111): This is the other cluster that has a corresponding cluster in the Specialized Philosophy of Economics. In this case, both clusters focus on methodological issues that are more connected with the day-to-day work of economists. They also represent only a small share of the articles. This time, the most-cited technical source on statistical inference is Edward Leamer (1978, 1983), and many keywords refer to this topic. The cluster includes discussions of economic theory, such as rational expectations (citing Keynes and Lucas) and Piero Sraffa's theory. We note that the *Journal of Economic Perspectives* is its top source of articles, almost tied with the *Cambridge Journal of Economics* as both published 11% of the articles in the cluster. The presence of the *Journal of Economic Perspectives* indicates that some of the content of this cluster is closer to the mainstream of economics.

History of Economics ($n = 107$): This cluster is unique in its emphasis on the pre-1940 history of economic thought, with numerous references to classics such as Smith (1776) and Marshall (1890) and heavy reliance throughout the period on Schumpeter, including his *History of Economic Analysis* (1954). Its most important sources of articles are historical journals such as *History of Political Economy* (20%) and the *European Journal of the History of Economic Thought* (14%).

Regarding temporal tendencies, two clusters exhibit extreme changes in their shares of articles (see Figure 11.5). First, Critical Realism, starting from almost nothing, grows quickly in the second half of the 1990s, reaches a plateau of around 25% of articles in the early 2000s, and then decreases slightly to settle at around one-fifth of the articles at the end of our period. Second, the share of Big M decreases by 30 percentage points over the period, going from the biggest cluster to roughly tied with Small m and History of Economics as the smallest cluster.

The four other clusters exhibit comparatively mild changes in article shares over the period. Small m and History of Economics are the most stable, with increases of only a few percentage points over the period. Institutional Economics experienced a mild downward trend and thus remained the biggest cluster for more than 20 years. Finally, Political Economy had an S-shape progression, finishing the period 10 percentage points higher than where it started.[18]

4.2.2 Discussion

How does JEL Economic Methodology compare to Specialized Philosophy of Economics? We find some similarities, but also some striking differences.

We already tried to direct attention to the primary similarity between the corpora by giving two clusters the same name in each of them: Small m and Big M. These labels refer to McCloskey's distinction between "the workaday utility of method with a small *m*" and "Methodology" with a capital M, which asks big questions about the status of economics as a science (McCloskey, 1998, p. 160; see also Hands, 2001, p. 255).[19] The Big M clusters in each corpus engage extensively with Friedman's 1953 essay, Blaug's Popperian interpretation of economics, and McCloskey's criticism of the big questions. Both clusters also see their relative importance diminish significantly between the 1990s and the late 2010s, which indicates that the relative disinterest in Big M already documented in the Specialized Philosophy of Economics (Hands, 2015) extends to the other economic methodology. With respect to the two Small m clusters, they both cover issues related to statistical inference. Furthermore, both have a low share of the articles.

Yet, even Big M and Small m exhibit dissimilarities across corpora. In Specialized Philosophy of Economics, the most-cited document in Big M by a large margin is Hausman's *Inexact and Separate Science* (1992), but it is little cited in JEL Economic Methodology. Other scholars associated with INEM, such as Hands and Reiss, follow the same pattern: important in Specialized Philosophy of Economics but of minor relevance in JEL Economic Methodology. Big M in JEL Economic Methodology stays closer to philosophical classics such as Popper and Kuhn and, furthermore, does not follow the same path through time toward a focus on the scientific status of models as its homologous cluster.

The two Small m clusters also have mostly a surface similarity. Even the challenges of statistical inference are treated differently: in Specialized Philosophy of Economics, it is strongly connected to the philosophy of causality with extensive citations of Haavelmo (1944), Pearl (2000), Spirtes et al. (2000), and Hoover (2001), while the key inspiration for JEL Economic Methodology is Leamer's approach (1983) to sensitivity testing. In addition, discussions of Lucas's rational expectations and Sraffa's neo-Ricardian economics figure prominently only in the Small m of

JEL Economic Methodology. One hypothesis that would explain this different focus is that specialized philosophers of economics face incentives to make interdisciplinary connections, which are easy with causality but less obvious for theories such as Lucas's and Sraffa's that are native to economics.

When we look at the other clusters, the differences between the two corpora grow even bigger. No cluster in the JEL corpus is associated with the philosophical topics of "action theory" and "ethics" (or normative social and political philosophy) (Hausman, 2008). In this sense, Economic Methodology as a JEL code is more restrictive than influential delimitations of philosophy of economics: it is, as its name suggests, focused on the third subject in Hausman's typology, the one associated with philosophy of science. Obviously, this focus does not imply the absence of sustained discussions of action theory and ethics in journals covered by EconLit, beyond *JEM* and *E&P*. As we already hinted in Section 4.1.2, our corpus of Specialized Philosophy of Economics has no monopoly over foundational issues in decision and game theories, and a similar point holds for the ethics and political philosophy of economics. However, economics, through the JEL codes, is not structured such that it is easy to individuate work strongly related to these subjects. They are dispersed in the JEL hierarchy under headings such as:[20]

- A13 Relation of Economics to Social Values.
- C70 Game Theory and Bargaining Theory: General.
- D01 Microeconomic Behavior: Underlying Principles.
- D6 Welfare Economics.

It is flagrant that the negotiations inside the economics profession that have defined and updated the JEL codes (Cherrier, 2017) are not conducive to clearly delineating the subject matter of Specialized Philosophy of Economics.

What our results indicate is rather the strong association of JEL Economic Methodology with heterodox approaches and with the history of economic thought. Heterodox approaches are central to three clusters: Institutional Economics, Critical Realism, and Political Economy. We also have a History of Economics cluster. None of these orientations is prevalent in Specialized Philosophy of Economics. JEL Economic Methodology thus reflects the hierarchy of the current JEL classification extremely strongly, which puts B4 Economic Methodology under B History of Economic Thought, Methodology, and Heterodox Approaches. As a result, JEL Economic Methodology also shows little interest in what has boomed in Specialized Philosophy of Economics: the cluster Behavioral Economics.[21]

These results put in perspective a general narrative about the philosophy (or methodology) of economics. According to this narrative, the philosophy of economics has not only moved away from Big M but also left behind the divide between neoclassical and heterodox economics:

> The bottom line is that almost all of the real "action" within contemporary economic methodology is in precisely . . . elements of the new, more pluralistic, mainstream. . . . Neoclassicism may not be dead, but it is no longer the focus of the cutting edge of methodological research – but then nor is heterodox economics. Neither neoclassical nor heterodox economics are the main focus of recent methodological inquiry.
>
> (Hands, 2015, p. 72)

This narrative is a neat example of the boundary work (Gieryn, 1983) internal to science. According to our study, it is a proper characterization of the field of Specialized Philosophy of Economics – a field whose structure Hands has contributed to as co-editor of the *Journal of Economic Methodology*. However, it leaves out much of what occurs in JEL Economic Methodology: for better or worse, a significant number of articles labeled Economic Methodology still take heterodox economics to be real action.

5. Conclusion

What is philosophy of economics? Our investigation leads us to the conclusion that there has been, for the last 30 years, at least two quite distinct philosophies of economics.

The field of Specialized Philosophy of Economics used to be well depicted by the threefold distinction between ethics and economics, action theory, and philosophy of science (Hausman, 2008), with the further precision that philosophy of science can ask either vast questions about the scientific character of economics or more narrow questions about the methodological challenges of economics – Big M versus Small m (McCloskey, 1998, p. 160). With the sudden and massive rise in interest in behavioral economics and similar approaches (experimental economics, neuroeconomics) around 2005, the map changed. In the last few years, Specialized Philosophy of Economics has been divided between a still strong ethics and economics cluster (which we call Moral Philosophy in Section 4.1) and three other subject areas: models and explanation (Big M), causal inference (Small m), and behavioral economics.

The other philosophy of economics, the one corresponding to JEL Economic Methodology, is strongly associated with criticisms of "mainstream economics" (with three clusters: Institutional Economics, Critical Realism, and Political Economy) and with pre-1945 history of economic thought (the History of Economics cluster). It has clusters that can be paired with Big M and Small m in the other corpus, but the pairs are far from identical twins.

The interpretive literature that we surveyed in our two discussion sections (4.1.2 and 4.2.2) overlooks the important differences between these two philosophies of economics. A perspective informed by the sociology of science can easily explain this neglect: the interpretations are written by and for members of the specialized field, those who belong to Specialized Philosophy of Economics. One value of the more data-driven approach used in this chapter is to remind members of a scientific field that, although they have delineated a region for themselves, what they have excluded does not necessarily become extinct.

Related Chapters

Grayot, J., Chapter 6 "Economic Agency and the Subpersonal Turn in Economics
Lecouteux, G., Chapter 4 "Behavioral Welfare Economics and Consumer Sovereignty"
Nagatsu, M., Chapter 24 "Experimentation in Economics"
Verreault-Julien, P., Chapter 22 "Explanation in Economics"

Notes

* Francois.Claveau@USherbrooke.ca, Université de Sherbrooke, Canada, Research Chair in Applied Epistemology and CIRST.

1 From www.aeaweb.org/econlit/jelCodes.php (last accessed October 2, 2020).

2 In a companion paper (Truc et al., 2020), we use a different technique (decade-long co-citation networks) on Specialized Philosophy of Economics. The subject matter discovered is highly similar, but not identical, to what we present here. A recent article also shows that economics, as compared to other scientific disciplines, has grown less interested in the philosophy of science since the 1980s (Khelfaoui et al., 2021).

3 See https://doi.org/10.5281/zenodo.4306372

4 This consensus is expressed by, among others, Hausman (2008, sec. 4), Mäki (2012, p. xv), and (Hands, 2015, p. 62). Needless to say there are now other journals in the field, including the *Erasmus Journal for Philosophy and Economics*. We made sure that these other journals are not included in our second corpus.

5 www.scopus.com/home.uri

6 We use the version hosted by EBSCO: www.ebsco.com/products/research-databases/econlitfull-text
7 We use the version hosted by the Observatoire des sciences et technologies: www.ost.uqam.ca/
8 www.aeaweb.org/econlit/ (last accessed October 6, 2020).
9 For instance, the *Journal of Economic Methodology* is indexed in Web of Science only from 2013 onward. The fact that it does not go back to 1994 (the first issue) is the reason why we use Scopus rather than Web of Science for Specialized Philosophy of Economics.
10 See Section 2.4 of the Technical Appendix for a table comparing the top 50 references in both corpora.
11 For the inspiration for the label, see Section 4.2.2.
12 McCloskey's book is the only top reference shared by Big M and Small m.
13 See Section 3.3.1 in our Technical Appendix for the full list of articles. For instance, the earliest article citing the *General Theory* is titled "Keynes's Theory of Probability and Its Relevance to His Economics: Three Theses" (Cottrell, 1993), and a more recent article is "Conventionalism, Coordination, and Mental Models: From Poincaré to Simon" (Koumakhov, 2014).
14 A similar threefold division has been endorsed recently by Campagnolo and Gharbi (2017) and Hédoin (2018). Scholars who use a more restrictive distinction tend to focus on the philosophy of science branch (e.g., Davis and Hands, 2011; Mäki, 2012; Ross, 2014).
15 See Section 3.4.1 in our Technical Appendix for details of this analysis.
16 In all decades, *Journal of Economic Theory* and *Games and Economic Behavior* take turns in first and second places. *Synthese* took over the third position from *Theory and Decision* in the 2010s
17 For the top sources of articles for each cluster, see Section 4.4. in our Technical Appendix.
18 There are also changes in the focus of clusters that can be gleaned from the changes in the most-cited documents (Table 11.2) and from the decade-by-decade changes in keywords and most frequent journal sources (both of these properties are in the Technical Appendix, Sections 4.2.2 and 4.4, respectively). Most notably, the heterogeneity of Political Economy discussed previously represents a temporal evolution: beginning with a Marxian focus in the 1990s, moving on to social ontology in the 2000s, and adding discussions of case studies and process tracing in the 2010s.
19 Although McCloskey used the label to criticize Big M, our borrowing of terms does not imply that we share McCloskey's opinion on the relative value of each type of inquiry
20 Note also that most methodological discussions are not classified with the JEL code Economic Methodology (B4 since the early 1990s). For instance, there is "C1 Econometric and Statistical Methods and Methodology: General."
21 As a clear indicator of the disparity, we can take citations of Kahneman: his *Econometrica* article with Tversky (1979) is the seventh most cited in Specialized Philosophy of Economics but is only 45th in the JEL Economic Methodology corpus. The gap is huge for his recent *Thinking, fast and slow* (Kahneman, 2011): 44th versus 638th. See Section 2.4 in the Technical Appendix for more comparisons.

Bibliography

Abbott, A. (2001). *Chaos of Disciplines*. University of Chicago Press, Chicago.

Allais, M. (1953). Le Comportement de l'Homme Rationnel devant le Risque: Critique des Postulats et Axiomes de l'Ecole Americaine. *Econometrica*, 21(4):503.

Angrist, J., Azoulay, P., Ellison, G., Hill, R., and Lu, S. F. (2020). Inside Job or Deep Impact? Extramural Citations and the Influence of Economic Scholarship. *Journal of Economic Literature*, 58(1):3–52.

Aumann, R. J. (1976). Agreeing to Disagree. *The Annals of Statistics*, 4(6):1236–1239. Publisher: Institute of Mathematical Statistics.

Blaug, M. (1980). *The Methodology of Economics, or, How Economists Explain*. Cambridge University Press, Cambridge.

Blaug, M. (1992). *The Methodology of Economics, or, How Economists Explain*. Cambridge Surveys of Economic Literature. Cambridge University Press, Cambridge; New York, 2nd ed.

Blondel, V. D., Guillaume, J. L., Lambiotte, R., and Lefebvre, E. (2008). Fast Unfolding of Communities in Large Networks. *Journal of Statistical Mechanics: Theory and Experiment*, 2008(10):P10008.

Boyack, K. W., Klavans, R., and Börner, K. (2005). Mapping the Backbone of Science. *Scientometrics*, 64(3):351–374.

Campagnolo, G. and Gharbi, J. S., editors (2017). *Philosophie économique: Un état des lieux*. Éditions Matériologiques, Paris.

Cherrier, B. (2017). Classifying Economics: A History of the JEL Codes. *Journal of Economic Literature*, 55(2):545–579.

Claveau, F., and Gingras, Y. (2016). Macrodynamics of Economics: A Bibliometric History. *History of Political Economy*, 48(4):551–592.

Colander, D., Holt, R., and Rosser, B. (2004). The Changing Face of Mainstream Economics. *Review of Political Economy*, 16(4):485–499.

Cole, S., Cole, J. R., and Dietrich, L. (1978). Measuring the Cognitive State of Scientific Disciplines. In Elkana, Y., Lederberg, J., Merton, R. K., Thackray, A., and Zuckerman, H., editors, *Toward a Metric of Science: The Advent of Science Indicators*, pages 209–252. John Wiley & Sons, New York.

Cottrell, A. (1993). Keynes's Theory of Probability and Its Relevance to His Economics: Three Theses. *Economics & Philosophy*, 9(1):25–51. Publisher: Cambridge University Press.

Davis, J. B. (2006). The Turn in Economics: Neoclassical Dominance to Mainstream Pluralism? *Journal of Institutional Economics*, 2(1):1.

Davis, J. B., and Hands, D. W., editors (2011). *The Elgar Companion to Recent Economic Methodology*. Edward Elgar, Cheltenham.

Deaton, A. (2010). Instruments, Randomization, and Learning About Development. *Journal of Economic Literature*, 48(2):424–455.

Friedman, M. (1953). *Essays in Positive Economics*. University of Chicago Press, Chicago.

George, A. L., and Bennett, A. (2007). *Case Studies and Theory Development in the Social Sciences*. MIT Press, Cambridge, MA. OCLC: 634382063.

Gieryn, T. F. (1983). Boundary-Work and the Demarcation of Science from Non-Science: Strains and Interests in Professional Ideologies of Scientists. *American Sociological Review*, 48(6):781–795.

Haavelmo, T. (1944). The Probability Approach in Econometrics. *Econometrica*, 12:iii–115.

Hands, D. W. (2001). *Reflection Without Rules: Economic Methodology and Contemporary Science Theory*. Cambridge University Press, New York.

Hands, D. W. (2015). Orthodox and Heterodox Economics in Recent Economic Methodology. *Erasmus Journal for Philosophy and Economics*, 8(1):61.

Hausman, D. M. (1992). *The Inexact and Separate Science of Economics*. Cambridge University Press, Cambridge; New York.

Hausman, D. M. (2008, Fall). Philosophy of Economics. In Zalta, E. N., editor, *The Stanford Encyclopedia of Philosophy (Fall 2008 Edition)*. Stanford University Press, Stanford.

Hédoin, C. (2018). Philosophy and Economics: Recent Issues and Perspectives: Introduction to the Special Issue. *Revue d'Économie Politique*, 128(2):177.

Hoover, K. D. (2001). *Causality in Macroeconomics*. Cambridge University Press, Cambridge.

Kahneman, D. (2011). *Thinking, Fast and Slow*. Penguin Books, London. OCLC: 798805166.

Kahneman, D. and Tversky, A. (1979). Prospect Theory: An Analysis of Decision Under Risk. *Econometrica*, 47(2):263.

Kessler, M. M. (1963). Bibliographic Coupling Between Scientific Papers. *American Documentation*, 14(1):10–25.

Keynes, J. M. (1936). *The General Theory of Employment, Interest and Money*. Palgrave Macmillan, London.

Khelfaoui, M., Gingras, Y., Lemoine, M., and Pradeu, T. (2021). The Visibility of Philosophy of Science in the Sciences, 1980–2018. *Synthese*, Forthcoming.

Koumakhov, R. (2014). Conventionalism, Coordination, and Mental Models: From Poincaré to Simon. *Journal of Economic Methodology*, 21(3):251–272. Publisher: Routledge. Eprint. https://doi.org/10.1080/1350178X.2014.939688.

Kuhn, T. S. (1962). *The Structure of Scientific Revolutions*. University of Chicago Press, Chicago, IL, 3rd ed.

Lawson, T. (1997). *Economics and Reality: Economics as Social Theory*. Routledge, London; New York.

Leamer, E. E. (1978). *Specification Searches: Ad Hoc Inference with Nonexperimental Data*. John Wiley & Sons, New York.

Leamer, E. E. (1983). Let's Take the Con Out of Econometrics. *American Economic Review*, 73(1):31–43.

Luce, R. D., and Raiffa, H. (1957). *Games and Decisions: Introduction and Critical Survey*. Dover Publications, New York.

Mäki, U., editor (2012). *Philosophy of Economics*. Handbook of the Philosophy of Science. Elsevier, Oxford, 1st ed.

Marshall, A. (1890). *Principles of Economics*. Palgrave Macmillan, New York. OCLC: 958386501.

McCloskey, D. N. (1985). *The Rhetoric of Economics*. University of Wisconsin Press, Madi son, WI.

McCloskey, D. N. (1998). *The Rhetoric of Economics*. University of Wisconsin Press, Madison, WI, 2nd ed.

Mireles-Flores, L. (2018). Recent Trends in Economic Methodology: A Literature Review. In Fiorito, L., Scheall, S., and Suprinyak, C. E., editors, *Research in the History of Economic Thought and Methodology*, volume 36, pages 93–126. Emerald Publishing Limited, Bingley.

Nelson, R. R., and Winter, S. G. (1982). *An Evolutionary Theory of Economic Change*. Belknap Press of Harvard University Press, Cambridge, MA.

Newman, M. E. J., and Girvan, M. (2004). Finding and Evaluating Community Structure In Networks. *Physical Review E*, 69(2):026113.

Noichl, M. (2019). Modeling the Structure of Recent Philosophy. *Synthese*. https://doi.org/10.1007/s11229-019-02390-8.

North, D. C. (1990). *Institutions, Institutional Change and Economic Performance*. Cambridge University Press, Cambridge.

Pearce, D. G. (1984). Rationalizable Strategic Behavior and the Problem of Perfection. *Econometrica: Journal of the Econometric Society*, 52(4):1029–1050. Publisher: JSTOR.

Pearl, J. (2000). *Causality: Models, Reasoning and Inference*. Cambridge University Press, Cambridge.

Popper, K. R. (1934). *The Logic of Scientific Discovery*. Routledge Classics. Routledge, London, repr. 2008 (twice) ed.

Rawls, J. (1971). *A Theory of Justice*. Oxford Paperbacks. Oxford University Press, Oxford. OCLC: 832501930.

Reiss, J. (2012). The Explanation Paradox. *Journal of Economic Methodology*, 19(1):43–62.

Robbins, L. (1935). *An Essay on the Nature and Significance of Economic Science*. Macmillan, London, 2nd ed.

Ross, D. (2014). *Philosophy of Economics*. Palgrave Macmillan, Basingstoke.

Rossetti, G., and Cazabet, R. (2018). Community Discovery in Dynamic Networks: A Survey. *ACM Computing Surveys*, 51(2):35:1–35:37.

Rutherford, M. (1994). *Institutions in Economics: The Old and the New Institutionalism*. Cambridge University Press, Cambridge.

Savage, L. J. (1954). *The Foundations of Statistics*. Dover Publications, New York, 2nd rev. ed.

Schumpeter, J. A. (1954). *History of Economic Analysis*. Allen & Unwin, London.

Smith, A. (1776). *The Wealth of Nations*. OCLC: 920454681.

Spirtes, P., Glymour, C., and Scheines, R. (2000). *Causation, Prediction, and Search*. MIT Press, Cambridge, MA, 2nd ed.

Truc, A., Claveau, F., and Santerre, O. (2020). Economic Methodology: A Bibliometric Perspective. *Journal of Economic Methodology*, 28, forthcoming.

Veblen, T. (1919). *The Place of Science in Modern Civilization and Other Essays*. Huebsch, New York.

Whitley, R. (2000). *The Intellectual and Social Organization of the Sciences*. Oxford University Press, Oxford.

Williamson, O. E. (1985). *The Economic Institutions of Capitalism*. Free Press, New York.

12
PHILOSOPHY OF AUSTRIAN ECONOMICS

Alexander Linsbichler

1. Précis: What Was and Is the Austrian School?

Carl Menger's *Principles of Economics* (1871/2004) is usually regarded as the founding document of the Austrian School of economics.[1] In the early phase around 1900, international dissemination and further advancement of the new economic and methodological ideas were, for the most part, due to Böhm-Bawerk and Wieser. In the 1930s, when Mises, Hayek, Machlup, Morgenstern, Haberler, and most other representatives of Austrian economics emigrated from Vienna, the School's center began to shift to the United States. There, Kirzner, Lachmann, Rothbard, Lavoie, and many others contributed to the further development and so-called "revival" of Austrian economics. Throughout the one and a half centuries of the Austrian School's existence, its position relative to the mainstream as well as its internal diversifications have changed considerably several times. Still, there are some (nearly consensual) demarcating traits of the Austrian School from Menger up to contemporary neo-Austrians of various stripes: methodological individualism, relatively thoroughgoing subjectivism, and an emphasis on the signaling function of market prices and price changes, the processual character of many relevant social phenomena, entrepreneurial discovery, and the heterogeneity of the capital structure.[2]

Austrian methodological, epistemological, and economic positions tend to instill skepticism toward precise quantitative predictability (see also Megger 2021 for the questions of determinism and free will). Rough "pattern predictions" and "explanations of the principle" are attainable even for complex phenomena, though (see e.g., Hayek 1952, 1955, 1967; Scheall 2015a). Because epistemological modesty reinforces a humble attitude regarding the malleability of social institutions as well, many Austrian economists are paragons of the "constrained vision" (Sowell 1987/2007). Coherently, Dekker (2016, 2020) characterizes the Austrian economists' role in society as humanist, accepting "students of civilization". As this label indicates, Austrian economics at its best incorporates institutional, political, sociological, psychological, and cultural considerations as well as legal theory: "nobody can be a great economist who is only an economist – and I am even tempted to add that the economist who is only an economist is likely to become a nuisance if not a positive danger" (Hayek 1956/1967: 123; see also Mises 1962: 3–4). Given this broad, inclusive conception of the discipline, perhaps Austrian economics should rather be called Austrian political economy.

Many stated characteristics of Austrian economics have a philosophical or methodological component. In the following eight sections, we will briefly discuss Austrian action theory and interpretative understanding, subjectivism, methodological individualism, ontological individualism, apriorism, essentialism, formal methods, and economic semantics.

DOI: 10.4324/9781315739793-15

Except for a few remarks, we will not touch upon the political philosophy, social philosophy, or historical, legal, and ethical treatises of Austrian economists. We treat Austrian economics as a scientific research program with a certain methodology, theories, and research interests. Although many Austrian economists have published on political philosophy, often advocating an array of libertarian positions ranging from anarchocapitalism to classical liberalism, we treat Austrian economics as, in principle, independent from any political position.[3] Indeed, an aspiration for value-free economics features prominently in the writings of many Austrians, according to which the economist qua economist "cannot advocate any course of action. As a citizen, however, he may, along with other citizens, try to decide upon the proper course of social policy" and use economic theory in those deliberations (Rothbard 1951: 946). The preceding is not to say, of course, that Austrian economists always succeed in separating scientific theory and ideological value judgment.

2. Understanding Action, the Austrian Way

Acting individuals in Austrian economics are conceived as active, creative problem-solvers, whose knowledge is incomplete. Lachmann even urges economics to consider that knowledge is often lacking altogether ("radical uncertainty"). In any case, for Austrians, knowledge is dispersed among agents and contains an interpretative element, and actors can commit errors in their reasoning, their interpretations, and their choices.[4]

Choices and decisions are a crucial element of Austrian economics. Ideally however, oftentimes

> the analytical unit is not the act of choice within a given ends-means framework. . . . [T]he unit of analysis is human action, a concept that includes the identification of the very ends-means framework within which efficient decision making must be exercised. . . . [T]he verb "to act" includes not only effective exploitation of all perceived net opportunities for gain, but also the discovery of those opportunities.
>
> (Kirzner 2001: 86–87)

Thus, agents are not just potentially ignorant about the value of some variables; they might even err by neglecting a relevant factor or failing to picture an option altogether. Consequently, agents can encounter real surprises, and market opportunities can remain undiscovered for a while. Accordingly, Austrian economics has been labeled the "economics of ignorance and coordination" (Aimar 2009) and the "economics of time and ignorance" (O'Driscoll and Rizzo 2015).

The Austrian demonstrated preference approach closely resembles the well-known revealed preference approach (see Vredenburgh, Chapter 5), but Austrians presume to be more attentive to a necessary interpretative element. Strictly speaking, all that observation and economic theory yield is the following: *if the observed behavior is an action, then the acting individual prefers something to something else in that moment.* Observations and economic theory are insufficient to tackle questions like: Is the observed behavior an action? What is preferred to what? Can we reasonably assume some constancy of that preference? Declarations of acting individuals about their motives cannot serve as trustworthy final answers, as Machlup (1969) wittily elucidates. To be sure, self-descriptions can serve indirectly as useful knowledge and can become the object of subsequent explanations themselves. The primary "method" for arriving at conjectures about the subjective preferences, beliefs, and meaning assignments of acting individuals, however, remains interpretative understanding (*Verstehen*).[5]

Because the meaning assignments of market participants play a central role in Austrian economics, so does interpretative understanding. On the basis of economic theory and observation exclusively, we would be clueless as to whether Romeo preferred suicide to eloping with Juliet, whether Amartya preferred the small apple to the big or preferred following the social norms of politeness to appearing greedy, whether a mother saving one of her two daughters from drowning preferred

Venus to Serena or rather preferred saving one child to saving none,[6] and whether Bobby lost the ball game due to his poor strategic choices or succeeded in achieving his secret goal of losing the game.

On a final note regarding Austrian action theory, the ultrathin conception of rationality in Austrian economics is a noteworthy difference from most other conceptions of rational action in economics and philosophy (see Stefánsson, Chapter 3; Grayot, Chapter 6; Lecouteux, Chapter 4). For most Austrian economists, action is by definition rational, that is, any purposeful employment of means to achieve chosen ends which is subject to some form of evaluation merits the label "rational". Consequently, descriptions of actions as rational or irrational are rare in Austrian economics (see, e.g., Pham 2017; Linsbichler 2021a, 2021d).

As an outlook to the sections that follow, if the "facts of the [Austrian] social sciences are what people believe and think" (Storr 2010), then methodological individualism and subjectivism are congenial to Austrian methodology.

3. Subjectivism

In order to explain exchange, relative prices, or indeed almost anything in economics, economists require a theory of value, that is, an explication of the concept of value and a theory about the principles according to which individuals value goods and services.

Objective value theories hold that goods can be and in fact are evaluated according to some objective standard. Consequently, people exchange goods of equal value, and the relative prices of goods reflect their relative objective values. By contrast, but encompassing objective value theories as a very special case, subjective theories of value hold that people value goods and services according to their (subjective) beliefs about whether these goods and services will satisfy their subjective preferences (see also Moscati, Chapter 2). Because today almost all economists maintain a subjective theory of value of some sort, subjectivism prima facie ceased to suffice as an informative distinguishing characteristic of Austrian economics.[7] Having said that, there are several layers of how subjective one's value theory is, and Austrian economists tend to champion more thoroughgoing versions of subjectivism.[8] Congruously, Hayek contends "that every important advance in economic theory during the last hundred years was a further step in the consistent application of subjectivism" (1952/1964: 31).

There are trends in the history of Austrian economics toward more thoroughgoing subjectivism. Menger's subjective theory is applicable to goods (including works of art and money), services, and labor and, hence, facilitates a uniform theory of relative prices. However, Menger's value theory still retains several objective features. For instance, he speaks of "human needs" instead of preferences or wants. Moreover, in order to be a good in Menger's sense, not only is a physical thing required to be believed to satisfy a need but the physical thing must also (objectively) have the property of being able to causally contribute to the satisfaction of the need. Otherwise, Menger (1871/2004: 51–55) speaks of an "imagined good". Finally, Menger focused on the subjective evaluations of consumers, and only Wieser developed the Austrian theory of opportunity costs, thereby extending subjectivism to production. Later, Wieser was reproached by Mises: "[Wieser] never really grasped the core of subjectivism, a limitation that caused him to make many unfortunate mistakes" (Mises 1940/2009: 28). Subsequently, although Mises' "consistent development of the subjectivist approach . . . has for a long time moved ahead of his contemporaries" (Hayek 1952/1964: 210), some of Mises' arguments in monopoly theory (see Costea 2003) and in the calculation debates (see Nemeth 1999; Uebel 2019) have been accused of containing assumptions that are untenable from Mises' own subjectivist stance. In some respects, Lachmann represents the pinnacle of subjectivity in the tradition of the Austrian School.[9] Particularly, Lachmann emphasizes that learning from past experience involves an inextricable interpretative element, and, more drastically, under the prevailing conditions of radical uncertainty, even if actors learn anything from the past, they only learn something about the past, not about the future. Consequently, not only evaluations but also expectations are entirely subjective.

Examples of implications for economic theory include subjectivist challenges to the existence of equilibrating tendencies and subjectivist capital theory. Pursuing Lachmann's approach, Garzarelli and Kuchar (2018) suggest that

> a consistently subjectivist theory of capital does not depend on the physical character of capital goods . . . what matters for a good to become capital is what an individual, such as an entrepreneur, imagines can be done with it.

Other layers of subjectivity are particularly relevant for welfare economics. Most Austrian economists object to quantifying utility and are wary of the constant preferences assumption. Most Austrian criticisms of the assumption of transitivity of preferences, rather, should be interpreted as criticism of the assumption of constancy as well (Hudik 2012). Furthermore, thoroughgoing subjectivism combined with ordinal utility denies the possibility of interpersonal utility comparisons, intertemporal utility comparisons, and aggregation of utilities of several individuals, thereby severely restricting the possibility of welfare economics.[10] Stringham (2010) discusses proxies to stand in for utility as a magnitude for welfare assessments: monetary income, migration patterns, and willingness to pay as estimated in cost-benefit analysis do not pass the test of thoroughgoing subjectivism.[11]

Systematically subjectivist Austrian economists accept only limited access to an actor's preferences: demonstrated preference. Without the constant preferences assumption, however, preferences are only demonstrated for one point in time. The ensuing welfare economics, based on thoroughgoing subjectivism and the implicit assumption of property rights, is mostly "negative" in the sense that

> [e]ach involuntary act of acquisition or interaction is Pareto Inferior. . . . the free market achieves the greatest social utility possible of any economic system. [Rothbard's (1956/1997)] achievement is no less than a rigorous proof . . . that the free market, without qualification, maximizes social welfare.
>
> (Herbener 1997: 106)

Note that "social utility" in that assessment is a technical term that is purely based on individually demonstrated preferences. It is a separate discussion whether interventionism and income redistribution are to be endorsed on other, non-(Austrian)economic grounds.

4. Methodological Individualism

The term "methodological individualism" was coined by Schumpeter (1908/1980), and the origin of the concept is often ascribed to M. Weber, two scholars in close contact with Austrian economists. Methodological individualism is a doctrine regarding explanations (Verreault-Julien, Chapter 22). It rejects organic conceptions of social organizations, and, in its strictest form, methodological individualism requires satisfactory explanations in the social sciences to explain social phenomena as the *unintended* outcome of intended individual actions (see, e.g., Menger 1883/1985: 127–159; Hayek 1946/1948, 1973/1998: 35–54).

Milford (2010) argues that it is precisely the combination of strict methodological individualism, a theory of subjective evaluations, and the equimarginal principle that constitutes the innovative core of Menger's research program.[12] A simple example of a social phenomenon is exchange. In a theory of objective evaluations, goods and services of equivalent value are exchanged, so in order to explain why some exchanges happen and others do not, a psychological motive such as A. Smith's "propensity to truck, barter and exchange one thing for another" (1776/1976: 29) needs to be invoked.[13] People exchange because they have the propensity to exchange. Although the explanandum might perhaps be true, such question-begging explanations could be given ad hoc for any social phenomenon and are not very instructive.[14] Moreover, this account leaves unexplained "why the two participants should not be willing to reverse the trade immediately" (Menger 1871/2004: 193). In contrast, a theory of subjective evaluations allows for an explanation of exchange as an *unintended* consequence. Say Eve has an orange and prefers apples to oranges and Francis has an apple and prefers oranges to apples; assume both Eve and Francis consciously recognize the opportunity to improve their preference satisfaction by an exchange. Then an exchange between Eve and Francis can be explained without recourse to an initial intention to exchange. Similarly, Hayek (1952/1964: 40–41) explains the emergence of a trail through a thicket: the only relevant goal of an individual is to pass through the thicket with the least possible effort. Thus, she chooses a route already somewhat trampled down, thereby further contributing to the emergence of a path – without intending to do so.

As a more sophisticated example, Menger (1871/2004) explains the emergence of money as an unintended outcome of intended individual actions – or, in Ferguson's and Hayek's words, "as product of human action but not the execution of any human design" (Ferguson 1767: 205). Note that Menger's theory does not preclude the possibility that some or even all "monies" in economic history are a product of human design, for example, of state design. Methodological individualism does not preclude the possibility of social institutions that are consciously designed. In such cases, the main task of the methodological individualist social scientist is to uncover and explain unintended side effects.

Other possibly illuminating examples are Austrian explanations of the business cycle and of the emergence and stability of a market order. From a strictly methodological individualist perspective, Hayek improves upon Mises insofar as Hayek explains the business cycle without taking recourse to the selfish intentions of central bankers or politicians as a factor contributing to booms and busts, and Mises does not. Similarly, Hayek improves upon Rothbard insofar as the latter employs a psychological hypothesis about the market participants' endorsement of the market order to explain its emergence and stability, and Hayek does not (see Long 2010: 54–56).

The strict version of methodological individualism discussed so far plays an eminent role in the writings of Menger, Hayek, and many other Austrian economists. Moreover, almost all Austrian economists at least proclaim to adhere to a weaker version of methodological individualism.[15] This weaker version only requires social phenomena to be explained as a result of individual action, no matter whether the result is intended or unintended. For instance, Ebeling's assessment that "Mises insisted upon a strict adherence to methodological individualism" (1990: xvi) is only accurate with respect to the weaker version of methodological individualism. Both forms of methodological individualism in effect require microfoundations and considerably restrict the scope of Austrian macroeconomics.[16]

5. Other Individualisms

Many Austrian economists also champion (i) political individualism and (ii) ontological individualism. They hold that (i) the primary objective of policy ought to be the individual's rights, well-being, opportunities, or freedoms. Against organic conceptions of social organizations, they hold that (ii) ultimately only human individuals exist, act, and are causally relevant in the social sphere, whereas social collectives such as nations, classes, sports clubs, and universities exist, act, think, and are causally relevant only through their constitutive individuals. Ontological individualism does not "deny that nations, states, municipalities, parties, religious communities, are real factors determining the course of human events" (Mises 1949/1998: 42). It merely insists that, regardless of whether one can really miss seeing the forest for the trees, one can never see a forest without trees. (Mises 1940: 33).

Kaufmann (1929), who was closely associated with the Austrian School, admonished against blurring the distinctions between logical-ontological, empirical,[17] methodological, and axiological-political individualism. Nevertheless, the term "methodological individualism" is regularly employed for political or ontological positions until today. It might be unusual for socialists and fascists to endorse methodological individualism; conversely, few liberals and libertarians endorse methodological collectivism or holism. These correlations are, however, psychologically or sociologically induced. Logically, methodological individualism and political individualism are independent.

As for the more intricate relation between ontological individualism and methodological individualism, there is an argument widely propagated not only by some Austrian economists stating that ontological individualism necessitates methodological individualism: if only individuals exist, think, act, and are causally relevant for social phenomena, then explanations of social phenomena (ideally) ought to start with individuals. Against this argument, Menger (1883/1985: 50–53) can be interpreted as rejecting any inference from the purported ontological structure of the universe to a specific methodological or epistemological position as committing a category mistake.[18] According to this reading of Menger (and because the reverse is trivial), methodological individualism and ontological individualism are logically independent too.

6. Apriorism

One characteristic of Austrian economics is the openly aprioristic character of at least parts of economic theory, that is, for the truth values of at least some parts of economic theory, experience is not considered a critical standard: some sentences of the theory are not to be tested, verified, falsified, confirmed, or corroborated by empirical means.

Extreme forms of apriorism are considered untenable in the light of modern philosophy of science. Consequently, the Austrian School's putatively extreme apriorism and alleged neglect of empirical work faces harsh criticism by economists and philosophers alike. Scheall (2017) as well as Zanotti and Cachanosky (2015) demur that untenable extreme apriorism has sometimes been invoked as a pretense to dismiss other ideas of Austrian economists *tout court*, perhaps too hastily on occasion. In fact, the extremeness of apriorism varies considerably between different branches of Austrian economics, and the exact nature of the apriorism of many prominent Austrian economists is subject to ongoing exegetical debates.[19] Scheall (2017) proposes a more fine-grained analysis to clarify these debates and assesses the extremeness of an aprioristic position along three different dimensions: (i) the extent of a priori knowledge, (ii) the kind of justification for a priori knowledge, and (iii) the purported certainty of a priori knowledge. As a tentative and rough result, we might array representatives of branches of Austrian economics in decreasing extremeness of apriorism as follows: Hoppe > Rothbard >> Mises >> Menger >> Hayek > Machlup > Lachmann.

However, even for Rothbard, who embraces extreme apriorism (1957), and Mises, whose method was labeled "perhaps the most anti-positivist and anti-empiricist approach to social science ever stated" (Milonakis and Fine 2009: 259), the extent of apriorism (i) is far narrower than many popular expositions of Austrian economics suggest. Even for the extreme apriorists Rothbard and Mises, the only a priori true part of economic theory is everything deducible from the fundamental axiom "Man acts", that is, *human individuals and only human individuals choose ends and employ means they consider suitable to attain these ends*. Auxiliary axioms like the disutility of labor are not a priori and neither are the sentences describing the value judgments, preferences, meaning assignments, and subjective beliefs of the acting individuals. Such empirical sentences are indispensable for each situational analysis and for each Austrian explanation and prediction (Linsbichler 2017: 52–55; Mises 1957/2005; Mäki 1990b). Paraphrasing Kant and Hansen, Roderick Long (2010: 50) trenchantly encapsulates that even the most extreme apriorists acknowledge an interdependency of aprioristic components ("praxeology" in the Mises-Rothbard branch of Austrian economics) and empirical components ("thymology"): "Praxeology without thymology is empty; thymology without praxeology is blind."

As for the kind of justification (ii) of a priori truth, the epistemological status most frequently attributed to the fundamental axiom is that of synthetic a priori in a Kantian tradition. Other construals of the a priori parts of Austrian economics include the following: Rothbard (see, e.g., 1973/1997) invokes a specific form of inner experience that guarantees the truth of the fundamental axiom. According to Hoppe (1995), the justification for the synthetic a priori of praxeology improves upon Kant.[20] Some of Mises' and Hayek's ideas about evolutionary effects on the human mind could be (mis)interpreted as unsuccessfully trying to provide justification for aprioristic elements of the theory (see, e.g., Mises 1962; Hayek 1988). However, even if these arguments successfully established that, for evolutionary reasons the human mind cannot avoid having certain beliefs, this result would only establish a genetic or psychological a priori and not a priori truth as required. Even if an individual could not avoid having certain empirical expectations, these expectations could still be disappointed.

Recent attempts to render some elements of Austrian economics a priori include Long's (2004, 2008, 2010) ingenious appropriation of Wittgenstein's philosophy of language and Frege's Platonism for a reformulation and defense of praxeology; an attempted vindication of Mises with a strong pragmatist flavor (Leeson and Boettke 2006); and the *Hamburger Deutung* (see, e.g., Puster 2014; Oliva Cordoba 2017) interprets the a priori elements as analytic, that is, true in virtue of meaning. Withal, conceptual analysis in the spirit of the *Hamburger Deutung* seems to deny the dependence of intersubjective concepts on language. Consequently, its ultimate aim is not the explication of expedient terminological conventions but the discovery and establishment of allegedly unique, correct concepts such as *the* concept of action. Like the *Hamburger Deutung*, Linsbichler (2017, 2021c; see also Lipski 2021) proposes to construe the a priori parts of Austrian economics as analytic, but he advocates conventionalism regarding the "ultra-refined grammar" (Hutchison 1998: 68) of economics.

7. Realism, Essentialism, and All That

Labels that are often attributed and self-attributed to Austrian economics are "realism," "anti-instrumentalism," "realisticness," and "essentialism." All four terms are sufficiently ambiguous to impair ensuing discussions severely. Mäki disentangles many terminological and conceptual confusions and argues that realism and anti-instrumentalism are appropriate philosophical positions for Austrian process theories of the market (Mäki 1990a, 1990b, 1992).

Qua realist, the typical Austrian economist claims that all terms postulated by her theory (including theoretical terms such as "goal," "preference," and "knowledge") do refer to existing entities. The scientific realism of the Austrian School is often portrayed as continuous with laypeoples' life-world realism. Phenomenologist Kaufmann (Linsbichler 2019), sociologist Schütz (Kurrild-Klitgaard 2001, 2003), and subsequently via Schütz perhaps even social constructivists Berger and Luckmann were strongly influenced by interpretative aspects of Austrian economics after all.

Qua "anti-instrumentalist", all sentences of the typical[21] Austrian theory have truth values, and the theories aim to give a truthful picture of what the world (including the unobservables) is like, instead of merely serving as useful instruments, and only as instruments, for whatever purposes there may be. For instance, Mäki (1997: 477) argues that, "what Menger calls exact types in economics can be interpreted as complex universals in the immanent realist sense, and what he calls exact laws are relations between these universals".

As for realisticness, Austrian economists' criticisms of idealizations (precisive abstractions) in economic theories and models are indeed ubiquitous.[22] In all theories and models that aim to describe or explain the world, Austrians reject idealizations and assumptions known to be false (Long 2006).[23] By contrast, (nonprecisive) abstractions are permitted and prominent in Austrian economics (and indeed unavoidable for almost any theory in empirical science); that is, if certain criteria are deemed irrelevant in a context, they can be left unspecified. Unfortunately, idealizations and abstractions are not always neatly distinguished. Not all formulations of economic theories explicitly specify whether they assert that, say, a public sector is actually absent or is negligible and thus left unspecified or whether the theory's domain is restricted to cases without a public sector.

The question of whether and in what sense Austrian economics is essentialist is perhaps even more convoluted than the question of realism as, for instance, the ongoing debates about whether Menger was an essentialist or an anti-essentialist indicate. Here, we can only provide a rough disambiguation of a few simplified forms of essentialism and sketch some appraisals of whether and in what sense Austrian economics is essentialist.

A very mild form of essentialism coincides with the conjunction of realism and anti-instrumentalism. J. O'Neill (1995) characterizes (Hayekian) Austrian economics as Aristotelian essentialist by focusing on the dispositional character of many purported properties of the market. O'Neill convincingly demonstrates that many attacks on essentialism misfire because they target much stronger versions of essentialism, which few scholars in fact defend. However, like most others', O'Neill's characterization that the "essential properties of an entity of a particular kind are those properties of the object that it must have if it is to be an object of that kind" (O'Neill 1995: 159) bypasses the crucial question of whether having an essential property is just an analytic truth and, if not, how to distinguish between essential and accidental properties.

Stronger versions of Aristotelian essentialism were explicated and criticized by a fellow traveler of the Austrian School, Karl Popper (1960/2000).[24] Essentialism as defined by Popper holds that ultimate explanations of appearances in terms of the underlying essences should be sought and can be found. Such ultimate explanations can be established with certainty or beyond any reasonable doubt, and they are neither in need nor capable of further explanation. To Mäki, "[i]t is obvious that some Austrian economists – most notably von Mises – accept [essentialism as defined by Popper]" (1990b: 339).[25] B. Smith (1990, 1996) by and large characterizes all of Austrian economics as essentialist in that sense, except for his attempt to integrate fallibilism with essentialism and apriorism. Milford's (2008, 2010, 2015) appraisal of essentialism in the Austrian School slightly dissents from these influential views: he admits and underlines that, in the interwar period, strongly essentialist positions as exemplified by Spann, Degenfeld-Schonburg, and the Austrian economists Wieser and Mayer indeed dominated economics at the University of Vienna, Austria. However, according to Milford, the branch of Austrian economics represented by Menger, Böhm-Bawerk, Mises, Haberler, Machlup, Hayek, and Morgenstern is, in our nomenclature, only mildly essentialist. Karl Menger rejects an interpretation of his father Carl Menger as a strong essentialist as well, and Hayek seconds him (see Schumacher and Scheall 2020; Diskussion 1972).

On top of essentialism as defined by Popper, an even stronger version of essentialism states that, via a specific form of intuition or introspection, we (or some genius economists) have infallible access to the truth about at least some essences. Rothbard (1976/1997: 65–71) and Hoppe (1995) seem to defend this extreme essentialism regarding the essence of human action. While some of Mises' remarks about introspection seem to hint in that direction as well, he harshly criticizes Spann for such overestimations of intuition and inner experience (Mises 1933/2003: 42–50; see also 1940: 17–19, 1957/2005: 36, 110).[26]

Strong versions of essentialism are not only relevant from an epistemological point of view but impact the kind of questions to be asked by economists. A strongly essentialist research program is often consumed by questions of origin, historical development, and the "essence" of concepts such as value or preference. Objective value theories are prone to be combined with essentialism. They invite one to ask: by what physical process did the goods acquire their (objective) value? Or what is the essential structure of human needs? The latter question is pursued by Wieser's "psychologistic" research program. Wieser (1884) heavily relies on introspection and on analysis of the alleged essences of value concepts in natural language.

By contrast, nonessentialist and mildly essentialist positions aim to find regularities and laws in the succession of phenomena. Mild essentialists add the postulate that such underlying laws governing both observable phenomena and unobservable entities do exist. Consider, for instance, Menger (1871/2004): even though he regularly speaks of the "Wesen" ("essence"), he maintains that just like the

> goods-character is nothing inherent in goods and not a property of goods, but merely a relationship between certain things and men, the things obviously ceasing to be goods with the disappearance of the relationship (p. 52) . . . value is . . . nothing inherent in goods, no property of them, nor an independent thing existing by itself. It is a judgment economizing men make (p. 120–121).

Consequently, in order to explain value, Menger's only mildly essentialist methodology aims to find laws and regularities governing the evaluating behavior of individuals.

8. Formal Methods

Austrian economics is almost invariably portrayed as being skeptical of or even hostile toward the use of formal methods, such as mathematics, statistics, and (modern) logic.[27] Indeed, classic tomes and contemporary journal publications, as well as textbooks, in Austrian economics predominantly consist of plain text without models, formulas, or equations in mathematical terms.

There are several pragmatic reasons for the absence of formal methods in Austrian economics: (i) Some central topics of Austrian economic theory, like meaning assignments, entrepreneurship, subjective interpretative knowledge, "radical uncertainty," the time structure of production, discreet processes, and institutional considerations, may be difficult to formalize at the current state of the development of formal methods and formalization techniques.[28] Perhaps "altogether new mathematics has to be invented in order to cope with manifold forms of economic problems" (Morgenstern 1963: 3). (ii) Formalization often (but not necessarily, as e.g. Klamer 1994 contends) involves simplifying assumptions and idealizations (see Jhun, Chapter 23), which can clash with Austrian economists' pleas for realisticness. (iii) Similarly, those econometric methods that comprise inductive inferences (Spanos, Chapter 29) are problematic from an Austrian perspective, because many Austrian economists hold inductive methods to be inapplicable outside the natural sciences. (iv) Inasmuch as Austrian economics is more concerned with broad public outreach than with scientific progress on highly specialized research questions, plain natural language has its advantages over formal languages. These and other pragmatic considerations block many approaches that are inadequate from an Austrian perspective. However, they are not sufficient to reject formalization of (parts of) Austrian economics per se.

Still, over and above pragmatic considerations, a principled dismissal of any use of mathematics or modern logic is often ascribed to the Austrian School, expressly by many neo-Austrian economists (see, e.g., Jaffe 1976: 521; Rothbard 1952/2009, 1956/1997, 1976/1997; Boettke 1996). Rothbard (1976/1997) maintains that because individual human behavior is imprecise, it should ideally be described by likewise imprecise natural language. Apart from this unconvincing contention, hardly any argument is given for a principled dismissal of all formal methods. Accordingly, Mayer (1998), himself an ardent critic of excessive formalism, blames Austrian economics for overstating its case against formal methods. Backhouse (2000: 40) even discerns that "no Austrian, to my knowledge, has ever explained why mathematics cannot be used alongside natural-language explanations."[29]

Indeed, otherwise cherished great names in the history of Austrian economics collaborated with mathematicians and mathematical economists in the Austrian Center for Business Cycle Research, in the Mathematical Colloquium conducted by K. Menger, in Mises' private seminar, and in the creation of game theory. Even though they rarely use formal methods themselves, Hayek (1952/1964) and Machlup (1991) speak highly of the prospects of (adequate) formal methods for (adequate) tasks in economics, and Mises praises K. Menger's formal paper (1936/1979).[30]

Contrary to the received view, most economists in the history of the Austrian School do not reject formalization per se. Those neo-Austrians who do, seem to rely on Wieser's most idiosyncratic philosophy of language and epistemology. While the pitfalls of formalization require continuous reflection as Austrian economists rightly underline, some parts of Austrian economics are presumably underformalized at the moment. In particular, the praxeological Mises-Rothbard branch of Austrian economics emphasizes the role of logic and complete deductive proofs but has hitherto eschewed the aid of modern symbolic logic. The latter has proven to be extremely helpful in detecting gaps and hidden assumptions in proofs in other disciplines, and it might do so in prospective praxeological investigations.[31]

9. Economic Semantics and the Future of Austrian Economics

Finally, Machlup's project *Economic Semantics* (1991) deserves a mention, because it can be located at the threshold of economics and philosophy. Machlup examines the history of economic thought in order to gather and analyze different definitions and meanings of one and the same term. Examples of ambiguous terms that have caused economists to misunderstand each other include 'equilibrium', 'disequilibrium', 'marginal product', 'marginal utility', 'structural change', 'microeconomics', 'macroeconomics', 'rational', 'Say's Law', 'savings', 'balance of payments', 'knowledge', 'methodology', and 'monopoly'. According to Hayek's kindred conceptual analysis, the use of the term 'social' is meaningless in many contexts, famously including ramblings about "social justice" (1957/1967, 1976). More recent progress in disambiguating and clarifying the meanings of terms is submitted by Klein (2012). Depending on the explication of concepts like entrepreneur, entrepreneurial error, and coordination, disputed propositions about equilibrating tendencies of markets become analytically true or empirical hypotheses (see also Selgin 1990).

Lavoie (1985) and Boettke (1998) recognize a more general pattern of misunderstandings between Austrian economists and mainstream economists due to equivocations. If this babel can be further alleviated by economic semantics, if Austrian apriorism is not as extreme as it is sometimes made out to be, and if formal methods cease to be anathema for Austrian economists, then more and more productive communication between the Austrian School and competing research programs becomes possible.[32]

Acknowledgments

I am grateful to Theo Anders, Brecht Arnaert, Erwin Dekker, David Gordon, Marek Hudik, Uskali Mäki, Karl Milford, Scott Scheall, and Rahim Taghizadegan for their valuable recommendations on a previous draft and to Reinhard Schumacher for our exchange on Karl Menger.

Related Chapters

Grayot, J., Chapter 6 "Economic Agency and the Subpersonal Turn in Economics"
Jhun, J., Chapter 23 "Modeling the Possible to Modeling the Actual"
Lecouteux, G., Chapter 4 "Behavioral Welfare Economics and Consumer Sovereignty"
Moscati, I., Chapter 2 "History of Utility Theory"
Spanos, A., Chapter 29 "Philosophy of Econometrics"
Stefánsson, H.O., Chapter 3 "The Economics and Philosophy of Risk"

Verreault-Julien, P., Chapter 22 "Explanation in Economics"
Vredenburgh, K., Chapter 5 "The Economic Concept of a Preference"
Jurgis Karpus and Mantas Radzvilas, Chapter 7 "Game Theory and Rational Reasoning"
Camilla Colombo and Francesco Guala, Chapter 8 "Institutions, Rationality, and Coordination"

Notes

1 For a relativization of Menger's departure from the German Historical School, see Streissler (1990).

2 For an outline of ten central features of the neo-Austrian School, see Boettke (2010). Medium-length introductions to Austrian economics include Holcombe (2014) and Kirzner (1960/1976: 146–185), with the latter focusing on foundational questions. The most popular introductory textbook is Heyne, Boettke, and Prychitko (2013); Schulak and Unterköfler (2011) provide a historically oriented introduction to the Austrian School for non-economists. More extensive takes on Austrian methodology and epistemology can be found in Martin (2015), Nozick (1977), Block (1980), and, focusing on the Misesian and Hayekian branches, respectively, Linsbichler (2017) and Caldwell (2004). The perceived split between a Mises-Rothbard branch and a Hayek-Kirzner branch of neo-Austrian economics is outlined by Salerno (2002); for an external perspective on the purported split, see also Wasserman (2016, 2019: 233–269). Against an overstatement of the differences, we sympathize with Boettke's dictum that, "the best reading of Mises is a Hayekian one and the best reading of Hayek is a Misesian one" (quoted in Horwitz 2004: 308).

3 In the first half of the 20th century, political positions in the Austrian School were more diverse than today. When W. Weber wrote a synoptic view of Austrian economics and economic policy before the rise of neo-Austrian economics in the United States, he considered "Manchester liberalism" to be a personal attitude of Mises but not a characteristic of most Austrian economists, let alone a conclusion based on scientific findings of the Austrian School (Weber 1949: 30). See also (Boettke 1995).

4 This makes rationality research a potential ally of Austrian economics. In contrast to many approaches in behavioral economics, however, Austrian economists tend to question not only the empirical adequacy of expected utility theory but also its normative appeal.

5 By trying to refine and extend the interpretative components of (Austrian) economics, Lavoie (1985/2011) initiated the "hermeneutics debate" within the Austrian School (see also Gordon 1986; Lavoie 1990; Harris 2016).

6 See B. O'Neill (2010) for an entertaining, more extreme example of the importance of framing the choice situation.

7 Sometimes "subjective value theory" and "marginal value theory" are used synonymously. This is unfortunate because, for example, in the German Historical School, there are subjective value theories that are not marginalist (or marginal utility is treated psychologically) and hence can only yield reservational price theories. For subjective value theories before Menger, see Priddat (1997), Milford (2012), and Oakley (1997). See also Ikeda and Yagi (2012).

8 See Stringham (2010) for an excellent breakdown of ten layers of subjectivism.

9 For Lachmann's position at the boundary of the Austrian School and the extension of the "subjectivist revolution," see Lachmann (1977), Storr (2017), Fiorito, Scheall, and Suprinyak (2019).

10 See, for example, Gordon (1993) for a meticulous critique of less consequently subjectivist fellow Austrians' welfare economics.

11 Wieser (1889/1993) aims to identify social value and money price, but he is well aware of and discusses a fundamental problem: such an identification rests on, among other things, the false assumption of equal purchasing power of all market participants. Wieser was heavily criticized by Mises (1949/1998: 205) for a tendency to equate objective money prices with subjective value. Given Mises's own concessions that money prices reflect social value modulo purchasing power at best, Linsbichler (2021a, 2021d) surmises that some of his unconditional propositions in the calculation debates ought to be qualified more carefully.

12 Milford (2008) identifies Hufeland as a precursor of Menger and Hayek, combining methodological individualism and a subjective theory of evaluations, but lacking the equimarginal principle. Whereas neoclassical economists obtain the equimarginal principle as a result of linear optimization, Menger asserts that it can be established as the result of observation (Milford 2012).

13 Similarly, A. Smith draws on "sympathy" and authors of the German Historical School on "Gemeinsinn" ("community spirit") to explain the peaceful stability of social institutions.

14 If people exchange because they intend to exchange, the real question becomes why people have these intentions. Subsequently, the research program becomes psychological, historical, and sociological. Thus,

methodological individualism is also a strategy to secure the autonomy of economics (or other social sciences) from psychology, history, and sociology. This is very much in line with the depsychologizing tendencies of some Austrian economists.

15 Some implicit aggregations are debatable, and one could question whether representative agents qualify for methodological individualism.

16 The details of the restriction of macroeconomics are controversial within the Austrian School. For instance, the most prominent representative of neo-Austrian macroeconomics (Garrison 2001) is contested from within the Austrian School (Hülsmann 2001). See also Wagner (2005, 2020), Horwitz (2000), and Cowen (1998).

17 As one example of a (broadly conceived) empirical problem: against accusations of "atomism," most Austrian economists by no means deny that the human mind may have an irreducibly social dimension. They are, like M. Weber but unlike Hobbes, "sophisticated methodological individualists" (Heath 2014). See also Di Iorio (2015).

18 More recently, Blaug (1992/2006: 45) concurs by declaring ontological individualism to be "trivially true" but denies any necessary implication for methodology.

19 See, e.g., Caldwell 2009; Scheall 2015b; Zanotti and Cachanosky 2015, 2017; Linsbichler 2017, 2021c.

20 Hoppe's argumentation ethics also claims to prove the a priori validity of the nonaggression principle and by implication that of anarchocapitalism. See, for example, Murphy and Callahan (2006) for a summary of and counterarguments to Hoppe's position.

21 Schumpeter's instrumentalism (Shionoya 2005; Milford and Cerman 2011) is one of the reasons for not considering him a full member of the Austrian School.

22 Hülsmann's claim that the Austrian School "has consistently adhered to the postulate of [realisticness]" (1999: 3) might be only slightly overstated. See Caplan (1999, 2001) for objections.

23 It is underappreciated how eminent idealizing assumptions and unrealistic models feature in Austrian economics, notably, the use of Robinsonades and thought experiments by Wieser (see Tokumaru 2016) and the use of "imaginary constructions to which nothing corresponds in reality" (Mises 1949/1998: 202–203). The main purpose of these unrealistic models and counterfactual scenarios, however, is not to describe the world but to highlight contradictions or to indicate hypotheses (see Linsbichler and da Cunha 2021).

24 Popper's "criticism of essentialism does not aim at establishing the nonexistence of essences" (1960/2000: 105). Indeed, Popper endorses realism and anti-instrumentalism, that is, mild essentialism. He even accepted the label "modified essentialism" for his view, albeit grudgingly (1957/1972).

25 See also Mäki (1997) for realism and anti-instrumentalism, that is, at least mild essentialism, in Menger's methodology.

26 See Schweinzer (2000) for a juxtaposition of Spann's essentialist intuitive universalism and mildly essentialist branches of Austrian economics.

27 See, for example, Wutscher, Murphy, and Block (2010) for a neo-Austrian critique of mathematics and modern logic in economics and K. Menger (1972) for a balanced analysis of potential benefits and pitfalls of formal methods in economics. K. Menger developed a decision theory ("logic") for ethical norms and social associations (1934/1974) – one of the first employments of formal models in the social sciences outside economics. Like K. Menger, Hudik (2015) and Linsbichler (2021b) explicitly suggest the compatibility of adequate formal methods and Austrian economics.

28 Rothbard (1973/1997) and others also claim that the functional relationships in mathematics are incapable of adequately dealing with cause and effect as involved in human action. However, various formal methods have been employed to elucidate and explicate the notion of causation employed in natural language.

29 One potential argumentative resource against translations from natural language to formal languages could be obtained by Wieser's (1884) epistemological position, according to which necessarily true knowledge about some phenomena is contained in the sound of the natural language of a people. Therefore, instead of studying these phenomena, "the scientific investigator is allowed to restrict herself to the analysis of language in order to determine the essential characteristics of a phenomenon" (Wieser 1884: 6, author's translation). Given this idiosyncratic epistemological position, arguments against translations from natural language into formal languages could be substantiated. Translations from one natural language into another turn out to be equally problematic though. Ironically, Wieser's role in the Austrian School is not held in high regard by most of those neo-Austrians who strongly object to formal methods in economics. See also Linsbichler 2021b.

30 Appropriately enough, it was Wieser's protégé, H. Mayer, who strongly advised against a publication.

31 See Oliva Cordoba (2017) for a rare example of the application of formal logic in praxeology.

32 For overall optimistic assessments of the contemporary significance and potential future of Austrian economics, see, for example, D'Amico and Martin (2019).

Bibliography

Aimar, T. (2009) *The Economics of Ignorance and Coordination: Subjectivism and the Austrian School of Economics*, Cheltenham: Edward Elgar.

Backhouse, R. (2000) "Austrian Economics and the Mainstream: View from the Boundary," *The Quarterly Journal of Austrian Economics* 3(2): 31–43.

Blaug, M. (1992/2006) *The Methodology of Economics: Or How Economists Explain*, Cambridge: Cambridge University Press.

Block, W. (1980) "On Robert Nozick's 'On Austrian Methodology'," *Inquiry* 23: 397–444.

Boettke, P.J. (1995) "Why Are There No Austrian Socialists? Ideology, Science and the Austrian School," *Journal of the History of Economic Thought* 17: 35–56.

Boettke, P.J. (1996) "What Is Wrong with Neoclassical Economics (and What Is Still Wrong with Austrian Economics)," in F. Foldvary (ed.) *Beyond Neoclassical Economics*, Cheltenham: Edward Elgar Publishing. Available at SSRN: https://ssrn.com/abstract=1530995

Boettke, P. J. (1998) "Economic Calculation: The Austrian Contribution to Political Economy," *Advances in Austrian Economics* 5: 131–158.

Boettke, P.J. (2010) "Introduction," in P.J. Boettke (ed.) *Handbook on Contemporary Austrian Economics* (pp. xi–xviii), Cheltenham, Northampton: Edward Elgar.

Caldwell, B. (2004) *Hayek's Challenge*, Chicago: The University of Chicago Press.

Caldwell, B. (2009) "A Skirmish in the Popper Wars: Hutchison Versus Caldwell on Hayek, Popper, Mises, and Methodology," *Journal of Economic Methodology* 16(3): 315–324.

Caplan, B. (1999) "The Austrian Search for Realistic Foundations," *Southern Economic Journal* 65(4): 823–838.

Caplan, B. (2001) "Probability, Common Sense, and Realism: A Reply to Hülsmann and Block," *The Quarterly Journal of Austrian Economics* 4(2): 69–86.

Costea, D. (2003) "A Critique of Mises's Theory of Monopoly Prices," *The Quarterly Journal of Austrian Economics* 6(3): 47–62.

Cowen, T. (1998) *Risk and Business Cycles: New and Old Austrian Perspectives*, London: Routledge.

D'Amico, D., and Martin, A. (eds.) (2019) *Assessing Austrian Economics: Advances in Austrian Economics*, vol. 24, Bingley: Emerald.

Dekker, E. (2016) *The Viennese Students of Civilization: The Meaning and Context of Austrian Economics Reconsidered*, New York: Cambridge University Press.

Dekker, E. (2020) "On Emancipators, Engineers, and Students: The Appropriate Attitude of the Economist," *The Review of Austrian Economics* 33: 55–68.

Di Iorio, F. (2015) *Cognitive Autonomy and Methodological Individualism: The Interpretative Foundations of Social Life*, Cham: Springer.

"Diskussion." (1972) *Zeitschrift für Nationalökonomie*, 32(1): 111–151.

Ebeling, R.M. (1990) "Introduction," in R.M. Ebeling (ed.) *Money, Method, and the Market Process: Essays by Ludwig Von Mises* (pp. ix–xxvi), Auburn: Praxeology Press of the Ludwig von Mises Institute.

Ferguson, A. (1767) *An Essay on the History of Civil Society*, London: Cadell, Creech, Bell.

Fiorito, L., Scheall, S., and Suprinyak, C.E. (eds.) (2019) *Research in the History of Economic Thought and Methodology. Volume 37B. Including A Symposium on Ludwig Lachmann*, Bingley: Emerald Publishing.

Garrison, R.W. (2001) *Time and Money: The Macroeconomics of Capital Structure. Foundations of the Market Economy*, London and New York: Routledge.

Garzarelli, G., and Kuchar, P. (2018) "Measurement versus Hermeneutics of Capital," *Storia Libera* 4(7): 191–199.

Gordon, D. (1986) *Hermeneutics Versus Austrian Economics*. Available at: https://mises.org/library/hermeneutics-versus-austrian-economics.

Gordon, D. (1993) "Toward a Deconstruction of Utility and Welfare Economics," *The Review of Austrian Economics* 6(2): 99–112.

Harris, J. (2016) "Gadamer, Lavoie, and Their Critics: The Hermeneutics Debate Revisited," *Journal of Markets & Morality* 19(1): 61–78.

Hayek, F.A. (1946/1948) "Individualism: True and False," in F.A. Hayek (ed.) *Individualism and Economic Order* (pp. 1–32), Chicago: The University of Chicago Press.

Hayek, F.A. (1952) *The Sensory Order*, Chicago: University of Chicago Press.

Hayek, F.A. (1952/1964) *The Counter-Revolution of Science: Studies in the Abuse of Reason*, London: Collier-Macmillan.

Hayek, F.A. (1955) "Degrees of Explanation," *The British Journal for the Philosophy of Science* 6(23): 209–225.

Hayek, F.A. (1956/1967) "The Dilemma of Specialization," in F.A. Hayek (ed.) *Studies in Philosophy, Politics and Economics* (pp. 122–132), Chicago: The University of Chicago Press.

Hayek, F.A. (1957/1967) "What's Social? What Does It Mean?" in F.A. Hayek (ed) *Studies in Philosophy, Politics and Economics* (pp. 237–247), Chicago: The University of Chicago Press.

Hayek, F.A. (1967) "The Theory of Complex Phenomena," in F.A. Hayek (ed.) *Studies in Philosophy, Politics and Economics* (pp. 22–42), Chicago: The University of Chicago Press.

Hayek, F.A. (1973/1998) *Law, Legislation and Liberty: A New Statement of the Liberal Principles of Justice and Political Economy*, London: Routledge.

Hayek, F.A. (1976) *The Mirage of Social Justice: Law, Legislation, and Liberty*, Vol. 2, Chicago: University of Chicago Press.

Hayek, F.A. (1988) *The Fatal Conceit: The Errors of Socialism*, edited by W. W. Bartley III, Chicago: University of Chicago Press.

Heath, J. (2014) "Methodological Individualism," *The Stanford Encyclopedia of Philosophy*. Available at: http://plato.stanford.edu/archives/fall2014/entries/methodological-individualism/.

Herbener, J.M. (1997) "The Pareto Rule and Welfare Economics," *The Review of Austrian Economics* 10(1): 79–106.

Heyne, P., Boettke, P.J., and Prychitko, D. (2013) *The Economic Way of Thinking*, 13th ed., Munich: Pearson.

Holcombe, R.G. (2014) *Advanced Introduction to the Austrian School of Economics*, Cheltenham: Edward Elgar.

Hoppe, H. (1995) *Economic Science and the Austrian Method*, Auburn: Mises Institute.

Horwitz, S. (2000) *Microfoundations and Macroeconomics: An Austrian Perspective*, London: Routledge.

Horwitz, S. (2004) "Monetary Calculation and the Unintended Extended Order: The Misesian Microfoundations of the Hayekian Great Society," *The Review of Austrian Economics* 17(4): 307–321.

Hudik, M. (2012) "Transitivity: A Comment on Block and Barnett," *The Quarterly Journal of Austrian Economics* 15(4): 456–462.

Hudik, M. (2015) "'Mises and Hayek Mathematized': Toward Mathematical Austrian Economics," in P.L. Bylund, D. Howden, and J.T. Salerno (eds.) *The Next Generation of Austrian Economics: Essays in Honor of Joseph T. Salerno* (pp. 105–122), Auburn: Mises Institute.

Hülsmann, J.G. (1999) "Economic Science and Neoclassicism," *The Quarterly Journal of Austrian Economics* 2(4): 3–20.

Hülsmann, J.G. (2001) "Garrisonian Macroeconomics," *The Quarterly Journal of Austrian Economics* 4(3): 33–41.

Hutchison, T.W. (1998) "Ultra-Deductivism from Nassau Senior to Lionel Robbins and Daniel Hausman," *Journal of Economic Methodology* 5(1): 43–91.

Ikeda, Y., and Yagi, K. (eds.) (2012) *Subjectivism and Objectivism in the History of Economic Thought*, London: Routledge.

Jaffe, W. (1976) "Menger, Jevons and Walras Dehomogenized," *Economic Inquiry* 14: 511–524.

Kaufmann, F. (1929) "Soziale Kollektiva," *Zeitschrift für Nationalökonomie* 1: 294–308.

Kirzner, I. (1960/1976) *The Economic Point of View: An Essay in the History of Economic Thought*, 2nd ed., Kansas City: Sheed and Ward.

Kirzner, I. (2001) *Ludwig von Mises: The Man and His Economics*, Wilmington: ISI Books.

Klamer, A. (1994) "Formalism in Twentieth-Century Economics," in P. Boettke (ed.) *The Elgar Companion to Austrian Economics* (pp. 48–53), Brookfield: Edward Elgar.

Klein, D. (2012) *Knowledge and Coordination: A Liberal Interpretation*, Oxford and New York: Oxford University Press.

Kurrild-Klitgaard, P. (2001) "On Rationality, Ideal Types and Economics: Alfred Schutz and the Austrian School," *The Review of Austrian Economics* 14(2–3): 119–143.

Kurrild-Klitgaard, P. (2003) "The Viennese Connection. Alfred Schutz and the Austrian School," *The Quarterly Journal of Austrian Economics* 6(2): 35–67.

Lachmann, L. (1977) *Capital, Expectations, and the Market Process: Essays on the Theory of the Market Economy*, Kansas City: Sheed Andrews and McMeel.

Lavoie, D. (1985) *Rivalry and Central Planning: The Socialist Calculation Debate Reconsidered*, Cambridge: Cambridge University Press.

Lavoie, D. (1985/2011) "The Interpretive Dimension of Economics: Science, Hermeneutics, and Praxeology," *The Review of Austrian Economics* 24: 91–128.

Lavoie, D. (ed.) (1990) *Economics and Hermeneutics*, New York: Routledge.

Leeson, P.T., and Boettke, P.J. (2006) "Was Mises Right?" *Review of Social Economy* 64(2): 247–265.

Linsbichler, A. (2017) *Was Ludwig von Mises a Conventionalist? A New Analysis of the Epistemology of the Austrian School of Economics*, Basingstoke: Palgrave Macmillan.

Linsbichler, A. (2019) "Felix Kaufmann – 'A Reasonable Positivist'?" in F. Stadler (ed.) *Ernst Mach – Life, Work, Influence* (pp. 709–719), Cham: Springer.

Linsbichler, A. (2021c) "Austrian Economics Without Extreme Apriorism: Construing the Fundamental Axiom of Praxeology as Analytic," *Synthese*, 198: 3359-3390. https://link.springer.com/article/10.1007/s11229-019-02150-8.
Linsbichler, A. (2021a) "Rationalities and Their Limits: Reconstructing Neurath's and Mises's Prerequisites in the Early Socialist Calculation Debates," *Research in the History of Economic Thought and Methodology*, 39B, : 95-128. https://doi.org/10.1108/S0743-41542021000039B00.
Linsbichler, A. (2021b) "Realisticness and Sprachgeist: The Troubled Relationship Between (Austrian) Economics and Mathematics revisited," Center for the History of Political Economy at Duke University Working Paper Series, 2021-15. https://papers.ssrn.com/sol3/papers.cfm?abstract_id=3897919.
Linsbichler, A. (2021d). Viennese Late Enlightenment and the Early Socialist Calculation Debates: Rationalities and Their Limits. Center for the History of Political Economy at Duke University Working Paper Series, 2021-16. https://papers.ssrn.com/sol3/papers.cfm?abstract_id=3904011
Linsbichler, A., and da Cunha, I.F. (2021) "Otto Neurath's Scientific Utopianism Revisited – A Refined Model for Utopias in Thought Experiments," Submitted.
Lipski, J. (2021). Austrian economics without extreme apriorism: A critical reply. Synthese (forthcoming). https://doi.org/10.1007/s11229-021-03249-7
Long, R. (2004) "Anti-Psychologism in Economics: Wittgenstein and Mises," *The Review of Austrian Economics* 17(4): 345–369.
Long, R. (2006) "Realism and Abstraction in Economics: Mises and Aristotle versus Friedman," *The Quarterly Journal of Austrian Economics* 9(3): 3–23.
Long, R. (2008) *Wittgenstein, Praxeology, and Frege's Three Realms*. Available at: www.praxeology.net/praxeo.htm on March 7, 2016.
Long, R. (2010) *Wittgenstein, Austrian Economics, and the Logic of Action: Praxeological Investigations*, Working Copy. Available at: http://praxeology.net/wiggy-draft.pdf on March 7, 2016.
Machlup, F. (1969) "If Matter Could Talk," in S. Morgenbesser, P. Suppes, and M. White (eds.) *Philosophy, Science, and Method* (pp. 286–305), New York: St. Martin's Press.
Machlup, F. (1991) *Economic Semantics*, 2nd ed., New Brunswick and London: Transaction Publishers.
Mäki, U. (1990a) "Mengerian Economics in Realist Perspective," *History of Political Economy* 22(annual supplement): 289–310.
Mäki, U. (1990b) "Scientific Realism and Austrian Explanation," *Review of Political Economy* 2(3): 310–344.
Mäki, U. (1992) "The Market as an Isolated Causal Process: A Metaphysical Ground for Realism," in B. Caldwell and S. Böhm (eds.) *Austrian Economics: Tensions and New Directions* (pp. 35–66), Boston: Springer.
Mäki, U. (1997) "Universals and the Methodenstreit: A Re-examination of Carl Menger's Conception of Economics as an Exact Science," *Studies in the History and Philosophy of Science* 28(3): 475–495.
Martin, A. (2015) "Austrian Methodology: A Review and Synthesis," in P.J. Boettke and C.J. Coyne (eds.) *The Oxford Handbook of Austrian Economics* (pp. 13–42), Oxford: Oxford University Press.
Mayer, T. (1998) "Boettke's Critique of Mainstream Economics: An Empiricist's Response," *Critical Review* 12(1–2): 151–171.
Megger, D. (2021). "Determinism, free will, and the Austrian School of Economics", Journal of Economic Methodology, 28(3): 304-321. DOI: 10.1080/1350178X.2021.1926528
Menger, C. (1871/2004) *Principles of Economics*, Auburn: Ludwig von Mises Institute.
Menger, C. (1883/1985) *Investigations into the Method of the Social Sciences with Special Reference to Economics*, New York and London: New York University Press.
Menger, K. (1934/1974) *Morality, Decision and Social Organizations: Toward a Logic of Ethics*, Dordrecht: D. Reidel.
Menger, K. (1936/1979) "Remarks on the Law of Diminishing Returns: A Study in Meta-Economics," in K. Menger (ed.) *Selected Papers in Logic and Foundations, Didactics, Economics, Vienna Circle Collection 10* (pp. 279–302), Dordrecht: Springer.
Menger, K. (1972) "Österreichischer Marginalismus und mathematische Ökonomie," *Zeitschrift für Nationalökonomie* 32: 19–28.
Milford, K. (2008) "Inductivism and Anti-Essentialism in Menger's Work," in G. Campagnolo and S. Haltmayer (eds.) *Carl Menger. Discussed on the Basis of New Findings* (pp. 59–86), Frankfurt A. M.: Lang.
Milford, K. (2010) "A Note on Menger's Problem Situation and Non-Essentialist Approach to Economics," in H. Hagemann, T. Nishizawa, and Y. Ikeda (eds.) *Austrian Economics in Transition: From Carl Menger to Friedrich Hayek* (pp. 154–175), New York: Palgrave Macmillan.
Milford, K. (2012) "The Empirical and Inductivist Economics of Professor Menger," in J. Backhaus (ed.) *Handbook of the History of Economic Thought* (pp. 415–436), Dordrecht: Springer.
Milford, K. (2015) "Zur Entwicklung der Volkswirtschaftslehre an der Universität Wien von 1763 bis 1976," in K. Fröschl, G. Müller, T. Olechowski, and B. Schmidt-Lauber (eds.) *Reflexive Innenansichten aus der*

Universität: Disziplinengeschichten zwischen Wissenschaft, Gesellschaft und Politik (pp. 341–354), Göttingen: V&R Unipress.

Milford, K., and Cerman, M. (2011) "Scheinsatzpositionen als Begründungsversuche der theoretischen Ökonomie," in P. Berger, P. Eigner, A. Resch (eds.) *Die vielen Gesichter des wirtschaftlichen Wandels* (pp. 55–82), Wien: LIT-Verlag.

Milonakis, D., and Fine, B. (2009) *From Political Economy to Economics Method, the Social and the Historical in the Evolution of Economic Theory*, New York: Routledge.

Mises, L. (1933/2003) *Epistemological Problems of Economics*, Auburn: Ludwig von Mises Institute.

Mises, L. (1940) *Nationalökonomie: Theorie des Handelns und Wirtschaftens*, Genf: Editions Union.

Mises, L. (1940/2009) *Memoirs*, Auburn: Ludwig von Mises Institute.

Mises, L. (1949/1998) *Human Action: A Treatise on Economics*, Auburn: Ludwig von Mises Institute.

Mises, L. (1957/2005) *Theory and History: An Interpretation of Social and Economic Evolution*, Indianapolis: Liberty Fund.

Mises, L. (1962) *The Ultimate Foundation of Economic Science: An Essay on Method*, Princeton: D. Van Nostrand.

Morgenstern, O. (1963) *Limits to the Uses of Mathematics in Economics*, Research Memorandum. Available at: https://apps.dtic.mil/dtic/tr/fulltext/u2/296935.pdf.

Murphy, R.P., and Callahan, G. (2006) "Hans-Hermann Hoppe's Argumentation Ethic: A Critique," *Journal of Libertarian Studies* 20(2): 53–64.

Nemeth, E. (1999) *Denken in Beziehungen – Beiträge zur Ortsbestimmung der Erkenntnisphilosophie*, habilitation thesis, University of Vienna, Vienna.

Nozick, R. (1977) "On Austrian Methodology," *Synthese* 36: 353–392.

Oakley, A. (1997) *The Foundations of Austrian Economics from Menger to Mises: A Critico-Historical Retrospective of Subjectivism*, Cheltenham: Edward Elgar.

O'Driscoll, G., and Rizzo, M. (2015) *Austrian Economics Re-examined. The Economics of Time and Ignorance*, London: Routledge.

Oliva Cordoba, M. (2017) "Uneasiness and Scarcity: An Analytic Approach towards Ludwig von Mises's Praxeology," *Axiomathes* 27: 521–529.

O'Neill, B. (2010) "Choice and Indifference: A Critique of the Strict Preference Approach," *The Quarterly Journal of Austrian Economics* 13(1): 71–98.

O'Neill, J. (1995) "Essences and Markets," *The Monist* 78(3): 258–275.

Pham, A. (2017) "Mainstream Economics and the Austrian School: Toward Reunification," *Erasmus Journal for Philosophy and Economics* 10(1): 41–63.

Popper, K. (1957/1972) "The Aim of Science," in K. Popper (ed.) *Objective Knowledge: An Evolutionary Approach* (pp. 191–205), Oxford: Clarendon Press.

Popper, K. (1960/2000) "Three Views Concerning Human Knowledge," in K. Popper (ed) *Conjectures and Refutations: The Growth of Scientific Knowledge* (pp. 97–119), London: Routledge.

Priddat, B. (ed.) (1997) *Wert, Meinung, Bedeutung: Die Tradition der subjektiven Wertlehre in der deutschen Nationalökonomie vor Menger*, Marburg: Metropolis-Verlag.

Puster, R. (2014) "Dualismen und ihre Hintergründe," in L. Mises (ed.) *Theorie und Geschichte: Eine Interpretation sozialer und wirtschaftlicher Entwicklung* (pp. 7–50), München: Akston.

Rothbard, M. (1951) "Praxeology: Reply to Mr. Schuller," *American Economic Review* 41(5): 943–946.

Rothbard, M. (1952/2009) "A Note on Mathematical Economics," Bettina Greaves Papers, Mises Archives at the Mises Institute, Auburn, Alabama, September 1. Available at: https://mises.org/library/note-mathematical-economics.

Rothbard, M. (1956/1997) "Toward a Reconstruction of Utility and Welfare Economics," in M. Rothbard (ed.) *The Logic of Action, Volume One. Method, Money and the Austrian School* (pp. 211–254), Cheltenham: Elgar.

Rothbard, M. (1957) "In Defense of 'Extreme Apriorism'," *Southern Economic Journal*: 314–320, January.

Rothbard, M. (1973/1997) "Praxeology as the Method of the Social Sciences," in M. Rothbard (ed.) *The Logic of Action, Volume One: Method, Money and the Austrian School* (pp. 28–57), Cheltenham: Elgar.

Rothbard, M. (1976/1997) "Praxeology: The Method of Austrian Economics," in M. Rothbard (ed.) *The Logic of Action, Volume One: Method, Money and the Austrian School* (pp. 59–79), Cheltenham: Elgar.

Salerno, J.T. (2002) "The Rebirth of Austrian Economics – In the Light of Austrian Economics," *The Quarterly Journal of Austrian Economics* 5(4): 111–128.

Scheall, S. (2015a) "Lesser Degrees of Explanation: Further Implications of F.A. Hayek's Methodology of Sciences of Complex Phenomena," *Erasmus Journal for Philosophy and Economics* 8(1): 42–60.

Scheall, S. (2015b) "Hayek the Apriorist?" *Journal of the History of Economic Thought* 37(1): 87–110.

Scheall, S. (2017) "What Is so Extreme About Mises's Extreme Apriorism?" *Journal of Economic Methodology* 24(3): 226–249.

Schulak, E.M., and Unterköfler, H. (2011) *The Austrian School of Economics: A History of Its Ideas, Ambassadors, and Institutions*, Auburn: Ludwig von Mises Institute.
Schumacher, R., and Scheall, S. (2020) "Karl Menger's Unfinished Biography of his Father: New Insights into Carl Menger's Life Through 1889," *CHOPE Working Paper*, No. 2020-01.
Schumpeter, J. (1908/1980) *Methodological Individualism*, Bruxelles: Institutum Europaeum.
Schweinzer, P. (2000) "Two Competing Paradigms in Austrian Economic Theory," *Notizie di Politeia* 16(59): 44–66.
Selgin, G. (1990) *Praxeology and Understanding: An Analysis of the Controversy in Austrian Economics*, Auburn: The Ludwig von Mises Institute.
Shionoya, Y. (2005) "Instrumentalism in Schumpeter's Economic Methodology," in Y. Shionoya (ed.) *The Soul of the German Historical School* (pp. 65–96), Boston: Springer.
Smith, A. (1776/1976) *An Inquiry into the Nature and Causes of the Wealth of Nations*, Chicago: University of Chicago Press.
Smith, B. (1990) "Aristotle, Menger, Mises: An Essay in the Metaphysics of Economics," *History of Political Economy* 22(annual supplement): 263–288.
Smith, B. (1996) "In Defense of Extreme (Fallibilistic) Apriorism," *Journal of Libertarian Studies* 12(1): 179–192.
Sowell, T. (1987/2007) *A Conflict of Visions: Ideological Origins of Political Struggles*, New York: Basic Books.
Storr, V.H. (2010) "The Facts of the Social Sciences Are What People Believe and Think," in P.J. Boettke (ed.) *Handbook on Contemporary Austrian Economics* (pp. 30–40), Cheltenham: Edward Elgar.
Storr, V.H. (2017) "Ludwig Lachmann's Peculiar Status within Austrian Economics," *Review of Austrian Economics* 32: 63–75.
Streissler, E. (1990) "Carl Menger, der deutsche Nationalökonom," in B.P. Priddat (ed.) *Wert, Meinung, Bedeutung: Die Tradition der subjektiven Wertlehre in der deutschen Nationalökonomie vor Menger* (pp. 33–88), Marburg: Metropolis-Verlag.
Stringham, E. (2010) "Economic Value and Cost are Subjective," in P.J. Boettke (ed.) *Handbook on Contemporary Austrian Economics* (pp. 43–66), Cheltenham: Edward Elgar.
Tokumaru, N. (2016) "From Gedankenexperiment to Social Economics. Wieser's Empiricism and the Social Sciences," in N. Tokumaru (ed.) *Social Preference, Institutions, and Distribution: An Experimental and Philosophical Approach* (pp. 133–154), Singapore: Springer.
Uebel, T. (2019) "Rationality and Pseudorationality in Political Economy: Neurath, Mises, Weber," in J. Cat and A.T. Tuboly (eds.) *Neurath Reconsidered: New Sources and Perspectives* (pp. 197–216), Cham: Springer.
Wagner, R. (2005) "Austrian Cycle Theory and the Prospect of a Coordinationist Macroeconomics," in J. Backhaus (ed.) *Modern Applications of Austrian Thought* (pp. 77–92), London: Routledge.
Wagner, R. (2020) *Macroeconomics as Systems Theory: Transcending the Micro-Macro Dichotomy*, Cham: Palgrave Macmillan.
Wasserman, J. (2016) "'Un-Austrian' Austrians? Haberler, Machlup, and Morgenstern, and the Post-Emigration Elaboration of Austrian Economics," *Research in the History of Economic Thought and Methodology* 34A: 93–124.
Wasserman, J. (2019) *The Marginal Revolutionaries: How Austrian Economists Fought the War of Ideas*, New Haven and London: Yale University Press.
Weber, W. (1949) *Wirtschaftswissenschaft und Wirtschaftspolitik in Österreich*, Wien: Springer-Verlag.
Wieser, F. (1884) *Über den Ursprung und die Hauptgesetze des wirthschaftlichen Wertes*, Wien: Hölder.
Wieser, F. (1889/1893) *Natural Value*, London and New York: Macmillan & Co.
Wutscher, R., Murphy, R.P., and Block, W. (2010) "Mathematics in Economics: An Austrian Methodological Critique," *Philosophical Investigations* 33(1): 44–66.
Zanotti, G., and Cachanosky, N. (2015) "Implications of Machlup's Interpretation of Mises's Epistemology," *Journal of the History of Economic Thought* 37(1): 111–138.
Zanotti, G., and Cachanosky, N. (2017) *What Is so Extreme About Mises's Extreme Apriorism? Reply to Scott Scheall.* SSRN. Available at: https://ssrn.com/abstract=2875122.

13
REPRESENTATION

Hsiang-Ke Chao

1. Introduction

Representation is omnipresent in science as well as in the ordinary business of life. We perhaps "use representations in nearly all our reasoning about the world" (Swoyer 1991: 449). Many things are used to represent: such as models, maps, miniatures, numbers, equations, sentences, words, simulations, graphs, diagrams, images, and more (Swoyer 1991; Giere 2004; Jhun, Chapter 23; Kuorikoski and Lehtinen, Chapter 26). Investigation into this issue has been a long-standing and important topic in the philosophy of science, and the same holds true for the philosophy of economics. Although the philosophical discussion of scientific representation is usually related to models, to which philosophers of economics contribute greatly, historical and contemporary economic practices provide a rich source for the analysis of economists' plural practices of representations. Consider the following two quotes:

> Regarding choice as a relation, we restate the problem at hand, if *R* [weak preference] is a complete, reflexive relation, then what conditions insure [*sic*] that there exists a real valued utility function which *represents R*.
>
> (Rader 1963: 229; emphasis added)

> Phillips curve, graphic *representation* of the economic relationship between the rate of unemployment (or the rate of change of unemployment) and the rate of change of money wages.
>
> (*Encyclopedia Britannica*; emphasis added)[1]

The preceding quotes suggest some key aspects of the nature and scope of scientific representation. First, representation is concerned with a relationship between the *representational medium* or *medium* (utility function; the Phillips curve) and the *target system* or *target* (weak preference; inflation-unemployment relationship). This can be roughly stated as

> *X* represents *Y*,

where *X* is the medium and *Y* is the target. This general statement is subject to modifications. According to Roman Frigg and James Nguyen's (2020) latest examination, a general framework of

 DOI: 10.4324/9781315739793-16

a philosophical account of representation must address certain problems and satisfy certain conditions, and they clearly delineate such problems and conditions throughout their book. While their account covers a great deal of scientific representation, *models* form the central theme, focusing on how they represent the target systems. In the preceding quotes, both utility functions and the Phillips curve are models for economists that conform not only to Frigg and Nguyen's account but also to the economic methodology of what Roger Backhouse (2007) called "representation through modeling."

However, models come with different *forms*. Because different forms of models play a dominant epistemic role in reasoning in economics (see Morgan 2012), the discussion of representation in economics could follow suit in terms of different forms of representational media. As indicated in the preceding quotes, Trout Rader's article reflects economists' search for a mathematical utility function in order to provide a numerical way to represent preferences. In contrast, *Britannica*'s definition of the Phillips curve indicates a diagrammatic representation of the trade-off between the rate of inflation and the unemployment rate. Recent studies on the history and philosophy of economics suggest that although models are viewed as providing surrogative reasoning, they have different forms and different modes of reasoning. Conversely, the form may dictate the mode of reasoning (Morgan 2012), so that a model's epistemic reasoning power can be form dependent (Chao 2018).

This kind of form dependence helps to classify various types of representation in economics and to understand their unique characteristics in terms of reasoning power. Therefore, this chapter discusses economic representation in terms of different forms and examines the nature and usages of economic representation from the perspectives of models, measurements, and diagrams.

2. Accounts of Representation

2.1 Representation-of vs. Representation-as

Nelson Goodman once put forward the "most naïve view of representation":

> *A* represents *B* if and only if *A* appreciably resembles *B*, or *A* represents *B* to the extent that *A* resembles *B*.
>
> (Goodman 1968: 3–4)

Goodman's naïve view of representation is based on resemblance, which is thought of as a natural and legitimate feature connecting two objects in a representational relationship. Subscribing to the requirement of resemblance, Ronald Giere's (1988, 1999, 2004) well-known, model-based approach calls for the property of *similarity* between the model and the target system. The *similarity view* of representation proposes that *X* represents *Y* if and only if *X* and *Y* are similar in relevant respects and to relevant degrees. However, where there is similarity, there is dissimilarity, as a model's representational relationship to the target system is usually restricted to certain aspects and degrees, which could lead to a vain conclusion because everything is similar to everything else. Also, similarity is symmetrical, while representation is usually asymmetrical (Goodman 1968; van Fraassen 2008). Moreover, similarity may not be the right criterion for successful representation, as in practice there has to be *distortion* in order for representation to be successful (van Fraassen 2008). The problem is to what degree *misrepresentation* (representation lacking in accuracy) is permitted in actual practice.

To improve the naïve view, we need to further distinguish between *representation-of* and *representation-as*. Representation-of characterizes the representation relationship as binary. In contrast, representation-as can be a ternary relationship:

> *X* represents *Y* as *Z*.

Caricature is a typical case of representation-as: a caricature represents Winston Churchill as a bulldog (Elgin's 2010 example); another represents King Louis-Philippe I as a pear (Morgan's 2012 example). Representation-as is offered as a better account for scientific representation, especially concerning how a scientific model represents its target system (Frigg and Nguyen 2017). Thomas Schelling's checkerboard model of segregation clearly contains this ternary representational relationship: his model represents the space in which the social phenomenon of segregation arises as a checkerboard.

If representation is regarded as the practice of representing, the role of *representer* has to be emphasized. Representation is a matter of *use*: it is about how the representer uses an object to represent the target system as something he or she intends to do. However, as Giere (2004) observes, because scientists are intentional agents, their practices should have a goal or purpose. Thus, to adopt his form of representation that *S* uses *X* to represent *Y* for purposes *P*, representation-as can be defined thus:

> *S* uses *X* to represent *Y* as *Z* for purposes *P*.

In sum, scientists' purposes can be manifold and various, but the general considerations are reasoning and inference. It is therefore essential that representation incorporates both the role and the purpose of the user (scientist). With reference to diagrammatic representation, Morgan expresses a similar point, that "[d]iagrams don't draw themselves . . . And nor do diagrams use themselves. Rather, diagrams are made and shared within a community of scientific users" (Morgan 2020: 234). With regard to the purpose, scientists use diagrams not just to visualize theoretical or empirical target systems but to reason with them as tools (Morgan 2020: 225).

2.2 Analogy and Misrepresentation

Although the philosophical accounts of representation emphasize the role of users and purposes, there is a question regarding whether the representability of the same representational medium, such as a model, varies due to a change in users and purposes. The "hydraulic Keynesianism" developed since the 1930s subsequently became the "orthodox" interpretation of Keynes' theory (Coddington 1976; Snowdon and Vane 2005: 70–71). But its models are regarded by post-Keynesian economists such as Joan Robinson as a "distortion" or "bastardization" of Keynes' original ideas (Snowdon and Vane 2005: 113) and are therefore not good representations of Keynesian theory. Given that distortion or idealization is also commonplace in modeling, misrepresentation is inevitable. Reiss once wrote that, "all models . . . misrepresent their targets" (Reiss 2013: 128). One kind of misrepresentation Reiss mentions concerns Mary Hesse's negative analogies: for instance, money does not have the property of wetness like the water in the Phillips Machine, yet if the Phillips Machine is justified by the user's purpose, we can say that the Phillips Machine may still be a good representation of the UK economy for a specific purpose (Reiss, Ibid.).[2]

The view of representation-as allows us more flexibility in interpreting those representations based on similarity. Specifically, it also refines our understanding of analogical models, because analogies are usually based on similarities between two systems in certain aspects and to certain degrees. Since Hesse's classic work on analogy and models, there has been a resurgence in the study of analogical reasoning in philosophy of science. However, the core issues are still whether a given model corresponds to what Hesse regards as an analogy, consisting of analogical relations with another model, or with the theoretical description of the world (Hesse 2000: 299), and whether it allows scientists to apply something familiar to their study and gain new insight. Hesse (1966) described the similarities in observable properties of two objects as a *material analogy* and analogy by the same mathematical form as *formal analogy*. Objects are formally analogous to one another if they have "the same mathematical formalism," meaning "similarity of mathematical structure" (Hesse 1953: 203). The difference between formal and material analogies may lie in abstractness vs. observableness and functions vs. properties. In practice, analogical models in economics benefit from both formally and materially analogical reasoning. Without an existing formal analogy, economists have long seen money as liquid (Hume), distinguishing between stock and flow variables in an analogy with water (Fisher 1896). The hydraulic metaphor and analogy allow economists to construct formal models, but while the formal models such as those of hydraulic Keynesianism are not constructed using the same mathematical forms as any particular theory of hydraulic mechanics, the mechanical analogy did inspire economists to construct a material, three-dimensional, hydraulic mechanical model, the Phillips Machine, to represent the Keynesian macroeconomy.

To rationalize the existence of Keynesian models in various forms, one can say that they share the same structure. The IS-LM diagram, the Phillips Machine, and other types of Keynesian models embed a structure equivalent to their algebraic counterparts. The maintenance of "the same mathematical form" in different contexts is interpreted by philosophers of science as evidence of structural realism during theory change (Worrall 1989), or the existence of computational templates (Humphreys 2002, 2004). The case of Keynesian models depicts a situation where models representing the same theory but in different forms have the same structure. From Patrick Suppes' (2002) reductionist perspective, they can be reduced to a set-theoretical entity expressing the fundamental structure shared by all models. This is the uniqueness theorem in Suppes' account of the representational theory of measurement that will be introduced in Section 4, but if we subscribe to the form-dependent view, each form would afford a specific way of reasoning so that its representational value is unique.

3. Models as Representation

3.1 From Bildtheorie to Model

Analogical reasoning in economics can be a result of interdisciplinary model transfer from other sciences. There are abundant examples in the history of economics that demonstrate models traveling from other disciplines. Morgan (1999) studied Irving Fisher's analogical models of monetary theory. Harro Maas (2005) did the same for 19th century political economist William Stanley Jevons' mechanical reasoning. Philip Mirowski (1989) has argued that the history of economics can be interpreted in terms of physics transfer, as economists rely on metaphors and analogies from physics in theory construction. In contrast, Marcel Boumans observed (Boumans 1993) that the work of Jan Tinbergen during the early 20th century belongs to a "limited physics transfer" as it involves only the "method of analogy of the mathematical form" that Tinbergen borrowed from physics in his modeling of business cycle phenomena.

Tinbergen was among the earliest economists to introduce the term "model" to economics, and he was one of the first-generation econometric model-builders. (For more on models in economics, see also Jhun, Chapter 23.) Trained as a physicist, Tinbergen adopted the methodology of a line of great physicists: James Clark Maxwell, Heinrich Hertz, Ludwig Boltzmann, and Paul Ehrenfest. They all used models (or *schemes*) to represent the target system based on model users' cognitive abilities to construct *Bilder* (images) of the world. Hertz wrote that the model-target relation is "precisely the same as the relation of the images which our mind forms of things to the things themselves" (quoted in Boumans 2005: 27). As Tinbergen adopted this *Bildtheorie* (picture theory) of science, it shows that economists only borrow from physics the same mathematical forms for building models to represent economic phenomena, as compared with van Fraassen's (2008) discussion of *Bildtheorie* that advocates an empiricist structuralism asserting that science represents only structure in science.

According to van Fraassen, what is essential to empiricist structuralism is the slogan, "all we know is structure." This is construed as follows:

> I. Science represents the empirical phenomena as embeddable in certain *abstract structures* (theoretical models).
> II. Those abstract structures are describable only up to structural isomorphism.
>
> (van Fraassen 2008: 238)

Van Fraassen is a representative of the *semantic view* of scientific theory (van Fraassen 1980, 1989). The semantic view contrasts with the *received view* in their focus on the mapping between two types of models representing the theory and the real world, respectively. The scheme of representation according to the semantic view is more clearly laid down by Giere, who held a realist conception in opposition to van Fraassen's empiricist stance. In order to understand scientific representation in the relationships between theories and the world, Giere drew a five-stage diagram to denote his model-based account of theories. The diagram shows a two-directional scheme. From the top down, scientists first use *principles and specific conditions*, which generate *representational models* at the next stage. In the other direction, analysis of the *world (including data)* generates *models of data*. These meet at a middle stage of *specific hypotheses and generalizations*, where representational models are mediated by models of data (Giere 2006: 60–61).

3.2 Dichotomies of Representation

Giere's schematic chart highlights the need to specify the difference between theoretical and empirical aspects of representation, corresponding to theoretical and empirical models, respectively, in scientific practice. The conventional view of the rational scientific process was to test a theoretical hypothesis via testing theoretical models against empirical data; thus, the distinction between theoretical and empirical models did not seem relevant. Not until Suppes argued for the importance of models of data, proposing a five-level hierarchy of empirical model building from the top down that includes *specific models*, *models of experiment*, *models of data*, *experimental design*, and *ceteris paribus conditions* (Suppes 1962: 259), did such a distinction draw the attention of philosophers of science. Economists, however, were already conscious of the theoretical-empirical model divide. Despite the possibility of various conceptions of what constitutes theoretical and empirical models, the divide not only shows the autonomy of models – that there is no one genre of model that entirely depends on theory or the world (Morgan and Morrison 1999) – but also emphasizes the need for classification of target-oriented representation. Accordingly, we can have models *representing theory* and models *representing the world* (Morgan and Morrison 1999).

Because models are independent of theory, there is a distinction between *direct* and *indirect* representation (Godfrey-Smith 2006; Weisberg 2007). *Abstract direct representation*, such as Dmitri Mendeleev's periodic table, aims to directly represent data or real-world phenomena without going through a secondary system. In contrast, model-building is an indirect representation, because models are built and used to represent not a specific, real target system but a hypothetical, imaginary one. Modelers take a detour to study real-world phenomena through their models. The Lotka-Volterra predator-prey model in biology and Schelling's segregation model in economics are considered by Michael Weisberg as examples of indirect representation. They also exhibit the three-stage procedure of scientific modeling proposed by Weisberg, in which the modeler does not consider an assessment of the relationship between the model and the target system until the final stage, if such an assessment is necessary (Weisberg 2007: 209).

The distinction between direct and indirect representation is also related to the ontology of the target. Direct representation aims at specific real targets, while indirect representation provides imagined or hypothetical systems. In extreme cases where a model does not have a target system at all, this is known as a *targetless model* (Frigg and Nguyen 2020: 13), yielding *targetless representation*.

The distinction between direct and indirect representation is not without criticism. Skeptics points out that there is no clear-cut separation between direct and indirect representation in the case studies used by the authors to exemplify such a distinction (Scholl and Räz 2013). Additionally, anything that uses "surrogates" to study real-world targets is inevitably indirect (Knuuttila and Loettgers 2017). Because Godfrey-Smith's and Weisberg's purpose is to stress the existence of different types of theorizing, the distinction between direct and indirect representation does not fully apply to economic modeling practice precisely because of the theoretical vs. empirical model divide. Empirical modeling, while not performed for the purpose of theorizing, can be a direct representation of the world. A better taxonomy would be to adopt Backhouse's (2007) *representation through modeling* mentioned previously and *representation without explicit modeling*. The latter refers to the description of economic phenomena by statements (e.g., noncliometric economic history) or statistical data (e.g., national income accounting), in which economic theory plays little or no role. Thus, nonexplicit modeling may cover a wide range of practices, including model-free activities and theory-free modeling (e.g., the vector autoregression (VAR) approach), which may both be regarded as direct representation.

4. Measurement as Representation

4.1 Representational Theory of Measurement

Formal or mathematical representation, being central to economic representation, seeks to find adequate mathematical functions to represent the structure and properties of the target system. Consider Gerard Debreu's (1954) classic paper on the use of a numerical function to represent a preference order: he seeks to define a real-value function that preserves the order of preferences, especially pondering whether we can find a numerical function to represent a complete order. Swoyer (1991: 451) identifies the *applications problem*: how an abstract theory can apply to a concrete reality. His solution is similar to the semantic view, proposing the practice of *structural representation* as follows: "the pattern of relations among the constituents of the represented phenomena is mirrored by the pattern of relations among the constitutions of the representation itself" (Swoyer 1991: 452).

While there are abundant applications and interpretations of economic models in terms of philosophical structuralism (see the survey in Chao 2009), it should be noted that economics has its own definitions and forms of structure, as exemplified by the methodology of econometric modeling from the structural econometric model to the Lucas critique of the New Classical School of macroeconomics (see also Spanos, Chapter 29). The present notion of structure in economics is a set of invariant relations under intervention, which is comparable to the recent invariance accounts of causal structure in the philosophy of science (Clarke, Chapter 21). When structuralists assert that representation is aimed at structure only, the claim does not necessarily mean the aim of preserving the invariant economic structure (see Chao 2009).

Swoyer's applications problem and its solution of structural representation can be best understood by the theory and practice of measurement, which he also regarded as an exemplar of his account. At the turn of the 20th century, Bertrand Russell already viewed measurement as an applications problem, describing it as:

> [m]easurement of magnitudes is, in its most general sense, any method by which a unique and reciprocal correspondence is established between all or some of the magnitudes of a kind and all or some of the numbers, integral, rational, or real, as the case may be.
>
> (Russell 1903: 176)

Or as S.S. Stevens, a pioneer of measurement theory, put it, measurement is to assign numerals to objects according to a rule – any rule (Stevens 1959: 19). However, for each type of numerical assignment, that is, measurement scale, a set of corresponding conditions needs to be satisfied in order to guarantee that the measurement is adequate. Swoyer's account is consistent with the representational theory of measurement, as represented by the three-volume set, *Foundations of Measurement*, by David Krantz, Duncan Luce, Suppes, and Amos Tversky (Krantz et al. 1971; Suppes et al. 1989; Luce et al. 1990). Although the representational theory of measurement, the dominant approach in theoretical investigation, has received criticism over a lack of accounting for the actual practice of measurement (Heilmann 2015), it does provide fruitful grist for understanding how measurement functions as representation and vice versa.

4.2 Solving the Applications Problem

Specifically, Swoyer's applications problem is consistent with what Suppes and Zinnes (1963) called the *representation problem* for a measurement procedure, whose general form is defined as to "characterize the formal properties of the empirical operations and relations used in the procedure and show that they are isomorphic to appropriately chosen numerical operations and relations" (Suppes and Zinnes 1963: 4–5). Accordingly, the notion of structure in the representational theory of measurement is usually referred to as *relational structure*, which is rooted in Alfred Tarski's concept of the *relational system* (Tarski 1954a, 1954b). Expressed set theoretically, a relational system $\boldsymbol{A} = \langle A, R_1, R_2, \ldots, R_n \rangle$, where A is a non-empty set of elements called the domain and $R_1, R_2, \ldots, R_n$ are relations on A. There is also a set of axioms characterizing R_i on A. A relational structure is defined in the same vein as $\boldsymbol{A}$. Both the target system to be measured and the numerical system applied to measure the target system are constituted as relational structures, known as the *empirical relational structure* and the *numerical relational structure*, respectively. If we let $\boldsymbol{A} = \langle A, R_1, R_2, \ldots, R_n \rangle$ be the empirical relational structure and $\boldsymbol{B} = \langle B, S_1, S_2, \ldots, S_n \rangle$ be the numerical relational structure, the process of measurement is equivalent to the representation problem (Suppes and Zinnes') and to the applications problem (Swoyer's). The application of $\boldsymbol{B}$ to $\boldsymbol{A}$ establishes a certain type of "morphism" between $\boldsymbol{A}$ and $\boldsymbol{B}$, so that we can construct a function f mapping $\boldsymbol{A}$ to $\boldsymbol{B}$. That is, f: $\boldsymbol{A} \rightarrow \boldsymbol{B}$.[3]

The key elements of representational theory are the representation theorem, the uniqueness theorem, and mapping or morphism. Representation theorems are required in order to secure a quantitative scale on the basis of qualitative empirical observations for a particular type of measurement. For example, a weak preference $\gtrsim$ can be represented by an ordinal utility function $u(x)$: $X \rightarrow R$, if and only if $\gtrsim$ satisfies the axioms of completeness, reflexivity, and transitivity. Uniqueness theorems are about *reduction* and *invariance*. When there is more than one representing model, reduction to a unique representation can be accomplished by defining a possible admissible transformation of a scale. Supposing there are two scales with the same structure, we can then establish an admissible transformation between them, indicating that the measurement is "meaningful" as it is unique up to the corresponding admissible transformation (Falmange and Narens 1983; Narens 1985; Narens and Luce 1987). Both representation and uniqueness theorems are related to a certain type of morphism. If we take isomorphism as an example, a relational structure $\boldsymbol{A} = \langle A, R_1, R_2, \ldots, R_n \rangle$ is isomorphic to a relational structure $\boldsymbol{B} = \langle B, S_1, S_2, \ldots, S_n \rangle$, if and only if there is a function f to establish one-to-one mapping between A and B and between R_i and S_i.[4]

To expand from the representational theory of measurement to scientific representation in general, a successful representation must satisfy certain conditions, such as representation theorems. (Cartwright 2008). Also, given the fact that there are abundant practices to prove the existence of representation theorems in economics, it can be said that, from the perspectives of philosophy and practices, representation theorems offer more. I have argued elsewhere (Chao 2014) that solving the applications problem by proving the existence of representation theorems is a way to justify the credible worlds problem (Sugden 2000, 2009). Credible worlds refer to an imaginary, parallel world created by a theoretical model, whose justification relies on how such an imaginary world is credible in the sense that the model can explain a particular real-world phenomenon. However, the problem is that, as a credible model does not intend to offer a testable hypothesis, it therefore lacks concrete connections to the real world: what Till Grüne-Yanoff (2009) describes as *world-linking conditions* or *world referentiality* in Chao (2014). Proof of representation theorems shows exactly how two relational structures are related to each other, hence justifying the adequacy of structural representation of a theoretical model for the target.

5. Diagrams as Representation

5.1 Diagrams and Graphs

The third type of the form of representation is visual representation. In economics, visually representational media take the form of tables (numerical and statistical charts), diagrams and graphs (supply-demand curves; Phillips curves; Harvard ABC Barometers), machines (the Phillips Machine; Irving Fisher's hydraulic model), and even films [Michael Polanyi's *Unemployment and Money* (Bíró 2020)]. Studies in visual representation have increased in the philosophy of science, as well as in the history and philosophy of economics.[5] Nowadays, visual representations occupy most of the space in undergraduate economics textbooks, but they largely disappear in favor of mathematical modeling in those required by more advanced students. However, diagrams have been common tools in science since the 19th century. We see the appearance of Michael Faraday's lines of force and James Clerk Maxwell's reciprocal diagrams at this time. Economic diagrams by pioneers such as Augustin Cournot, William Stanley Jevons, and Alfred Marshall also emerged during the same period. In Alfred Flux's entries for Palgrave's *Dictionary of Political Economy*, the graphical method is a method of representation for statistical investigations of economic phenomena (Flux 1912b; see also Marshall 1885). Flux's entry "Diagrams" (Flux 1912a), while beginning by proclaiming that diagrammatic representation is the best form for the purpose of "conveying readily to the mind of general facts contained in a table of figures," actually covers more space on Marshall's supply and demand curves.

This historical information suggests that economists have long been aware of and interested in using and distinguishing between different types of diagrammatic representations according to what they wish to represent. One classification still pertinent today was made by Henry Cunynghame, Marshall's pupil. In his book *A Geometrical Political Economy*, published in 1904, Cunynghame distinguished between *law-curves* and *fact-curves*. Fact-curves "present in a visual form a series of facts" (Cunynghame, 1904: 14). Law-curves represent economic laws (Ibid.: 21). The essence of fact-curves is *accuracy in detail*, whereas law-curves aim for *accuracy in conception*. Hence, when a law-curve is drawn, its truth does not depend on the accuracy of the drawing, which merely substitutes for a group of concepts (Ibid.).

5.2 Three Kinds of Space

Law-curves and fact-curves can be seen as representing the world and theory, respectively; thus, they also correspond to theoretical models and empirical models. However, diagrammatic form provides a distinct mode of reasoning, rather than operating only as translations of the algebraic models of the same sort.

The key characteristic of diagrams is *space*. Diagrams are intended to be used to represent the spatial relations of the target system in its two-dimensional space. While economists may think the reasoning power of diagrams is limited exactly because of the restriction imposed by its two-dimensional space, as recent philosophy of science studies demonstrate, diagrams are epistemically and methodologically valuable because they afford various notions of spatial relations, allowing economists to imagine the world and reason with it. Morgan (2020), following the classification proposed in Jill Larkin and Herbert Simon's (1987) classic paper, distinguishes three types of diagram: *real*, *ideal*, and *artificial*. Diagrams such as pulley systems and maps can describe real spatial systems. Geometric diagrams describe ideal spatial systems written in mathematics. Diagrams in artificial space (what Larkin and Simon called "artificial diagrams") do not have an actual spatial arrangement (Larkin and Simon 1987: 93), but are products of the scientist's creation of representation. Economic diagrams, represented by supply-and-demand curves and time-series graphs, generally belong to the category diagrams in artificial space, meaning that they are thought to deviate from diagrams depicting real space.

However, there are cases in which the geometrical properties of diagrams matter for economic interpretations, where economists seek to build a correspondence between geometrical and economic properties so that properties transforming from one domain to the other are meaningful. Price elasticity is the slope of the demand curve; surplus is the area under the demand curve. Marshall observed that, in order to represent a demand of unitary elasticity, the demand curve must appear as a rectangular hyperbola. To meet Marshall's need, Cunynghame thus invented a *hyperbolagraph*, a "beautiful machine for constructing a series of [rectangular hyperbolas] with the same asymptotes."[6] This suggests that geometrical properties can inspire economists toward a new way of reasoning by providing a guide of idealization. When geometrical idealization is applied in studying real space, such as in spatial economics, economists use geometrical diagrams and reason into them to derive a model that represents the real-world spatial relations as in the ideal geometrical shape displayed in their model, finally creating diagrams in artificial space. Models in location theory are formulated as idealized geometric shapes, such as concentric rings [Von Thünen's (1966) *The Isolated State*], triangles [Alfred Weber's (1929) industrial locations], and hexagons [Walter Christaller's (1966) central place theory]. Christaller, for example, derived his theory from "games with maps": he connected cities of equal size with straight lines and measured their lengths; the resulting shapes then became "crystallized as six-sided figures (hexagons)" (Christaller 1972: 607). The mapping between ideal geometrical shape and real spatial system further allowed Christaller to not only theorize three distinct patterns of settlement under different causal conditions but also implement an "ideal" regional plan based on the "geometrical schema" laid down by central place theory in the German-occupied East during the Second World War.[7]

These examples are among many practices of diagrammatic reasoning in economics.[8] They also demonstrate that the methodology of economic diagrams exhibits various types of reasoning. Morgan's (2020) study of theoretical and empirical diagrams focuses on investigating the diagrams used in inductive and deductive modes of reasoning. The empirical graphs use inductive logic for statistical thinking. This is what Boumans (2016) calls *graph-based inductive reasoning*, indicating that empirical graphs can not only display data but also be used as reasoning tools to infer or predict. On the other hand, the theoretical diagrams such as supply and demand curves employ deductive logic and can be used as tools for thought experiments. Morgan thus distinguishes between *inductive visuality* – making things visible that were not visible before by "the process of inducing sense out of a collection of bits and pieces that are not so obviously related or not previously understood to be so" (Ibid.: 228) – and *visual deduction* – reasoning with theoretical diagrams. The use of such deductive reasoning with diagrams "enables scientists to explore the content of their theories, suggest new hypotheses or close off others, and so forth" (Ibid.: 242). Yet, it has to be noted that Morgan does not indicate that these two modes of diagrammatic reasoning are exclusive, as there are cases in which economists use both inductive and deductive modes of reasoning. The point is to determine how economists tell stories about the world according to their diagrams, in specific, or models, in general. This *model narrative* functions "*both to take apart and explore the world in the model, and to put together and make coherent accounts of the world that the model represents*" (Morgan 2012: 246; original emphasis). So she notes that diagrams come with keys, such as vocabularies or symbols referring to economic variables, as an essential component of model narratives.

6. Conclusion

In scientific practice, representation is not for representing per se but for reasoning and inference. The preceding discussion suggests that economists model, measure, and visualize their target systems in order to reason with and into them.

The discussion in this chapter has provided some more cases drawn from the philosophy of science and practices of economics, suggesting a pluralistic view of economic representation. Regardless of how models, measurements, or diagrams function as representation, their roles serving as reasoning tools are form dependent.

Acknowledgments

I am grateful to Julian Reiss for his invitation to contribute to this book and his encouraging comments. This work was supported by Taiwan's Ministry of Science and Technology under grant number 108–2420-H-007–012-MY5.

Related Chapters

Clarke, C., Chapter 21 "Causal Contributions in Economics"
Jhun, J., Chapter 23 "Modeling the Possible to Modeling the Actual"
Kuorikoski, J., and Lehtinen, A., Chapter 26 "Computer Simulations in Economics"
Spanos, A., Chapter 29 "Philosophy of Econometrics"

Notes

1 www.britannica.com/topic/Phillips-curve. Retrieved 1/1/2021.
2 Morgan (2012) argues that a negative analogy can have a positive role in inspiring scientists to create a new world by reasoning within the model.
3 See Roberts (1980) for various types of morphism.
4 See Chao (2009) and Reiss (2013) for further discussion.
5 See, for example, the special issue of *East Asian Science, Technology and Society* (2020) 14(2), edited by Chao and Maas.
6 Letter from Alfred Marshall to F.Y. Edgeworth, March 9, 1881 (Whitaker 1996: 134).
7 See Chao (2018, 2020) for further discussion.
8 Recent studies of the history and philosophy of economic diagrams include, among others, Giraud (2010), Maas (2012), Boumans (2016), and Chao and Maas (2017).

Bibliography

Backhouse, R. E. (2007) "Representation in Economics," in M. Boumans (ed.) *Measurement in Economics: A Handbook*: 135–152, Amsterdam: Academic Press.
Bíró, G. (2020) "Michael Polanyi's Neutral Keynesianism and the First Economics Film, 1933 to 1945," *Journal of the History of Economic Thought* 42(3): 335–356.
Boumans, M. (1993) "Paul Ehrenfest and Jan Tinbergen: A Case of Limited Physics Transfer," *History of Political Economy* 25(supplement): 131–156.
Boumans, M. (2005) *How Economists Model the World into Numbers*, London: Routledge.

Boumans, M. (2016) "Graph-Based Inductive Reasoning," *Studies in History and Philosophy of Science Part A* 59: 1–10.
Cartwright, N. (2008) "In Praise of the Representation Theorem," in M. Frauchiger and W.K. Essler (eds.) *Representation, Evidence, and Justification: Themes from Suppes*: 83–90, Frankfurt: Ontos.
Chao, H.-K. (2009) *Representation and Structure in Economics: The Methodology of Econometric Models of the Consumption Function*, London: Routledge.
Chao, H.-K. (2014) "Models and Credibility," *Philosophy of the Social Sciences* 44(5): 588–605.
Chao, H.-K. (2018) "Shaping Space Through Diagrams: The Case of the History of Location Theory," *Research in the History of Economic Thought and Methodology* 36(B): 59–72.
Chao, H.-K. (2020) "Representation and Idealization: Diagrammatic Models in the Early Studies of the Spatial Structure of Periodic Markets in Rural China," *East Asian Science, Technology and Society* 14(2): 253–277.
Chao, H.-K., and Maas, H. (2017) "Engines of Discovery: Jevons and Marshall on the Methods of Graphs and Diagrams," *Research in the History of Economic Thought and Methodology* 35(A): 35–61.
Chao, H.-K., and Maas, H. (2020) "Thinking and Acting with Diagrams," *East Asian Science, Technology and Society* 14(2): 191–197.
Christaller, W. (1966) *Central Places in Southern Germany* (trans. Carlisle W. Baskin), Englewood Cliffs, NJ: Prentice-Hall.
Christaller, W. (1972) "How I Discovered the Theory of Central Places: A Report About the Origin of Central Places," in P.W. English and R.C. Mayfield (eds.) *Man, Space, and Environment: Concepts in Contemporary Human Geography*: 601–610, New York: Oxford University Press.
Coddington, A. (1976) "Keynesian Economics: The Search for First Principles," *Journal of Economic Literature* 14(4): 1258–1273.
Cunynghame, H. H. (1904) *A Geometrical Political Economy: Being an Elementary Treatise on the Method of Explaining Some of the Theories of Pure Economic Science by Means of Diagrams*, Oxford: Clarendon Press.
Debreu, G. (1954) "Representation of a Preference of Ordering by a Numerical Function," in M. Thrall, R. C. Davis, and C. H. Coombs (eds.) *Decision Processes*: 159–165, New York: John Wiley and Sons.
Elgin, C. Z. (2010) "Telling Instances," in R. Frigg and M.C. Hunter (eds.) *Beyond Mimesis and Convention: Representation in Art and Science*: 1–18, Berlin and New York: Springer.
Fisher, I. (1896) "What Is Capital?" *The Economic Journal* 6(24): 509–534.
Falmange, J.-C., and Narens, L. (1983) "Scales and Meaningfulness of Quantitative Laws," *Synthese* 55: 287–325.
Frigg, R., and Nguyen, J. (2017) "Scientific Representation Is Representation-as," in H.-K. Chao and J. Reiss (eds.) *Philosophy of Science in Practice: Nancy Cartwright and the Natural of Scientific Reasoning:* 149–179, Cham, Switzerland: Springer.
Frigg, R., and Nguyen, J. (2020) *Modelling Nature: An Opinionated Introduction to Scientific Representation*, Cham: Springer.
Flux, A.W. (1912a) "Diagrams," in R.H.I. Palgrave (ed.) *Dictionary of Political Economy*, Vol. I: 574–576, London: Macmillan.
Flux, A.W. (1912b) "Graphic Method," in R.H.I. Palgrave (ed.) *Dictionary of Political Economy*, Vol. II: 251–255, London: Macmillan.
Giere, R.N. (1988) *Explaining Science: A Cognitive Approach*, Chicago: University of Chicago Press.
Giere, R.N. (1999) "Using Models to Represent Reality," in L. Magnani, N.J. Nersessian, and P. Thagard (eds.) *Model-Based Reasoning in Scientific Discovery*: 41–57, Dordrecht: Kluwer.
Giere, R.N. (2004) "How Models Are Used to Represent Reality," *Philosophy of Science* 71(5): 742–752.
Giere, R.N. (2006) *Scientific Perspectivism*, Chicago: University of Chicago Press.
Giraud, Y.B. (2010) "The Changing Place of Visual Representation in Economics: Paul Samuelson Between Principle and Strategy, 1941–1955," *Journal of the History of Economic Thought* 32(2): 175–197.
Godfrey-Smith, P. (2006) "The Strategy of Model-Based Science," *Biology and Philosophy* 21(5): 725–740.
Goodman, N. (1968) *Languages of Art: An Approach to a Theory of Symbols*, Indianapolis: Bobbs-Merrill.
Grüne-Yanoff, T. (2009) "Learning from Minimal Economic Models," *Erkenntnis* 70(1): 81–99.
Heilmann, C. (2015) "A New Interpretation of the Representational Theory of Measurement," *Philosophy of Science* 82(5): 787–797.
Hesse, M. (1953) "Models in Physics," *British Journal for the Philosophy of Science* 4(15): 198–204.
Hesse, M. (1966) *Models and Analogies in Science*, Norte Dame, IN: Notre Dame University Press.
Hesse, M. (2000) "Models and Analogy," in W.H. Newton-Smith (ed.) *A Companion to the Philosophy of Science*: 299–307, Oxford: Blackwell.
Humphreys, P. (2002) "Computational Models," *Proceedings of the Philosophy of Science Association* 2002(3): S1–S11.
Humphreys, P. (2004) *Extending Ourselves: Computational Science, Empiricism, and Scientific Method*, Oxford: Oxford University Press.

Knuuttila, T., and Loettgers, A. (2017) "Modelling as Indirect Representation? The Lotka – Volterra Model Revisited," *British Journal for the Philosophy of Science* 68(4): 1007–1036.

Krantz, D.H., Luce, R.D., Suppes, P., and Tversky, A. (1971) *Foundations of Measurement, vol. 1: Additive and Polynomial Representations*, New York: Academic Press.

Larkin, J.H., and Simon, H.A. (1987) "Why A Diagram Is (Sometimes) Worth Ten Thousand Words," *Cognitive Science* 11(1): 65–100.

Luce, R.D., Krantz, D.H., Suppes, P., and Tversky, A. (1990) *Foundations of Measurement, vol. 3: Representation, Axiomatization, and Invariance*, San Diego, CA: Academic Press.

Maas, H. (2005) *William Stanley Jevons and the Making of Modern Economics*, Cambridge: Cambridge University Press.

Maas, H. (2012) "The Photographic Lens: Graphs and the Changing Practices of Victorian Economists," in M. Hewitt (ed.) *The Victorian World*: 500–518, London: Routledge.

Marshall, A. (1885) "On the Graphic Method of Statistics," *Journal of the Statistical Society of London*: 251–260.

Mirowski, P. (1989) *More Heat than Light: Economics as Social Physics, Physics as Nature's Economics*, Cambridge: Cambridge University Press.

Morgan, M.S. (1999) "Learning from Models," in M.S. Morgan and M. Morrison (eds.) *Models as Mediators: Perspectives on Natural and Social Science*: 347–388, Cambridge: Cambridge University Press.

Morgan, M.S. (2012) *The World in the Model*, Cambridge: Cambridge University Press.

Morgan, M.S. (2020) "Inducing Visibility and Visual Deduction," *East Asian Science, Technology and Society* 14(2): 225–252.

Morgan, M.S., and Morrison, M. (eds.) (1999) *Models as Mediators: Perspectives on Natural and Social Science*, Cambridge: Cambridge University Press.

Narens, L. (1985) *Abstract Measurement Theory*, Cambridge, MA: MIT Press.

Narens, L., and Luce, R.D. (1987) "Meaningfulness and invariance," in J. Eatwell, M. Milgate, and P. Newman (eds.) *The New Palgrave: A Dictionary of Economics*, vol. 3: 417–421, London: Macmillan.

Rader, T. (1963) "The Existence of a Utility Function to Represent Preferences," *The Review of Economic Studies* 30(3): 229–232.

Reiss, J. (2013) *Philosophy of Economics: A Contemporary Introduction*, New York: Routledge.

Roberts, F. (1980) "On Luce's Theory of Meaningfulness," *Philosophy of Science* 47(3): 424–433.

Russell, B. (1903) *The Principles of Mathematics*, Cambridge: Cambridge University Press.

Scholl, R., and Räz, T. (2013) "Modeling Causal Structures: Volterra's Struggle and Darwin's Success," *European Journal for Philosophy of Science* 3(1): 115–132.

Snowdon, B., and Vane, H.R. (2005) *Modern Macroeconomics: Its Origins, Development and Current State*, Cheltenham: Edward Elgar.

Stevens, S.S. (1959) "Measurement, Psychophysics and Utility," in C.W. Churchman and P. Ratoosh (eds.) *Measurement: Definitions and Theories*: 18–63, New York: Wiley.

Sugden, R. (2000) "Credible Worlds: The Status of Theoretical Models in Economics," *Journal of Economic Methodology* 7(1): 1–31.

Sugden, R. (2009) "Credible Worlds, Capacities and Mechanisms," *Erkenntnis* 70: 3–27.

Suppes, P. (1962) "Models of Data," in E. Nagel, P. Suppes, and A. Tarski (eds.) *Logic, Methodology and Philosophy of Science: Proceedings of the 1960 International Congress*: 252–261, Stanford: Stanford University Press.

Suppes, P. (2002) *Representation and Invariance of Scientific Structures*, Stanford: CSLI Publications.

Suppes, P., Krantz, D.H., Luce, R.D., and Tversky, A. (eds.) (1989) *Foundations of Measurement, vol. II: Geometrical, Threshold, and Probabilistic Representations*, New York: Academic Press.

Suppes, P., and Zinnes, J. (1963) "Basic Measurement Theory," in D. Luce and R. Bush (eds.) *Handbook of Mathematical Psychology*, vol. I: 1–76, New York: John Wiley and Sons.

Swoyer, C. (1991) "Structural Representation and Surrogative Reasoning," *Synthese* 87(3): 449–508.

Tarski, A. (1954a) "Contributions to the Theory of Models I," *Indagationes Mathematicae* 16: 26–32.

Tarski, A. (1954b) "Contributions to the Theory of Models II," *Indagationes Mathematicae* 16: 582–588.

Van Fraassen, B.C. (1980) *The Scientific Image*, Oxford: Oxford University Press.

Van Fraassen, B.C. (1989) *Law and Symmetry*, Oxford: Oxford University Press.

Van Fraassen, B.C. (2008) *Scientific Representation: Paradoxes of Perspective*, Oxford: Oxford University Press.

Von Thünen, J.H. (1966) *Von Thünen's Isolated State* (trans. C.M. Wartenberg), Oxford: Pergamon Press.

Weber, A. (1929) *Alfred Weber's Theory of the Location of Industries* (trans. C. J. Friedrich), Chicago: University of Chicago Press.

Weisberg, M. (2007) "Who Is a Modeler?" *British Journal for the Philosophy of Science* 58: 207–233.

Whitaker, J.K. (1996) *The Correspondence of Alfred Marshall, Economist*, Cambridge: Cambridge University Press.

Worrall, J. (1989) "Structural Realism: The Best of Both Worlds?" *Dialectica* 43(1–2): 99–124.

14

FINANCE AND FINANCIAL ECONOMICS

A Philosophy of Science Perspective

Melissa Vergara-Fernández and Boudewijn de Bruin

1. Introduction

Finance, from the perspective of the philosophy of science, is largely *terra incognita*. In contrast to social studies scholars, philosophers of science have been rather indifferent to the study of finance. An obvious starting point, from a philosophical perspective, is thus to ask what is distinctive about finance that has led to this indifference. One answer could be that the historical roots of economics lie in theorizing about the world and thereby understanding it, whereas those of finance lie in solving practical problems. Economics is a science; finance is workmanship.

But that cannot be the whole story. Economics and finance have too much shared history, at least recently. Take modern portfolio theory (MPT), with the mean-variance portfolio model, the efficient market hypothesis (EMH), and the capital asset pricing model (CAPM) as its main constituents. This accomplishment is taken by most historians of finance to be the watershed between "old finance" and "new finance" precisely because it established important areas in finance on a model-based footing, very much like the rest of economics. Or consider the institutions involved: the Cowles Commission, together with Carnegie Tech (later Carnegie Mellon University), the University of Chicago, and the Massachusetts Institute of Technology (MIT), shaped not only much of economics but also new finance (Bernstein 1993; MacKenzie 2006: Chapter 2).

This shared history of economics and finance is one of the reasons why financial economics deserves philosophical scrutiny. Furthermore, while financial economics is a young subdiscipline, it is of high importance: it studies the financial markets and their institutions. In fact, it actively shapes them and does so arguably to a greater extent than other scientific disciplines might shape their own object of study. We shall see that if we look at what drove the big innovations in financial economics, the connection with practice (industry, regulators, supervisory authorities, and so on) is clearly present. This is arguably the reason why the social studies literature has devoted so much attention to what is called the *performativity* of financial economics. We think this is an important issue. But we also hope to show that it is far from the only topic a philosopher of science should find interesting.

For obvious reasons, it is impossible to cover the entire field of financial economics in this chapter. We have thus opted for selecting some key elements of modern finance that we think should generate philosophical interest (see De Bruin et al. 2020 for a discussion of money and finance). We also offer a case study on a central result from finance, a model by Modigliani and Miller, that has attracted some earlier attention by philosophers, where we address the explanatoriness of unrealistic models.

 DOI: 10.4324/9781315739793-17

2. Key Elements of Finance

2.1. The Joint Hypothesis Problem

Two core elements of financial economics are the efficient market hypothesis (EMH) and the capital asset pricing model (CAPM). Taken together, they pose an important question about how theories are, and can be, tested, as well as about the assumptions necessary to do so. The EMH states that the price of any asset at any point in time fully reflects all available information (Fama 1970). The hypothesis can be seen as motivated by an equilibrium argument to the effect that rational traders, maximizing their expected utility on the basis of the best information available, would drive out *noise traders* (the minority of irrational traders) through arbitrage, if a market were not efficient. An illustration is the well-known *January effect*, according to which stock prices increase in the first week of the year. Following the logic of the EMH, this trend should disappear as soon as traders notice it, and indeed, there is evidence that the January effect and similar phenomena have disappeared once they became common knowledge (Thaler 1987).

The significance of the EMH is difficult to overstate. It tells us that there is no agent in the economy who can systematically "beat" the market. There is nothing they can know that asset prices do not already fully reflect. If the primary role of capital markets is the efficient allocation of capital stock, it is a desirable feature that prices fully reflect the available information, for only then can the allocation be efficient. The January effect, according to the EMH, will not happen systematically. The question is, then, whether the EMH can be tested empirically.

This is hard, as Fama (1970) observed. The definition of the EMH "is so general that it has no empirically testable implications" (Fama 1970: 384). In order for the EMH to be tested, the process of price formation must be specified in detail. In other words, "[w]e can't test whether the market does what it is supposed to do unless we specify what it is supposed to do" (Fama 2014: 1467).

At least in principle, the CAPM tells us what the market is supposed to do. It measures the market risk of an asset and prices that risk (on the concept of risk in economics, see Stefánsson, Chapter 3). A key idea behind it is that rational investors need not care about the *specific* risk attached to specific assets, as this risk can be diversified away by investing in a broader portfolio of assets. Instead, the CAPM states that the only risk to be priced is the one that cannot so be eliminated. It also states that, in equilibrium, there is a linear relationship between this undiversifiable risk and expected returns. A test of the EMH, therefore, is to determine whether the determinants of expected returns implied by the CAPM are indeed observed in actual returns. The problem, however, is that if actual returns do not conform to the predictions of the CAPM, we cannot tell whether it is due to the fact that the markets are inefficient or whether the CAPM is a poor model of market equilibrium. This is the *joint hypothesis problem*.

While this problem is not a textbook case of underdetermination, where competing theories are underdetermined by the data, rendering the test indecisive, it is clear that the testability of "the two pillars" or "Siamese twins" of asset pricing, as Fama (2014) calls them, is at stake. It might tempt philosophers to revisit the Duhem–Quine thesis and the problem of underdetermination altogether. The material, we venture, is certainly more interesting than similar problems in game theory (Hausman 2005; Karpus and Radzvilas, Chapter 7) and macroeconomics (Cross 1982) because, unlike game theorists, financial economists were keenly aware of the issue, describing it as a "problem" or a "research opportunity" (Campbell 2014).

2.2. Event Studies

How the profession has dealt with the lack of testability of two of its most substantive achievements is also worthy of philosophical attention. It led to the development of a new (and Nobel

Prize-winning) method: the event study. An event study examines the effects of a particular event (e.g., an oil spill disaster) on the price of certain assets (e.g., shares in oil companies). The first event study, by Fama et al. (1969), examined the effects of stock splits on share prices. The number of published event studies in economics may well run to over 10,000 to date (not only in finance but also in accounting). Unlike other widespread methods such as randomized controlled trials, to our knowledge no philosopher of science has so far looked at event studies.

Event studies are not only interesting because they are explicitly targeting a Duhem–Quine type of predicament. Their development also underscores our finance-as-a-practice view, with potential relevance to the philosophical discussion about non-evidentialism and the non-epistemic value of models. Here is our story. Modern finance would look different (or would have developed more slowly) if it had not been spurred by substantial funding from Merrill Lynch, for instance. In the 1960s, this bank contributed tens of thousands of dollars to establish a Center for Research in Security Prices (CRSP) at the University of Chicago, the aim of which was exactly what its name suggests. But as Fama (2017) writes in an anniversary article of the *Journal of Political Economy*, there was a worry that while the bank would benefit greatly from making available high-quality asset price data, mainstream economists would not sufficiently appreciate the value of the research conducted at the Center. The founder of the Center, James Lorie, therefore suggested that Fama conduct research on stock splits. And this led to the birth of the event study.

2.3. *Performativity*

MacKenzie (2006) uses the term performativity to refer to what happens when the practical use of some aspect of economics makes the relevant economic processes more similar to economic theory. A key example of performativity is the Black–Scholes option-pricing model (more appropriately also including the name of Robert Merton). An option is the right to buy (call option) or sell (put option) a particular underlying asset, typically a piece of stock, at a stated price within a specific time frame. The thought behind the Black–Scholes model, which has sufficient prima facie plausibility, is that one should be able to determine the "right" price of an option solely on the basis of relevant information concerning the underlying asset. Technical details aside, Black–Scholes accomplishes this by allowing one to determine the price of an option on the basis of a few variables, such as the underlying asset's price, its volatility, and the risk-free rate.

Yet, the model was not very accurate when actual option prices were compared with the prices predicted by the model. Only after the model was published (and Black–Scholes price sheets circulated among traders) did option prices converge to what should be expected on the basis of the model. This tempted social studies of science scholars to see Black–Scholes as a paradigmatic case of performativity.

We cannot give a full evaluation of the cogency of their argument here, but there is considerable opportunity for philosophical analysis. For instance, it may help to analyze the relation between theory (the Black–Scholes model) and practice (observed option pricing) as one between norms and behavior. A similar idea has been defended by Guala (2016). He suggested that option prices as determined by Black–Scholes can figure as coordination devices, just as people conform with certain traffic rules. This makes the traffic laws quite accurate as "descriptions" of observed behavior. So, when traders start using Black–Scholes as a guidebook, observed behavior will converge to theory.

Furthermore, relevant facts have not yet been taken into account in the performativity discussions. For instance, traders Haug and Taleb (2011) have argued that historical evidence of trading methods suggest that traders do not use Black–Scholes. Similarly, quoting extensively from Niederhoffer (1997), Phoa et al. (2007) detail how traders use an array of techniques to help decision-making, which is best compared with a mechanical engineer using astrology and necromancy alongside

Newtonian physics. Potentially more interesting than performativity may be, therefore, the observation that practitioners often use patently contradictory financial theories at the same time.

Use of the methods from analytic philosophy would allow us to define and study performativity with greater conceptual, and perhaps formal, precision. This would not just help us to better understand the logic of the Black–Scholes model but also allow us to assess the plausibility of claims for performativity or self-fulfillingness in other branches of finance, including agency theory and corporate governance (Marti and Gond 2018), as well as the EMH and the CAPM.

2.4. Benchmarks for Evaluation

Our finance-as-a-practice approach may suggest that concepts, theories, and models are used for a much larger variety of purposes than in other branches of economics. Philosophers have been concerned with the question of whether models are explanatory (Jhun, Chapter 23; Verreault-Julien, Chapter 22). In finance, these models may, however, play many different roles. Hindriks (2008, 2013) considers the 1958 Modigliani and Miller model, an early result in finance that is the topic of our case study. Hindriks uses this model to introduce what he calls "explanation by relaxation." The model states that the way a corporation is financed (that is, the proportion of debt versus equity) does not affect its market value. This was a highly surprising and decidedly unrealistic result, given that debt was long considered the preferable way to fund a firm, for instance, because it suggests greater trustworthiness and stability on the part of the firm's management. The validity of the result depends, however, on the assumption that there is no taxation. Hindriks therefore argues that the function of the model is rather to explain how taxes might matter: subsequent results did include differential taxation of stocks and bonds (relaxing the assumptions of the original model), and this shows how taxes matter.

But our finance-as-a-practice approach opens our eyes to another, complementary way in which these models are used in the finance industry: as a benchmark or normative guideline. Here is the idea. When a market fails to satisfy the conditions of the EMH, regulators may conceive of that as not so much the failure of theory but rather as a failure of the market. This is not a "saving the phenomena" approach where theory is maintained coûte que coûte. Rather, failure may have a moral or political connotation, such as when an inefficient market is seen as one in which certain participants are offered "unjust" opportunities for arbitration because of informational asymmetries. Or it may have a more instrumental type of connotation: the financial industry has, for instance, witnessed an array of technologies that make information provision increasingly smooth (thereby making the market increasingly efficient), ranging from the semaphore (really!) and the ticker tape over telegraph lines to the internet and high-frequency trading. The EMH here is a benchmark against which to evaluate information and communication opportunities. We can witness a similar benchmarking use of the CAPM (or more complex variants thereof). Such models underlie, for instance, arguments to adjudicate claims about the performance of fund managers. This is because the sole fact that a fund generated high returns does not mean it was managed well (just as losses do not mean it was managed badly), and an assessment should also take into account the level of risk the manager took. That is where the CAPM and its ilk come into play.

2.5. Ideology and Science

Some authors associate the EMH (or modern finance altogether) with a pro-business ideology of deregulation. Indeed, as we have already noted, Merrill Lynch contributed substantial funding to the development of financial economics at the University of Chicago in the 1960s. And in the 1940s, William Mellon had already offered an endowment to Carnegie Tech to establish a business school that would, more indirectly, play a role in shaping modern finance. Also, some forms of deregulation are more easily defended using modern finance than old finance, and some representatives of modern finance do indeed favor deregulation.

However, to begin with, we should caution against what seems quite popular in some corners: to associate modern finance with regressive views of justice. Perhaps the biggest progressive development in finance, index funds as developed by Jack Bogle's Vanguard, can be seen as having contributed considerably to making financial services available to people with low or modest income and wealth. Yet, it is exactly this innovation that owes its existence to the EMH; the logic of index funds is that if markets are efficient, there is no hope for active investors to achieve higher risk-adjusted returns. Consequently, individuals would be wasting their money if they paid someone to manage their funds.

More fundamentally perhaps, it is unclear what the direction of causation is supposed to be between ideology and theory. Someone believing the EMH on the basis that it supports their ideology would be forming beliefs in a nonevidentialist way. Work on nonevidentialism or pragmatism in epistemology would help to elucidate this. Someone embracing a deregulation ideology solely on the basis of the EMH would, on the other hand, commit a naturalistic fallacy, or more plausibly their argument for deregulation would have to be construed as enthymematic, as it leaves unspecified the normative ideal that they think deregulation would help to realize.

Conceptual clarification is dearly needed here. We suggest the following as a default starting position: it is plausible to assume that the ultimate normative ideal that drives arguments for (or against) deregulation is that of a fair and cost-effective distribution of financial resources. Keep this normative ideal constant, and then see how policy recommendations change when theory changes. If one's empirical theory is 1960s modern finance, the advice may well be deregulation. Equally, if one's empirical theory is 21st-century behavioral finance, it may well be something like liberal paternalism. This does not mean, however, that modern finance and behavioral finance subscribe to or entail different ideologies; it would be equally odd to attribute different ideologies to 1960s and 21st-century food science, even though nutrition advice has radically changed in the last 50 years.

While we realize that we have only scratched the surface here and that our choice of topics is necessarily arbitrary, we hope that we have shown that finance and financial economics are interesting territory for philosophers to explore. It is now time to move to our case study.

3. Modigliani–Miller: Models and Epistemic Import

In 1958, Franco Modigliani and Merton Miller published the first of a series of papers in which they introduced a number of propositions about the cost of capital for firms, their dividend policy, and their debt/equity ratio. They demonstrated that the decisions of a firm about how to fund its activities, be it by issuing debt or by issuing equity, are irrelevant to the firm's market valuation (Modigliani and Miller 1958). The choice has no effect on the market's valuation of the firm. Their argument relied on the concept of arbitrage by noting that, if the value of the firm depended on the debt/equity ratio, there would be arbitrage opportunities for investors: they would have a "free lunch." They would be able to increase their returns without incurring higher costs. This is an unsustainable equilibrium.

The propositions are striking for at least two reasons: first, because many of the assumptions under which the result holds are unrealistic. As we mentioned earlier, taxation is assumed to play no role, though it is clear that differential taxation schemes for debt and equity do matter. Second, at the time, the propositions seemed to go against everything that was known about how firms could fund their activities. Equity still had a poor reputation by dint of the market crash of 1929 and the subsequent Great Depression: in contrast to debtholders, in the case of bankruptcy stockholders are not paid. Debt was therefore considered safer than equity. And yet, too much debt would make a corporation look risky in the eyes of potential investors and creditors. The intuition was therefore that there had to be an optimum balance between the two forms of acquiring capital. By contrast, Modigliani and Miller argued that any combination of the two would have no effect on the firm's market valuation. Their contribution became a cornerstone of corporate finance and asset pricing.

3.1. Explanation by Relaxation

This kind of result is naturally of much interest to philosophers. What is the use of a model with patently false assumptions and implications? And how could it become a cornerstone in financial economics?

Hindriks (2008, 2013) took a stab at offering an answer with this model and argued for a specific method of explanation, namely, explanation by relaxation (see also Jhun, Chapter 23). He maintains that the model can be explanatory despite the unrealisticness of its assumptions and implications. If some of the assumptions are relaxed (for instance, to include differential tax treatment of debt and equity), the result obtained by Modigliani and Miller fails to hold. Hindriks therefore claims that this is explanatory because it allows us to see that taxes do matter; they are a factor in preventing the Modigliani–Miller result from holding. By relaxing assumptions and obtaining results that are consistent with reality, we are able to explain that the factors in the assumptions being relaxed do play a role.

Hindriks's motivation appears to be the worry that, under Hausman's (1992) philosophical account of explanation, economics models that are too idealized, such as Modigliani and Miller's, seem not to have any explanatory value. Hindriks considers it "implausible that, by their own lights, most of the models [economists] have proposed cannot even be used as the point of departure for potential explanations" (Ibid. 2013: 525). He seems to think that, if models cannot be the starting point of an explanation, then there is no use for them. With his method of explanation by relaxation, the Modigliani–Miller result is vindicated: it explains by relaxing assumptions.

A great deal of the philosophical literature on economic models has indeed focused on the explanatoriness of models. It has addressed models' capacity to make us learn (Claveau and Vergara-Fernández 2015; Grüne-Yanoff 2009), to explain (Aydinonat 2018; Reiss 2012), to yield understanding (Verreault-Julien 2017; Ylikoski and Aydinonat 2014), and to identify robust causal mechanisms to understand economic phenomena (Kuorikoski et al. 2010). But model building is not justified for its epistemic virtues alone. Indeed, some authors are skeptical of the epistemic benefits of models (Alexandrova and Northcott 2013). Some argue that models are only capable of serving a heuristic role as providing open formulae (Alexandrova 2008): mere causal hypotheses that have yet to be empirically verified in order to be used in explanations. Others have argued that they allow conceptual exploration (Hausman 1992).

3.2. The Search for Consistency

Rather than attempt to settle the matter here as to what the epistemic benefits of models are, we want to highlight that models may have other important purposes besides the strictly epistemic ones. Notwithstanding potential epistemic interests, the relevance of Modigliani and Miller's (1958) model is related to the values that motivated the contribution in the first place. The assessment of models through the lens of the values that motivate them offers important insights that would be overlooked if the focus remained on the actual epistemic payoff of models. There are two values in particular that help us understand the relevance the Modigliani–Miller model had for financial economics.

First, there was the motivation to bring consistency to the microeconomic and macroeconomic treatments of the problem of firm valuation. Indeed, the contribution of Modigliani and Miller was part of a long-term project that encompassed the question of the cost of capital and the implications for the firm's decision-making process and aggregate investment. It began in 1949 as the

Expectations and Business Fluctuations project, which Modigliani was asked to supervise upon joining the faculty of the University of Illinois. The research involved empirical and theoretical work on business expectations and their influence on aggregate economic behavior (Rancan 2020: Chapter 4). Modigliani and Miller's treatment of the problem would allow further theoretical developments in rational investment and financial policy under uncertainty.

The question Modigliani and Miller (1958) pose is the following: what is the cost of capital for a firm when the income stream of a particular investment is uncertain? They take particular issue with the way in which the problem had been treated by economic theorists. The traditional assumption had been that the cost of capital of a firm, regardless of whether it is financed through debt or equity, is simply the riskless rate of interest, as if it yielded sure streams. The question of how risk affected the cost of capital had been eschewed or treated in an ad hoc way, namely, by superimposing a risk discount on the results under sure streams. And while Modigliani and Miller admit that the ad hoc way had been helpful in addressing "the grosser aspects of capital accumulation and economic fluctuations" (Ibid. 1958: 262), in which Modigliani in particular was interested, they did claim that "at the macroeconomic level there are ample grounds for doubting that the rate of interest has as large and as direct an influence on the rate of investment as this analysis would lead us to believe" (Ibid.: 262–263). In the Keynesian model, on which Modigliani had worked, aggregate investment is written as a function of the riskless rate of interest. This same rate of interest appears, too, in the liquidity preference equation.

As a way to incorporate the uncertainty, their proposal was to tackle the question by finding a rational investment policy that maximizes the market value of the firm instead of one that maximizes profits. The problem, however, was that no theory of the effect of financial structure on market valuations was available, nor could these effects be inferred from available data (Ibid. 1958: 264). Prior to writing the article, Modigliani and Miller had dealt with the question from different angles: Modigliani from a purely analytical perspective and Miller from an empirical one, unsuccessfully trying to establish a correlation between debt/stock ratio and firm value.

Ultimately, more than giving an explanation of the way in which actual firms were funded in the 1950s, their result was meant to demonstrate that a problem that was generally seen to be solved "within" the firm (by the financial specialist and perhaps the managerial economist) with the use of only old ad hoc finance machinery, could be answered using the tools of the economic theorist.

3.3. Settling a Debate

To establish consistency between the micro and macro treatments is related to another value that seems to have driven the contribution of the two economists: the intent to settle a methodological debate that was taking place within Carnegie Tech, the institution with which they were affiliated. As mentioned earlier, in 1948, William Mellon offered a $6 million endowment to Carnegie Tech to establish the Graduate School of Industrial Administration (GSIA). The new leaders of the school, who included Herbert Simon, saw US business education at the time "as a wasteland of vocationalism that needed to be transformed into science-based professionalism" (Simon 1996: 139). Finance was mostly descriptive of financial instruments and institutions. The "chief book of finance," *The Financial Policy of Corporations*, first published in 1919 (Sewing 1919), focused on describing the workings of corporations and regulatory schemes, often with many historical asides, and had no mathematics beyond simple arithmetic. The GSIA aimed to establish a modern management science on the basis of a strong interdisciplinary and empirical approach to the study of firms' behavior (Rancan 2020: Chapter 4). The hiring of Modigliani and Miller at Carnegie was part of that interdisciplinary effort.

But there was resistance. Traditional scholars, in particular, whose approach to corporate finance was mostly description of the institutional setup were defiant. David Durand, for instance, a well-known and respected representative of old finance, took issue with Modigliani and Miller because he thought that, although the arbitrage mechanism was at work, the real-world institutions posed restrictions for investors, which would not allow such arbitrage (MacKenzie 2006: Chapter 2). Scholars such as Durand were among the first to complain about modern finance lacking realisticness. Modigliani and Miller were thus keen to show that the "science-based professionalism" that Simon had in mind was to be found in modern economic theory.

The point Modigliani and Miller (1958) were precisely trying to make was the following: they were interested in arguing that an understanding of capital structure required an analytical framework that would allow an understanding of firm decisions as part of the larger economic setup. The analytical framework of microeconomics in terms of arbitrage and equilibrium suggested that the question of firm funding "was not really an issue."

> The paper was meant to upset my colleagues in finance by arguing that the core issue that received most attention in corporation finance, namely finding out what exactly is the optimum capital structure, was not really an issue. It didn't make any difference. To be sure, it might make a difference if there were taxes. If so, you would have to approach the problem precisely in that way and ask what is the effect of taxes and why do they make a difference.
>
> (Modigliani 2009: 126)

3.4. *Epistemic and Non-epistemic Values*

We read Modigliani's quote as underscoring our view that it can be useful to be sensitive to the fact that models do not necessarily have only epistemic goals. In particular, the relevance of a model might be better assessed by noting the values that drive its building in the first place. Previously, we argued that there were two values at play: an epistemic one, to establish consistency between theoretical frameworks, and a non-epistemic one, to settle an institutional battle within the GSIA to establish the methodological framework that would give its much sought-after scientific status.

Some might want to argue that the motivation of Modigliani and Miller was methodological and consequently still epistemic, namely, to demonstrate the superiority of the modern finance framework over old finance. But, if the ultimate purpose was to win an institutional battle at Carnegie Tech, does it still count as epistemic? We think the answer is not obviously affirmative. Some might also be tempted to dismiss Modigliani's reminiscence as spurious, subtracting plausibility from our claim. But our claim is not historical. It is sufficient for us to entertain his remark as plausible in order to suggest that the very motivations of model building need not always be purely epistemic.

Furthermore, similar concerns can be found elsewhere in economics. Robert Aumann's (1985) defense of the expected utility approach against Herbert Simon's (1947) satisficing, for instance, may also be amplified by strategic, non-epistemic reasons behind the model. The role of such reasons has been acknowledged in the literature on values in science (e.g., Diekmann and Peterson 2013; Douglas 2000, 2009; Baujard, Chapter 15; Reiss, Chapter 16). An apt metaphor employed by Elliott (2017) is that values "weave" themselves into scientific practice like the weaving of a tapestry, for instance, when it comes to choosing research topics and questions or the goals of scientific inquiry. Consideration of these aspects allows us to understand better why Modigliani and Miller's model in particular, as well as the others that followed, proved to be so influential in the discipline. A purely epistemic characterization in terms of the explanatoriness of the model leaves much unaccounted for.

More generally, an understanding of not only the epistemic contributions models make but also the values that drive their building offers us a more comprehensive understanding of the modeling practice. Such an understanding allows for a better potential dialogue between philosophers and practitioners and a better assessment of the epistemic risks involved in doing science (e.g., Douglas 2011; Elliott and Richards 2017), and it contributes to the political philosophy of science urged by Douglas (2018).

4. Conclusion

In this chapter, we have made an attempt to highlight some features of financial economics that are of potential interest to philosophers of science. We have argued that the traditional key elements of finance (the efficient market hypothesis, the capital asset pricing model, and the Black–Scholes model) merit greater philosophical attention. They give rise to issues such as performativity and underdetermination that go to the core of the traditional philosophy of science. They also call for addressing questions that have to do with the non-epistemic value of models and the political or ideological values inherent in science, which have occupied philosophers more recently.

Perhaps some readers wish we had added other items to our survey. Others may have found our case study too quick to be immediately plausible. We are keenly aware of these and other potential limitations. Our ambition with this chapter was precisely to kindle interest in finance and financial economics from philosophers of science, hoping that the issues we treated here will be revisited.

Related Chapters

Baujard, A., Chapter 15 "Values in Welfare Economics"
Jhun, J., Chapter 23 "Modeling the Possible to Modeling the Actual"
Karpus, J., and Radzvilas, M., Chapter 7 "Game Theory and Rational Reasoning"
Reiss, J., Chapter 16 "Measurement and Value Judgments"
Stefánsson, H.O., Chapter 3 "The Economics and Philosophy of Risk"
Verreault-Julien, P., Chapter 22 "Explanation in Economics"

Bibliography

Alexandrova, A. (2008) "Making Models Count," *Philosophy of Science* 75(3): 383–404.
Alexandrova, A., and Northcott, R. (2013) "It's Just a Feeling: Why Economic Models Do Not Explain," *Journal of Economic Methodology* 20(3): 262–267.
Aumann, R.J. (1985) "What Is Game Theory Trying to Accomplish," in K. Arrow and S. Honkapohja (eds.) *Frontiers of Economics*, Oxford: Blackwell: 5–46.
Aydinonat, N.E. (2018) "The Diversity of Models as a Means to Better Explanations in Economics," *Journal of Economic Methodology* 25(3): 237–251.
Bernstein, P.L. (1993) *Capital Ideas: The Improbable Origins of Modern Wall Street*, New York: Free Press.
Campbell, J.Y. (2014) "Empirical Asset Pricing: Eugene Fama, Lars Peter Hansen, and Robert Shiller: Empirical asset pricing," *The Scandinavian Journal of Economics* 116(3): 593–634.
Claveau, F., and Vergara Fernández, M. (2015) "Epistemic Contributions of Models: Conditions for Propositional Learning," *Perspectives on Science:* 405–423.
Cross, R. (1982) "The Duhem-Quine Thesis, Lakatos and the Appraisal of Theories in Macroeconomics," *The Economic Journal* 92(366): 320–340.
De Bruin, B., Herzog, L., O'Neill, M., and Sandberg, J. (2020, Winter) "Philosophy of Money and Finance," in E.N. Zalta (ed.) *The Stanford Encyclopedia of Philosophy*, Metaphysics Research Lab, Stanford: Stanford University Press.
Diekmann, S., and Peterson, M. (2013) "The Role of Non-Epistemic Values in Engineering Models," *Science and Engineering Ethics* 19(1): 207–218.
Douglas, H. (2000) "Inductive Risk and Values in Science," *Philosophy of Science* 67(4): 559–579.
Douglas, H. (2009) *Science, Policy, and the Value-Free Ideal*, Pittsburgh: University of Pittsburgh Press.

Douglas, H. (2011) "Facts, Values and Objectivity," in I. Jarvie and J. Zamora-Bonilla (eds.) *The Sage Handbook of the Philosophy of Social Sciences*, Los Angeles: Sage Publications.
Douglas, H. (2018) "From Tapestry to Loom: Broadening the Perspective on Values in Science," *Philosophy, Theory, and Practice in Biology* 10(008).
Elliott, K. (2017) *A Tapestry of Values*, New York: Oxford University Press.
Elliott, K. and Richards, T. (eds.) (2017) *Exploring Inductive Risk: Case Studies of Values in Science*, New York: Oxford University Press.
Fama, E.F. (1970) "Efficient Capital Markets: A Review of Theory and Empirical Work," *Journal of Finance* 25(2): 383–417.
Fama, E.F. (2014) "Two Pillars of Asset Pricing," *American Economic Review* 104(6): 1467–1485.
Fama, E.F. (2017) "Finance at the University of Chicago," *Journal of Political Economy* 125(6): 1790–1799.
Fama, E.F., Fisher, L., Jensen, M.C., and Roll, R. (1969) "The Adjustment of Stock Prices to New Information," *International Economic Review* 10(1): 1–21.
Grüne-Yanoff, T. (2009) "Learning from Minimal Economic Models," *Erkenntnis* 70(1): 81–99.
Guala, F. (2016) "Performativity Rationalized," in I. Boldyrev and E. Svetlova (eds.) *Enacting Dismal Science*, London: Palgrave Macmillan: 29–52.
Haug, E.G., & Taleb, N.N. (2011) "Option traders use (very) sophisticated heuristics, never the Black–Scholes–Merton formula," *Journal of Economic Behavior & Organization* 77(2): 97–106.
Hausman, D.M. (1992) *The Inexact and Separate Science of Economics*, Cambridge: Cambridge University Press.
Hausman, D.M. (2005) " 'Testing Game Theory," *Journal of Economic Methodology* 12(2): 211–223.
Hindriks, F. (2008) "False Models as Explanatory Engines," *Philosophy of the Social Sciences* 38(3): 334–360.
Hindriks, F. (2013) "Explanation, Understanding, and Unrealistic Models," *Studies in History and Philosophy of Science Part A* 44(3): 523–531.
Kuorikoski, J., Lehtinen, A., and Marchionni, C. (2010) "Economic Modelling as Robustness Analysis," *British Journal for the Philosophy of Science* 61(3): 541–567.
MacKenzie, D. (2006) *An Engine, not a Camera: How Financial Models Shape Markets*, Cambridge, MA: MIT Press.
Marti, E., and Gond, J.P. (2018) "When Do Theories Become Self-Fulfilling? Exploring the Boundary Conditions of Performativity," *Academy of Management Review* 43(3): 487–508.
Modigliani, F. (2009) "Ruminations on My Professional Life," in W. Breit and B.T. Hirsch (eds.) *Lives of the Laureates: Twenty-Three Nobel Economists*, Cambridge, MA: MIT Press: 5th ed.
Modigliani, F., and Miller, M.H. (1958) "The Cost of Capital, Corporation Finance and the Theory of Investment," *American Economic Review* 48(3): 261–297.
Niederhoffer, V. (1997) *The Education of a Speculator*, New York: Wiley.
Phoa, W., Focardi, S.M., and Fabozzi, F.J. (2007) "How Do Conflicting Theories About Financial Markets Coexist?" *Journal of Post Keynesian Economics* 29(3): 363–391.
Rancan, A. (2020) *Franco Modigliani and Keynesian Economics*, Abingdon: Routledge.
Reiss, J. (2012) "The Explanation Paradox," *Journal of Economic Methodology* 19(1): 43–62.
Verreault-Julien, P. (2017) "Non-Causal Understanding with Economic Models: The Case of General Equilibrium," *Journal of Economic Methodology* 24(3): 297–317.
Sewing, A.S. (1919) *The Financial Policy of Corporations*, New York: Ronald Press Company.
Simon, H.A. (1947) *Administration Behavior: Study of Decision-Making Processes in Administrative Organization*, London: Palgrave Macmillan.
Simon, H.A. (1996) *Models of My Life*, Cambridge, MA: MIT Press.
Thaler, R.H. (1987) "Anomalies: The January Effect," *Journal of Economic Perspectives* 1(1): 197–201.
Ylikoski, P., and Aydinonat, N.E. (2014) "Understanding with Theoretical Models," *Journal of Economic Methodology* 21(1): 19–36.

PART IV

Values

15

VALUES IN WELFARE ECONOMICS

Antoinette Baujard

1. Introduction

Welfare economics provides a general theoretical framework intended to be used to evaluate social states and to assist in public decision-making, with the underlying aim of improving social welfare. In terms of content, welfare economics draws heavily from microeconomics, which notably furnishes its two fundamental theorems, as well as the basis for cost-benefit or equity analyses. Welfare economics is thus used to evaluate the consequences of alternative situations or public policies as regards social welfare, generally considering social welfare as tightly linked to individual well-being.

The standard approach to social welfare in welfare economics is *welfarist*, that is, social welfare is thought to depend only on individual utility and on no other information. It is fair to say that the term "welfarism" – notably introduced by Hicks (1959) and formally defined and popularized by Amartya Sen (1977, 1979a, 1979b) – was intended precisely as a tool to critique the use of welfarism in welfare economics. There are indeed major issues in welfare economics connected to the welfarist framework, including the link between theory and practice, the definition of social welfare, and the foundations of the judgments used in welfare economics. While a substantial number of distinct definitions of welfarism exist, each associated with specific lines of criticism or debate, philosophical approaches to welfare economics have in common the questioning of which information is to be judged relevant or legitimate for the determination of social welfare, and they seek in particular to tackle the hot issue of value judgments. The assessment of welfarism ultimately belongs to the wider debates regarding the axiological neutrality of science (see Reiss and Sprenger 2020) and the possibility of a demarcation between positive and normative economics (see Reiss, Chapter 16).

Hence, the present discussion focuses on whether welfare economics is a normative science and how welfare economics should tackle normative objectives such as social welfare, given that promoting social welfare is its main goal. As Atkinson (2009: 791) recalled,

> economists frequently make judgments about economic welfare, but there is today little discussion of the foundations of welfare economics. It is assumed either that there is unanimity of interests, or that there is general acceptance of utilitarianism. This means that economics cannot address many key policy issues and that important differences in ethical views cannot be recognized.

DOI: 10.4324/9781315739793-19

There are indeed several approaches to the issue of values in welfare economics, reflecting distinct lines of argumentation, and philosophical inquiry calls upon us to classify these approaches. Drawing on Mongin (2006), we present and assess the principal positions on the spectrum between the extreme view that welfare economics is entirely neutral and the counterview that it is an entirely ideological practice. The aim is to set out what is at stake for each of these positions: rather than pretending that specific literatures exist corresponding to each of the views canvassed here, we instead focus on their inner rationales and key consequences. For the purposes of analysis, we single out for discussion four archetypal positions: value neutrality (Section 2), the value confinement ideal (Section 3), the transparency requirement (Section 4), and the value entanglement claim (Section 5). This classification is meant to help us better understand not only how the welfarist framework is defined and why it has been called into question but more generally how each proposition in welfare economics fares with the issue of value neutrality and how it tackles the problem of ethical value judgments.

2. The Value-Neutrality Claim

2.1 Objectivity

Economics presents itself as a science in the mold of the natural sciences, and one of the objectivity requirements associated with such scientific ambition is that economics should be neutral with respect to judgments concerning ethical values. Seeing ethics as a matter of mere convention, subjectivity, or metaphysics, Robbins (1932) claims it is not liable to proof by observation or introspection, and he defends the influential view that ethics falls outside the scope of science – and hence of economics. In particular, there is no test that can be employed "in comparing the satisfaction of different people," and intercomparisons of utilities "cannot be justified by appeal to any kind of positive science," such that "it would be totally illegitimate to argue" that any recommendation may be warranted by economics. Thus, he concludes, "propositions involving 'ought' are on an entirely different plane from propositions involving 'is'" (Robbins 1932: 140–143). Economics should be neutral toward different ends and cannot pronounce on the validity of ultimate judgments of value (Robbins 1932: 147). The two areas of inquiry, economics and ethics, should therefore be considered disjointed and at no time should economists hold ethical values (for a discussion of the relationship between economics and ethics, see White, Chapter 17).

2.2 Behaviorism

The efforts of economics to establish itself as a value-neutral science have had deep and regrettable consequences for the conditions, the existence, and the reach of welfare economics. The exclusion of normative considerations and the focus on neutral observable phenomena have had direct consequences for the interpretation and the properties of individual utilities (Baujard 2017). Hedonic or moral utilities, in contrast with choices, are not observable. In revealed preference theory, utility is simply the numerical representation of choices, that is, the ranking of alternatives derived from observed choice situations. Hence, microeconomics, and subsequently welfare economics, has focused on utility under such a behavioral interpretation. Within such an interpretation, it is meaningless to talk about the intensity of utility or the comparison of utility between different individuals, such that welfare economics must as a consequence focus on ordinal and noncomparable utilities.

At the collective level, the only meaningful criterion for the ranking of social states at the collective level on the basis of ordinal noncomparable utility is the Pareto criterion.[1] According to the Pareto criterion, if everybody is at least equally well off in a state with the policy as without, and at least one individual is strictly better off with the policy, then the social state is better with the policy than without it. In every case where decisions may impact different individuals in a heterogeneous way, that is, where there are both losers and winners, welfare economics is not able to derive recommendations concerning whether the policy should be adopted. These situations are not comparable according to the Pareto criterion.

Thus, in most cases, the banishment of ethical values, and of interpersonal comparisons of utility in particular, automatically impedes the use of any normative premises and, hence, any prescriptive assertions: no recommendations that enable us to decide among policies could be derived from allegedly value-neutral welfare economics (Hicks 1939; Little 1950).

2.3 The Potential Pareto Criterion

Welfare economics has not – to say the least – attained such a desired state of value neutrality yet, nor has it remained content to debar itself from prescriptive judgment.

Kaldor (1939) and Hicks (1939) developed certain alternative methods in welfare economics designed to circumvent the preclusion of recommendations, appealing to the Weberian notion of the separation of the roles and tasks of politics and scientists. Imagine that losers lose less than winners win, and imagine that transfers from the former to the latter are likely to elicit an improvement that may be unanimously acclaimed. In such a case, everybody is likely to be better off with the policy than without it, provided the transfers are actually implemented. Economists qua economists are able to assert that the policy is making a potentially universal improvement, while politicians are empowered to decide whether the transfers should or should not be effected. The separation of tasks between economists and politicians is preserved here and recommendations may be proffered, but it is now questionable whether welfare economics still lives up to its ambition to issue recommendations without detouring through ethical judgments.

> To say that a policy which meets the Kaldor-Hicks criterion increases the "efficiency" of society is, in effect, to recommend it. Whereas if the value judgments implicit in the criterion are barred, it is unlikely to find favour with many people. . . . Compensation tests, consumers' and producers' surpluses suffer not only from the distributional complications common to comparisons based on such tests but also from difficulties in their measurement, largely owing to their essentially partial character.
>
> (Mishan 1960: 250–251)

Some even conclude that, in its ambition to produce value-neutral recommendations, welfare economics should be considered as a failure (Chipman and Moore 1978: 548, 581).

From the perspective of the history of welfare economics, this debate on the place of ethical values within welfare economics has driven the evolution of the discipline from the old to the new welfare economics and from welfare economics to contemporary theories of equity (Baujard 2017). But from a philosophical perspective, these two observations should come as no surprise. As a consequence of Hume's guillotine (see Reiss, Chapter 16), no recommendations can be formulated without normative premises, and hence value neutrality impedes the very recommendations that were the *raison d'être* of welfare economics. Conversely, any recommendation must derive from some normative premises; hence, the pretension of producing value-neutral recommendations is inconsistent. Insofar as the aim of welfare economics is evaluation or recommendation, it is constrained to suppose that there is such a thing as a substantial notion of "good" or "better."

Among the views that countenance normative premises in economics, we may distinguish two versions of an intermediate neutrality claim: the value confinement ideal and the transparency requirement.

3. The Value Confinement Ideal

Rather than targeting the chimeric ambition of value neutrality, economics may seek to associate itself with a value-free *ideal*, that is, to seek to minimize the importance of ethical values in scientific reasoning. In practice, such a search for "more" neutrality rather than "less" amounts to confining oneself to a reduced number of ethical principles, which, although they are admittedly normative, should not generally be considered controversial.

3.1 A Consensual Focus on Utility

With the emergence of modern standard microeconomics in the interwar and Cold War periods, individual utility has come to be cautiously associated with subjective ordinal preferences. This concept of utility does not convey any substantial definition of well-being: it derives only from what individuals themselves judge to be relevant and valuable. This focus on subjectivity conforms with the respect for "consumer sovereignty" and manifests a strong resistance to paternalism (Amadae 2003; Desmarais-Tremblay 2020a, 2021), having emerged at a moment in history when freedom, individualism, and market competition appeared as the alternatives to fascism and communism. Except for the individuals concerned, there is no reason why anybody should be entitled to say what is best for people. By trusting individuals' own ability to define their own version of well-being, economists would at least succeed in avoiding taking any stance in this regard themselves. Utility for microeconomics is defined in terms of subjective, ordinal, and noncomparable preferences; in order to fit with the value-containment ideal, welfare economics must also focus on this information. Note, however, that the assumption that subjective utility amounts to substantial well-being, or that it even satisfactorily reveals well-being, requires that individuals are sufficiently consistent, that their tastes and values are constant over the period studied, and that they are rational in seeking out the best strategies to serve their well-being. If these conditions are not met, as notably brought to light by behavioral economics, the assumption that subjective utility properly reveals real well-being remains debatable (see Rossi, Chapter 18, and Lecouteux, Chapter 4).

3.2 Welfarism

By focusing on individual utility, the value-containment ideal entails that welfare economics is welfarist, in the sense that the welfare of the community depends on the welfare of the individuals comprising it and nothing else, with the further restriction that individual utility is nothing but the numerical representation of subjective, ordinal, noncomparable preferences. Under this definition, welfarism appears to be the only source of ethical values in welfare economics.

This implies, on the one hand, *ethical individualism*: a social state is assessed only on the basis of how that state affects individuals, to the exclusion of any other source of ethical values. We cannot assign intrinsic importance to social phenomena, collective objects, or externalities apart from their individual parts.

On the other hand, welfarism supposes a stable focus on a given theory of individual utility. Welfare economics has long defended the superiority of subjective ordinal utility instead of its alternative. But note that the selection of one notion of well-being could, nevertheless, be considered as a significant normative choice. Each notion is consistent with the formal welfarist framework while also setting specific constraints upon it; it corresponds to distinct social theories of justice. Well-being could designate utility,[2] primary goods, resources, advantages, opportunities, capabilities, etc. (see Section 4 in this chapter, and Rossi, Chapter 18).

Hence, within the value-free ideal, the normativity is imported not only through the use of the welfarist framework itself but also through the choice of a given theory of well-being, insofar as there are indeed a number of alternative potential theories of well-being.

3.3 *Paretianism*

Because welfare economics is required to derive recommendations at the collective level, there ought also to be a collective ethical principle besides that of welfarism. The Pareto criterion (strictly speaking) ultimately seems a reasonable candidate for the value-containment claim, because it does not require any greater ethical load than the simple statement that improving individual well-being (whatever it is) is a good thing; hence, it claims no more than welfarism as such (see the next section on formal welfarism). The statement that individuals would be better off with than without a policy, with no losers, ought to be a matter of consensus, insofar as nobody has any reasonable interest in rejecting the claim and individual interest itself is considered as valuable.

However, because almost any public policy generates both losers and winners, adjudication for or against the policy implies a trade-off between different parties with diverging interests. In such a context, the Pareto criterion is mute due to the exclusion of interpersonal comparisons and, more generally, due to the exclusion of any further significant ethical commitment. Like the value-neutrality claim, the value-confinement claim fails to allow welfare economics to generate recommendations.

4. The Transparency Requirement

Any normative assertion requires some normative premises; in their absence, no recommendation may be formulated. The search for neutrality, or even more neutrality, in welfare economics is nothing but an illusion. And because value judgments are needed, the only alternative is to accept them as such, which first and foremost requires that we circumvent the difficulties induced by the role of values in economics.

Among the difficulties with the role of values in science – and economics is no exception in this regard – the possibility that the scientist's values might influence the outcome of her research is a significant source of skepticism about the reliability of scientific research outcomes. Given that the scientist is only a specific individual, the potential role of her emotions, private interests, personal values, or illegitimate pressures may engender distrust of her particular scientific assertions. By contrast, scientific analysis is considered to be reliable when assertions are void of any subjective bias on the part of those who formulate them. The goal of neutrality as regards values thus ought to be discarded; we should rather support the view that scientific assertions should be invariant to the individuality of different scientists.

The second difficulty with ethical values in science is that any debate on the desirability or appropriateness of *ends* for a society properly pertains to the role of elected officials within the domain of politics (whose actors we may call *politicians*), rather than the domain of science (whose producers we may call *scientists*, among whom number the economists). Science has no legitimacy to decide upon political values (e.g. Robbins 1932; Sugden 2004). As remarked in passing earlier, this echoes the famous thesis defended by Max Weber (1904) regarding the separation of tasks between politicians and scientists. However, given a set of political values a priori, social science (and welfare economics in particular) may be able to provide insightful recommendations on the best strategies to reach the ends decided upon by politicians: economics "is incapable of deciding the desirability of different ends. . . . It makes clear to us the implications of the different ends we may choose" (Robbins 1932: 152). The politicians' ends, once identified, should be able to be taken as given by economists. In other words, values should be given transparently by politicians and treated neutrally by scientists, such that any other set of scientists under the influence of different subjective biases would be able to derive the same conclusion.

As a provisional conclusion on this version of the nonneutrality view, there are three conditions that must be met for welfare economics to respect scientific standards while also engaging with value judgments: value transparency, intersubjective neutrality, and separation of tasks. The view deriving from these three requirements, which we call "the transparency requirement," comes with certain consequences.

4.1 Demarcation Among a Diversity of Potential Values

First, value judgments should be made transparent, not least because they are inescapable. Robbins (1932: 156) stated that, in the matter of policies, we need to choose among ends, and for this, "economics brings the solvent of knowledge. It enables us to conceive the far-reaching implications of alternative possibilities of policy. It does not, and it cannot, enable us to evade the necessity of choosing between alternatives." Little, for instance, also affirms that value judgments, and in particular judgments about distribution, whatever they are, cannot be avoided in welfare economics, but they should at least be made explicit: "Since we believe that the essential purpose of the economics of wealth, happiness, or welfare is to make recommendations, and to influence people, it follows that it should be put on an explicit, and not merely an implicit value basis" (Little 1950: 116; see also Mishan 1960).

The transparency standard implicitly assumes there is a diversity of a priori equally acceptable ethical value judgments. The task of normative economics is "to examine the consequences of different ethical positions" (Atkinson 2009: 791). This definition manifests a sharp and acknowledged contrast with the common underlying suppositions that there may be welfare recommendations without any ethical commitments, that such a thing as a consensual ethical position exists, or that we could rely on a more decisive ethical position, for example, on the utilitarianism that is sometimes employed by economists without any debate or reflection. As Atkinson (2009: 803) remarks,

> Many of the ambiguities and disagreements stem not from differences of view about how the economy works but about the criteria to be applied when making judgments. . . . People can legitimately reach different conclusions because they apply different theories of justice. This may seem self-evident to non-economists, but the economics profession in recent years has tended either to assume away welfare judgements or to assume that there is a general agreement.

He goes on to regret "the disappearance from economics of discussion of the principles underlying normative statements" (Atkinson 2001: 193). Hence, we first need to take for granted that there is a diversity of acceptable value judgments; the role of economics is to derive the subsequent recommendations and unveil the consequences of given value judgments.

Diversity comes with the need to be explicit about which ethical judgment has been selected, and this requires the demarcation of facts and values. If demarcation were possible, we could then factor out the descriptive and the evaluative components, as suggested by Hare (1952). Yet, certain judgments are not straightforwardly and exclusively prescriptive or evaluative: to say that some behavior is "rude" or "cruel" entails both descriptive and evaluative judgments. Hare (1952), rather, proposed that such statements should be considered to be entirely descriptive, at least if we agree that we can judge an action to be rude, say, if it conforms to some pregiven norms of rudeness society: we then need only describe such "compliance" to the norm. Similarly, we could describe certain notions of fairness as equity, or certain versions of utilitarianism, in terms of compliance to a norm, such that the consideration of these ethical values becomes just another descriptive ingredient included in our judgment (see Wintein and Heilmann, Chapter 19). The transparency of values, then, is the other side of the demarcation claim.

4.2 The Quantifying Device of Intersubjective Neutrality

Second, the means by which we make value judgments explicit should be introduced into economics in a manner that is itself neutral. Intersubjective neutrality may be obtained through devices that are able to formalize the normative criteria: this involves quantifying them and, in particular, assigning a list of desirable normative criteria to these tools (and *only* to them).

Equity and welfare theories, henceforth called the "social welfare approach," have been developed in the context of the Bergson-Samuelson school of the New Welfare Economics and in the wake of social choice theory. The social welfare approach seeks to analyze situations and rank them according to clear normative criteria (Adler 2019). Social welfare functions are tools in theoretical welfare economics, whose currency is not income or wealth but rather well-being and social welfare. The social welfare approach is characterized by two components: on the one hand, it assigns to each individual some inclusive measure of well-being that is supposed to depend on every welfare-relevant dimension; for instance, well-being is defined as subjective utility, which ultimately depends on one's own consumption, opportunity, or some objective index of well-being (see Rossi, Chapter 18). On the other hand, it provides a rule to rank these lists of measures at a collective level, taking into account a number of normative criteria of aggregation, for example, utilitarian vs. egalitarian. This allows the policy analyst to represent and rank each possible outcome of a policy for different contexts or for different policy choices. Indeed, a social welfare function depends both on the normative choices concerning the relevant information about every individual's well-being and on how to aggregate the list of individuals' well-being into a collective judgment.

If we allow that some normative ingredients are amenable to being embedded within the tools of economics without importing any bias, the normative load of the social welfare function can then be assimilated to the ethical interpretation of those ingredients, typically as derived from some well-established philosophical theory. A specific approach today commonly called "axiomatics," which is typical of normative economics, aims precisely at identifying these ingredients and, conversely, at choosing the proper devices given the desirable ingredients. At a high level of generality, axiomatics allows the deductive formalization of a given theory, whose propositions belong either to primary conditions called axioms or to derived propositions called theorems. Applied to welfare economics, it consists of the following steps: the primary conditions (including normative premises and descriptive elements) that collective evaluative rules should ideally satisfy are first captured by formal language. Then we describe, by deduction, the logical consequences of the association of the different conditions as the set of rules able to satisfy them exactly. If this set is empty, we have proven an impossibility result, which is interesting in itself as a means to highlight the inconsistency of the desired conditions; if this set is not empty, there is a theorem that characterizes a solution.

The deductive part is either true or false: it can be proven or confirmed, but it is not a matter of debate. The formal language does not convey any meaningful interpretation at all, at least until the axiomatics are given an external anchor point, for example, an external theory able to make sense of the symbols (Mongin 2003: 101). Some premises, which should originate only from the politicians, may be value laden, but their normativity is only conveyed not transformed by the deductive process conducted by the scientist: "the axiomatization would allow us to disentangle the logical inference from the interpretations, and hence to exercise greater control over the latter than any other formalization process would" (Mongin 2003: 121, author's translation). As a consequence of this clear separation of interpretation on the one hand and formal deduction on the other, who the scientist is becomes irrelevant, and the axiomatic approach is thus supposed to guarantee the neutrality of the treatment of the normative ingredients.

Just as Hare considered that rude was only a descriptive judgment because it implied some compliance with the norm defining rudeness, Fleurbaey (1996) considers the axiomatic approach to welfare and equity as entirely positive insofar as it does not require any personal commitment from the researcher. For instance, this approach enables Fleurbaey, qua scientist, to explain the consequences of a utilitarian theory in a given context just as any committed utilitarian would do, although he, as a person, would certainly value a greater dose of egalitarianism.

4.3 Separation of Tasks

Third, the transparency requirement supposes that the legitimacy of a given value judgment can differ depending on the perspective: judgments are of equal value from the scientific point of view, even while from the political point of view their value and social acceptability sharply vary.

The selection from among different potential normative criteria should not be completed by scientists but by those who have legitimacy to perform this function – hence, either the persons themselves or those who are representative of their interests (whom we previously called politicians, after Weber). There is a diversity of possible views here, which formal devices may help us to objectivize and disentangle. In the archetypal transparency requirement, therefore, we observe a three-stage process of reasoning: politicians choose ethical values; scientists associate the politicians' values (and no others) within the social welfare functions through axiomatics; and policy analysts apply the chosen social welfare functions in the given context and derive normative conclusions. The use of axiomatics explicates the normative load of a chosen social welfare function; the application of this social welfare function to a specific situation then enables us to generate an evaluative or prescriptive judgment, which closely derives from the chosen values but does not depend on the scientist. From this it follows that a similar situation may be judged differently by different philosophical theories, but equally by different analysts considering a given theory. A given sponsor may ask different scientists and still get the same "neutral" answer to her normative question.

5. The Entanglement Claim

The model offered by contemporary normative economics seems to meet the transparency requirement, although certain debates concerning the actual possibility of demarcation may still persist. Some, indeed, defend the thesis of an irreducible entanglement of facts and values; as a consequence, the transparency of the normative load of any scientific assertion is not fully attainable or will be potentially misleading.

5.1 The Case of Epistemic Values

According to Putnam (2002), values pervade scientific assertions. Descriptions always depend on the values or norms scientists may need to include in making their statements. He concludes that there is no such thing as a pure description of a reality waiting to be discovered by scientists and that scientists' statements necessarily always include some normative content.

This recalls the argument made by Rudner (1953) that scientists are constrained to make value judgments: he underlines that "the scientist as scientist accepts or rejects hypotheses," which presupposes "the *necessary* selection of a confidence level or interval" (Rudner 1953: 2–3) and, hence, the application of epistemic values. And this is indeed desirable, as it is the function of scientists in a society to uphold such epistemic value judgments. To fail to be aware of this is "to leave an essential aspect of the production of knowledge out of control" and, hence, what we need is a "science of ethics" (Rudner 1953: 6): "A science of ethics is a necessary requirement if science's progress toward objectivity is to be continuous. . . . A first step is surely comprised of the reflective self-awareness of the scientist in making the value judgements he must make."

Any tool that is able to make the values included in science transparent would be a positive step in the direction of building a science of ethics. This is precisely what was proposed in the previous section of this chapter: axiomatics is a device for transparency, and formal welfarism is the framework that allows a systematic analysis in welfare economics in particular. In formal welfarism, we describe the normative content of an ethical claim on the basis of two ingredients: the normative choice of a theory of individual well-being on the one hand, and the normative choice of a specific aggregating device on the other. A full description of the normative load of an assertion with no bias only holds conditionally upon the requirement that these two ingredients are independent of each other, however; otherwise, the dependency between the two levels would import other unexpected normative issues.[3]

And they are indeed not independent, because the aggregation rule enforces or requires certain properties of the informational basis: the use of a utilitarian sum requires cardinal utilities, and, conversely, ordinal utilities are compatible only with the Pareto criterion (Baujard 2017). Pursuing this line of thought, in providing a systematic analysis of this dependency in the case of voting rules, I have considered the individual informational basis as the voter's preferences as captured through a given form of ballot – which may be either the single name of a candidate, a list of approved names, names associated with nominal or cardinal grades for various given scales, etc. – and the aggregative part as the aggregative component of the voting rule – which may be the sum, the mean, or the median (Baujard 2015). While in a welfarist framework the analysis of the normative load of a voting rule should be independently based on these two successive steps, I have shown that the ballot information depends on and influences the aggregative rule used through a mechanical effect, for example, certain aggregative procedures are only compatible with certain forms of ballots. The dependency also obtains through psychological and behavioral effects: the strategic incentives or the ability for expression induced by the aggregative device, for instance, modifies the voter's expression of her preferences (see notably Baujard et al. 2018, 2020); hence, the ballot is not given independently of the voter's preferences but also depends on the aggregative device.

As a consequence of the dependency between the two stages in formal welfarism, the possibility of demarcation is disrupted even in the case of axiomatics. Instead of concluding that there is an irreducible entanglement, some claim rather that it shifts the problem onward and propose to modify the target of the axiomatic analysis: Ceron and Gonzalez (2021) propose to include the two levels simultaneously in their axiomatic analysis and to undertake a new research program in this regard. It is too early to say whether axiomatics may reveal itself to be the science of ethics that is likely to achieve a full normative analysis in this sense, but we can still assert that, as a device to factor out the descriptive and evaluative components of assertions at this stage, it is a good candidate to reduce the impact of the entanglement problem.

5.2 The Contextual Dependency of Facts and Values

Distinguishing between "thick" and "thin" concepts, Williams (1995) observes that thin judgment admits only evaluative content (good or bad, right or wrong) and remains very general, while a thick concept combines evaluative and nonevaluative descriptions (cruel, generous, courageous) and implies some description of the context. But Williams also observes that such a description can never be objective, as it always requires a perspective from which one wants to look at the world;[4] hence, he supports a relativistic thesis. Putnam (2002: 34–45) questions his relativist conclusion and rather supports the view that because in thick concepts the evaluative and descriptive aspects are intertwined, there is an irreducible dependency between values and facts.

Sen (1967) insists on the importance of distinguishing "compulsive" and "noncompulsive" judgments among the diversity of value judgments. Compulsive judgments are imperative prescriptions, that is, those that must be done whatever happens; noncompulsive evaluations are not absolutely obligatory and may be neglected, for example, for lack of other potentially relevant information concerning the context. He then introduces a distinction between "basic" and "nonbasic" statements. Some judgments may be basic if they always hold whatever the context: "you should not kill, whatever happens." Sen, however, very much doubts that any judgment can ever be considered as nonbasic, and this doubt especially concerns those judgments likely to be relevant for welfare economics. Indeed it is hard to make sense of assertions such as, "one should lower taxes, in every situation" or "the local government should build a swimming pool, whatever the public finance and the tastes of the population." By contrast, after a thorough descriptive analysis of the economic, social, and cultural situation, it may be meaningful to assert that, "in this specific case, it would serve aim *A* or conform with value *B* to lower taxes," or that, "considering the financial situation and the project, considering the cultural and sports policy goals of the new elected officials, considering the expected economic, social, and personal benefits of the pool set out in model z of agency β, building a swimming pool would provide more social benefits than less." As these examples illustrate, all evaluative statements depend in some sense on descriptive judgments. Conversely, descriptions are chosen on the basis of the specific aim of the value judgment embedded in the evaluation. Sen (1980) called this "description as choice," stating that any description supposes an active process of selection of some specific relevant information among an ocean of potentially relevant information. The description, hence, depends on this selection, which is driven by some values and goals.

Those values and goals should certainly not be swept under the carpet. They may even be specified as transparently as possible, as I have previously claimed in applying the "description as choice" argument to the axiomatic approach of formal welfarism (Baujard 2013). We said previously that the use of axiomatics is able to strive toward being value free as it conveys values that are not held by the scientist: this proposal might be acceptable if confined within a theory. Nevertheless, in the case of economics expertise, when applying the formal analysis to specific contexts, experts need to include goals and values when describing relevant information concerning the context. The choice of description is intertwined with the choice of values. To go beyond the thesis of entanglement, therefore, we need not only a science of ethics but also a science of the art of choosing the right models and data in the context of expertise. This is yet to come, and until then, the entanglement claim, at least insofar as it concerns welfare economics in the making, still has a robust future.

6. Conclusion

Whether welfare economics is or is not value laden is not a matter of debate: because welfare economics is not liable to issue any recommendations without a prior reference to values, whether epistemic or ethical, it must be seen as pervaded by values. But, depending on how the debate over ethical values has been approached – whether from the value-confinement ideal, the value-transparency requirement, or the entanglement claim – certain important restrictions and developments have taken place. Let us recognize that the neutrality claim is still very present in the economists' beliefs. The value-confinement ideal has led to a strong restriction of focus to ordinal utilities, a narrowing of the number of value judgments, and, potentially, the silent inclusion of certain other ethical judgments. It is fair to say that the axiomatic devices elaborated in the transparency requirement as a means to make values transparent and clearly demarcate them from descriptive statements have not yet achieved generalized application in applied welfare economics; nevertheless, it seems to have constituted a first step in the reduction – if not the resolution – of the issues raised by the entanglement claim.

Now that we have established the different rationales as to how values may be considered within welfare economics, the major question for welfare economics, namely, what social welfare is, can be studied with fresh eyes. Being directly related to values, welfare economics is first required to define or decide what social welfare depends on and which values should be considered as legitimate in this process. The choice of the relevant description of the social states entails an ethical commitment, which appears to be a fundamentally political issue. This chapter has intended to contribute to the clarification of the debate in this regard.

Related Chapters

Hausman, D., Chapter 31 "Quantifying Health"
Lecouteux, G., Chapter 4 "Behavioral Welfare Economics and Consumer Sovereignty"
Reiss, J., Chapter 16 "Measurement and Value Judgments"
Rossi, M., Chapter 18 "Well-Being"
Wintein, S., and Heilmann, C., Chapter 19 "Fairness and Fair Division"

Notes

1 Notice that, throughout the history of welfare economics, the Pareto criterion has been considered by economists as both a positive and a normative view. Berthonnet and Declite (2014) have shown that its use evolved from a normative to a positive concept in the course of the second half of the 20th century.
2 Utility on the one hand may refer to a state of mind. Hedonic theories, as in classical utilitarianism, consider well-being as the experience of happiness, as the balance between pains and pleasures, or as flourishing. This notion of well-being has been seen as insufficiently measurable or comparable to be serviceable for the new welfare economics. An alternative is to see utility as the mere numerical representation of preferences: if individual i prefers x to y, this means her utility is higher with x than with y. Under the revealed preference theory, i prefers x to y if and only if she chooses x when she has the opportunity to choose among x and y. Philosophers would require that preferences be rational, informed, and based on true beliefs (see Chapter 18 by Rossi on well-being). When utility is interpreted on the basis of preferences alone, it is only ordinal and noncomparable. On the other hand, utility may refer to a state of the world, for example, the level of individual income, the list of private goods and public amenities to which an individual has access, the number of kilometers that must be traversed in order to access water. Such states may be described and measured similarly by different external observers. In this respect, capabilities appear to be an individual basis of information that is objectively measurable, albeit distinct for each individual, and that may be used as the individual well-being ingredient in the formal welfarist framework.
3 Gharbi and Meinard (2017) use a similar argument when, reflecting on the fact that formal welfarism has pretentions to neutrality, they maintain that the dependency of the two stages compromises this neutrality.
4 By contrast, Sen (1993, 2009) considers this fact as the context for forming an objective positional view, at least if it can still be made context dependent although personally invariant.

Bibliography

Adler, M. D. (2019) *Measuring Social Welfare: An Introduction*, Oxford: Oxford University Press.
Amadae, S. M. (2003) *Rationalizing Capitalist Democracy: The Cold War Origins of Rational Choice Liberalism*, Chicago: University of Chicago Press.
Atkinson, A. B. (2001) "The Strange Disappearance of Welfare Economics," *Kyklos* 54(2/3): 193–206.
Atkinson, A. B. (2009) "Factor Shares: The Principal Problem of Political Economy?" *Oxford Review of Economic Policy* 25(1): 3–16.
Baujard, A. (2013) "Value Judgments and Economics Expertise," Working Paper GATE L-SE, WP 1314. (ftp://ftp.gate.cnrs.fr/RePEc/2013/1314.pdflink).
Baujard, A. (2015) *Le bien-être et les valeurs en économie: Perspectives historique, expérimentale et philosophique*, Mémoire d'Habilitation à diriger des recherches, Lyon: Université de Lyon.
Baujard, A. (2017) "L'économie du bien-être est morte. Vive l'économie du bien-être!" in *Philosophie économique, Editions Matériologiques*, ch. 2: 77–128.
Baujard, A., Gavrel, F., Igersheim, H., Laslier, J. F., and Lebon, I. (2018) "How Voters Use Grade Scales in Evaluative Voting," *European Journal of Political Economy* 55: 14–28.

Baujard, A., Igersheim, H., and Lebon, I. (2021) "Some Regrettable Grading Scale Effects Under Different Versions of Evaluative Voting," *Social Choice and Welfare*, 56: 803-834.

Berthonnet, I., and Declite, T. (2014) "Pareto-Optimality or Pareto-Efficiency: Same Concept, Different Names? An Analysis Over a Century of Economic Literature," *Research in the History of Economic Thought and Methodology* 32: 129–145.

Ceron, F., and Gonzalez, S. (2021) "Approval Voting Without Ballot Restrictions," *Theoretical Economics* 16(3): 759–775.

Chipman, J.S., and Moore, J.C. (1978) "The New Welfare Economics 1939–1974," *International Economic Review* 19(3): 547–584.

Desmarais-Tremblay, M. (2020) "W.H. Hutt and the Conceptualization of Consumers' Sovereignty," *Oxford Economic Papers* 72(4): 1050–1071.

Desmarais-Tremblay, M. (2021) "Paternalism and the Public Household. On the Domestic Origins of Public Economics," *History of Political Economy* 53(2): 179–211.

Fleurbaey, M. (1996) *Théories économiques de la justice*, Paris: Economica.

Gharbi, J. -S., and Meinard, Y. (2017) Welfarism and Ethical Neutrality. CNRS Working Paper. Online: https://www.gate.cnrs.fr/IMG/pdf/gharbi_meinard_-_welfarism_and_ethical_neutrality_-_saint-etienne.pdf

Hare, R. M. (1952) *The Language of Morals*, Oxford: Clarendon Press.

Hicks, J. (1959) *Essays in World Economics*, Oxford: The Clarendon Press.

Hicks, J. R. (1939) "The Foundations of Welfare Economics," *Economic Journal* 49: 696–712.

Kaldor, N. (1939) "Welfare Propositions of Economics and Interpersonal Comparisons of Utility," *Economic Journal* 49: 549–552.

Little, I. (1950/1957) *A Critique of Welfare Economics*, Oxford: Oxford University Press.

Mishan, E.J. (1960/1965) "A Survey of Welfare Economics, 1939–1959," *Economic Journal* 70: 197–265, published in 1965 by Macmillan.

Mongin, P. (2003) "L'axiomatisation et les théories économiques," *Revue Economique* 54(1): 99–138.

Mongin, P. (2006) "Value Judgments and Value Neutrality in Economics," *Economica* 73: 257–286.

Putnam, H. (2002) *The Collapse of the Fact/Value Dichotomy and Other Essays*, Cambridge: Harvard University Press.

Reiss, J., and Sprenger, J. (2020) "Scientific Objectivity," *The Stanford Encyclopedia of Philosophy*, Winter Edition, Edward N. Zalta (ed.). (https://plato.stanford.edu/archives/win2020/entries/scientific-objectivity/).

Robbins, L. (1932/1984) *An Essay on the Nature and Significance of Economic Science*, London: Macmillan.

Rudner, R. (1953) "The Scientist qua Scientist Makes Value Judgments," *Philosophy of Science* 20(1): 1–6.

Sen, A.K. (1993) "Internal Consistency of Choice," *Econometrica* 61(3): 495–521.

Sen, A.K. (1967) "The Nature and Classes of Prescriptive Judgments," *The Philosophical Quarterly* 17(66): 42–62.

Sen, A.K. (1977) "On Weights and Measures: Informational Constraints in Social Welfare Analysis," *Econometrica* 45(7): 1539–1572. Also in A.K. Sen (1982), *Choice, Welfare and Measurement*, Cambridge: MIT Press.

Sen, A.K. (1979a) "Personal Utilities and Public Judgements: Or What's Wrong With Welfare Economics?" *Economic Journal* 89(355): 537–558.

Sen, A.K. (1979b) "Utilitarianism and Welfarism," *The Journal of Philosophy* 76(9): 463–489.

Sen, A.K. (1980–81) "Plural Utilities," *Proceedings of the Aristotelian Society* 81: 193–215.

Sen, A.K. (2009) *The Idea of Justice*, Cambridge, MA: Harvard University Press.

Sugden, R. (2004) "The Opportunity Criterion: Consumer Sovereignty Without the Assumption of Coherent Preferences," *American Economic Review* 94(4): 1014–1033.

Weber, M. (1904/1959) "'Objectivity' in Social Science and Social Policy," in *The Methodology of the Social Sciences*, Free Press.

Williams, B. (1995) "Truth in Ethics," *Ratio* 8(3): 227–236.

16
MEASUREMENT AND VALUE JUDGMENTS

Julian Reiss

1. Introduction

Value judgments are all over the place in economics. Economists make a value judgment when they call one institution "efficient" and another "second-best" (Dupré 2007; see also Baujard, Chapter 15, for value judgments in welfare economics). They make value judgments when they decide to pursue this rather than that research project as "important" or "significant." As Gunnar Myrdal put it (Myrdal 2017/1954: xli):

> This implicit belief in the existence of a body of scientific knowledge acquired independently of all valuations is, as I now see it, naive empiricism. Facts do not organize themselves into concepts and theories just by being looked at; indeed, except within the framework of concepts and theories, there are no scientific facts but only chaos. There is an inescapable *a priori* element in all scientific work. Questions must be asked before answers can be given. The questions are an expression of our interest in the world, they are at bottom valuations. Valuations are thus necessarily involved already at the stage when we observe facts and carry on theoretical analysis, and not only at the stage when we draw political inferences from facts and valuations.

The defense of this or that climate change mitigation policy as "economically sound" is based on value judgments incorporated into economic models of climate change (Stern 2006; Nordhaus 2008).

There are, then, numerous sources of "value-laden" economics that are more or less obvious. There is also a long-standing view according to which value judgments do not affect all areas of economic practice. For example, in an early and influential paper, Amartya Sen argued that economists' *actions* (such as the actions of choosing a research question, investigating it, and publicizing the fruits of one's research) "must be value-based in a way that the evaluation of [*accounts*] need not be" (Sen 1983: 87). With "accounts" Sen refers to descriptions and explanations of economic phenomena and gives the mean consumption basket of the British consumer as a (descriptive) statement of the standard of living in Britain (Ibid.: 98) and monetarism as an explanatory/causal account (Ibid.: 92) as explicit examples.

Taking descriptive accounts of the inflation rate as its main case study, this chapter goes beyond what Sen argues in his 1983 paper. While he may well be right that the evaluation of descriptive and

DOI: 10.4324/9781315739793-20

explanatory accounts *need not be* value-based in a way that the evaluation of economists' actions is, I maintain that in practice it is hard to eschew value judgments in the construction and evaluation of accounts of economic phenomena. One reason is that the distinction Sen draws between the evaluation of the *truth* of an account as opposed to the evaluation of its *goodness* is not straightforward in practice. While it is often possible to determine whether a statement such as, "The inflation rate in our country is *x*% according to index such-and-such," is true, there is little point in doing so unless one also has a way to determine whether the measurement procedure is valid. But that cannot be done without a clear idea of what the purpose of measuring the quantity is, and many measurement purposes are inextricably linked with normative questions about the good life and the good society. In other words, the evaluations of the *truth* of certain descriptive and explanatory statements entail an endorsement of value judgments.

2. The Measurement of Inflation

The measurement of inflation – of the development of the "value of money" over time – is of enormous scholarly and practical importance. The scholarly importance is due to the fact that all longitudinal studies that use time-series data on "real" variables, such as "real GDP growth" or "real interest rates" or "real consumption," require an inflation index in order to deflate the observable nominal counterparts. The practical importance stems from the indexation of many contracts and payments to popular measures of inflation, such as the Austrian consumer price index (A-CPI). Examples of A-CPI-indexed payments include rental payments and payments of alimony. The A-CPI is often also the basis for wage negotiations.

None of this would matter a great deal if inflation were straightforwardly observable or, failing that, its measurement were uncontested. Alas, it is not. Controversies surrounding the measurement of inflation are almost as old as the consumer price index itself, and news outlets publish reports that "felt inflation" diverges from "measured inflation" on a regular basis (often coinciding with the wage negotiation cycle). Price measurement matters. Differences in the details of measurement procedures, for example, about the composition of the basket of goods that determines the structure of the index, the treatment of quality changes, the weighting of households, and the index number formula can make significant differences in the values the index produces. Especially when the inflation rate is relatively low (the Eurozone rate has been, with just a few exceptions, fairly close to 2%, the rate targeted by the European Central Bank, since the 1990s), decisions about how to construct the index can then have economically significant consequences for both economic analysis and the economy.

John Neville Keynes, father of the better known John Maynard Keynes, introduced a tripartite distinction between positive economics, normative economics, and the art of economics (Keynes 1890/1999: Ch. 2). According to Keynes, a positive science is a body of systematized knowledge concerning *what is*; a normative science is a body of systematized knowledge concerning *what ought to be* (and therefore concerned with the ideal as distinguished from the actual); and an art is a system of rules for the attainment of a given end. Today it is more common merely to distinguish positive and normative economics, keeping the definition of positive economics in place but extending normative economics to cover the art as well [see Samuelson and Nordhaus (2009) for the more recent, twofold distinction and Colander (1992) for a lament about the "lost art of economics"].

Importantly, there is not just a *distinction* between a science that describes what is and one that considers what ought to be. According to the received view in economics, positive economics is "in principle independent of any particular ethical position or normative judgments" (Friedman 1953: 4). Thus, while normative economics and the art of economics are dependent on the conclusions of positive economics (e.g., because policy recommendations must partly be based on predictions about the consequences of implementing a policy), positive economics proceeds in an objective, value-free manner.

A long-standing tradition in economics maintains that value judgments are purely subjective. For example, as Lionel Robbins wrote in his *Essay on the Nature and Significance of Economic Science* (Robbins 1932: 134):

> Now, as regards the first type of difference [of opinion], neither Economics nor any other science can provide any solvent. If we disagree about ends it is a case of thy blood or mine – or live and let live, according to the importance of the difference, or the relative strength of our opponents.

In the essay cited earlier, Friedman says something very similar. More recently, Gregory Mankiw uses a somewhat more conciliatory tone but agrees that normative conclusions are based on subjective points of view (Mankiw 2017: 27):

> By contrast, evaluating normative statements involves values as well as facts. [The] statement ["The government should raise the minimum wage"] cannot be judged using data alone. Deciding what is good or bad policy is not just a matter of science. It also involves our views on ethics, religion, and political philosophy.

Thus, positive economics on the one hand and normative economics and the art of economics on the other differ not only with respect to their subject matter (what is vs what ought to be) but also with respect to their respective sources of knowledge (evidence vs opinions) and with respect to their degree of trustworthiness (objective vs subjective). We refer to this view that knowledge of the facts is, in principle, independent of value judgments and is of a qualitatively different character from knowledge of values as the *fact/value dichotomy*.

These two claims – that inflation measurement is contested and the fact/value dichotomy – form the dual backdrop against which this chapter proceeds.

There are numerous inflation indices, such as the consumer price index, the wholesale price index, the industrial output price index, the gross domestic product (GDP) deflator, the retail price index in the United Kingdom, and so on. Because of its practical importance (see previous discussion), widespread use, and relevance, this chapter will focus on the consumer price index (CPI).

The CPI measures the price level for a weighted average basket of goods and services purchased by households. To give a very simple example, if people consume 25% goods (G) and 75% services (S) and the prices of goods rise by 5% but those of services by 10%, then the change in the price *level* is $\text{weight}_G \times \text{price}_G + \text{weight}_S \times \text{price}_S = 0.25 \times 5\% + 0.75 \times 10\% = 8.75\%$.

A price index is fully accurate only if nothing changes in the economy but the prices. Unfortunately, this is not even approximately true. When prices change, people substitute cheaper goods for more expensive goods, thus increasing the weights of the goods that have become (relatively) cheaper. People's tastes change. The quality of goods and services changes. New goods and services appear in the market, and old goods and services vanish. New kinds of retail outlets are introduced, replacing older forms of retailing. The social, cultural, and natural environment changes.

For none of these changes is there a fully satisfactory treatment within the concept of a price index. Consider the substitution effect. Suppose that people, because services have become relatively more expensive, buy more goods and fewer services, so that the weights change to 30% and 70%, respectively. We can now compute not one but indefinitely many indices: one using the weights from the base year (which leads to the so-called Laspeyres index), one using the weights from the current year (which leads to the Paasche index), and any number of indices that use some average of weights, such as the geometric mean between the Laspeyres and Paasche indices [which Irving Fisher called the "ideal index; see Fisher (1922)]. The Paasche index would yield an inflation rate of 8.5%. It is sometimes said that the Laspeyres index overstates the inflation rate (e.g., Schultze and Mackie 2002: 21ff.). By substituting cheaper goods for more expensive goods, people can maintain the same standard of living. The use of base-year weights, as the Laspeyres index does, means to ignore the possibility of reacting to price changes and therefore to overstate inflation according to this view. A similar argument can be made that the Paasche index *under*states inflation. There is thus some justification in using an index such as Fisher's ideal index.

However, two tacit assumptions have been made, both of which are highly controversial. First, it is assumed that the CPI measures the "cost for maintaining a constant standard of living," which is very different from the level of prices. It is by no means clear that this is the right concept behind the CPI (Deaton 1998). Second, it is assumed that the change in weights is exclusively due to the substitution effect. But, of course, there may be all sorts of reasons why people change their shopping patterns (changes in income, tastes, environment, etc.), and the ideal index does not capture any of these effects.

Quality changes have been referred to as the "house-to-house combat of price measurement" (Shapiro and Wilcox 1996). The reason is that quality changes raise the question of whether any given price change is due to the change in quality or due to inflation. If the new iPhone costs 50% more than the previous model but has a variety of new features, some of which constitute improvements, how much of the 50% is due to the change in quality and how much is a pure price change? There are numerous methods to deal with the problem, but each method has limitations and drawbacks (Hulten 1997). It has been suggested that the quality change problem is unsolvable (Deaton 1998).

Apart from these and other technical problems, there is the more fundamental issue that the CPI measures the *average* level of prices, which may be meaningful to no one. Each household has different shopping patterns and therefore experiences price changes differently. The weights used in the CPI are driven by the economically very active segment of the population, but the measure is used, for instance, to index pension payments. Old people and poor people potentially face very different price vectors if they are unable to drive or benefit from online commerce. It is therefore not surprising that the CPI has been a highly contested and politicized construct since its birth [for its history in the United States, see Stapleford (2007)].

3. The Fact/Value Dichotomy and Its Collapse

David Hume provided the first systematic defense of the fact/value dichotomy in modern philosophy. According to Hume, all true statements fall into one of two categories: relations of ideas and matters of fact. Mathematical and logical truths (tautologies) belong in the former category and are ascertainable through reason; empirical truths belong in the latter category and are ascertainable through observation. This idea has come to be known as "Hume's fork" (e.g., Dicker 1998: Ch. 2). Moral claims are of neither kind and therefore cannot be true nor false. Hume is also famous for arguing that an "ought" (a normative statement) cannot be derived from an "is" (a positive statement).[1]

The contemporary debate originates in the logical empiricists' quest for a criterion of cognitive significance. All extralogical statements had to be verifiable (empirically testable) in order to be meaningful. Because moral claims were not verifiable, they were once more neither true nor false but expressions of approval and disapproval (Ayer 1936/1971).

An important step toward the collapse of the fact/value dichotomy was made by W.V.O. Quine when he showed the logical empiricists' version of Hume's fork, the distinction between analytical and synthetic statements, and the verifiability criterion to be untenable (Quine 1953). Without a sharp separation between analytical and synthetic statements, and without a viable definition of what a "fact" is, the fact/value dichotomy no longer seemed compelling (Putnam 2002).

Within the philosophy of science, a first crack in the structure of the value-free ideal (the idea that scientific reasoning should not be affected by value judgments) was an article published in the same year as Quine's that argued that value judgments influence hypothesis testing (Rudner 1953). No matter how much evidence we collect, the decision to accept or reject a hypothesis is always risky. When the evidence, on balance, speaks in favor of a hypothesis, we might accept it or wait until we can be more certain. Either way, we can make a mistake. But the consequences between the different errors are often different. To come to optimal decisions, then, requires an evaluation of which consequences are more palatable. This cannot be done without value judgments.

While Rudner's argument has received some criticism (e.g., Jeffrey 1956; Levi 1960), Heather Douglas pointed out that hypothesis acceptance is only one of a number of stages of the scientific process in which value judgments enter (Douglas 2000). Many decisions in the process of scientific inquiry may conceal implicit value judgments: the design of an experiment, the methodology for conducting it, the characterization of the data, the choice of a statistical method for processing and analyzing data, the interpretational process findings, etc. None of these methodological decisions could be made without consideration of the possible consequences that could occur.

Although the debate continues, most philosophers of science have moved on to accepting value-ladenness as a given and addressing the issue of how best to manage values. One cluster of proposals centers around the idea of public engagement in science. Elliott (2017) argues that scientists should be as transparent as possible about the value judgments they make and, if possible, incorporate values that are representative of major social and ethical priorities. He identifies public engagement as a powerful means to achieve these ends and distinguishes among community-based, bottom-up approaches, formal top-down approaches, approaches that promote engagement between interdisciplinary groups of scholars with diverse backgrounds, and approaches that focus on engagement between different groups of people and the laws, institutions, and policies that influence scientific research. I refer to these proposals as "Deweyan value management strategies" after John Dewey's defense of the democratization of science (Dewey 1954/2012).

An alternative kind of proposal is to replace the value-free ideal with a "social value management ideal" after Helen Longino (1990, 2002), who accepts the influence of values on science as long as there are appropriate venues for criticism, scientists are responsive to criticism, there are publicly recognized evidential standards, and the scientific community is inclusive (Wray 1999; Anderson 2004; Rolin 2011). In economics, Gebhard Kirchgässner has defended a similar view (Kirchgässner 2003). I refer to these proposals as "Popperian value management strategies," as they regard the objectivity of science to be constituted by its ability to effectively promote criticism (Popper 1976).

Both Deweyan and Popperian proposals should be understood as at best solution sketches as they are strongly influenced by case studies, the lessons of which may not apply elsewhere, and as they raise a host of follow-up issues. It is not clear, for instance, why science being more representative in terms of demographics should improve scientific conclusions and the handling of values in science. Given that (a) people often disagree about values but (b) scientists are expected to provide unambiguous answers to questions concerning which policies or technologies are safe and effective, it does not seem as though democratizing science would improve its ability to play that role.

4. Fact/Value Entanglement in Economics and in Inflation Measurement in Particular

Max Weber famously argued that, although social science was necessarily value-laden in that it investigated phenomena that have cultural *significance* – a value-laden term – the social scientist could proceed objectively in the sense that answers about the causes of these phenomena are not dependent on individual researchers' idiosyncrasies, nor does the individual researcher decide whether a phenomenon is culturally significant; this is a question concerning values, but not (necessarily) the social scientist's values (Weber 1904/1949). One of the main issues in the *Werturteilsstreit* that erupted a few years after Weber published his essay was precisely about the role of social scientists in policy advice: Weber argued that the scientist qua scientist should offer only information about effective means but not opinions about the desirability of ends, and his opponents advocated a broader role for the social scientist, which included giving normative advice [a view that was echoed more recently by British economist Anthony Atkinson; see Atkinson (2001)].

Joseph Schumpeter was less optimistic than Weber that the selection of facts to be investigated could proceed without the scientist's own bias affecting his or her choice, and he noted the possible influence of ideology on setting standards for hypothesis acceptance (Schumpeter 1949). A further reason that value judgments affect the conclusions of positive economics is due to the fact that economics builds on the theory of rationality at its core, which, despite many economists' protestations, makes substantial claims about what kinds of behavior count as rational and irrational (Broome 1991: Ch. 5; Hausman and McPherson 2006: Ch. 4; Reiss 2013: Ch. 3).

Finally, and most relevantly for the present project, value judgments enter through the formation of concepts. Bernard Williams calls notions whose meanings mix descriptive and evaluative components "thick ethical concepts" (Williams 1985/2011: 143). Examples include *treachery*, *promise*, *brutality*, and *courage*. He argues that attempts to separate the descriptive from the evaluative are bound to distort meanings unacceptably. There is no way to rid economics of such concepts without changing the nature of the science (Mongin 2006).[2]

Consumer price inflation is a thick concept in the sense that both descriptive and evaluative judgments enter the measurement procedure. That this should be so is not surprising because inflation is generally seen to be a bad thing,[3] and so our answer to the question, "What is the inflation rate?" matters a great deal to human interests.[4]

Value judgments enter the measurement procedure at numerous stages. The first is a fundamental decision about measurement purpose: because there is no one way to measure inflation, the adequacy of the procedure must be evaluated in light of the purpose to which it is put. The CPI is used for numerous purposes, such as (Schultze and Mackie 2002: 192) the following:

- As a compensation measure to calculate how much is needed to reimburse recipients of social security and other public transfer payments against changes in the cost of living and for formal or informal use in wage setting.
- For inflation indexation in private contracts.
- As a measure of inflation for inflation-indexed treasury bonds.
- As a measure with which to index the income tax system to keep it inflation neutral.
- As an output deflator for separating changes in gross domestic product (GDP) and its components into changes in prices and changes in real output.
- As an inflation yardstick for the Federal Reserve and other macroeconomic policymakers.

Amartya Sen argues that the fact that the goodness of an account (and of a measurement procedure, we might add) has to be judged in light of the purpose for which the account (or the measurement procedure) is made makes the evaluation necessarily value based, but in a way that is unproblematic (Sen 1983: 102f.):

> More importantly, insofar as statements or accounts are judged to be good from a specified point of view, viz., that of a particular use-interest, the judgement is rather like describing

> a knife to be a good knife to cut bread. The value element is not fundamental here, since the goodness is seen as an instrumental merit.

I disagree with Sen about this point. In an ideal world with unlimited resources and cognitive capacities, economists could develop as many indices as there are purposes, and policymakers and the general public could pick and choose. But in our world, in which resources and cognitive capacities are scarce, it is the economist who has to make choices. Because, with limited funds, the number of indices that are regularly measured must be limited, decisions that are adequate for one purpose rather than another make an implicit judgment about what purposes are more important. This matters particularly when different groups in the population face significantly different price vectors, and the measurement purpose is to keep the value of certain payments (such as rents, pensions, or alimony) constant.

Second is the concept behind the construct. In their review of the US CPI, the Boskin commission's main recommendation was that the CPI should measure a "cost-of-living index" (Boskin et al. 1996). This recommendation is hardly innocuous, partly because the choice to frame scientific information in one way rather than another is driven by value judgments (Elliott 2017: Ch. 6) and partly because the specific choice made here is based on the economic theory of index numbers (e.g., Diewert 2004), which imports numerous value judgments related to neoclassical economic theory. For example, a consumer who chooses a new good over an old one, when the old good is still available, is assumed to prefer the new good and his or her standard of living therefore improves. More generally, standard of living is conceptualized as utility, which in turn is understood as preference satisfaction, all of which is highly controversial (e.g., Crisp 2008). An argument in favor of equating well-being or the standard of living with (actual) preference satisfaction is that doing so respects consumer autonomy more than alternative theories of well-being. An argument against equating the two is that doing so makes it difficult to maintain that people sometimes desire things that are bad for them, which is plausible to say the least. Accounts that equate well-being with "laundered" or "tutored" or "rational" preferences solve the latter problem (as it can be argued that some of the things people actually prefer may well be bad for them, but they would not prefer these things if they were fully rational) at the expense of opening the door to charges of paternalism (Reiss 2013: Ch. 12). Debates such as these are normative to the teeth.

Third, choices have to be made about the extent to which new goods, goods whose quality has changed, new distribution channels, and so on are "comparable" to the goods and distributions channels they replace. If we focus on changes in the quality of goods here, the first thing to note is that the issue is massive. For the US CPI, it has been estimated that about 4% of price quotations on average involve a replacement item *each month*. Because some items are replaced more than once during a year, this translates into an annual replacement rate of about 30% for items in the CPI (Moulton and Moses 1997). Importantly, when an item is either temporarily or permanently unavailable, the decision has to be made whether an available similar item is a "comparable replacement." That decision involves a value judgment, for instance, about whether or not a consumer benefits from the change.

Fourth, in the CPI, household budgets are weighted by their share in aggregate expenditure. The CPI has therefore been called a "plutocratic index" because richer households count more than poorer ones (Prais 1959). An alternative would be to compute a "democratic index" in which all households are weighted equally. Once more, it is a value judgment that a plutocratic index is the more appropriate one. It has been calculated that the household for which the plutocratic weights are correct lies at the 75th percentile of the expenditure distribution for 1990 (Deaton 1998). When inequality is large, the CPI is unrepresentative of the cost of living for the great majority of households.

In the paper referred to previously, Sen distinguishes between assessing the *truth* of an account and assessing its *goodness*. One way to understand the distinction is to invoke Paul Grice's maxims of effective communication (Grice 1975). Apart from being truthful (Grice's maxim of quality), Grice maintains that conversation partners can reasonably expect each other to be as informative as required (maxim of quantity), to be relevant (maxim of relation), and to be perspicuous (maxim of manner). What Sen calls a good account is essentially one that satisfies Grice's maxims of quantity, relation, and manner.

Quantity, relation, and manner all depend on the accepted purpose of the conversation. If someone asks what to buy to make hollandaise sauce, I should say eggs, butter, lemon, salt, and pepper and not specify Sicilian lemon, Hawaiian Alaea sea salt, or 221.056 g of butter or use sodium chloride for salt. Truth and goodness sometimes pull in different directions. If someone asks me how old I am, I am truthful if I say "over 18," but that will not be a good account of my age unless I want to buy alcohol or a ticket to an adult movie. By contrast, a negative answer to "Do I look fat?" will serve most purposes even if not always truthful.

Sen's distinction is therefore entirely valid in principle but, I would like to argue, not always easy to uphold in the context of statements that involve economic indicators. There is little point in saying that the inflation rate is such-and-such unless one accepts the measurement procedure as valid. But to accept the measurement procedure as valid commits one not only to a specific measurement purpose (which in turn commits one to a judgment of that purpose as significant and appropriate) but also to a number of additional value judgments. When it comes to statements involving economic indicators, truth and goodness are therefore entangled.

5. Other Economic Indicators

Naturally, consumer price inflation is not alone in its mixing of descriptive and normative components. Let us briefly look at two further economic indicators: the unemployment rate and economic product. Much like inflation, the unemployment rate appears to be objectively and straightforwardly measurable – after all, what is the unemployment rate but the number of unemployed persons divided by the number of persons in the workforce – but appearances deceive greatly here too. The International Labour Organization (ILO), whose definition is used all around the world, defines a person as unemployed when he or she is out of work and is currently looking and available for work. But not everyone to whom the definition applies is counted, and precisely who is counted varies from country to country. In the United States, persons under 16, those confined to institutions such as nursing homes and prisons, or persons on active duty in the armed forces are excluded. The precise specification matters. Using US standards, for example, the Canadian unemployment rate would be about 1% lower than the country's official rate says it is (Flaherty 2012: 35). Now that child labor is banned or at least severely restricted in developed countries, excluding persons under 16 seems plausible enough. However, there is no natural cutoff point (why not 15 or 18), and the expectations concerning a young person's activity are indubitably influenced by societal norms.

The other aspect of the definition of unemployment that is strongly influenced by normative expectations concerns the effort a person must put forth in order to count as "looking for work." Does asking around in one's neighborhood suffice? Or reading the newspaper? As people rely on internet media more and more, job ads in newspapers lose significance. But should someone be regarded as having left the labor force because they do not have an internet connection? In some countries, a person has to be registered with a government agency (such as the UK Jobcentre) in order to count as unemployed.

Economic product is another widely discussed quantity that is as important as its measurement is controversial (Stiglitz et al. 2010; Coyle 2014). In early editions of his best-selling textbook, the economist Paul Samuelson joked that GDP falls when a man marries his maid. The serious kernel of truth in this is that two nations can produce the exact same goods and services but organize their exchange differently – one nation has a higher degree of market integration, whereas in the other more is produced in households – and consequently they will wind up with different GDPs. Most certainly it is not the case that everything of value is produced for the market so that market prices can be used as a measure of value. But nonmarket production by households and governments and black-market production are difficult to estimate, and decisions about their inclusion and how to estimate them necessarily involve value judgments. The same is true of production processes that involve externalities such as environmental degradation that do not have a market price.

6. Conclusions

In economics, judgments of matters of fact and value judgments are deeply entangled. Economists cannot hope even to describe certain simple economic "facts" without taking a stance about the good life and the good society. What this chapter tries to show is that economic indicators require substantial background assumptions, not only about facts (e.g., whether or not consumers make their decisions according to the rational choice model given by economic theory) but also about values (e.g., whether or not a given quality change constitutes a consumer benefit), as well as the purposes addressed by the measurement (e.g., whether an inflation indicator is used for indexing purposes or for macroeconomic analysis). Those who maintain that descriptive and explanatory accounts of economic phenomena can be value free are therefore wrong, at least insofar as these accounts make use of economic indicators, such as those surveyed in this chapter.

Related Chapter

Baujard, A., Chapter 15 "Values in Welfare Economics"

Notes

1 This idea has also come to be known as Hume's guillotine (Black 1964).
2 *Efficiency* is a prime example of a thick ethical concept in economics. To call a situation efficient provides descriptive information – that markets clear – and also an evaluation – that this is a desirable state of affairs. Even if some economists might refuse to acknowledge the implicit normative judgment, it is made is unambiguous in the context of policy advice (Dupré 2007: 36–37).
3 That the negative sentiment might not be shared by debtors does not invalidate the claim that inflation mixes descriptive and evaluative components. Compare "politically correct," which clearly fuses description and evaluation, even though the evaluation differs between different groups of people.
4 Compare Gunnar Myrdal:

> There is no way of studying social reality other than from the viewpoint of human ideals. A "disinterested social science" has never existed and, for logical reasons, cannot exist. The value connotations of our main concepts represent our interest in a matter, give direction to our thoughts and significance to our inferences. It poses the questions without which there are no answers.
>
> (Myrdal 1958: 1)

Bibliography

Anderson, Elizabeth 2004. "Uses of Value Judgments in Science: A General Argument, with Lessons from a Case Study of Feminist Research on Divorce." *Hypatia* **19**: 1–24.
Atkinson, Anthony 2001. "The Strange Disappearance of Welfare Economics." *Kyklos* **54**(2–3): 193–206.
Ayer, Alfred 1936/1971. *Language, Truth and Logic*. London, Penguin Books.
Black, Max 1964. "The Gap Between 'Is' and 'Should'." *The Philosophical Review* **73**(2): 165–181.

Boskin, Michael, Ellen Dulberger, Robert Gordon, Zvi Griliches and Dale Jorgensen 1996. *Final Report of the Advisory Commission to Study the Consumer Price Index*. Washington, DC, U.S. Government Printing Office.

Broome, John 1991. *Weighing Goods: Equality, Uncertainty and Time*. Oxford, Blackwell.

Colander, David 1992. "The Lost Art of Economics." *Journal of Economic Perspectives* **6**(3): 191–198.

Coyle, Diana 2014. *GDP: A Brief But Affectionate History*. Princeton, NJ, Princeton University Press.

Crisp, Roger 2008. Well-Being. *The Stanford Encyclopedia of Philosophy*. Edward N. Zalta, Ed. Stanford, Stanford University Press.

Deaton, Angus 1998. "Getting Prices Right: What Should Be Done?" *Journal of Economic Perspectives* **12**(1): 37–46.

Dewey, John 1954/2012. *The Public and Its Problems: An Essay in Political Inquiry*. University Park, PA, Penn State University Press.

Dicker, Georges 1998. *Hume's Epistemology and Metaphysics: An Introduction*. London, Routledge.

Diewert, W. Erwin 2004. The Economic Approach to Index Number Theory: The Single Household Case. *Consumer Price Index Manual: Theory and Practice*. International Labour Organization, Ed. Geneva, ILO Statistical Office.

Douglas, Heather 2000. "Inductive Risk and Values in Science." *Philosophy of Science* **67**(4): 559–579.

Dupré, John 2007. Fact and Value. *Value-Free Science? Ideals and Illusions*. Harold Kincaid, John Dupré and Alison Wylie, Eds. Oxford, Oxford University Press: 27–41.

Elliott, Kevin 2017. *A Tapestry of Values: An Introduction to Values in Science*. Oxford, Oxford University Press.

Fisher, Irving 1922. *The Making of Index Numbers: A Study of Their Variety, Tests and Reliability*. Boston, MA, Houghton Mifflin.

Flaherty, James M. 2012. *Jobs, Growth, and Long-Term Prosperity: Economic Action Plan 2012* Ottawa, ON, Public Works and Government Services Canada.

Friedman, Milton 1953. The Methodology of Positive Economics. *Essays in Positive Economics*. Chicago, University of Chicago Press.

Grice, Paul 1975. Logic and Conversation. *Syntax and Semantics*. Vol. 3. P. Cole and J.L. Morgan, Eds. New York, Academic Press.

Hausman, Daniel M. and Michael S. McPherson 2006. *Economic Analysis, Moral Philosophy, and Public Policy*. 2nd Ed. New York, Cambridge University Press.

Hulten, Charles 1997. "Quality Change in the CPI." *Federal Reserve Bank of St. Louis Review* **79**(3): 87–100.

Jeffrey, Richard 1956. "Valuation and Acceptance of Scientific Hypotheses." *Philosophy of Science* **22**: 237–246.

Keynes, John Neville 1890/1999. *The Scope and Method of Political Economy*. Kitchener, ON, Batoche Books.

Kirchgässner, Gebhard 2003. Empirical Economic Research and Economic Policy Advice: Some Remarks. *Economic Policy Issues for the Next Decade*. Karl Aiginger and Gernot Hutschenreiter, Eds. New York, NY, Springer: 265–288.

Levi, Isaac 1960. "Must the Scientist Make Value Judgments?" *Journal of Philosophy* **57**: 345–357.

Longino, Helen 1990. *Science as Social Knowledge: Values and Objectivity in Scientific Inquiry*. Princeton, NJ, Princeton University Press.

Longino, Helen 2002. *The Fate of Knowledge*. Princeton, NJ, Princeton University Press.

Mankiw, Gregory 2017. *Principles of Economics*. 8th Ed. Boston, MA, Cengage Learning.

Mongin, Philippe 2006. "Value Judgments and Value Neutrality in Economics." *Economica* **73**: 257–286.

Moulton, Brent and Karin Moses 1997. "Addressing the Quality Change Issue in the Consumer Price Index." *Brookings Papers on Economic Activity* **1**: 305–349.

Myrdal, Gunnar 1958. *Value in Social Theory*. London, Routledge.

Myrdal, Gunnar 2017/1954. *The Political Element in the Development of Economic Theory*. Abingdon, Routledge.

Nordhaus, William D. 2008. *A Question of Balance: Weighing the Options on Global Warming Policies*. New Haven and London, Yale University Press.

Popper, Karl 1976. On the Logic of the Social Sciences. *The Positivist Dispute in German Sociology*. Theodor Adorno, Hans Albert, Ralf Dahrendorf et al., Eds. London, Heinemann: 87–104.

Prais, Sigmund 1959. "Whose Cost of Living?" *Review of Economic Statistics* **26**(2): 126–134.

Putnam, Hilary 2002. *The Collapse of the Fact/Value Dichotomy and Other Essays*. Cambridge, MA, Harvard University Press.

Quine, Willard van Orman 1953. Two Dogmas of Empiricism. *From a Logical Point of View*. Willard van Orman Quine, Ed. Cambridge, MA, Harvard University Press: 20–46.

Reiss, Julian 2013. *Philosophy of Economics: A Contemporary Introduction*. New York, Routledge.

Robbins, Lionel 1932. *Essay on the Nature and Significance of Economic Science*. Toronto, ON, Macmillan.

Rolin, Kristina 2011. Contextualism in Feminist Epistemology and Philosophy of Science. *Feminist Epistemology and Philosophy of Science: Power in Knowledge*. Heidi Grasswick, Ed. Dordrecht, Springer: 25–44.

Rudner, Richard 1953. "The Scientist Qua Scientist Makes Value Judgments." *Philosophy of Science* **20**(1): 1–6.
Samuelson, Paul and William Nordhaus 2009. *Economics*. 19th Ed. Boston, MA, McGraw Hill, Irwin.
Schultze, Charles and Christopher Mackie, Eds. 2002. *At What Price? Conceptualizing and Measuring Cost-of-Living and Price Indexes*. Washington, DC, National Academy Press.
Schumpeter, Joseph 1949. "Science and Ideology." *American Economic Review* **39**: 345–359.
Sen, Amartya 1983. Accounts, Actions and Values: Objectivity of Social Science. *Social Theory and Political Practice*. Chris Lloyd, Ed. Oxford, Clarendon Press.
Shapiro, Matthew and David Wilcox 1996. *Mismeasurement in the Consumer Price Index: An Evaluation*. NBER Working Paper Series. Cambridge, MA, NBER.
Stapleford, Thomas 2007. *The Cost of Living in America: A Political History of Economic Statistics, 1880–2000*. New York, Cambridge University Press.
Stern, Nicholas H. 2006. *The Economics of Climate Change: The Stern Review*. Cambridge, Cambridge University Press.
Stiglitz, Joseph E., Amartya Sen and Jean-Paul Fitoussi 2010. *Mismeasuring Our Lives: Why GDP Doesn't Add Up*. New York, New Press.
Weber, Max 1904/1949. 'Objectivity' in Social Science and Social Policy. *The Methodology of the Social Sciences*. Edward Shils and Henry Finch, Eds. New York, Free Press: 49–112.
Williams, Bernard 1985/2011. *Ethics and the Limits of Philosophy*. London and New York, Routledge.
Wray, K. Brad 1999. "A Defense of Longino's Social Epistemology." *Philosophy of Science* **66**(3): 538–552.

17

REFLECTIONS ON THE STATE OF ECONOMICS AND ETHICS

Mark D. White

1. Introduction

Economics and ethics is difficult to discern as a distinct and independent field of inquiry. Unlike most other fields of study in economics, there is no professional association representing it and only one journal (*Éthique et économique/Ethics and Economics*) devoted to it; scholarship in the area is found in journals and conferences of the methodology and philosophy of economics, broader multidisciplinary groupings (such as philosophy, politics, and economics or PPE), and heterodox economics groups (such as the Association for Social Economics, which explicitly cites a focus on ethics and values in its mission statement). Compared to more formal, quantitative work in economics, research in economics and ethics is more often found in book form: in addition to original monographs, some of which are found in book series (such as *On Ethics and Economics* from Rowman and Littlefield International), there are book-length overviews that can serve as textbooks for advanced undergraduate or graduate courses (Sen 1987; Wight 2015; Hausman, McPherson, and Satz 2016), as well as two handbooks (Peil and van Staveren 2009; White 2019) that survey the field.

For a field that literally dates back to the origin of modern economics, the lack of scholarly focus on economics and ethics in the modern day is perplexing. One reason for this may be found in the nature of the field itself, especially as compared to other subfields in economics. It is not like economics of the law or the family, in which economic reasoning is brought to bear on topics more often associated with other disciplines, nor is it like financial economics or international trade, narrower topics that fit squarely within economics as it is traditionally understood. Economics and ethics is more like the relationship between economics and mathematics, wherein the latter is seen by some as an essential and indispensable tool to understanding and advancing the former and by others as wholly irrelevant. Perhaps an even better comparison is the relationship between economics and politics: some think of this more as the intersection of two distinct disciplines, while others regard politics as ever present and embedded in the very language of economics, as reflected in the term *political economy* by which economics in general was once known.[1]

These comparisons provide a useful way to think about the dichotomy within economics and ethics. Is ethics an external topic from which economics can benefit and to which it might contribute, but at the discretion of economists satisfied with the state and progress of their discipline? Or is ethics an intrinsic and pervasive aspect of economics that has gone neglected for the past 100 years to the detriment of the field (despite the measures of success it has shown)? The answers to these questions, reflecting the disparate attitudes that economists take toward ethics, help to explain the

DOI: 10.4324/9781315739793-21

bifurcated nature of the work that is gathered under that umbrella term, as well as the scholars working in each part.

2. Two Aspects of Economics and Ethics

Appropriately, this dichotomy can be understood in terms of the work of Adam Smith, the moral philosopher who is better known as the father of modern economics. Smith scholars speak of "das Adam Smith problem," which refers to the apparent inconsistency between the outline for an ethical society he laid out in his 1759 book *The Theory of Moral Sentiments* and his more analytical description of a market economy in 1776's *The Wealth of Nations*.[2] Those who emphasize such a conflict see Smith's ethics as contradicting or interfering with how he presents the market economy running ostensibly on self-interest, while others see no inconsistency, understanding Smith's market economy as simply one part of society as a whole, a part that *can* operate on self-interest alone but does not *need* to. The first group sees ethics as a distraction, irrelevant to the "pure" analysis of economics, and the second group sees economics as embedded in a civil society that relies on moral sentiments and behavior, even if the economy could, in theory, operate without them.

The first group has dominated modern economics since the marginalist revolution, which severed economics from its intuitive and almost literary origins and heralded its transformation into the formal language of mathematics (see also Moscati, Chapter 2). Although this move is often regarded as severing economics from its ethical origins as well, the actual effect was to fasten its sail to a single mast: that of classical utilitarianism, by which economic phenomena were reduced to mathematical variables that could be combined algebraically and then maximized. This brought economics squarely into line with Jeremy Bentham's "hedonic calculus" (1789), by which the greatest excess of pleasure over pain was to be pursued (or total utility was to be maximized). This was simple to translate into mathematics, whether investigating how individuals maximize their utility when choosing consumption bundles, employment offers, or marriage prospects; how firms maximize their profits when setting prices, outputs, or charitable donations; or how governments maximize a social welfare function when making fiscal, monetary, or regulatory policy.

Despite its roots in classical utilitarianism, mainstream economics claims to be a value-free science because it does not acknowledge the ethical principles inherent in its mathematical processes. However, there is nothing ethically neutral about declaring personal utility (or preference satisfaction), profit, or social utility the sole focus of decision-making, to the exclusion of other ethical concepts like justice, equality, or rights. There is nothing ethically neutral about summing individual utilities into an aggregate and then maximizing the sum, regardless of distributional effects. And there is nothing ethically neutral about one group of agents assuming it has the right to make decisions in the interest of aggregate utility on behalf of other agents, whose rights are minimized or ignored. Yet, these are all taken to be logical implications of the mathematical techniques of mainstream economics because economists are trained to use these tools without being taught their foundations, much less their ethical implications (Dolfsma and Negru 2019). Furthermore, the tremendous success of economics as an academic field of study, as well as a resource for business and government, provides little incentive for economists to reflect on the ethical foundations of their field. Instead, they are often hostile to any suggestion that economics needs a more explicit consideration of ethics or that it needs to incorporate a wider range of ethical theories, falling back on the values of parsimony and tractability (an ethical valuation, of course) and the presumed but illusory objectivity of mathematical techniques.

Mainstream economics' attitude toward ethics as a methodological intrusion or distraction results in the first of two general approaches to economics and ethics: the analysis of ethical behavior using mainstream economic techniques. We can call this approach *accommodationist* because it attempts to explain all behavior that is not obviously self-interested by using models that explain self-interested behavior. This is done by either explaining all behavior as ultimately self-interested in some way or expanding the agent's objective function beyond self-interest while leaving the maximization calculus unchanged. Examples of the former include the selfish child who behaves kindly toward their family in order to gain some strategic advantage (Becker 1981) and the profit-maximizing firm that applies the same cost-benefit analysis to prosocial behavior as it does to all its business decisions, engaging in them if the benefit from the resulting goodwill justifies its cost. In general, this approach seeks to explain behavior that is anomalous in terms of maximizing self-interest in the short run by showing how it achieves that result in the long term and is therefore consistent with utility maximization as it is traditionally understood (see also Vromen, Chapter 9).

Such models fail, however, to explain behavior that is advantageous to the agent in neither the short nor the long run, such as tipping at restaurants one is unlikely to visit again, voting in large elections in which one person's vote has an infinitesimally small effect, or general acts of generosity with no expectation of reciprocation or goodwill. In such cases, economists may expand the understanding of self-interest beyond the typical utility enjoyed from consumption (or the wealth that makes it possible) to include prosocial attitudes or feelings. Prominent examples include the "warm glow" used to explain altruistic behavior (Andreoni 1990), preferences for fairness or norm-following (Rabin 1993), or altruistic preference orderings in general (Margolis 1984). All of these explanations fit nicely with the constrained utility-maximization (or preference-satisfaction) paradigm of mainstream economics by using the formal understanding of preference as rankings of options with no specific psychological basis, in which an agent's preferences may be ranked along the lines of simple self-interest, "enlightened" self-interest including prosocial sentiments and concerns, or even full-blown altruism. Each successive option in this list stretches the intuitive understanding of what economic agents maximize, but they are all consistent with formal modeling techniques and, more broadly, with the scientific principle of testing a model to see how many observed phenomena it can explain before it fails.

The choice of prosocial attitudes or preferences in order to solve an anomaly is nakedly ad hoc and only serves to highlight the extent to which economists regard the assumption of self-interest as self-evident rather than an important value judgment in and of itself. In theoretical work, any exception to the self-interest assumption is regarded as a deviation from the norm that needs to be justified; in empirical work, self-interest is always the null hypothesis that research aims to reject (which it often does, as shown in Fehr and Schmidt 2006). Even evolutionary research that demonstrates how altruistic sentiments and behavior develop (Bowles and Gintis 2013) takes self-interest as its "natural" starting point. Despite the tremendous volume of research from various perspectives that supports the nonanomalous nature of altruistic behavior, the standard assumption among economists remains self-interest, with little if any acknowledgment of the value judgment inherent therein.

The accommodationist approach to economics and ethics can explain a great deal of ethical behavior, but it does so solely within a utilitarian framework, which is restrictive in both descriptive and prescriptive terms. As John Hicks wrote, "If one is a utilitarian in philosophy, one has a perfect right to be a utilitarian in one's economics. But if one is not . . . one also has the right to an economics free from utilitarian assumptions" (1939: 18). Accordingly, the second approach to economics and ethics is more methodological and critical in nature, questioning economics' ethical foundations in classical utilitarianism and exploring ways that other schools of moral philosophy can be incorporated into economic analysis, regardless of the changes to mainstream economic analysis this demands. Such changes are often required because other approaches to ethics, such as deontology and virtue ethics, are qualitative and do not lend themselves as easily to mathematization as utilitarianism does. While many mainstream economists work in the accommodationist version of economics and ethics, testing the bounds of traditional models, the critical version tends to be dominated by heterodox economists – such as social economists, feminist economists, and radical political economists – and philosophers, all of whom are more willing to challenge mainstream economic techniques and practices. Also, in terms of positive economics, many of these scholars are less devoted to the positivist value of prediction, instead favoring explanation and understanding, although all of these values are supported by including ethical frameworks that better reflect the thinking of real-world economic actors. In terms of normative economics, critical voices in economics and ethics question the sole focus of policy being aggregate welfare, perhaps the most direct legacy of the field's utilitarian roots and one that is again largely unchallenged by most mainstream economists, as a focus on maximizing welfare "seems" obvious, natural, and even objective and scientific (see also Baujard, Chapter 15, and Reiss, Chapter 16).[3]

For the rest of this chapter, I will survey the various ways that ethical approaches other than utilitarianism have been incorporated into economic theory, policy, and practice; the extent to which they demand changes in established mainstream techniques; and the state of the field in terms of where it stands with respect to them.

3. Positive Economics

In his classic 1979 paper "Rational Fools," Amartya Sen explained how commitment can change the nature of agents' choices by introducing a new type of constraint motivated by the agents themselves, reflecting a principle or moral value, rather than by material circumstances imposed on them from outside.[4] This seminal contribution is representative of deontology, which stands as the ethical system that is the most obvious alternative to utilitarianism.

Sometimes defined simply in opposition to consequentialism, *deontology* focuses on the moral quality of actions themselves, which depends on an intrinsic property of them, rather than their outcomes in particular instances. The properties that determine the moral quality of an action can be intuitive, as in the deontology of W.D. Ross (1930), or derived from some basic principle, such as dignity in the work of the most well-known deontologist, Immanuel Kant. To Kant (1785), the inherent dignity of rational beings implies the ability to follow the dictates of morality over their own self-interest and the influence of others, a capacity known as *autonomy*, which entitles them to an inalienable respect from fellow persons as well as from their government. Dignity and autonomy also ground Kant's famous (or infamous) categorical imperative, which tests possible maxims of action to determine whether acting on them is morally permissible or impermissible (wrong). If an action is declared wrong by the categorical imperative, a duty to refrain from that action is generated, and this duty must be followed out of respect for the moral law that grounds it rather than any benefit that may result from it, material or otherwise.

In terms of economics, the effect of Kantian deontology on the ethical behavior of agents depends on the two types of duties, perfect and imperfect, generated by the categorical imperative. *Perfect duties* are those that forbid a certain action and for that reason are usually negative duties; these are the familiar "thou shalt not" commands, including duties not to kill, steal, or lie, all actions that are rejected by the categorical imperative. These are also called *strict duties* in that they do not admit any exceptions for inclinations or preferences (even if altruistic). For instance, there is no exception to the duty not to kill, even for "good reason," unless that exception was included in the proposed maxim itself and was approved by the categorical imperative (as might be done for killing in self-defense or the defense of others). *Imperfect duties* are those that forbid a certain type of inaction and therefore prompt certain behavior (and are often positive duties); the best example of this is the duty of beneficence, which requires that agents adopt an attitude of giving aid and acting on it when appropriate. This language implies that imperfect duties are also *wide duties*, which offer latitude in their execution in terms of how, when, and to what extent beneficence is practiced, opening the door for balancing this duty with other concerns, including agents' own interests (which they have an imperfect duty to promote as well).

Another way to look at the two types of duties is that perfect duties are constraints on action (similar to Sen's commitment) and imperfect duties provide reasons for action.[5] Understood this way, both types of duties have analogues to the standard economic model of choice: perfect duties sit alongside resource constraints regarding income and time, while imperfect duties can be included among preferences as additional options for choice. All included, agents make Kantian economic decisions by choosing the highest ranked options out of their preferences and imperfect duties that are possible or permissible according to both resource and moral constraints (White 2011).

According to this method of incorporating Kantian ethics into economics, the basic structure of constrained preference satisfaction is preserved, with the addition of perfect duties to the constraint set and imperfect duties to the preference ranking, which itself is determined by the agent's faculty of judgment that orders imperfect duties against each other and preferences (White 2015a). Although this modeling approach is somewhat accommodationist, it nonetheless challenges the way agents structure their options as well as how they understand constraints; as with Sen's commitment, agents must choose to recognize perfect duties (out of respect for the moral law), whereas resource constraints are imposed on them. As discussed earlier, this is only perceived as a challenge to the extent that self-interest is regarded as the more natural assumption, but agents in economic models are normally assumed to follow basic moral constraints even when they are not acknowledged as such. In simple models of market exchange, buyers and sellers are assumed to be honest traders – except in the economics of crime, which only confirms that immoral behavior is regarded as an anomaly. Also, resource constraints are binding only to the degree that agents are unwilling to violate morality; they could always steal to get more income or shirk in their job to get more time. The fact that moral behavior is taken for granted in economic models shows that an ethics beyond utilitarianism has always been a part of economics; a deontological approach just makes this aspect of economic behavior explicit and allows economists to explain compliance as well as deviation.

Although deontology provides a more direct contrast to utilitarianism, virtue ethics poses a stronger challenge to both, as well as the nature of economic models of choice themselves – which is ironic given that, in recent years, Adam Smith himself has come to be regarded as a virtue ethicist as well as a moral sentimentalist (McCloskey 2008; Otteson 2016; Hanley 2017).[6] The term *virtue ethics* covers a broad range of ideas, including the thoughts of Aristotle, the Stoics, the Epicureans, and even Confucius, but their common focus is on the character of agents rather than their actions or the consequences thereof (both central concerns of traditional choice models).[7] In the most well-known virtue ethics, that of Aristotle (350 BCE), ethical agents have virtuous character traits – such as honesty, courage, and generosity – that in turn lead them to perform good acts. A person is recommended to cultivate these virtues and put them into action, using judgment to determine where, when, and how much to do so in any particular situation. Viewed this way, the virtue ethics of Aristotle comments more on the overall purpose and motivation of choice rather than exactly how it is made (van Staveren 2001), although practical judgment (*phronêsis*) could be understood as taking the form of ranking and maximization after the proper goals of action are determined by one's virtues (Yuengert 2012), similar to the way it allows Kantian imperfect duty to be worked into economic choice.[8] Other schools of virtue ethics make similar contributions, such as the Stoic insight that some goods should be considered as *indifferent*, irrelevant to ethical decision-making, which would imply a trivial impact on the process of economic choice (Baker 2009). Finally, virtue ethics is not limited to writers from antiquity: the more specific and contemporary *ethics of care* has been used extensively by feminist economists to analyze behavior motivated by prosocial attitudes, not only in the family or community but in business as well (Nelson 2011).

4. Normative Economics

Compared to positive economics, the prospects for working other ethical systems into normative economics (or welfare economics) in an accommodationist way are fewer, because welfare economics is essentially operationalized utilitarianism. Whether one uses social welfare functions or cost-benefit analysis, the aim of welfare economics is to maximize total utility, or the sum of individual utilities, which reflects both the best and the worst aspects of utilitarianism. On the one hand, the operation of summation reflects the moral equality at the heart of utilitarianism (and shared by many deontologists), in which each person's utility counts the same as every other person's, regardless of class, religion, race, or gender.[9] On the other hand, summation also implies substitutability among persons, so that one person's utility is no more valuable to the sum than another's. As John Rawls (1971: 27) pointed out, utilitarianism "does not take seriously the distinction between persons," rendering them interchangeable and valuable only to the extent that they contribute to total utility.[10]

The problem with substitutability reveals itself most starkly in Kaldor-Hicks efficiency, the version of cost-benefit analysis that is used to test incremental changes in policy or regulation. The Kaldor-Hicks test declares a policy change to be efficient – and therefore recommended – if the benefits it generates (for the "winners") are larger than the costs it imposes (on the "losers"). Although this is a clear good from the viewpoint of utilitarianism, the fact that such a policy arrives at its positive net benefit only by directly and consciously harming others offends Kant's dictum, expressed in one of the versions of his categorical imperative (1785: 429), that persons should be treated "always at the same time as an end and never simply as a means" to someone else's end, in this case the "winners" from the proposed change.

Economists typically justify Kaldor-Hicks changes by citing the potential for compensation to address the harm, which they usually leave to policymakers. However, not only does Kantian respect demand that compensation be built into a proposal before it is deemed acceptable – implying that, if compensation is prohibitively costly to include, this should count against the "efficiency" of the proposal – it also demands that consent be secured from those negatively affected (even if compensated). This criticism also extends to the stricter standard of Pareto improvement, which requires that a policy change make at one least one party better off while making no party worse off. Typically, the judgments of who is made better or worse off are not made by those affected, nor reflected in granted consent, but rather by external agents making those judgments on their behalf (White 2009). Presumptions of maintenance or improvements in persons' interests on the part of external observers cannot take the place of consent on the part of the affected persons themselves.

There is innovative work by economists and philosophers in an accommodationist vein that acknowledges these difficulties and suggests revisions to address them without abandoning utilitarian welfare economics altogether, including seminal work by Little (1957) and Sen (1982) as well as more recent contributions by Fleurbaey (2008) and Adler (2011). However, there are also many approaches to policy issues that reject utilitarianism altogether in favor of other valuable ends such as equality, justice, or capabilities (or combinations thereof), which are more difficult to accommodate within traditional conceptions of welfare economics because they serve as constraints (at the least) on welfare maximization.

Equality – or, more prevalently, inequality – is the most frequently discussed of these topics, even more so since the 2008 financial downturn, especially inequality in income, wealth, or living standards. Students in introductory economics are usually introduced to the trade-off between efficiency and equality; even if some consider this a false dichotomy or that the two ideals must be balanced somehow, the relationship between them is rarely discussed in terms of the ethical roots of the two concepts. In terms of the preceding discussion, equality is not utilitarian because the total sum of utilities is not the primary concern and substitutability between individuals is rejected (giving more weight and protection to the well-being of the less fortunate). Equality can be considered a form of consequentialism in general: outcomes are what matter, but in a relative sense instead of, or in addition to, an absolute sense. While equality (or inequality) has been examined by prominent economists, both mainstream (Atkinson 2015) and heterodox (Piketty 2014), the rich philosophical literature on egalitarianism is rarely referenced, nor are the ethical foundations for egalitarianism itself (Arneson 2013).

Alongside equality, there is also substantial work by economists and philosophers on the topic of justice in economics, a broader discussion (often drawing upon Rawls 1971) that often brings in issues of inequality along with fairness and well-being (Kolm 1971; Sen 2009). Unlike Nozick (1974), these justice theorists seek not to replace utilitarian welfare economics altogether but to make it more just and humane. Closely related to both justice and equality is the capabilities approach developed by Amartya Sen and Martha Nussbaum (1993), which maintains that persons rely on certain capabilities or "their real opportunities to do and be what they have reason to value," which enable them to have meaningful lives (Robeyns 2016). According to proponents, these capabilities, which include not only basic sustenance needs such as food and shelter but also literacy, free speech, and democratic participation, should be protected and promoted by the state to generate a more inclusive and holistic version of well-being (Stiglitz, Sen, and Fitoussi 2010) as expressed in the United Nations Human Development Index, which is explicitly based on the capabilities approach (Fukuda-Parr 2003).

5. Final Comments

This chapter has surveyed a wide range of work being done in economics and ethics, either to improve mainstream economic technique based on utilitarianism or to broaden its range by supplementing it (or replacing it) with other ethical perspectives. However, most of this work remains on the fringes of mainstream economics if not exclusively in heterodox economics, PPE, or philosophy circles. Positive economics in an accommodationist vein is most often seen in the work of behavioral economists, who are well-known for relaxing mainstream assumptions to better explain observed phenomena. However, even this approach has been criticized for being *too* accommodating: "rather uncritically accept[ing] the rules of axiomatic decision theory as the norm for all rational behavior" (Gigerenzer 2015: 365) and failing to recognize when observed behavior demands more significant changes to modeling techniques.[11] In terms of normative economics, the application of ethical concepts such as equality, justice, and capabilities has had more purchase, although more so in policy circles and popular literature than in scholarly economics publications, where they would have more influence on future generations of academic economists through graduate training and mentorship.

On the bright side, aside from the application of moral philosophy to economics, which this chapter has implicitly considered the "core" of economics and ethics, there is a much broader range of literature involving the interaction between the two fields. For example, many topics in economics, such as health, labor, race and gender, and the environment, are inherently ethical in nonutilitarian ways, and discussions of them necessarily involve ethics concepts (at varying degrees of specificity).[12] The ethical behavior of economists themselves, occasionally a topic of reflection (Buchanan 1964), has received renewed attention of late (DeMartino 2011; DeMartino and McCloskey 2016), primarily due to the push for codes of conduct in professional associations across the academy, but especially in economics due to the financially lucrative nature of much applied research.[13]

Many topics associated with economics have also been subjected to ethical scrutiny of late. The application of market principles to the exchange of certain goods, such as drugs and bodily organs, has been criticized from various ethical perspectives by prominent philosophers such as Elizabeth Anderson (1993), Debra Satz (2010), and Michael Sandel (2012). The market system itself, always a topic of ethical debate, has received renewed attention hand-in-hand with increases in wealth inequality and high-profile examples of financial corruption among business and government leaders. *Are Markets Moral?* is actually the title of two recent edited volumes (Skidelsky and Skidelsky 2015; Melzer and Kautz 2018), but the theme is omnipresent in both the scholarly and popular literatures at the moment (see also Binder, Chapter 33).

The ethical interrogation of the market and its interactions with the state and society, rather than technical issues regarding the incorporation of moral philosophy in economic theory, may be the future of economics and ethics, which would bring the field around nicely to the original contributions of Adam Smith and would help to demonstrate to general audiences the importance of ethics to economics. Nonetheless, economic theory has progressed since the 18th century, and the highly formalized and mathematicized nature of modern mainstream economics also merits reflection, criticism, and improvement, along the lines surveyed in this chapter, to develop both a positive economics that is able to describe and predict the full range of motivations of human behavior and a normative economics that can better understand the rich nature of human well-being and pursue ideals of justice and equality along with it.

Related Chapters

Baujard, Chapter 15 "Values in Welfare Economics"
Binder, Chapter 33 "Freedom and Markets"
Moscati, Chapter 2 "History of Utility Theory"
Reiss, Chapter 16 "Measurement and Value Judgments"
Vromen, Chapter 9 "*As If* Social Preference Models"

Notes

1 For background on this term, see Groenewegen (1987).
2 See, for instance, Tribe (2008).
3 I use the terms *positive* and *normative economics* to provide common reference points despite the problems with them identified by Putnam (2002), which is also relevant to the previous discussion of hidden value judgments.
4 See Minkler (2008) for an elaboration of this point.
5 Accordingly, perfect duties are sometimes known as *duties of action*, while imperfect duties are *duties of ends*.
6 For an overview of virtue ethics, see Hursthouse and Pettigrove (2018).
7 For recent overviews, see Bruni and Sugden (2013), Bielskis and Knight (2015), and Baker and White (2016).
8 This is not an accident, as there are many similarities between Kant and virtue ethics; see White (2016) and references therein.
9 This is not to imply that all effects on utility are to be treated equally, an assumption on which the economic analysis of externalities is based; see White (2015b).
10 For more on the problems with utilitarianism from an economist's point of view (as well as others), see Sen and Williams (1982).
11 See also White (2017) and references therein.
12 On the other hand, law and economics and the economics of the family are inherently ethical as well, but those literatures rarely invoke ethics beyond the implicit utilitarianism of mainstream economic theory.
13 Fortunately, scholarship in economics and ethics has never had cause or opportunity for accusations of financial corruption.

Bibliography

Adler, M.D. (2011) *Well-Being and Fair Distribution: Beyond Cost-Benefit Analysis*, Oxford: Oxford University Press.

Anderson, E. (1993) *Value in Ethics and Economics*, Cambridge, MA: Harvard University Press.

Andreoni, J. (1990) "Impure Altruism and Donations to Public Goods: A Theory of Warm-Glow Giving," *Economic Journal* 100: 464–477.

Aristotle (350 BCE) *Nicomachean Ethics*, trans. W.D. Ross. Available at http://classics.mit.edu/Aristotle/nicomachaen.html.

Arneson, R. (2013) "Egalitarianism," in Edward N. Zalta (ed.), *The Stanford Encyclopedia of Philosophy*. Available at https://plato.stanford.edu/archives/sum2013/entries/egalitarianism/.

Atkinson, A.B. (2015) *Inequality: What Can Be Done?* Cambridge, MA: Harvard University Press.
Baker, J.A. (2009) "Virtue and Behavior," *Review of Social Economy* 67: 3–24.
Baker, J.A., and White, M.D. (eds.) (2016) *Economics and the Virtues: Building a New Moral Foundation*, Oxford: Oxford University Press.
Becker, G.S. (1981) *A Treatise on the Family*, Cambridge, MA: Harvard University Press.
Bentham, J. (1789) *An Introduction to the Principles of Morals and Legislation*, London: T. Payne and Son.
Bielskis, A., and Knight, K. (eds.) (2015) *Virtue and Economy: Essays on Morality and Markets*, London: Routledge.
Bowles, S., and Gintis, H. (2013) *A Cooperative Species: Human Reciprocity and Its Evolution*, Princeton, NJ: Princeton University Press.
Bruni, L., and Sugden, R. (2013) "Reclaiming Virtue Ethics for Economics," *Journal of Economic Perspectives* 27: 141–164.
Buchanan, J.M. (1964) "What Should Economists Do?" *Southern Economic Journal* 30: 213–222.
DeMartino, G.F. (2011) *The Economist's Oath: On the Need for the Content of Professional Economic Ethics*, Oxford: Oxford University Press.
DeMartino, G.F., and McCloskey, D.N. (eds.) (2016) *The Oxford Handbook of Professional Economic Ethics*, Oxford: Oxford University Press.
Dolfsma, W., and Negru, I. (eds.) (2019) *The Ethical Formation of Economists*, London: Routledge.
Fehr, E., and Schmidt, K.N. (2006) "The Economics of Fairness, Reciprocity and Altruism – Experimental Evidence and New Theories," in S. Kolm and J.M. Ythier (eds.), *Handbook of the Economics of Giving, Altruism and Reciprocity, vol. I*, Dordrecht: Elsevier: 615–691.
Fleurbaey, M. (2008) *Fairness, Responsibility, and Welfare*, Oxford: Oxford University Press.
Fukuda-Parr, S. (2003) "The Human Development Paradigm: Operationalizing Sen's Ideas on Capabilities," *Feminist Economics* 9: 301–317.
Gigerenzer, G. (2015) "On the Supposed Evidence for Libertarian Paternalism," *Review of Philosophy and Psychology* 6: 361–383.
Groenewegen, P. (1987) "'Political Economy' and 'Economics'," in J. Eatwell, M. Milgate, and P. Newman (eds.) *The World of Economics*, New York: Palgrave: 556–562.
Hanley, R.P. (2017) "Is Smith a Real Virtue Ethicist?" in A.J.G. Sison, G.R. Beabout, and I. Ferrero (eds.) *Handbook of Virtue Ethics in Business and Management*, Dordrecht: Springer: 119–125.
Hausman, D.M., McPherson, M.S., and Satz, D. (2016) *Economic Analysis, Moral Philosophy, and Public Policy*, 3rd ed. Cambridge: Cambridge University Press.
Hicks, J.R. (1939) *Value and Capital*, Oxford: Clarendon Press.
Hursthouse, R., and Pettigrove, G. (2018) "Virtue Ethics," in Edward N. Zalta (ed.), *The Stanford Encyclopedia of Philosophy*. Available at https://plato.stanford.edu/archives/win2018/entries/ethics-virtue/.
Kant, I. (1785) *Grounding for the Metaphysics of Morals*, trans. James W. Ellington, 1993 ed., Indianapolis: Hackett.
Kolm, S.-C. (1971) *Justice and Equity*, trans. Harold F. See, 1997 ed., Cambridge, MA: The MIT Press.
Little, I.M.D. (1957) *A Critique of Welfare Economics*, 2nd ed., Oxford: Clarendon Press.
Margolis, H. (1984) *Selfishness, Altruism, and Rationality*, Chicago: University of Chicago Press.
McCloskey, D. (2008) "Adam Smith, the Last of the Former Virtue Ethicists," *History of Political Economy* 40: 43–71.
Melzer, A.M., and Kautz, S.J. (2018) *Are Markets Moral?* Philadelphia: University of Pennsylvania Press.
Minkler, L. (2008) *Integrity and Agreement: Economics When Principles Also Matter*, Ann Arbor: University of Michigan Press.
Nelson, J.A. (2011) "Care Ethics and Markets: A View from Feminist Economics," in M. Hamington and M. Sanders-Staudt (eds.) *Applying Care Ethics to Business*, Dordrecht: Springer: 35–53.
Nozick, R. (1974) *Anarchy, State, and Utopia*, New York: Basic Books.
Nussbaum, M., and Sen, A. (eds.) (1993) *The Quality of Life*, Oxford: Clarendon Press.
Otteson, J. (2016) "Adam Smith on Virtue, Prosperity, and Justice," in J.A. Baker and M.D. White (eds.) *Economics and the Virtues: Building a New Moral Foundation*, Oxford: Oxford University Press: 72–93.
Peil, J., and van Staveren, I. (eds.) (2009) *Handbook of Economics and Ethics*, Cheltenham: Edward Elgar.
Piketty, T. (2014) *Capital in the Twenty-First Century*, Cambridge, MA: Harvard University Press.
Putnam, H. (2002) *The Collapse of the Fact/Value Dichotomy and Other Essays*, Cambridge, MA: Harvard University Press.
Rabin, M. (1993) "Incorporating Fairness into Game Theory and Economics," *American Economic Review* 83: 1281–1302.
Rawls, J. (1971) *A Theory of Justice*, Cambridge, MA: Harvard University Press.
Robeyns, I. (2016) "The Capability Approach," in Edward N. Zalta (ed.), *The Stanford Encyclopedia of Philosophy*. Available at https://plato.stanford.edu/archives/win2016/entries/capability-approach/.

Ross, W.D. (1930) *The Right and the Good*, Oxford: Oxford University Press.
Sandel, M. (2012) *What Money Can't Buy: The Moral Limits of Markets*, New York: Farrar, Straus and Giroux.
Satz, D. (2010) *Why Some Things Should Not Be for Sale: The Moral Limits of Markets*, Oxford: Oxford University Press.
Sen, A.K. (1977) "Rational Fools: A Critique of the Behavioral Foundations of Economic Theory," *Philosophy & Public Affairs* 6: 317–344.
Sen, A.K. (1987) *On Ethics and Economics*, Oxford: Blackwell.
Sen, A.K. (2009) *The Idea of Justice*, Cambridge, MA: The Belknap Press.
Sen, A.K., and Williams, B. (eds.) (1982) *Utilitarianism and Beyond*, Cambridge: Cambridge University Press.
Skidelsky, E., and Skidelsky, R. (2015) *Are Markets Moral?* New York: Palgrave.
Stiglitz, J.E., Sen, A.K., and Fitoussi, J. (2010) *Mismeasuring Our Lives: Why GDP Doesn't Add Up*, New York: New Press.
Tribe, K. (2008) " 'Das Adam Smith Problem' and the Origins of Modern Smith Scholarship," *History of European Ideas* 34: 514–525.
van Staveren, I. (2001) *The Values of Economics: An Aristotelian Perspective*, Abingdon: Routledge.
White, M.D. (2009) "Pareto, Consent, and Respect for Dignity: A Kantian Perspective," *Review of Social Economy* 67: 49–70.
White, M.D. (2011) *Kantian Ethics and Economics: Autonomy, Dignity, and Character*, Stanford, CA: Stanford University Press.
White, M.D. (2015a) "Judgment: Balancing Principle and Policy," *Review of Social Economy* 73: 223–241.
White, M.D. (2015b) "On the Relevance of Wrongfulness to the Concept of Externalities," *Œconomia* 5: 313–329.
White, M.D. (2016) "The Virtues of a Kantian Economics," in J.A. Baker and M.D. White (eds.), *Economics and the Virtues: Building a New Moral Foundation*, Oxford: Oxford University Press: 94–115.
White, M.D. (2017) "Preferences All the Way Down: Questioning the Neoclassical Foundations of Behavioral Economics and Libertarian Paternalism," *Œconomia* 7: 353–373.
White, M.D. (ed.) (2019) *The Oxford Handbook of Ethics and Economics*, Oxford: Oxford University Press.
Wight, J.B. (2015) *Ethics in Economics: An Introduction to Moral Frameworks*, Stanford, CA: Stanford University Press.
Yuengert, A. (2012) *Approximating Prudence: Aristotelian Practical Wisdom and Economic Models of Choice*, New York: Palgrave Macmillan.

18
WELL-BEING

Mauro Rossi

1. Introduction

Interest in the topic of individual and societal well-being (or welfare)[1] has soared among philosophers and economists over the last quarter of a century. While there are certainly several factors contributing to this trend, two seem especially salient. First, the increasing levels of inequality within developed countries and across the globe, exacerbated by the global financial crisis of 2008, have put well-being at the forefront of the public debate. Relatedly, the increasing dissatisfaction with traditional economic indicators, such as GDP, has pushed scholars from different disciplines to think about new bases for assessing how well or how badly societies fare.

The aim of this chapter is to examine the most foundational question about well-being, namely, that of its nature. What is well-being? What does it consist in? In Section 3, I review the main philosophical theories of well-being: mental state theories (Section 3.1), preference satisfaction theories (Section 3.2), objective list theories (Section 3.3), and perfectionist theories (Section 3.4). Before doing that, I make some preliminary remarks on the concept of well-being in Section 2.[2]

2. The Concept of Well-Being

When contemporary philosophers enquire about the nature of well-being, they engage in first-order theorizing about it. This involves elaborating and discussing *substantive* theories of well-being. Yet, in order to understand what these theories are theories *of*, that is, in order to understand what these philosophers are talking about and disagreeing upon when they offer competing accounts of well-being, we need to have some grasp of the *concept* of well-being. This requires us to engage in second-order theorizing, akin to what moral philosophers do when they enquire about the meaning of moral terms such as right and wrong.

In everyday discourse, the concept of well-being is often considered to be synonymous with the concept of happiness. However, it is more and more common in philosophy to distinguish the two. Happiness is understood as a psychological concept, namely, the concept of a favorable psychological state (or combination of favorable psychological states), while well-being is understood as an evaluative concept, namely, the concept of the life that is *good for* the individual who lives it.

In order to have a grasp of the concept of well-being, we then need to have a grasp of the concept of "goodness for." To begin with, the concept of goodness for is the concept of a specific kind of value: prudential value. Thus, to say that an item is good for an individual is equivalent to saying

 DOI: 10.4324/9781315739793-22

that it is prudentially valuable for that individual. We can further elucidate the concept of goodness for by linking it to similar evaluative concepts. For instance, we can say that an item is good for an individual if and only if it benefits that individual, if it is to the individual's own advantage, or if it is in the individual's self-interest to have it. This allows us to appreciate some important points. First, the concept of goodness for is distinct from the concept of goodness *simpliciter* (or absolute goodness). The concept of goodness *simpliciter* is the concept of an impersonal (or subject-independent) value. Instead, when we say that an item is good for an individual, we say that that item stands in a particular relation (e.g. the benefiting relation) to a particular individual. This point is often expressed by saying that the concept of goodness for is the concept of a personal (or subject-relative or subject-dependent) value. Second, to say that an item is good *for* an individual is not the same as saying that that item is good (*simpliciter*) *according* to that individual. That is, the concept of goodness for is not the concept of what the individual *believes* to be good *simpliciter*. It is the concept of a specific kind of value. Third, the concept of goodness for is also distinct from the concepts of other kinds of value, such as the concepts of moral value and aesthetic value. Thus, to say that an item is good for an individual does not entail that this item is morally (or aesthetically) good – nor vice versa.

All of this has some important implications for research on well-being. When we enquire about well-being, we enquire about the prudentially good life, that is, the life that is good *for* the individual living it. This is not the same as enquiring about the morally good life, the aesthetically good life, or the life that is good for an individual to live from the point of view of justice. Importantly, as this point is often misunderstood, the concept of the prudentially good life is also not the same as the concept of the good life *tout court* (i.e. the life that is good *simpliciter*).[3]

3. Substantive Theories of Well-Being

Substantive theories purport to offer an account of what well-being consists in. Typically, this involves addressing the following questions. (i) What items are noninstrumentally good for an individual? (ii) What properties make these items noninstrumentally good for the individual? (iii) How do these items determine the overall well-being of an individual?

Let us consider each of these questions in more detail. The first is an *enumerative* question: it can be reformulated as the question of *which* items are finally good for the individual. The contrast here is between final versus instrumental prudential goods. The former are items that are good for the individual for their own sake or as ends. The latter are items that are good for the individual for the sake of something else, that is, as means to obtain other items that are finally good for the individual. Substantive theories aim to identify which items are finally good for the individual. More specifically, they aim to identify which items are *nonderivatively* finally good for the individual. Some items may indeed be finally good for an individual only in a derivative way. This happens, for instance, when an item is a specification of a more general item that is nonderivatively finally good for the individual (e.g. olfactory pleasures as a kind of pleasure). By contrast, an item that is nonderivatively finally good for an individual is an item that is finally good for the individual in its own right. Or, as it is sometimes put, it is a *basic* prudential good.[4]

The second question is an *explanatory* question: it asks *why* certain items are finally good for an individual or, equivalently, in virtue of what these items are finally good for the individual. This question concerns the ultimate explanatory grounds for each particular fact about well-being. To identify these grounds requires identification of the properties that make certain items finally good for an individual or, as it is sometimes put, their good for–making properties.

Finally, the third question asks how the overall *degree of well-being* is determined. In order to address this question, we need to know not just which items are finally good for an individual but also which items are finally *bad for* an individual (and why). A well-being theory must then specify how to determine the relative prudential value of the different instances of these items and the overall level of the individual's well-being, that is, how well, or how badly, the individual's life goes for them.

In the rest of this section, I will consider four types of substantive theories of well-being: mental state theories, preference satisfaction theories, objective list theories, and perfectionist theories.

3.1 Mental State Theories

According to mental state theories (MSTs henceforth), well-being consists in the net balance of some positive and negative mental states. I will start by presenting the historically most popular MST of well-being, that is, hedonism. Next, I will consider some alternative MSTs. Finally, I will discuss the main attractions of, and objections to, MSTs.

The main tenets of hedonism can be summarized as follows. Pleasures are the only items that are finally good for an individual. Displeasures are the only items that are finally bad for an individual. Pleasures are finally good for an individual by virtue of the fact that they are pleasant. Displeasures are finally bad for an individual by virtue of the fact that they are unpleasant. An individual's level of well-being is determined by their net balance of pleasures and displeasures.

Two elements in this characterization must be further specified. First, what are pleasures and displeasures? Second, how exactly does their balance determine an individual's overall level of well-being?

Consider the first question. (For simplicity, I shall only focus on pleasures.) For a start, we can say that a pleasure is any mental state that possesses the property of being pleasant. So, to understand what pleasures are, we need to have an account of pleasantness. Roughly speaking, there are two main views of pleasantness: internalist views, according to which pleasantness consists in a phenomenal quality intrinsic to the mental state,[5] and externalist views, according to which a mental state's pleasantness consists in having a favorable attitude (broadly construed) toward that mental state or toward its object.[6]

Consider now the second question. The standard view makes two claims. First, the prudential value of each pleasure and displeasure is a function of its intensity and duration. Second, the overall prudential value of a life is determined by summing the prudential value of each individual pleasure and displeasure.[7]

As mentioned earlier, there are other MSTs of well-being. To contrast them with hedonism, it is useful to consider one possible route by which one can come to endorse hedonism. This consists in accepting the following propositions: (i) well-being is exclusively determined by facts about the individual's mind; (ii) the only facts about the individual's mind that matter for well-being are facts about their happiness; (iii) happiness consists in the net balance of pleasures and displeasures; (iv) therefore, well-being is exclusively determined by the net balance of pleasures and displeasures.[8]

All defenders of MSTs accept (i). So, in this scenario, one may defend a *non*-hedonist MST by rejecting either (ii) or (iii). For instance, a MS theorist may argue that, although a hedonistic theory of happiness is correct, well-being does not depend only (or even at all) on the individual's happiness. There are other mental states that matter for well-being in addition to (or in substitution of) pleasures and displeasures, such as, for example, self-understanding, compassion, the experience of novelty, and so on (see van der Deijl 2019). Alternatively, an MS theorist may argue that, although well-being does exclusively depend on the individual's happiness, happiness does not consist in the balance of pleasures and displeasures. There are two competing theories of happiness: life satisfaction, according to which happiness consists in an attitude of satisfaction toward one's life (Sumner 1996), and the emotional state theory, according to which happiness consists in a positive balance of affective states such as emotions, moods, and mood propensities (Haybron 2008). If one accepts either of these theories, in addition to (i) and (ii), then one is led, respectively, to a life satisfaction theory of well-being and to an emotional state theory of well-being. Both these approaches figure prominently in the fields of happiness studies and the economics of happiness, together with the hedonic approach.[9]

MSTs of well-being share two main attractions. First, they are intuitively appealing. Paradigmatically, lives that are high in well-being are lives that contain a favorable balance of positive and negative mental states. Second, MSTs are explanatorily powerful. Here is an example. It is widely accepted, though not uncontroversial, that only sentient beings can have a well-being. MSTs explain why this is true. The reason is that well-being consists in the net balance of mental states that only sentient beings possess. Here is another example. Many well-being scholars accept the so-called "experience requirement," that is, the claim that in order for something to contribute to an individual's well-being, it must affect the individual's experience in one way or another. MSTs explain why this requirement holds. The reason is that well-being consists in the net balance of mental states that possess a phenomenal character and are, thus, "experienced" by the individual. Anything that contributes to well-being does so by causing, or being the object of, one of these mental states.

Two main objections have been raised against MSTs. The first is sometimes known as the "base pleasures objection". While this objection is typically raised against hedonism, it applies, *mutatis mutandis*, to all the MSTs just discussed. The idea is that an individual may experience pleasures in relation to objects that are either immoral or worthless. These are kinds of base pleasures. If all pleasures matter for an individual's well-being, then base pleasures contribute to their well-being too. Some scholars balk at this conclusion because they think that base pleasures can never be good for an individual.

Three main strategies have been pursued to neutralize this objection. One consists in claiming that only pleasures taken in relation to moral or worthwhile objects are good for an individual. Another is to hold that the prudential value of pleasures depends not just on their quantitative features but also, and most importantly, on their quality (Mill 1863). The last strategy consists in biting the bullet and insisting that base pleasures, although morally bad or worthless, are nonetheless good for the individual.

The second main objection against MSTs is the so-called "experience machine objection" (Nozick 1974). Suppose we could enter a machine that stimulates our brain in such a way as to produce only positive mental states. If mental states are all that matter for well-being, then we should conclude that our well-being is very high when in the machine, as high as if these mental states were produced by experiences in the real world. To many, this conclusion is deeply counterintuitive. The experience machine objection has generated a large literature over the years, discussing several possible ways to counter the objection.[10] Perhaps the most promising strategy consists in biting the bullet and accepting the conclusion of the thought experiment, while offering a debunking explanation of why that conclusion seemed so counterintuitive in the first instance.

3.2 Preference Satisfaction Theories

The main idea underlying the preference satisfaction theories of well-being (PSTs henceforth) is that an individual's well-being depends exclusively on the satisfaction of their preferences, where a preference for x over y is satisfied if and only if x is the case and is frustrated if and only if x is not the case. There are two main variants of this theory: object preferentialism and satisfaction preferentialism. According the former, the only items that are finally good for an individual are the *objects* of the individual's noninstrumental preferences, that is, the items that the individual desires for their own sake. What makes these items finally good is that they are objects of the individual's preferences. According to the latter, what is finally good for an individual is the *satisfaction* of their preferences or, equivalently, the compound state of affairs of their preferring x to y and x being the case. What makes this state of affairs finally good for the individual is that it involves a correspondence between the individual's preferences and the world. The difference between these two versions of the theory is subtle, but, as Krister Bykvist (2016) for one has shown, it is relevant for the assessment of the arguments for and against PSTs.[11]

Once again, two elements must be clarified in order to complete the characterization of the theory. First, what are preferences? Second, how is the overall level of well-being determined?

Let us start with the second question. The standard view is that the prudential value of the satisfaction of an individual's preference for *x* over *y* is determined as a function of the degree of the individual's preference for *x*, typically measured by an interval utility function representing the individual's preferences. If we assume that the degree of preference for *x* corresponds to the strength with which the individual desires *x*, then it follows that the prudential value of the satisfaction of an individual's preference for *x* over *y* is a function of the individual's strength of desire for *x*.[12] The overall level of the individual's well-being is then typically calculated as the sum of the prudential value of each preference satisfaction.

Let us go back to the first question. According to the most prominent view, preferences are choice dispositions (see also Vredenburgh, Chapter 5). Thus, to prefer *x* to *y* is equivalent to being disposed to choose *x* rather than *y*. Daniel M. Hausman (2012) has proposed a different account of preferences, arguing that it better describes the concept of preference that is *actually* used in economics. According to Hausman, preferences are total subjective comparative evaluations, that is, evaluations of two options *x* and *y*, which an individual forms by considering everything they find relevant to compare *x* and *y*. This view of preferences brings PSTs closer to a more recent theory of well-being, that is, the value-fulfillment theory of well-being, according to which well-being consists in the fulfillment of the individual's values (Tiberius 2018).

Like MSTs, PSTs are intuitively appealing. To say that well-being consists in getting what you want has a ring of plausibility. In addition, PSTs avoid the experience machine objection, for they maintain that people typically want not just the *experience* of doing various things but to *actually do* those things. Another powerful argument in favor of PSTs is that they best capture the requirement that a well-being theory be non-alienating. It seems that if well-being concerns what is good *for* an individual, it must not leave the individual cold. As Peter Railton forcefully puts it, "[i]t would be an intolerably alienated conception of someone's good to imagine that it might fail in any way to engage him" (2003: 47). The non-alienation requirement often leads to subjectivism about well-being, according to which an item must be favored by the individual in order to be finally good for them. PSTs seem to be paradigms of subjectivist theories. As such, they seem to fully capture the non-alienation requirement. Note, however, that this argument supports only object preferentialism because, according to satisfaction preferentialism, the explanatory ground for the prudential value of preference satisfactions is not that they are *themselves* favored by the individual but rather that they involve a correspondence between the world and the individual's preferences.

Over the years, PSTs have been subject to a battery of objections. The first is that actual preferences are sometimes ill-informed or based on false beliefs (e.g. when a person decides not to use a vaccine because they mistakenly believe it causes autism); in other cases, the actual preferences are irrational (e.g. when they manifest some failure of means-ends rationality). In yet other cases, the actual preferences are formed through defective processes (e.g. under conditions of oppression that are incompatible with individual autonomy, as is the case for many with "adaptive preferences"). In all these circumstances, satisfaction of the individual's preferences does not seem to contribute to their well-being. The standard move, here, is to claim that what matters for well-being are not the individual's actual preferences, but their ideal preferences – more specifically, the preferences they would have were they instrumentally rational, well informed, and sufficiently autonomous.[13]

However, this move is ineffective against other kinds of objections. One has to do with the scope of PSTs. An individual can have other-regarding preferences (e.g. that a stranger will get the job of their dreams) or preferences for temporally or spatially remote states of affairs (e.g. that alien civilizations will eventually be discovered). Their satisfaction does not seem to have any impact on the individual's well-being. There are two main strategies to counter this objection: one consists in restricting the theory to preferences for objects that make necessary reference to the individual (Overvold 1980). The other consists in adding an experience requirement, according to which only preferences whose satisfaction affects the individual's experience contribute to the individual's well-being.

A third objection is that an individual, even when fully informed and instrumentally rational, may have preferences for immoral, degrading, or simply valueless objects (e.g. for counting blades of grass in a park[14]). This is the equivalent of the base pleasure objection raised with respect to MSTs and is indeed addressed in similar ways by PS theorists.

A fourth objection is that the move to ideal preferences violates the non-alienation requirement, as a fully informed and rational individual may have preferences for things that leave their actual self completely unmoved. One possible reply to this objection is to move from ideal preferences to the preferences of an *ideal advisor* and to say that what matters for well-being is what a fully informed and instrumentally rational advisor would want for their actual, nonideal self. This move is sometimes attacked on the grounds that it renders PSTs explanatorily inadequate. To illustrate, let us observe that an ideal advisor may want plenty of things that have nothing to do with the well-being of their actual counterpart (e.g. they may want the actual self to be honest, even if this costs them their career). So, perhaps a qualification is needed: what matters for well-being is what an ideal advisor would want out of benevolence. However, this renders the explanation circular: insofar as benevolence involves a concern for the individual's well-being, it amounts to saying that well-being consists in what an ideal advisor would want for their actual self out of concern for their well-being.

3.3 Objective List Theories

Objective list theories (OLTs henceforth) are a family of theories that share two elements. First, they typically hold that there is a plurality of items that are finally good for the individual, hence the term "list" theories. Second, they deny that for an item to be finally good for an individual, it must be favored by the individual. That is, they deny the defining tenet of subjectivism, hence the term "objective" theories. Of these elements, only the second is invariant among OLTs. Pluralism about prudential goods is typical, but not constitutive, of OLTs. A theory that includes only one item in the list may still count as an OLT, provided that the explanation of why that item is finally good for the individual does not make reference to the individual favoring it. This implies that OLTs may partly overlap with some of the approaches examined so far; for example, on this understanding, internalist views of hedonism and satisfaction preferentialism count as OLTs.[15]

There are a variety of OLTs, differing with respect to the prudential goods that are included in the list. To give two (other) examples: according to John Finnis (1980), the list includes life, knowledge, play, aesthetic experience, sociability, practical reasonableness, and religion; according to Guy Fletcher (2013), the list instead includes achievement, friendship, happiness, pleasure, self-respect, and virtue.

As we have seen, a well-being theory must fulfill two other tasks: it must explain why these items are finally good for an individual and how the overall degree of well-being is determined. Here is where we encounter the main objections against OLTs. Consider the first task. Some scholars have attacked OLTs by claiming that they give *no* explanation of why certain items are on the list. Note that this is not a principled objection. An OL theorist can satisfy the explanatory requirement in two ways. On the one hand, they can argue that there is a common explanation as to why the items in the list are prudentially valuable. For instance, they can say that what makes these items finally good for an individual is that they manifest and exercise distinctively human capacities. This leads us to a perfectionist theory of well-being, which I will discuss in the next subsection. On the other hand, an OL theorist can argue that there are several good for–making properties, potentially one for each item in the list. For instance, they may hold that pleasure is finally good for an individual by virtue of its pleasantness, whereas achievement is finally good for an individual by virtue of the effort it involves. When the latter strategy is chosen, another objection is typically raised. If there are several good for–making properties that have nothing in common, then the explanation that OLTs provide as to why certain items are prudentially good is arbitrary. However, this charge is hard to sustain. On the one hand, the fact that OLTs identify a plurality of distinct reasons as to why certain items are prudentially good does not render, by itself, their explanation arbitrary. On the other hand, if the objection is simply an objection against explanatory pluralism, then it begs the question against OLTs.

What remains true is that not all contemporary OLTs have addressed these concerns in a satisfactory way. The same can be said with respect to the last task that OLTs must complete, namely, clarifying how to determine the overall level of an individual's well-being. This requires offering a list of prudential "bads," in addition to the list of prudential goods, and explaining how prudential goods and bads should be weighted so as to determine the overall level of well-being. Explanatorily pluralistic OLTs are often attacked as being at a fundamental disadvantage in this regard in comparison to explanatorily monistic theories. Once again, however, this is not a principled objection. The determination of how the prudential value of a life depends on different good for–making properties is, in principle, no more difficult than determining how the prudential value of a life depends on different elements (e.g. intensity, duration, quality) of a single good for–making property (e.g. pleasantness).

One final objection often raised against OLTs is that, qua objective theories, they violate the non-alienation requirement. OLTs have two main replies. The first is simply to reject the requirement. The second is to argue that each prudential good in the list requires some form of engagement from the individual in order for it to be fully realized (e.g. friendship requires an affective and motivational investment).[16] As such, they do not leave the individual cold. If that is the case, then OLTs can satisfy the spirit of the non-alienation requirement, even if not the letter.

Despite these objections, OLTs generally have good press. The explanatory pluralism of typical OLTs is the main source of their attraction. For one, it matches the intuition, shared by many, that things like knowledge, friendship, and virtue are good for an individual in their own right, not just because they cause pleasant experiences (as with hedonism) or because they are objects of the individual's preferences (as with object preferentialism). OLTs also avoid some of the main objections raised against competing approaches, most notably the experience machine objection. Because other goods matter for well-being in addition to mental states, OLTs can conclude that a life in the machine is prudentially inferior to an experientially identical life outside the machine.

3.4 Perfectionist Theories

According to perfectionist theories (PTs henceforth), an individual's well-being depends on the development and exercise of the capacities that are distinctive of the individual's nature. There are two ways of spelling out the notion of an individual's nature. The first, which has its roots in the Aristotelian tradition, says that, insofar as human beings are concerned, an individual's nature is simply their nature as a human being. This is the standard way of presenting PTs. The second, non-Aristotelian way ties the notion of an individual's nature more closely to the particular physical and psychological constitution of each individual. This is the notion at work in nonstandard perfectionist approaches to well-being, such as Daniel Haybron's (2008) self-fulfillment theory. Having made this distinction, for reasons of space I will only focus on standard PTs.

We can summarize their main tenets as follows. The only thing that is finally good for an individual (belonging to the human species) is the development and exercise of their distinctively human capacities. What makes the development and exercise of these capacities finally good for an individual is that they are constitutive of human nature. In this sense, we can say that the development and exercise of these capacities are finally good for the individual because they fulfill the individual's human nature. It follows from this that, in order to be complete, PTs must provide an account of human nature. I will consider this issue shortly. Before doing that, let me point out that a life lived according to distinctively human capacities will involve certain specific activities.[17] A complete PT thus must also identify which activities manifest the development and exercise of each capacity. It is likely that the list of relevant activities will include many of the items that figure in standard OLTs, such as knowledge, friendship, achievement, and so on. Note, however, that on a perfectionist account, these items are finally good for the individual only *derivatively*, as manifestations of human capacities whose exercise is nonderivatively finally good for an individual.

From this brief characterization, we can already appreciate the main attractions of PTs. The idea that well-being consists in nature fulfillment is intuitively appealing. PTs also provide us with a neat way to distinguish the well-being of human beings from the well-being of other nonhuman animals, which is determined by referring to each animal species. Finally, PTs provide a principled and unified explanation of why the items listed by OLTs are (derivatively) finally good for an individual.

Let us go back to the task of providing an account of human nature. This is where the problem begins for PTs.[18] There are two main approaches. One holds that human nature is constituted by the capacities that are unique to humans. The other holds that human nature is constituted by the capacities that are essential to humans (i.e. that no humans can lack). Both approaches appear to generate some unwanted results. For example, some capacities that are deemed to be central to well-being, such as practical rationality, may be neither unique (e.g. some alien species or nonhuman animals may also possess this capacity) nor essential to humans (e.g. some severely disabled individuals may lack this capacity). If so, PTs entail, counterintuitively by their own standards, that practical rationality is not finally good for the individual.

PTs face a second objection. Recall that well-being theories must specify how the overall level of an individual's well-being is determined. This requires having an account of prudential bads and of how these are to be weighed against prudential goods. PTs are sometimes deficient in this respect. That said, it is not impossible to come up with a perfectionist account of degrees of well-being. For example, one may hold that the only thing that is finally bad for an individual is the diminishment of their distinctively human capacities,[19] and that the overall level of an individual's well-being is a function of how much and/or how significantly the relevant capacities are exercised or diminished.[20] Still, PTs are not off the hook yet, for they seem to have trouble accounting for the prudential badness of pain. To begin with, the capacity for pain is neither unique nor essential to humans. If so, it appears that pain is not constitutive of human nature and thereby is not bad for the individual in itself, but only instrumentally. Some find this conclusion counterintuitive.[21] One may think that the solution is to adopt an account of human nature that turns the capacity to experience pain into a distinctively human capacity. However, this will not do – on the contrary. Such an account implies that an episode of extreme headache is finally good for an individual, because it involves exercising their distinctively human capacity to experience pain. Relatedly, a painkiller is (instrumentally) bad for the individual because it hinders the exercise of their capacity to experience pain.

3.4.1 The Capability Approach

At this stage, it is useful to say a few words about an approach that has been highly influential in a variety of fields, that is, the capability approach, originally proposed and developed by Amartya Sen (1985, 1992, 2009) and Martha Nussbaum (1988, 2000, 2011). The capability approach is often presented as a flexible framework that can be used for the evaluation of social institutions and the design of public policies. What interests us here, however, is whether the capability approach can also provide us with an *independent* theory of well-being.

Let me start by clarifying the two notions at the heart of the capability approach, namely, the notions of functionings and capabilities. Functionings are simply "beings and doings," that is, states the individual may be in (e.g. being well-nourished, being in lockdown, being a philosopher) or things they may do (e.g. writing an article, participating in Zoom meetings, pirating online software). Capabilities are the individual's opportunities to function in certain ways, that is, what the individual *can* be and do. In Sen's own words, capabilities refer to "the substantive freedom to achieve alternative functioning combinations" (Sen 1999: 40).

The next thing to clarify is what matters for well-being, whether functionings or capabilities. When the capability approach is deployed in the context of theories of distributive justice, most scholars think that we should primarily care about capabilities or a mixture of capabilities and functionings. By contrast, when it comes to well-being, the literature is pretty much consensual in taking functionings as the central element. It is indeed customary to identify functionings with "achieved well-being" and capabilities with "well-being opportunities."

We need to specify exactly *which* functionings matter for well-being. Sen has traditionally been reluctant to offer a fixed list of relevant functionings. Instead, Nussbaum has identified ten central capabilities, which generate a corresponding list of central functionings: life; health; bodily integrity; senses, imagination, and thought; emotions; practical reason; affiliation; play; relations with other species; and control over one's environment.

When it comes to well-being, these things are supposed to be good in themselves for the individual. The question is *why*. Only after we address this question can we be in a position to assess whether the capability approach offers an independent theory of well-being. Unfortunately, the answers are not always clear or persuasive. In recent writings (especially), Sen claims that the relevant functionings are those we have "reason to value" (e.g. Sen 2009: 231–232). If this is what makes them prudentially good, however, the capability approach is simply a (reason-based) version – in fact, a precursor – of the value-fulfillment theory of well-being.[22] As for Nussbaum, in earlier writings (1988), she connects the notion of functionings to that of human nature. This seems to reduce the capability approach to a version of perfectionism. Unlike the PTs seen earlier, however, Nussbaum conceives the notion of human nature as an evaluative notion, rather than as a descriptive one. According to her Aristotelian account, in order to establish what human nature is, we need to look at the "evaluative beliefs of the many and the wise" (Ibid. 1988: 177). As Hurka, for one, has suggested (2016: 396), this seems to imply that what makes certain functionings finally good for an individual is the fact that they are so judged by the wise (*phronimoi*), which, as an explanation of the ultimate grounds of well-being, is less than fully convincing. More recently (2011), Nussbaum has tied her central capabilities to human dignity. When applied to well-being, the idea is that certain functionings are finally good for the individual because they are central to human dignity. Note that dignity is typically invoked to explain what an individual is owed from the moral point of view or from the point of view of justice. Arguably, however, the domains of morality and justice do not perfectly overlap with the domain of prudence. If so, it is doubtful that Nussbaum's appeal to dignity provides an adequate foundation for a capability-based theory *of well-being*, rather than for a theory of justice.

4. Conclusion

In this chapter, I have provided an overview of the most important features, attractions, and problems of the main philosophical theories of well-being. Needless to say, defenders of these theories have offered, and continue to offer, various rebuttals and refinements of their theories in response to the objections raised against them. Some have also proposed hybrid theories, combining elements from different approaches, which I have not discussed here for reasons of space. Hopefully, this quick sketch is enough to show the breadth and complexity of the debate about the nature of well-being.

Related Chapter

Vredenburgh, Chapter 5 "The Economic Concept of a Preference"

Notes

1 I will use these terms interchangeably in this chapter.
2 There are other important questions about well-being that deserve close attention. One is the question of what to do with well-being. In other words, what role should well-being play in moral and political decision-making? Related questions concern the measurement and comparisons of well-being. How should well-being be measured? What are reliable indicators of well-being? Is it possible to make intrapersonal and interpersonal comparisons of well-being in a scientifically justified way? How? For reasons of space, I will not consider these questions in this chapter.
3 The previous considerations help us to demarcate the concept of goodness for from similar evaluative concepts. In order to provide a full understanding of the concept of goodness for, some philosophers have moved one step further and offered a conceptual analysis of goodness for, that is, an analysis of goodness for in terms of simpler, and hopefully better understood, concepts or in terms of concepts that are regarded as more fundamental. There are a few competing analyses currently on offer. For an overview, see Campbell (2016).
4 For simplicity, in what follows I will omit the qualification "basic" when talking about final prudential goods.
5 Internalist views of pleasantness come in two main varieties: distinctive feeling views, according to which pleasantness consists in a distinctive kind of feeling common to all pleasures (e.g., Moore 1903; Brink 1989; Bramble 2011), and hedonic tone views, according to which pleasantness consists in a determinable kind of feeling, which admits of different specifications (e.g. Kagan 1992; Crisp 2006; Smuts 2011).
6 Externalist views also come in different varieties. For instance, according to conative views, pleasantness consists in the desire that that mental state continues (e.g. Heathwood 2007). According to evaluativist views, pleasantness consists in a perceptual evaluation of that mental state's object as good or as good for the individual (cf. Cutter and Tye 2011; Bain 2013).
7 Clearly, however, other options are possible and have indeed been explored with respect to both of these claims.
8 Note, however, that this is not the only route to hedonism about well-being. In particular, one might reject hedonism about happiness (e.g. by holding that happiness consists in life satisfaction) but still accept hedonism about well-being (e.g. by holding that happiness is not the mental state that matters for well-being).
9 See Haybron (2016) for an overview.
10 See Fletcher (2016b) and Hawkins (2016) for overviews.
11 See also Rabinowicz and Österberg (1996).
12 On this account, the satisfaction of an individual's preference for x over y contributes positively to the individual's well-being only if the individual desires x with positive strength; it contributes negatively insofar as the individual desires x with negative strength or, equivalently, if the individual is averse to x, despite preferring x to y. It follows that frustrating an individual's preferences is not necessarily bad for them, because they may not be averse to $\neg x$.
13 For an alternative reply to these objections, which preserves the formulation of the PST in terms of actual desires, see Heathwood (2005).
14 See Rawls (1971).
15 See also Fletcher (2016b: 49–51).
16 See Fletcher (2013).
17 On this point, see also Dorsey (2010) and Bradford (2016).
18 As a methodological requirement, such an account must be generated without appealing to facts about human well-being, on pain of circularity.
19 See Fletcher (2016b: 86).
20 See Bradford (2016).
21 Similar problems arise for PTs when accounting for the prudential goodness of pleasure.
22 Alternatively, if "what we have a reason to value" is the same as "what is objectively valuable" (either *simpliciter* or for the individual), then the capability approach to well-being reduces to a version of the OLT.

Bibliography

Bain, D. (2013) "What Makes Pains Unpleasant?" *Philosophical Studies* 166(1): 60–89.
Bradford, G. (2016) "Perfectionism," in G. Fletcher (ed.) *The Routledge Handbook of Philosophy of Well-Being*: 124–134, London: Routledge.

Bramble, B. (2011) "The Distinctive Feeling Theory of Pleasure," *Philosophical Studies* 162(2): 201–217.
Brink, D. (1989) *Moral Realism and the Foundations of Ethics*, Cambridge: Cambridge University Press.
Bykvist, K. (2016) "Preference-Based Views of Well-Being," in M. D. Adler and M. Fleurbaey (eds.) *The Oxford Handbook of Well-Being and Public Policy*: 321–346, Oxford: Oxford University Press.
Campbell, S. M. (2016) "The Concept of Well-Being," in G. Fletcher (ed.) *The Routledge Handbook of Philosophy of Well-Being*: 402–413, London: Routledge.
Crisp, R. (2006) *Reasons and the Good*, Oxford: Oxford University Press.
Cutter, B. and Tye, M. (2011) "Tracking Representationalism and the Painfulness of Pain," *Philosophical Issues* 21: 90–109.
Dorsey, D. (2010) "Three Arguments for Perfectionism," *Noûs* 44: 59–79.
Finnis, J. (1980) *Natural Law and Natural Rights*, Oxford: Clarendon Press.
Fletcher, G. (2013) "A Fresh Start for the Objective-List Theory of Well-Being," *Utilitas* 25: 206–220.
Fletcher, G. (2016b) *The Philosophy of Well-Being: An Introduction*, London: Routledge.
Hausman, D. (2012) *Preference, Value, Choice, and Welfare*, Cambridge: Cambridge University Press.
Hawkins, J. (2016) "The Experience Machine and the Experience Requirement," in G. Fletcher (ed.) *The Routledge Handbook of Philosophy of Well-Being*: 355–365, London: Routledge.
Haybron, D. (2008) *The Pursuit of Unhappiness*, Oxford: Oxford University Press.
Haybron, D. (2016) "Mental State Approaches to Well-Being," in M. D. Adler and M. Fleurbaey (eds.) *The Oxford Handbook of Well-Being and Public Policy*: 347–378, Oxford: Oxford University Press.
Heathwood, C. (2005) "The Problem of Defective Desires," *Australasian Journal of Philosophy* 83: 487–504.
Heathwood, C. (2007) "The Reduction of Sensory Pleasure to Desire," *Philosophical Studies* 133: 23–44.
Hurka, T. (2016) "Objective Goods," in M. D. Adler and M. Fleurbaey (eds.) *The Oxford Handbook of Well-Being and Public Policy*: 379–402, Oxford: Oxford University Press.
Kagan, S. (1992) "The Limits of Well-Being," *Social Philosophy and Policy* 9(2): 169–189.
Mill, J. S. (1863) *Utilitarianism*, London: Parker, Son, and Bourne.
Moore, G.E. (1903/1993) *Principia Ethica*, T. Baldwin (ed.), Cambridge: Cambridge University Press.
Nozick, R. (1974) *Anarchy, State, and Utopia*, New York: Basic Books.
Nussbaum, M. (1988) "Nature, Function, and Capability: Aristotle on Political Distribution," *Oxford Studies in Ancient Philosophy, Supplementary Volume* 6: 145–184.
Nussbaum, M. (2000) *Women and Human Development: The Capabilities Approach*, New York: Cambridge University Press.
Nussbaum, M. (2011) *Creating Capabilities: The Human Development Approach*, Cambridge, MA: Harvard University Press.
Overvold, M. (1980) "Self-Interest and the Concept of Self-Sacrifice," *Canadian Journal of Philosophy* 10: 105–118.
Rabinowicz, W. and Österberg, J. (1996) "Value Based on Preferences: On Two Interpretations of Preference Utilitarianism," *Economics and Philosophy* 12: 1–27.
Railton, P. (2003) *Facts, Values, and Norms: Essays Towards a Morality of Consequence*, Cambridge: Cambridge University Press.
Rawls, J. (1971) *A Theory of Justice*, Cambridge, MA: Harvard University Press.
Sen, A. K. (1985) *Commodities and Capabilities*, Amsterdam: North-Holland.
Sen, A. K. (1992) *Inequality Re-Examined*, Oxford: Clarendon Press.
Sen, A. K. (1999) *Development as Freedom*, New York: Knopf.
Sen, A. K. (2009) *The Idea of Justice*, New York: Penguin.
Smuts, A. (2011) "The Feels Good Theory of Pleasure," *Philosophical Studies* 155(2): 241–265.
Sumner, W. (1996) *Welfare, Happiness, and Ethics*, Oxford: Clarendon Press.
Tiberius, V. (2018) *Well-Being as Value Fulfilment*, Oxford: Oxford University Press.
van der Deijl, W. (2019) "Is Pleasure All That Is Good About Experience?" *Philosophical Studies* 176: 1769–1787.

19
FAIRNESS AND FAIR DIVISION

Stefan Wintein and Conrad Heilmann

1. Introduction

Fairness is a central value concept in both philosophy and economics. It is ubiquitous in contributions to ethics and political philosophy and a key concern in many areas of economic theory. Philosophers and economists alike frequently employ specific conceptions of fairness in order to develop theories centered on other concepts, such as equality, welfare, and justice. A prominent example is Rawls (1971), who conceptualized justice *as* fairness.

Yet, fairness *itself* "is a central, but under-theorized, notion in moral and political philosophy" (Saunders 2010:41). Indeed, Carr (2000:3) observes: "rarely if ever does one find a theoretical work of any sort devoted exclusively or largely to understanding what it means to be fair or unfair." And while the words "fair" and "fairness" are used in many contexts, both in everyday life and in philosophy and economics, quite often they are not fully defined and are employed in a somewhat loose, general way. In relation to this, Brad Hooker has issued the following challenge:

> I believe "fair" is often used in [a] broad sense. But the broad usage seems to me unfortunate. We already have terms signifying the verdicts of all-things-considered moral reasoning. Terms signifying the verdicts of all-things-considered moral reasoning include "morally justified", "morally legitimate", "morally right" and "morally best". Don't we want "fair" to have a distinctive and thus narrower meaning?
>
> (Hooker 2005:332)

In this chapter, we review philosophical and economic theories of fairness that have contributed to give affirmative, and substantive, answers to this challenge by Hooker. Our overall message is straightforward: we show that *fair division theories* in philosophy and economics have much to offer for substantiating the conceptual content of fairness. Doing so, we demonstrate that a specific type of fair division theories is well suited for this task: theories that promote understanding fairness as a *substantive, local,* and *objective* concept. We also suggest that philosophical and economic theories in this area have much to offer to one another. Although developed by and large in isolation from each other, they are surprisingly complementary.

In Section 2, we make precise the idea of fairness as a distinct value concept and introduce several key notions for the concept of fairness, including distinguishing between substantive and formal fairness, local and global fairness, and objective and subjective fairness. In Section 3, we review

DOI: 10.4324/9781315739793-23

philosophical fair division theories that build on John Broome's (1990) influential account of fairness. In Section 4, we review economic fair division theories that analyze fair division by modeling them as claims problems and as cooperative games. Section 5 focuses on open challenges for both the philosophical and the economic fair division theory regarding the central notion of a *claim*. Section 6 concludes.

2. Fair Division

A good starting point to locate our discussion of fairness as a distinct moral value is an infamous example from Diamond (1967), displayed in Table 19.1. There are two equiprobable states of nature, states 1 and 2, and two alternative actions, A and B, that a social planner might take. The actions affect two individuals, Ann and Bob: for example, in state 1, action A leads to a utility of 1 for Ann and 0 for Bob.

If state 1 occurs, the results of A and B are the same, whereas if state 2 occurs, the results are symmetrical. It then follows from *the sure thing principle*[1] that the social planner should be *indifferent* between A and B. However, whereas A results in utility distribution (1, 0) with certainty, action B renders distributions (1, 0) and (0, 1) equally probable. Diamond uses this observation to argue that the preferences of the social planner violate the sure thing principle: the planner should *not* be indifferent, as the principle has it, but rather should prefer B to A as that action is *fairer*.

But why, exactly, is it that B is fairer? Diamond suggests two answers to that question:

1. **Distributive answer**. B is fairest because it equally distributes total expected utility: the total expected utility of both A and B is 1, but B yields expected utilities of 0.5 for both Ann and Bob and so distributes total expected utility equally.
2. **Procedural answer**. B is fairest because it distributes utilities via a fair procedure: an equal chance lottery.

Broome (1984) argues that both answers are wanting, along the following lines. First, Broome dismisses the distributive answer by arguing that *expected* utility is not a good to which the prima facie plausible principle that "*ceteris paribus*, the more equally a total amount of good is distributed, the fairer" applies. Although that principle may very well be applicable to equalizing *utilities*, Broome (1984:626) stresses that "an expected utility is not at all the same sort of thing as utility, so what applies to one does not necessarily apply to the other." Second, Broome fully acknowledges that *sometimes* it is fairest to distribute a good via lottery. However, that is not *always* the case, and, as Broome convincingly shows, the decision matrix of Diamond's example cannot distinguish cases from which it is from cases in which it is not. Hence, Diamond's procedural answer is flawed, as it cannot be inferred from Table 19.1 that action B corresponds with a fair procedure.

Although the distributive and procedural answers are flawed, they do appeal to important truisms about fairness: *sometimes* it is fairest to equally divide a good, and *sometimes* it is fairest to distribute a good via lottery. But when, and why, exactly? These questions cannot be answered within the

Table 19.1 Diamond's example

	State 1	*State 2*
Action A	(1, 0)	(1, 0)
Action B	(1, 0)	(0, 1)

choice-theoretic framework of Diamond's example. Rather, they have to be answered by a theory of *fairness*, that is, a theory of the concept of fairness *itself*.

Fairness, as a key value concept in philosophy and economics, has been discussed in a variety of ways. For the remainder of the chapter, we will focus on philosophical and economic theories that understand fairness as a *substantive*, *local*, and *objective* concept. But before doing so, we clarify these terms.

2.1 Substantive and Formal Fairness

In everyday life, the idea of fairness and fair treatment is often brought up in relation to legal matters, be it court proceedings, contracts, or the application of rules. "Fairness" here often means something like equal treatment of equals under the law or evenhandedness in applying rules and regulations. But, as any kind of rule or law, irrespective of its content, can be applied consistently, this appeal to fairness is merely *formal*. In order to analyze fairness as a *distinct* value, it is helpful to focus on *substantive fairness* (see also Ferguson, Chapter 10).

2.2 Local and Global Fairness

Fairness theorizing is often concerned with problems of a large scale, such as regarding societal structures and institutional arrangements. We follow Peyton Young in reserving the term "global fairness" for such matters:

> Fairness in [a] global sense is concerned with the proper distribution of resources, rights, duties, opportunities, and obligations in society at large. This grand theme has animated political philosophers since antiquity, from Plato's and Aristotle's conceptions of the ideal state, to the social contract theories of Hobbes, Locke, and Rousseau, to the more modern theories of Rawls, Nozick and Walzer. I shall refer to these as theories of *social justice*.
>
> (Young 1994:xi)

No doubt, theories of social justice need to be "fair." However, we think that for studying what fairness *is*, it is more fruitful to turn our attention to problems at a much more local scale. For instance, how to fairly divide the household chores? How to fairly divide the remaining assets of a firm after a bankruptcy? Or, for a concrete example:

> **Kidney**. Ann and Bob both need a kidney transplant in order to survive, but there is only one kidney available. If given to Ann, she gains 21 years of life, while Bob gains 20 years of life if given the kidney. How should we allocate the kidney?

This chapter reviews theories in philosophy and economics that analyze fairness in terms of (local) *fair division problems* such as "Kidney." We concur with Young that

> All of these [fair division problems] can be and are solved without invoking theories of social justice. I am not saying that these theories are unimportant; they are of the utmost importance. What I am saying is that it is possible to analyze the meaning of [local fairness] without resolving what social justice means in the large.
>
> (Young 1994:xi)

Many fairness-related accounts in ethics and political philosophy, as well as in economics, are geared toward analyzing global, rather than local, fairness. Approaches that deal with large-scale fairness problems often touch on assessing the social states of affairs with regard to many important ethical concerns, such as welfare and inequality [see, for example, Adler (2012), Elster (1992), and Voorhoeve, Chapter 34]. Not only is this true of theories of distributive and retributive justice (e.g. Roemer 1996; Miller 2017), it is also true of approaches in economics. Consider, for instance, the analysis of Roth et al. (2004) on how to design a mechanism for a fair distribution of donated organs (such as kidneys). The complexities in determining the correct institutional setup for a "globally" fair kidney market across a whole country stand in contrast to the simple, singular fair division problem introduced previously, "Kidney." In the remainder of the chapter, we will focus on local fairness and investigate the concept of fairness by analyzing fair division problems like "Kidney."

2.3 Objective and Subjective Fairness

There is a straightforward sense in which fairness always has a subjective component: through the individuals concerned that might feel a certain arrangement is fair or unfair. And many of the key approaches to fairness in economics are based on individual preferences. For one, the concept of individuals having "no envy" for each other's position plays a canonical role in the subjective equity approach to fairness (reviewed by Thomson 2011).[2] For another, there are newer theories related to behavioral economics that analyze the fairness considerations by individuals with respect to inequality aversion and reciprocity (see Vromen, Chapter 9). In contrast, many approaches in philosophy, as well as certain microeconomics literature to be discussed in Section 4, analyze fairness by turning "a blind eye to the wishes and preferences of the parties involved" (Rescher 2002:31). Such "objective" (nonsubjective) approaches to fairness aim to ground the meaning of fairness by appealing to notions other than preferences, most notably that of a *claim*, as discussed in Section 3. In this chapter, we will focus on these objective, claim-based approaches.

We will thus review "fair division" theories in philosophy and economics that use the analysis of fair division problems in order to explore fairness understood mainly as a *substantive*, *local*, and *objective* concept. Classification of their aims in this way does not preclude that they may also make certain formal assumptions, or that they might also be used to explore global fairness questions, or that they have subjective elements to them. Still, what these theories have in common is that they are (or can be) used to explore the meaning of fairness as a distinct moral concept, while accentuating the substantive, local, and objective aspects of fairness. We aim to show that the potential interplay and links between these different philosophical and economic theories are interesting and that this interplay can also be productive in addressing ongoing challenges in spelling out the meaning of fairness.

3. Broomean Fair Division Theories

The most influential philosophical theory of fair division, developed by John Broome (1990), can be summarized in the following slogan:

> **Broomean formula**: *Fairness requires that claims are satisfied in proportion to their strength.*

To illustrate the theory behind the formula, we show how "Kidney" is analyzed via Broome's theory.

To give the kidney to Ann will have the best *consequences*: she will live another 21 years (as opposed to Bob, who will only live another 20 years). But to give the kidney to Ann seems *unfair* to Bob. According to Broome, Ann and Bob have equally strong *claims* to the kidney, as they both need the kidney to survive. Claims are a *specific type* of reason as to why a person should receive a good: "duties owed to the person herself," as Broome puts it. As fairness requires the satisfaction of claims in proportion to their strength, perfect fairness can only be achieved by "destroying" the kidney, so that Ann's and Bob's equally strong claims receive equal satisfaction: none. Doing so, however, is clearly unacceptable in terms of the consequences. For "Kidney," Broome advocates for the following solution. Allocation of the kidney via a coin toss gives Ann and Bob an equal *chance* of getting the kidney, which generates *some* fairness ("surrogate satisfaction" as Broome puts it) and which has better consequences than letting two persons die. A coin toss is neither the best nor the fairest thing to do, but in striking a proper balance between *fairness* and *goodness*, it is the *right* thing to do. Or so Broome would argue.

The Broomean formula can be interpreted as a straightforward development of the more general Aristotelian formula (*The Nicomachean Ethics,* Aristotle 2009).

> **Aristotelian formula:** *Fairness requires that equals should be treated equally, and unequals unequally, in proportion to relevant similarities and differences.*

In Aristotle's view, fairness is thus the equal treatment of equals (which in Broome is subsumed under the proportional satisfaction principle) as well as the demand to take into account the "relevant" similarities and differences in a proportional way. The Broomean concept of a claim can thus be seen as a more precise, and demanding, way to spell out the vague requirement in the Aristotelian formula.

For cases with indivisible goods, most authors agree that when competing claims to the good are equally strong, fairness requires dividing the good via an equal chance lottery.[3] Disagreements abound, however, about what fairness requires when claims are *not* equally strong. Hooker (2005) argues that Broome is committed to use *weighted lotteries* for such cases – with weights being determined by claim strengths – and that this commitment is problematic. For instance, consider "Unequal Kidney", where Ann needs the kidney for only a very slight improvement in her otherwise perfect life, while Bob needs it for survival. Many agree with Hooker that it is appropriate to let Bob's stronger claim win rather than to set up a lottery where there is a slight chance that the kidney would be given to Ann in the end.[4] Lazenby (2014) develops a Broomean theory of fairness in which, for cases like "Unequal Kidney," fairness indeed requires that "the stronger claim should win." Wintein and Heilmann (2018) invoke *apportionment theory*[5] – originally developed to fairly allocate indivisible parliamentary seats after elections – in order to avoid the use of weighted lotteries. Also, Gerard Vong has proposed certain refinements and extensions of Broome's theory of fairness on the basis of his analysis of consecutive lotteries (Vong 2015) and lotteries that benefit different, potentially *overlapping groups* of individuals (Vong 2020).

Broome (1990:87) writes that, "Sometimes a lottery is the fairest way of distributing a good, and my theory explains, better than any other theory I know, why this is so." Previously, we illustrated that, even though the Broomean *formula* is widely endorsed, quite a few authors disagree that Broome's *theory* best explains the fairness of lotteries.

Broome *stipulates* that fairness requires proportionality, and he justifies this stipulation by the way in which it accounts for the fairness of lotteries for allocating indivisible goods. However, Broome's theory also applies to problems with divisible good, such as the following:

> **Owing Money**. Ann, Bob, and Carla have deposited €10, €20, and €30, respectively, into the bank. After bankruptcy, the liquidation value of the bank is €24. How should this money be divided?

Cases like "Owing Money" are also analyzed in economics: either as *claims problems* or as *cooperative games*. In the next section, we briefly discuss these approaches and explain that they allow for a study of proportionality that goes beyond stipulation.

4. Fair Division in Claims Problems and Cooperative Games

4.1 Fair Division in Claims Problems

Fair division problems like "Owing Money" are paradigmatic for the mathematical and economic literature[6] on so-called *claims problems*.

> **Claims problem**. A claims problem, $C = (E, N, c)$, consists of an amount of good E, called the estate, a set of agents N, and a claims vector c specifying the amount $c_i \geq 0$ of the estate E to which agent i has a claim and is such that the sum of all $c_i \geq E$.

In "Owing Money," the estate E = €24, and the respective claims by Ann, Bob, and Carla are €10, €20, and €30.

> **Division rule**. A division rule r is a function that maps each claims problem (E, N, c) to an allocation x such that $x_i \leq c_i$ for each agent i and $\sum x_i \leq E$.

According to this definition, a division rule is not necessarily efficient or fair, but is simply an assignment of a part of the estate to each agent, such that no agent receives more than their claim. Consider the following allocations for "Owing Money" for three different division rules.

P awards shares proportional to claims, whereas CEA equalizes awards as much as possible without giving any agent more than their claim. CEL first calculates the difference between the sum of all claims (€60) and the estate E (€24) to determine the *joint loss* L (€36), which is then equally shared among all agents without awarding any agent a negative amount. Apart from these division rules, multitudes of others have been proposed in the literature.

> The best-known rule is the proportional rule, which chooses awards proportional to claims. Proportionality is often taken as the definition of fairness . . . but we will challenge this position and start from more elementary considerations.
>
> (Thomson 2003:250)

Indeed, in this literature, division rules are studied and compared on the basis of their elementary properties or *axioms*. In particular, to *characterize* a division rule is to show that the rule is the *only* rule that satisfies certain desirable axioms. For example, Young (1988) characterizes P as follows:

> The proportional rule P is the only division rule that satisfies the following axioms: Efficiency, Equal Treatment of Equals, Self-Duality, and Composition.

Efficiency says that the division rule allocates all of the estate, whereas *equal treatment of equals* says that agents with the same claims receive the same amount. Now, *efficiency* and *equal treatment of equals* are shared by many division rules, so there is no unique division rule satisfying them. The *self-duality*

Table 19.2 Allocations for "Owing Money" in different division rules

Division rules	*Ann*	*Bob*	*Carla*
Proportional rule (P)	4	8	12
Constrained equalized awards (CEA)	8	8	8
Constrained equalized losses (CEL)	0	7	17

axiom needs some more explanation. It relies on the *loss problem* $C_L = (L, N, c)$, which is obtained from a claims problem $C = (E, N, c)$ by replacing its estate E with the joint loss L. A division rule r is *self-dual* when it divides the estate in C in the same way as it divides the joint loss in C_L, that is, when $r(C) = c - r(C_L)$ for each claims problem C. For P, it makes no difference to the allocation whether the proportional shares are calculated for the estate or for the joint loss; it is, hence, *self-dual.* This self-duality holds for neither CEA nor CEL (however, as can be easily verified, they are dual rules with respect to *each other*). Finally, *composition* is a technical property that prevents the partition of fair division problems into smaller ones to make a difference in the allocation.[7]

Now, the preceding discussion testifies that Young's characterization is not to be understood as an analysis of P in terms of more basic *fairness* axioms. For sure, *equal treatment of equals* can be understood as such. But *composition* clearly cannot. And although *self-duality* has normative appeal – as one might think it signifies the absence of a certain kind of bias – it does not seem to provide a strong reason for underpinning the normative appeal of proportionality. Moreover, there are other rules that belong to the class of division rules that satisfy *efficiency*, *equal treatment of equals*, and *self-duality*: for instance, the Talmud rule (Aumann and Maschler 1985) and the run-to-the-bank (RTB) rule (O'Neill 1982). As such, proportionality does not look so special in this framework, which is an interesting contrast to the philosophical literature (see also Heilmann and Wintein 2017).

4.2 Fair Division in Cooperative Games

A substantive literature that is closely related to the claims problem literature analyzes problems such as "Owing Money" as *cooperative games*,[8] starting with O'Neill (1982).

> **Cooperative game**. A cooperative game (N, v) consists of a set of agents N and a *characteristic function* v that specifies, for each group of agents $S \subseteq N$, the value that S can *guarantee* itself.

In "Owing Money," the group that consists of Bob and Carla can guarantee itself 14 as that is what is left after all agents outside the group, Ann in this case, are fully reimbursed. This we denote as $v(\{\text{Bob,Carla}\}) = 14$. The complete cooperative game induced by "Owing Money," then, is as follows:

$$v(\emptyset) = 0,\ v(\{\text{Ann}\}) = 0,\ v(\{\text{Bob}\}) = 0,\ v(\{\text{Carla}\}) = 0,\ v(\{\text{Ann,Bob}\}) = 0,$$
$$v(\{\text{Ann,Carla}\}) = 4,\ v(\{\text{Bob,Carla}\}) = 14,\ v(\{\text{Ann,Bob,Carla}\}) = 24$$

Whereas division rules allocate the estate in a claims problem, *solution values* allocate "the value of the grand coalition," $v(N)$, among the agents in N.

> **Solution value**. A solution value φ is a function that maps each cooperative game (N, v) to an allocation x of $v(N)$ such that $\sum x_i \leq v(N)$.

Many solution values exist and are (also axiomatically) studied in cooperative game theory. Solution values and their axiom are discussed and evaluated in terms of their "fairness." Without a doubt, the best-known solution value is the *Shapley value* (1953), which has been heralded by Moulin (2004) as the "single most important contribution by game theory to distributive justice." More generally, the Shapley value is often referred to as yielding "fair" allocations.

The Shapley value proposes an allocation of $v(N)$ by giving each agent their average marginal contribution realized over all possible orders in which the grand coalition is formed. To illustrate, consider Table 19.3.

Table 19.3 Allocation for "Owing Money" under the Shapley value

Order	*Marginal contribution Ann*	*Marginal contribution Bob*	*Marginal contribution Carla*
Ann, Bob, Carla	0	0	24
Ann, Carla, Bob	0	20	4
Bob, Ann, Carla	0	0	24
Bob, Carla, Ann	10	0	14
Carla, Ann, Bob	4	20	0
Carla, Bob, Ann	10	14	0
Sum	*24*	*54*	*66*
Shapley value	*4*	*9*	*11*

One way in which the grand coalition can be formed is in the order Carla, Bob, Ann. Carla enters first, which gives her a marginal contribution of $v(\{\text{Carla}\}) - v(\varnothing) = 0 - 0 = 0$. Then Bob joins, realizing a marginal contribution of $v(\{\text{Bob, Carla}\}) - v(\{\text{Carla}\}) = 14$. Finally, Ann joins and her marginal contribution of doing so is $v(\{\text{Ann, Bob, Carla}\}) - v(\{\text{Bob, Carla}\}) = 10$. By taking the average marginal contribution that the agents realize over all orders, the Shapley allocation recommends (4, 9, 11) on the basis of the cooperative game induced by "Owing Money." Note that this allocation differs from that recommended by the proportional rule.

So, we have two ways to divide the liquidation value in "Owing Money." First, we can model "Owing Money" as a claims problem r to which we apply a division rule. Second, we can model "Owing Money" as a cooperative game to which we apply a solution value φ . More generally, any claims problem C can be analyzed as a cooperative game v_C in which a group S can guarantee itself that amount that is not claimed by the agents outside of S: $v_C(S) = max\{0, E - \sum c_i\}$.

The correspondence between claims problems and cooperative games raises the interesting question of whether there is a similar correspondence between division rules and solution values. A division rule r is *game theoretic* when there is a solution value φ such that, for any claims problem C, applying r to C yields the same allocation as applying φ to the corresponding v_C. Quite a few division rules are game theoretic. In particular, the RTB rule, mentioned earlier, is game theoretic and corresponds with the Shapley value. *The proportional rule* P, *however, is not.* This is easily seen by supposing that, in "Owing Money," Carla's claim is 50 rather than 30, all else being equal. Now, the cooperative game that corresponds with this "adjusted Owing Money" is the very same as the game that corresponds with "Owing Money." Hence, any solution value must recommend the same allocation for "Owing Money" as for its adjustment. The proportional rule P, however, allots 12 to Carla in "Owing Money" and 15 in its adjustment.

Rules that *have* a game-theoretic counterpart are robust with respect to how the underlying fair division problem is modeled – that is, whether as a claims problem or as a cooperative game. The proportional rule P, then, is not robust. Now, one may not be too impressed by this lack of robustness by arguing that it is *obvious* that we should realize an allocation for "Owing Money" by modeling it as a claims problem,[9] to which we then apply P. However, irrespective of the value of this argument, not all fair division problems are like "Owing Money."

> **Gloves**. Ann owns one left and two right gloves; Bob owns three left gloves and one right glove, and Carla owns one right glove. Each full pair of gloves that is brought to the market can be, and is, sold for €1. Ann, Bob, and Carla can go to the market individually, in pairs, or together. When they all go together, how should their joint revenue be divided?

In "Gloves," Bob and Carla can, by pooling their gloves, guarantee themselves revenues of €2. More generally, "Gloves" gives rise to the following cooperative game:

$$v(\emptyset) = 0,\ v(\{\text{Ann}\}) = 1,\ v(\{\text{Bob}\}) = 1,\ v(\{\text{Carla}\}) = 0,$$
$$v(\{\text{Ann,Bob}\}) = 3,\ v(\{\text{Ann,Carla}\}) = 1,\ v(\{\text{Bob,Carla}\}) = 2,\ v(\{\text{Ann,Bob,Carla}\}) = 4.$$

"Gloves" is a fair division problem within the scope of the substantive, local, and objective conception of fairness that is at stake in this chapter. "Gloves" is naturally modeled as a cooperative game, but not as a claims problem. Hence, fair division in "Gloves" cannot proceed via the proportional rule P. Moreover, Broomean theories of fairness do not tell us how to *be* fair in situations such as "Gloves." Now, an allocation of the joint revenues in "Gloves" *can* be obtained by applying a solution value to the "Gloves" game. For instance, the Shapley value recommends, as the reader may care to verify, the division of the €4 in "Gloves" by allocating 1.5 to Ann, 2 to Bob and 0.5 to Carla.

For "Gloves," the Shapley allocation is intuitively fair: it comes naturally to conceive of the value of a single glove as 0.5. The power of cooperative game theory, however, is that it can guide fair division in areas where intuition is less firm and where neither Broomean theories of fairness nor the proportional division rule is applicable. We have only mentioned the Shapley value in this chapter, but many solution values exist. Which solution value best captures, for which type of fair division problem, the requirement of fairness understood as "proportional to claims"? Which axioms of the proportional rule P have counterparts as axioms for solution values, and to what extent do such axioms motivate a choice for one solution value over another? Admittedly, these are far-reaching questions. And yet, we think that these questions have to be addressed by any mature theory of the substantive, local, and objective notion of fairness.

The fundamental nature of these questions also testifies to the potential of cooperative game theory, which is often overlooked in favor of non-cooperative game theory in philosophical applications. One possible explanation for philosophers favoring non-cooperative over cooperative game theory is that cooperative game theory is often interpreted as a theory of (rational) *coalition formation*. The formation of coalitions is ultimately determined by the behavior of rational individual agents whose sole goal is preference satisfaction. But that behavior is described by non-cooperative game theory. In this view, ultimately and fundamentally, non-cooperative game theory is all the game theory we need. Although the coalitional formation interpretation may be *one* possible interpretation of cooperative game theory, in this chapter, we have used a claims-based interpretation for the analysis of fairness.

5. The Notion of Claims

In this section, we review a number of ongoing challenges in the philosophical and economic fair division literature that loosely centers on the interpretation and application of the notion of a *claim*.

Recall that a claim is a specific *type* of reason as to why a person should receive a good, to be contrasted with teleological reasons and side constraints. Claims are "duties owed to the person herself," as Broome puts it, but he does not seek to offer an account of the nature of claims. As such, Broome's theory of fairness is incomplete, but this is not something that should count against the theory. For, as Piller (2017:216) notes:

> This kind of incompleteness might not matter. Any theory will have to leave some questions open. What is left open here does not take us into unfamiliar territory, because we understand talk of claims pre-theoretically.

The Broomean fairness literature by and large[10] relies on an intuitive understanding of claims talk. Thus far, a detailed account of the sources of claims and how they work in moral deliberations has not been developed. However, there are quite a few issues surrounding the notion of a claim whose resolution does not require a full-fledged account of the nature of claims, some of which we review in this section.

5.1 Comparative and Noncomparative Fairness

For "Owing Money," it seems intuitively clear that we should realize allocation (4, 8, 12), as the proportional rule (cf. Table 19.2) has it. Now, although (4, 8, 12) is also fair according to Broome, it is not the only such allocation. For fairness is, in Broome's theory, a strictly comparative value: any allocation in which the claims of Ann, Bob, and Carla are satisfied in proportion to their strength is fair. For instance, (1, 2, 3) is just as fair as (4, 8, 12). All things considered, we should realize (4, 8, 12), but this allocation is not required by fairness itself. Or so Broome would argue. However, pace Broome it has been argued[11] that fairness also has a noncomparative requirement, which demands the satisfaction of claims as such and according to which fairness requires the realization of (4, 8, 12) for "Owing Money." Although quite a few authors have appealed to the noncomparative requirement of fairness, a proper account of this requirement, in particular its relation to the comparative requirement, is still lacking in the literature.

5.2 Claim Amounts, Strengths, and How To Be Fair

Some authors say that,[12] in "Owing Money," Bob has claim to an *amount* of 24 that is twice as *strong* as Ann's claim to 24. Others say that Bob has a claim to an *amount* of 20 that is equally strong as Ann's claim to an *amount* of 10. At any rate, each claim has, in addition to its *strength*, an *amount*. Now, the Broomean formula does not mention "amounts" and, more generally, neither does Broome's theory. In addition, as Curtis (2014) observes, Broome's theory does not tell us how to *be* fair, as it does not come with a concrete allocation rule either for allocating a divisible or for allocating an indivisible good. Curtis develops a theory that does tell us how to be fair, but his theory neglects claim *strength*.[13] The economic claims literature (cf. Section 4) provides us with many ways "to be fair" but, likewise, neglects the strength dimension of claims. How to divide fairly while taking claim strengths and amounts into consideration is, as of yet, an open question.

5.3 (Un)fairness Without Claims

The preceding two issues are refinements of the notion of a claim, intended to foster the development of a Broomean, claims-based notion of fairness. Tomlin (2012), however, is critical of an account of fairness that is (solely) based on claims. He does this by presenting cases in which there are no claims but where, nevertheless, a good is divided unfairly. As an example, he considers the case of a father who takes one of his two daughters for a ride in a sports car but not the other. The father acted unfairly, while neither of his daughters has a claim to be taken for a ride. According to Tomlin, this shows that there are cases of (un)fairness without claims, which cannot be accounted for by Broomean theories as these understand fairness to be function of *claims*. We think, however, that Tomlin's cases are best analyzed as cases without claims in which the allocating agent (e.g. the father) violates desiderata of subjective equity such as the no-envy principle mentioned in Section 3.

These issues – how to analyze situations, such as "Gloves," without obvious identifiable claims, comparative and noncomparative fairness, the relations between the amounts and strengths of claims, and (un)fairness without claims – strike us as some of the main ongoing challenges that the philosophical and economic fair division literature faces. To make progress on them will reap conceptual progress on fairness theorizing.

6. Concluding Remarks

Fairness is one of the most important concepts in Western philosophy and plays a crucial role in economic theory too. In this chapter, we have reviewed so-called "fair division" theories in philosophy and economics that aim at exploring fairness. We have suggested that their *substantive, local,* and *objective* character is conducive to identifying and investigating underlying principles of fairness: for instance, the key notions of proportionality and claims, as well as their axiomatic and game-theoretic foundations. More work is needed in order to reap the benefits of the obvious complementarities between the philosophical and economic approaches within this area of fairness research – let alone exploring how fair division–driven research on fairness can inform and challenge research related to fairness problems of a more complex, global scale. Doing so will also allow fairness theorists to make vital contributions to *broader* moral theorizing.

Although fairness is a central value concept in both philosophy and economics, it is not the only such concept, as we already saw in "Kidney." In this chapter, we concentrated on theories of fairness *itself.* However, a theory of fairness will, ultimately, need to be subsumed under a broader moral theory. The nature of this moral theory is, by and large, independent of the nature of the theory of fairness: the requirements of fairness might be *deontological,* for instance, but the requirements of one's ultimate moral theory need not be so too. Indeed, Broome (1991) himself embeds his theory of fairness in a broader, *consequentialist,* moral theory that respects the *sure thing principle.* For, to come full circle, Broome ultimately thinks that by writing the fairness of an action in its possible outcomes, Diamond's example is no threat to that principle. A discussion of the relations between fairness and Broome's, or any other broader, moral theory goes far beyond this review of philosophical and economic approaches to fairness as a distinct value concept.

Related Chapters

Ferguson, Chapter 10 "Exploitation and Consumption"
Stefánsson, Chapter 3 "The Economics and Philosophy of Risk"
Voorhoeve, Chapter 34 "Policy Evaluation Under Severe Uncertainty: A Cautious, Egalitarian Approach"
Vromen, Chapter 9 "*As If* Social Preference Models"

Notes

1 See Stefánsson, Chapter 3.
2 The key concept of "no envy" ' for the subjective equity literature is from Tinbergen (1930/2021) (see Wintein and Heilmann 2021) and was further developed by Foley (1967) and Varian (1975). Modern treatments can be found in both Brams and Taylor (1996) and Thomson (2011). Fleurbaey (2008) and Fleurbaey and Maniquet (2011) have developed theories of welfare by using concepts from the subjective equity fairness literature.
3 However, see Henning (2015) for an argument that neither fairness nor any other moral value requires equal chance lotteries in the case of equal claims.
4 For example, Lazenby 2014, Kirkpatrick and Eastwood (2015), and Piller (2017) all agree that fairness does not require holding a weighted lottery in "Unequal Kidney." However, by carefully distinguishing between outcome and lottery fairness, Piller (2017) forcefully argues, pace Hooker, that Broome's theory does not recommend a weighted lottery for "Unequal Kidney."
5 See Balinski and Young (2001) for an overview.
6 See Thomson (2003, 2015, 2019) for overviews.
7 For a comprehensive treatment of the axiomatic derivation of the division rules discussed here, consult Herrero and Villar (2001).
8 See Peleg and Sudhölter (2007) for an overview of cooperative game theory.

9 But see Wintein and Heilmann (2020) for an argument in favor of modeling "Owing Money" as a cooperative game that appeals to "aggregativity."
10 See Kirkpatrick and Eastwood (2015) and Sharadin (2016) for rebuttals of that view.
11 See, for example, Saunders (2010), Hooker (2005), Curtis (2014), or Vong (2018).
12 See, for example, Paseau and Saunders (2015) and Morrow (2017).
13 See Wintein and Heilmann (2018) for a detailed argument.

Bibliography

Adler, M. D. (2012). *Well-Being and Fair Distribution: Beyond Cost Benefit Analysis*. Oxford: Oxford University Press.
Aristotle. *The Nicomachean Ethics*. Eds. W. D. Ross and L. Brown. Oxford: Oxford University Press, 2009.
Aumann, R. J., & Maschler, M. (1985). Game theoretic analysis of a bankruptcy problem from the Talmud. *Journal of Economic Theory*, 36, 195–213.
Balinski, M. L., & Young, H. P. (2001). *Fair Representation: Meeting the Ideal of One Man, One Vote* (2nd ed.). Washington, DC: Brookings Institution.
Brams, S. J., & Taylor, A. D. (1996). *Fair Division: From Cake-Cutting to Dispute Resolution*. New York: Cambridge University Press.
Broome, J. (1984). Uncertainty and fairness. *The Economic Journal*, 94(375), 624–632.
Broome, J. (1990). Fairness. *Proceedings of the Aristotelian Society*, 91, 87–101.
Broome, J. (1991). *Weighing Goods: Equality, Uncertainty and Time*. Oxford: Wiley-Blackwell.
Carr, C. L. (2000). *On Fairness*. London: Routledge.
Curtis, B. L. (2014). To be fair. *Analysis* 74: 47–57.
Diamond, P. A. (1967). Cardinal welfare, individualistic ethics, and interpersonal comparison of utility: Comment. *The Journal of Political Economy*, 75(5), 765.
Elster, J. (1992). *Local Justice: How Institutions Allocate Scarce Goods and Necessary Burdens*. Cambridge: Cambridge University Press.
Fleurbaey, M. (2008). *Fairness, Responsibility, and Welfare*. Oxford: Oxford University Press.
Fleurbaey, M., & Maniquet, F. (2011). *A Theory of Fairness and Social Welfare*. Cambridge: Cambridge University Press.
Foley, D. K. (1967). Resource allocation and the public sector. *Yale Economic Essays,* 7, 45–98.
Heilmann, C., & Wintein, S. (2017). How to be fairer. *Synthese,* 194, 3475–3499.
Henning, T. (2015). From choice to chance? Saving people, fairness, and lotteries. *Philosophical Review,* 24, 169–206.
Herrero, C., & Villar, A. (2001). The three Musketeers: Four classical solutions to bankruptcy problems. *Mathematical Social Sciences*, 42, 307–328.
Hooker, B. (2005). Fairness. *Ethical Theory and Moral Practice,* 8, 329–352.
Kirkpatrick, J. R., & Eastwood, N. (2015). Broome's theory of fairness and the problem of quantifying the strengths of claims. *Utilitas,* 27, 82–91.
Lazenby, H. (2014). Broome on fairness and lotteries. *Utilitas,* 26, 331–345.
Miller, D. (2017). Justice. *The Stanford Encyclopedia of Philosophy* (Fall 2017 Edition), Edward N. Zalta (ed.), https://plato.stanford.edu/archives/fall2017/entries/justice/.
Morrow, D. (2017). Fairness in allocating the global emissions budget. *Environmental Values,* 26, 669–691.
Moulin, H. J. (2004). *Fair Division and Collective Welfare*. Cambridge and London: MIT Press.
O'Neill, B. (1982). A problem of rights arbitration from the Talmud. *Mathematical Social Sciences*, 2, 345–371.
Paseau, A. C., & Saunders, B. (2015). Fairness and aggregation. *Utilitas*, 27, 460–469.
Peleg, B., & Sudhölter, P. (2007). *Introduction to the Theory of Cooperative Games*. Boston: Kluwer Academic.
Piller, C. (2017). Treating Broome fairly. *Utilitas,* 29, 214–238.
Rawls, J. (1971). *A Theory of Justice*. Oxford: Oxford University Press.
Rescher, N. (2002). *Fairness Theory & Practice of Distributive Justice*. London: Taylor and Francis.
Roemer, J. E. (1996). *Theories of Distributive Justice*. Harvard: Harvard University Press.
Roth, A. E., Sönmez, T., & Ünver, M. U. (2004). Kidney exchange. *Quarterly Journal of Economics,* 119(2), 457–488.
Saunders, B. (2010). Fairness between competing claims. *Res Publica,* 16, 41–55.
Shapley, L. S. (1953). A value for n-person games. In H. W. Kuhn & A. W. Tucker (Eds.), *Contributions to the Theory* (pp. 307–317), Annals of mathematical studies v. 28. Princeton: Princeton University Press.
Sharadin, N. (2016). Fairness and the strengths of agents' claims. *Utilitas,* 28(3), 347–360.

Thomson, W. (2003). Axiomatic and game-theoretic analysis of bankruptcy and taxation problems: A survey. *Mathematical Social Sciences,* 45, 249–297.

Thomson, W. (2011). Fair allocation rules. In K. J. Arrow, A. K. Sen, & K. Suzumura (Eds.), *Handbook of Social Choice and Welfare* (pp. 393–506). Amsterdam: Elsevier.

Thomson, W. (2015). Axiomatic and game-theoretic analysis of bankruptcy and taxation problems: An update. *Mathematical Social Sciences,* 74, 41–59.

Thomson, W. (2019). *How to Divide When There Isn't Enough. From Aristotle, the Talmud, and Maimonides to the Axiomatics of Resource Allocation.* Cambridge: Cambridge University Press.

Tinbergen (1930/2021). Mathematical psychology. *Erasmus Journal for Philosophy and Economics*, 14(1), 210–221.

Tomlin, P. (2012). On fairness and claims. *Utilitas*, 24, 200–213.

Varian, H. R. (1975). Distributive justice, welfare economics and the theory of fairness. *Philosophy and Public Affairs,* 4, 223–247.

Vong, G. (2015). Fairness, benefiting by lottery and the chancy satisfaction of moral claims. *Utilitas,* 27, 470–486.

Vong, G. (2018). Measuring a neglected type of lottery unfairness. *Economics and Philosophy,* 34, 67–86.

Vong, G. (2020). Weighing up weighted lotteries: Scarcity, overlap cases, and fair inequalities of chance. *Ethics*, 130(3), 320–348.

Wintein, S., & Heilmann, C. (2018). Dividing the indivisible: Apportionment and philosophical theories of fairness. *Philosophy, Politics and Economics,* 17(1), 51–74.

Wintein, S., & Heilmann, C. (2020). Theories of fairness and aggregation. *Erkenntnis,* 85, 715–738.

Wintein, S., & Heilmann, C. (2021). No envy: Jan Tinbergen on fairness. *Erasmus Journal for Philosophy and Economics*, 4(1), 222–245.

Young, H. P. (1988). Distributive justice in taxation. *Journal of Economic Theory*, 43, 321–335.

Young, H. P. (1994). *Equity: In Theory and Practice.* Princeton: Princeton University Press.

PART V

Causality and Explanation

20
CAUSALITY AND PROBABILITY

Tobias Henschen

1. Introduction

When investigating causes, economists stand in one of roughly two traditions: the tradition of understanding efficient causes as raising the probability of their effects or the tradition of understanding them as causally dependent on instrumental variables (or "instruments").[1] While the first tradition goes back to Hume, the second tradition has its roots in some of the work of the early econometricians (Haavelmo and Simon). The second tradition is younger than the first, but unlike the first tradition, the second tradition is at least compatible with Aristotelian approaches to efficient causation: with approaches that involve firm ontological commitments to powers, tendencies, or capacities.[2]

The present chapter will be concerned with the first tradition almost exclusively (I will only touch upon the second tradition in Sections 6 and 7; for a more detailed discussion, see Clarke, Chapter 21). The chapter will briefly present and discuss the probability theories of causality of Suppes and Granger (Sections 2 and 3) and introduce Zellner's idea of using causal laws to determine the relevance of the variables and lags to be included in a model representing relations of Granger causality (Section 4). It will then present and discuss causal Bayes nets theory (Section 5) and emphasize that knowledge of causes that raise the probability of their effects can be employed for purposes of prediction, but less so for purposes of policy analysis (Section 6). It will finally mention a number of problems that are potentially inherent to attempts to infer causality in the sense of the second tradition from probabilities (Section 7).

2. Suppes on Genuine Causation

While Hume required constant conjunction of cause and effect, probability approaches to causality are content to understand causes as raising the probability of their effects. They say that $X = x$ causes $Y = y$ if the conditional probability of $Y = y$ given $X = x$ is greater than the unconditional probability of $Y = y$. Formally: $P(Y = y \mid X = x) > P(Y = y)$, where $X, Y, \ldots$ are random variables, that is, functions from a sample or state space into a range of values, where lowercase letters $x, y, \ldots$ denote the values that $X, Y, \ldots$ can take, and where P is a probability measure over the power set of that sample space, that is, a function from that power set into the set of real numbers such that the Kolmogorov axioms are satisfied.

The power set of the sample space may also be understood as the set of propositions saying that $X = x$, $Y = y$, ... Instead of propositions, probability approaches to causality usually speak of events:

DOI: 10.4324/9781315739793-25

the event A of X attaining the value x, the event B of Y attaining the value y, ... Suppes (1970: 12) interprets events as "instantaneous," that is, as occurring at a particular point in time, and he includes their time of occurrence in their formal characterization. So for him, $P(A_t)$ refers to the probability of the event A occurring at time t, where "A occurs at time t" means as much as "X attains value x at time t." Suppes (1970: 24) understands "cause" as "genuine cause" and defines "genuine cause" as a "prima facie cause that is not spurious." Thus, in order to understand his definition of "cause," one needs to understand his definitions of "prima facie cause" and "spurious cause."

His definition of prima facie cause is as follows (cf. Suppes 1970: 12):

(C_{PF}) B'_t is a prima facie cause of A_t iff (i) $t' < t$, (ii) $P(B'_t) > 0$, and (iii) $P(A_t \mid B'_t) > P(A_t)$.

Condition (iii) requires that causes increase the probability of their effect, and condition (ii) is needed because in the definition of conditional probability – $P(A_t \mid B'_t) = P(A_t \wedge B'_t)/P(B'_t)$ – $P(B'_t)$ is the denominator and because the denominator must not be equal to zero. Condition (i) implies that B'_t occurs earlier than A_t in time. Why does Suppes introduce that condition? One answer is that the relation "increases the probability of" is symmetric because $P(A_t \mid B'_t) > P(A_t)$ is equivalent to $P(B'_t \mid A_t) > P(B'_t)$, that the relation "causes" is asymmetric, and that temporality is capable of turning the relation "increases the probability of" into an asymmetric one. A second answer is that the Humean tradition, in which Suppes stands, holds that causality is intrinsically linked to temporality.

Suppes' definition of spurious cause is as follows (Suppes 1970: 21–22):

(C_S) B'_t is a spurious cause of A_t iff B'_t is a prima facie cause of A_t, and there is a $t'' < t'$ and an event C''_t such that (i) C''_t precedes B'_t, (ii) $P(B'_t \wedge C''_t) > 0$, and (iii) $P(A_t \mid B'_t \wedge C''_t) = P(A_t \mid C''_t)$.

In other words, B'_t is a spurious cause of A_t iff B'_t is a prima facie cause of A_t, C''_t precedes B'_t, and C''_t "screens off" A_t from B'_t. The notion of a spurious cause is needed to rule out cases in which prima facie causes do not represent genuine causes. A falling barometer, for instance, is a prima facie cause, but not a genuine cause, of an upcoming storm. Atmospheric pressure that precedes both the falling barometer and the upcoming storm screens off the upcoming storm from the falling barometer.

(C_S) is not the only definition of spurious causation that Suppes (1970: 21–28) brings into play, and in addition to prima facie cause and spurious cause, he defines "direct cause," "sufficient cause," and "negative cause." But a consideration of these definitions lies beyond the purposes of this chapter. More immediately relevant to these purposes is a consideration of the problems that Suppes' account of genuine causation faces and that require specific solutions. These problems are of essentially two kinds: they both suggest that condition (iii) of (C_{PF}) cannot be a necessary condition for B'_t causing A_t.

The first problem is that it seems that B'_t can turn out to be a cause of A_t even though $P(A_t \mid B'_t) < P(A_t)$. This problem can be illustrated by an example that Suppes (1970: 41) himself discusses. The example is that of a golfer with moderate skill who makes a shot that hits a limb of a tree close to the green and is thereby deflected directly into the hole for a spectacular birdie. If A_t is the event of making a birdie and B'_t the earlier event of hitting the limb, we will say that B'_t causes A_t. But we will also say that $P(A_t \mid B'_t) < P(A_t)$: the probability of his making a birdie is low, and the probability of his making a birdie given that the ball hits the branch is even lower.

Does the example show that condition (iii) of (C_{PF}) cannot qualify as a necessary condition for B'_t causing A_t? Suppes (1970: 42–43) argues for a negative answer. He argues that definition (C_{PF}) can be defended if condition (iii) is relativized to background information K'_t:

(C_{PF}') B_t' is a prima facie cause of A_t iff (i) $B_t' \wedge K_t'$ precedes A_t, (ii) $P(B_t' \wedge K_t') > 0$, and (iii) $P(A_t | B_t' \wedge K_t') > P(A_t | K_t')$.

Thus, if K_t' is, for example, the event of the shot being deflected at a specific angle, then the probability that the golfer will make a birdie, given that the ball hits the branch and is deflected at a specific angle, might well be higher than the probability of his making a birdie. Suppes (1970: 42) adds that such relativization to background knowledge "can be useful, especially in theoretical contexts."

The second problem is a fact about probabilities that is well-known to statisticians and is often referred to as "Simpson's paradox." The fact is that any association between two variables that holds in a given population – $P(Y = y | X = x) > P(Y = y)$, $P(Y = y | X = x) < P(Y = y)$ or $P(Y = y | X = x) = P(X = x)$ – can be reversed in a subpopulation by finding a third variable that is correlated with both. Consider, for instance, the population of all Germans. For the population of all Germans, the conditional probability of developing heart disease, given that an individual smokes, is *higher* than the unconditional probability of developing heart disease. But for a subpopulation of Germans in which all smokers exercise, the conditional probability of developing heart disease, given that an individual smokes, is *lower* than the unconditional probability of developing heart disease – at least if exercise is more effective in preventing heart disease than smoking is in causing it.

The fact itself is not a paradox. But Cartwright (1979: 421) points out that the paradox arises if we define causation of $Y = y$ by $X = x$ in terms of $P(Y = y | X = x) > P(Y = y)$. If we define causation of $Y = y$ by $X = x$ in terms of $P(Y = y | X = x) > P(Y = y)$, then causation of $Y = y$ by $X = x$ will depend on the population that we select when establishing $P(Y = y | X = x) > P(Y = y)$. At the same time, we have the strong intuition that causation should be independent of specific populations. Cartwright (1979: 423) proposes to dissolve the paradox by conditioning $Y = y$ on the set of "all alternative causal factors" of $Y = y$. By conditioning $Y = y$ on such a set, Cartwright renders Suppes' definition of genuine causation circular: causal vocabulary would show up in both the *definiendum* and the *definiens*. But some philosophers (e.g. Woodward 2003: 104–105; Hoover 2001: 42) hold that noncircularity is not absolutely necessary.

3. Granger Causality

Perhaps the most influential explicit approach to causality in economics is that of Granger (1969, 1980). Like Suppes, Granger stands in the Humean tradition of understanding causes as raising the probability of their effect; and, like Suppes, he believes that causality is intrinsically linked to temporality. But unlike Suppes, Granger (1980: 330, notation modified) defines causation as a relation between variables:

(*GC*) X_t Granger-causes Y_{t+1} if and only if $P(Y_{t+1} = y_{t+1} | \Omega_t = \omega_t) \neq P(Y_{t+1} = y_{t+1} | \Omega_t = \omega_t - X_t = x_t)$,

where Ω_t is the infinite universe of variables dated t and earlier. The temporal ordering of X_t and Y_{t+1} guarantees that the relation between X_t and Y_{t+1} is asymmetric, and by conditioning on $\Omega_t = \omega_t$, (*GC*) is immunized against circularity, spuriousness, and the problem that causes might lower the probability of their effects.

Spohn (2012: 442) points out that it is "literally meaningless and an abuse of language" to speak of variables themselves as causing other variables. "X_t causes Y_{t+1}" may mean either "$X_t = x_t$ causes $Y_{t+1} = y_{t+1}$" or "Y_{t+1} causally depends on X_t," where the causal dependence of Y_{t+1} on X_t is understood as a relation that obtains between X_t and Y_{t+1} if some event $X_t = x_t$ causes some event $Y_{t+1} = y_{t+1}$.[3] The context of time series econometrics suggests that (*GC*) is to be read in the first sense (cf. Spohn 1983: 85–86). The phrase "X_t Granger-causes Y_{t+1}" will be retained in the remainder of this chapter because economists and econometricians have become accustomed to its use. It should be kept in mind, however, that the phrase is to be understood as synonymous with "$X_t = x_t$ causes $Y_{t+1} = y_{t+1}$."

Granger (1980: 336) himself points out that (*GC*) is not "operational" because practical implementations cannot cope with an infinite number of variables with an infinite number of lags. But econometricians think that, in order to test for "Granger causality," they need to select only the relevant variables and only the relevant number of lags. Sims (1972), for instance, uses two variables (for money and GNP) and four future and eight past lags to show that money Granger-causes GNP and not the other way around. Later, as part of a general critique of the practice of using a priori theory to identify instrumental variables, Sims (1980a) advocates vector autoregression (VAR), which generalizes Granger causality to the multivariate case. The following two-equation model, for instance, is a VAR model for two variables and one lag:

(1) $y_{t+1} = \alpha_{11}y_t + \alpha_{12}x_t + \varepsilon_{1t+1}$
(2) $x_{t+1} = \alpha_{21}y_t + \alpha_{22}x_t + \varepsilon_{2t+1}$

where the α_{ij} are parameters and the ε_{it+1} are random error terms. X_t is said to Granger-cause Y_{t+1} if $\alpha_{12} \neq 0$, and Y_t is said to Granger-cause X_{t+1} if $\alpha_{21} \neq 0$.

While definition (*GC*) avoids some of the problems that competing definitions face (circularity, spuriousness, the problem of causes that lower the probability of their effects), objections have been raised to the implementation of (*GC*), that is, to empirical procedures of testing for Granger causality. Hoover (1993: 700–705) lists three problems that stand in the way of a temporal ordering of cause and effect in macroeconomics. The first problem is that, in macroeconomics, it is difficult to rule out contemporaneous causality because data most often are reported annually or quarterly. Hoover (1993: 702) cites Granger as suggesting that contemporaneous causality could be ruled out if data were sampled at fine enough intervals. But Hoover (1993: 702) responds that, "such finer and finer intervals would exacerbate certain conceptual difficulties in the foundations of economics," and he cites gross national product (GNP) as an example: "There are hours during the day when there is no production; does GNP fall to nought in those hours and grow astronomically when production resumes? Such wild fluctuations in GNP are economically meaningless."

The second problem is that there are hidden variables that (like expectations) cannot be included among the regressors in VAR models, even though they are likely to be causally relevant. And the third problem is that economic theory (no matter which) provides reasonably persuasive accounts of steady states, that is, of hypothetical economic configurations that feature constant rates, quantities, and growth rates and that are timeless in the sense that they result if time is allowed to run on to infinity. Hoover (1993: 705) admits that proponents of Granger causality might respond that, "if macroeconomics cannot be beat into that mold [of temporal ordering], so much the worse for macroeconomics." But Hoover (1993: 706) also argues that, in macroeconomics, causal questions like, "Will interest rates rise if the Fed sells $50 million worth of treasury bonds?" are sensible and well formulated and that our concepts of causality need to be suitable for their formulation and interpretation.

Another prominent objection that has been raised to Granger-causality tests says that it is impossible to select the relevant number of variables and lags without (explicit or implicit) reliance on economic theory or background knowledge. Sims' subsequent work on the relation of Granger causality between money and GNP indicates why this objection is important. When he included four variables (money, GNP, domestic prices, and nominal interest rates) and 12 past lags in a VAR model, the previously mentioned result of money Granger-causing GNP no longer obtained.[4] A relation of Granger causality thus crucially depends on the number of variables and lags that are deemed to be relevant. And who is to determine the relevance of variables and lags and how?

4. Zellner on Causal Laws

Zellner (1979, 1988) can be read as responding to the preceding question when he defines causality in terms of "predictability according to a law or set of laws."[5] He claims that laws may be deterministic or stochastic, qualitative or quantitative, micro or macro, resulting from controlled or uncontrolled experiments, involving simultaneous or nonsimultaneous relations, and so on. He also claims that the only restrictions that need to be placed on laws relate to logical and mathematical consistency and to the ability to explain past data and experience and predict future data and experience. While these restrictions are not "severe," they imply that (auto)regressions cannot qualify as laws because they "do not provide understanding and explanation and often involve confusing association or correlation with causality" (Zellner 1988: 9).

Sketching a rudimentary theory of the psychology of scientific discovery, Zellner (1988: 9–12) suggests that the discovery of laws proceeds in roughly three steps. In a first step, the mind produces ideas using observed past data, known theories, and future knowable data as inputs. In a second step, the mind selects a specific idea or "phenomenon" and develops a theory (or model) that is capable of explaining the phenomenon and yielding predictions. The third step is that of demonstrating that the theory really explains what it purports to explain. That demonstration requires the use of new data to test the theory and its implications, such as predictions. Whenever a demonstration succeeds, the degree of reasonable belief in the theory increases. This degree of reasonable belief corresponds to the posterior probability that can be assigned to the theory and computed using Bayes' theorem: $P(H|E) = P(E|H) \times P(H)/P(E)$, where H is a proposition summarizing the theory and E is an "evidential proposition" referring to new data that can be used to test H.[6] Zellner (1988: 16) says that "a theory can be termed a causal law" if the posterior probability that can be assigned to it is "very high, reflecting much outstanding and broad-ranging performance in explanation and prediction."

Zellner can be read as responding to the question of how to determine the relevance of variables and lags because causal laws may include well-confirmed theories about the strength of the parameters that can be included in a VAR model. If that strength happens to be among the phenomena that the conscious mind decides to investigate, the mind aims to develop an appropriate model or theory H that is capable of quantifying and explaining that strength. Once H is developed, it can be subjected to a Bayesian updating procedure in which a prior probability is assigned to H, the likelihood of E given H is evaluated, and data E are collected to compute the posterior probability of H in accordance with Bayes' theorem. The posterior probability of H then serves as its prior probability when new data E are collected to test H (or any of its implications) again. Once the posterior probability of H is "very high," H can be viewed as a causal law that supports decisions about the relevance of the variables and lags to be included in a VAR model: the greater the strength of a parameter, the more relevant its corresponding (lagged) variable.

5. Causal Bayes Nets Theory

One final probability approach to causality is causal Bayes nets theory. Causal Bayes nets theory was first developed outside economics [substantially foreshadowed in Spohn (1980) and then developed in detail by Spirtes, Glymour, and Scheines (1993) and Pearl (2000)] but was applied in economics and econometrics soon after (Bessler and Lee 2002; Demiralp and Hoover 2003). Unlike the approaches of Suppes and Granger, causal Bayes nets theory is primarily interested in relations of causal dependence and analyzes causal relations irrespective of any temporal ordering. It consequently focuses on relations of *direct* causal dependence more explicitly.

At the center of causal Bayes nets theory[7] is the notion of a directed, acyclic graph (DAG). A DAG is a tuple $\langle \rightarrow, V \rangle$, where $\mathbf{V}$ is a non-empty finite set of preselected variables and $\rightarrow$ is an acyclic relation on $\mathbf{V}$: there are no variables $X, \ldots, Y \in \mathbf{V}$ such that $X \rightarrow \ldots \rightarrow Y$ and $Y \rightarrow X$.

A DAG is a *causal* graph if the arrow (→) can be interpreted as representing a relation of direct causal dependence between the variables in **V**. In order to understand the notion of direct causal dependence that is involved here, one needs to become acquainted with a bit of graph-theoretical notation and the three axioms that determine the relation between causality and probability according to causal Bayes nets theory.

Consider the graph-theoretical notation first. In a DAG, $X \in \mathbf{V}$ is said to be

- a *parent* of $Y \in \mathbf{V}$ if and only if $X \rightarrow Y$ (the set of parents of Y is denoted by $\mathbf{pa}(Y)$).
- a *child* of $Y \in \mathbf{V}$ if and only if Y is a parent of X.
- an *ancestor* of $Y \in \mathbf{V}$ if and only if there are $X, \ldots, Y \in \mathbf{V}$ such that $X \rightarrow \ldots \rightarrow Y$ (the set of ancestors of Y is denoted by $\mathbf{an}(Y)$).
- a *descendant* of $Y \in \mathbf{V}$ if and only if Y is an ancestor of X.
- a *nondescendant* of $Y \in \mathbf{V}$ if and only $X \neq Y$ and X is not a descendant of Y (the set of nondescendants of Y is denoted by $\mathbf{nd}(Y)$).

Now turn to the three axioms (cf. Spirtes, Glymour, and Scheines 1993: 29–32). Let á→, **V**ñ be a causal graph and P a probability measure over the power set of the sample space, and let $\perp_p$ stand for probabilistic independence. Then P satisfies the so-called

- Causal Markov condition if and only if for all $X \in \mathbf{V}$ $X \perp_p \mathbf{nd}(X) - \mathbf{pa}(X)/\mathbf{pa}(X)$.
- Causal minimality condition if and only if for all $X \in \mathbf{V}$ $\mathbf{pa}(X)$ is the smallest subset of variable set $\mathbf{Y}$ such that $X \perp_p \mathbf{nd}(X) - \mathbf{Y}/\mathbf{Y}$.
- Causal faithfulness condition if and only if for all subsets $\mathbf{X}$, $\mathbf{Y}$, $\mathbf{Z}$ of $\mathbf{V}$ $\mathbf{X} \perp_p \mathbf{Y}/\mathbf{Z}$ holds only if $\mathbf{X} \perp_p \mathbf{Y}/\mathbf{Z}$ is entailed by P's satisfaction of the causal Markov and minimality conditions.

Informally, the causal Markov condition says that the parents of X screen off X from all other nondescendants of X. The causal minimality condition says that P would no longer satisfy the causal Markov condition if any of the parents of X were excluded from $\mathbf{pa}(X)$; it requires that there be exactly one minimal set of parents of X that screens off X from all its other nondescendants. Finally, the faithfulness condition says that there are no accidental conditional independencies: that all of the conditional independencies that the causal Markov and minimality conditions make reference to reflect relations of causal dependence.

If P satisfies the causal Markov, minimality, and faithfulness conditions and $\langle\rightarrow, \mathbf{V}\rangle$ is a causal graph, then P combines with $\langle\rightarrow, \mathbf{V}\rangle$ to form a causal Bayes net. As an example of a causal Bayes net, consider the graph in Figure 20.1 and imagine that you are worried about the competitiveness (X_4) of your firm and that you ponder it in terms of productivity (X_1), cost reduction (X_2), value creation (X_3), and the probabilistic independencies that you think obtain between these variables.

Then the causal Markov condition entails that $X_2 \perp_p X_3/X_1$ (X_2 and X_3 are probabilistically independent, given their common cause X_1) and that $X_4 \perp_p X_1/\{X_2, X_3\}$ (X_2 and X_3 screen off X_4 from X_1). The minimality condition entails that it is not the case that $X_2 \perp_p X_3$ (otherwise $\{X_1\}$ would not be the minimal set given that X_2 is independent of its nondescendant X_3 and vice versa) and it is not the case that $X_4 \perp_p X_2/X_3$ or $X_4 \perp_p X_3/X_2$ (X_2 and X_3 must make a difference, given the other). Finally, the faithfulness condition requires that probabilistic dependencies do not disappear when there are causal chains: that it is not the case that $X_4 \perp_p X_1/X_2$, $X_4 \perp_p X_1/X_3$, or $X_4 \perp_p X_1$.

Spirtes, Glymour, and Scheines make it clear that they do not expect the three axioms to hold universally. They point out that the causal Markov condition might be violated in quantum physics and that the causal faithfulness condition is violated on occasion (in the foregoing example it would be violated if $X_4 \perp_p X_1$ because the direct influences of X_2 and X_3 cancel each other out). But they also say of the three axioms that, "their importance – if not their truth – is evidenced by the fact that

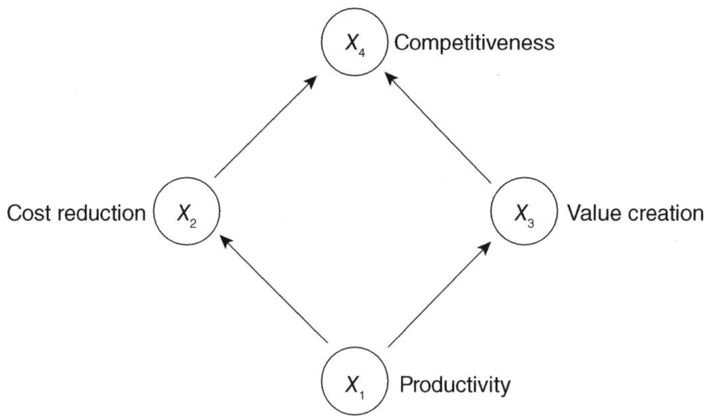

Figure 20.1 An example of a causal Bayes net

nearly every statistical model with a causal significance we have come upon in the social scientific literature satisfies all three" (Spirtes, Glymour, and Scheines 1993: 53). What they could have stated more clearly is that, in order to satisfy the three axioms, a statistical model or set of variables needs to be causally sufficient: it needs to include each proximate common cause of any two variables in **V**; otherwise the probabilistic independencies will inadequately reflect relations of direct causal dependence.

Spohn (2012: 501) points out that causal sufficiency might be difficult to achieve. The common causes of any two variables in **V** might go back as far as the big bang or simply slip off our radar, especially when they are hidden, that is, nonmeasurable and causally relevant. Hoover (2001: 168) analyzes the repercussions of this difficulty for the case of economics. He argues that the faithfulness condition might be violated whenever expectations operate because expectations are hidden and take positions in causal relations that might fail to be reflected by conditional independencies. Hoover (2001: 167) argues, moreover, that macroeconomics poses "systematic threats to the Causal Markov Condition" because the "search for an unmeasured conditioning variable may end in the crossing of the micro/macro border before an appropriate conditioning variable could be located."

Spirtes, Glymour, and Scheines refrain from defining causation explicitly and prefer to understand conditional independencies as reflecting relations of direct causal dependence. Spohn (2012: 508–509), in contrast, proposes to define direct causal dependence in terms of the conditional independencies. He proposes, more specifically, to say that Y causally depends on X directly if and only if not $Y \perp_p X/\mathbf{nd}(Y) - X$, that is, if and only if it is not the case that Y is probabilistically independent of X given all the nondescendants of Y except X. He emphasizes that this definition is problematic because it relativizes the notion of direct causal dependence to a set **V** of preselected variables: change that set and the conditional independencies will change too, and with them relations of direct causation. But he also suggests that the problem can be solved by derelativizing the notion of direct causal dependence, that is, by defining it for a "universal frame" or universal set of variables.

6. Policy or Prediction?

Sections 3 and 4 called attention to the problem that economists cannot establish the claim that X_t Granger-causes Y_{t+1} unless they manage to include in a VAR model only the relevant number of variables and lags. Assume that, despite this problem, they manage to establish the claim that X_t Granger-causes Y_{t+1}. Can they now predict the value that Y_{t+1} is going to attain if they know the value of X_t? Can they predict, for instance, the value that GNP will attain in $t + 1$ if they know the value that money takes in t? Most economists believe that the answer is positive. Granger (1969: 428) suggests that prediction is in fact the principal purpose of searching for relations of Granger causality. And in statistics, there are standard procedures for computing the expected value of Y_{t+1} when the values of the other variables and lags in the model are given. Economists might not be able to predict the exact value of Y_{t+1} (e.g. GNP), but they can state the probability with which Y_{t+1} can be expected to attain a specific value.

An entirely different question is whether economists can predict the value that Y_{t+1} *would* attain *if* they were to *control* X_t to a specific value. Again assume that they know that X_t (standing, for example, for money) Granger-causes Y_{t+1} (standing, for example, for GNP): does that imply that they know the value that Y_{t+1} would attain if they managed to set X_t to a specific value? Most economists agree that the answer is negative. In order to see that the answer is negative, consider again equations (1) and (2) in Section 3. In order to be able to predict the value that Y is going to attain in $t + 1$, one needs to condition equation (1) on the observations of X and Y in t and take the expectation of Y_{t+1}:

$$(3)\quad E(Y_{t+1} \mid y_t, x_t) = \alpha_{11}y_t + \alpha_{12}x_t + E(E_{1t+1} \mid y_t, x_t)$$

But in order to be able to predict the value that Y_{t+1} would attain if X_t were controlled to x_t, one would need to condition equation (1) on the observations of X and Y in t and take the expectation of a *counterfactual* quantity. The expectation of that quantity is calculated in the same way as in equation (3). But in order to understand that quantity as counterfactual, one would need to understand the relation between X_t and Y_{t+1} as causal in the sense of the second tradition mentioned in the Introduction: one would need to assume that there is an instrumental variable I_t (standing, for example, for the federal funds rate) that causes X_t, that causes Y_{t+1} only via X_t, and that is not caused by E_{1t+1}. One would need to interpret equation (1) as a structural equation (and not as a regression equation) and E_{1t+1} as encompassing omitted variables that cause Y_{t+1} (and not as a regression error).[8]

Thus, knowledge that X_t Granger-causes Y_{t+1} is not sufficient for (does not imply) knowledge of the value that Y_{t+1} would take if X_t were controlled to x_t. Might one perhaps say that knowledge that X_t Granger-causes Y_{t+1} is *necessary* for knowledge of the value that Y_{t+1} would take if X_t were controlled to x_t? Unfortunately, the answer is still negative. In order to see that the answer is negative, consider the following model of structural equations:

$$(4)\quad y_{t+1} = \theta x_{t+1} + \beta_{11}y_t + \beta_{12}x_t + v_{1t+1}$$
$$(5)\quad x_{t+1} = \gamma y_{t+1} + \beta_{21}y_t + \beta_{22}x_t + v_{2t+1}$$

where θ, γ, and β_{ij} represent parameters and the N_{it+1} structural errors, that is, errors encompassing omitted variables that are causally relevant. To solve the current values out of these equations yields the reduced form equations, which coincide with equations (1) and (2) such that $\alpha_{11} = (\beta_{11} + \theta\beta_{21})/(1 - \theta\gamma)$, $\alpha_{12} = (\beta_{12} + \theta\beta_{22})/(1 - \theta\gamma)$, $\alpha_{21} = (\gamma\beta_{11} + \beta_{21})/(1 - \theta\gamma)$, $\alpha_{22} = (\gamma\beta_{12} + \beta_{22})/(1 - \theta\gamma)$, $\varepsilon_{1t} = (v_{1t} + \theta v_{2t})/(1 - \theta\gamma)$, and $\varepsilon_{2t} = (\gamma v_{1t} + \theta v_{2t})(1 - \theta\gamma)$. In order for Granger causality (or knowledge thereof) to qualify as a necessary condition of causality in the sense of the second tradition (or knowledge thereof), α_{12} in equation (1) would need to be unequal to zero. But Jacobs, Leamer, and Ward (1979: 402–405) show (for a similar model) that there are cases in which α_{12} is equal to zero: cases in which, for example, $\beta_{12} = -\theta\beta_{22}$. And Hoover (2001: 152–153) points out that these cases are not among the exotic ones that economists can neglect with a clear conscience.

While the question relating to the value that Y_{t+1} is going to attain if the value of X_t is reported to be x_t arises in contexts of forecasting, the question relating to the value that Y_{t+1} would attain if X_t were set to x_t by intervention arises in contexts of policy analysis. It goes without saying that if we complement our knowledge of causality in the sense of the second tradition with knowledge of Granger causality, it is likely to be helpful in both contexts. And perhaps knowledge of causality in the sense of the second tradition yields better predictions than knowledge of Granger causality (cf. Pearl 2000: 31). But the decisive point of the foregoing analysis is that policy analysis requires knowledge of causality in the sense of the second tradition.

Many economists believe that policy analysis is the ultimate justification for the study of economics (cf. e.g. Hoover 2001: 1), and that belief might explain why some of them hold that only the second tradition deals with causality in the strict sense of the term. Sargent (1977: 216), for instance, states that, "Granger's definition of a causal relation does *not*, in general, coincide with the economists' usual definition of one: namely, a relation that is invariant to interventions in the form of imposed changes in the processes governing the causal variables." In econometric textbook expositions of the concept of causality, one is likewise likely to find the observation that, "Granger causality is not causality as it is usually understood" (Maddala and Lahiri 2009: 390). (For a discussion of an alternative methodology for underwriting policy claims, see Khosrowi, Chapter 27.)

7. Common Effects and Common Causes

The result of the preceding section has been that (knowledge of) Granger causality is neither a necessary nor a sufficient condition of (knowledge of) causality in the sense of the second tradition. Does that result generalize to the claim that (knowledge of) causality in the sense of the second tradition can *never* be inferred from (knowledge of) probabilities? Hoover (2009: 501) defends a negative answer when suggesting that, "some causal claims may be supported by facts about probability models that do not depend on assumptions about the truth of these very same causal claims." The causal claims that he discusses include the claim that Z causally depends on both X and Y and the claim that X and Y causally depend on Z. The primary purpose of the present and final section is to point to the problems that are potentially inherent in attempts to infer these claims from probability models.

It is, of course, impossible to observe the relations of causal dependence that might (or might not) obtain between X, Y, and Z directly. But one might be able to observe realizations of X, Y, and Z. And Hoover thinks that it is possible to specify an adequate probability model for these realizations independently of any assumptions about the causal relations that might (or might not) obtain between X, Y, and Z. In some of his work, Hoover (2001: 214–217) advocates for the application of London School of Economics (LSE) methodology to specify adequate probability models. LSE methodology operates by (i) specifying a deliberately overfitting general model, (ii) subjecting the general model to a battery of diagnostic (or misspecification) tests (i.e. tests for normality of residuals, absence of autocorrelation, absence of heteroscedasticity, and stability of coefficients), (iii) testing for various restrictions (in particular, for the restriction that a set of coefficients is equal to the zero vector) in order to simplify the general model, and (iv) subjecting the simplified model to a battery of diagnostic tests. If the simplified model passes these tests, LSE methodology continues by repeating steps i–iv, that is, by using the simplified model as a general model, by subjecting that model to a battery of diagnostic tests, etc. Simplification is complete if any further simplification either fails any of the diagnostic tests or turns out to be statistically invalid as a restriction of the more general model.

Let us assume that the application of LSE methodology has resulted in the following normal model of X, Y, and Z (cf. Hoover 2009: 502, notation modified):

$$(X, Y, Z) \sim N(\mu_X, \mu_Y, \mu_Z, \sigma^2_X, \sigma^2_Y, \sigma^2_Z, \rho_{XY}, \rho_{XZ}, \rho_{YZ})$$

where μ_X, μ_Y, and μ_Z are the three means, σ^2_X, σ^2_Y, and σ^2_Z are the three variances, and ρ_{XY}, ρ_{XZ}, and ρ_{YZ} are the three covariances or population correlations of the model. Hoover argues that the model supports the claim that Z causally depends on both X and Y if it satisfies the antecedent of the common effect principle and that it supports the claim that X and Y causally depend on Z if it satisfies the antecedent of the common cause principle. The two principles can be restated as follows (cf. Hoover 2009):

> **Principle of the common effect**: If X and Y are probabilistically independent conditional on some set of variables (possibly the null set) excluding Z, but they are probabilistically dependent conditional on Z, then Z causally depends on both X and Y (then Z forms an unshielded collider on the path XZY).
>
> **Principle of the common cause**: If X and Y are probabilistically dependent conditional on some set of variables (possibly the null set) excluding Z, but they are probabilistically independent conditional on Z, then X and Y causally depend on Z.

Hoover argues, more specifically, that the normal model of X, Y, and Z supports the claim that Z causally depends on both X and Y if $\rho_{XY} = 0$ and $\rho_{XY|Z} \neq 0$ and that it supports the claim that X and Y causally depend on Z if $\rho_{XY} \neq 0$ and $\rho_{XY|Z} = 0$.

There are three problems that are potentially inherent in attempts to infer these claims from probability models. The first problem is that, in practice, LSE methodology might be incapable of implementation without data mining, which Mayo (1996: 316–317) characterizes as data used for double duty, that is, as the use of data to arrive at a claim (e.g. at the claim that Z causally depends on both X and Y or that X and Y causally depend on Z) in such a way that the claim is constrained to satisfy some criterion (e.g. the absence of misspecification) and that the same data are regarded as supplying evidence in support of the same claim. Spanos (2000), however, argues that there are problematic and nonproblematic cases of data mining.

The second problem is that Hoover's claim that an adequate probability model can be specified independently of any causal assumptions might not be accurate. If there are hidden variables (i.e. variables that cannot be measured and are known to be causally relevant), then these variables cannot be included in a deliberately overfitting general model and the model resulting from the application of LSE methodology cannot be said to be adequate.[9] But even if the probability model can be said to be adequate, there will be the third problem that neither principle obtains in cases in which $\rho_{XY} \neq 0$ denotes a nonsense correlation like that between higher than average sea levels and higher than average bread prices (Sober 2001: 332) or that between cumulative rainfall in Scotland and inflation (Hendry 1980: 17–20). It would be absurd to ask for the variable that causally depends on X and Y or the variable on which X and Y causally depend if X and Y were correlated in a way that does not make any sense.

Hoover (2003, 2009) responds to this problem by distinguishing stationary and nonstationary time series that provide values for X and Y and by arguing that nonstationary time series are not subject to the common cause principle unless they are co-integrated. Time series are nonstationary if they grow over time and do not have a fixed (or "stationary") mean. They are co-integrated if each of them is $I(1)$, that is, integrated of order 1, and if there is a linear combination of them that is $I(0)$, that is, integrated of order 0, where time series or linear combinations of them are $I(d)$, that is, integrated of order d if they must be differentiated d times to be made stationary.

Hoover's response is convincing to the extent that it explains why neither the common effect principle nor the common cause principle obtains in cases in which $r_{XY} \neq 0$ denotes a nonsense correlation: nonsense correlations are correlations between nonstationary time series that are not co-integrated.[10] It is worth mentioning, however, that it is not always easy to test for co-integration. Johansen (1988) has developed an empirical procedure that can be applied to test for co-integration, but Cheung and Lai (1993) point to several finite-sample shortcomings of that procedure, and Pagan (1995) points to difficulties in interpreting co-integration relationships that stem from the fact that Johansen's procedure involves estimations of reduced form equations.

Related Chapters

Clarke, C., Chapter 21 "Causal Contributions in Economics"
Khosrowi, D., Chapter 27 "Evidence-Based Policy"

Notes

1 An instrumental (or intervention) variable is a variable on which not only the putative cause causally depends but also the putative effect (via the putative cause) and which does not causally depend on the putative effect or any other variable on which the putative effect causally depends (cf. e.g. Woodward 2003: 98).
2 Hoover (2001: 100), for instance, stands in the second tradition and characterizes his account of causality as "not inconsistent" with that of Cartwright (1999: 50), who is sympathetic to probability theories of causality but holds that (high) conditional probabilities only manifest capacities or "nomological machines."
3 Instead of relations of "causal dependence," theorists sometimes speak of relations of "type-level causation." Both ways of speaking refer to relations between variables (e.g. to the relation between income and consumption in general) and not to relations between events (i.e. not to relations like that between the event of US income attaining a specific value in Q4 2019 and the event of US consumption attaining a specific value in Q4 2019).
4 The new result stated that money accounted for only 4% of the variance in GNP (cf. Sims 1980b).
5 Zellner (1979: 12, 1988: 7) points out that he adopts that definition from Herbert Feigl.
6 Compare Norton (2011) for a concise and thorough discussion of the problems pertaining to the Bayesian updating procedure.
7 Much of the notation that the present section uses to describe causal Bayes nets theory is borrowed from Spohn (2012: section 14.8).
8 One would need to interpret E_{1t+1}, more specifically, as encompassing omitted variables that adopt certain values and cause Y_{t+1} in $t + 1$ or earlier.
9 Compare Henschen (2018: section 5) for an elaboration of this second problem.
10 Compare Reiss (2015: chap. 8) for a more critical discussion of Hoover's response.

Bibliography

Bessler, D.A. and Lee, S. (2002) "Money and Prices: U.S. Data 1869–1914 (a Study with Directed Graphs)," *Empirical Economics* 27(3): 427–446.
Cartwright, N. (1979) "Causal Laws and Effective Strategies," *Nous* 13(4): 419–437.
Cartwright, N. (1999) *The Dappled World*, Cambridge: Cambridge University Press.
Cheung, Y.-W. and Lai, K.S. (1993) "Finite-Sample Sizes of Johansen's Likelihood Ratio Tests for Cointegration," *Oxford Bulletin of Economics and Statistics* 55: 313–328.
Demiralp, S. and Hoover, K.D. (2003) "Searching for the Causal Structure of a Vector Autoregression," *Oxford Bulletin of Economics and Statistics* 65: 745–767.
Granger, C.W.J. (1969) "Investigating Causal Relations by Econometric Models and Cross-Spectrum Methods," *Econometrica* 37(3): 424–438.
Granger, C.W.J. (1980) "Testing for Causality: A Personal Viewpoint," *Journal of Economic Dynamics and Control* 2(4): 329–352.
Hendry, D. (1980) "Econometrics – Alchemy or Science?" *Economica* 47(188): 387–406.
Henschen, T. (2018) "The In-Principle Inconclusiveness of Causal Evidence in Macroeconomics," *European Journal for Philosophy of Science* 8: 709–733.
Hoover, K.D. (1993) "Causality and Temporal Order in Macroeconomics or Why Even Economists Don't Know How to Get Causes from Probabilities," *The British Journal for Philosophy of Science* 44(4): 693–710.
Hoover, K.D. (2001) *Causality in Macroeconomics*, Cambridge: Cambridge University Press.
Hoover, K.D. (2003) "Nonstationary Time Series, Cointegration, and the Principle of Common Cause," *The British Journal for Philosophy of Science* 54: 527–551.
Hoover, K.D. (2009) "Probability and Structure in Econometric Models," in C. Glymour et al. (eds.) *Logic, Methodology, and Philosophy of Science*, London: College Publications: 497–513.
Jacobs, R.L., Leamer, E.E., and Ward, M.P. (1979) "Difficulties with Testing for Causation," *Economic Inquiry* 17: 401–413.
Johansen, S. (1988) "Statistical Analysis of Cointegration Vectors," *Journal of Economic Dynamics and Control* 12: 231–254.

Maddala, G.S. and Lahiri, K. (⁴2009) *Introduction to Econometrics*, Chichester: Wiley & Sons.
Mayo, D.G. (1996) *Error and the Growth of Experimental Knowledge*, Chicago: University of Chicago Press.
Norton, J.D. (2011) "Challenges to Bayesian Confirmation Theory," in P.S. Bandyopadhyay and M.R. Forster (eds.) *Handbook of the Philosophy of Science, Vol. 7: Philosophy of Statistics*, Amsterdam: Elsevier.
Pagan, A. (1995) "Three Methodologies: An Update," in L. Oxley et al. (eds.) *Surveys in Econometrics*, Oxford: Basil Blackwell: 30–41.
Pearl, J. (2000) *Causality: Models, Reasoning, and Inference* Cambridge, MA: Cambridge University Press.
Reiss, J. (2015) *Causation, Evidence, and Inference*, London: Routledge.
Sargent, T.J. (1977) "Response to Gordon and Ando," in C.A. Sims (ed.) *New Methods in Business Cycle Research*, Minneapolis: Federal Reserve Bank of Minneapolis.
Sims, C.A. (1972) "Money, Income and Causality," *American Economic Review* 62(4): 540–552.
Sims, C.A. (1980a) "Macroeconomics and Reality," *Econometrica* 48: 1–48.
Sims, C.A. (1980b) "Comparison of Interwar and Postwar Business Cycles: Monetarism Reconsidered," *The American Economic Review* 70(2): 250–257.
Sober, E. (2001) "Venetian Sea Levels, British Bread Prices, and the Principle of the Common Cause," *The British Journal for the Philosophy of Science* 52: 331–346.
Spanos, A. (2000) "Revisiting Data Mining: 'Hunting' with or without a License," *Journal of Economic Methodology* 7(2): 231–264.
Spirtes, P., Glymour, C., and Scheines, R. (1993) *Causation, Prediction and Search*, New York: Springer.
Spohn, W. (1980) "Stochastic Independence, Causal Independence, and Shieldability," *Journal of Philosophical Logic* 9: 73–99.
Spohn, W. (1983) "Probabilistic Causality: From Hume via Suppes to Granger," in M.C. Galavotti and G. Gambetta (eds.) *Causalità e modelli probabilistici*, Bologna: Cooperativa Libraria Universitaria.
Spohn, W. (2012) *The Laws of Belief*, Oxford: Oxford University Press.
Suppes, P. (1970) *A Probabilistic Theory of Causality*, Amsterdam: North-Holland.
Woodward, J. (2003) *Making Things Happen: A Causal Theory of Explanation*, Oxford: Oxford University Press.
Zellner, A. (1979) "Causality and Econometrics," *Carnegie-Rochester Conference Series on Public Policy* 10(1): 9–54.
Zellner, A. (1988) "Causality and Causal Laws in Economics," *Journal of Econometrics* 39: 7–21.

21
CAUSAL CONTRIBUTIONS IN ECONOMICS

Christopher Clarke

1. Introduction

This chapter explores the idea of one variable making a causal contribution to another variable and how this idea applies to economics. It also explores the related concept of what-if questions in economics. In particular, it contrasts the modular theory of causal contributions and what-if questions (advocated by interventionists) with the ceteris paribus theory (advocated by Jim Heckman and others). It notes a problem with the modular theory raised by Nancy Cartwright, and it notes how, according to the ceteris paribus theory, causal contributions and what-if questions are often indeterminate in economics. (For a discussion of probabilistic theories of causation and their use in economics, see Henschen, Chapter 20.)

2. Causal Contributions and What Ifs

It is not uncommon for economists to say that one variable made a causal contribution to another variable: the low price of lumber made a positive causal contribution to the high demand for lumber; a large class size made a negative causal contribution to a child's educational attainment. Similarly, it is not uncommon for economists to answer "what if things had been different?" questions about hypothetical scenarios. What would the demand for lumber have been if the price of lumber had been high? What would this child's educational attainment have been if the size of her class had been low? This chapter is about these two concepts (causal contributions and what-if questions) and how they apply to economics.

The chapter will examine two theories of causal contributions: the modular theory (advocated by Judea Pearl and by interventionists such as Jim Woodward) and the ceteris paribus theory (defended by Jim Heckman and others). Because both of these theories posit a tight connection between causal contributions and the answers to what-if questions, these theories also serve as theories of what-if questions as well. These two theories contrast with Nancy Cartwright's approach to causal contributions, according to which (a) no explicit theory of causal contributions is possible, and (b) there is a weaker connection between causal contributions and the answers to what-if questions (Cartwright 1989, 2007). Because Cartwright does not offer an explicit theory of causal contributions, I will not discuss her approach in this chapter. All I will say is that, the more problems one finds for the modular and ceteris paribus theories of causal contributions, the more attractive Cartwright's "no theory" approach to causal contributions becomes. I also will not discuss Hoover's (2001, 2011, 2013) theory of causation

DOI: 10.4324/9781315739793-26

in economics, because Hoover's theory does not define causal contributions quantitatively and because it does not give a recipe for answering what-if questions. Instead, Hoover's theory is qualitative: it is a theory of when one variable is a cause of another variable. Limitations of space prevent me from discussing Stephen LeRoy's theory (2016, n.d.), which I see as an important variant of Heckman's ceteris paribus theory. See also Julian Reiss (2012, 2009) for a discussion of what-if questions in the social sciences more broadly and some alternative approaches to them not considered in this chapter.

This chapter will proceed as follows. Section 3 sets things up by distinguishing between direct causal contributions and overall causal contributions and by defining the difference between an external variable and an internal variable. Section 4 lays out the modular theory of causal contributions. Section 5 notes some problems with the modular theory when it is applied to economics. The most important problem is Cartwright's argument that modularity fails for complex social systems. Sections 6 and 7 develop my preferred version of the ceteris paribus theory.

I will illustrate these two theories (i.e., the modular theory and the ceteris paribus theory) by using two toy models, one of educational attainment and another of supply and demand. To keep an already complex discussion as simple as possible, I will not include any disturbance terms in these models. In other words, the models I am discussing do not have probability distributions attached to them. The discussion in this chapter can be extended to probabilistic econometric models, however, by treating these disturbance terms as additional external variables.

3. Key Concepts

To talk about causal contributions, economists find it useful to label some variables in their models as "external variables" and to label other variables as "internal variables." Some economists also find it useful to talk about the "direct causes" of a variable and the "direct causal contribution" that one variable makes to another. This section will illustrate these four concepts. To do so, I will present a model of educational attainment; I will then abstract from this concrete example to give a precise definition of an external variable.

3.1 Direct Causal Contributions

The first equation that defines the model of educational attainment is $Y = \gamma_v V + \gamma_w W + \gamma_1 X_1$. This equation is to be interpreted as saying that, for any given child, there are three things that directly causally contributed to that child's educational attainment Y : the number of other children in the child's class V, the hours that the child spends on extracurricular activities W, and the educational policy X_1 enacted by the local or regional educational authority responsible for the child. The coefficients γ_v, γ_w, and γ_1 each denote an unknown constant – a positive or negative number that does not vary across the children in the population that we are studying. For example, γ_v is an unknown constant that describes the strength of the direct causal contribution that class size V makes to educational attainment Y. Each extra member of a child's class directly contributed γ_v extra units to that child's educational attainment.

The second equation that defines the model is $V = v_1 X_1 + v_2 X_2$. This equation is to be interpreted as saying that, for any given child, there are two things that directly contribute to that child's class size V : regional educational policy X_1 and the child's parental income X_2. Again v_1 and v_2 denote unknown constants that describe the strength of these direct causal contributions.

The final equation that defines the model is $W = \omega_2 X_2 + \omega_3 X_3$. This equation is to be interpreted as saying that, for any given child, there are two things that directly contribute to that child's extracurricular activities W : the child's parental income X_2 and the child's attitude toward education X_3. Again, ω_2 and ω_3 denote unknown constants that describe the strength of these direct causal contributions.

3.2 *Direct Causes*

I will call these equations *direct-causes equations* because they purport to describe direct causal contributions. One can depict what these equations say about direct causes by drawing a diagram. Specifically, whenever a variable makes a direct causal contribution to a second variable, one says that the first variable directly causes the second variable, and one draws an arrow starting at the first variable and ending at the second variable. See Figure 21.1.

Here, class size V and extracurricular activities W are each direct causes of attainment Y ; parental income X_2 is an indirect cause of attainment Y , via both class size V and extracurricular activities W as intermediaries; learning attitude X_3 is an indirect cause of attainment Y , via extracurricular activities W as an intermediary; and education policy X_1 is a direct cause of attainment Y , and it is also an indirect cause of attainment Y , via class size V as an intermediary. (Of course, the notion of a direct cause is relative to the variables that one includes in one's model. If, for example, one excluded V and W from our model, then X_2 and X_3 would become direct causes of Y .)

This notion of direct causation and a direct causal contribution is meant to be intuitive, and many theorists would say that this notion cannot be reduced or defined in terms of any more fundamental notions. It is worth noting that one exception is Woodward (2003a), who provides the following definition of direct causation. Roughly: X_1 is a direct cause of Y if and only if, were X_1 to take a different value (from the value it actually took) but all the other variables in the model (other than Y) were to take the values they actually took, then Y would take a different value (from the value Y actually took).

3.3 *Hypothetical Differences in the X's*

The three equations that define the educational attainment model do not just describe the values that these variables $\{V, W, Y, X_1, X_2, X_3\}$ actually took in the population of children being studied. These three equations are also to be interpreted as describing the values, for any child in this population, that these variables $\{V, W, Y, X_1, X_2, X_3\}$ would have taken under any hypothetical scenario in which the X variables had differed (taking values different from the values that the X variables actually took). Thus, they answer "What if the X's had differed?" questions. Take, for example, a hypothetical scenario in which education policy X_1 had taken value 5 instead, parental income X_2 had taken value 8 instead, and learning attitude X_3 had taken value 2 instead. Under this hypothetical scenario, the child's class size V would have been $5v_1 + 8v_2$, according to the equation $V = v_1 X_1 + v_2 X_2$, on this interpretation of the equation. In short, the equations that define the model not only make correct predictions for the scenario that actually occurred but they also make correct predictions about what would have occurred under hypothetical differences in the X variables in the model.

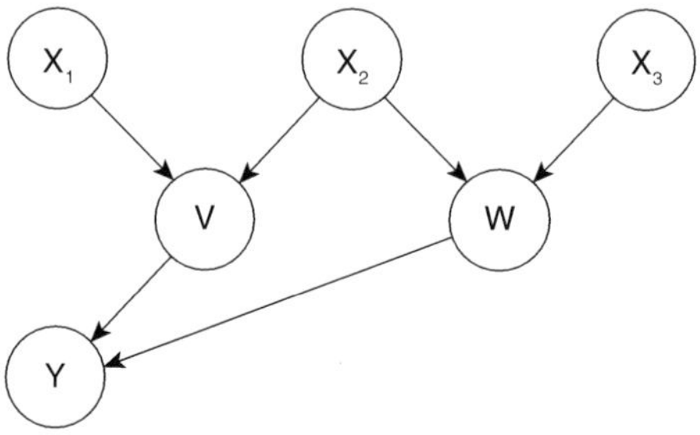

Figure 21.1 Direct causes

Note that one can substitute the first two equations that define the educational attainment model into the third equation to yield $Y = \gamma_v[v_1X_1 + v_2X_2] + \gamma_w[\omega_2X_2 + \omega_3X_3] + \gamma_1X_1$. If we tidy up, we get $Y = (\gamma_v v_1 + \gamma_1)X_1 + (\gamma_v v_2 + \gamma_w\omega_2)X_2 + \gamma_w\omega_3X_3$. But, when a set of equations makes correct predictions under some hypothetical scenario, then any equation that is derived mathematically from those equations will also make correct predictions under that hypothetical scenario. Thus, the following equations make correct predictions under hypothetical differences in the X variables in the model:

$$V = v_1X_1 + v_2X_2$$

$$W = \omega_2X_2 + \omega_3X_3$$

$$Y = (\gamma_v v_1 + \gamma_1)X_1 + (\gamma_v v_2 + \gamma_w\omega_2)X_2 + \gamma_w\omega_3X_3$$

3.4 External Variables Versus Internal Variables

To divide the variables in one's economic model into external variables $\{X_1, X_2, X_3\}$ and internal variables $\{V, W, Y\}$ is to say something about how to interpret the equations that define one's economic model. It is to say the following:

> *External variables predict internal variables under hypothetical differences in the external variables.* For each internal variable in the model, one can derive (from the equations that define the model) an equation that expresses this internal variable purely as a function of one or more external variables. Any such equation derived from the model will make correct predictions (about the value this internal variable takes) under hypothetical differences in the external variables in the model.
>
> *External variables cause internal variables but not vice versa.* Each of the external variables appearing in such an equation is a cause of the internal variable in question. But no internal variable is a cause of any external variable.
>
> *Variation freedom of external variables.* An external variable taking a given value does not preclude any other external variable from taking a given value. More precisely, if x_1 denotes a possible value of external variable X_1, and if x_2 denotes a possible value of external variable X_2, and if x_3 denotes a possible value for external variable X_3, for example, then it is possible for $X_1 = x_1$ and $X_2 = x_2$ and $X_3 = x_3$ to hold in any single case. By "possible" I mean both "consistent with the equations that define the model" and also something like "consistent with the system working as it normally does." In this respect, neither the model nor the system itself places strong restrictions on the value that an external variable can take, given the values of the other external variables.

The basic idea is that the model describes how the external variables causally determine the values of the internal variables, but it says nothing about the causes of the external variables themselves. Note that, as I have defined it here, the concept of an external versus internal variable is a different from the concept of an exogenous versus endogenous variable.[1]

4. The Modular Theory of Causal Contributions

With these concepts in hand, we can now describe the first theory of causal contributions and of what-if questions, which I call the "modular" theory. The modular theory is defended by Pearl (2009: 22–32, 70, 205–207) and Woodward (2003b). Woodward calls this theory the "interventionist" theory, but I find this metaphorical talk of "interventions" somewhat misleading so I will avoid it here. The modular theory is sometimes attributed to Haavelmo (1943), for example, by Pearl (2009: 365). There is also a broad similarity between the modular theory and Simon's (1953) theory (for a discussion see Cartwright 2007: 252).

The intuitive idea behind modularity is that direct-causes equations are "modular": if one were to "intervene" in the system to "break" one of the direct-causes equations, such as $V = v_1 X_1 + v_2 X_2$, for example, this intervention would still leave all of the other direct-causes equations intact. Thus, if one were to intervene in the system to set V equal to 10, for example, this intervention would not change the value of any of the external X variables, nor would it change the other direct-causes equations $W = \omega_2 X_2 + \omega_3 X_3$ and $Y = \gamma_v V + \gamma_w W + \gamma_1 X_1$. Given this, one can calculate what would happen to Y, for example, if internal variable V were different.

This talk of "interventions breaking equations" is metaphorical. So let me give a more rigorous description of the recipe that the modular theory suggests for answering what-if questions with respect to the educational attainment model. In the educational attainment model, the first step in the recipe is to write down the values $\{x_1, x_2, x_3, v, w, y\}$ that each of the variables $\{X_1, X_2, X_3, V, W, Y\}$ actually took in the case of a particular child. For example, let's take a child (called Menno) for whom

$$x_1 = 10$$

$$x_2 = 3$$

$$x_3 = 4$$

$$v = 4x_1 + x_2 = 43$$

$$w = \frac{1}{2}x_2 + 2x_3 = 9.5$$

$$y = \frac{1}{2}v + 2w + 5x_1 = 90.5$$

(For ease of I illustration, I've filled in the unknown values of the constants $v_1, v_2, \omega_2, \omega_3, \gamma_v, \gamma_w, \gamma_1$ with some specific values, namely, $4, 1, \frac{1}{2}, 2, \frac{1}{2}, 2, 5$.) The second step is to consider the hypothetical scenario in which the education policy X_1 in Menno's region had been 9 units, for example (instead of its actual value of 10 units). How should one calculate the values of all of the other variables under this hypothetical scenario in which X_1 differs? The modular theory endorses a principle called "modularity" (Pearl 2009: 22–32, 69). Modularity makes precise the rough idea that "interventions" on a set of variables C will leave all of the other external variables and direct-causes equations "intact":

> **Modularity**. Imagine that I want to evaluate what would occur in any hypothetical scenario of the form: if variable C_1 had instead taken value c'_1 (any value I choose), and variable C_2 had instead taken value c'_2 (any value I choose). This is how to do it:

a. For any external variable X (other than C_1 or C_2), the value that variable X would take in this hypothetical scenario is equal to the value that X took in the actual scenario.
b. For any internal variable Y (other than C_1 or C_2), the value that variable Y would take in this hypothetical scenario is correctly predicted by the equation that (in the actual scenario) specifies the direct causes of Y.
c. Variable C_1 takes the value c'_1 and variable C_2 takes the value c'_2, of course.

To understand what modularity means, look at how one can use it to calculate the values $\{x'_1, x'_2, x'_3, v', w', y'\}$ that each of the variables $\{X_1, X_2, X_3, V, W, Y\}$ would have taken, in Menno's case, under the hypothetical scenario in which $X_1 = 9$:

$x'_1 = 9$ according to (c) from modularity
$x'_2 = 3$ according to (a) from modularity
$x'_3 = 4$ according to (a) from modularity
$v' = 4x'_1 + x'_2 = 39$ according to (b) from modularity

$w' = \frac{1}{2}x'_2 + 2x'_3 = 9.5$ according to (b) from modularity

$y' = \frac{1}{2}v' + 2w' + 5x'_1 = 83.5$ according to (b) from modularity

The modular theory then adds that

Causal contributions match hypothetical differences:

> Whenever q denotes the value that variable Q actually took in a particular case, and p denotes the value that variable P actually took; and
> whenever q' denotes the value that Q would have taken under the hypothetical scenario in which P had taken the value p' instead;
> then P taking the value p (rather than taking value p') made an overall causal contribution to variable Q in the case in question of $q - q'$ units.

This tells us that the overall causal contribution that education policy X_1 taking value 10 (rather than taking value 9) made to this child's educational attainment is $y' - y = 90.5 - 83.5 = 7$ units. (Contrast this overall causal contribution with the direct causal contribution of education policy X_1 to educational attainment Y, namely, 5 units. The overall contribution differs from the direct contribution, of course, because education policy X_1 also makes an indirect contribution to educational attainment Y, namely, via class size V.)

This illustrates how the modular theory can be used to calculate the overall causal contribution that an external variable made to an internal variable. More controversially, the modular theory can also be used to calculate the overall causal contribution that any internal variable made to any other internal variable – and equally to calculate the value of any internal variable in any hypothetical scenarios in which one or more internal variables are hypothesized to differ. For example, one can calculate the values $\{x''_1, x''_2, x''_3, v'', w'', y''\}$ that each of the variables $\{X_1, X_2, X_3, V, W, Y\}$ would have taken, in Menno's case, under the hypothetical scenario in which V is 1 unit less (than its actual value of 43):

$x''_1 = 10$ according to (a) from modularity
$x''_2 = 3$ according to (a) from modularity
$x''_3 = 4$ according to (a) from modularity

$v'' = 43 - 1 = 42$ according to (c) from modularity

$w'' = \frac{1}{2}x''_2 + 2x''_3 = 9.5$ according to (b) from modularity

$y'' = \frac{1}{2}v'' + 2w'' + 5x''_1 = 90$ according to (b) from modularity

This tells us that the overall causal contribution that class size being 43 (rather than 42) made to this child's educational attainment is $y' - y = 90.5 - 90 = .5$ units.

This is Pearl and Woodward's modular theory of overall causal contributions. Their theory allows one to calculate the overall causal contribution that any variable in the model made to any other variable in the model. Similarly, modularity also allows one to predict the value that any variable would have taken under hypothetical differences to one or more of the other variables in the model. Note that the modular theory relies on direct-causes equations as an input. It presupposes that, for each internal variable, the model supplies us with exactly one equation that describes the direct causes of that variable.

5. Problems for the Modular Theory in Economics

The modular theory is popular in the sciences in general, but it is much less popular in economics in particular. To see why this is, consider the economic model of supply and demand:

Demand equation: $Q = \alpha P + \alpha_1 X_1 + \alpha_2 X_2$
Supply equation: $Q = \beta P + \beta_1 X_1 + \beta_3 X_3 + \beta_4 X_4$

Imagine that the first equation (the demand equation) describes the quantity of lumber Q that is produced in a given period. (This model assumes that the market for lumber is in equilibrium: the quantity of lumber produced Q is the same as the quantity of lumber Q that is purchased in that period.) The demand equation relates this quantity Q to the price P at which purchasers can buy lumber during this period, the price X_1 at which purchasers can buy brick during this period, and X_2 the overall income of consumers in the economy. The second equation (the supply equation) relates quantity Q to the price P at which producers can sell lumber during this period, the price X_1 at which producers can sell brick during this period, the technological conditions X_3 that determine how easy it is to produce lumber, and the technological conditions X_4 that determine how easy it is to produce brick. $\alpha, \alpha_1, \alpha_2, \beta, \beta_1, \beta_3$, and β_4 are unknown constants that do not vary across economies (in the population of market economies that we are studying).

To apply the modular theory to this model, we need direct-causes equations. But, as the supply and demand equations currently stand, there is a problem with interpreting them as direct-causes equations. Note that, as they stand, both equations have Q on the left-hand side. So, if we interpret each equation in the model as describing the direct causes of the left-hand side variable in the equation, the result is two contradictory stories about the direct causes of Q. The demand equation says that $\{P, X_1, X_2\}$ are the only direct causes of Q ; the supply equation says that $\{P, X_1, X_3, X_4\}$ are the only direct causes of Q. Even worse, consider a hypothetical scenario in which P differs – for example, the hypothetical scenario in which P takes a value one unit less (than the value P actually took). These contradictory stories about the direct causes of Q lead to an incoherent story about the value that Q would take under this hypothetical scenario, one can show. If we assume that the demand equation correctly describes the direct causes of Q, modularity says that the demand equation would hold under this hypothetical scenario. But modularity also says that none of the X variables would differ under this hypothetical scenario. It follows that Q would be α units less under this hypothetical scenario (than the value that Q actually took). In contrast, however, if one assumes that the supply equation also correctly describes the direct causes of Q, then by the exact same logic we can conclude that Q would be β units less under this hypothetical scenario. So, unless $\alpha = \beta$, modularity issues in an incoherent description of the value that Q would take under this hypothetical scenario.

This problem is easily fixed, however, by changing our interpretation of the equations in the supply-demand model. One option is to interpret the demand equation as describing the direct causes of Q and to interpret the supply equation as describing the direct causes of P. To work with this interpretation, one re-expresses the supply equation in a mathematically equivalent form.

Namely: There are some (unknown) values of constants $\alpha, \alpha_1, \alpha_2, \beta, \beta_1, \beta_3$, and β_4, such that for any economy (in the population being studied) the following two equations describe the direct causal contributions made to Q and P, respectively:

$$Q = \alpha P + \alpha_1 X_1 + \alpha_2 X_2$$

$$P = -(1/\beta)Q + (\beta_1/\beta)X_1 + (\beta_3/\beta)X_3 + (\beta_4/\beta)X_4$$

This interpretation of the supply and demand equations clears up the issue of what directly causes what: $\{P, X_1, X_2\}$ are the direct causes of Q, and $\{Q, X_1, X_3, X_4\}$ are the direct causes of P. (Note the "mutual causation" in which P causes Q and Q causes P. This mutual causation may sound weird, but at least it is not logically contradictory.)

This interpretation also allows the modular theory to issue in a coherent description of what would happen under the hypothetical scenario in which P, for example, had taken a value p' one unit less (than the value p that P actually took). Imagine for illustration that $x_1 = 8$, $x_2 = 3$, $x_3 = 4$, and $x_4 = 9$ are the values that the external variables actually took in the economy in question. Modularity says that the values $\{x'_1, x'_2, x'_3, x'_4, p', q'\}$ that the variables $\{X_1, X_2, X_3, X_4, P, Q\}$ would have taken, in the case of this particular economy, under the hypothetical scenario in which $P = p - 1$, are as follows:

$x'_1 = 8$ according to (a) from modularity
$x'_2 = 3$ according to (a) from modularity
$x'_3 = 4$ according to (a) from modularity
$x'_4 = 9$ according to (a) from modularity
$q' = \alpha p' + \alpha_1 x'_1 + \alpha_2 x'_2$ according to the demand equation and (b) from modularity
$p' = p - 1$ according to (c) from modularity

Because the value of Q in the actual scenario is given by $q = \alpha p + \alpha_1 x_1 + \alpha_2 x_2$, as per the demand equation, it follows that $q - q' = \alpha$, one can calculate. Because the modular theory says that causal contributions match hypothetical differences, it follows that P taking value p (rather than $p - 1$) made a causal contribution to Q in this particular economy of α units. In this respect, the causal contribution that price P makes to quantity Q can be "read off" the demand equation (in which α is the coefficient of the P variable).

Note that under the preceding hypothetical scenario, the supply equation is violated.[2] So, under this hypothetical scenario, the supply side of the economy is not working as it normally does. In effect, this hypothetical scenario is that in which the government has nationalized the production of lumber, fixed the price of lumber at $p - 1$, and guaranteed to produce as much lumber as was needed to keep up with demand. That is to say, this hypothetical scenario describes a government monopoly on lumber production.

However, an alternative (and equally well-motivated) interpretation of the supply and demand model is instead to interpret the demand equation as describing the direct causes of P and to interpret the supply equation as describing the direct causes of Q. To work with this interpretation, one instead re-expresses the demand equation in a mathematically equivalent form.

Namely: There are some (unknown) values of constants $\alpha, \alpha_1, \alpha_2, \beta, \beta_1, \beta_3$, and β_4, such that for any economy (in the population being studied) the following two equations describe the direct causal contributions made to P and Q, respectively:

$$P = -(1/\alpha)Q + (\alpha_1/\alpha)X_1 + (\alpha_2/\alpha)X_2$$

$$Q = \beta P + \beta_1 X_1 + \beta_3 X_3 + \beta_4 X_4$$

In this interpretation of the supply and demand equations, $\{P, X_1, X_3, X_4\}$ are the direct causes of Q, and $\{Q, X_1, X_2\}$ are the direct causes of P. This alternative interpretation issues in an alternative answer to the question of the value that Q would have taken in this particular economy, if P had taken a value p' one unit less (than the value p that P actually took). Modularity says that the values $\{x'_1, x'_2, x'_3, x'_4, p', q'\}$ that the variables $\{X_1, X_2, X_3, X_4, P, Q\}$ would have taken, in the case of this particular economy, under the hypothetical scenario in which $P = p - 1$, are the following:

$x'_1 = 8$ according to (a) from modularity
$x'_2 = 3$ according to (a) from modularity
$x'_3 = 4$ according to (a) from modularity
$x'_4 = 9$ according to (a) from modularity
$p' = p - 1$ according to (c) from modularity
$q' = \beta p' + \beta_1 x'_1 + \beta_3 x'_3 + \beta_4 x'_4$ according to (b) from modularity

Because the value of Q in the actual scenario is given by $q = \beta p + \beta_1 x_1 + \beta_3 x_3 + \beta_4 x_4$, as per the supply equation, it follows that $q - q' = \beta$, one can calculate. So, in this alternative interpretation of what the supply and demand model means, the modular theory says that P taking value p (rather than $p - 1$) made a causal contribution to Q in this particular economy of β units. In this respect, the causal contribution that price P makes to quantity Q can be "read off" the supply equation (in which β is the coefficient of the P variable).

Note that, under the preceding hypothetical scenario, the demand equation is violated.[3] So, under this hypothetical scenario, the demand side of the economy is not working as it normally does. In effect, this hypothetical scenario is that in which the government has banned the direct sale of lumber to lumber purchasers and has instead insisted that the producers of lumber sell only to the government at a fixed price of $p - 1$, with the government guaranteeing to buy as much as the producers are willing to produce. That is to say, this hypothetical scenario is a government monopsony on lumber purchase.

This illustrates how, when applying the modular theory, one needs to make a judgment call about what the direct causes of each internal variable are. And for the supply and demand system, there seem to be two equally well-motivated judgment calls here – with each judgment call issuing in a distinct measure of the causal contribution that P made to Q.

Now that we have fixed this minor problem, however, a major problem remains: when economists ask of a particular market economy, "What value would quantity Q have taken if the price P had taken the value $p - 1$ instead?" they often are not interested in hypothetical scenarios in which $P = p - 1$ arose via a noncompetitive arrangement, such as a government monopoly on lumber production or a government monopsony on lumber sales. This is simply not the hypothetical scenario in which most economists are interested. Rather, most economists are interested in the normal workings of the market economy as a competitive system. So, they are interested in a hypothetical scenario in which $P = p - 1$ arose from a competitive arrangement between buyers and between producers. Therefore, the modular theory, when applied to the supply-demand model, is answering a question that economists are not usually interested in. (An analogy might help here: when asking what would have happened if the steering wheel in a car had been rotated right by 90 degrees, one is usually interested in what would have happened if this had occurred with the car working normally. One is not usually interested in what would have happened if this had occurred via someone detaching the steering wheel from the car and then rotating the steering wheel by 90 degrees.)

This major problem for the modularity theory has been pressed most forcefully by Cartwright (2007). For Pearl's response, see Pearl (2009: 106, 363–365, 374–378).

6. The General Supply-Demand Equation

To explore the supply and demand system in more depth, it will be useful to derive several consequences from the supply and demand equations. To do this, multiply the demand equation by any constant λ, and multiply the supply equation by any constant μ. This yields

$$\lambda Q = \lambda \alpha P + \lambda \alpha_1 X_1 + \lambda \alpha_2 X_2$$

$$\mu Q = \mu \beta P + \mu \beta_1 X_1 + \mu \beta_3 X_3 + \mu \beta_4 X_4$$

If we add these two equations together, we get

$$(\lambda + \mu) Q = (\lambda \alpha + \mu \beta) P + (\lambda \alpha_1 + \mu \beta_1) X_1 + \lambda \alpha_2 X_2 + \mu \beta_3 X_3 + \mu \beta_4 X_4$$

Division by $\lambda + \mu$ gives what I will call the *general supply-demand equation*, which combines the information from both the supply and the demand equations:

$$Q = \frac{\lambda \alpha + \mu \beta}{\lambda + \mu} P + \frac{\lambda \alpha_1 + \mu \beta_1}{\lambda + \mu} X_1 + \frac{\lambda \alpha_2}{\lambda + \mu} X_2 + \frac{\mu \beta_3}{\lambda + \mu} X_3 + \frac{\mu \beta_4}{\lambda + \mu} X_4$$

One can derive various useful facts from this general supply-demand equation by choosing particular values for λ and μ. First, when one lets $\mu = -\alpha$ and $\lambda = \beta$ in the general supply-demand equation, one derives the more specific equation:

$$Q = \frac{\beta \alpha_1 - \alpha \beta_1}{\beta - \alpha} X_1 + \frac{\beta \alpha_2}{\beta - \alpha} X_2 - \frac{\alpha \beta_3}{\beta - \alpha} X_3 - \frac{\alpha \beta_4}{\beta - \alpha} X_4$$

Because each of $\{X_1, X_2, X_3, X_4\}$ is an external variable and the preceding function of Q is derived from our model, the definition of external variables from Section 3 says that each of $\{X_1, X_2, X_3, X_4\}$ is a cause of Q – although not necessarily a direct cause of Q. Second, because $\{X_1, X_2, X_3, X_4\}$ are each external variables, Q must be an internal variable, otherwise the variation-freedom condition on external variables would fail (again see Section 3).

Third, when one lets $\lambda = -1$ and $\mu = 1$ (and divides by $\alpha - \beta$ rather than by $\lambda + \mu$), one derives the more specific equation:

$$P = \frac{\beta_1 - \alpha_1}{\alpha - \beta} X_1 - \frac{\alpha_2}{\alpha - \beta} X_2 + \frac{\beta_3}{\alpha - \beta} X_3 + \frac{\beta_4}{\alpha - \beta} X_4$$

It will be absolutely crucial for the discussion that follows to note from this equation: given that the supply and demand equations hold, the values of $\{X_1, X_2, X_3, X_4\}$ together predict the value that P takes. Fourth, it follows from this that P is an internal variable that is caused by each of $\{X_1, X_2, X_3, X_4\}$.

7. The Ceteris Paribus Theory

The problem for the modular theory that I discussed in Section 5 motivates the search for an alternative theory of overall causal contributions and of what-if hypotheticals. This section will develop an alternative theory, which I will call the *ceteris paribus theory* and which I take to be in the spirit of Heckman's theory (Heckman 2000, 2005; Heckman and Vytlacil 2007), although there are a number of ambiguities in Heckman's own theory that make it unclear whether Heckman would endorse the ceteris paribus theory as I formulate it.

Heckman's theory does not require us to make any assumptions about direct causes. And so, unlike the previous sections, I will no longer assume anything about the direct causes of P and of Q. Instead, I will assume only that (a) the external variables in the supply-demand model are $\{X_1, X_2, X_3, X_4\}$ and (b) the supply equation and the demand equation correctly predict the values of P and Q under hypothetical differences in these external variables. In virtue of this, the supply and demand equations are assumed to be "externally stable," to coin a phrase. It follows, as I pointed out in the last section, that $\{X_1, X_2, X_3, X_4\}$ are each causes of Q and are each causes of P. I will also assume, as most economists do, that c) P is a cause of Q. After all, without this assumption, discussion of the causal contribution that P makes to Q is meaningless.

With these assumptions in hand, let's now consider a hypothetical scenario under which P takes a value one unit less (than P took in the actual scenario). One might then be tempted to reason (naively) as follows. Note the variables $\{P, X_1, X_2\}$ on the right-hand side of the demand equation. These variables are each a cause of the variable Q on the left-hand side of the demand equation. But one might assume that, under a hypothetical scenario in which P differs, each of the other causes in this set $\{P, X_1, X_2\}$ would take the same value (as it took in the actual scenario). That is to say, one might assume that X_1 and X_2 do not differ under this hypothetical scenario. If one also assumes that the demand equation correctly predicts what would happen under this hypothetical scenario, it follows that, under this hypothetical scenario, Q would have taken the value $q' = \alpha(p-1) + \alpha_1 x_1 + \alpha_2 x_2$. But, because Q actually took the value $q = \alpha p + \alpha_1 x_1 + \alpha_2 x_2$, it follows that $q - q' = \alpha$. And, because causal contributions match hypothetical differences, one assumes, α is the causal contribution that an extra unit of P made to Q in this particular economy.

I will call the general idea here the *extremely naive ceteris paribus theory*:

> Whenever (I) $Q = q(P, O)$ expresses Q as an externally stable function of P and some other variables O; and
> whenever (II) P and O are each causes of Q; and
> whenever o denotes the values that these other variables O actually took;
> then, under the hypothetical scenario in which P had instead taken the value p', O would have taken the value o and Q would have taken the value $q' = q(p', o)$.

Because causal contributions match hypothetical differences, P taking value p (rather than p') made an overall causal contribution to variable Q in the case in question of $q - q'$ units.

I use the label *ceteris paribus* – all else being equal – to mark the fact that this theory uses hypothetical scenarios in which these other causes O take the values that they actually take. (It is also worth noting that, according to the ceteris paribus theory, facts about what would happen in a hypothetical scenario in which P is different are relative to the variable Q on which one chooses to focus on as an outcome variable.)

Why is this theory extremely naive? Consider the case in which a bodybuilder is trying to gain muscle mass. Imagine that muscle mass is caused by gym activity and by protein consumed, in accordance with the equation $\text{Mass} = 3\text{Gym} + 4\text{Protein}$. Imagine also that gym activity is also a cause of protein consumption, in accordance with the equation $\text{Protein} = 2\text{Gym}$. Note that the extremely naive ceteris paribus theory mistakenly entails that the overall contribution that an extra unit of Gym makes to Mass is 3 units. But this is incorrect: 3 is the merely the direct causal contribution that Gym makes to Mass; there is also the indirect contribution that Gym makes to Mass through Protein consumption as an intermediary. To calculate the overall causal contribution, note that $\text{Mass} = 3\text{Gym} + 4(2\text{Gym}) = 11\text{Gym}$.

It is easy to fix this problem, of course. One improves the ceteris paribus theory by adding to it the condition that the ceteris paribus theory only applies:

> Whenever (III) the cause in question (for example, P or Gym) is not a cause of any of the other variables O.

This improved theory fixes the problem. $\text{Mass} = 3\text{Gym} + 4\text{Protein}$ fails the condition of application III of the improved theory, because Gym is a cause of Protein.

What does this improved theory say about the supply and demand system? Because P is an internal variable, our definition of internal variables in Section 3 tells us that P is not a cause of X_1 or X_2. And so the improved theory can be applied to the demand equation $Q = \alpha P + \alpha_1 X_1 + \alpha_2 X_2$ to calculate that an extra unit of P makes an overall contribution of α units to Q. (But, because X_1 and X_2 are causes of P, condition III says that the improved theory cannot be applied to the demand equation. Thus, condition III prevents one from drawing the conclusion that an extra unit of X_1 makes an overall contribution of α_1 units to Q.)

I call this improved theory the *somewhat naive ceteris paribus theory*. This is because this ceteris paribus theory still faces a major problem. To see this problem, recall the general supply-demand equation from Section 6.

$$Q = \frac{\lambda\alpha + \mu\beta}{\lambda + \mu} P + \frac{\lambda\alpha_1 + \mu\beta_1}{\lambda + \mu} X_1 + \frac{\lambda\alpha_2}{\lambda + \mu} X_2 + \frac{\mu\beta_3}{\lambda + \mu} X_3 + \frac{\mu\beta_4}{\lambda + \mu} X_4$$

This equation is externally stable, because it follows from two externally stable equations. By virtue of this, the equation satisfies condition I from the somewhat naive ceteris paribus theory. But recall that the previous section established that these other variables $O = \{X_1, X_2, X_3, X_4\}$ are each causes of Q. And recall that we are assuming that P is a cause of Q. And so, by virtue of this, condition II is satisfied too. But, P is an internal variable, as shown in Section 6. And it follows from our definition of an internal variable that P does not cause any of $O = \{X_1, X_2, X_3, X_4\}$, because they are all external variables. So, by virtue of this, condition III is satisfied too. So, the general supply-demand equation satisfies conditions I–III for applying the somewhat naive ceteris paribus theory. The result is that $(\lambda\alpha + \mu\beta)/(\lambda + \mu)$ is a correct description of the causal contribution that each extra unit of P makes to Q. But note that λ and μ can take any values that one likes, and conditions I–III are still satisfied. And so $(\lambda\alpha + \mu\beta)/(\lambda + \mu)$ can be any value that one likes. Therefore, the causal contribution of P to Q is correctly described by any number that one likes, positive or negative, according to the somewhat naive ceteris paribus theory. That it is maximally indeterminate is the unwelcome conclusion.

How might one further improve the ceteris paribus theory to avoid this unwelcome conclusion? Let's say that, whenever both the supply and the demand equations hold, the economy is "working normally" as a competitive economy. Given this, one might improve the ceteris paribus theory by stipulating that the theory only applies to hypothetical scenarios in which the economy is working normally. Namely, one might add the following condition:

> Whenever (IV) there is a logically possible hypothetical scenario in which P takes value p', the other variables O take value o, and the system is working normally.

This normal workings condition can be motivated independently from the desire to avoid the previous unwelcome conclusion: at the end of Section 5, I suggested that economists are typically interested in hypothetical scenarios in which there is competition both between buyers and between producers. When modeling competitive economies, economists are not typically interested in hypothetical scenarios in which the government has imposed a monopoly on lumber production or a monopsony on lumber purchases, for example. That is to say, they are interested only in hypothetical cases in which the economy is working normally.

To see the implications of this "normal workings" condition, remember from Section 6 that, given that the supply and demand equations hold, the values of the other variables $O=\{X_1,X_2,X_3,X_4\}$ predict the value that P takes. So, there is no logically possible hypothetical scenario in which (a) P is one unit less (than in the actual scenario), (b) all the other variables $O=\{X_1,X_2,X_3,X_4\}$ take the same values (as they took in the actual scenario), and (c) the system is working normally. And so the hypothetical scenario in which P differs, but in which all the other variables $O=\{X_1,X_2,X_3,X_4\}$ remain the same, fails the normal workings condition. So the set of other variables $O=\{X_1,X_2,X_3,X_4\}$ fails condition IV. And so, unlike the somewhat naive ceteris paribus theory, the normal workings ceteris paribus theory does not issue in the unwelcome conclusion that – for any value of λ and μ that we like – the causal contribution that each extra unit of P makes to Q is correctly described by $(\lambda\alpha+\mu\beta)/(\lambda+\mu)$. That is to say, it does not issue in the conclusion that this causal contribution is maximally indeterminate.

Now that we have said that, consider the more specific equation that results when we let $\mu=-\alpha_1$ and $\lambda=\beta_1$ in the general supply-demand equation:

$$Q=\frac{\beta_1\alpha-\alpha_1\beta}{\beta_1-\alpha_1}P+\frac{\beta_1\alpha_2}{\beta_1-\alpha_1}X_2-\frac{\alpha_1\beta_3}{\beta_1-\alpha_1}X_3-\frac{\alpha_1\beta_4}{\beta_1-\alpha_1}X_4$$

These specific choices of μ and λ ensure that the coefficient for the X_1 term in the general supply-demand equation is zero, and so it eliminates X_1 from the general supply-demand equation. So, the other variables O in this more specific equation are $O=\{X_2,X_3,X_4\}$. But it is possible for P to differ (from its actual value) and for these other variables $O=\{X_2,X_3,X_4\}$ to take the same values (as they actually took) and for the economy to work as normal. Therefore, the normal workings ceteris paribus theory applies to this more specific equation, an equation in which the other variables are $O=\{X_2,X_3,X_4\}$. The theory says that $(\beta_1\alpha-\alpha_1\beta)/(\beta_1-\alpha_1)$ is a correct description of the overall causal contribution that an extra unit of P made to Q.

Similarly, if we let $\mu=0$, the more specific equation that results from the general supply-demand equation is just the demand equation itself $Q=\alpha P+\alpha_1X_1+\alpha_2X_2$. This specific choice of μ ensures that the coefficients for both the X_3 and X_4 terms in the general supply-demand equation are zero, and so it eliminates X_3 and X_4 from the general supply-demand equation. So the other variables O in this more specific equation are $O=\{X_1,X_2\}$. But it is possible for P to differ (from its actual value) and for the other variables $O=\{X_1,X_2\}$ to take the same values (as they actually took) and for the economy to work normally. Therefore, the normal workings ceteris paribus theory applies to this more specific equation, namely, the demand equation, an equation for which the other variables are $O=\{X_1,X_2\}$. The theory says that α is also a correct description of the overall causal contribution that one unit of P made to Q.

Similarly, if we let $\lambda=0$, the more specific equation that results from the general supply-demand equation is just the supply equation itself $Q=\beta P+\beta_1X_1+\beta_3X_3+\beta_4X_4$. This specific choice of λ ensures that the coefficient for the X_2 term in the general supply-demand equation is zero, and so it eliminates X_2 from the general supply-demand equation. So, the other variables O in this more specific equation are $O=\{X_1,X_3,X_4\}$. But it is possible for P to differ (from its actual value) and for these other variables $O=\{X_1,X_3,X_4\}$ to take the same values (as they actually took) and for the economy to work normally. Therefore, the normal workings ceteris paribus theory applies to this more specific equation, namely, the supply equation, an equation for which $O=\{X_1,X_3,X_4\}$.

The theory says that β is also a correct description of the overall causal contribution that one unit of P made to Q.

Further inspection shows that there are no other choices of λ and μ that eliminate any of the X's from the general supply-demand equation. However, only when one finds a function for Q in which one has eliminated one of the X's from the right-hand side of the function is it possible for P to differ while the other variables O on the right-hand side of the function take the same values. And so there are only three ways to apply the normal workings ceteris paribus theory to the supply and demand system. The first way is to apply it with $O = \{X_2, X_3, X_4\}$ to show that $(\beta_1\alpha - \alpha_1\beta)/(\beta_1 - \alpha_1)$ is a correct description of the overall causal contribution that one unit of P made to Q. The second way is to apply it with $O = \{X_1, X_2\}$ to show that α is also a correct description of this overall causal contribution too. The third way is to apply it with $O = \{X_1, X_3, X_4\}$ to show that β is also a correct description. Thus, for the normal workings ceteris paribus theory, causal contributions are relative to the choice of O. (Compare and contrast the modular theory, which said that there is only one correct description, namely, β or α, depending on what one judges the direct causes of Q to be.)

In sum, I have explained and motivated the *normal ceteris paribus theory*:

> Whenever (I) $Q = q(P,O)$ expresses Q as an externally stable function of P and some other variables O ; and
> whenever (II) P and O are each causes of Q ; and
> whenever (III) P is not a cause of any of the other variables O ; and
> whenever o denotes the values that these other variables O actually took; and
> whenever (IV) there is a logically possible hypothetical scenario in which P takes value p', and O takes value o, and the system is working normally,
> then, under the hypothetical scenario in which P instead took the value p', O would have taken the value o and Q would have taken the value $q' = q(p',o)$. This answer is relative to one's choices of O and Q.

Because causal contributions match hypothetical differences, P taking value p (rather than p') made an overall causal contribution to variable Q in the case in question of $q - q'$ units. This answer is relative to one's choices of O and Q.

Thus, when examining hypothetical scenarios in which P differs, the normal ceteris paribus theory takes a different approach from the modular theory. On the one hand, the normal ceteris paribus theory considers hypothetical scenarios in which the system is working normally, scenarios for example in which both the supply and demand equations hold. The modular theory, on the other hand, considers situations in which one of these two equations fails and so the economy is not a fully competitive market economy. We have already seen how this leads to different conclusions: the normal ceteris paribus theory says that $(\beta_1\alpha - \alpha_1\beta)/(\beta_1 - \alpha_1)$ is a correct description of the causal contribution of P to Q, whereas the modular theory denies this.

To further understand the differences between these two theories, let's return to the educational attainment model, and let's say that the educational system is working normally if and only if the three equations in the model all hold:

$$V = v_1X_1 + v_2X_2$$

$$W = \omega_2X_2 + \omega_3X_3$$

$$Y = \gamma_vV + \gamma_wW + \gamma_1X_1$$

Now, it follows from the first equation here that that $\lambda V - \lambda v_1 X_1 - \lambda v_2 X_2 = 0$ holds for any value of λ we like. But we have already established that $Y = (\gamma_v v_1 + \gamma_1) X_1 + (\gamma_v v_2 + \gamma_w \omega_2) X_2 + \gamma_w \omega_3 X_3$ follows from these equations. If we add the former equation to the latter, we get, for any value of λ, the general equation

$$Y = \lambda V + ([\gamma_v - \lambda] v_1 + \gamma_1) X_1 + ([\gamma_v - \lambda] v_2 + \gamma_w \omega_2) X_2 + \gamma_w \omega_3 X_3$$

If one chooses $\lambda = \gamma_v + \gamma_1 / v_1$, then the more specific equation that results from this general equation is one in which the X_1 term is eliminated:

$$Y = \left(\gamma_v + \frac{\gamma_1}{v_1} \right) V + \left(\gamma_w \omega_2 - \frac{\gamma_1 v_2}{v_1} \right) X_2 + \gamma_w \omega_3 X_3 .$$

This equation is externally stable, because it follows from two externally stable equations. By virtue of this, the equation satisfies condition I from the normal ceteris paribus theory. But $\{V, X_2, X_3\}$ are each causes of Y, and so condition II is satisfied also. But, because V is an internal variable, it follows from our definition of an internal variable that V does not cause any of the external variables $\{X_2, X_3\}$. By virtue of V not causing X_2 or X_3, condition III is satisfied also. But there is a hypothetical scenario in which X_2 and X_3 each take the same values (as they took in the actual scenario), but in which V takes a value one unit lower (than it took in the actual scenario) and in which the system works normally. (Under this hypothetical scenario, X_1 takes a value $1/v_1$ units lower than it actually took.) By virtue of this, condition IV is satisfied also. So, the normal ceteris paribus theory applies to this equation. The result is that $\gamma_v + \gamma_1 / v_1$ is a correct description of the overall causal contribution that an extra unit of V makes to Y, that is to say, relative to $O = \{X_2, X_3\}$.

However, if instead one chooses $\lambda = \gamma_v + \gamma_w \omega_2 / v_2$, then the more specific equation that results from this general equation is one in which the X_2 term is eliminated:

$$Y = \left(\gamma_v + \frac{\gamma_w \omega_2}{v_2} \right) V + \left(\gamma_1 - \frac{\gamma_w \omega_2 v_1}{v_2} \right) X_1 + \gamma_w \omega_3 X_3$$

But there is a hypothetical scenario in which X_1 and X_3 each take the same values (as they took in the actual scenario), but in which V takes a value one unit lower (than it took in the actual scenario) and in which the system works normally. (Under this hypothetical scenario, X_2 takes a value $1/v_2$ units lower than it actually took.) So, by the same logic, the normal ceteris paribus theory applies to this equation. The theory says that $\lambda = \gamma_v + \gamma_w \omega_2 / v_2$ is also a correct description of the overall causal contribution that an extra unit of V makes to Y, that is to say, relative to $O = \{X_1, X_3\}$.

However, what if instead one considers our original equation $Y = \gamma_v V + \gamma_w W + \gamma_1 X_1$? Note that there is a hypothetical scenario in which W and X_1 each take the same values (as they took in the actual scenario), but in which V takes a value one unit lower (than it took in the actual scenario) and in which the system is working normally. (Under this hypothetical scenario, X_2 takes a value $1/v_2$ units lower than it actually took, and X_3 takes a value $\omega_2 / \omega_3 v_2$ units higher than it actually took.) By virtue of this, condition IV is satisfied. Let's also assume that V does not cause W. By virtue of this, condition III is satisfied also. Let's also assume that W is a cause of Y. By virtue of this, condition II is satisfied also. So the normal ceteris paribus theory applies to this equation. The theory says that the causal contribution that an extra unit of V made to Y was γ_v units, that is to say, relative to $O = \{W, X_1\}$.

This illustrates how the normal ceteris paribus theory differs from the modular theory, which says that γ_v is the only correct description of this causal contribution.

8. Conclusion

This chapter has contrasted two theories of causal contributions and of what-if questions: the modular theory and the ceteris paribus theory. The modular theory requires information about direct causal contributions as an input, and it faces Cartwright's objection that (arguably) it interprets causal contributions and what-if questions in a way that makes them uninteresting to economists. The ceteris paribus theory only requires information about which variables are external variables (and which equations are stable under differences in the external variables). But it entails that causal contributions are often relative to one's choice of "other variables," the variables that one imagines "holding fixed" while one imagines the cause in question varying.

Related Chapter

Henschen, T., Chapter 20 "Causality and Probability"

Notes

1 In the most common definition of exogeneity, exogeneity is a concept that applies to models in which each equation contains a "disturbance term," for example, the U term in the equation $Y = \gamma X + U$. Exogeneity claims that the mathematical expectation $E(U \mid X)$ is equal to $E(U)$. See Engle, Hendry, and Richard (1983) for a classic discussion.

2 Because the supply equation does hold in the actual scenario, we have $q = \beta p + \beta_1 x_1 + \beta_3 x_3 + \beta_4 x_4$, and so $(q-\alpha)+\alpha = \beta + \beta(p-1) + \beta_1 x_1 + \beta_3 x_3 + \beta_4 x_4$. By substitution, we have $q' + \alpha = \beta + \beta p' + \beta_1 x'_1 + \beta_3 x'_3 + \beta_4 x'_4$, and so $q' \neq \beta p' + \beta_1 x'_1 + \beta_3 x'_3 + \beta_4 x'_4$, unless $\alpha = \beta$.

3 Because the demand equation does hold in the actual scenario, we have $q = \alpha p + \alpha_1 x_1 + \alpha_2 x_2$, and so $(q-\beta)+\beta = \alpha + \alpha(p-1) + \alpha_1 x_1 + \alpha_2 x_2$. By substitution, we have $q' + \beta = \alpha + \alpha p' + \alpha_1 x'_1 + \alpha_2 x'_2$, and so $q' \neq \alpha p' + \alpha_1 x'_1 + \alpha_2 x'_2$, unless $\alpha = \beta$.

Bibliography

Cartwright, N. (1989) *Nature's Capacities and Their Measurement*, Oxford: Oxford University Press.

Cartwright, N. (2007) *Hunting Causes and Using Them: Approaches in Philosophy and Economics*, Cambridge; New York: Cambridge University Press.

Engle, R.F., Hendry, D.F., and Richard, J.-F. (1983) "Exogeneity," *Econometrica* 51: 277–304. https://doi.org/10.2307/1911990.

Haavelmo, T. (1943) "The Statistical Implications of a System of Simultaneous Equations," *Econometrica* 11: 1–12. https://doi.org/10.2307/1905714.

Heckman, J.J. (2000) "Causal Parameters and Policy Analysis in Economics: A Twentieth Century Retrospective," *The Quarterly Journal of Economics* 115: 45–97.

Heckman, J.J. (2005) "The Scientific Model of Causality," *Sociological Methodology* 35: 1–97. https://doi.org/10.1111/j.0081-1750.2006.00164.x.

Heckman, J.J., and Vytlacil, E.J. (2007) "Chapter 70 Econometric Evaluation of Social Programs, Part I: Causalmodels, Structural Models and Econometric Policy Evaluation," in *Handbook of Econometrics* 6: 4779–4874. Elsevier. https://doi.org/10.1016/s1573-4412(07)06070-9.

Hoover, K.D. (2001) *Causality in Macroeconomics*, Cambridge: Cambridge University Press.

Hoover, K.D. (2011) "Counterfactuals and Causal Structure," in P. Mckay Illari, F. Russo, and J. Williamson (eds.) *Causality in the Sciences*, Oxford University Press. https://doi.org/10.1093/acprof:oso/9780199574131.001.0001.

Hoover, K.D. (2013) "Identity, Structure, and Causal Representation in Scientific Models," in H. Chao, S. Chen, and R.L. Millstein (eds.) *Mechanism and Causality in Biology and Economics*: 35–57, Dordrecht: Springer Netherlands. https://doi.org/10.1007/978-94-007-2454-9_3.

LeRoy, S.F. (2016) "Implementation-Neutral Causation," *Economics and Philosophy* 32: 121–142. https://doi.org/10.1017/S0266267115000280.

LeRoy, S.F. (n.d.) "Implementation-Neutral Causation in Structural Models," 22.

Pearl, J. (2009) *Causality: Models, Reasoning, and Inference*, 2nd ed. New York: Cambridge University Press.

Reiss, J. (2009) "Counterfactuals, Thought Experiments, and Singular Causal Analysis in History," *Philosophy of Science* 76: 712–723.

Reiss, J. (2012) "Counterfactuals," in H. Kincaid (ed.) *The Oxford Handbook of Philosophy of Social Science*, Oxford; New York: Oxford University Press.

Simon, H.A. (1953) "Causal Ordering and Identifiability," in W.C. Hood and T.C. Koopmans (eds.) *Studies in Econometric Method. Cowles Commission for Research in Economics, Monograph No. 14*, 4974, John Wiley & Sons.

Woodward, J. (2003a) *Making Things Happen: A Theory of Causal Explanation*, Oxford: Oxford University Press.

Woodward, J. (2003b) *Making Things Happen: A Theory of Causal Explanation*, Oxford University Press. https://doi.org/10.1093/0195155270.001.0001/acprof-9780195155273.

22

EXPLANATION IN ECONOMICS

Philippe Verreault-Julien

1. Introduction

"Much of economics is positive: It just tries to explain how the economy works" (Mankiw 2018: 28). Notwithstanding the potentially contentious distinction between positive and normative economics, Mankiw makes clear that economics aims to *explain* economic phenomena. This was not always the case. Milton Friedman's (in)famous methodological foray into the use of unrealistic assumptions downplayed the role of explanation and had a lasting influence on subsequent economic methodology. According to him, the "ultimate goal" of economic theory is to yield "valid and meaningful (i.e. not truistic) predictions about phenomena not yet observed" (Milton Friedman 1953: 7). To achieve that goal, Friedman contended, one does not need "realistic" assumptions. As we can infer a true conclusion from false premises, false assumptions can yield true predictions.

Friedman's view has often been labeled as a form of instrumentalism because it appears to favor the practical goal of prediction (Blaug 1992; Boland 1979; Caldwell 1994; Hausman 1998; Reiss 2012a).[1] What Friedman's position also seemed to imply was that economics *should not* aim to explain economic phenomena. Insofar as explanation requires truth, then to waive the need for realistic – that is, (approximately) true – assumptions appears to imply forgoing explanation.[2] One major impetus for the "realism program" in economic methodology has thus been to show how economics, despite appearances, is committed to some form of truth (Mäki 1992, 2000, 2009a, 2012). Hausman (1998; see also Reiss 2012a) argues that, compared to the traditional instrumentalism-realism debate, the main issue at stake in economics is a question concerning its goals: should they be only practical (instrumentalism), or should they also be epistemic (realism)? In particular, should economics pursue the epistemic goal of explanation?[3]

Today, explanation is a widely recognized aim of economics. Banerjee and Duflo (2005: 478) maintain that "[n]on-aggregative growth models thus seem to have the potential to explain why poor countries remain poor," and Chetty et al.'s (2016: 287) "findings suggest that part of the explanation [for gender gaps in adulthood] may instead lie in the growth of residential segregation, income inequality, and the fraction of children raised in single-parent households." Like Mankiw, economists do not shun the language of explanation. The question, therefore, is not so much whether they consider that explanation is a legitimate aim: it is. That said, still few discussions in the literature on economic methodology *explicitly* concern explanation. The goal of this chapter is not to give a precise account of whether economics succeeds at explaining nor of how it may do so. Instead, its goal is to show that, often implicitly, some key methodological discussions are best understood as indirect debates

 DOI: 10.4324/9781315739793-27

about explanation in economics. By that, I mean that disputes about, for instance, causal inference (Clarke, Chapter 21; Henschen, Chapter 20), idealizations (Chao, Chapter 13; Jhun, Chapter 23), or microfoundations are debates about whether and how economics (should) explains. In turn, I believe this sheds light on the methodological issues economics faces.

This chapter is separated into three sections. In the next section, I examine issues that concern the *type* of explanation. Then, I discuss the problem of *idealizations and model-based* explanation. In the penultimate section, I address the question of the *levels* of explanation.

2. What Type of Explanation?

Hempel and Oppenheim (1948; see also Hempel 1965) argued that all scientific explanations have the form of an argument and subsumed their explanandum under a scientific law. Their main model was the deductive-nomological (D-N model). The D-N model became the received view on explanation for the following decades. A corollary of the D-N model is that a science devoid of laws would never be able to explain. Applied to economics, if economics cannot have laws, then it cannot explain. Accordingly, economic methodologists set forth to find laws in economics and, more generally, in the social sciences (e.g. Hausman 1981; Kincaid 1996; Mcintyre 1998; Rosenberg 1976).

Although economics is replete with alleged laws (the law of supply and demand, Engel's law, Okun's law, etc.), whether those are genuine laws remains a contentious issue (e.g. Blaug 1992; Hardt 2017; Hausman 1992; Jhun 2017; Kincaid 2004; Roberts 2004). One reason for this is that economic laws are seldom universal generalizations. Even the law of demand, which is arguably quite robust, has exceptions in certain circumstances, for example, with luxury goods. To safeguard laws in economics, one defense has been to argue that economic laws are "inexact" in the sense of not entailing universal regularities (e.g. Cartwright 1995; Hausman 1992). Two related ways of spelling out the inexactness of laws have been in terms of tendencies and ceteris paribus laws. Tendencies, which go back to Mill (e.g. Mill 1843), are causes that produce a characteristic effect in the absence of disturbing factors (Reiss 2013a). The law of demand may hold as a rule, but other factors may prevent it from acting. Ceteris paribus laws are supplemented with hedge clauses that specify under which conditions the laws hold. So, the law of demand would always hold, but only in some particular circumstances. The ceteris paribus clause hedges the explanation against potential disturbing factors and other adverse contexts.[4] However, neither account garnered wide approval. In that respect, economics is not exceptional, and whether there are laws across the sciences is controversial, physics included (e.g. Cartwright 1983).

Furthermore, there was a second significant problem with laws and the D-N model that concerned the direction of explanation. Using laws, we can derive the value of the explanans (what explains) with the explanandum (what is explained) and the initial conditions. For instance, one can explain the length of a flagpole's shadow by appealing to the flagpole's length, the angle with the sun, and laws about the rectilinear propagation of light. Using that same information, one can also derive the length of the flagpole. But the shadow's length does not *explain* the flagpole's length (Bromberger 1966). Explanations are asymmetric: the explanans explain the explanandum, but the reverse is not true. This suggests that a different notion than laws should be at the center of our accounts of explanation. Causes have that asymmetric feature. A cause brings about its effect; the effect does not bring about its cause. So, the natural step was to develop an account of explanation based on causes (Salmon 1984, 1998; Strevens 2008; Woodward 2003).

As Hausman (2009) observes, economic methodologists have followed this trend, and the interest in laws has waned over the years. Nowadays, most discussions revolve around the neighboring notion of causation. If one favors the D-N model of explanation, then one has to find laws in economics. Similarly, if one prefers the causal account, then one has to show that economics explains by citing the causes of phenomena. Discussions about causal inference in economics are concomitant with developments concerning the nature of scientific explanation. The current dominant view is that economics aims to provide (broadly construed) causal explanations (e.g. Cartwright 2007; Hausman 2009; Hoover 2001a). While it is beyond the scope of this chapter to give a complete overview of the issues surrounding causal inference in economics (for a more detailed discussion, see Clarke, Chapter 21, and Henschen, Chapter 20), two noteworthy questions that originate from this literature are the following:

1. Should we privilege a particular account of causation?
2. Are causes necessary for explanation, or only sufficient?

We may agree that economics should provide causal explanations but disagree on what form these explanations should take. Causal explanations can appeal, for instance, to mechanisms (e.g. Hedström and Ylikoski 2010; S. L. Morgan and Winship 2014) or causal laws (e.g. Hausman 1992; Henschen 2015). And sometimes these concepts are themselves ambiguous. For example, mechanisms can be used to refer to a simple causal relation, a mediating variable, or an underlying structure (Reiss 2013a, 104ff.). So basically, the question is whether there is a single best notion of causality that economics should follow for the purpose of explanation, or whether pluralism is to be favored (e.g. Maziarz and Mróz 2019; Reiss 2009).

The other question is whether citing causes is necessary for explanation in economics. Because causal explanation was the dominant account of explanation for several decades, the necessity of *causal* explanation became the de facto position (Reutlinger 2017). Following the recent interest in noncausal explanation in the sciences (e.g. Lange 2017; Reutlinger and Saatsi 2018), some have examined the possibility that economics provides mathematical explanations (Hardt 2017; Verreault-Julien 2017). Both authors use Lange's (2013) account of distinctively mathematical explanations to study cases in economics. In a nutshell, distinctively mathematical explanations explain by showing how the explanandum is to be expected, but by using generalizations that are modally stronger than ordinary causal ones. Hardt is skeptical about their prevalence in economics. Looking at a particular case, Verreault-Julien (2017) argues that the Arrow and Debreu (1954) model of general equilibrium provided a "how-possibly" explanation (see Section 3). But either way, so far no one has posited that there are cases of *how-actually* mathematical explanation in economics.

There is also a long tradition that investigates whether rational choice theory, broadly construed, is explanatory (e.g. Davidson 1963; Fumagalli 2020; Satz and Ferejohn 1994; Vredenburgh 2020). Economics invokes *preferences* to explain people's choices (Vredenburgh, Chapter 5). If I chose to play tennis, it is because I had a preference, all things considered, for tennis over the alternatives (e.g. miniature golf). Explanation with preferences has a lot of intuitive appeal because it seems very similar to folk psychological explanations of action (Rosenberg 2015, ch. 3). We see people acting a certain way and infer their beliefs and desires. These beliefs and desires thus explain their actions.

One interesting feature of rational choice explanations is that it is unclear whether they are a bona fide type of explanation or just a subspecies of ordinary causal explanations. Indeed, one can view reasons for actions as causes (Davidson 1963). If my preference for bananas is responsible for my buying them, my preference *caused* it. However, some interpretations of revealed preference theory do not appear to be amenable to causal explanation (Fumagalli 2020; Hands 2013b; Vredenburgh 2020). For instance, Binmore holds that the use of revealed preference theory implies giving up "any pretension to be offering a causal explanation" of people's behavior (Binmore 2009: 20). If the theory is only a systematic description of choice behavior and *does not* postulate the existence of beliefs or desires, it would indeed seem odd to say that someone's choices would cause their choices.

Whether or not preferences should be understood solely in behavioral terms is controversial (e.g. Angner 2018; Bradley 2017; Clarke 2016; Dietrich and List 2016; Hausman 2012; Guala 2019; Vredenburgh, Chapter 5; Thoma forthcoming). For one, Hausman (2012, 36ff.) maintains that rational choice theory must make additional commitments if it is to do any explanatory work. According to him, choices depend on preferences over objects, beliefs about their availability, and constraints.[5] So, if I have a preference for bananas over cantaloupe, I will only buy cantaloupe if I believe that bananas are unavailable and that cantaloupe is available, and if cantaloupe is in fact available. And if the cantaloupe is available, but I do not believe it is, I may not even bother to go to the market. Thus, I will not choose to get cantaloupe. Guala (2019), for instance, rejects a strictly mentalist interpretation and instead favors a dispositional view of preferences, according to which they have a multiply realizable causal basis. The same behavior (preferences) within or across people may originate from different causal bases. What standard rational choice theory does when explaining with preferences is simply to bracket the causal basis, not necessarily to reject that there is one.

Another proposal that downplays the role of causation in explanation is that economics explains via *unification*. The main idea is that science explains by subsuming phenomena under a small set of explanatory principles. Unification has a controversial status in the general philosophy of science (Michael Friedman 1974; Kitcher 1981; Schurz 1999; cf. Gijsbers 2007; Roche and Sober 2017; Weber and Van Dyck 2002). One perennial difficulty has been to provide acceptable criteria for genuine explanatory unification. It is always possible to come up with a theory that unifies everything in the sense of being able to derive phenomena with it. But that theory would not necessarily capture actual, "real," patterns. In the context of economics, Mäki (2001) claims that proper explanatory unification should be *ontological* and not merely *derivational*. It should show the ontological unity behind phenomena and not merely provide a common formal framework. One colorful way of conveying a similar concern comes from Reiss, who says that attributing unifying power to economic theory "is therefore like saying to express economic ideas in Italian is unifying" (2012b: 59). Nonetheless, there are some recent defenses of unificationism in economics. Vredenburgh (2020) argues that if revealed preference theory explains, then unificationism is a sound interpretation of the reasons why. However, according to her, whether it actually unifies is still an open question. Fumagalli (2020) defends that stronger position and claims that "thin" rational choice theory unifies by identifying stringent constraints that accurately describe choice patterns without making any assumptions on the underlying neural or psychological substrates.

As the previous discussion should make clear, there is not one single agreed upon interpretation of how economics explains – or *should* explain. Although the causal account of explanation is the current dominant explanatory strategy, there have been various attempts (e.g. via preferences or unification) to spell out the explanatory power of economics differently.

3. Idealizations and Model-Based Explanation

Another area where explanation is lurking concerns the status of highly idealized models. Ever since Friedman's (1953) controversial essay, "unrealistic assumptions" in economics has been a major and continuous source of controversy. Contemporary discussions about unrealistic assumptions have switched to discussions about modeling and idealizations (Chao, Chapter 13; Jhun, Chapter 23). There are two reasons for this. First, although economics is arguably more empirical than it was (Einav and Levin 2014; Hamermesh 2013) a couple of decades ago, theoretical models are ubiquitous in economics to the point that, "training in economics consists essentially of learning a sequence of models" (Rodrik 2015: 10). To understand explanation in economics, one thus had better look at models. Second, many regard "idealization" to be a more precise and less metaphysically charged label for "unrealistic assumptions." Methodologists have been interested in how models systematically and deeply abstract, simplify, or distort – idealize – explananda and explanantia. In other words, models *mis*represent in various ways the very things that they are supposed to explain and be explained. This is problematic insofar as prevalent accounts of explanation hold that explanation is *factive*.[6] This means that successful explanations need to identify (approximately) true actual explanantia and explananda. For instance, if I want to explain why unemployment increased in Canada in 2020 and I cite positive growth as the cause, I am not providing a correct explanation because growth was, as a matter of fact, negative. Similarly, models that contain idealizations misrepresent reality and appear to run contrary to the demand for factive explanations.

Reiss's (2012b, 2013b) discussion of the "explanation paradox" shows well that apparent debates about highly idealized models are, in fact, debates about whether said models satisfy the factivity requirement. Slightly reformulated, the paradox is as follows:

1. Models are highly idealized; they misrepresent reality.
2. Explanations are factive.
3. Models explain phenomena.

Reiss maintains that we have good reasons to believe in the truth of these statements, taken individually. Jointly, however, they are contradictory. If models do not satisfy the factivity requirement, how could they explain? Regardless of one's views on the paradox's genuineness, his analysis reveals how the literature has been addressing this problem from different angles. In response to the first statement, some hold that despite their idealizations, this does not entail that models misrepresent (e.g. Cartwright 1989, 1998, 2007; Hausman 1992; Mäki 1992, 2009a, 2011; Rol 2013). They may represent faithfully the explanatory factors and, therefore, the factivity of explanation is safeguarded. Others reject the factivity requirement. Faithful representation is not necessary; subjective judgments of similarity may be sufficient for models to explain (Sugden 2013, see also 2009, 2011b).[7] Finally, others qualify the third statement and argue that, despite intuitions to the contrary, models do not actually explain. The more pessimistic say that the explanations that models provide are illusory and that economists are simply mistaken about their model's explanatoriness (Alexandrova 2008; Alexandrova and Northcott 2013; Northcott and Alexandrova 2015). The more optimistic say that they have a different purpose, for example, to provide how-possibly explanations (Aydinonat 2007; Grüne-Yanoff 2013b; Grüne-Yanoff and Verreault-Julien 2021; Kuorikoski and Ylikoski 2015; Verreault-Julien 2017; Ylikoski and Aydinonat 2014). These how-possibly explanations may fulfill epistemic purposes, such as prompting learning or improving our understanding, but they fall short of actually explaining phenomena.

All these strands of the literature try, in their own way, to deal with the factivity of explanation. If explanation were not factive, idealizations would not pose a particular problem and we would be more willing to accept economists' explanations. As of now, the jury is still out and no position has achieved full consensus. Hence, in that sense, Reiss's explanation paradox remains unsolved. This should not be totally surprising insofar as similar discussions are taking place in other sciences, for instance, physics or biology (e.g. Bokulich 2011; Jebeile and Kennedy 2015; Knuuttila and Loettgers 2017; Morrison 2015; Rohwer and Rice 2013). Economics is not exceptional. This also suggests that answers about model-based explanation in economics may be found in the general philosophy of science literature or in the philosophy of other sciences (Hands 2019).

That said, it is worth expanding on the third resolution to the puzzle, namely, to reject that models explain. Unfortunately, there is often ambiguity about the use of the term "explanatory" (cf. Marchionni 2017). Is it a success term, that is, meaning that explanatory models *actually* explain? Is it a term that refers to the explanatory *potential* of models, namely, that they could actually explain if some conditions were met? Or is it just a functional term connoting that models may be *used* for explanation in some unspecified sense? To compound the difficulty, within the same usage there may be ambiguity concerning the conditions for explanatory success. For example, Sugden (2013) claims that economic models actually explain, but his conditions for explanatory success are also less demanding. Methodologists thus run the risk of talking past each other when examining whether economic models are explanatory.

That said, one assumption shared by many participants in the general debate is that models afford understanding only insofar as they provide how-actually explanations (HAEs) of phenomena (see Marchionni 2017; Verreault-Julien 2019b). HAEs have true (vs false) and actual (vs possible) explanantia and explananda. This assumption seems to impose the following dilemma: either models explain (in the how-actually sense) and they are epistemically valuable because of the understanding that they afford, or they do not explain and thus have at best limited epistemic value. As we have seen, to reconcile the highly idealized nature of economic models and the factivity of explanation has proven to be difficult. Yet, methodologists are also typically reluctant to deny any form of epistemic value to theoretical modeling. They are between a rock and a hard place.

One way methodologists have sought to get out of this dilemma is by questioning the source and nature of the epistemic benefits science affords. That explanations afford understanding is uncontroversial (e.g. Michael Friedman 1974). When we grasp an explanation of a given phenomenon, we *understand why* that phenomenon occurred. This raises two questions. First, can we have understanding *without* explanation? Perhaps what matters is the epistemic benefit we obtain, not necessarily *how* we obtain it (Lipton 2009). Second, is understanding the only epistemic benefit models can afford? Even if we grant that models do not explain, and thus do not afford understanding, they may not be epistemically idle. We may get something else from them. In both cases, this would allow sidestepping the demand for factive explanations.

Let us first look at the second question: is understanding the only epistemic (i.e. not merely heuristic) benefit models may provide? Some have claimed that models help us *learn* about the world (e.g. Claveau and Vergara Fernández 2015; Grüne-Yanoff 2009; M.S. Morgan 1999). For instance, Grüne-Yanoff (2009) argues that models may prompt learning by changing our confidence about impossibility claims about the world.[8] Whether learning is a categorically different epistemic benefit than understanding is an open question. Claveau and Vergara Fernández (2015) have provided the most substantial characterization of learning, but its cashing out in epistemological terms makes it susceptible to subsumption under the more widely discussed and accepted notions of knowledge and understanding (see, e.g., Khalifa 2017). At any rate, learning as a distinct epistemological category has not yet gathered a lot of traction.

This brings us back to first question: is it possible to have understanding without explanation (see Lipton 2009)? This is what the discussion on how-possibly explanations (HPEs) aims to demonstrate. HPEs provide information about *possible* explanations of phenomena (Verreault-Julien 2019a).[9] For instance, one may say that globalization possibly explains rising inequality in the United States (Aydinonat 2018; Rodrik 2015); it is an HPE of the phenomenon. Many economic models appear to provide HPEs. Paradigmatic examples discussed in the literature are Akerlof's (1970) market for lemons or the checkerboard model (Schelling 1971, 1978). These models do not seem to provide HAEs of real-world phenomena (cf. Sugden 2000, 2013), yet they give reasons to believe that they are possible explanations worthy of consideration. Crucially, the possible explanations also appear to provide epistemic benefits; economists build them because they believe the explanations will help them understand phenomena of interest.[10] Methodologists (e.g. Aydinonat 2007; Grüne-Yanoff 2013b, 2013a; Kuorikoski and Ylikoski 2015; Verreault-Julien 2017; Ylikoski and Aydinonat 2014) have thus tried to show that HPEs are not mere "just so stories" but that they are epistemically valuable. For example, Ylikoski and Aydinonat argue that theoretical models like the checkerboard model provide understanding because they allow us to answer counterfactual "what-if-things-had-been-different" questions. What matters to understanding, they claim, is the modal information models provide, not whether they actually explain (see also Kuorikoski and Ylikoski 2015; Verreault-Julien 2019b). Hence, if economic models provide HPEs, then this may show how we can have understanding with them even when they do not explain qua HAEs.

The view that economic models offer HPEs has some advantages. It explains why models *appear* to provide explanations, and by showing that it is not epistemically vacuous, it also explains why economists would engage in that practice. However, more work needs to be done to specify under what conditions HPEs are successful and epistemically valuable (Grüne-Yanoff and Verreault-Julien 2021). Moreover, it still denies that many models actually explain, a conclusion at odds with what some practicing economists believe (e.g. Sugden 2000, 2009, 2011a, 2013). Of course, relaxation of the factivity requirement would make explanations more common. But in the philosophy of science, factivity is well entrenched and largely accepted. If we consider that philosophers overwhelmingly espouse scientific realism (Bourget and Chalmers 2014), it is perhaps unsurprising that most of them have not targeted factivity itself.[11] Reiss (2013b, see also 2012a) suggested that an instrumentalist account of explanation might do the trick, but he also granted that economics' predictive and policy successes are dim. In any case, there is no evident alternative in sight.

4. Levels of Explanation

What is economics a science *of*? What phenomena does economics purport to explain? For classical economics, it was the study of the production, consumption, and distribution of national wealth. Following the development of marginalism, it became more individualistic. Robbins's (1935) definition of economics as a study of the optimizing behavior of individuals came to dominate and shape the discipline in profound ways, notably its axiomatization (Backhouse and Medema 2009a, 2009c). However, it appears that economics is not only concerned with human behavior in a strict sense.

> Economics is also studied on various levels. We can study the decisions of individual households and firms. Or we can study the interaction of households and firms in markets for specific goods and services. Or we can study the operation of the economy as a whole, which is the sum of the activities of all these decision makers in all these markets.
>
> (Mankiw 2018: 26–27)

Economics is traditionally divided into two branches, microeconomics and macroeconomics, which investigate these different levels.[12] Microeconomics examines how individuals, households, and firms make economic decisions and interact in the market. Macroeconomics studies economies as a whole and aggregate phenomena such as business cycles, growth, or inflation.

At first glance, micro and macro are two relatively independent fields. They study different objects and, presumably, their methods accordingly differ. In fact, as Hoover (2010, 2015) observes, economists widely hold that macroeconomics needs *microfoundations*. This view maintains that macroeconomics, and thus macroeconomic phenomena, can and should be reduced to microeconomics. The microfoundations program entails that all phenomena, be they micro or macro, ultimately need to be explained in terms of the economic (optimizing) behavior of individual agents.

So, what the microfoundations program does is to deny that there are two (or more) independent levels of explanation. Everything we say about aggregates such as employment, growth, or inflation can and should be reduced to individual action. The position has an ontological and a methodological dimension. Ontologically, it is true that, for example, employment "depends on" the existence of individuals (Hoover 2010). There would be no rate of unemployment without people seeking work. Methodologically, the argument is that if macroeconomic phenomena depend on intentional action, which in a sense they at least partially do, then the only proper level of explanation is at that level. Social explanations should thus provide an account of how the individual level brings about the social level. In a nutshell, because only individuals exist, explanations cannot and *should not* dispense citing them.

The call for microfoundations is thus a form of methodological individualism (Zahle and Kincaid 2019): the general view that explanations of social phenomena should be in terms of individuals.[13] There are several issues with this position. Hoover (2015; see also Kirman 1992) argues that the standard implementation of microfoundations in terms of a representative agent is deeply flawed. Because economists obviously do not – and cannot – know the preferences of every single agent in the economy, they instead posit a single – "representative" – agent that faces economy-wide constraints and decisions. But if it is not possible, even in principle, to implement the microfoundations program, why should we hold on to it? A more principled way of denying the need for microfoundations is to say that holistic explanations, namely, explanations in terms of social structures or aggregates, may sometimes be adequate, if not preferable. For instance, Hoover (e.g. 2001b) argues that there is causal autonomy at the macroeconomic level. In fact, the causal relations we find at the macro level may be more invariant than those at the micro level. Because people's choices will heavily depend on contextual factors, we may only find invariant relationships above the individual level. Stable macro relationships do not depend on the particular makeup of individuals.

But even if we agree with the spirit of the microfoundations program and the Robbins definition, its standard implementation has faced different challenges. First, is economics really only about *individual* choice behavior? Second, even if this is so, what is the best way to explain it? These methodological questions are fundamentally questions about the explanatory targets and strategies of economics. Crucially, this suggests that the "levels of explanation" issue Mankiw's earlier quote pointed out is, in fact, twofold: at what level(s) can economics' explanantia *and* explananda be located?

One way of explaining people's economic choices is to cite their preferences. But within the standard approach, preferences are only summaries of choices that satisfy rationality assumptions. Rationality thus comes to be a foundational explanatory principle (e.g. Herfeld 2021; Lagueux 2010). Importantly, the standard approach does not require any psychological assumptions. But what if people, as a matter of fact, violate the rationality assumptions? In a nutshell, what if people are not rational? There is a substantial body of evidence indicating that people fail to act on their alleged preferences or choose inconsistently (Thaler 2016; Lecouteux, Chapter 4). If economics' goal is not only to predict but also to explain economic decision-making qua human behavior, this suggests it should do so by faithfully identifying on what it depends.

This is precisely what some strands of behavioral economics aim to do by providing "psychologically plausible foundations" (Angner 2019: 5). In that sense, it pushes even further the need for microfoundations: why stop at people's choices and not go deeper down to the personal and subpersonal levels? Economics should not be mindless, but mind*ful* (Camerer 2008). That research at the interface between economics, psychology, and cognitive science aims to explain the same explananda, namely, people's choices, but departs from the standard approach by proposing to locate economic explanantia at a different level. Among behavioral economics, some hold that psychological mechanisms such as heuristics and biases (e.g. Kahneman 2011) should play a prominent role in explaining choices, while others (e.g. Camerer, Loewenstein, and Prelec 2005) suggest opening the black box of the brain and embracing neuroscience. This is often cashed out in terms of *mechanisms* (Craver and Alexandrova 2008). Mechanisms may tell us the underlying causes of a given phenomenon. Consequently, the goal should be to determine the psychological and neurological mechanisms responsible for people's choices.

Some economists and methodologists have been skeptical of the current or potential value of deeper, psychologically plausible foundations. From economics, one notable dismissal of neuroeconomics, in particular, and psychology, more generally, is due to Gul and Pesendorfer (2008). According to them, the questions economics and psychology purport to answer are different and thus require different types of evidence. What standard economics does – and should do – is to describe these choices in a way that allows for extrapolation.[14] Typically, this involves representing choice behavior as maximizing utility under constraints. Crucially, this does not require making any substantial assumptions about people's psychological or physiological makeup. As a result, the argument goes, for the purpose of describing choices, psychological evidence is irrelevant to economics; only choice behavior is relevant. In the more methodological camp, Fumagalli (2011, 2014, 2017) also challenges the explanatory relevance of neuroscience for economics. In particular, he points out that the use of neural findings may also come at a cost because neuroscientists and economists often have different modeling goals. Thus, these findings may not always be relevant for explaining the phenomena in which economists are typically interested in, namely, choice behavior.

Another way of resisting the behavioral critique is to deny that economics primarily aims to explain *individual* choice. Rather, the proper explananda of economics are the patterns of social interaction that markets mediate. For instance, Ross (2014), one recent proponent of that view, maintains that most economic choice happens at a "supra-individual" scale and that informational differences within markets are central to economics.[15] If economics is indeed about market-level phenomena and not individual decision-making, then this prima facie suggests that knowledge of what influences particular agents to choose *X* over *Y* may not be relevant for our understanding of socially aggregated choices. In fact, Herfeld (2018) argues, demands for more psychological realism and methodological individualism may simply be misplaced. But even if we accept that the explananda of economics are not individual choices, this does not necessarily imply that psychological or neural findings cannot be relevant. Indeed, some have submitted that choice need not be solely located in the brain and that those findings may inform the features of choice that are external to agents (Herrmann-Pillath 2012; Ross 2011; Petracca 2020).

The "level of explanation" problem thus raises two main sets of questions. First, at what level should the explanans be? Are good explanations those that cite underlying mechanisms, or are behavioral generalizations sufficient? Advocates of neuroeconomics are those who – for now – go the deepest; traditional methodological individualists aim for the meso level (namely, an intermediate level(s) between the micro and macro); and macroeconomics sometimes locates the explanans at the level of aggregate variables. Second, what is the appropriate level of the explanandum? Should economics aim to explain individual decision-making, the interactions between individuals, or market-level phenomena? It is important to note that the combination of these two issues may lead to very different explanatory strategies. Behavioral economists commonly aim to explain individual decision-making (explanandum) and hold that, to do so, we need to identify the underlying mechanisms (explanans). Neoclassical economists usually reject the need for underlying mechanisms (explanans), but whether it is only about market phenomena or individual choices (explanandum) is debatable. And it is possible to blend these strategies. For instance, nothing a priori prevents the use of neural findings to explain social-level phenomena (see Harbecke and Herrmann-Pillath 2020).

5. Conclusions

Backhouse and Medema (2009b: 231) say that, "adhering to a specific definition [of economics] may constrain the problems that economists believe it is legitimate to tackle and the methods by which they choose to tackle them." Debates about explanation in economics are debates about the aims of economics and the value of its achievements. Should it explain or not? Can economics be epistemically valuable even if it falls short of explaining the actual world? To Backhouse and Medema's point, we could add that the adoption of a specific account of explanation may also constrain what economics ends up being about. What are the explananda of economics? Is it a science of market-level phenomena, or should it foray into individual decision-making? And what are its explanantia? Does economics need to ground its explanations on neuroscience, or can it explain by merely citing macroeconomic variables? Does it need to find laws, or are causal generalizations sufficient? Should explanations in economics fulfill the factivity requirement?

As is perhaps clear by now, there is no widespread agreement on answers to these questions. But they also raise interesting issues of division of labor. Who should set the explanatory criteria, practicing economists or philosophers? And among the philosophers, should they look up to the general philosophy of science, or is there really a distinct, separate way of explaining in economics? And should we trust economists when they claim the conditions have been satisfied? Naturalistically inclined philosophers would not want to attribute systematic illusory understanding to the discipline, but economists or philosophers qua methodologists should also not shy away from criticizing when criticism is due (Hausman 2009).

Generalizing Marchionni's (2017) claim about model-based explanation in economics, we could say that the two key problems of explanation in economics simpliciter are the following:

1. What are the conditions for successful explanation?
2. Have these conditions been met?

Even if they may be more salient in the context of models, these problems cut across methodological issues in economics. And my contention is that an examination of these issues through the prism of explanation may help us progress on the route to solving them.

Acknowledgments

I would like to thank Roberto Fumagalli, James Grayot, Ina Jäntgen, Julian Reiss, and all of the amazing people in the Protective Belt seminar at the London School of Economics for helpful suggestions, critiques, and feedback on previous versions of the chapter. I acknowledge support from the *Fonds de recherche du Québec – Société et culture* (FRQSC).

Related Chapters

Chao, H., Chapter 13 "Representation"
Clarke, C., Chapter 21 "Causal Contributions in Economics"
Henschen, T., Chapter 20 "Causality and Probability"
Jhun, J., Chapter 23 "Modeling the Possible to Modeling the Actual"
Lecouteux, G., Chapter 4 "Behavioral Welfare Economics and Consumer Sovereignty"
Vredenburgh, K., Chapter 5 "The Economic Concept of a Preference"

Notes

1 For dissenting – realist – interpretations of Friedman, see Hoover (2009) and Mäki (2009b).
2 Notably, Milton Friedman (1953) uses "explain" throughout the paper in scare quotes.
3 Reiss (2012a) holds that one can be an instrumentalist and still aim for explanations if explanations do not require truth. See Section 3.
4 However, Reiss (2013a) argued that *ceteris paribus* rather means "when other factors are absent" or "other things being right."
5 Hausman also notes that these factors can sometimes have an influence on one another. So, this is a simplified picture of the standard model.
6 Notable exceptions are Achinstein (1983) and Cartwright (1983).
7 For discussions outside of economics, see, for example, Bokulich (2011, 2012).
8 Fumagalli (2015, 2016) rejects that minimal models in the sense of Grüne-Yanoff (2009) may prompt learning.
9 Here, "possible" should be understood broadly. Some HPEs may have *im*possible explanantia or explananda. There are various accounts of HPEs (e.g. Bokulich 2014; Dray 1957; Forber 2010; Hempel 1965; Resnik 1991), but one common thread is that HPEs are different from HAEs. HPEs are also sometimes called "potential explanations" (e.g. Hempel 1965).
10 Sometimes, they do not even aim to explain actual phenomena (Sugden 2011a). This also does not assume that *all* HPEs are built with epistemic goals in mind. Naturally, sociological factors may also be at play. It simply assumes that many of these paradigmatic cases are epistemically driven.

11 Whether *understanding* is factive is the subject of a lively debate (e.g. Doyle et al. 2019; Elgin 2007; Frigg and Nguyen 2021; Khalifa 2020; Lawler 2021; Rice 2021; De Regt 2017).
12 See Ylikoski (2014) for the potentially misleading use of "levels." See Fumagalli (2011, 2017) for a discussion of levels in the context of neuroeconomic modeling.
13 As Hodgson (2007) argues, it is often a rather vague methodological prescription. See Zahle and Collin (2014) and Ylikoski (2017) for recent discussions.
14 Whether we should read Gul and Pesendorfer (2008) along instrumentalist lines is open to interpretation (Hands 2013a).
15 See, for example, Hayek (1955, 1967) for early defenses of similar positions.

Bibliography

Achinstein, P. (1983) *The Nature of Explanation*, New York: Oxford University Press.

Akerlof, G.A. (1970) "The Market for 'Lemons': Quality Uncertainty and the Market Mechanism," *Quarterly Journal of Economics* 84(3): 488–500.

Alexandrova, A. (2008) "Making Models Count," *Philosophy of Science* 75(3): 383–404.

Alexandrova, A., and Northcott, R. (2013) "It's Just a Feeling: Why Economic Models Do Not Explain," *Journal of Economic Methodology* 20(3): 262–267. https://doi.org/10.1080/1350178X.2013.828873.

Angner, E. (2018) "What Preferences Really Are," *Philosophy of Science* 85(4): 660–681. https://doi.org/10.1086/699193.

Angner, E. (2019) "We're All Behavioral Economists Now," *Journal of Economic Methodology* 26(3): 195–207.

Arrow, K.J., and Debreu, G. (1954) "Existence of an Equilibrium for a Competitive Economy," *Econometrica* 22(3): 265–290.

Aydinonat, N.E. (2007) "Models, Conjectures and Exploration: An Analysis of Schelling's Checkerboard Model of Residential Segregation," *Journal of Economic Methodology* 14(4): 429–454.

Aydinonat, N.E. (2018) "The Diversity of Models as a Means to Better Explanations in Economics," *Journal of Economic Methodology* 25(3): 237–251. https://doi.org/10.1080/1350178X.2018.1488478.

Backhouse, R.E., and Medema, S.G. (2009a) "Defining Economics: The Long Road to Acceptance of the Robbins Definition," *Economica* 76: 805–820. https://doi.org/10.1111/j.1468-0335.2009.00789.x.

Backhouse, R.E., and Medema, S.G. (2009b) "Retrospectives: On the Definition of Economics," *The Journal of Economic Perspectives* 23(1): 221–234.

Backhouse, R.E., and Medema, S.G. (2009c) "Robbins's Essay and the Axiomatization of Economics," *Journal of the History of Economic Thought* 31(4): 485–499. https://doi.org/10.1017/S1053837209990277.

Banerjee, A.V., and Duflo, E. (2005) "Growth Theory Through the Lens of Development Economics," in P. Aghion and S.N. Durlauf (eds.) *Handbook of Economic Growth*, Vol. 1A: 473–552. Amsterdam: Elsevier. https://doi.org/10.1016/S1574-0684(05)01007-5.

Binmore, K. (2009) *Rational Decisions*, Princeton: Princeton University Press.

Blaug, M. (1992) *The Methodology of Economics: Or How Economists Explain*, 2nd ed., Cambridge: Cambridge University Press.

Bokulich, A. (2011) "How Scientific Models Can Explain," *Synthese* 180(1): 33–45.

Bokulich, A. (2012) "Distinguishing Explanatory from Nonexplanatory Fictions," *Philosophy of Science* 79(5): 725–737. https://doi.org/10.1086/667991.

Bokulich, A. (2014) "How the Tiger Bush Got Its Stripes: 'How Possibly' vs. 'How Actually' Model Explanations," *The Monist* 97(3): 321–338. https://doi.org/10.5840/monist201497321.

Boland, L.A. (1979) "A Critique of Friedman's Critics," *Journal of Economic Literature* 17(2): 503–522.

Bourget, D., and Chalmers, D.J. (2014) "What Do Philosophers Believe?" *Philosophical Studies* 170(3): 465–500. https://doi.org/10.1007/s11098-013-0259-7.

Bradley, R. (2017) *Decision Theory with a Human Face*, Cambridge: Cambridge University Press.

Bromberger, S. (1966) "Why-Questions," in R.G. Colodny (ed.) *Mind and Cosmos: Essays in Contemporary Science and Philosophy*: 86–111. Pittsburgh: Pittsburgh University Press.

Caldwell, B.J. (1994) *Beyond Positivism: Economic Methodology in the Twentieth Century*, revised ed., London: Routledge.

Camerer, C. (2008) "The Case for Mindful Economics," in A. Caplin and A. Schotter (eds.) *The Foundations of Positive and Normative Economics*: 43–69. Oxford: Oxford University Press.

Camerer, C., Loewenstein, G., and Prelec, D. (2005) "Neuroeconomics: How Neuroscience Can Inform Economics," *Journal of Economic Literature* 43(1): 9–64.

Cartwright, N. (1983) *How the Laws of Physics Lie*, Oxford: Oxford University Press.
Cartwright, N. (1989) *Nature's Capacities and Their Measurement*, Oxford: Oxford University Press.
Cartwright, N. (1995) "'Ceteris Paribus' Laws and Socio-Economic Machines," *The Monist* 78(3): 276–294.
Cartwright, N. (1998) "Capacities," in D.W. Hands, J.B. Davis and U. Mäki (eds.) *The Handbook of Economic Methodology*: 45–48. Cheltenham, UK; Northampton, MA: Edward Elgar.
Cartwright, N. (2007) *Hunting Causes and Using Them: Approaches in Philosophy and Economics*, Cambridge: Cambridge University Press.
Chetty, R., Hendren, N., Lin, F., Majerovitz, J., and Scuderi, B. (2016) "Childhood Environment and Gender Gaps in Adulthood," *American Economic Review* 106(5): 282–288. https://doi.org/10.1257/aer.p20161073.
Clarke, C. (2016) "Preferences and Positivist Methodology in Economics," *Philosophy of Science* 83(2): 192–212. https://doi.org/10.1086/684958.
Claveau, F., and Vergara Fernández, M. (2015) "Epistemic Contributions of Models: Conditions for Propositional Learning," *Perspectives on Science* 23(4): 405–423. https://doi.org/10.1162/POSC_a_00181.
Craver, C.F., and Alexandrova, A. (2008) "No Revolution Necessary: Neural Mechanisms for Economics," *Economics and Philosophy* 24(Special Issue 03): 381–406. https://doi.org/10.1017/S0266267108002034.
Davidson, D. (1963) "Actions, Reasons, and Causes," *The Journal of Philosophy* 60(23): 685–700. https://doi.org/10.2307/2023177.
De Regt, H.W. (2017) *Understanding Scientific Understanding*, New York: Oxford University Press.
Dietrich, F., and List, C. (2016) "Mentalism Versus Behaviourism in Economics: A Philosophy-of-Science Perspective," *Economics & Philosophy* 32(2): 249–281. https://doi.org/10.1017/S0266267115000462.
Doyle, Y., Egan, S., Graham, N., and Khalifa, K. (2019) "Non-Factive Understanding: A Statement and Defense," *Journal for General Philosophy of Science*, 50: 345-365. https://doi.org/10.1007/s10838-019-09469-3.
Dray, W.H. (1957) *Laws and Explanation in History*, Oxford: Clarendon Press.
Einav, L., and Levin, J. (2014) "Economics in the Age of Big Data," *Science* 346 (6210). https://doi.org/10.1126/science.1243089.
Elgin, C.Z. (2007) "Understanding and the Facts," *Philosophical Studies* 132(1): 33–42.
Forber, P. (2010) "Confirmation and Explaining How Possible," *Studies in History and Philosophy of Science Part C: Studies in History and Philosophy of Biological and Biomedical Sciences* 41(1): 32–40. https://doi.org/10.1016/j.shpsc.2009.12.006.
Friedman, Michael. (1974) "Explanation and Scientific Understanding," *Journal of Philosophy* 71(1): 5–19.
Friedman, Milton. (1953) "The Methodology of Positive Economics," in *Essays in Positive Economics*: 3–43. Chicago: University of Chicago Press.
Frigg, R., and Nguyen, J. (2021) "Mirrors Without Warnings," *Synthese* 198: 2427–2447. https://doi.org/10.1007/s11229-019-02222-9.
Fumagalli, R. (2011) "On the Neural Enrichment of Economic Models: Tractability, Trade-Offs and Multiple Levels of Description," *Biology & Philosophy* 26(5): 617–635. https://doi.org/10.1007/s10539-011-9272-4.
Fumagalli, R. (2014) "Neural Findings and Economic Models: Why Brains Have Limited Relevance for Economics," *Philosophy of the Social Sciences* 44(5): 606–629. https://doi.org/10.1177/0048393114530948.
Fumagalli, R. (2015) "No Learning from Minimal Models," *Philosophy of Science* 82(5): 798–809. https://doi.org/10.1086/683281.
Fumagalli, R. (2016) "Why We Cannot Learn from Minimal Models," *Erkenntnis* 81(3): 433–455. https://doi.org/10.1007/s10670-015-9749-7.
Fumagalli, R. (2017) "On the Neural Enrichment of Economic Models: Recasting the Challenge," *Biology & Philosophy* 32(2): 201–220. https://doi.org/10.1007/s10539-016-9546-y.
Fumagalli, R. (2020) "How Thin Rational Choice Theory Explains Choices," *Studies in History and Philosophy of Science Part A* 83: 63–74. https://doi.org/10.1016/j.shpsa.2020.03.003.
Gijsbers, V. (2007) "Why Unification Is Neither Necessary Nor Sufficient for Explanation," *Philosophy of Science* 74(4): 481–500.
Grüne-Yanoff, T. (2009) "Learning from Minimal Economic Models," *Erkenntnis* 70(1): 81–99.
Grüne-Yanoff, T. (2013a) "Appraising Models Nonrepresentationally," *Philosophy of Science* 80(5): 850–861. https://doi.org/10.1086/673893.
Grüne-Yanoff, T. (2013b) "Genuineness Resolved: A Reply to Reiss' Purported Paradox," *Journal of Economic Methodology* 20(3): 255–261. https://doi.org/10.1080/1350178X.2013.828866.
Grüne-Yanoff, T., and Verreault-Julien, P. (2021) "How-Possibly Explanations in Economics: Anything Goes?" *Journal of Economic Methodology* 28(1): 114–123. https://doi.org/10.1080/1350178X.2020.1868779.
Guala, F. (2019) "Preferences: Neither Behavioural nor Mental," *Economics & Philosophy* 35(3): 383–401. https://doi.org/10.1017/S0266267118000512.

Gul, F., and Pesendorfer, W. (2008) "The Case for Mindless Economics," in A. Caplin and A. Schotter (eds.) *The Foundations of Positive and Normative Economics*: 3–39, Oxford: Oxford University Press.

Hamermesh, D.S. (2013) "Six Decades of Top Economics Publishing: Who and How?" *Journal of Economic Literature* 51(1): 162–172. https://doi.org/10.1257/jel.51.1.162.

Hands, D.W. (2013a) "GP08 Is the New F53: Gul and Pesendorfer's Methodological Essay from the Viewpoint of Blaug's Popperian Methodology," in M. Boumans and M. Klaes (eds.) *Mark Blaug: Rebel with Many Causes*: 245–266, Cheltenham, UK: Edward Elgar.

Hands, D.W. (2013b) "Foundations of Contemporary Revealed Preference Theory," *Erkenntnis* 78(5): 1081–1108. https://doi.org/10.1007/s10670-012-9395-2.

Hands, D.W. (2019) "Economic Methodology in the Twenty-First Century (So Far): Some Post-Reflection Reflections," SSRN Scholarly Paper ID 3464759. Rochester, NY: Social Science Research Network. https://papers.ssrn.com/abstract=3464759.

Harbecke, J., and Herrmann-Pillath, C. (eds.) (2020) *Social Neuroeconomics: Mechanistic Integration of the Neurosciences and the Social Sciences*, Milton Park: Routledge.

Hardt, Ł. (2017) *Economics Without Laws: Towards a New Philosophy of Economics*, Cham: Palgrave Macmillan.

Hausman, D.M. (1981) *Capital, Profits, and Prices: An Essay in the Philosophy of Economics*, New York: Columbia University Press.

Hausman, D.M. (1992) *The Inexact and Separate Science of Economics*, Cambridge: Cambridge University Press.

Hausman, D.M. (1998) "Problems with Realism in Economics," *Economics and Philosophy* 14(02): 185–213.

Hausman, D.M. (2009) "Laws, Causation, and Economic Methodology," in H. Kincaid and D. Ross (eds.) *The Oxford Handbook of Philosophy of Economics*: 35–54. New York: Oxford University Press.

Hausman, D.M. (2012) *Preference, Value, Choice, and Welfare*, Cambridge: Cambridge University Press.

Hayek, F.A. (1955) "Degrees of Explanation," *The British Journal for the Philosophy of Science* 6(23): 209–225. https://doi.org/10.1093/bjps/VI.23.209.

Hayek, F.A. (1967) "The Theory of Complex Phenomena," in *Studies in Philosophy, Politics and Economics*: 22–42. Chicago: University of Chicago Press.

Hedström, P., and Ylikoski, P. (2010) "Causal Mechanisms in the Social Sciences," *Annual Review of Sociology* 36: 49–67.

Hempel, C.G. (1965) "Aspects of Scientific Explanation," in *Aspects of Scientific Explanation: And Other Essays in the Philosophy of Science*: 331–497. New York: Free Press.

Hempel, C.G., and Oppenheim, P. (1948) "Studies in the Logic of Explanation," *Philosophy of Science* 15(2): 135–175.

Henschen, T. (2015) "Ceteris Paribus Conditions and the Interventionist Account of Causality," *Synthese* 192(10): 3297–3311. https://doi.org/10.1007/s11229-015-0703-7.

Herfeld, C. (2018) "Explaining Patterns, Not Details: Reevaluating Rational Choice Models in Light of Their Explananda," *Journal of Economic Methodology* 25(2): 179–209. https://doi.org/10.1080/1350178X.2018.1427882.

Herfeld, C. (2021) "Understanding the Rationality Principle in Economics as a Functional a Priori Principle," *Synthese* 198(14): 3329–3358. https://doi.org/10.1007/s11229-020-02730-z.

Herrmann-Pillath, C. (2012) "Towards an Externalist Neuroeconomics: Dual Selves, Signs, and Choice," *Journal of Neuroscience, Psychology, and Economics* 5(1): 38–61. https://doi.org/10.1037/a0026882.

Hodgson, G.M. (2007) "Meanings of Methodological Individualism," *Journal of Economic Methodology* 14(2): 211–226. https://doi.org/10.1080/13501780701394094.

Hoover, K.D. (2001a) *Causality in Macroeconomics*, Cambridge: Cambridge University Press.

Hoover, K.D. (2001b) *The Methodology of Empirical Macroeconomics*, Cambridge: Cambridge University Press.

Hoover, K.D. (2009) "Milton Friedman's Stance: The Methodology of Causal Realism," in U. Mäki (ed.) *The Methodology of Positive Economics: Reflections on the Milton Friedman Legacy*: 303–320, Cambridge: Cambridge University Press.

Hoover, K.D. (2010) "Idealizing Reduction: The Microfoundations of Macroeconomics," *Erkenntnis* 73(3): 329–347.

Hoover, K.D. (2015) "Reductionism in Economics: Intentionality and Eschatological Justification in the Microfoundations of Macroeconomics," *Philosophy of Science* 82(4): 689–711. https://doi.org/10.1086/682917.

Jebeile, J., and Kennedy, A.G. (2015) "Explaining with Models: The Role of Idealizations," *International Studies in the Philosophy of Science* 29(4): 383–392. https://doi.org/10.1080/02698595.2015.1195143.

Jhun, J.S. (2017) "What's the Point of Ceteris Paribus? Or, How to Understand Supply and Demand Curves," *Philosophy of Science* 85(2): 271–292. https://doi.org/10.1086/696385.

Kahneman, D. (2011) *Thinking, Fast and Slow*, New York: Farrar, Straus and Giroux.

Khalifa, K. (2017) *Understanding, Explanation, and Scientific Knowledge*, Cambridge: Cambridge University Press.

Khalifa, K. (2020) "Understanding, Truth, and Epistemic Goals," *Philosophy of Science* 87(5): 944–956. https://doi.org/10.1086/710545.

Kincaid, H. (1996) *Philosophical Foundations of the Social Sciences: Analyzing Controversies in Social Research*, Cambridge: Cambridge University Press.

Kincaid, H. (2004) "There Are Laws in the Social Sciences," in C. Hitchcock (ed.) *Contemporary Debates in Philosophy of Science*: 168–186, Malden, MA: Blackwell.

Kirman, A.P. (1992) "Whom or What Does the Representative Individual Represent?," *Journal of Economic Perspectives* 6(2): 117–136. https://doi.org/10.1257/jep.6.2.117.

Kitcher, P. (1981) "Explanatory Unification," *Philosophy of Science* 48(4): 507–531.

Knuuttila, T., and Loettgers, A. (2017) "Modelling as Indirect Representation? The Lotka – Volterra Model Revisited," *The British Journal for the Philosophy of Science* 68(4): 1007–1036. https://doi.org/10.1093/bjps/axv055.

Kuorikoski, J., and Ylikoski, P. (2015) "External Representations and Scientific Understanding," *Synthese* 192(12): 3817–3837. http://link.springer.com/article/10.1007/s11229-014-0591-2.

Lagueux, M. (2010) *Rationality and Explanation in Economics*, New York: Routledge.

Lange, M. (2013) "What Makes a Scientific Explanation Distinctively Mathematical?' *The British Journal for the Philosophy of Science* 64(3): 485–511. https://doi.org/10.1093/bjps/axs012.

Lange, M. (2017) *Because Without Cause: Non-Causal Explanations in Science and Mathematics*, New York: Oxford University Press.

Lawler, I. (2021) "Scientific Understanding and Felicitous Legitimate Falsehoods," *Synthese* 198: 6859–6887. https://doi.org/10.1007/s11229-019-02495-0.

Lipton, P. (2009) "Understanding Without Explanation," in H.W. De Regt, S. Leonelli, and K. Eigner (eds.) *Scientific Understanding. Philosophical Perspectives*: 43–63, Pittsburgh: University of Pittsburgh Press.

Mäki, U. (1992) "On the Method of Isolation in Economics," *Poznan Studies in the Philosophy of the Sciences and the Humanities* 26: 19–54.

Mäki, U. (2000) "Reclaiming Relevant Realism," *Journal of Economic Methodology* 7(1): 109–125. https://doi.org/10.1080/135017800362266.

Mäki, U. (2001) "Explanatory Unification Double and Doubtful," *Philosophy of the Social Sciences* 31(4): 488–506. https://doi.org/10.1177/004839310103100402.

Mäki, U. (2009a) "MISSing the World. Models as Isolations and Credible Surrogate Systems," *Erkenntnis* 70(1): 29–43. https://doi.org/10.1007/s10670-008-9135-9.

Mäki, U. (2009b) "Unrealistic Assumptions and Unnecessary Confusions: Rereading and Rewriting F53 as a Realist Statement," in U. Mäki (ed.) *The Methodology of Positive Economics: Reflections on the Milton Friedman Legacy*: 90–116, Cambridge: Cambridge University Press.

Mäki, U. (2011) "Models and the Locus of Their Truth," *Synthese* 180(1): 47–63.

Mäki, U. (2012) "Realism and Antirealism about Economics," in U. Mäki (ed.) *Philosophy of Economics*: 49–87, Oxford: North Holland.

Mankiw, N.G. (2018) *Principles of Economics*, 8th ed. Boston, MA: Cengage Learning.

Marchionni, C. (2017) "What Is the Problem with Model-Based Explanation in Economics?' *Disputatio* 9(47): 603–630. https://doi.org/10.1515/disp-2017-0020.

Maziarz, M., and Mróz, R. (2019) "Response to Henschen: Causal Pluralism in Macroeconomics," *Journal of Economic Methodology* 27(2): 164–178. https://doi.org/10.1080/1350178X.2019.1675897.

Mcintyre, L.C. (1998) *Laws And Explanation In The Social Sciences: Defending a Science of Human Behavior*, Boulder, CO: Westview Press.

Mill, J.S. (1843) *A System of Logic*, London: John W. Parker, West Strand.

Morgan, M.S. (1999) "Learning from Models," in M. Morrison and M.S. Morgan (eds.) *Models as Mediators: Perspectives on Natural and Social Science*: 347–388, Cambridge: Cambridge University Press.

Morgan, S.L., and Winship, C. (2014) *Counterfactuals and Causal Inference: Methods and Principles for Social Research*, 2nd ed., New York: Cambridge University Press.

Morrison, M. (2015) *Reconstructing Reality: Models, Mathematics, and Simulations*, Oxford: Oxford University Press.

Northcott, R., and Alexandrova, A. (2015) "Prisoner's Dilemma Doesn't Explain Much," in M. Peterson (ed.) *The Prisoner's Dilemma*: 64–84, Cambridge: Cambridge University Press.

Petracca, E. (2020) "Neuroeconomics Beyond the Brain: Some Externalist Notions of Choice," *Journal of Economic Methodology* 27(4): 275–291. https://doi.org/10.1080/1350178X.2020.1789690.

Reiss, J. (2009) "Causation in the Social Sciences: Evidence, Inference, and Purpose," *Philosophy of the Social Sciences* 39(1): 20–40.

Reiss, J. (2012a) "Idealization and the Aims of Economics: Three Cheers for Instrumentalism," *Economics and Philosophy* 28(3): 363–383.

Reiss, J. (2012b) "The Explanation Paradox," *Journal of Economic Methodology* 19(1): 43–62. https://doi.org/10.1080/1350178X.2012.661069.

Reiss, J. (2013a) *Philosophy of Economics: A Contemporary Introduction*, New York: Routledge.

Reiss, J. (2013b) "The Explanation Paradox Redux," *Journal of Economic Methodology* 20(3): 280–292. https://doi.org/10.1080/1350178X.2013.828874.

Resnik, D.B. (1991) "How-Possibly Explanations in Biology," *Acta Biotheoretica* 39(2): 141–149. https://doi.org/10.1007/BF00046596.

Reutlinger, A. (2017) "Explanation Beyond Causation? New Directions in the Philosophy of Scientific Explanation," *Philosophy Compass* 12(2): 1–11. https://doi.org/10.1111/phc3.12395.

Reutlinger, A, and Saatsi, J. (eds.) 2018) *Explanation Beyond Causation: Philosophical Perspectives on Non-Causal Explanations*, Oxford: Oxford University Press.

Rice, C. (2021) "Understanding Realism," *Synthese* 198: 4097–4121. https://doi.org/10.1007/s11229-019-02331-5.

Robbins, L. (1935) *An Essay on the Nature and Significance of Economic Science*, 2nd ed., London: Palgrave Macmillan.

Roberts, J.T. (2004) "There Are No Laws of the Social Sciences," in C. Hitchcock (ed.) *Contemporary Debates in Philosophy of Science*: 151–167, Malden, MA: Blackwell.

Roche, W., and Sober, E. (2017) "Explanation = Unification? A New Criticism of Friedman's Theory and a Reply to an Old One," *Philosophy of Science* 84(3): 391–413. https://doi.org/10.1086/692140.

Rodrik, D. (2015) *Economics Rules: The Rights and Wrongs of the Dismal Science*, New York: W. W. Norton & Company.

Rohwer, Y., and Rice, C. (2013) "Hypothetical Pattern Idealization and Explanatory Models," *Philosophy of Science* 80(3): 334–355. https://doi.org/10.1086/671399.

Rol, M. (2013) "Reply to Julian Reiss," *Journal of Economic Methodology* 20(3): 244–249. https://doi.org/10.1080/1350178X.2013.828870.

Rosenberg, A. (1976) *Microeconomic Laws: A Philosophical Analysis*, Pittsburgh: University of Pittsburgh Press.

Rosenberg, A. (2015) *Philosophy of Social Science*, 5th ed., Boulder, CO: Westview Press.

Ross, D. (2011) "Neuroeconomics and Economic Methodology," in J.B. Davis and D.W. Hands (eds.) *The Elgar Companion to Recent Economic Methodology*: 61–93. Cheltenham, UK; Northampton, MA: Edward Elgar.

Ross, D. (2014) *Philosophy of Economics*, Hampshire, UK: Palgrave Macmillan.

Salmon, W.C. (1984) *Scientific Explanation and the Causal Structure of the World*, Princeton: Princeton University Press.

Salmon, W.C. (1998) *Causality and Explanation*, Oxford: Oxford University Press.

Satz, D., and Ferejohn, J. (1994) "Rational Choice and Social Theory," *The Journal of Philosophy* 91(2): 71–87.

Schelling, T.C. (1971) "Dynamic Models of Segregation," *Journal of Mathematical Sociology* 1: 143–186.

Schelling, T.C. (1978) *Micromotives and Macrobehavior*, New York: W. W. Norton & Company.

Schurz, G. (1999) "Explanation as Unification," *Synthese* 120(1): 95–114. https://doi.org/10.1023/A:1005214721929.

Strevens, M. (2008) *Depth: An Account of Scientific Explanation*, Cambridge, MA: Harvard University Press.

Sugden, R. (2000) "Credible Worlds: The Status of Theoretical Models in Economics," *Journal of Economic Methodology* 7(1): 1–31.

Sugden, R. (2009) "Credible Worlds, Capacities and Mechanisms," *Erkenntnis* 70(1): 3–27. https://doi.org/10.1007/s10670-008-9134-x.

Sugden, R. (2011a) "Explanations in Search of Observations," *Biology and Philosophy* 26(5): 717–736. https://link.springer.com/article/10.1007/s10539-011-9280-4.

Sugden, R. (2011b) "Salience, Inductive Reasoning and the Emergence of Conventions," *Journal of Economic Behavior & Organization*, The Dynamics of Institutions in Perspectives: Alternative Conceptions and Future Challenges, 79(1): 35–47. https://doi.org/10.1016/j.jebo.2011.01.026.

Sugden, R. (2013) "How Fictional Accounts Can Explain," *Journal of Economic Methodology* 20(3): 237–243. https://doi.org/10.1080/1350178X.2013.828872.

Thaler, R.H. (2016) "Behavioral Economics: Past, Present, and Future," *American Economic Review* 106(7): 1577–1600. https://doi.org/10.1257/aer.106.7.1577.

Thoma, J. (forthcoming) "Folk Psychology and the Interpretation of Decision Theory," *Ergo*.

Verreault-Julien, P. (2017) "Non-Causal Understanding with Economic Models: The Case of General Equilibrium," *Journal of Economic Methodology* 24(3): 297–317. https://doi.org/10.1080/1350178X.2017.1335424.

Verreault-Julien, P. (2019a) "How Could Models Possibly Provide How-Possibly Explanations?' *Studies in History and Philosophy of Science Part A* 73: 22–33. https://doi.org/10.1016/j.shpsa.2018.06.008.

Verreault-Julien, P. (2019b) "Understanding Does Not Depend on (Causal) Explanation," *European Journal for Philosophy of Science* 9(2): 18. https://doi.org/10.1007/s13194-018-0240-6.

Vredenburgh, K. (2020) "A Unificationist Defence of Revealed Preferences," *Economics & Philosophy* 36(1): 149–169. https://doi.org/10.1017/S0266267118000524.

Weber, E., and Van Dyck, M. (2002) "Unification and Explanation," *Synthese* 131(1): 145–154. https://doi.org/10.1023/A:1015005529380.

Woodward, J. (2003) *Making Things Happen. A Theory of Causal Explanation*, New York: Oxford University Press.

Ylikoski, P. (2014) "Rethinking Micro-Macro Relations," in J. Zahle and F. Collin (eds.) *Rethinking the Individualism-Holism Debate*: 117–135, Dordrecht: Springer.

Ylikoski, P. (2017) "Methodological Individualism," in L. McIntyre and A. Rosenberg (eds.) *The Routledge Companion to Philosophy of Social Science*: 135–146, New York: Taylor & Francis.

Ylikoski, P., and Aydinonat, N.E. (2014) "Understanding with Theoretical Models," *Journal of Economic Methodology* 21(1): 19–36. https://doi.org/10.1080/1350178X.2014.886470.

Zahle, J., and Collin, F. (eds.) 2014) *Rethinking the Individualism-Holism Debate: Essays in the Philosophy of Social Science*, Cham: Springer.

Zahle, J., and Kincaid, H. (2019) "Why Be a Methodological Individualist?' *Synthese* 196(2): 655–675. https://doi.org/10.1007/s11229-017-1523-8.

23
MODELING THE POSSIBLE TO MODELING THE ACTUAL

Jennifer S. Jhun

1. Introductory Remarks

In his 2004 address to the Econometrica society (published later in 2006 in its flagship journal), Ariel Rubenstein puzzled over his vocation as an economist: "my greatest dilemma is between my attraction to economic theory, on the one hand, and my doubts about its relevance, on the other" (Rubinstein 2006: 866). He concludes that the economist's use of models is not much different from an author's use of fables and that the economic theorist is (in some wonderful sense) a storyteller.

> A theory, like a good fable, identifies a number of themes and elucidates them. We perform thought exercises that are only loosely connected to reality and that have been stripped of most of their real-life characteristics. However, in a good model, as in a good fable, something significant remains.
>
> (Ibid.: 881)

When the significant epistemic upshot is meant to be causal knowledge, how does one proceed?[1],[2] One is tempted to respond in the following way: first de-idealize, and then identify similarity relations between the model and target systems. Roughly, the former attempts to identify the information that was missing from or incorrect in the model, while the latter attempts to find what relevant information *was* captured. I take it as granted that models on their own only give, at best, how-possibly explanations (Verreault-Julien, Chapter 22) in some broad sense – and therefore one needs to de-idealize and identify similarity relations in order for those models to apply to the real world and provide how-actually explanations.[3] This chapter will consider how, in practice, that transition can happen.

Whatever one learns about in a given model, this knowledge only carries over to knowledge about the target system if the appropriate kinds of relationships hold between the two (Chao, Chapter 13). Part of the policymaker's job is to find out when such hypothetical claims actually do hold – that is, when the conditions stipulated by the models are instantiated (to a good approximation, whatever that means) in the real world, and sometimes the model needs some tinkering before this can be successfully done. When we think about real practices, it becomes clearer that something more complicated than simply de-idealizing and identifying similarity relations is going on. Models do not generally fit their purported real-world targets out of the box, nor does it suffice to simply "add in" the missing information.

 DOI: 10.4324/9781315739793-28

We begin by surveying some of the prominent work available in the literature discussing idealized models. To connect them to their real-world targets is not straightforward, though, at all. We then consider how a policymaking body like the Federal Reserve in the United States concocts its forecasts and conducts policy analysis. We suggest envisioning the process of constructing how-actually explanations as that of constructing credible narratives, appealing especially on work by Morgan (2001, 2017).

2. Idealized Models

The strongest form of this model-target relation is isomorphism; given that this standard is unrealistic, some authors have spoken of similarity instead. Here we consider a handful of positions commenting on what the bridge between the model and the world is supposed to look like. We wish to note that none of these quite takes the approach glossed in the previous section: that to move from a how-possibly explanation to a how-actually explanation requires de-idealization and then the identification of similarity relations (Northcott, Chapter 28).

Consider the isolationist view of models: Cartwright (1999) claims that, among other things, most of our knowledge consists of ceteris paribus laws that fail to hold universally, but hold only in certain circumstances, barring outside interference. Furthermore, she maintains that it is not laws but "capacities" that truly have an explanatory role in scientific inquiry (Ibid.: 49). It is when things thrown together in a certain way and are shielded from outside influences that laws may do some descriptive work. By conceiving of economic models as "nomological machines" in thought experiments, we are meant to be able to delineate these causal features – the "capacities" – at play that give rise to what we call laws.[4] These models are highly idealized, identifying only some causal factors at play (and ignoring others) in the world. For such a model, it is not a matter of de-idealizing, but finding where it fits.

On the constructivist side, the view that emphasizes models as the kind of things we build (and which may even be fictional), the credible worlds account by Sugden (2000) reigns as paradigm.[5] This view treats models as parallel worlds on their own but analogous to ours. There is a similarity relation between the model and the target phenomenon, and inferences from the model are even more reliable "the greater the extent to which we can understand the relevant model as a description of how the world *could* be" (Ibid.: 24, original emphasis). How to establish this relationship, however, is open ended. Referring to Banerjee's (1992) paper on herding behavior, Sugden (2009) notes that Banerjee couches his model within a larger, but not unintuitive, story about how people choose to eat at certain restaurants.

> Very informally, [Banerjee] invites us to consult our experience . . . to conclude that what is going on in his model world is in some way similar to that experience. And that is it: we are left to draw the appropriate conclusions.
>
> (Ibid.: 9–10)

While not literally true, models – via an imaginative effort on our part as modelers – bear some sort of resemblance without being identical (or isomorphic) to the target. But the model itself has an autonomous status:

> We recognize . . . that the model world *could be* real – that it describes a state of affairs that is *credible*, given what we know (or think we know) about the general laws governing events in the real world. On this view, the model is not so much an abstraction from reality as a parallel reality. The model world is not constructed by starting with the real world and stripping out complicating factors . . . the one is not a *simplification* of the other.
>
> (Sugden 2000: 25)

Sugden emphasizes the notion of credibility: "we see Schelling's checkerboard cities as *possible cities*, alongside real cities like New York and Philadelphia. We see Akerlof's used-car market as a *possible market*, alongside real markets such as the real market for used cars in a particular city" (Ibid.: 25). These possible worlds are considered "as instances of some category, some of whose instances actually exist in the real world." If both the possible world and the actual world are instances of the same class, then they must share some relevant similar features: "forces or tendencies which connect *real* causes (asymmetric information, mildly segregationist preferences) to *real* effects (sub-optimal volumes of trade, sharp segregation)" (Ibid.: 12). The emphasis here is on the analogical relationship the model bears to its potential targets, rather than de-idealization.

The fictionalist school of thought, plausibly a species of constructivism, goes even further: models have their own internal logic whether or not they represent anything out in the world. Frigg (2010) rightly points out that models need not take representation to be their primary aim at all. We can speak of a fictional character truthfully (i.e. within the story) as being tall or short, despicable or appealing, etc., without any correspondence to an external world; furthermore,[6]

> models, like literary fictions, are not *defined* in contrast to truth. In elementary particle physics, for instance, a scenario is often proposed simply as a suggestion worth considering and only later, when all the details are worked out, the question is asked whether this scenario bears an interesting relation to what happens in nature, and if so what the relation is.
> (Ibid.: 260)

While a model is conceived as like a fictional story, it serves as a "prop" that sanctions our imaginative reasoning about hypothetical objects – one that we can undertake without reference to a target system (though, of course, one could go on to do so). Models themselves are akin to stories or fables; they provide a point upon which to anchor some bit of analogical reasoning to worldly phenomena later down the road. A more extensive story about how a model relates to the world is found in Frigg and Nguyen (2016), who propose the DEKI account (which stands for **d**enotation, **e**xemplification, **k**eying up, and **i**mputation). Imagined systems denote targets when certain exemplified properties in the model are imputed to properties of the target via a key that helps bridge them.

A maneuver like stipulating interpretive keys is one way of spelling out how one might secure a how-actually story. Elsewhere, Morgan and Knuuttila (2012) have documented extensively the different kinds of idealizations that there are in economics, and in a 2019 paper they critically examine what it is that de-idealization could even be.[7] Some of these are rather sophisticated maneuvers. For instance, in the case of what they call "resituation," or making a model applicable to a context, they find that this may involve radical change to the initial model template. This change may even be conceptual. For example, "the supply-and-demand model had to be reinterpreted when it was moved from the market for goods to the market for labor, prompting the concept of 'voluntary unemployment'" (Knuuttila and Morgan 2019: 654). So the work that a scientist has to do to bring this alignment between model and target system about may vary. A fairly simple supply-demand model might do for some economic analyses. For example, this task can be characterized as identifying a domain of application for a particular model (suitably interpreted – that is, the parameters ought to be meaningful). Other, more complex, scenarios may require substantial adjustments.

What is especially salient in the aforementioned works is that to do the extra work to make a model applicable to a real-world target at all is a rather flexible affair, and the process is underdetermined by the model and the target. For instance, one thing that seems quite obvious is that de-idealization, construed as simply adding in information that was omitted or ignored the first time around, is not an adequate account of how someone goes about constructing a model that can yield how-actually explanations. This is not to say that to supplement a baseline model with additional relevant information is never called for – it often is – but the process by which this happens is not straightforward.[8] As one might expect, in macroeconomic policymaking it is often a rather complicated story.

3. Building Bridges via Narrative Construction: The Federal Reserve

This section documents a few key details about how the US Federal Reserve (the Fed) attempts its forecasting and policy analysis goals. One thing that is striking is that the Fed, in addition to a number of other central banks, is explicit about its use of expert *judgment* in its forecasting practices. And the implementation of judgment makes it difficult to spell out what the model-target relation is supposed to be.

The core domestic policy model in use at the Federal Reserve is currently a large-scale, New Keynesian, general equilibrium, econometric model called FRB/US (pronounced "furbus"), which the Federal Reserve is careful to distinguish from dynamic stochastic general equilibrium (DSGE) models (on DSGE models, see Kuorikoski and Lehtinen, Chapter 26). The FRB/US replaced its predecessor, the MPS model (an acronym for the Massachusetts Institute of Technology, the University of Pennsylvania, and the Social Science Research Council), which had been developed in the 1960s and was based around the IS/LM/Phillips curve. The FRB/US model was developed later in the 1990s and is used in conjunction with a number of other models at the Federal Reserve, such as FRB/WORLD and FRB/MCM (a multicountry model), an open, multicountry DSGE model SIGMA, and a medium-scale, closed-economy model EDO.

The Federal Open Market Committee (FOMC) makes decisions about monetary policy and effects such policies by influencing the money supply. There are seven governors and twelve Federal Reserve Bank presidents. The FOMC itself is the governors plus five presidents, who take turns serving on the committee. While the FOMC is a voting bloc, all twelve presidents participate in the discussion. So, despite the fact that only some presidents vote, decisions on how to conduct open-market operations are largely reached by consensus. The FOMC makes its recommendations to the Open Market Desk at the New York Federal Reserve, which strategically buys and/or sells the appropriate number of securities, thus manipulating the federal funds rate.

The FOMC is scheduled to meet eight times per year. One of the highlights of the FOMC meeting is the discussion of the precirculated Tealbook. Before 2010, the FOMC was issued the Greenbook and the Bluebook, which were merged to form today's Tealbook. The Tealbook comes in two parts: A ("Economic and Financial Conditions: Current Situation and Outlook") and B ("Monetary Policies: Strategies and Alternatives"). Together, these documents summarize and analyze the state of both the US and foreign economies, in addition to containing the staff forecast. A number of difference scenarios are considered, as well as multiple specific policy options.

As of Sims' writing in 2002, when the Tealbook was not yet the Tealbook, the forecasting process began

> with a small group (around four people) meeting to set the forecast "top line" – values for GDP growth and for key financial variables, including the Federal Funds rate. The next stage is generation of forecasts for their variables by the sectoral experts. The expert forecasts are fed through the FRBUS model to generate residuals, and the results of this exercise are considered at a subsequent meeting. Feedback can occur in both directions between model forecasts and subjective forecasts, as well as back to the top line numbers.
>
> (Sims 2002: 4)

The process is an iterative one, requiring quite a bit of back-and-forth between sectoral experts and an overseer (the forecast coordinator) until there is convergence. Reifschneider et al. (1997) describe this process as a " 'human Gauss-Siedel algorithm,' iterating between coordinator and sectoral analysts until convergence is achieved" (p. 10). The sectoral experts consult a number of different sources of evidence, including "econometric models of their sector, surveys, anecdotal evidence, and his or her own judgment of the impact of developments that cannot be captured by other tools" (Canales-Kriljenko et al. 2006: 13). They work together "within the context of agreed-upon conditioning assumptions," which as Meyer (1997) stated include "a path for short-term interest rates, fiscal policy, oil prices, and foreign economic policies." These forecasts are then aggregated, and additional iterations are done to ensure consistency with incoming data and of the macroeconomic framework in general.[9]

The workhorse FRB/US model anchors a collective enquiry that requires cooperation and coordination. That the forecasts it informs are called "judgmental" emphasizes how crucial it is that they inform the use of and are shaped by expertise.[10],[11] Even though the Tealbook forecast is not itself the FRB/US forecast, FRB/US is then in turn is adjusted via the use of add-factors to mimic it in order to further go on to run counterfactual simulations for different scenarios.

The process of getting a model to exhibit the relevant similarity relations requires quite a bit of legwork, often supplemented by *other* models (all of which are, to some degree, idealized) and off-model information. Policymakers stitch this information together in formal and informal ways. One way to account for this patching together project is to turn to a different conception of explanation that one finds, for instance, in the historical sciences and that Morgan (2001, 2017) and Morgan and Wise (2017) bring to the fore: narrative explanation. And this suits the purpose of policymaking nicely. For policymaking purposes, the point of using a model (or rather, models) is that it is something that both enables and constrains the production of a coherent, credible narrative.

Models do not do very much by themselves. According to Morgan (2001), the theoretical model needs to be accompanied by a narrative in order to be saying anything about the real world, as "when we use the model to discuss specific cases, we also rely on the complementary explanatory power of narrative" (p. 378). This construction of narrative refers to an epistemic process of integrating various, sometimes quite disparate, bits of information:

> Narrative ordering refers to the way a scientist brings similar and conflicting elements into contact with each other; the ways that interrelations are revealed and established; the modes of interleaving; and the process of creating an overall picture in which all their pieces of investigation have a place.
>
> (Morgan 2017: 11)

As we have seen in the case of the Tealbook forecasts, sometimes even the construction of the model itself is also buttressed by narrative – it is not the case that narrative is called for only once a complete model is available. As Boumans (1999, 2004) carefully documents, models in economics tend to need to pull many different ingredients together – some empirical, some theoretical, some ideological, and so on. Model building, according to Boumans (1999), is akin to baking a cake without a particular recipe (p. 67).

Part of the central model's purpose is to be a coordinating platform upon which to do these things. Kuorikoski and Lehtinen (2018) claim that when we think about dynamic stochastic general equilibrium (DSGE) models, which are often the main models in macroeconomic policy at central banks (the United States is a bit peculiar in this regard by using the semistructural FRB/US instead as its main model), "such models work more like platforms for integrating expert judgments than alternative models capturing single or a few key causal mechanisms" (p. 257).[12] This holds for the FRB/US as well (though it is not the only model in use at the Federal Reserve, nor is it true that it is at the forefront *all the time* for all the different kinds of analyses one might want to undertake).[13]

The ultimate goal is to formulate a coherent narrative in order to guide policy actions. If we think a narrative is a credible one, we expect it to help us accomplish policy interventions successfully. To this end, it seems reasonable to suppose that economists would have a handle on the causal structure of the economy.[14] The hope is that one has built a model wherein the causal relationships depicted (or, more broadly, identified in the narrative that is shaped around the model) correspond to causal relations in the world (for a criticism of this view, see Northcott, Chapter 28). At least, we expect this in the relevant domain of application, which may mean an economy of some size or another on some time scale or other. Or perhaps, in different words: that the mechanism depicted in the model corresponds to an economic mechanism of interest.[15],[16] For instance, Akinci et al. (2017) assert that a DSGE model "allows us to explain the source of economic fluctuations (shocks) and the key causal relationships between different components of the economy" (p. 2).[17] While the FRB/US is a semi-structural model (and thus – some argue – distinct from a structural model like DSGE), it seems to be attempting something similar.

A disclaimer: none of this indicates whether or not the FRB/US is successful at what it aims to do. Further questions include: what are the standards we use to assess whether FRB/US is the kind of model that reliably captures the relevant causal relations to a good approximation, given the aims of the policymaker? Does it get enough right in order to be successful? As we have said, FRB/US is not, strictly speaking, a structural model like traditional New Keynesian models, and even those have identification and specification problems. A semistructural model identifies "a sub-set of parameters and/or mechanisms rather than full counterfactuals" (Blundell 2017: 1). But they are more flexible in that they "impose fewer restrictions on the data than these structural models," and interestingly enough they have the added benefit of "thus improving the robustness of the results in case of specification errors" (Castillo and Florián 2019: 4).[18]

A glance at the modifications made to the last vintage of FRB/US shows that it includes the elimination of energy as a factor of production, not because it has no role to play in the economy but because "the benefits of this capability have always been minor if not negligible," and it has the added benefit of cutting down on the costs of modeling (Laforte 2018). Another modification is the aggregation of nonresidential investment as a bloc rather than disaggregated components, as "Our experience over the past decade indicates that the presence of disaggregated components of investment has never been crucial, while the costs of maintaining the disaggregation have been a noticeable burden" (Ibid.). So there is, at least sometimes, a trade-off between the usefulness of the model and increasing representational accuracy. Part of this trade-off could probably be attributed to the model's aim to identify relevant difference-making features. Because a successful model captures *relevant* causal structure, this does not require some kind of causal completeness in that every causal factor must individually be captured in the model.[19],[20]

Even in the FRB/US model, causality cannot be read off just from looking at the individual equations (even equations on their own do not specify directionality of cause, nor is everything obviously apt for causal interpretation). The equations in the FRB/US model have different roles to play. Some are behavioral (i.e. refer to agent expectations), some are drawn from the New Keynesian Phillips curve, and some are identities. The first two are classes of optimizing equations; the last one is not (i.e. sometimes it requires making sense of the relationship between lower and higher level aggregates). And finally, because FRB/US is so large (it contains about 300 equations, about 50 of which are considered "core" or behavioral), it cannot be estimated all at once. Recall that the Federal Reserve staff forecasting process is a collaborative process between a number of sectoral experts with a forecast coordinator. Portions of the model – for example, the optimization-based equations – are investigated via submodels characterized by vector autoregressions.

> Estimation of the optimization-based equations involves the estimation of a set of independent sub-models, each of which typically combines one of the structural equations with a condensed model of the overall economy that features a VAR. Projections of the VAR provide proxies for the explicit expectations terms in the structural equation. Each VAR model shares a *core* set of macro variables. . . . *Auxiliary* variables are added to individual VARs as needed to form proxies for expectations of variables not in the core set.
>
> (Brayton et al. 2014)

All this goes to show that it takes a great deal of work to get some kind of causal information out of a model. Models do not suffice on their own as representational items – but model construction and use in practice is a process that does aim at representation. This might explain why economists may not see their judgmental work as merely – or even mainly – supplementing the flaws of a particular model. Sims (2002) interviews a number of economists who work at central banks and finds the following:

> One hypothesis is that the models are flawed descriptions of the economy (which is certainly true) and that the expert judgment of seasoned economists allows more subtle and accurate understandings of the economy to be brought to bear. None of the economists I talked to at these central banks expressed this view.
>
> Instead, they claimed that the subjective forecasters mainly provide a more accurate picture of the current state of the economy than can easily be provided by a single quantitative model.
>
> (pp. 20–21)

The way to bridge the model-target gap is not algorithmic, nor would it do to think of one as the faint but recognizable reflection of the other. In fact, it also means that the similarity relations that hold do not look any way in particular across the board. In this respect, we are in agreement with Giere (2010): "I doubt that there exists any uniquely justifiable measure of this type" (p. 64).[21]

4. Concluding Remarks

Models are tools for identifying relevant causal relationships that are apt for intervention – they facilitate hypothetical and counterfactual reasoning. After all, FRB/US is used not only to forecast but to analyze alternative scenarios as well. There is no algorithmic route from the model that provides a how-possibly explanation to the model that provides a how-actually explanation. This is largely because we do not conceive of the how-possible model as initially impoverished, eventually redeemable via incorporation of the additional information needed to make a match with the target system. For instance, we do not (always) merely add in extra factors in order to get the model to imply or accord with a bit of data. Rather, that model is an integral part, even if it may end up being modified, in a larger narrative practice that aims to construct a coherent account of the relevant causal structure at hand.

One way to continue this discussion moving forward to supplement our observations is to appeal to the richness of narrative explanatory strategies. Such strategies enable us to flexibly make sense of the complex causal system that is the economy in a way that makes space for and acknowledges the use of expert judgment in spelling out how a model could be used to describe actual targets.[22] Indeed, Morgan's (2001, 2017) work on narrative can be given the slogan of conceiving of narrative as a "sense-making enterprise."[23] Importantly, narrative construction accommodates that there is no particular algorithmic way of moving from the how-possibly to the how-actually model. Given what economic modeling in practice looks like, we suggest taking as crucial the role of narrative as something that informs model construction and enables models to be applied to real-world contexts.

Acknowledgments

I am grateful to Federico Ravenna for helpful and interesting discussions.

Related Chapters

Chao, H., Chapter 13 "Representation"
Kuorikoski, J., and Lehtinen, A, Chapter 26 "Computer Simulations in Economics"
Northcott, R., Chapter 28 "Economic Theory and Empirical Science"
Verreault-Julien, P., Chapter 22 "Explanation in Economics"

Notes

1 In this chapter, I will focus my attention on models that provide causal explanations specifically for the purpose of guiding policy interventions. Therefore, I do not address in detail models that might do other things for other purposes, such as reduced-form models that are used for forecasting, nor do I discuss the distinction and relationship between theories and models.

2 Models in economics come in a wide variety and vary in what kind of epistemic product they offer, so they cannot be assessed in a uniform way. For example, Blanchard (2018) identifies at least five salient types that are used in policymaking: dynamic stochastic general equilibrium (DSGE) models, foundational models, policy models, toy models, and forecasting models.

3 For a more extensive discussion of the distinction between how-actually and how-possibly explanations, see Brandon (1990), Bokulich, (2014), Forber (2010), and Reydon (2012) – though with the disclaimer that these papers are not focused on socioeconomic phenomena. Other authors in the fray include Aydinonat (2007), Craver (2006), Forber (2012), Grüne-Yanoff (2009, 2013), Rohwer and Rice (2013), Verreault-Julien (2017), and Ylikoski and Aydinonat (2014).

4 This is, in some respects, similar to Mäki (2009), where models are both tools of isolation and surrogate systems capable of representation.

5 See Hardt (2016, 2017) and Knuuttila (2009) for an elaboration of the isolationist versus constructivist distinction.

6 See also Toon (2012) and Contessa (2010).

7 They identify at least four projects: "recomposing, reformulating, concretizing, and situating" (p. 657).

8 For instance, Nowak (1994) terms it "concretization."

9 See also Robertson (2000).

10 In a working paper, Kisinbay et al. (2006: 13) state:

> Sectoral expertise and judgment play an important role in some central banks for short-term forecasting. A macroeconomic forecast based on judgment is built up in a fully coordinated way from sectoral forecasts provided by sectoral experts. This is a full macroeconomic forecast as an alternative or a complement to a model-based one.

11 While the staff forecast is meant to be "uncontaminated," that is, it does not involve input from policymakers (i.e. the FOMC members), Edison and Marquez (2000) locate several instances in the past that indicate that there is more interaction than might be assumed.

12 See, for a contrasting take, Ylikoski and Aydinonat (2014), who emphasize thinking in terms of families of models, rather than isolated models on their own.

13 For instance, in a panel on modeling at central banks, John Roberts (2016) of the Federal Reserve Board of Governors noted that, while in the medium run the Fed would use FRB/US, for longer term forecasting

the core model would be a New Keynesian three-equation model distinct from FRB/US (though calibrated to it in various ways).

14 This suggests a kind of causation that would be in line with what authors such as Woodward (2003) and Hoover (2011) might have suggested.

15 I am glossing over the difference and relationship between causal explanation and mechanistic explanation here. But I take it that mechanistic explanation presupposes knowing something about causes.

16 Reifschneider et al. (1999) indicate that FRB/US is supposed to articulate the monetary transmission mechanism, though it does not make all channels explicit.

17 Importantly, they specify that it is "the model's microfoundations [that] provide a framework for understanding economic conditions" (p. 2).

18 See Hirakata et al. (2019) for a characterization of the difference between structural models like DSGE models and semistructural ones like FRB/US.

19 Maybe even a partial isomorphism will do. See Pincock (2005) here for a discussion.

20 For a formalization of the notion of partial isomorphism, see French (1999). For a more detailed account of how to apply Giere to economic cases, see also Hoover (2012).

21 Giere is also speaking specifically in terms of a perspectival view of scientific models, and we are sympathetic with that view generally speaking.

22 A special issue of *Studies in the History and Philosophy of Science*, titled "Narrative in Science" (2017) and edited by both Morgan and Wise, elaborates on this in a variety of ways.

23 See also Svetlova (2013) for a case study in financial valuation.

Bibliography

Akinci, O., Cai, M., Gupta, A., Li, P., and Tambalotti, A. (2017) Appendix to "The New York Fed DSGE Model Forecast: DSGE Model Q & A". Retrieved at: www.newyorkfed.org/medialibrary/media/research/blog/2017/LSE_dsge-forecast-appendix_Nov-2017

Aydinonat, N.E. (2007) "Models, Conjectures and Exploration: An Analysis of Schelling's Checkerboard Model of Residential Segregation," *Journal of Economic Methodology* 14(4): 429–454.

Banerjee, A. (1992) "A Simple Model of Herd Behavior," *Quarterly Journal of Economics* 107: 797–817.

Blanchard, O. (2018) "On the Future of Macroeconomic Models," *Oxford Review of Economic Policy* 34(1–2): 43–54.

Blundell, R. (2017) "What Have We Learned from Structural Models?" *American Economic Review* 107(5): 287–292.

Bokulich, A. (2014) "How the Tiger Bush Got Its Stripes: 'How Possibly' vs. 'How Actually' Model Explanations," *The Monist* 97(3): 321–338.

Boumans, M. (1999) "Built-in Justification," in M.S. Morgan and M. Morrison (eds.) *Models as Mediators*, Cambridge: Cambridge University Press: 66–96.

Boumans, M. (2004) *How Economists Model the World into Numbers*, London: Routledge.

Brandon, R. (1990) *Adaptation and Environment*, Princeton: Princeton University Press.

Brayton, F., Laubach, T., and Reifschneider, D. (2014) "The FRB/US Model: A Tool for Macroeconomic Policy Analysis," *FEDS Notes*, Washington, DC: Board of Governors of the Federal Reserve System. Retrieved at: https://doi.org/10.17016/2380-7172.0012

Canales-Kriljenko, J.I., Kisinbay, T., Maino, R., and Parrado, E. (2006) "Setting the Operational Framework for Producing Inflation Forecasts," IMF Working Paper No. 06/122. Available at SSRN: https://ssrn-com.eur.idm.oclc.org/abstract=910687

Cartwright, N. (1999) *The Dappled World: A Study of the Boundaries of Science*, Cambridge: Cambridge University Press.

Castillo, L., and Florián, D. (2019) "Measuring the Output Gap, Potential Output Growth and Natural Interest Rate from a Semi-Structural Dynamic Model for Peru," *Working Papers (No. 2019–012)*, Banco Central de Reserva del Peru.

Contessa, G. (2010) "Scientific Models and Fictional Objects," *Synthese* 172(2): 215–229.

Craver, C.F. (2006) "When Mechanistic Models Explain," *Synthese* 153(3): 355–376.

Edison, H.J., and Marquez, J. (2000) "US Monetary Policy and Econometric Modeling: Tales from the FOMC transcripts 1984–1991," in F. den Butter and M. Morgan (eds.) *Empirical Models and Policy-Making: Interactions and* Institutions, London: Routledge: 187–205.

Forber, P. (2010) "Confirmation and Explaining how Possible," *Studies in History and Philosophy of Biological and Biomedical Sciences* 41: 32–40.

Forber, P. (2012) "Conjecture and Explanation: A Reply to Reydon," *Studies in History and Philosophy of Science Part C: Studies in History and Philosophy of Biological and Biomedical Sciences* 43(1): 298–301.

French, S. (1999) "Models and Mathematics in Physics: The Role of Group Theory," in M. Redhead, J. Butterfield, and C. Pagonis (eds.) *From Physics to Philosophy*, Cambridge: Cambridge University Press: 187–207.

Frigg, R. (2010) "Fiction and Scientific Representation," in R. Frigg and M. Hunter (eds.) *Beyond Mimesis and Convention: Representation in Art and Science*, Dordrecht: Springer: 97–138.

Frigg, R., and Nguyen, J. (2016). "The Fiction View of Models Reloaded," *The Monist* 99(3): 225–242.

Giere, R.N. (2009) "Why Scientific Models Should Not be Regarded as Works of Fiction," in M. Suárez (ed.) *Fictions in Science: Philosophical Essays on Modeling and Idealization*, New York: Routledge: 248–258.

Giere, R.N. (2010). *Scientific Perspectivism*, Chicago: University of Chicago Press.

Grüne-Yanoff, T. (2009) "Learning from Minimal Economic Models," *Erkenntnis* 70(1): 81–99.

Grüne-Yanoff, T. (2011) "Isolation Is Not Characteristic of Models," *International Studies in the Philosophy of Science* 25(2): 1–19.

Grüne-Yanoff, T. (2013) "Appraising Models Nonrepresentationally," *Philosophy of Science* 80(5): 850–861.

Hardt, Ł. (2016) "Between Isolations and Constructions: Economic Models as Believable Worlds," in B. Rodopi, G. Borbone and K. Brzechczyn (eds.) *Idealization XIV: Models in Science*, Boston: Brill Rodopi: 130–160.

Hardt, Ł. (2017) *Economics Without Laws: Towards a New Philosophy of Economics*, London: Palgrave Macmillan.

Hirakata, N., Kan, K., Kanafuji, A., Kido, Y., Kishaba, Y., Murakoshi, T., and Shinohara, T. (2019) *The Quarterly Japanese Economic Model (Q-JEM): 2019 version* (No. 19-E-7), Bank of Japan.

Hoover, K.D. (2011) "Counterfactuals and Causal Structure," in P.M. Illari, F. Russo, and J. Williamson (eds.) *Causality in the Sciences*, Oxford: Oxford University Press: 338–360.

Hoover, K.D. (2012) "Pragmatism, Perspectival Realism, and Econometrics," in A. Lehtinen, J. Kuorikoski, and P. Ylikoski (eds.) *Economics for Real: Uskali Mäki and the Place of Truth in Economics*.

Kisinbay, T., Parrado, E., Maino, R., and Canales-Kriljenko, J.I. (2006) "Setting the Operational Framework for Producing Inflation Forecasts," *IMF Working Paper* No. 06/122.

Knuuttila, T. (2009) "Isolating Representations Versus Credible Constructions? Economic Modelling in Theory and Practicem," *Erkenntnis* 70: 59–80.

Knuuttila, T., and Morgan, M.S. (2019) "Deidealization: No Easy Reversals," *Philosophy of Science* 86(4): 641–661.

Kuorikoski, J., and Lehtinen, A. (2018) "Model Selection in Macroeconomics: DSGE and ad hocness," *Journal of Economic Methodology* 25(3): 252–264.

Laforte, J-P. (2018) "Overview of the Changes to the FRB/US Model (2018)," *FEDS Notes*. Washington: Board of Governors of the Federal Reserve System, December 7, 2018, https://doi.org/10.17016/2380-7172.2306.

Mäki, U. (2009) "Missing the World. Models as Isolations and Credible Surrogate Systems," *Erkenntnis* 70(1): 29–43.

Meyer, L.H. (1997) "The Role for Structural Macroeconomic Models," *Remarks at the AEA Panel on Monetary and Fiscal Policy*, New Orleans, Louisiana.

Morgan, M.S. (2001) "Models, Stories and the Economic World," *Journal of Economic Methodology* 8(3): 361–384.

Morgan, M.S. (2017) "Narrative Ordering and Explanation," *Studies in History and Philosophy of Science* Part A, 62: 86–97.

Morgan, M.S., and Knuuttila, T. (2012) "Models and Modelling in Economics," in U. Mäki (ed.) *Philosophy of Economics*. Amsterdam: Elsevier: 49–87.

Morgan, M.S., and Wise, M.N. (2017) "Narrative Science and Narrative Knowing. Introduction to Special Issue on Narrative Science," *Studies in History and Philosophy of Science* Part A, 62: 1–5.

Nowak, L. (1994) "The Idealization Methodology and Econometrics," in B. Hamminga and N. De Marchi (eds.) *Idealization VI: Idealization in Economics*. Amsterdam: Rodopi: 303–336.

Pincock, C. (2005) "Overextending Partial Structures: Idealization and Abstraction," *Philosophy of Science* 72(5): 1248–1259.

Reifschneider, D.L., Stockton, D.J., and Wilcox, D.W. (1997) "Econometric Models and the Monetary Policy Process," *Carnegie-Rochester Conference Series on Public Policy* 47: 1–37.

Reifschneider, D.L., Tetlow, R.J., and Williams, J. (1999) "Aggregate Disturbances, Monetary Policy, and the Macroeconomy: The FRB/US Perspective," *Federal Reserve Bulletin*, Board of Governors of the Federal Reserve System (U.S.), issue January: 1–19.

Reydon, T.A. (2012) "How-Possibly Explanations as Genuine Explanations and Helpful Heuristics: A Comment on Forber," *Studies in History and Philosophy of Science Part C: Studies in History and Philosophy of Biological and Biomedical Sciences* 43(1): 302–310.

Roberts, J. (2016) Panel discussion on uses of models at central banks. Presented at the conference "DSGE models and Forecasting" at the European Central Bank. Frankfurt, Germany.

Robertson, J.C. (2000) "Central Bank Forecasting: An International Comparison," *Economic Review-Federal Reserve Bank of Atlanta* 85(2): 21–32.

Rohwer, Y., and Rice, C. (2013) "Hypothetical Pattern Idealization and Explanatory Models," *Philosophy of Science* 80(3): 334–355.

Sims, C.A. (2002) "The Role of Models and Probabilities in the Monetary Policy Process," *Brookings Papers on Economic Activity* 2002(2): 1–40.

Sugden, R. (2000) "Credible Worlds: The Status of Theoretical Models in Economics," *Journal of Economic Methodology* 7(1): 1–31.

Sugden, R. (2009) "Credible Worlds, Capacities and Mechanisms," *Erkenntnis* 70(1): 3–27.

Svetlova, E. (2013) "De-Idealization by Commentary: The Case of Financial Valuation Models," *Synthese* 190(2): 321–337.

Toon, A. (2012) *Models as Make-Believe: Imagination, Fiction and Scientific Representation*, Basingstoke: Palgrave Macmillan.

Verreault-Julien, P. (2017) "Non-Causal Understanding with Economic Models: The Case of General Equilibrium," *Journal of Economic Methodology* 24(3): 297–317.

Woodward, J. (2003) *Making Things Happen*, Oxford: Oxford University Press.

Ylikoski, P., and Aydinonat, N.E. (2014) "Understanding with Theoretical Models," *Journal of Economic Methodology* 21(1): 19–36.

PART VI

Experimentation and Simulation

24
EXPERIMENTATION IN ECONOMICS

Michiru Nagatsu

1. Introduction

Güth and Kliemt (2017) note that, "[t]o what extent the philosopher regards the toolbox of experimental economics as well as the results created by its use as philosophically relevant depends obviously on the fundamental conception of philosophy she endorses." In this chapter, however, I shall not start from any fundamental conception of philosophy, nor shall I argue for any particular one drawing on experimental results (cf. Rubin et al. 2019). Instead, I will describe two main ways in which the methodology of experimental economics has been interesting philosophically, namely, as an embodiment of the logic of inductive inferences and as a field in which interdisciplinary relations between economics and psychology become salient.

I will start by introducing two typologies of economics experiments in the next section. The typologies are meant to give the reader an overview of experimentation in economics, but they are also intended to reveal different epistemic and practical interests of experimental economists. In Sections 3 and 4, I turn to the philosophical relevance of the methodology of experimental economics. Section 3 briefly outlines how a general normative theory of inductive inferences, more specifically, the severe testing approach, can be abstracted from the practice. Section 4 zooms in and discusses discrepancies in practices, which are often associated with the differences between economics and psychology, and how to reconcile these differences. Section 5 concludes the chapter with a summary of the argument. As illustrations, I will draw on several experimental paradigms, such as a public goods game, a double auction, bargaining games, endowment effect experiments, and a market entry game (see, e.g., Camerer et al. 2003; Bardsley et al. 2010; Dhami 2016; Jacquemet and l'Haridon 2018, for details of these games).

2. Overview: Typologies of Experiments in Economics

Before proceeding, it will be useful to provide a few typologies for distinguishing different kinds of experiments in economics. Because the experiments are not a natural kind, there is no single correct way to do this. I will introduce two typologies in each subsection coming from the philosophy of science and science and technology studies, respectively. These typologies reveal the different epistemic and nonepistemic interests underlying experiments in economics.

DOI: 10.4324/9781315739793-30

2.1 The Standard Typology

Economic experiments primarily concern economic agents' incentivized – motivated and consequential – choices and their aggregate outcomes. Because types of motivations and consequences are different in different contexts, it is customary to categorize economic experiments by the type of context in which those choices are made: decision-theoretic, game-theoretic, and market experiments. They correspond to distinct theoretical frameworks that are used to model them (Roth 1993). Table 24.1 summarizes these types in columns.

Decision-theoretic experiments concern individual choices that affect one's own pecuniary outcomes, while game-theoretic and market experiments concern choices that affect one's own as well as others' outcomes. An imperfect but intuitive way to distinguish these experiments is to look at the number of participants required: a decision-theoretic experiment can be conducted, in principle, with one participant, exposing her to a set of risky or intertemporal decision-problems. A larger subject pool is required for reasons related to statistical significance and representativeness. Independent from those statistical reasons, a game-theoretic experiment requires at least two participants, whose decisions are consequential to each others' pecuniary outcomes.[1] A market experiment requires more than two participants, although how many are required depends on the market that is of interest. For example, if the experiment is about a duopoly market, then the number of participants can be as few as two.

In terms of the theoretical models underlying the experiments (the first row in Table 24.1), decision-theoretic experiments are based on models of individual choice, such as expected utility theory and the discounted utility model. The distinction between game-theoretic and market experiments is not so clear in this sense, because game theory (both non-cooperative and cooperative variants) is also essential for theoretical modeling of market experiments. The distinction becomes clearer, however, once one considers the target constructs of measurement (the second row of Table 24.1). In game-theoretic experiments, the experimenter's interests are typically individual attributes, such as preferences and strategic rationality: do participants care only about their own pecuniary gains and losses, or do they also care about those of others? What is the depth of their strategic reasoning? In their focus on individual properties, game-theoretic experiments are similar to decision-theoretic ones. In market experiments, in contrast, the focus is on system-level properties, such as the efficiency of an experimental market with respect to competitive prices or the strategy-proofness of certain auction rules: do those rules encourage participants to state their true valuation of goods, or do they incentivize participants to strategically deviate from them? These are informational and allocational properties of an experimental system as a whole, consisting of agents endowed with particular information and constrained by rules defining their actions and interactions.

Table 24.1 The three-part typology of experiments in economics

Dimension\type	*Decision-theoretic*	*Game-theoretic*	*Market*
1. Theoretical models	Expected utility theory, discounted utility model	Non-cooperative games (Nash play; selfishness)	Matching and auction theory (e.g. Vickrey auction)
2. Measured constructs	Risk preferences, time preferences, subjective probability	Social preferences, strategic reasoning, expectations	Market efficiency, robustness, strategy-proofness
3. Well-established phenomena ("exhibits")	Preference reversals, Allais' paradox	"Fair" offers in the ultimatum game, decline of contributions in the public goods game	Convergence on equilibrium prices in Smith's double auction
4. Traditions	Testers		Builders

Guala's (2007) distinction between "the tester's tradition" and "the builder's tradition" roughly corresponds to the focus on system properties and the focus on individual properties, respectively, in experimental economics (the fourth row in Table 24.1). I will follow this terminology after making one qualification: not all experiments on individual properties are about testing theoretical hypotheses. Bardsley et al. (2010) argue that a lot of experimental economists' effort goes to establishing phenomena – what Daniel Kahneman once called "the bottled phenomena" – and analyzing their behavior. Sugden (2005) uses the term *exhibit* to refer to an experimental design that reliably produces an interesting phenomenon (the third row in Table 24.1). An important function of this terminology is to make a distinction between two related but distinct practices, namely, producing a phenomenon and explaining it. Experimenters may disagree over what explains a particular phenomenon, but they disagree less over the fact that such a phenomenon can be produced reliably. In this theory-independent sense, the decision-theoretic experiments that demonstrate Allais' paradox and the double auction experiments of Vernon Smith that demonstrate the convergence on competitive equilibrium prices and quantities of traded goods are both exhibits, although the former seems to refute the received theory (expected utility theory), while the latter seems to confirm it (the efficient market hypothesis). With this proviso in mind, the distinction between testers and builders is useful in contrasting two distinct loci of epistemic interests in economic experiments, namely, the individual and system properties. Of course, because the former is part of the building blocks of any economic system, the builders have to pay attention to the individual properties to the extent that they matter to the design of the system. This concern is most salient in the public goods game, in which the two traditions intersect.

Example 1: Public goods game

A public goods game is an experiment in which multiple players ($n \geq 2$) independently choose how to allocate the experimentally endowed money into private and public investments, which yield the payoff (π_i) defined as follows:

$$\pi_i = e_i - c_i + \frac{a\Sigma_k c_k}{N} \tag{1}$$

where $N > a > 1$ or, equivalently, $1 > \frac{a}{N} > \frac{1}{N}$. In words, each individual (i) is endowed with a certain amount of money (e_i), a fraction of which (c_i) she can contribute to the public investment ($e_i \geq c_i \geq 0$). Everyone's contribution is aggregated ($\Sigma_k c_k$), then multiplied by a factor a, and finally divided equally by all the participants (N), regardless of their individual contributions. The condition $a > 1$ makes the public investment profitable as a collective endeavor, while the condition $N > a$ makes it always individually more profitable if one contributes nothing. Notice that equation (1) represents the individual perspective: e_i stays in her pocket as it is – by factor 1 – whereas the contribution benefits her only by the factor $\frac{a}{N} < 1$ (*marginal per capita return* or MPCR). For example, an experiment with four players with $a = 2$ satisfies these conditions. These conditions constitute what experimental economists call a *voluntary contribution mechanism* (or VCM).

Public goods games are an instructive experimental paradigm often used to illustrate how experiments in economics are conducted (e.g. see Guala 2009, 2012) for at least two reasons. First, they capture the features of ubiquitous social dilemmas in everyday life and therefore help the reader grasp its incentive structure.[2] Second, and more importantly, it is a hybrid experiment in which the tester's and the builder's traditions intersect. On the one hand, the game can be interpreted as a many-player, many-strategy variation of the well-known prisoner's dilemma game, which is represented as a two-by-two normal form game with two players with two strategies. In this view, the properties of individual players, such as their beliefs, preferences, and strategic rationality can be the focus of the experiment. On the other hand, the VCM can be interpreted as an institutional arrangement to provide a public good. Although the standard theory recommends the use of involuntary measures such as taxation rather than the VCM for the provision of public goods, the latter captures the strategic situations underlying many economically important decentralized arrangements in the management of common resource pools, for instance. Because of its prevalence and centrality in people's economic lives, the builder's tradition has taken the paradigm seriously, trying to understand its system-level properties: how should the group be formed? Should communication be allowed and, if so, what information? How many rounds should the players play? Should they be allowed to punish free riders? The "shoulds" in these questions indicate the underlying design goal of the builder's tradition, namely, to promote more voluntary provision of public goods.

Public goods games can be a tricky example, however, because of their dual character. In this experimental paradigm, one of the key tasks for the builder who wishes to induce the voluntary provision of public goods (without changing the game structure itself significantly, that is) is to understand and exploit the individual properties of the participants, in particular those who do not conform to the standard models of choice, such as *conditional* preferences for cooperation, *strong reciprocity*, and *team reasoning*.

In contrast, in a typical market design experiment, beliefs, social preferences, and nonstandard strategic reasoning are carefully suppressed. For example, consider Smith's double auction.

Example 2: Double auction

In this experiment, an equal number of buyers and sellers are given different, predetermined reservation prices of a unit of an experimental commodity: for buyers in terms of willingness to pay (WTP, highest payable price) and for sellers in terms of willingness to accept (WTA, lowest acceptable price). The buyers and sellers then negotiate bilaterally to make an agreement for trade, and this is repeated in several rounds. A buyer (she) and a seller (he) can both make a profit if they manage to trade the commodity lower than her WTP and higher than his WTA, whereas how much profit each makes depends on the agreed-upon price.

One of the important rules of this experimental market is that a trade that creates negative profit is not accepted (zero profit is acceptable). This rule effectively eliminates the possibility that a participant could altruistically benefit the other trading partner. Another important rule is that each participant knows only her or his own WTP or WTA, so it is impossible to know the size of the collective surplus (the pie) from a potential trade (which is defined as the difference between her WTP and his WTA). So not only can a trader not make his or her own choice altruistic from a subjective point of view but a pair of traders also cannot establish an intersubjective understanding of what constitutes a fair deal. In addition, neither the pair nor the buyers nor the sellers are given any team frame nor collective consequences, so participants have no reason to team reason. These rules effectively eliminate motivations other than making as much profit as possible as an individual. It is not that the participants are selfish, but rather that the experiment is designed such that they behave as if they were, so that the experimenter does not have to rely on the complex motivations underlying interpersonal transactions to achieve design goals. In other auction experiments too, the key design task is to make sure that revealing one's own true valuation of a good is the dominant strategy for all of the participants, that is, regardless of what others do.

In sum, although market experiments such as Smith's double auction and public goods games share an interest in the design of efficient institutions, their routes to get there are rather different. The latter try to understand and exploit nonstandard behavior for the common good (voluntary provision of public goods), whereas the former try to eliminate it for another type of common good (maximizing collective surplus from trades). This is why I characterize the latter as having aspects of both tester's and builder's traditions: in public goods games, the tester's interest in demonstrating or explaining anomalies of human behavior and builder's interest in establishing that robust systems converge.

In order to understand the difference between the two traditions, it is instructive to look at another famous game-theoretic experiment, the ultimatum game (for a discussion, see Vromen, Chapter 9).

Example 3: The ultimatum game

An ultimatum game is a simple two-person, two-move game with the following setup. The proposer is endowed with some amount of money, let's say €10, and proposes to give some of it, $10 \geq x > 0$, to the responder, while keeping the rest $(10 - x)$. The responder has two choices, to either accept or reject the offer. If he accepts, then $\pi_p = 10 - X$ euro and $\pi_R = x$ euro. If he rejects, then both receive nothing $(\pi_p = \pi_R = 0)$.

Notice that this game can be interpreted as zeroing in on the situation that a pair in Smith's double auction faces after failing to make a deal with all of the other participants. Let's assume that the seller's WTA is €50 and the buyer's WTP is €60. The potential surplus from this trade is €10, and any proposal from either side is a proposal to divide it in a particular way. After some haggling over the right price, one trader makes a final, take-it-or-leave-it proposal at some point. An ultimatum game artificially isolates this last part of the bargaining process. As I said, however, Smith's traders do not know the size of the pie because the other's WTA or WTP is unknown. In contrast, the standard ultimatum game makes the size of the pie common knowledge, making sharing a salient frame. It also makes the pair more interdependent by removing outside options. Ultimatum games clearly belong to the tester's tradition because the focus is on isolating and understanding individual properties, in particular the participants'' other-regarding preferences. Although this is a game-theoretic experiment, the strategic aspect is kept to a minimum to focus on the preferences: because the game involves only two moves, the experimenter can assume common knowledge between both players about the implications of their choices. Specifically, because the responder clearly sees that acceptance always gives him more profit than rejection $(x > 0)$, his rejection must be motivated by something other than material gain, for example, anger at what he perceives as an unfair offer from the proposer.

As the contrast between Examples 2 and 3 shows, the testers are interested in revealing and measuring nonstandard or behavioral characteristics of individuals, whereas the builders tend to suppress these to focus on the behavior of experimental systems. Example 1 is a special case in that the experimental paradigm is useful for both traditions. Before we come back to the distinction between the tester's and builder's traditions later on in Section 4, let us briefly review how the standard typology can be situated in a wider context in which economics experiments are practiced.

2.2 From the Lab to the Field and to the Wild

The recent rise of *field experiments* in economics and other social sciences motivates another typology, defined along the dimension of laboratory vs. field experiments (e.g. Harrison and List 2004; Charness et al. 2013). Such a typology highlights a systematic way in which naturalism increases from the lab to field experiments. In principle, one can bring any of the three types of experiments (decision-theoretic, game-theoretic, or market experiments) from the lab to the field, to different degrees. And these experiments can address a range of epistemic interests from comparative measurements of some individual properties (e.g. social preferences) to tests of theoretical hypotheses (e.g. Gneezy et al. 2012). See Nagatsu and Favereau (2020), Favereau and Nagatsu (2020), and Favereau's chapter in this volume for a more detailed discussion on field experiments in economics (Favereau, Chapter 25).

Whereas field experiments still address epistemic goals (measurement and causal inference) through controlled variations, the notion of economic experimentation can be extended further to address nonepistemic interests, such as political persuasion and institutional reform. From this perspective, science and technology studies (STS) construe experiments as sociotechnological devices to construct and interact with reality. STS scholars thus de-emphasize the lab-field and controlled-uncontrolled divides, considering some activities "in the wild" as experimentation also. Muniesa and Callon (2007), for example, argue that economics experiments participate in the co-production of knowledge and governance, whether it is inside or outside of the laboratory walls. Table 24.2 summarizes the typology of Muniesa and Callon (2007) in columns and their dimensions in rows (row 4 shows their examples).

What Muniesa and Callon call platform experiments are not experiments in the standard sense, but more like public simulations with nonhuman subjects (e.g. commercial products and numbers in equations and computer programs). *In vivo* experiments are not experiments in the standard sense either, because they are characterized as lacking control, without even a random allocation of the subjects into treatment and control groups. They are experiments in a more nontechnical sense of involving trials and errors on the part of the experimenters and participants. This lack of emphasis on epistemically distinctive features of experiments, such as causal inference through direct and indirect control of variables, is motivated by interest in the unique ways in which economics experiments not only inform policy but also *perform* it by their very model-building practices (see e.g. Van Egmond and Zeiss 2010).

Table 24.2 A threefold typology of economics experiments*

Dimension\typology	*Laboratory*	*Platform*	*In vivo*
1. Location (materials)	Lab closed	Hybrid	Open in the wild
2. Manipulation (operations)	Imposition of experimental protocols	Simulation-by-modeling, simulation-by-testing	Injection of intervention into a black box
3. Demonstration (acceptance)	Academic publications => limited	Stakeholder engagement =>high. politicized	Maximal stakeholder engagement
4. Example	Elicitation of willingness to pay for GMO-free food products by Vickery auction	Optimization models for electricity market reform in France, French consumerist magazines' product tests	Reform of stock exchange rules in the Paris Bourse

*Based on Muniesa and Callon (2007).

Muniesa and Callon's (2007) typology allows us to understand the builder's tradition in experimental economics in a wider context. The builder is not only interested in building cognitively desirable systems in the lab but also interested in the design and construction of the sociotechnical systems that govern our economic lives. In fact, all three of these types of experiments are utilized in both episodes that Guala (2005) uses to illustrate the builder's tradition: the design of the auction of bandwidths by the US Federal Communications Commission (FCC) and the design of the auction of oil leases in the Outer Continental Shelf (OCS) of the Gulf of Mexico. In these highly applied policy and management contexts, the experimenter does not stay in the laboratory, from which she reports experimental results and suggests their policy implications; she goes out into the wild, interacting with stakeholders and sometimes becoming one of the participants in the system she herself helped build, as in the cases of auction design by game theorists.

In sum, whereas the standard typology identifies basic categories of laboratory experiments with specific interests in studying individual and/or system-level properties of a particular experimental paradigm, the extended typology relaxes the philosophical notion of experimentation associated with controlled variations. The extended typology highlights that the builders use wider methods by which to involve stakeholders and to co-produce experimental knowledge and governance practices. Thus, sometimes we need to pay attention not only to a range of experimenters' epistemic interests but also to the practical and even political interests of involved stakeholders (see, e.g., Mirowski and Nik-Khah 2007).

3. Philosophical Interests: The Logic of Inductive Inferences

But let us come back to *the philosopher's interests* in studying these experiments. An understanding of the different interests underlying them is surely one, which motivated our overview of the typologies in the last section. In this and the following sections, I will describe in more detail two main methodological interests and continue to add some of the experimental paradigms as illustrations. I will divide those interests into high level and low level and start with the former.

Perhaps one of the most prominent reasons why economics experiments interest philosophers of science is due to their methods to achieve reliable inductive inferences through systematic and controlled variations of experimental conditions. Guala (2012) thus sees experimental economics as a practice from which a general normative theory of inductive inferences can be abstracted. In this view, the experimental method is essentially "an attempt to investigate the causal influence of separate factors working in isolation" (Guala 2012, 613). Specifically, when the experimenter varies only one factor in the experimental and control conditions (denoted as X_e and X_c, respectively, or simply x and its absence), while holding all of the other factors (denoted as K) constant, then the difference between the outcomes of the two conditions (denoted as $Y_e - Y_c$) can be reliably attributed to the difference between the two conditions, namely, the experimental treatment x. Guala (2012) argues that this *model of the perfectly controlled experiment* captures the normative essence of various inferential strategies that experimental economists use.

Now consider a simple causal hypothesis H: the proposer's preference for the fair distribution of income (X) causes him to propose to the responder an equal division of the pie (Y) in the ultimatum game ($\neg H$ denotes its negation). The model of the perfectly controlled experiment implies that, in a good experiment, namely, an experiment in which the experimenter controls for the background conditions (K) well, (a) the observed values of the variables X and Y are correlated if H, *and* (b) they are not correlated if $\neg H$. Denote the confirming observation as E, and the disconfirming observation as $\neg E$. The experiment is a *severe test* of H if and only if the experimenter is likely to observe (a) E if H *and* (b) $\neg E$ if $\neg H$. The test is severe in the sense that E supports H more than in the case in which E would be observed had H been false (see Spanos, Chapter 29). Is the ultimatum game a severe test of our H? It is not, because X – the proposer's preference for a fair distribution of income – is not observable and not operationalized, that is, we do not observe variations in X. Specifically, there is another possibility that the fair offer is caused by the proposer's fear of the responder's rejection that would lead him to earn nothing. In order to test this possibility, one can compare the original game with a dictator game.

Example 4: The dictator game

The dictator game is the same as the ultimatum game (Example 3), except that the responder has no say in the game and, therefore, the proposer has no reason to fear that his minimum offer will be rejected.

Comparison of the observations from the two games is considered as a more severe test of H than its test in the ultimatum game because the former introduces the likelihood of observing $\neg E$ if $\neg H$. Of course, this controlled variation may introduce other uncontrolled, confounding factors, compromising its severity as a test of H (List 2007; Bardsley 2008). Nevertheless, a general lesson here is that severe testing guides an iterative process of experimentation, as well as the design of and inferences from single experiments.

Guala (2012) also emphasizes that a hypothesis that can be severely tested in an experiment is usually very specific and local (e.g. fair offers in bargaining games are robust and not due to a chance event), rather than high-level theoretical hypotheses or explanations (e.g. that the fairness concern causes fair offers in bargaining situations, or that this class of games elicits the latent and general construct of the "fairness" of individuals). This is to say that the logic of severe testing guides not only theory-testing experiments but also exhibits experiments, namely, the kind of experiments that are mostly concerned with establishing robust phenomena.

In sum, from a high-level perspective, economics experiments are interesting because philosophers can extract an important normative principle of inductive inferences, such as severe testing. [See Guala (2012, 3.3) for more elaboration of the severe test approach in contrast to other accounts of inductive inferences.]

4. Philosophical Interests: Methodological Divergence and Convergence Between Economics and Psychology

At a certain level of abstraction, philosophical accounts of causal inferences make explicit common, normative, methodological principles that guide a wide range of experimental practices. This type of abstraction addresses one type of philosophical interests but leaves another unsatisfied. That is: can we find more specific normative standards to adjudicate experimenters' disagreements? The typologies we reviewed in Section 2 suggest that the normative methodological standards may be different depending on one's interests. But these typologies are not sufficient when philosophers want to understand and reconcile controversies in which experimenters with apparently converging epistemic interests disagree over what should be the right account of a specific phenomenon or the right approach to investigating that type of phenomenon.

Controversies of this type are most salient in the debates in behavioral economics, whose central methods include experiments (Lecouteux, Chapter 4). Behavioral economics is a kind of interfield between economics and psychology, and many practitioners have discussed the differences between the two disciplines (e.g. Simon 1986; Kahneman 1988; Smith 1991; Lewin 1996; Rabin 1998, 2002; Hertwig and Ortmann 2001). Part of the core difference is, to use our terminology, that psychology is associated with the tester's tradition and economics with the builder's. The former is interested in the individual-level properties of decision-makers, mostly operating in decision-theoretic and game-theoretic experiments, while the latter is interested in the aggregate-level properties of interactive systems, mostly dealing with game-theoretic and market experiments (see Table 24.1). However, there are some cases in which these interests converge, as I have illustrated with public goods experiments in Section 2. In this section, I will discuss two more cases, mostly drawing on Kahneman (1988). Both cases are market experiments, which Kahneman (1988) takes to jointly demonstrate the limits of psychologists' contributions to economics. I update Kahneman's assessment, suggesting that there is room for further convergence between economics and psychology, drawing on the findings from more recent experiments.

4.1 Psychology Explains the Market

The first case is a series of famous experiments on endowment effects (Kahneman 1988; Kahneman et al. 1990, 1991). Endowment effects refer to the phenomenon in which one's measure of willingness to accept (WTA) in a seller's position is higher than one's measure of willingness to pay (WTP) in a buyer's position for the same good. In standard economic analysis, WTA and WTP are assumed to be approximately the same, such that mere ownership does not confer any psychic benefit or reluctance to trade. Recall Smith's double auction (Example 2), in which the experimenter assigns both buyers and sellers predetermined WTPs and WTAs for a unit of the experimental commodity. This manipulation is called the *induced value technique*. Under this control, the WTP of a buyer who is told that a unit is worth €5 for him will likely be €5, and so is the WTA of a seller who is told that a unit costs her €5. This will not change whether the same participant is assigned the role of a seller or a buyer. Is this experiment a severe test of the hypothesis that WTA = WTP? It is not. Rather, the experimental design ensures that this equality holds. In order to test this hypothesis, another design is needed.

Example 5: Double auction with a random allocation technique

Kahneman and colleagues devised a double auction experiment similar to Smith's but using a *random allocation technique*. In this design, the experimenter does not induce or impose values of a good to the participants, but instead assigns them randomly into a seller or a buyer role, by giving a random half of the participants goods such as coffee mugs and pens with a university logo (worth roughly $5). This way those who receive the good become potential sellers, and those who do not are potential buyers. Then individuals from both groups can meet and negotiate bilaterally to agree on a trade, as in Smith's double auction (see Kahneman et al. 1990; Dhami 2016, 217–235).

The key idea is that because this allocation is random, there is a 50/50 chance that a good is given to someone who values it more (and less) than the other participants. If WTA = WTP for all individuals, then approximately one-half of the goods will be traded. We do not know the exact shapes of the supply and demand curves, unlike in the experiment with the induced value technique, but we can expect that they will be "mirror images of each other" (Kahneman 1988, 15), leaving the volume of trade approximately one-half of the number of the distributed goods. The result, however, is that the actual volume of trade is about 50% of the prediction (for a more detailed discussion of randomized trials in economics, see Khosrowi, Chapter 27).

As Kahneman (1988) notes, this is not a refutation of WTA = WTP in all commodity markets; in fact, this equality holds up well in some situations, and not others, with an unclear boundary between the two types of situations. However, these series of experiments demonstrate that potential individual-level psychological causes of the discrepancy – such as "loss aversion, or ambiguity in the value of the good in conjunction with anticipated regret" (Kahneman 1988, 16) – may predictably affect the aggregate-level outcomes, such as the volume of trades. This is a vindication of the relevance of psychological factors to economics.

4.2 Psychology Does Not Explain the Market

Kahneman (1988) illustrates another market experiment that is in stark contrast to the experiments on endowment effects. He dubs it an $N^\star$ game, but the game is more commonly known as a market entry game.

Example 6: The N*/market entry game

The $N^\star$ game is an n-player symmetric coordination game without communication: the market is profitable for entrants, but the marginal profit from entry decreases as the number of entrants increases, and beyond a certain market capacity (denoted by $N^\star$) profit becomes negative. One can think of it as an n-person variation of the game of chicken (or the hawk-dove game). In the original experiment, $n = 15$ and N^* was changed over a period of repetition within the range $12 > N^\star > 3$; the payoff to each person was \$0.25 if one did not enter the market, and $\$[0.25 + 0.5(N^\star - E)]$ if one did, where E is the number of total entrants. If $E = N^\star$ – if the number of actual entrants equals the capacity – both entrants and nonentrants receive the same \$0.25 payoff. To Kahneman's great surprise, E quickly converged to $N^\star$ in a few rounds and stayed within the range $N^\star + 1 \geq E \geq N^\star - 1$ in the vast majority of trials. This is the implication of a mixed-strategy Nash equilibrium: each player decides to enter with a probability such that the expected payoff from entry equals that from nonentry – and is indifferent between entering and not entering in a steady state. The aggregate outcome from such individual strategies will result in $E \approx N^*$ (see Rapoport and Seale 2008).

What made Kahneman think that the result was "almost like magic" is not that the equilibrium result was reached. He had observed that in a variation of the experiments on endowment effects. Rather, what was "bewildering" was that "[t]he equilibrium outcome (which would be generated by the optimal policies of rational players) was produced in this case by a group of excited and confused people, who simply did not know what they were doing" (Kahneman 1988, 12). In other words, there is a causal gap between the aggregate phenomenon (the Nash equilibrium) and individual behavior (a mixture of non-Nash plays). The two lessons Kahneman learned from this experiment are (a) that the cognitive psychologist "has essentially nothing of interest to contribute" and (b) "that his bag of intellectual tools lack the powerful instrument of equilibrium explanations" (Kahneman 1988, 13). The second lesson is trivially true if game theory is monopolized by economics (cf. Nagatsu and Lisciandra 2021), but the first one is more substantial, which I will examine.

In fact, the result of the $N^\star$ game experiment, conducted by Kahneman and the economists Richard Thaler and James Brander, has never been published in a peer-reviewed journal of economics or psychology. One can speculate that the reason why this was not published is because the message did not favor their agenda of promoting behavioral economics, and the priority was instead given to publishing results from endowment effects experiments (Kahneman et al. 1990), as well as ultimatum and dictator games (Kahneman et al. 1986a, 1986b), both of which highlight the violation of the standard economics predictions while offering psychological explanations. Another explanation, which is compatible with the first, is that Kahneman really felt, as he recounts (Kahneman 1988), that psychology had little to contribute to the understanding of the equilibrium results in market entry games.[3] In any case, more recent results from market entry games show that cognitive psychology *is* relevant to the understanding of market entry games. Amnon Rapoport and his colleagues have conducted a series of market entry games since 1995, and they find (a) that when learning is allowed by design, individual behavior also converges on some individual-specific behavioral rules (for example, conditioning one's entrance decision on some cutoff market capacity $c^{\star}$) and (b) that the distribution of different cutoff rules is sufficient for generating the equilibrium results (Rapoport and Seale 2008). In particular, the study of (a) is informed by the theory of short-term memory and learning, which psychologists have developed and which also informed behavioral game theory (see Camerer 2003, chapter 3). So, it is not generally true that cognitive psychology has no potential contribution here. The relevant causal mechanisms underlying the equilibrium results concern both the individual (learning of heuristics) and the aggregate (combination of heterogeneous behavioral patterns), and the former is a psychological phenomenon. Moreover, some behavioral economists (e.g. Dhami 2016) contend that the type (b) explanation is an alternative, more realistic explanation than the "as if" explanation by mixed-strategy Nash equilibrium. So, the fact that psychologists do not have "the powerful instrument of equilibrium explanations" might not even be the fundamental obstacle for psychologists to contribute to the study of the aggregate phenomenon.

4.3 Economics and Psychology Reconsidered

The last point is most clearly demonstrated by recent developments in decision-theoretic experiments, in which the aggregate-level data are not explained by the Nash equilibrium because they are not the result of interactive decision-making. However, this does not mean that the explanations of the results from these experiments are exhausted by individual-level psychological mechanisms. The outcome of a risky-choice experiment, for example, can be explained as resulting from either (a) the average behavior of one type of decision-maker (e.g. following expected utility theory, prospect theory, and so on) or (b) the combination of the behaviors of these heterogeneous types of decision-makers. The results of a decision-theoretic experiment can even be an outcome of the mixture of risky choice and intertemporal choice, that is, caused by both risk and the time preferences of any given individual decision-maker (Andersen et al. 2008). When the experimenter tries to test the truth of one model of choice against another, (a) is implicitly assumed (model selection test). But the experimenter can also explicitly test this assumption by making a structural model of the data-generating processes, assuming that multiple types of decision-makers exist, or that multiple types of decision-making mechanisms operate inside one individual, or both (model specification test). As a statistical technique to do this, the maximum likelihood estimation of such a structural model with a mixture specification is used (Harrison 2019). This approach to explicitly addressing the heterogeneity of data-generating processes in experimental economics is called *behavioral econometrics* (Andersen et al. 2010) or *experimetrics* (Moffatt 2016). As it demonstrates, even in non-game-theoretic and non-market experiments, explicit modeling of how individual-level choices give rise to aggregate-level data seems crucial for better understanding experimental results.

In particular, this approach can lead researchers to explain individual-level decision-making mechanisms in a way that goes beyond the standard utility maximization modeling framework (see also Grayot, Chapter 6). Andersen et al. (2014), for example, illustrate how a nonmaximization, dual-process model of individual risky choice can explain the experimental results using the behavioral econometrics approach. This is significant methodological progress from the psychological perspective too, given that the continuous dependence on the as if models of utility maximization has been one of the main complaints about behavioral economics by some psychologists (e.g. Berg and Gigerenzer 2010).

To summarize this section, Kahneman (1988) takes the endowment effect experiment to illustrate a situation in which psychology can directly explain economic phenomena, whereas the N^* game illustrates another situation in which psychology has no contribution to make. Drawing on the recent experimental results and methodological developments in experimental economics, I reevaluated this assessment, which was also revisited by Kahneman in his Nobel Prize biography (Kahneman 2003). Put simply, my assessment is that Kahneman (1988) was too pessimistic about psychology's contribution to economics. Moreover, this pessimistic assessment was based on the contingent dichotomy between psychology as responsible for the explanation of individual choices and economics for the aggregate choice data. This dichotomy has been challenged both empirically and methodologically.

5. Conclusion

In this chapter, I have provided an overview of diverse experimental practices in economics, by way of reviewing two typologies of economics experiments (Section 2). These typologies highlight that different experimental practices are motivated by different epistemic and nonepistemic interests, such as investigating individual- and system-level properties of experimental systems, extrapolating experimental results to nonexperimental setups, evaluating policy, and constructing a new socio-technological system in the wild with stakeholders. The philosopher who is interested in a normative theory of inductive inferences can glean from these experimental practices the logic of inductive inferences, such as the severe testing methodology, among others (Section 3). At the same time, philosophical interests, on a finer level, call for some explanation and evaluation of the existing controversies in experimental economics. I focused on a general question, "does economics need psychology?" to which different economists and psychologists would give different answers. To situate this question in the context of experimental economics, I examined Kahneman's (1988) take on the bounds between economics and psychology, which draws on two market experiments he has conducted, one famous and the other lesser known in behavioral economics (Section 4). Drawing on the recent developments in these and other experiments, I argued for a kind of symmetrical convergence between psychological and economic perspectives in experimental economics. Although behavioral economics has highlighted a particularly dramatic way in which psychology can be directly relevant to the study of economic phenomena (as in the endowment effect experiment), there is much more potential for psychological and economic perspectives to inform each other in experimental economics. I have briefly mentioned the use of the theory of short-term memory and learning in behavioral game theory and the use of a nonoptimization model of individual choice in decision-theoretic experiments.

I said *symmetrical* convergence because these developments point to the limit of framing the debate as one-sided, as in the question "does economics need psychology?" At least in some important class of economics experiments in which the interests in the individual- and aggregate-level phenomena converge, it seems that psychology also needs economics, as much as the latter needs it.

Acknowledgments

I thank Francesco Guala, Judith Favereau, and Julian Reiss for providing valuable feedback on the early drafts of this chapter and James Blander and Amnon Rapoport for generously sharing their insights on the market entry game via email and Zoom, respectively. All remaining mistakes are mine. The author is not aware of any potential conflict of interest in this research.

Funding

This research is conducted as part of the project Model-building across disciplinary boundaries: Economics, Ecology, and Psychology (2016–2021), funded by the Academy of Finland (No. 294545).

Related Chapters

Favereau, J., Chapter 25 "Field Experiments"
Grayot, J., Chapter 6 "Economic Agency and the Subpersonal Turn in Economics"
Khosrowi, D., Chapter 27 "Evidence-Based Policy"
Lecouteux, G., Chapter 4 "Behavioral Welfare Economics and Consumer Sovereignty"
Spanos, A., Chapter 29 "Philosophy of Econometrics"
Vromen, J., Chapter 9 "*As If* Social Preference Models"

Notes

1 The dictator game (see Example 4) is an exception in the sense that one of the two players does not make any choice. But for the experiment to count as game theoretic, the presence of that passive player is needed.
2 This does not mean, however, that experimental subjects immediately understand the structure of the game, because experimental games are often presented in a very context-neutral fashion.
3 James Blander points out that one reason why the N^* game project was not completed was timing: Thaler's visit to the University of British Columbia (UBC) in 1984–1985 ended, and Kahneman left UBC the following academic year. But Blander also mentions that "we had not really found a good way to demonstrate the key insight we were trying to identify" (email correspondence with the author, May 25, 2020).

Bibliography

Andersen, S., Harrison, G. W., Lau, M. I., and Rutström, E. E. (2008). Eliciting risk and time preferences. *Econometrica*, 76(3):583–618.
Andersen, S., Harrison, G. W., Lau, M. I., and Rutström, E. E. (2010). Behavioral econometrics for psychologists. *Journal of Economic Psychology*, 31(4):553–576.
Andersen, S., Harrison, G. W., Lau, M. I., and Rutström, E. E. (2014). Dual criteria decisions. *Journal of Economic Psychology*, 41:101–113. From Dual Processes to Multiple Selves: Implications for Economic Behavior.
Bardsley, N. (2008). Dictator game giving: Altruism or artefact? *Experimental Economics*, 11:122–133.
Bardsley, N., Cubitt, R., Loomes, G., Moffat, P., Starmer, C., and Sugden, R. (2010). *Experimental economics: Rethinking the rules*. Princeton University Press, Princeton, NJ.
Berg, N. and Gigerenzer, G. (2010). As-if behavioral economics: Neoclassical economics in disguise? *History of Economic Ideas*, 18(1):133–166.
Camerer, C., Issacharoff, S., Loewenstein, G., O'Donoghue, T., and Rabin, M. (2003). Regulation for conservatives: Behavioral economics and the case for 'asymmetric paternalism'. *University of Pennsylvania Law Review*, 151(3):1211–1254.
Camerer, C. F. (2003). *Behavioral Game Theory*. Princeton University Press, Princeton, NJ.
Charness, G., Gneezy, U., and Kuhn, M. A. (2013). Experimental methods: Extra-laboratory experiments – extending the reach of experimental economics. *Journal of Economic Behavior & Organization*, 91(0):93–100.
Dhami, S. (2016). *The Foundations of Behavioral Economic Analysis*. Oxford University Press, Oxford.
Favereau, J. and Nagatsu, M. (2020). Holding back from theory: Limits and methodological alternatives of randomized field experiments in development economics. *Journal of Economic Methodology*, 0(0):1–21.
Gneezy, U., List, J., and Price, M. K. (2012). Toward an understanding of why people discriminate: Evidence from a series of natural field experiments. Working Paper 17855, National Bureau of Economic Research.
Guala, F. (2005). *The Methodology of Experimental Economics*. Cambridge University Press, Cambridge, England.
Guala, F. (2007). How to do things with experimental economics. In MacKenzie, D., Muniesa, F., and Siu, L., editors, *Do Economist Make Markets? On the Performativity of Economics*, chapter 5, pages 128–162. Princeton University Press, Princeton, NJ.
Guala, F. (2009). Methodological issues in experimental design and interpretation. In Ross, D. and Kincaid, H., editors, *The Oxford handbook of philosophy of economics*. Oxford University Press, Oxford.

Guala, F. (2012). Experimentation in economics. In Mäki, U., editor, *Philosophy of Economics*, Handbook of the Philosophy of Science, pages 597–640. North-Holland, Amsterdam.
Güth, W. and Kliemt, H. (2017). Experimental economics – a philosophical perspective. In *Oxford Handbooks Online*, pages 1–33. Oxford University Press, Oxford.
Harrison, G. W. (2019). The methodologies of behavioral econometrics. In Nagatsu, M. and Ruzzene, A., editors, *Contemporary Philosophy and Social Science: An Interdisciplinary Dialogue*, chapter 4, pages 107–137. Bloomsbury Academic.
Harrison, G. W. and List, J. A. (2004). Field experiments. *Journal of Economic Literature*, 42(4):1009–1055.
Hertwig, R. and Ortmann, A. (2001). Experimental practices in economics: A methodological challenge for psychologists? *Behavioral and Brain Sciences*, 24:383–451.
Jacquemet, N. and l'Haridon, O. (2018). *Experimental Economics*. Cambridge University Press, Cambridge.
Kahneman, D. (1988). Experimental economics: A psychological perspective. In Tietz, R., Albers, W., and Selten, R., editors, *Bounded Rational Behavior in Experimental Games and Markets*, pages 11–20. Springer-Verlag, Berlin.
Kahneman, D. (2003). Biographical. Nobelprize.org.
Kahneman, D., Knetsch, J. L., and Thaler, R. H. (1986a). Fairness as a constraint on profit seeking: Entitlements in the market. *The American Economic Review*, 76(4):728–741.
Kahneman, D., Knetsch, J. L., and Thaler, R. H. (1986b). Fairness and the assumptions of economics. *The Journal of Business*, 59(4):S285–S300.
Kahneman, D., Knetsch, J. L., and Thaler, R. H. (1990). Experimental tests of the endowment effect and the Coase theorem. *Journal of Political Economy*, 98(6):1325–1348.
Kahneman, D., Knetsch, J. L., and Thaler, R. H. (1991). Anomalies: The endowment effect, loss aversion, and status quo bias. *Journal of Economic Perspectives*, 5(1):193–206.
Lewin, S. B. (1996). Economics and psychology: Lessons for our own day from the early twentieth century. *Journal of Economic Literature*, 34(3):1293–1323.
List, J. A. (2007). On the interpretation of giving in dictator games. *Journal of Political Economy*, 115(3):482–493.
Mirowski, P. and Nik-Khah, E. (2007). Markets made flesh: Performativity and a problem in science studies, augmented with consideration of the fcc auctions. In MacKenzie, D., Muniesa, F., and Siu, L., editors, *Do Economist Make Markets? On the Performativity of Economics*, chapter 7, pages 190–224. Princeton University Press, Princeton, NJ.
Moffatt, P. G. (2016). *Experimetrics: Econometrics for Experimental Economics*. Palgrave Macmillan, London.
Muniesa, F. and Callon, M. (2007). Economic experiments and the construction of markets. In MacKenzie, D., Muniesa, F., and Siu, L., editors, *Do Economist Make Markets? On the Performativity of Economics*, chapter 6, pages 163–189. Princeton University Press, Princeton, NJ.
Nagatsu, M. and Favereau, J. (2020). Two strands of field experiments in economics: A historical-methodological analysis. *Philosophy of the Social Sciences*, 50(1):45–77.
Nagatsu, M. and Lisciandra, C. (2021). Why is behavioral game theory a game for economists? The concept of beliefs in equilibrium. In Egashira, S., Taishido, M., Hands, W., and Mäki, U., editors, *A Genealogy of Self-interest in Economics*. Springer, New York.
Rabin, M. (1998). Psychology and economics. *Journal of Economic Literature*, 36(1):11–46.
Rabin, M. (2002). A perspective on psychology and economics. *European Economic Review*, 46:657–685.
Rapoport, A. and Seale, D. A. (2008). Coordination success in non-cooperative large group market entry games. In Plott, C. R. and Smith, V. L., editors, *Handbook of Experimental Economics Results*, volume 1, chapter 34, pages 273–295. Amsterdam: North-Holland.
Roth, A. E. (1993). The early history of experimental economics. *Journal of the History of Economic Thought*, 15(2):184–209.
Rubin, H., O'Connor, C., and Bruner, J. (2019). Experimental economics for philosophers. In Fischer, E. and Curtis, M., editors, *Methodological Advances in Experimental Philosophy*, Advances in experimental philosophy, pages 175–206. London: Bloomsbury Publishing.
Simon, H. A. (1986). Rationality in psychology and economics. *The Journal of Business*, 59(4):S209–S224.
Smith, V. L. (1991). Rational choice: The contrast between economics and psychology. *Journal of Political Economy*, 99(4):877–897.
Sugden, R. (2005). Experiments as exhibits and experiments as tests. *Journal of Economic Methodology*, 12(2):291–302.
Van Egmond, S. and Zeiss, R. (2010). Modeling for policy science-based models as performative boundary objects for Dutch policy making. *Science & Technology Studies*, 23(1):58–78.

25
FIELD EXPERIMENTS

Judith Favereau

1. Introduction

The 2019 Nobel Prize in Economic Sciences, awarded to Abhijit Banerjee, Esther Duflo, and Michael Kremer, has acknowledged the importance of field experiments in economics, and more specifically the importance of randomized field experiments (RFEs) in development economics. Historically, there have been two strands of field experiments: one that draws from laboratory experiments and the other that draws from social field experiments more broadly (Nagatsu and Favereau, 2020). These social field experiments evaluate large-scale public policies and often explicitly rely on a theoretical framework. Social field experiments aim to simultaneously test a public policy and a theoretical framework. RFEs in development economics are based on social field experiments, although they change significant dimensions of these experiments. Indeed, they aim to test local development policy and do not rely on any theoretical framework. This change of scale, as well as the lack of any explicit theoretical framework in the study, changes the methodological challenge that experiments usually face, which is that of validity. The literature on experimentation often distinguishes between internal and external validity.[1] Internal validity is the validity of the experimental result within the context of the particular experiment. This validity tests whether the experiment highlights any causal inference. External validity is the validity of the experimental result outside the frame of the experiment. This validity emphasizes whether the experimental result is applicable to another context. For instance, when an experiment evaluates a local development program, does it imply that a similar result would be obtained in a region other than the one of the experiment? Social field experiments conducted on a large scale that rely on a theoretical framework are often considered to have weak internal validity and a stronger external validity. In contrast, proponents of RFEs in development economics insist on the strong internal validity of these experiments, while critics point out their weak external validity. In this sense, RFEs reframe the methodological challenges of field experiments in economics. Moreover, they also emphasize two distinct issues of external validity: artificiality[2] and generalizability. Indeed, field experiments inspired by the lab are often described as artificial and too detached from the real world, whereas RFEs might suffer from difficulties related to generalizing the results to other contexts. (For a further discussion of lab experiments in economics, see Nagatsu, Chapter 24.)

This chapter attempts to highlight these methodological challenges for RFEs. I will try do this by showing that the methodological challenges that RFEs face are all embedded in the notion of "the field." I will rely on the notion of the field as recently defined by Boumans (2015). The field refers

DOI: 10.4324/9781315739793-31

to an environment that is messy and complex. Moreover, the field helps to define social sciences. This stands in opposition to the laboratory, which is used in the natural sciences. The laboratory offers a controlled and clean environment. In such an environment, one can produce reliable causal inferences. My claim in this chapter is that recent field experiments in economics, namely, RFEs, have succeeded in making the field vanish: they are field experiments devoid of a messy and complex environment. Therefore, they almost become field experiments conducted in a laboratory. The field in which they take place has become a laboratory: an environment that is fully controlled from which one can draw reliable causal inferences. However, in keeping with the metaphor, within such a ghost field, such reliable causal inferences are restricted to the laboratory. This is another way of framing the struggle between internal and external validity within field experiments, and particularly within RFEs. Transformation of the field into a lab enables RFEs to produce reliable causal inferences, guaranteeing that they have strong internal validity. However, this transformation weakens the researcher's ability to extrapolate from these causal inferences and apply the results to other environments. I will therefore call for alternatives that could restore the field to RFEs, which will ensure that RFEs keep their internal validity while strengthening their external one.

Section 2 presents the history of field experiments and gives some examples that illustrate the diversity of these experiments. Section 3 concentrates on the most recent iteration of these experiments, that is to say, RFEs in development economics, and highlights the main challenges of RFEs and changes from previous experiments (such as the lack of theory, the change of scale, and the field as a lab). Section 4 suggests that RFEs could be combined with qualitative studies in order to reintegrate some aspects of the field. Section 5 concludes.

2. Field Experiments in Economics: A Historical Overview

Field experiments are vast and diverse and, as such, are hard to define. Harrison and List (2004) have provided a taxonomy to define field experiments and to distinguish them from laboratory experiments. This taxonomy helps to define the first strand of field experiments in economics (Nagatsu and Favereau, 2020), which draws on laboratory experiments and applies the main principles of these experiments to field experiments. However, field experiments in economics also draw from a second source: social field experiments. This chapter concentrates on this second strand. List (2006a) and List and Metcalfe (2015) have offered a useful distinction to understand what field experiments in this second strand are, which is the distinction between naturally occurring data and controlled data. On the basis of this distinction, List and Metcalfe (2015) have defined field experiments as lying on a spectrum between laboratory and natural experiments. Such a spectrum follows Harrison and List (2004)'s typology. As Figure 25.1 highlights, at the extreme left end of the spectrum lie the laboratory experiments, which are characterized by fully controlled data. At the other extreme of the spectrum are those experiments that use naturally occurring data. The left spectrum relates to the first strand of field experiments in economics, while the right one relates to the second strand. The experiments in which data occur naturally are natural field experiments and natural experiments.[3]

Artifactual field experiments mimic the laboratory, except that the subjects are nonstandard, which means that they are not economics students. Framed field experiments are, according to Levitt and List (2009), a type of social experiment. Greenberg and Shroder (2004), who have compiled the largest report of all social experiments that have been conducted, define a social field experiment as having four characteristics. A social field experiment is an experiment that aims to (1) assess the impact of (2) a political intervention and (3) to collect data on such a political intervention. In order to properly collect data, the participants of the experiment are (4) randomly assigned into at least two groups. The participants of one of these two groups receive the political intervention that is being assessed, while the other group does not receive the intervention. Such a design allows for the comparison of the two groups and, thus, allows researchers to identify the

Controlled data			Naturally occurring data	
Lab	AFE	FFE	NFE	NE PSM IV STR

Notes: Lab: lab experiment; AFE: artefactual field experiment; FFE: framed field experiment; NFE: natural field experiment; NE: natural experiment; PSM: propensity score estimation; IV: instrumental variables estimation; STR: structural modelling.

Figure 25.1 Spectrum of empirical methods

Source: List and Metcalfe (2015)

impact of the intervention. The random assignment also provides another advantage: it removes the selection bias, therefore offering reliable results.[4] These social experiments focus on evaluating public policies. Indeed, the primary objective of these experiments is to "speak to policy-makers" (Greenberg and Shroder, 2004: 4).[5] A framed field experiment is, according to Levitt and List (2009), a social experiment in which the subjects are aware of the randomization. A natural field experiment is a framed field experiment in which the subjects are neither aware that they are part of the experiment nor aware that they have been randomly assigned to one group. Finally, a natural experiment is an experiment in which exogeneous changes, for example, a change in the law, mimic a social experiment and in which the subjects do not know they are being observed (Carpenter, Harrison, and List, 2005; Meyer, 1995). In addition, Diaz, Jimenez-Buedo, and Teira (2015) have discussed the history of field and quasi-field experiments in medicine and social sciences. They highlight that the major difference between the two is the way in which the intervention is assigned to the individuals: randomized in the field experiment and not randomized in the quasi-field experiment.

The New Jersey Income Maintenance experiment is often considered to be the first social experiment conducted in the field of economics (Levitt and List, 2009).[6] This experiment was aimed at testing a specific economic hypothesis on the negative income tax, as well as its political implications. The idea of a negative income tax was developed by Milton Friedman (1962) and proposed that, over a certain threshold, households have to pay taxes, while under this threshold households receive subsidies. The threshold thus allows for policymakers to distinguish between positive and negative taxes. This experiment was conducted by Heather Ross from 1968 to 1972 and constituted her PhD dissertation for the Massachusetts Institute of Technology. In her dissertation, Ross wanted to investigate new tools to reliably assess the impact of a political intervention that is directly based on economic theory. Ross suggested that, to do this, an RFE should be conducted. In addition to the experiment, the participants had to answer a questionnaire every three months. The results of the experiment have shown that a negative tax does create incentives for people who receive them to work, or at least it does not provide any incentives for people to refrain from looking for a job (as some economic theories would have supposed). More than 235 social field experiments evaluating public policy programs have been conducted during the second half of the 20th century [Greenberg and Shroder (2004) offer a comprehensive overview of these experiments]. Labor economics was one of the privileged subfields of economics in which these social experiments were implemented. For instance, in 1986, during the Reagan administration, a vast job program was evaluated using an RFE: the Job Training Partnership Act Title II-A (Greenberg and Shroder, 2004). This experiment is the paradigm case used by Heckman (2010) and Heckman, Clement, and Smith (1997) to question the power of social evaluations in contrast to structural econometrics. List and Rasul (2010) have offered a recent overview of these field experiments in labor economics.

In the area of natural field experiments, Levitt and List (2009) have argued that Ashraf, Karlan, and Yin's (2006) experiment is emblematic.[7] In partnership with the Green Bank of Caraga in the Philippines, the researchers constructed a saving commitment product, which restricted the client's access to their own savings. Half of the clients, randomly chosen, benefited from a new contract, named Save, Earn, Enjoy Deposits, which was actually the saving commitment product that restricted access to savings. The other half of the clients were either in the control group or in the marketing group, which received visits from officials promoting the benefits of the saving product. Ashraf, Karlan, and Yin (2006) found that the treatment group's savings increased significantly, leading them to argue that the saving product could generate lasting and substantial changes in saving behavior. This experiment is classified as a natural field experiment because the subjects were not aware that they were part of the experiment nor that they had been randomly selected to be a certain group. Finally, List (2006b) is an example of a natural experiment. List (2006b) analyzed data from a television show called "Friend or Foe?" According to List (2006b), this show was similar to the prisoner's dilemma. In the show, people work together to earn money, and then they play a one-shot prisoner's dilemma game. The money they can earn in this last step ranges from $200 to more than $22,000. List (2006b) concluded that the participants' reactions in the show were similar to those that the discrimination model would have predicted. This experiment is a natural one, because the experimenters did not intervene in the research. The intervention is an exogeneous one, namely, the show. The show participants did not know that they were being observed by List (2006b).

These three experiments offer an overview of what field experiments are and help to highlight some of their differences, as well as their different methodologies and designs.[8] They are all concerned with different topics, ranging from taxation and savings to discrimination. List and Metcalfe (2015) offer an overview of the different domains of field experiments in developed countries. They list field experiments on human capital and wages, air pollution, payment compliance, public goods, and savings. Indeed, most field experiments are conducted in the subfield of labor economics.

3. Randomized Experiments: When the Field Vanished

At the beginning of the 21st century, field experiments underwent an important methodological change, primarily in the field of development economics. Indeed, following the development of evidence-based medicine, which occurred a decade earlier in that field, field experiments in development economics became the privileged tool for the development of evidence-based policy. In 2003, Abhijit Banerjee, Esther Duflo, and Sendhil Mullainthan created the Jameel Abdul Latif Poverty Action Lab (J-PAL) at the Massachusetts Institute of Technology. The goal of this laboratory is to base the fight against poverty on evidence. RFEs, in a manner similar to randomized controlled trials in medicine, are often considered to be the methodological gold standard, and, more importantly, they are at the top of the evidence hierarchy.[9] In other words, RFEs are the keystone of evidence-based policies. (For a detailed discussion of evidence-based policy, see Khosrowi, Chapter 27.) They produce the evidence on which decisions will then be based. Thereby, RFEs in economics today are the byproduct of social field experiments and evidence-based movements.

This combination of social experiments and evidence-based movements has substantially changed field experiments in economics. The first change is the move away from testing theories. For instance, Duflo (2006) has emphasized that theory is not a strong basis for policymaking. Moreover, Banerjee (2005) has argued that theories are contradictory, at least in behavioral economics, and create chaos. The aim of these new types of field experiments is, therefore, to move away from theory. Their more important aim is to assess the impact of public policies, particularly in developing countries. Indeed, according to Banerjee and Duflo (2011), neither researchers nor development aid agencies know what is efficient in the fight against poverty. As such, there are no clear guidelines on what steps to take to eradicate poverty. RFEs are thus systematically promoted by J-PAL's researchers to assess the impact of development programs. The second major change is the change in scale of these experiments. In social field experiments, discussed in the previous section, field experiments assessed policy on a large scale. However, RFEs in development economics are done on a small scale. According to Banerjee and Duflo (2011), the accumulation of changes at the margin will lead to a quiet revolution, a world without extreme poverty. Banerjee and Duflo (2011) have argued passionately against what they call "political economy." Political economy, according to Banerjee and Duflo (2011), relates to the work of Daron Acemoglu and Jonathan Robinson (2012). Acemoglu and Robinson (2012) emphasize that the development process is an institutional process. They also insist on the need to grasp the "big picture" to understand development processes.

RFEs in development economics therefore are now a dominant tool.[10] Indeed, upon its creation in 2004, the J-PAL had conducted 21 RFEs, while this number today is 1094.[11] The systematic promotion of RFEs, especially in development economics, has led to what Harrison (2013) terms "methodological intolerance." This methodological intolerance imposes that field experiments should only be randomized ones. As List and Metcalfe (2015) argue, field experiments are not necessarily randomized experiments. The randomization part is not mandatory, for several reasons. Ziliak (2014), Heckman (2010, 1992), and Heckman and Smith (1995) point to statistical reasons. Ortmann (2005) and Harrison (2005, 2014) argue that the issue of control does not vanish with RFEs; it simply takes other forms. List (2006a) calls for bridges between field experiments. Harrison (2005, 2014) warns that an experimental design should serve a research purpose; therefore, different research questions imply different experimental designs. One should, thus, benefit from the plurality of field experiment designs rather than simply promoting one.

Let me now illustrate one of these RFEs, as doing so will help me highlight the methodological challenges of these field experiments and highlight how they differ from previous ones. This is the RFE conducted by Blattman, Jamison, and Sheridan (see Blattman, Jamison, and Sheridan, 2017). It was aimed at testing the impact of cognitive behavioral therapy and cash transfers on "high risk young men." Blattman, Jamison, and Sheridan (2017) first emphasized that, in developing countries and in fragile states, young men with no real economic and social opportunity might engage in criminal activities, leading to social instability and threatening economic growth. The experiment was implemented in Monrovia, the capital of Liberia, jointly with a nonprofit organization called the Network for Empowerment and Progressive Initiative (NEPI). The NEPI recruited 1,000 young men aged between 18 and 35 years who were considered "high risk" to be part of the experiment. A total of 999 young men were enrolled in the experiment. Half of them were randomly assigned to eight weeks of cognitive behavioral therapy. At the end of therapy, the full sample of 999 young men were again randomly assigned into two groups: one in which the young men benefited from an unconditional cash transfer of US$200 and the other group in which the young men did not receive the cash transfer. The experimental results show that therapy had a positive impact on both the young men's behavior and their beliefs. The unconditional transfer did not have any impact. However, the unconditional transfer combined with the therapy generated a higher impact than the therapy alone. Last, both the therapy and unconditional transfer did not have any impact on the men's long-term economic outcomes.

It is difficult to explain these results on the basis of the RFE alone, namely, to highlight the mechanisms behind such results. Indeed, without considering a theoretical framework, how can one highlight such mechanisms? Moreover, because the RFEs are conducted on a small scale, how can one scale up the program? Most of the criticisms against RFEs revolve around these two issues. Such criticisms come from development economics (Deaton, 2010, 2020; Ravallion, 2009; Rodrik, 2008; Acemoglu, 2010, Basu, 2014; Barrett and Carter, 2010), experimental economics (Harrison, 2011, 2013), econometrics (Heckman, 1992; Heckman and Smith, 1995; Leamer, 2010), the philosophy of science (Cartwright, 2007, 2009a, 2009b, 2010; Cartwright and Hardie, 2012; Teira and Reiss, 2013; Teira, 2013; Davis, 2013), and, more recently, economics and philosophy jointly (Cartwright and Deaton, 2018a, 2018b). As Deaton (2010: 451) frames it, the RFEs' results are a "black box test of 'what works':" one knows whether a program is working but does not know *why* the program is working. This black box expresses the trade-off that might exist between the internal and external validity of RFEs.[12] As seen in the previous section, the random assignment reduces the selection bias of the two groups. Selection bias occurs when the difference in the results of the two groups is not due to the treatment but is due instead to the different characteristics of the individuals in the two groups. The random assignment enables researchers to remove such a bias, guaranteeing the internal validity of RFEs. However, in doing so, the random assignment masks the individual and social characteristics of the sample. According to Deaton (2010), this masking leads to the black box, which relates to the external validity issue. Indeed, the individual and social characteristics of the individuals that are masked by the random assignment makes it difficult to hypothesize the potential mechanisms behind a treatment. Deaton (2010) frames this issue around the one of heterogeneity (see also, Harrison, 2011, 2014; Heckman, 1992, 2010; Heckman and Smith, 1995; Heckman et al., 1997, 1998; Leamer, 2010 on this issue). RFEs offer an average of the treatment effect for the two groups. From an RFE alone, one cannot access the distribution of the treatment effect. In other words, one does not know how the participants interact with the treatment. This distribution could offer valuable insights into the mechanisms behind the RFE results.[13] The existence of such a black box threatens the external validity of RFEs.

My claim is that, in masking social and individual characteristics, RFEs make the field vanish. Indeed, the social and individual characteristics, which are made invisible by the random assignment, are the central aspect of the field, as well as of the complex and messy environment in which the experiment takes place. Therefore, RFEs create a laboratory in the field. In other words, it is now possible to obtain an artificially clean and controlled environment and to impose it on the field. The issue with this is that such an artificially clean and controlled environment does not offer any clues for understanding the results that are obtained, as it has removed the field. The field encapsulates all of these social and individual characteristics in a messy and complex environment. Without it, one struggles to come up with explanations based on the results of RFEs. Therefore, it seems that what is needed is for the field to be restored.

4. Restoring the Field

Some of the researchers who have criticized RFEs have proposed alternatives to accessing the underlying mechanisms of the RFEs' results. In other words, they have proposed alternatives to understanding *why* the program tested is working or not. For instance, in development economics, various researchers (Deaton, 2010; Ravallion, 2009; Rodrik, 2008; Acemoglu, 2010; Basu, 2014; Barrett and Carter, 2010) have insisted on the need for theory to understand why a development program is working. In particular, Acemoglu (2010), Deaton (2010), Harrison (2011, 2013), Heckman (1992), Heckman and Smith (1995), Heckman, Clement, and Smith (1997), Heckman et al. (1998), and Leamer (2010) have emphasized the importance of structural estimation in econometrics to highlight the causal channels at play in an experiment. The results of RFEs are usually expressed in reduced-form econometrics and, as such, are detached from other factors, and their interactions with these other factors are not defined. The philosophical literature, especially Cartwright and Hardie (2012), has emphasized that, on the one hand, one needs to proceed in the abstract in defining the causal inferences at play. On the other hand, one needs to proceed in the concrete in highlighting the causal mechanisms at play when successfully applying the tested program on the experimental population. J-PAL's researchers, such as Banerjee, Chassang, and Snowberg (2017), have also proposed alternatives. According to Banerjee, Chassang, and Snowberg (2017), in order to increase an RFE's external validity, one should focus on structured speculation – that is, speculation on why and how the program tested could work somewhere else. Building on these alternatives, Favereau and

Nagatsu (2020; Nagatsu and Favereau 2020) propose a methodological framework based on a series of experiments that could strengthen the external validity of RFEs. More specifically, and based on Harrison and List (2004) and Bardsley et al. (2010), the aim of this framework is to combine laboratory field experiments with RFEs. List (2006a), in a similar vein, proposes that laboratory and natural experiments should be combined. Harrison, Lau, and Rutström (2015) and Meyer (1995) have also insisted on the complementarity between lab and field experiments. Dufwenberg and Harrison (2008) have emphasized that field experiments in economics arose from the combination of field and laboratory experiments, as Bohm's (1972) experiment highlights. The environment of the laboratory enables one to know precisely what variable to control [see Harrison (2005} on control in different experimental frames]. In that sense, it becomes possible a posteriori to unpack plausible mechanisms at play behind the results of RFEs and to test them in the laboratory.

Based on this methodological framework and on previous historical overviews, I would like to suggest possible ways to reintroduce the field by combining RFEs with qualitative studies at the design stage. For that purpose, let me first contrast RFEs with natural experiments. As seen in the previous section, natural experiments are, according to Harrison and List (2004), field experiments in which an exogeneous change mimics that of social experiments and in which the participants do not know they are being observed. Shadish, Cook, and Campbell (2002) define natural experiments in a similar manner: natural field experiments are experiments in which subjects are randomized without being aware of it. In the first case, the researchers do not intervene, while in the second one they do. Rosenzweig and Wolpin (2000) distinguish between natural experiments and what they call "natural-natural experiments." The latter type of experiments are natural experiments as defined by Harrison and List (2004) or by Shadish, Cook, and Campbell (2002) but that use instrumental variables. The use of Maimonides' rule by Lavy and Pischcke is an illustration of such a natural-natural experiment [see Reiss (2013) for an analysis of this rule]. All of these natural experiments involve an intervention, be it from the researchers themselves or an exogeneous one.

Qualitative studies are not an experimental method, because there is no direct, explicit intervention. I attempt to relax one more aspect, that of intervention. Indeed, qualitative studies are free from the experimenters' intervention, free from exogeneous intervention, and free from the use of instrumental variables. In conducting qualitative studies, researchers do not intervene in the field and do not clean it or control it. In this sense, qualitative studies might help to restore the field that was lost in RFEs. They would offer the social and individual characteristics that have been removed because of the random assignment of RFEs. They would also emphasize the messy and complex environment of the field. This methodological alternative goes hand in hand with the one proposed in Nagatsu and Favereau (2020) and Favereau and Nagatsu (2020), as well as with the different calls for complementarity between lab and field experiments (e.g., Harrison, Lau, and Rutström, 2015; Meyer, 1995; List, 2006a). The goal is to utilize qualitative studies to unpack RFEs. This gives a twofold benefit. First, as already emphasized, qualitative studies enable access to the field and to the social and individual characteristics. In that sense, they represent a way to restore the field, which was removed in RFEs. This might help to strengthen the external validity of RFEs. Second, the use of qualitative studies in RFEs might reinforce the reliability of the researcher's observations. In that sense, qualitative studies might also benefit from the strong internal validity of RFEs.

Let me now try to illustrate how this can work in practice, using the example of the RFE on the effects of cognitive behavioral therapy and cash transfer on diminishing the crime level of young men in Liberia. As seen in the previous section, it may be difficult to understand *why* the cognitive therapy was efficient, *why* the unconditional cash transfer alone did not have any impact, and finally *why* the therapy combined with the unconditional transfer was even more efficient. The application of qualitative studies to this RFE would help in answering these questions. Indeed, qualitative studies could take the form of the first proper observation of the field, in which the RFE would be implemented afterward. Blattman, Jamison, and Sheridan (2017) worked closely with the NEPI. The

NEPI consists of field-workers who knew some of the young men and their histories beforehand. They directly recruited the 999 young men. In this sense, the NEPI represents a valuable resource that would be able to outline the crucial individual and social characteristics of these young men before implementing the RFE. In addition, the NEPI, as a nonprofit organization that is based in Monrovia and works daily in the city, has crucial information about the social environment in which the young men live. It also benefits from having a broader understanding of Liberia. A qualitative study conducted jointly with the NEPI on the social, environmental, and individual characteristics of the young men who would be taking part in the RFE would benefit the researchers with its insights, and it would highlight the factors needed to understand why the program worked in a certain way. In other words, it would enable researchers to highlight potential mechanisms as well as to understand these mechanisms. Such a study could take the form, as is often the case with RFEs, of a systematic and broad baseline survey. In their RFE, Blattman, Jamison, and Sheridan (2017) did ask questions in their baseline survey pertaining to the marriage status of the young men, their earnings, their occupation, their drug usage, whether they worked in small businesses, high-skilled business, or agriculture, whether they had ever engaged in any illegal activities, whether they were homeless, and whether they had ever committed a robbery. This baseline survey is already something one might rely on to understand the mechanisms behind the experimental results. What I suggest is that, in the combination of a qualitative study with a RFE, such a baseline survey would be much more developed and systematic and would account for proper fieldwork. Doing so would offer insights into the mechanisms at play behind the RFE. In addition, one could conduct "intensive qualitative case studies" (Shadish, Cook, and Campbell, 2002: 500). Indeed, Blattman, Jamison, and Sheridan (2017) conducted several interviews before and after the RFE. They also interviewed the field-workers, such as the NEPI workers. However, such interviews were not done systematically and there is not much information on the interviews in the published paper. These interviews represent crucial material that is needed to restore the disappeared field. Thus, the RFE conducted by Blattman, Jamison, and Sheridan (2017) might open promising doors. However, to truly open doors to access the field, qualitative studies should systematically be included in RFEs. Thus, RFEs in development economics should develop this natural fieldwork more explicitly, clearly, and systematically.

5. Conclusion

In attempting to highlight the methodological challenges that field experiments in economics face nowadays, I have concentrated on the notion of the field. I aimed to highlight that economics should take the field seriously and find ways to properly integrate it into experiments. For this purpose, I first gave some definitions and examples of prominent field experiments in economics, referring to the commonly used taxonomy of field experiments (e.g. Harrison and List, 2004; Bardsley et al., 2010). I concentrated on the "naturally occurring data" aspect and, as such, on natural experiments as defined in economics (List and Reiley, 2007; List, 2006a; List and Metcalfe, 2015). This enabled me to distinguish within these natural experiments between natural experiments per se and natural-natural experiments. This highlights the central aspect of field experiments: intervention. On the basis of this framework, I focused on the most recent and popular field experiments in economics: RFEs, as institutionalized by the J-PAL in development economics. I then highlighted the most striking changes that RFEs introduce compared to previous field experiments in social sciences: the change in scale and the lack of theory. These changes are also the foundation of the central methodological challenges faced by RFEs. Indeed, due to the refutation of a theoretical basis and the focus on small scales, the J-PAL's RFEs tend to remove the field and, with it, any crucial information it carries. This is why, in a f step, I attempted to reintroduce the field by proposing a combination of qualitative studies and RFEs. By conducting these three steps and giving a taxonomy of natural experiments, I simultaneously aimed at another goal, that of offering an overview of field experiments in economics.

Related Chapters

Khosrowi, D., Chapter 27 "Evidence-Based Policy"
Nagatsu, M., Chapter 24 "Experimentation in Economics"

Notes

1 See Heukelom (2011) for a history of the validity concept in economics.
2 See Jimenez-Buedo and Guala (2016) on the notion of artificiality for experiments in economics.
3 List and Metcalfe (2015) concentrate on empirical methods. Thus, propensity score estimation, instrumental variables estimation, and structural modeling, which are included in Figure 25.1, relate to econometric techniques and are not experiments per se.
4 For an analysis of randomization and selection bias, see Heckman et al. (1998). James Heckman and Jeffrey Smith (1995: 88–89) have shown that, instead of removing the selection bias, randomized experiments only balance it between the two groups. See also Worall (2002) for a philosophical analysis of the selection bias.
5 Greenberg and Shroder's (2004) definition excludes many experiments conducted in economics that do not satisfy (2) and (3). Ferber and Hirsch (1982) define field social experiments in a manner very similar to Greenberg and Shroder (2004) but clearly relate them to the domain of economics. Ferber and Hirsch (1982) suggest that a social field experiment evaluates the impact of both economic and social political intervention. Their definition of a social field experiment is as follows:

> A publicly funded study that incorporates a rigorous statistical design and whose experimental aspects are applied over a period of time to one or more segments of a human population, with *the aim of evaluating the aggregate economic and social effects of the experimental treatments.*
>
> (Ferber and Hirsch, 1982: 7, emphasis added)

Ferber and Hirsch (1982) insist on public findings, highlighting the fact that such experiments are extremely costly because most of them were conducted on a large scale.
6 Levitt and List (2009) define a prehistory of field experiments. In this prehistory, they go back to the work of Pasteur in medicine and the work of Fisher and Neyman in agriculture. Fisher (1935) defines the experimental design of randomized field experiments as well as its statistical rigor. The aim of Fisher was to apply this experimental design to agriculture. Ziliak (2014) nuances such a prehistory by insisting on the role of "Student." According to Ziliak (2014) this role is too often neglected, whereas Heckman's (1992) and Heckman and Smith's (1995) work have continuity with the one of "Student," both insisting on the absence of randomization as a necessity to conduct social evaluation.
7 Ashraf, Karlan, and Yin (2006: 636) also define their experiments as natural field experiments. Moreover, in doing so they refer to Harrison and List (2004) typology.
8 See Gerber and Green (2012) for a study of the different design for field experiments.
9 Cartwright (2009a) develops and discusses such an evidence hierarchy; see also Cartwright (2007, 2009b). Cartwright and Deaton (2018a, 2018b) discuss the internal validity of RFEs, highlighting that it is not as strong as suggested by J-PAL researchers.
10 Of course, other types of field experiments occur in development economics; see, for example, the discussion of Cardenas and Carpenter (2005).
11 The J-PAL classifies those experiments in different sectors: (1) agriculture, (2) crime, violence, and conflict, (3) education, (4) environment, energy, and climate change, (5) finance, (6) firm, (7) gender, (8) health, (9) labor markets, and (10) political economy and governance. Very often, RFEs are concerned with several of these sectors at once. For instance, when Cohen and Dupas (2010) conduct a RFE to determine whether bed nets should be fully subsidized or not, they target pregnant women. As such, this experiment is dealing with both health and gender. Moreover, when Dupas and Robinson (2013) assess the impact of a savings device in order to increase savings toward preventative care health products, they are dealing with both finance and health (https://www.povertyactionlab.org/fr/evaluations, last consulted September 8, 2021).
12 The trade-off between internal and external validity has been studied, for example, by Jiménez-Buedo and Miller (2010), Jiménez-Buedo (2011), and Heukelom (2011), leading sometimes to calls "against external

validity" Reiss (2018) or against both types of validity Jimenez-Buedo (2020). Roe and Just (2009) analyze the trade-off between external and internal validity within field experiments, fieldwork, and field data.

13 Econometrics methods (see, for example, Crump et al., 2008; Athey and Imbens, 2017) and, more recently, machine learning modeling have been proposed by J-PAL researchers to access such heterogeneity afterward (see Chernozhukov et al., 2018; Duflo, 2018). In both cases, J-PAL researchers target the potential heterogeneity in separating the distribution of the sample. Nonetheless, as Deaton (2010) highlights, the heterogeneity problem is not an issue that technique alone can tackle:

> What this should tell us is that the heterogeneity is *not* a technical problem but a symptom of something deeper, which is the failure to specify causal models of the processes we are examining. Technique is never a substitute for the business of doing economics.
>
> (Deaton, 2010: 452, original emphasis)

Bibliography

Acemoglu, D. (2010) "Theory, General Equilibrium, and Political Economy in Development Economics," *Journal of Economic Perspectives* 24(3): 17–32.

Acemoglu, D., and Robinson, J. (2012) *Why Nations Fail, the Origins of Power, Prosperity, and Poverty*, New-York: Crown Business.

Ashraf, N., Karlan, D., and Yin, W. (2006) "Tying Odysseus to the Mast: Evidence from a Commitment Savings Product in the Philippines," *Quarterly Journal of Economics* 121(2): 635–672.

Athey, S., and Imbens, G. (2017) "The Econometrics of Randomized Experiments," in A. Banerjee and E. Duflo (eds.) *Handbook of Field Experiments:* 73–140, North-Holland: Elsevier.

Banerjee, A. (2005) "'New Development Economics' and the Challenge to Theory," *Economic and Political Weekly* 40(40): 4340–4344.

Banerjee, A., Chassang, S., and Snowberg, E. (2017) "Decision Theoretic Approaches to Experiment Design and External Validity," in A. Banerjee and E. Duflo (eds.) *Handbook of Field Experiments:* 141–174, North-Holland: Elsevier.

Banerjee, A., and Duflo, E. (2011) *Poor Economics: A Radical Rethinking of the Way to Fight Global Poverty*, Boston: Public Affairs.

Bardsley, N., Cubitt, R., Loomes, G., Moffat, P., Starmer, C., and Sugden, R. (2010) *Experimental Economics: Rethinking the Rules*, Princeton: Princeton University Press.

Barrett, C., and Carter, M. (2010) "The Power and the Pitfalls of Experiments in Development Economics: Some Non-random Reflections," *Applied Economic Perspective and Policy* 32(4): 515–548.

Basu, K. (2014) "Randomisation, Causality and the Role of Reasoned Intuition," *Oxford Development Studies* 42(4): 455–472.

Blattman, C., Jamison, J., and Sheridan, M. (2017) "Reducing Crime and Violence: Experimental Evidence from Cognitive Behavioral Therapy in Liberia," *American Economic Review* 17(4): 1165–1206.

Bohm, P. (1972) "Estimating the Demand for Public Goods: An Experiment," *European Economic Review* 3: 111–130.

Boumans, M. (2015) *Science Outside the Laboratory. Measurement in Field Science and Economics*, Oxford: Oxford University Press.

Cardenas, J.C., and Carpenter, J. (2005) "Three Themes on Field Experiments and Economic Development," in J. Carpenter, G.W. Harrison and J.A. List (eds.) *Field Experiments in Economics*, Research in Experimental Economics, Volume 10: 71–97, Oxford: Elsevier.

Carpenter, J., Harrison, G., and List, J. (2005) "Field Experiments in Economics: An Introduction," in J. Carpenter, G.W. Harrison and J.A. List (eds.) *Field Experiments in Economics*, Research in Experimental Economics, Volume 10: 1–16, Oxford: Elsevier.

Cartwright, N. (2007) "Are RCT's the Gold Standard?" *Biosocieties* 2(1): 11–20.

Cartwright, N. (2009a) "Evidence-based Policy: Where is our Theory of Evidence," *Journal of Children's Services* 4(4): 6–14.

Cartwright, N. (2009b) "What is This Thing Called Efficacy?" in Mantzavinos (ed.) *Philosophy of the Social Science. Philosophical Theory and Scientific Practice*, Cambridge: Cambridge University Press.

Cartwright, N. (2010) "What are Randomised Controlled Trials Good for?" *Philosophical Studies* 147(1): 59–70.

Cartwright, N., and Deaton, A. (2018a) "Reflections on Randomized Controlled Trials," *Social Science & Medicine* 210: 86–90.

Cartwright, N., and Deaton, A. (2018b) "Understanding and Misunderstanding Randomized Controlled Trials," *Social Science & Medicine* 210: 2–21.

Cartwright, N., and Hardie, J. (2012) *Evidence-Based Policy: A Practical Guide to Doing It Better*, Oxford: Oxford University Press.

Chernozhukov, V., Chetverikov, D., Demirer, M., Duflo, E., Hansen, C., Newey, W., and Robins, J. (2018) "Double/Debiased Machine Learning for Treatment and Structural Parameters," *The Econometrics Journal* 21(1): C1–C68.

Cohen, J., and Dupas, P. (2010) "Free Distribution or Cost-Sharing? Evidence from a Randomized Malaria Prevention Experiment," *Quarterly Journal of Economics* 125(1): 1–45.

Crump, R., Hotz, J., Imbens, G., and Mitnik, O. (2008) "Nonparametric Tests for Treatment Effect Heterogeneity," *Review of Economics and Statistics* 90(3): 389–405.

Davis, J. (2013) "Economics Imperialism under the Impact of Psychology: The Case of Behavioral Development Economics," *Œconomia* 3(1): 119–138.

Deaton, A. (2010) "Instruments, Randomization, and Learning about Development," *Journal of Economic Literature* 48(2): 424–455.

Deaton, A. (2020) "Randomization in the Tropics Revisited: A Theme and Eleven Variations," in F. Bédécarrats, I. Guérin, and F. Roubaud, (eds.) *Randomized Controlled Trials in the Field of Development: A Critical Perspective*, Oxford: Oxford University Press.

Diaz, A., Jimenez-Buedo, M., and Teira, D. (2015) "History of Quasi-and Field Experiments," in J. Wright (ed.) *International Encyclopedia of the Social and Behavioral Sciences* (2nd edition): 736–741, North Holland: Elsevier.

Duflo, E. (2006) "Field Experiments in Development Economics," in R. Blundell, W. Newey and T. Person (eds.) *Advances in Economics and Econometrics*, Cambridge: Cambridge University Press.

Duflo, E. (2018) "*Machinistas Meet Randomistas: Useful ML Tools for Empirical Researchers*," Summer Institute Master Lectures, National Bureau of Economic Research.

Dufwenberg, M., and Harrison, G. (2008) "Peter Bohm: Father of Field Experiments," *Experimental Economics*11(3): 213–220.

Dupas, P., and Robinson, J. (2013) "Why Don't the Poor Save More? Evidence from Health Savings Experiments," *American Economic Review* 103(4): 1138–1171.

Favereau, J., and Nagatsu, M. (2020) "Holding Back from Theory: Limits and Methodological Alternatives of Randomized Field Experiments in Development Economics," *Journal of Economic Methodology*, Forthcoming.

Ferber, R., and Hirsch, W. (1982) *Social Experimentation and Economic Policy*, Cambridge: Cambridge University Press.

Fisher, R. (1935/1960) *The Design of Experiment* (7th edition), New York: Hafner Publishing Company.

Friedman, M. (1962) *Capitalism and Freedom*, Chicago: University of Chicago Press.

Gerber, A.S., and Green, D.P. (2012) *Field Experiments: Design, Analysis, and Interpretation*, New York: W.W. Norton.

Greenberg, D., and Shroder, M. (2004) *The Digest of Social Experiments* (3rd edition), Washington, DC: The Urban Institute Press.

Harrison, G. (2005) "Field Experiments and Control," in J. Carpenter, G.W. Harrison, and J.A. List (eds.) *Field Experiments in Economics*, Research in Experimental Economics, Volume 10: 17–50. Oxford: Elsevier.

Harrison, G. (2011) "Randomization and its Discontents," *Journal of African Economies* 20(4): 626–652.

Harrison, G. (2013) "Field Experiments and Methodological Intolerance," *Journal of Economic Methodology* 20(2): 103–117.

Harrison, G. (2014) "Cautionary Notes on the Use of Field Experiments to Address Policy Issues," *Oxford Review of Economic Policy* 30(4): 753–763.

Harrison, G., Lau, M., and Rutström, E. (2015) "Theory, Experimental Design and Econometrics Are Complementary (And So Are Lab and Field Experiments)," in G. Frechette and A. Schotter (eds.) *Handbook of Experimental Economic Methodology*: 296–338, New York: Oxford University Press.

Harrison, G., and List, J. (2004) "Field Experiments," *Journal of Economic Literature* 42(4): 1009–1055.

Heckman, J. (1992) "Randomization and Social Policy Evaluation," in C.F. Manski and I. Garfinkel (eds.) *Evaluating Welfare and Training Programs*: 201–230, Boston, MA: Harvard University Press.

Heckman, J. (2010) "Building Bridges Between Structural and Program Evaluations Approaches to Evaluating Policy," *Journal of Economic Literature* 48(2): 356–398.

Heckman, J., Clement, N., and Smith, J. (1997) "Making the Most Out of the Programme Evaluations and Social Experiments: Accounting for Heterogeneity in Programme Impact," *The Review of Economic Studies* 64(4): 487–535.

Heckman, J., Ichimura, H., Smith, J., and Todd, P. (1998) "Characterizing Selection Bias Using Experimental Data," *Econometrica* 66(5): 1017–1098.

Heckman, J., and Smith, J. (1995) "Assessing the Case for Social Experiments," *Journal of Economic Perspectives* 9(2): 85–110.

Heukelom, F. (2011) "How Validity Travelled to Economic Experimenting," *Journal of Economic Methodology* 18(1): 13–28.
Jiménez-Buedo, M. (2011) "Conceptual Tools for Assessing Experiments: Some Well-Entrenched Confusions regarding the Internal/External Validity Distinction," *Journal of Economic Methodology* 18(3): 271–282.
Jimenez-Buedo, M., and Guala, F. (2016) "Artificiality, Reactivity, and Demand Effects in Experimental Economics," *Philosophy of the Social Sciences* 46(1): 3–23.
Jiménez-Buedo, M., and Miller, L. (2010) "Why a Trade-off? The Relationship between the External and Internal Validity of Experiments," *Theoria* 5(3): 301–321.
Leamer, E. (2010) "Tantalus on The Road to Asymptopia," *Journal of Economic Perspectives* 24(2): 31–46.
Levitt, S., and List, J. (2009) "Field Experiments in Economics: The Past, the Present, and the Future," *European Economic Review* 53(1): 1–18.
List, J. (2006a) "Field Experiments: A Bridge between Lab and Naturally Occurring Data," *Advances in Economic Analysis & Policy* 6(2): 1–45.
List, J. (2006b) "Friend or Foe? A Natural Experiment of the Prisoner's Dilemma," *Review of Economics and Statistics* 88(3): 463–471.
List, J., and Metcalfe, R. (2015) "Field Experiments in the Developed World: An Introduction," *Oxford Review of Economic Policy* 30(4): 585–596.
List, J., and Rasul, I. (2010) "Field Experiments in Labor Economics," in O. Ashenfelter and D. Card (eds.) *Handbook of Labour Economics*: 103–228, North Holland: Elsevier.
List, J., and Reiley, D. (2007) "Fields Experiments," in *The New Palgrave Dictionary of Economics*, London: Macmillan.
Meyer, B. (1995) "Natural and Quasi-Experiments in Economics," *Journal of Business & Economic Statistics* 13(2): 151–161.
Nagatsu, M., and Favereau, J. (2020) "Two Strands of Field Experiments in Economics: A Historical-Methodological Analysis," *Philosophy of the Social Sciences* 50(1): 45–77.
Ortmann, A. (2005) "Field Experiments in Economics: Some Methodological Caveats," in J. Carpenter, G.W. Harrison and J.A. List (eds.) *Field Experiments in Economics*, Research in Experimental Economics, Volume 10: 51–70, Oxford: Elsevier.
Ravallion, M. (2009) "Should the Randomistas Rule?" *The Economist' Voice, Berkeley Electronic Press* 6(2): 1–6.
Reiss, J. (2013) *Philosophy of Economics: A Contemporary Introduction*, London: Routledge.
Reiss, J. (2018) "Against External Validity," *Synthese* 196 (8): 3103–3121.
Rodrik, D. (2008) "The New Development Economics: We Shall Experiment, but How Shall We Learn?" in J. Cohen and W. Easterly (eds.) *What Works in Development, Thinking Big and Thinking Small*: 24–47, Washington DC: Brookings Institution Press.
Roe, B., and Just, D. (2009) "Internal and External Validity in Economics Research: Tradeoffs between Experiments, Field Experiments, Natural Experiments and Field Data," *American Journal of Agricultural Economics* 91(5): 1266–1271.
Rosenzweig, M., and Wolpin, K. (2000) "Natural Experiments," *Journal of Economic Literature* 38(4): 827–874.
Shadish, W., Cook, T.D., and Campbell, D.T. (2002) *Experimental and Quasi-Experimental Designs for Generalized Causal Inference*, Boston: Houghton Mifflin.
Teira, D. (2013) "Blinding and the Non-Interference Assumption in Medical and Social Trials," *Philosophy of the Social Sciences* 43(3): 358–372.
Teira, D., and Reiss, J. (2013) "Causality, Impartiality and Evidence-Based Policy," in H.-K. Chao, S.-T. Chen and R.L. Millstein (eds.) *Mechanism and Causality in Biology and Economics*: 207–224, New York: Springer.
Worall, J. (2002) "What Evidence in Evidence-Based Medicine," *Philosophy of Science* 69(3): 316–330.
Ziliak, S. (2014) "Balanced versus Randomized Field Experiments in Economics: Why W. S. Gosset aka 'Student' Matters," *Review of Behavioral Economics* 1: 167–208.

26
COMPUTER SIMULATIONS IN ECONOMICS

Aki Lehtinen and Jaakko Kuorikoski

1. Introduction

Economics investigates the consequences of interlinked individual decisions within specific institutional frameworks such as markets. As the idealizations required to make models of interdependent decision-making under multiple constraints analytically tractable are unavoidably heroic, it would seem an obvious advantage to start with theoretically and empirically more palatable assumptions about the individuals and their institutional environment and let the computer worry about determining the consequences of those assumptions. Furthermore, many other applied fields of science routinely run computer simulations to evaluate the effects of possible interventions and policies. As the social science with most political clout, should it not be expected that virtual experiments about possible economic policies would be central to economic practice?

The financial crisis brought two key constructs necessary for the tractability of central economic model templates into critical focus: the representative agent and equilibrium. Together the ubiquitous use of the representative agent and the equilibrium assumption arguably preempted inquiries into the effects of different heterogeneities, biases, herding effects, in particular, and endogenously generated crises in general. The failure of standard economic models to foresee or (for a long time) even analyze the crisis constituted for many a fundamental crisis in economic theory (e.g., Kirman 2010, 2016; Stiglitz 2018). A natural way to implement more realistic behavioral assumptions, heterogeneities, imperfect information, interdependencies, and out-of-equilibrium dynamics is by computer simulation.

There are four main kinds of simulation: discretizations, microsimulations, Monte Carlo, and agent-based simulations (see Gilbert and Troitzsch (1999) for a detailed description of these methods). Of these, the first three are widely and increasingly used in economics, while the fourth, albeit also being used more and more, continues to face methodological resistance. Boumans (2020), however, argues that simulations are already widespread in economics and charges methodologists for lagging behind in describing the change. Most of the arguments in philosophy of science on simulation in economics concern agent-based models and Monte Carlo. The reason might relate to the context in which the different kinds of simulations are used. Discretizations are mainly used in macroeconomics, and microsimulations are used in policy design. The epistemic role of discretization qua simulation is minuscule compared to other methodological issues, and while microsimulations do raise philosophical questions, thus far these have been treated in specialized outlets.

DOI: 10.4324/9781315739793-32

The lackluster reception of simulations can be contrasted with the relatively rapid spread of experimental methods, first in terms of behavioral economics (see Nagatsu, Chapter 24) and now in terms of natural and field experiments emphasized by the proponents of the credibility revolution (see Favereau, Chapter 25). Furthermore, economics is certainly an increasingly *computational* science. As the profession has grown increasingly data driven in what has become known as the credibility revolution, many undergraduate programs now put as much emphasis on learning R as they do on the basics of demand theory. The resistance to simulations, therefore, is clearly not solely due to any general methodological conservativeness in economics.

In this chapter, we first review central debates in the emerging philosophy of simulation subfield. After that, we will briefly discuss key types of simulation in economics: Monte Carlo methods, dynamic stochastic general equilibrium models, which constitute the mainstream in current macroeconomics, and the more marginal subfield of agent-based computational economics. As we will see, the general philosophical questions concerning simulation take very distinct forms in the context of economics. We argue that the methodological peculiarities present in all of these cases provide us with interesting lessons about the way in which the role of theory is conceived in economics.

2. Philosophical Questions in the Use of Simulations

Is there a specific "epistemic kind" of computer simulations with distinctive epistemic properties and problems? In a provocative opening article for a special issue of *Synthese*, Roman Frigg and Julian Reiss (2008) set the challenge for the emerging philosophy of simulation to explicate what novel philosophical issues simulations pose that are not common to all scientific modeling. Frigg and Reiss argue that the epistemological, semantic, and ontological questions pertaining to computer simulations do not differ from those concerning models in general and that simulations do not call for a "new philosophy of science." Although computer simulations certainly share many general methodological questions with analytically solvable models, the philosophical literature has delved into issues ranging from the implications of discretization (Lenhard 2019) all the way to the possible demise of anthropocentric epistemology (Humphreys 2009).

We begin by reviewing the debate on the definition of computer simulation as a way of locating putative features that might philosophically distinguish simulations from other models. Intuitively, not all computational exercises count as simulations, as some are simply, well, computations. Furthermore, not all simulations are carried out with computers. Physical analogue simulations like wind tunnels seem to have epistemological characteristics that render them distinct from ordinary physical experiments (see Trenholme 1994; Dardashti et al. 2017; Durán 2017 for accounts of analog simulations). Although the consensus seems to be that there is something distinct about simulations, not surprisingly no agreement has been reached on what exactly that distinct feature is.

2.1 What Is a Computer Simulation?

Paul Humphreys (1991) originally defined computer simulations simply as any computer-implemented method used to explore properties of mathematical models without analytical solutions. As Durán (2021) points out, this is in line with a long tradition of interpreting simulations in terms of solving intractable mathematical problems. This would tie the definition of computer simulation very closely to (1) (a set of) existing mathematical models and (2) whether it allows for closed-form solutions. The first constraint is problematic because not all computer simulations, such as cellular automata and agent-based models, are direct computational realizations of existing mathematical models. The second constraint is problematic because it is not clear why the mathematical fact of not having an analytical solution would necessarily correspond to a categorical difference in the way a model represents the modeled system.

Partly due to these concerns, Stephan Hartmann (1996) suggested that a simulation is a process imitating a process. This definition emphasizes both the representational function and the *dynamic* nature of simulations. Simulations are always simulations *of* something, and they represent something *unfolding* through time. This falls within the second major tradition of conceptualizing simulations in the sciences (Durán 2021). This definition is also applicable to physical analogue simulations more broadly. Hughes (1999), Humphreys (2004), and El Skaf and Imbert (2013), among others, have questioned whether time and dynamics are really essential to simulation. They agree on the importance of representation and the processual nature, however, and propose that simulations trace a trajectory of a (mathematical) system in its state space. Most often this is a trajectory along the time dimension, but not necessarily.

Although most simulations of *economic phenomena* include such a dynamic aspect, even this more abstract definition rules out an important class of computational techniques in economics that many consider to be simulations: Monte Carlo methods. We consider Monte Carlo methods more closely in Section 3.1.

2.2 The Epistemology of Computer Simulation

The debate about the definition of simulation is only interesting if there is an interesting and distinct "epistemic kind" to be defined. The question of the putative special epistemic status of computer simulations is motivated, on the one hand, by the similarity of simulation to experimentation and the consequent possibility of uncovering truly surprising and novel results and, on the other hand, by the seemingly unavoidable fact that computer simulations are "nothing more" than mere models with no direct causal interaction with the modeled reality.

The epistemology of computer simulations also depends on what the simulation is used for. Here, we discuss only "scientific" uses and leave out, for example, purely pedagogical functions. Yet, even this leaves a great number of rather distinct roles in economics. Computer simulations are used in forecasting (including nowcasting), the evaluation of policy scenarios, theoretical modeling, market design, and, depending on where the lines of simulation are drawn, various forms of data analysis.

Furthermore, the use of computer simulations involves several distinctive epistemological questions pertaining to the functioning of the computer simulation as a system in its own right, such as whether the program is doing what it is supposed to do (that there are no errors in the code) and whether the digitization introduces biases into the computation (e.g., truncation or rounding errors). Many of these questions belong squarely within the domain of computer science (e.g., to "stability theory"). We will not discuss this literature because it is vast and because we are not aware of any economic simulations in which verification could be done formally (see, e.g., Beisbart and Saam (2019) for some contributions to this literature). The philosophical question is whether these, or some other features of simulation, render computer simulations epistemologically distinct from analytically solvable models, analogue simulations, or experiments.

At first glance, the practice of simulation is often strikingly similar to that of "material" experimentation. Like an experiment, a simulation is first assembled and then left to run "on its own." Like an experiment, a simulation yields not conclusions but masses of raw data requiring further analysis and interpretation. Like experimentation, simulation practice involves looking for errors in the procedure, benchmarks for what kind of results ought to emerge, and so on. As Francesco Guala (2002) points out, both forms of inquiry require distinct judgments of internal and external validity. In macroeconomics, the use of simulations is often characterized as numerical experimentation, and Reiss (2011) even defends the use of simulations in economics by arguing that they should be used because they provide experimental data that are otherwise lacking in economics (see Norton and Suppe (2001) for a similar argument in climate science). Accordingly, Winsberg (2001, 2003, 2010) argued that the epistemology of simulation is motley and that it is self-vindicating in the same way as that of the experimental sciences.

Guala (2002) formulated what has become known as the *materiality thesis*: simulations are inferior to experiments in that the former cannot experiment with the material basis of the target system itself. Parker (2009) challenged the materiality thesis by arguing that what is relevant for the epistemic evaluation of simulations is relevant similarity and that material similarity is not always the relevant kind of similarity (see also Winsberg 2009). When formal similarity is relevant instead of material, simulations and experiments seem to be on a par. Parker also argued that the wider epistemic unit of simulation study, which includes all of the practices around constructing the simulation model, counts as a material experiment. A computer running a program is a physical system, and simulations thus are also experiments on a physical system.

Nevertheless, even if the user is experimenting *on* this physical system, the user is not running an experiment *about* the physical system (Durán 2013, 2018: 64–68). Norton and Suppe (2001) have argued that because, in running the simulation, the computer can *realize* the same abstract structure as the target system, it can function as an experimental stand-in for its target in a very concrete sense. This claim, however, seems questionable as at least all digital simulation essentially involves numerical approximation and numerous individual runs, rather than direct realization of mathematical structures (Imbert 2017).

Morrison (2009, 2015) argues that because simulations are in fact used as measurement devices, they should also be counted as experiments. Morrison, as well as Massimi and Bhimji (2015), provides examples of measurements in physics in which the data are practically impossible to interpret without simulation. Measurement often requires simulation in turning the raw data into a data model usable for making inferences about the target (see also Durán 2013). Morrison does not need to commit to a questionable view of measurement that does not require a direct physical causal connection to the measured quantity to make this epistemic claim, however. We will discuss simulations in the analysis of data later.

If the materiality of the computer and the surface features of the experimental praxis are irrelevant to the "deep epistemology" of simulation, perhaps simulations are more analogous to thought experiments or even should be conceived as computerized arguments? Claus Beisbart and John Norton (Beisbart and Norton 2012; Beisbart 2018) argue that computer simulations are simply computer-aided arguments: a single execution of a command by the computer is a logical inference step, and even a run of a complex simulation program therefore is nothing more than a massively long series of such steps. In this sense, a simulation (run) is a computerized argument. Even if the praxis of using, say, Monte Carlo techniques has many experiment-like features from the standpoint of the user, it does not invalidate this basic ontological and epistemological point. Simulation is computerized inference, not experimentation.

If this is correct, then this limits the epistemic reach of simulations. As Beisbart (2018) claims, "Simulations implement a model that entails the results of the simulation. The simulations can thus not refute these very assumptions. Nor can they refute other assumptions, unless the model of the simulations has independent support" (p. 191). For Beisbart, simulations are *overcontrolled*, meaning that there is nothing left for nature to say because all of the relevant causal information is already in the computer code. Morgan (2002, 2003, 2005; see also Giere 2009) puts this in the following way: that although simulations can surprise just like experiments, they can never *confound*. In other words, given that the computer simulation can only take into account causal factors that are explicitly written in the programming code, it cannot take into account confounders, namely, causal factors that have an effect on the phenomenon of interest but that the experimenter does not know about or does not know that they have such effects.

There are, in fact, two interrelated philosophical questions in the discussion that compares experiments and simulations. (1) Are simulations to be evaluated epistemically as experiments, expressions of theory, arguments, a new kind of mathematics, or *sui generis*? (2) Are simulations epistemically on a par with experiments? It is clear that even if the practice of simulation were admittedly comparable to experimentation, this would not yet be sufficient for giving simulations the probative force of experiments. What is the purpose of asking whether simulations and experiments are "on a par"? Is it to provide guidance for scientists in choosing between these methods? It is commonplace that simulations are heavily used especially when other methods cannot be employed in the first place. Roush (2019) argues, however, that this is irrelevant:

> That there are questions for which the simulation we are able to do is more reliable than any experiment we can do gives no reason to deny the superiority of a comparable experiment that we cannot, or cannot yet, do.
>
> (p. 4889)

One must thus ask, what is the relevant epistemic situation in which one can compare them? The epistemic situation determines what the researchers know about the world and the applicability of their methods (Achinstein 2001). Roush (2019) argues that, in comparing the two, one must start from an epistemic situation in which one has a given question about the actual world to which one does not know the answer. One is then asked to make a choice, and Roush argues that one should choose an experiment if the correct answer is determined in part by something one does not know. If the arguments for the epistemic superiority of experiments are to have a normative punch, one would have to come up with circumstances in which it is possible to conduct both an experiment and a simulation (see also Parke 2014).

The problem is that, despite the barrage of arguments for the superiority of experiments, it is very difficult to apply such arguments to actual cases from science. Perhaps the superiority question is ill-posed and we should start asking different questions. However, the discussion has not been useless. The supporters of the superiority thesis have contributed by describing the various limitations to the probative force of simulations, and the defenders of simulations have shown various ways in which simulations usefully contribute to empirical research.

2.3 Epistemic Opacity and Understanding

Even if we accept that what the computer does is a long series of deductive steps and that the content of the results cannot go beyond the content of the assumptions (barring considerations of truncation, etc.), to treat a single run as an argument is not very enlightening from the epistemological perspective, as any such run is *epistemically opaque* to the user: the relationship between the stipulated initial conditions and the simulation result cannot be "grasped" by a cognitively unaided human being (Humphreys 2004: 147–150; Lenhard 2006). Even if the simulation results were, in some sense, already built into the program, it is impossible to deny that the results are often novel to the simulator. This brings us to the questions of novelty and understanding.

Barberousse and Vorms (2014) point out that any interesting sense of novelty in simulation results should be separated altogether from that of surprise; both computations and experiments can produce previously unknown, yet not really surprising results. Furthermore, even though what the simulation does is to "unfold" the logical content of the programmed computational model, computer simulations can clearly produce surprising novelty in terms of results that are *qualitatively* different from the assumptions of the computational model (El Skaf and Imbert 2013). Many agent-based models especially produce phenomena that are, in some sense, *emergent* relative to the model assumptions. Paul Humphreys (2004) has defined such qualitative novelty as conceptual emergence: a result R is conceptually emergent relative to a conceptual framework F when its adequate description or representation requires a conceptual apparatus that is not in F. Note that this characterization renders novelty to be relative to the concepts used to describe the results.

A further and distinct question from the novelty of simulation results is whether simulations can provide explanations of the modeled phenomena in the same way that analytical models do. Simulations are subject to considerably milder analytic tractability constraints and, hence, can do away with many of the distorting idealizations and tractability assumptions. However, the very fact that a simulation model can do away with such assumptions often makes the simulation model itself difficult to understand. Complex simulations can increase predictive power, but is our understanding improved by replacing a puzzling phenomenon with its puzzling simulation?

Whether simulations are somehow explanatorily special depends, to some degree, on which theory of explanation one favors. Proponents of agent-based simulations usually favor a causal-mechanistic conception of explanations and argue that social mechanisms can only be adequately modeled by agent-based models (although Grüne-Yanoff (2009) denies that agent-based simulations could provide causal-mechanistic explanations). Social simulationist Joshua Epstein crystallized the appeal of agent-based *generative* explanations in his motto, "If you didn't grow it, you didn't explain it" (1999; see Davis 2018). Even though economists are usually committed to some form of methodological individualism, they have not embraced this idea of generative explanations in economics. Lehtinen and Kuorikoski (2007) argued that an important reason for mainstream economists' resistance to agent-based simulations is their implicit adherence to nonmechanistic criteria of understanding, and specifically to a conception of economic understanding in line with Kitcher's unificationist model of explanation: economic understanding is constituted by deriving results using a small set of stringent economic argument patterns (analytic model templates). In agent-based simulations, the derivation part of this activity is outsourced to the computer, and the modeling assumptions may not resemble the premises in these argument patterns.

We will next survey the most important uses of simulations in economics and the more specific philosophical questions related to them.

3. Simulations in Economics

3.1 Simulating Data and Monte Carlo

The preceding discussions have diverted attention from important differences between different kinds of simulations. Note that the vast majority of data that economists use for the purpose of testing their theories are observational, not experimental. Hence, in economics the more relevant difference is between observational data and data generated with a simulation (Reiss 2011). The distinctive methodological questions related to simulations that concern data manipulation and analysis may have important consequences for genuine substantive questions.

Let us first consider an example from macroeconomics. According to the real business cycle (RBC) theorists in the 1990s, macroeconomic fluctuations are caused by technology shocks. RBC theorists provided empirical evidence for this claim using specific data-analysis techniques. Their argument was that their vector autoregression (VAR) model fit the data better when technology shocks were added as a regressor. (See Henschen, Chapter 20, on VAR.) Hoover and Salyer (1998) used a simulation to construct simulated data sets to show that the increase in fit provided by the technology shocks was entirely due to the specific statistical methods used by the RBC theorists, irrespective of whether or not the data were generated with a process including technology shocks. The conclusion is that the specific data-analysis technique is unreliable because it seemingly indicates a statistical relationship between X and Y, even when we know that X is not there. We could not have known this by looking at empirical data because we cannot control whether the true data-generating process (DGP) contains X – this is what the empirical research tries to find out in the first place. Simulated data are thus necessary for this kind of counterfactual analysis.

Monte Carlo experiments often study the properties of statistical distributions and statistical research tools and concepts. We saw earlier why Monte Carlo simulations are so prevalent in econometrics: econometricians and statisticians are constantly developing new statistical tools for analyzing and processing data, but how do we know whether, say, a proposed estimator performs adequately? As these techniques have grown more complex and computationally taxing, in practice the only way to test such performance is to generate simulated data and then see whether the estimator finds the right characteristics of the data. One cannot use empirical data for this purpose because their DGP usually cannot be precisely known. In contrast, because the simulated DGP is created by the modeler herself, it can be used as a benchmark in evaluating the performance of estimators: overcontrol is necessary for this kind of study. (See Spanos, Chapter 29, on the philosophy of econometrics.)

As Winsberg (2015) notes, the standard definitions of simulation that emphasize mimicking a target system with a computational model do not quite do justice to Monte Carlo methods. Monte Carlo simulations often do not mimic any spatiotemporal objects or processes, and the randomness on which the method is based is not normally meant to be a claim about the object or process of interest (Beisbart and Norton 2012; Grüne-Yanoff and Weirich 2010). Grüne-Yanoff and Weirich (2010) argue that, as Monte Carlo methods lack the mimicking aspect, they should be counted as calculations not simulations.

The randomness is typically the result of using a *pseudorandom number generator* (PRNG), an algorithm that gives rise to a complicated deterministic process that produces data mimicking the distributional properties of genuine random processes. Thus, there is also a mimicking relation in Monte Carlo methods, but it holds between the generated data and a probability distribution. Nevertheless, mere mimicking should not be sufficient for distinguishing simulations from calculations, as one simply typing 5 + 7 on Matlab and producing the resulting datum 12 may be said to mimic the result of writing 5 + 7 on a piece of paper but, clearly, performing this calculation on Matlab does not count as a simulation.

Is the question of whether Monte Carlo should be considered a simulation merely a terminological one? One way to consider what is relevant with definitions is to determine which aspects of a method are epistemically important. The aforementioned mimicking relation between the data generated by a Monte Carlo method and the distributional properties of a mathematical object is only relevant if it fails, and it can fail only in those cases in which the difference between genuinely random and pseudorandom numbers makes a difference. Monte Carlo methods are quite multifaceted, however, in that what is being mimicked with a model that embeds the PRNG varies. The mimicandum can be at least a spatiotemporal target system (see Galison 1996), a data-generating process for a variable, the distributional properties of empirical data, and a mathematical function (as in most applications of Markov Chain Monte Carlo). This suggests that some applications of Monte Carlo should be counted as simulations, whereas some are mere calculations.

We propose that the relevant difference lies in whether the correct performance of the PRNG along with the other deductive capabilities of the computer is sufficient for the epistemic evaluation of the model. If it is, the method counts as a computation. If one also needs to consider whether the *model* that embeds the PRNG correctly mimics its target, the method counts as simulation. Here we are using the word "target" to mean whatever a model represents. Consider, for example, a Monte Carlo study that endeavors to model a data-generating process that in reality contains a systematic bias. The model generates simulated data by using a description of the data-generating process that uses a normal distribution from a PRNG. Clearly, it is not sufficient to provide epistemic justification to this model by appealing to the fact that its PRNG correctly mimics the normal distribution. One also has to consider whether the bias as well as other aspects of the DGP are correctly modeled.

This is not the case with Monte Carlo methods that count as computation. Consider, for example, calculation of the value of π with a Monte Carlo method that uses the uniform distribution (see, e.g., Grüne-Yanoff and Weirich (2010) for a simple description). The correctness of this calculation depends on how precise the calculation must be. If it does not need to be very precise, the epistemic performance is guaranteed as long as the pseudorandom numbers from the PRNG are not too far from the underlying analytic distribution and the computer is not making any mistakes in the calculation.

3.2 DSGE

Whereas Monte Carlo methods were argued to be the most prevalent form of simulation in economics, dynamic stochastic general equilibrium (DSGE) models are arguably the most influential ones, in terms of both theory and policy. They are also controversial, and, as with Monte Carlo, their popularity is accompanied by an insistence on viewing them as simply computational methods and downplaying their role as true simulations.

The DSGE modeling strategy stems from combining Kydland and Prescott's (1982) real business cycle model with added New Keynesian assumptions about wage setting, imperfect competition, and sticky pricing. The main reason for resorting to computer simulation is that because the whole economy is to be represented in the model, the systems of equations are not analytically solvable because of excessive complexity. This complexity has been seen as necessary because of the demand for microfoundations, which in turn is taken as a necessary condition for a macroeconomic model to function in policy analysis. The New Keynesian add-ons have been introduced to remedy the dramatic empirical shortcomings of the RBC model built on rational expectations and the representative consumer. Nevertheless, despite these fixes, whether the core DSGE still fundamentally misrepresents the most important structural macroeconomic relations remains a contested issue (see Kuorikoski and Lehtinen 2018).

One of the biggest changes in the last decade is that DSGE modelers are now frantically developing models in which the assumption of a single representative agent is replaced with two or three different representative agents to model important heterogeneities (e.g., Kaplan et al. 2018; Ravn and Sterk 2021). This has had important methodological consequences. Authors are now often reporting that they have simplified the model because otherwise it would take too much time to compute the results. This reflects the fact that the models have become so complex that the modelers are facing computational trade-offs between making more realistic assumptions concerning heterogeneous agents and less realistic assumptions concerning other aspects of the model. More importantly, the loss of analytical tractability makes it difficult to figure out which features of the models are really making a difference in the results (e.g., Acharya and Dogra 2020).

Another interesting aspect of current DSGE modeling is that there is very little critical discussion about the implications of the discretization of the underlying analytical model (Velupillai and Zambelli (2011) provide some remarks). Johannes Lenhard (2019: 33) argues that because real numbers must be represented by truncated values in such models, the information lost in truncation may lead to major errors when the procedure is iterated a large number of times. Lenhard is using climate modeling as a case study, and he criticizes "a common and influential belief about simulation models based on the incorrect idea that the discrete versions of models depend completely on the theoretical models" (Ibid., 24). Economists working with DSGE models seem to share this belief. Indeed, macroeconomists seem to accept this kind of computation *precisely because* it does not have any independent epistemic contribution in their models (see also Lehtinen and Kuorikoski 2007; Lenhard 2019: 137). We are not arguing that it would be important to analyze the role of truncation errors in DSGE models. These models have so many other more serious problems that discussing the problems of discretization might merely misorient the efforts to make them better.

3.3 Agent-Based Macroeconomics

For many, the inability to predict and analyze the financial crisis constitutes a damning indictment for the representative agent and rational expectations underlying the DSGE paradigm. After the crisis, agent-based macroeconomic models have become much more popular than before. Agent-based (AB) models provide much more flexibility in modeling heterogeneity, interaction with limited information, and computational capacities (e.g., Borrill and Tesfatsion 2011). There are now several groups engaging in AB macro modeling, and many of them no longer feel the need to discuss methodology. Instead, they just produce their models. This is a sign that the agent-based approach is taking off in an important way. Furthermore, some eminent economists like Joseph Stiglitz are now using AB models (Caiani et al. 2016), and the chief economist of the Bank of England is writing methodological papers in favor of them (Haldane and Turrell 2018, 2019). In addition, there are plenty of papers marketing the agent-based methodology in macroeconomics (Fagiolo and Roventini 2017; Caverzasi and Russo 2018; Dilaver et al. 2018; Dosi and Roventini 2019)

Yet, while there are plenty of AB macro papers being published, we have not seen a single one at the very top of the journal hierarchy. We will now look into aspects of AB models that many macroeconomists consider unattractive. Comparison of the reception of DSGE simulations, which can be appreciated within the first tradition of viewing simulations as computational solutions to intractable sets of equations, and agent-based macro models, which more clearly embody the second tradition of viewing simulations as imitations of processes (Durán 2021), sheds light on how economists see the proper place of computer simulation in their field.

Windrum et al. (2007) presented four interrelated categories of criticisms of AB models:

1. There is little or no understanding of the connection among the set of highly heterogeneous models that have been developed.
2. Lack of comparability between the models that have been developed. With many degrees of freedom, almost any simulation output can be generated by an AB model.
3. The lack of standardized techniques for analyzing and constructing AB models.
4. Empirical validation of AB models is difficult or is currently lacking.

Let us consider these criticisms in reverse order. Although many early agent-based models in macroeconomics were not tested with empirical data, we do not know of any argument to the effect that it would be intrinsically harder to empirically validate simulation models than analytical models. After all, it took more than two decades to develop the Kydland and Prescott (1982) model into one that can be estimated and that provides at least a reasonable fit to empirical data (Smets and Wouters 2003). Empirical validation of models also includes making predictions about the future development of the economy. In this respect, agent-based models are still unsatisfactory: we do not know of any agent-based models that are competitive in forecasting comparisons and tournaments. On the other hand, methods of estimating agent-based models are being developed (e.g., Delli Gatti and Grazzini 2020), and it might only be a matter of time before agent-based models mature sufficiently to be used in forecasting too (see Fagiolo et al. (2019) for a philosophically oriented account of these developments).

The lack of standardized techniques for developing agent-based models is also, at least partly, a contingent feature of their current state of development. Practically all DSGE modelers use the same program (Dynare) to discretize their analytical models, and as the community of agent-based modelers grows, it may well develop a similar specialized language to specifically study macroeconomic AB models.

In contrast, the first two criticisms point to deeper difficulties in agent-based modeling. The flexibility of AB modeling is also its most problematic characteristic [as acknowledged by agent-based modelers themselves, e.g., LeBaron and Tesfatsion (2008)]. Consider, for example, de Grauwe's (2011) model. This agent-based model is able to generate macroeconomic fluctuations endogenously. Given that the financial crisis of 2008–2009 could not be explained with DSGE models at the time, this could be taken as a major achievement. The problem, however, is that this model, just like many other agent-based models, provides sufficient but not necessary conditions for a result (e.g., Tubaro 2011). "Growing" the crisis simply does not suffice as an explanation because it leaves open the possibility that the result could have been obtained with different assumptions (see also Silverman 2018). This is why a demonstration of the robustness of the results is particularly crucial for agent-based models (e.g., Muldoon 2007; Durán and Formanek 2018).

More generally, given that agent-based models are more opaque than other kinds of simulation, it is important to be able to make systematic comparisons between different models. This kind of comparability is important in order to solve what Lehtinen (2021) calls "Duhemian problems"; as similar macro outcomes may be the result of several different individual behaviors and several possible mechanisms translating such behaviors into macro outcomes, it is important to be able to see how any given modification to the model affects the outcomes. The solution of Duhemian problems requires comparability among models and, thus, some common elements in a family of models. From this perspective, heterogeneity among the agent-based models is inexcusable when it is combined with the ease with which one can generate different results with agent-based models. It is no wonder that DSGE macroeconomists consider engaging in agent-based macro as a "walk on the wild side" (see Napoletano 2018).

Before we see how the agent-based macroeconomists have reacted to these difficulties, it is useful to consider a perspective from the natural sciences. Lenhard and Winsberg have argued (Lenhard and Winsberg 2010; Lenhard 2017) that it is practically impossible to solve Duhemian problems in climate modeling, which is also based on discretizations (for a dissenting view, see Jebeile and Ardourel (2019)). They argue that one can only see the effects of changing a module in the results concerning the whole globe. These models also require the calibration of a large number of parameters, they exhibit important feedback loops between model parts, and the parts are knit together with ad hoc kluges. Whatever the plausibility of these arguments is in the context of climate modeling, they are surely not less plausible in macroeconomics. The main difference between climate models and macroeconomic models is that climate models are partly based on established physical theory that is not questioned by anyone, whereas DSGE macro is based on "microeconomic" theory (of intertemporal utility maximization) that is commonly taken to be false, even by those who argue in favor of DSGE models (e.g., Christiano et al. 2018).

Such problems indicate that it is very difficult to solve Duhemian problems with a single model. Macroeconomists proceed to solve Duhemian problems by studying a benchmark model (see especially Vines and Wills 2018): the DSGE model provides a benchmark in the sense that it contains elements known to all researchers, and the macrolevel consequences of modifications and additions to the benchmark therefore remain mostly tractable.

Agent-based modelers have taken the criticism that their models are not comparable with each other or with the DSGE models seriously. Some have tried to provide a stripped-down version of what they consider to be the consensus way of diverging from the DSGE models, even labeling the resulting model a "benchmark" (Lengnick 2013; Caiani et al. 2016). Dawid and Delli Gatti (2018) discover an emerging consensus in their review of agent-based macroeconomics. Dawid et al. (2019) provide extensive documentation on one of the main agent-based macro models so as to facilitate using and replicating it. Finally, Gobbi and Grazzini (2019) provide a bridge between DSGE and agent-based approaches by constructing a model that is solved with agent interaction, but otherwise employs all of the standard assumptions of DSGE models. They show that as long as one uses rational expectations with intertemporal maximization and so on, the results of the AB model are highly similar to the DSGE benchmark. This suggests that the assumption of an instantaneous general equilibrium does not drive the results.

Even though all of these efforts will surely help to make agent-based models more acceptable to broader audiences, some obstacles remain. DSGE models were widely adopted by major central banks between 2004 and 2011. Central banks require first, that their macro models can provide a systematic causal account of what is happening in the economy and what would happen if various policies were to be implemented, and second, that they can predict the future at least as well as other models. The first DSGE model that is commonly thought to be good enough was that of Smets and Wouters (2003). At present, agent-based macro models are almost, but not quite, good enough in these respects for these purposes. Moreover, central bank economists must be able to demonstrate the economic mechanisms at work in the model in such a way that the decision-makers do not need to trust the modelers but rather can see for themselves how the model comes up with its results – the model has to provide a coherent economic story and agent-based models are not always transparent in this way.

4. Conclusions: Simulation and Theoretical Progress in Economics

Paul Humphreys (2009) stated that the growing importance of computational methods within most fields of science forces us to fundamentally reconsider the traditional anthropocentric epistemology, in which knowledge claims are, in the end, evaluated in terms of the perspective and cognitive capacities of human agents. The reception of computational methods in economics can be seen as a conservative reaction to this *anthropocentric predicament.* Simulation methods that can be conceptualized simply in terms of computational solutions to analytically intractable mathematical problems (Durán's first tradition of understanding simulation) are readily accepted in the mainstream methodological palette, whereas simulations that are more about directly mimicking dynamic processes in the modeled phenomena rather than computational extensions of existing theory (Durán's second tradition) face methodological resistance.

Simulation is thus accepted as a computational tool for calculating the consequences of economic theory, but theory building itself is still seen as lying solely in the purview of the mind of the human economist. Many economists have been taught to consider theory solely as a matter of analytical mathematics. Consider, for example, Lucas:

> I loved the Foundations. Like so many others in my cohort, I internalized its view that if I couldn't formulate a problem in economic theory mathematically, I didn't know what I was doing. I came to the position that mathematical analysis is not one of the many ways of doing economic theory: it is the only way. Economic theory is mathematical analysis. Everything else is just pictures and talk.
>
> (Lucas 2001: 9)

From this point of view, the fact that simulations do not have axioms or theorems, and that they look more like experimentation, generates resistance among economists to engage in them (Fontana 2006). This also means that conceptually emergent results from agent-based simulations cannot easily be accepted into theory as there is, by definition, no way to derive them from the axioms.

We hypothesize that this is also an important difference between the role of simulations in physics and in economics. In physics there is plenty of trust in physical theory as an accurate description of physical phenomena, and computer simulations built on this theory can therefore be regarded as good, or even superior, substitutes for material experiments (along the second tradition). In economics, theory is seen probably for good reasons more as a tool for thinking about rather than a literally true description of economic behavior. Econophysics is an interesting comparison case in this respect, but we cannot pursue this project here (however, see, e.g., Schinckus and Jovanovic 2013 and Jhun, Chapter 23).

Humphreys (2009) also outlined two possible ways in which the anthropocentric predicament can develop further. In the hybrid scenario, the role of the human cognitive agent remains epistemologically essential, and the computational aids need to be developed in such a way that respects human cognitive limitations. Economists accept the hybrid scenario in data analysis, forecasting, and policy analysis, but not yet in theory development. In the automated scenario, the computational aids are no longer built with human limitations in mind and science becomes fully automated. Although much has been said about the revolutionary nature of artificial intelligence (AI) and big data in the sciences in general, it remains to be seen how the mainstream will react to this challenge in their own field.

Related Chapters

Favereau, J., Chapter 25 "Field Experiments"
Henschen, T., Chapter 20 "Causality and Probability"
Jhun, J., Chapter 23 "Modeling the Possible to Modeling the Actual"
Nagatsu, M., Chapter 24 "Experimentation in Economics"
Spanos, A., Chapter 29 "Philosophy of Econometrics"

Bibliography

Acharya, S. and Dogra, K. (2020) "Understanding HANK: Insights from a PRANK," *Econometrica* 88(3): 1113–1158.

Achinstein, P. (2001) *The Book of Evidence*, New York; Oxford: Oxford University Press.

Barberousse, A. and Vorms, M. (2014) "About the Warrants of Computer-Based Empirical Knowledge," *Synthese* 191(15): 3595–3620.

Beisbart, C. (2018) "Are Computer Simulations Experiments? And if Not, how are they Related to each Other?" *European Journal for Philosophy of Science* 8(2): 171–204.

Beisbart, C. and Norton, J.D. (2012) "Why Monte Carlo Simulations are Inferences and Not Experiments," *International Studies in the Philosophy of Science* 26(4): 403–422.

Beisbart, C. and Saam, N.J. (2019) *Computer Simulation Validation*, Cham: Springer International Publishing AG.

Borrill, P.L. and Tesfatsion, L. (2011) "Agent-Based Modeling: The Right Mathematics for the Social Sciences?" in J. Davis and D.W. Hands (eds.) *The Elgar Companion to Recent Economic Methodology*, Cheltenham: Edward Elgar Publishing.

Boumans, M. (2020) "Simulation and Economic Methodology," in W. Dolfsma, D.W. Hands and R. McMaster (eds.) *History, Methodology and Identity for a 21st Century Social Economics*, New York: Routledge: 41–50.

Caiani, A., Godin, A., Caverzasi, E., Gallegati, M., Kinsella, S. and Stiglitz, J.E. (2016) "Agent Based-Stock Flow Consistent Macroeconomics: Towards a Benchmark Model," *Journal of Economic Dynamics and Control* 69: 375–408.

Caverzasi, E. and Russo, A. (2018) "Toward a New Microfounded Macroeconomics in the Wake of the Crisis," *Industrial and Corporate Change* 27(6): 999–1014.

Christiano, L., Eichenbaum, M. and Trabandt, M. (2018) "On DSGE Models," *Journal of Economic Perspectives* 32(3): 113–140.

Dardashti, R., Thébault, K.P.Y. and Winsberg, E. (2017) "Confirmation Via Analogue Simulation: What Dumb Holes could Tell Us about Gravity," *The British Journal for the Philosophy of Science* 68(1): 55–89.

Davis, J.B. (2018) "Agent-Based Modeling's Open Methodology Approach: Simulation, Reflexivity, and Abduction," *OEconomia* 8(8–4): 509–529.

Dawid, H. and Delli Gatti, D. (2018) "Agent-Based Macroeconomics," in C. Hommes and B. LeBaron (eds.) *Handbook of Computational Economics, Vol. 4*, Elsevier: 63–156.

Dawid, H., Harting, P., van der Hoog, S. and Neugart, M. (2019) "Macroeconomics with Heterogeneous Agent Models: Fostering Transparency, Reproducibility and Replication," *Journal of Evolutionary Economics* 29(1): 467–538.

De Grauwe, P. (2011) "Animal Spirits and Monetary Policy," *Economic Theory* 47(2): 423–457.

Delli Gatti, D. and Grazzini, J. (2020) "Rising to the Challenge: Bayesian Estimation and Forecasting Techniques for Macroeconomic Agent Based Models," *Journal of Economic Behavior & Organization* 178: 875–902.
Dilaver, Ö., Calvert Jump, R. and Levine, P. (2018) "Agent-Based Macroeconomics and Dynamic Stochastic General Equilibrium Models: Where do we Go from here?" *Journal of Economic Surveys* 32(4): 1134–1159.
Dosi, G. and Roventini, A. (2019) "More is Different . . . and Complex! The Case for Agent-Based Macroeconomics," *Journal of Evolutionary Economics* 29(1): 1–37.
Durán, J.M. (2013) "The Use of the 'Materiality Argument' in the Literature on Computer Simulations," in E. Arnold and J.M. Durán (eds.) *Computer Simulations and the Changing Face of Scientific Experimentation*, Cambridge: Cambridge Academic Publishers.
Durán, J.M. (2017) "Varieties of Simulations: From the Analogue to the Digital," in M.M. Resch, A. Kaminski and P. Gehring (eds.) *The Science and Art of Simulation I: Exploring Understanding Knowing*, Cham: Springer: 175–192.
Durán, J.M. (2018) *Computer Simulations in Science and Engineering*, Cham: Springer International Publishing AG.
Durán, J.M. (2021) "A Formal Framework for Computer Simulations: Surveying the Historical Record and Finding their Philosophical Roots," *Philosophy & Technology* 34: 105–127.
Durán, J.M. and Formanek, N. (2018) "Grounds for Trust: Essential Epistemic Opacity and Computational Reliabilism," *Minds and Machines* 28(4): 645–666.
El Skaf, R. and Imbert, C. (2013) "Unfolding in the Empirical Sciences: Experiments, Thought Experiments and Computer Simulations," *Synthese* 190(16): 3451–3474.
Epstein, J.M. (1999) "Agent-Based Computational Models and Generative Social Science," *Complexity* 4(5): 41–60.
Fagiolo, G., Guerini, M., Lamperti, F., Moneta, A. and Roventini, A. (2019) "Validation of Agent-Based Models in Economics and Finance," in C. Beisbart and N.J. Saam (eds.) *Computer Simulation Validation. Fundamental Concepts, Methodological Frameworks, and Philosophical Perspectives,* Heidelberg: Springer International Publishing: 763–787.
Fagiolo, G. and Roventini, A. (2017) "Macroeconomic Policy in DSGE and Agent-Based Models Redux: New Developments and Challenges Ahead," *Journal of Artificial Societies and Social Simulation* 20(1): 1.
Fontana, M. (2006) "Computer Simulations, Mathematics and Economics," *International Review of Economics* 53(1): 96–123.
Frigg, R. and Reiss, J. (2008) "The Philosophy of Simulation: Hot New Issues Or Same Old Stew?" *Synthese* 169(3): 593–613.
Galison, P. (1996) "Computer Simulations and the Trading Zone," in P. Galison and D.J. Stump (eds.) *The Disunity of Science*, Stanford: Stanford University Press: 118–157.
Giere, R.N. (2009) "Is Computer Simulation Changing the Face of Experimentation?" *Philosophical Studies* 143(1): 59–62.
Gilbert, N. and Troitzsch, K.G. (1999) *Simulation for the Social Scientist*, Buckingham; Philadelphia, PA: Open University Press.
Gobbi, A. and Grazzini, J. (2019) "A Basic New Keynesian DSGE Model with Dispersed Information: An Agent-Based Approach," *Journal of Economic Behavior & Organization* 157(C): 101–116.
Grüne-Yanoff, T. (2009) "The Explanatory Potential of Artificial Societies," *Synthese* 169: 539–555.
Grüne-Yanoff, T. and Weirich, P. (2010) "The Philosophy and Epistemology of Simulation: A Review," *Simulation & Gaming* 41(1): 20–50.
Guala, F. (2002) "Models, Simulations, and Experiments," in L. Magnani and N. Nersessian (eds.) *Model-Based Reasoning*, Boston: Springer: 59–74.
Haldane, A.G. and Turrell, A.E. (2018) "An Interdisciplinary Model for Macroeconomics," *Oxford Review of Economic Policy* 34(1–2): 219–251.
Haldane, A.G. and Turrell, A.E. (2019) "Drawing on Different Disciplines: Macroeconomic Agent-Based Models," *Journal of Evolutionary Economics* 29(1): 39–66.
Hartmann, S. (1996) "The World as a Process: Simulations in the Natural and Social Sciences," in R. Hegselmann, U. Mueller and K. Troitzsch (eds.) *Modelling and Simulation in the Social Sciences from the Philosophy of Science Point of View*, Dordrecht: Kluwer: 77–100.
Hoover, K.D. and Salyer, K.D. (1998) "Technology Shocks or Coloured Noise? Why Real-Business-Cycle Models Cannot Explain Actual Business Cycles," *Review of Political Economy* 10(3): 299–327.
Hughes, R.I.G. (1999) "The Ising Model, Computer Simulation, and Universal Physics," in M.S. Morgan and M. Morrison (eds.) *Models as Mediators: Perspectives on Natural and Social Science*, Cambridge; New York: Cambridge University Press: 97–145.
Humphreys, P. (1991) "Computer Simulations," in A. Fine, M. Forbes and L. Wessels (eds.) *PSA 1990*, East Lansing, MI: Philosophy of Science Association: 497–506.

Humphreys, P. (2004) *Extending Ourselves: Computational Science, Empiricism, and Scientific Method*, Oxford; New York: Oxford University Press.
Humphreys, P. (2009) "The Philosophical Novelty of Computer Simulation Methods," *Synthese* 169(3): 615–626.
Imbert, C. (2017) "Computer Simulations and Computational Models in Science," in *Springer Handbook of Model-Based Science*, Cham: Springer: 735–781.
Jebeile, J. and Ardourel, V. (2019) "Verification and Validation of Simulations Against Holism," *Minds and Machines* 29: 149–168.
Kaplan, G., Moll, B. and Violante, G.L. (2018) "Monetary Policy According to HANK," *American Economic Review* 108(3): 697–743.
Kirman, A.P. (2010) "The Economic Crisis is a Crisis for Economic Theory," *History CESinfo Economic Studies* 56(4): 498–535.
Kirman, A.P. (2016) "Complexity and Economic Policy: A Paradigm Shift Or a Change in Perspective? A Review Essay on David Colander and Roland Kupers's Complexity and the Art of Public Policy," *Journal of Economic Literature* 54(2): 534–572.
Kuorikoski, J. and Lehtinen, A. (2018) "Model Selection in Macroeconomics: DSGE and Ad Hocness," *Journal of Economic Methodology* 25(3): 252–264.
Kydland, F. and Prescott, E. (1982) "Time to Build and Aggregate Fluctuations," *Econometrica* 50(6): 1345–1370.
LeBaron, B. and Tesfatsion, L. (2008) "Modeling Macroeconomies as Open-Ended Dynamic Systems of Interacting Agents," *The American Economic Review* 98(2), Papers and Proceedings of the One Hundred Twentieth Annual Meeting of the American Economic Association: 246–250.
Lehtinen, A. (forthcoming) Core Models in Macroeconomics, in H. Kincaid and D. Ross (eds.) *Modern Guide to Philosophy of Economics*, Cheltenham: Edward Elgar: 254–283.
Lehtinen, A. and Kuorikoski, J. (2007) "Computing the Perfect Model: Why do Economists Shun Simulation?" *Philosophy of Science* 74(3): 304–329.
Lengnick, M. (2013) "Agent-Based Macroeconomics: A Baseline Model," *Journal of Economic Behavior & Organization* 86: 102–120.
Lenhard, J. (2006) "Surprised by a Nanowire: Simulation, Control, and Understanding," *Philosophy of Science* 73(5): 605–616.
Lenhard, J. (2017) "The Demon's Fallacy: Simulation Modeling and a New Style of Reasoning," in *The Science and Art of Simulation I*, Cham: Springer: 137–151.
Lenhard, J. (2019) *Calculated Surprises: A Philosophy of Computer Simulation*, Oxford: Oxford University Press.
Lenhard, J. and Winsberg, E. (2010) "Holism, Entrenchment, and the Future of Climate Model Pluralism," *Studies in History and Philosophy of Science Part B: Studies in History and Philosophy of Modern Physics* 41(3): 253–262.
Lucas, R. (2001). Professional Memoir. http://home.uchicago.edu
Massimi, M. and Bhimji, W. (2015) "Computer Simulations and Experiments: The Case of the Higgs Boson," *Studies in History and Philosophy of Science Part B: Studies in History and Philosophy of Modern Physics* 51: 71–81.
Morgan, M.S. (2002) "Model Experiments and Models in Experiments," in L. Magnani and N. Nersessian (eds.) *Model-Based Reasoning: Science, Technology, Values*, Dordrecht: Kluwer Academic//Plenum Publisher: 41–58.
Morgan, M.S. (2003) "Experiments without Material Intervention. Model Experiments, Virtual Experiments, and Virtually Experiments," in H. Radder (ed.) *The Philosophy of Scientific Experimentation*, Pittsburgh: University of Pittsburgh Press: 216–233.
Morgan, M.S. (2005) "Experiments Versus Models: New Phenomena, Inference and Surprise," *The Journal of Economic Methodology* 12(2): 317–329.
Morrison, M. (2009) "Models, Measurement and Computer Simulation: The Changing Face of Experimentation," *Philosophical Studies* 143(1): 33–57.
Morrison, M. (2015) *Reconstructing Reality: Models, Mathematics, and Simulations*, New York: Oxford University Press.
Muldoon, R. (2007) "Robust Simulations," *Philosophy of Science* 74(5): 873–883.
Napoletano, M. (2018) "A Short Walk on the Wild Side: Agent-Based Models and their Implications for Macroeconomic Analysis," *Revue de l'OFCE* 157(3): 257–281.
Norton, S.D. and Suppe, F. (2001) "Why Atmospheric Modeling is Good Science," in C.A. Miller and P. Edwards (eds.) *Changing the Atmosphere*, Cambridge, MA: MIT Press.
Parke, E.C. (2014) "Experiments, Simulations, and Epistemic Privilege," *Philosophy of Science* 81(4): 516–536.
Parker, W.S. (2009) "Does Matter really Matter? Computer Simulations, Experiments, and Materiality," *Synthese* 269(3): 483–496.

Ravn, M. and Sterk, V. (2021) "Macroeconomic Fluctuations with HANK & SAM: An Analytical Approach," *Journal of the European Economic Association,* 19(2): 1162–1202..
Reiss, J. (2011) "A Plea for (Good) Simulations: Nudging Economics Toward an Experimental Science," *Simulation & Gaming* 42(2): 243–264.
Roush, S. (2019) "The Epistemic Superiority of Experiment to Simulation," *Synthese* 195: 4883–4906.
Schinckus, C. and Jovanovic, F. (2013) "Towards a Transdisciplinary Econophysics," *Journal of Economic Methodology* 20(2): 164–183.
Silverman, E. (2018) *Methodological Investigations in Agent-Based Modelling: With Applications for the Social Sciences*, Cham: Springer Open.
Smets, F. and Wouters, R. (2003) "An Estimated Dynamic Stochastic General Equilibrium Model of the Euro Area," *Journal of the European Economic Association* 1(5): 1123–1175.
Stiglitz, J.E. (2018) "Where Modern Macroeconomics Went Wrong," *Oxford Review of Economic Policy* 34(1–2): 70–106.
Trenholme, R. (1994) "Analog Simulation," *Philosophy of Science* 61(1): 115–131.
Tubaro, P. (2011) "Computational Economics," in J. Davis and D.W. Hands (eds.) *The Elgar Companion to Recent Economic Methodology*, Cheltenham: Edward Elgar: 209–227.
Velupillai, K.V. and Zambelli, S. (2011) "Computing in economics," in John Davis and D. Wade Hands (eds.) *The Elgar Companion to Recent Economic Methodology*, Cheltenham: Edward Elgar: 259–298.
Vines, D. and Wills, S. (2018) "The Rebuilding Macroeconomic Theory Project: An Analytical Assessment," *Oxford Review of Economic Policy* 34(1–2): 1–42.
Windrum, P., Fagiolo, G. and Moneta, A. (2007) "Empirical Validation of Agent-Based Models: Alternatives and Prospects," *Journal of Artificial Societies and Social Simulation* 10(2).
Winsberg, E. (2001) "Simulations, Models, and Theories: Complex Physical Systems and their Representations," *Philosophy of Science* 68(3): 442–454.
Winsberg, E. (2003) "Simulated Experiments: Methodology for a Virtual World," *Philosophy of Science* 70(1): 105–125.
Winsberg, E. (2009) "Computer Simulation and the Philosophy of Science," *Philosophy Compass* 4(5): 835–845.
Winsberg, E. (2010) *Science in the Age of Computer Simulation*, Chicago, IL; London: University of Chicago Press.
Winsberg, E. (2015) "Computer Simulations in Science," in Edward N. Zalta (ed.) *The Stanford Encyclopedia of Philosophy* Summer 2015 edn, Metaphysics Research Lab, Stanford University.

27
EVIDENCE-BASED POLICY

Donal Khosrowi

1. Introduction

Public policymakers and institutional decision-makers routinely face questions about whether interventions "work": does universal basic income improve people's welfare and stimulate entrepreneurial activity? Do gated alleyways reduce burglaries or merely shift the crime burden to neighboring communities? What is the most cost-effective way to improve students' reading abilities? These are empirical questions that seem best answered by looking at the world, rather than trusting speculations about what will be effective.

Evidence-based policy (EBP) is a movement that concretizes this intuition. It maintains that policy should be based on evidence of "what works." Not any evidence will do, however. Following on the heels of its intellectual progenitor, evidence-based medicine (EBM; see Evidence-Based Medicine Working Group 1992; Sackett et al. 1996), EBP insists on the use of high-quality evidence produced in accordance with rigorous methodological standards. Though intuitively compelling, EBP has attracted significant criticism from methodologists, political scientists, and philosophers (see, for instance, Cartwright et al. 2009; Cartwright 2013a; Reiss 2013; Strassheim and Kettunen 2014; Muller 2015; Parkhurst 2017; Deaton and Cartwright 2018a; Favereau and Nagatsu 2020).

This chapter provides a critical overview of EBP through a philosophical lens, reviewing and discussing some of the most pressing challenges that EBP faces and outlining some proposals for improving it. Section 2 provides a brief overview of EBP and distinguishes a broader and narrower understanding of it. Section 3 reviews existing criticisms, two of which are considered in detail. The first elaborates how EBP struggles with *extrapolation*, that is, the use of evidence from study populations to make inferences about the effects of policies on novel target populations. The second maintains that EBP's methodological tenets are deeply entwined with moral and political values, which can threaten EBP's promise to promote objectivity in policymaking. Finally, Section 4 considers some proposals for how EBP could be improved going forward and concludes the discussion.

2. What Is EBP?

2.1 Broad and Narrow EBP

With EBP proliferating in various policy areas, there are many ways to spell out what exactly it amounts to. Not all of these can be discussed here, but to help organize our thinking, it is useful to draw a provisional distinction between a narrow and a broad understanding of EBP.

 DOI: 10.4324/9781315739793-33

Broad EBP simply emphasizes that policy should be informed by evidence, but no *general* criteria are put in place to govern what kinds of evidence should be sought or how to use them (for a more general discussion of the use of evidence in economics, see Northcott, Chapter 28). Importantly, there is no requirement that evidence should speak directly to whether policies are *effective*; evidence could simply be used to monitor certain policy variables, for instance. To use a fringe example, the gathering of data on whether the plankton concentration in a marine ecosystem is within a certain desirable range could count as an evidence-based way of informing marine ecology management (see, e.g., Addison et al. 2018). Here, evidence guides real-world decision-making, but it is not used to determine the impacts of specific interventions, nor are there strict guidelines for what kinds of methods and evidence are good enough to inform decision-making.

By contrast, *narrow EBP*, which is the focus of this chapter, concentrates primarily on learning which policies "work" and applies concrete strictures on what evidence is good enough for this purpose. In doing so, narrow EBP focuses on evidence from high-quality *effectiveness studies*, in particular randomized controlled trials (RCTs), which are widely considered the best method for determining the effectiveness of policy interventions. Results from these studies are often (1) amalgamated in *meta-analyses* that compute an overall best estimate of a policy effect (Haynes et al. 2012) and (2) collated in *systematic reviews* and other evidence syntheses that grade available evidence according to quality and summarize it to provide a broader picture. While narrow EBP is far from a unified paradigm (see Head 2010, 2016), several general features help to characterize it in more detail.

Narrow EBP is advocated, governed, and conducted by a wide range of institutions, collaborations, and research networks (see Parkhurst 2017, ch.8), such as the Campbell and Cochrane Collaboration, the GRADE and CONSORT working groups, and others.[1] These are complemented by more specific governmental institutions focusing on EBP in particular areas, such as the US Department of Education's What Works Clearinghouse or the UK's eight What Works Centres (Cabinet Office 2013), which cover a wide range of policy areas including health, education, policing, and local economic growth. Finally, there are also numerous nongovernmental organizations (NGOs), academic and private institutions, and research centers, such as 3ie and J-PAL, who champion the EBP approach in areas such as international development (see Duflo and Kremer 2005; Banerjee and Duflo 2009).

These institutions perform a variety of functions: they offer general guidelines and concrete assistance to evaluators conducting effectiveness studies and meta-analyses; they produce systematic reviews that survey and summarize the existing evidence base and grade it according to quality; and they disseminate information about the (cost-) effectiveness of different interventions and the strength of the evidence underwriting these assessments. Importantly, while many of these activities involve backward-looking policy evaluation, a substantial portion of the evidence produced and summarized is supposed to help decision-makers implement policies in new environments. Ideally, decision-makers and practitioners, often termed "users" or "consumers," can go "shopping" for evidence collated in so-called "warehouses," "libraries of evidence," or "toolkits," which provide off-the-shelf information to help address common policy issues.

In performing these functions, a distinctive feature of narrow EBP is its reliance on rigorous methodological guidelines and so-called *evidence hierarchies*, which rank the quality of different kinds of evidence and the methods used to produce them (Nutley et al. 2013). While available hierarchies differ in their details, they largely follow the same blueprint. RCTs (and meta-analyses thereof) rank the highest; the fact that RCTs involve experimental control is thought to make them the most reliable for determining a policy's effects. Climbing down the ladder, one finds quasi-experimental and observational approaches, such as matching methods and simpler multivariate regression-based studies. Due to a lack of experimental control, these study types face more severe concerns about the *risk of bias*, that is, whether they can properly distinguish the effect of a policy from other things that can influence an outcome at the same time. Finally, evidence hierarchies bottom out with the least credible kinds of studies and evidence, for example, cohort studies, qualitative case-control studies, and expert judgment, which are considered to be even more prone to bias or are not believed to help determine policy effectiveness at all.

When analysts build systematic reviews of evidence pertaining to the effectiveness of particular interventions, they use these hierarchies and more specific evidence-grading guidelines as exclusion and ranking criteria. Studies exhibiting a risk of bias are discounted or even excluded when determined to be below a certain level of quality. This *manualization* is supposed to streamline evidence production and use; ensure that rigorous standards are applied in synthesizing evidence; and make the criteria underlying evidence synthesis more transparent in the pursuit of promoting accountability and objectivity in evidence-based decision-making. With these general features in place, let us consider in more detail why RCTs are often at the top of evidence hierarchies.

2.2 Gold Standards

In the production of evidence that is informative for decision-making, it is important to obtain evidence of the *causal effects* of policies. Without knowledge of what causes what, it is unlikely that our policy interventions will be successful. However, the demand for evidence of causal effects presents a formidable epistemic challenge.

Consider an example: do gated alleyways reduce burglaries (Sidebottom et al. 2018; see Cowen and Cartwright (2019) for a detailed analysis)? To answer this question, we could compare the incidence of burglaries in gated and ungated neighborhoods. Yet, even if we found that gated neighborhoods experienced fewer burglaries than ungated ones, it is not obvious whether this difference is an effect of alley gates or rather of some *confounding factor* (also *confounder*) that induces a spurious correlation between alley gates and burglary rates. Perhaps those neighborhoods that tend to have gates installed are targeted less by burglars regardless of gates, for example, because people are more concerned about burglaries and hence are more watchful or there is more video surveillance. We might also compare the same sample of neighborhoods before and after gates are installed. Yet, even if we observed that the incidence of burglaries decreased after gates had been installed, this could be due to a variety of other reasons, such as a change in police activity.

In each of these cases, there is a worry about obtaining a *biased* measurement of the effect we are interested in, either because alley gates do not have any effect at all and something else is responsible for any observed differences between gated and ungated neighborhoods or because the effect of alley gates is muddled together with other things that happen simultaneously. Clearly, if our estimates of policy effects are to be informative for decision-making, we need to ensure that we obtain *unbiased* estimates, that is, measurements that capture only the effects of our policy and nothing else.

The standard framework underlying attempts to accomplish this is the *potential outcomes framework* (Neyman 1923; Rubin 1974; Holland 1986). When we attempt to identify a causal effect, our aim is to compare two states of the world that are alike in all respects except for the cause, intervention, or treatment of interest. More specifically, an *individual treatment effect* (ITE) is defined as the difference between the outcome Y of a unit u's (say, a neighborhood or an individual) in two states: a factual state $Y_t(u)$ where the unit is "treated" (say, where a gate is installed) and a *counterfactual* state $Y_c(u)$ where the unit is "untreated" and all else is equal. The *fundamental problem of causal inference* (Holland 1986), however, is that we can never observe both states for the same unit at the same time. So, how can we measure causal effects at all?

RCTs offer a deceptively simple solution by randomly allocating units to (at least) two groups: the *treatment group*, which receives a treatment (e.g. alley gates), and the *control group*, which does not (or receives some alternative treatment, think of placebos in medical trials). Randomization promises to mitigate bias because it helps to ensure that the net effects of all confounding factors are balanced between the two groups. For instance, by randomly allocating neighborhoods from a given sample to the treatment group (receiving gates) and the control group (not receiving gates), we can ensure that the net effects of policing and watchfulness on burglary rates are the same for both groups. Importantly, while any two *specific* neighborhoods might still differ in how confounders influence their outcomes, randomization helps make sure that these differences wash out on *average*. So, when measuring the difference in the means of the outcome between treatment and control groups, we get an unbiased estimate of the *average treatment effect* (ATE) of an intervention (at least in expectation – more on this shortly).

Quasi-experimental methods that do not involve the experimentally controlled assignment of treatment status (e.g. instrumental variables, regression discontinuity, differences-in-differences, and matching methods) can sometimes achieve similarly credible estimates of treatment effects. But while there has been increasing enthusiasm for these methods in empirical microeconomics (see Angrist and Pischke 2010) and beyond, EBP's methodological guidelines insist that they are not as credible as RCTs because they require a host of assumptions that are more difficult to support by reference to features of the study design than is the case for RCTs (see Deaton and Cartwright 2018a).

For instance, matching methods (Rosenbaum and Rubin 1983) purposely select units from a population so that they differ only in their treatment status but are similar in all other respects, particularly in regard to potential confounders. In our alley gate example, we could match gated and ungated neighborhoods on the level of policing, watchfulness, and video surveillance and then compare them with respect to burglary rates. Importantly, however, the features on which units are matched must exhaust all features that can relevantly influence the outcome, which is often difficult to support. RCTs, by contrast, are argued to be applicable without the knowledge of potential confounders and to generally require fewer substantive assumptions. By virtue of these features, RCTs are believed to be more credible than other study designs and are often touted as the "gold standard" for clarifying policy effectiveness.

To summarize, while broader versions of EBP may be open to using various kinds of evidence to inform policy, narrow EBP insists on more rigorous methodological standards for what evidence is sufficiently credible. This insistence is supposed to underwrite two important promises: first, that we can build evidence libraries collating credible and ready-to-use evidence that speaks to policy issues of interest to decision-makers. Second, that this evidence, by virtue of its credibility, can push back on the role that individuals' values and convictions play in deciding which policies should be implemented, thus promoting objectivity, transparency, and accountability in policymaking (Nutley 2003: 3; Abraham et al. 2017: 60). Let us turn to some of the challenges that have been leveled against narrow EBP and consider how they cast doubt on whether it can deliver on its promises.

3. Challenges for EBP

Narrow EBP faces a wide range of (1) methodological as well as (2) value-related and practical challenges. Not all of these can be discussed here, so I will offer brief overviews of both kinds, each followed by a more detailed look at what I consider to be their most pressing instances.

3.1 Methodological Challenges

Methodological challenges take issue with the central methodological tenets of EBP, in particular evidence hierarchies proclaiming the superiority of RCTs (see Heckman 1992; Pawson 2006; Scriven 2008; Deaton 2009, 2010; Deaton and Cartwright 2018a and other articles in the same issue). One of the key concerns is that, on closer inspection, RCTs in fact require a whole array of substantive background assumptions, which are not always satisfied and can be difficult to validate.

First, the balance of confounders between treatment and control groups that randomization is supposed to achieve only obtains *in expectation* and not necessarily on any particular measurement (see Deaton and Cartwright 2018a: 4–6 for a discussion; see also Leamer 1983, 2010; Cartwright 2007; see Worrall 2002, 2007 for similar concerns about RCTs in EBM). In other words, while RCTs can provide unbiased effect estimates when results are averaged over repeated measurements, on any single occasion there may still be substantial background differences between groups that can distort an effect measure. Although this can be remedied by inspecting the balance of confounders and rerandomizing if necessary, doing so raises concerns similar to those faced by nonrandomized alternatives: one needs to know which confounders (or combinations thereof; see Fuller 2019) need to be balanced. This has led some to conclude that the assumptions required by RCTs are no less problematic in practice than those required by other methods (see Muller 2015; Bruhn and McKenzie 2009).

Second, there are a host of additional concerns about how bias can creep into RCTs even if randomization is successful (see Deaton and Cartwright 2018a for an overview). These focus on how units are selected into trials; attrition during a trial (e.g. individuals dropping out); the blinding of participants, administrators, and evaluators; spillover and equilibrium effects; and many other issues. For instance, a central assumption supposedly facilitated by randomization is that units' potential outcomes are independent of treatment status; for example, how much an individual will benefit from an intervention should not influence whether they are assigned to the treatment or the control group. This assumption is undermined when units nonrandomly leave a trial in a way that correlates with their potential outcomes, for example, low-crime neighborhoods could ultimately resist having inconvenient gates installed and drop out of a trial, which could yield an upward-biased effect estimate for the overall population. Moreover, in many cases it will be important that units are blinded to their treatment status: for instance, individuals aware of participating in an alley gate trial could unintentionally become more watchful once gates are installed, thus inadvertently affecting the outcome and biasing the effect estimate. Similarly, the effects experienced by treated units can sometimes spill over to untreated ones, for instance, when gated and ungated neighborhoods are geographically close and burglars are deterred from attempting burglaries in the whole area rather than just where gates are installed. Relatedly, some interventions, when implemented on a large scale, can change not only the values of particular variables but also more fundamental structural features of the causal setup one is seeking to meddle with (see Lucas 1976); think would-be burglars turned violent robbers because burglary becomes too cumbersome.

A third important concern about RCTs maintains that, even if they are helpful in successfully identifying causal effects, they still leave unclear *how* the effect of interest came about, for example, by which *mechanism* or *process* an intervention worked. Such knowledge can be crucial for understanding why and how a policy is effective or not, how affected individuals experience its effects, and how a policy might be improved. For instance, we could imagine a case where alley gates are effective in reducing burglaries, not because they physically prevent access to back doors but because an increased demand for gates happens to create job opportunities for skilled would-be burglars, something that could also be achieved in other, socially more desirable and more sustainable ways. The point here is that without ancillary analyses tracing the mechanisms and building theories of how interventions work, RCTs may not be informative enough for designing, deploying, and maintaining policy interventions; the effects they estimate will remain a "black box" that tells us too little about how policies work (see Heckman 2010 for positive proposals).

The preceding concerns largely target the *internal validity* of RCTs (Guala 2010), that is, their ability to successfully measure what they seek to measure in a particular context. We now take a more detailed look at challenges that focus on *external validity*, that is, problems encountered in reasoning beyond a particular study context (see also Favereau, Chapter 25).

3.2 Extrapolation: Getting From A to B Without Walking All the Way

As outlined earlier, a major promise of EBP is that we can build libraries of evidence, that is, collections of expertly curated and ready-to-use evidence on a variety of policy options targeting problems routinely faced by policymakers.

This promise comes under pressure when we recognize that the populations studied in trials and the eventual target populations of interest to policymakers can often differ in important ways (Vivalt 2020), so to conclude that what works in a study population A will also work in a target population B is often simply implausible (Steel 2009, 2010; Cartwright 2013b; Fuller 2019; Reiss 2019). But if, on their own, the only thing that evidence libraries can do for us is tell us what happened in a number of study populations, then why should we bother building these libraries at all? To make the evidence collated in our libraries useful, we need a theory of how to let it speak to questions about our eventual policy targets, that is, a theory of how to *extrapolate* from available effectiveness evidence.[2]

There are two ideas that can help us overcome problems of extrapolation: first, not all differences between populations matter. If we can support that populations are sufficiently similar in relevant respects, we might still be entitled to draw well-supported conclusions about a novel target. Second, even if populations differ relevantly, we might nevertheless be able to account for *how* these differences bear on the effects to be expected in a target.

There is now a menu of different approaches to extrapolation that draw on these ideas. Perhaps the most general is Cartwright's *Argument Theory of Evidence* (2013a), which maintains that inferences about the effects of policies in new environments should be cast in terms of valid and sound *effectiveness arguments*. "It works here, therefore it works there" is not a valid argument, for instance, and any methodological rigor exercised in producing evidence is undermined if one relies on bad arguments when putting it to use (Cartwright and Stegenga 2011; Cartwright and Hardie 2012).

According to Cartwright, a useful way to think about building better arguments is in terms of *causal principles* and *causal support factors*. Causal principles represent the causal arrangements that connect an intervention to an outcome variable. These arrangements need to be similar between populations for an intervention that works in *A* to also work in *B*: think of burglars in *B* who prefer front door access and are unlikely to be hindered by alley gates. Support factors are factors that interact with an intervention and need to be suitably realized for an intervention to yield its envisioned effects: think of alley gates that only work when people are willing to lock them. In making an inference to a new target, one needs to learn whether similar causal principles are at work in *A* and *B*, which support factors are important for an effect, and whether they are suitably realized in *B*. The following sketch illustrates how we could integrate these ideas into an effectiveness argument (adapted from Cartwright 2013a: 14):

P1: *X* plays a causal role in the production of *Y* in *A*.
P2: *X* can play a causal role in the production of *Y* in *B* *if* it does so in *A* *and* the support factors necessary for *X* to produce *Y* are present in *B*.
P3: The support factors necessary for *X* to produce *Y* are present in *B*.
C: Therefore, *X* can play a causal role in the production of *Y* in *B*.

Cartwright stresses that the only thing we get from an RCT is **P1** but that **P1** alone is not enough to infer **C**. **P2** is needed to ensure that the causal principles are similar (or indeed the same), and it clarifies the importance of support factors. **P3** ensures that these support factors are indeed present in the target. Importantly, both premises must be true, and to offer support or warrant for their truth we must invoke additional resources, including strong background theory, extensive causal knowledge of the study and target populations, etc.

Cartwright's Argument Theory provides general constraints on evidence use by emphasizing that the quality of evidence is not all that matters (i.e. how well-supported **P1** is): plenty of additional resources are needed to make this evidence speak compellingly to questions of interest to us. At the same time, the Argument Theory mainly provides a high-level account of how warranting conclusions about new targets should proceed. It tells us that good arguments are needed, including which general kinds of premises they might involve, but not what these arguments would look like in more concrete and more involved cases [but see Cartwright and Hardie (2012) for more detailed proposals]. Importantly, the exemplary arguments used to illustrate the Argument Theory (such as the preceding) also do not tell us what to do in cases where populations differ relevantly. While these are not principled shortcomings, we still need additional strategies that can help us to spell out more concrete and sophisticated recipes for extrapolation. Let us look at some candidates that can help us make progress on this front.

Reweighting strategies (Hotz et al. 2005; Crump et al. 2008; Bareinboim and Pearl 2012, 2016; see also Athey and Imbens 2017; van Eersel et al. 2019; see Duflo 2018 for related machine learning–based methods) aim to permit extrapolation even when populations differ in relevant ways. Say the effect of X on Y depends on an individual's age Z, that is, Z is a so-called *moderating variable* that can amplify or diminish the effect (Baron and Kenny 1986). Suppose further that two populations A and B differ in their Z distribution, so the X-Y effect is likely to differ between them. Then, despite this difference, if we can capture *how* the effect depends on Z, we can reweight the effect measured in A by the observed Z distribution in B to correctly predict the effect of interest there.

Hotz et al. (2005) provide an approach that articulates this idea through a simple but general reweighting formula. Bareinboim and Pearl's (2012, 2016) *causal graph-based approach* is more involved, allowing a wider range of more sophisticated inferences. In doing so, it requires that we write down a *structural causal model*, that is, a system of equations describing how variables hang together causally, and a corresponding graphical causal model (called a *directed acyclic graph*, DAG) that encodes these relationships [see Scheines (1997) and Pearl (2009 ch.1) for introductions and Henschen, Chapter 20, for a discussion]. Together with a powerful calculus, this framework helps derive formulae that permit more involved extrapolations, including in cases where populations differ in several ways at once and where it is important to accommodate which of these differences matter and how.

Both approaches involve extensive assumptions to license the inferences they can enable. For instance, Hotz et al.'s (2005) approach requires that we have an extensive grasp of what the important moderating variables are (Muller 2013, 2014, 2015). Moreover, it requires that study and target populations exhibit a wide range of causally relevant similarities, including at the level of the structure of causal mechanisms (Khosrowi 2019a). For instance, the adjustment of an effect to accommodate age differences between populations only works if the *way in which* age meddles with an effect is similar between the populations. Bareinboim and Pearl's approach involves even stronger assumptions (see Hyttinen et al. 2015; Deaton and Cartwright 2018b). So, while reweighting approaches enable a wide range of more sophisticated extrapolations, they also require more support to *justify* these inferences, that is, extensive background knowledge and supplementary empirical evidence to help clarify important similarities and differences between populations.

This requirement creates two problems: first, the acquisition of such support can be epistemically demanding. Especially in social sciences, we rarely find sufficiently developed causal knowledge to confidently assert, for instance, that the causal mechanisms governing an outcome in two populations are similar. A second, more pernicious, problem is the *extrapolator's circle* (LaFollette and Shanks 1996; Steel 2009). In a nutshell, the supplementary knowledge about the target required for an extrapolation should not be so extensive that we could identify an effect in the target on the basis of this knowledge *alone*. For instance, if we need to implement a policy *in a target* to learn whether the mechanisms governing its effects are similar between populations, we could simply measure the policy effect of interest there, thus, disappointingly, rendering the evidence from the study population redundant to our conclusion. The extrapolator's circle is a serious challenge for any strategy for extrapolation: in mapping out ways to make a leap from *A* to *B*, we need to avoid walking all the way to *B* first, as otherwise there will be no leap to be made (see Khosrowi (2021) for a broader elaboration of the problem).

Steel (2009, 2010) offers detailed proposals to overcome the extrapolator's circle in biomedical sciences. His *comparative process tracing* strategy outlines how, by focusing on clarifying certain downstream similarities between populations, we can avoid learning about the target in its full causal detail. However, others remain skeptical about whether the extrapolator's circle is indeed evaded (Reiss 2010) and whether Steel's approach can be helpful for extrapolation in EBP, unless a much wider range of evidence than is ordinarily used is admitted to bear on issues of causally relevant similarities and differences (Khosrowi 2019a).

In sum, there are a number of promising approaches to extrapolation. General accounts, such as Cartwright's, stress the importance of making crucial assumptions explicit and adequately supporting them. More specific strategies help detail which inferences are feasible in principle and what particular assumptions we need to bet on. However, while the inference templates licensed by these approaches are promising, there is still a persistent lack of concrete recipes for *supporting* these inferences. And while some authors have argued that existing strategies have solved the problem of extrapolation, at least in the abstract (Marcellesi 2015), it remains doubtful whether they are sufficient to overcome concrete real-world problems of extrapolation. These strategies tell us which assumptions are needed, but they do not provide a compelling story as to how these assumptions could be underwritten in practice without falling prey to the extrapolator's circle. Let us now turn to a second set of challenges that put additional pressure on the principled promises of EBP.

3.3 *Practical and Value-Related Challenges*

The second set of challenges has two strands: practical and value-related. First, various authors have voiced concerns about the practical feasibility of EBP as ideally envisioned. They worry that a simplistic template of EBP, where policy issues are identified and evidence is sought to help resolve them, rests on a naïve understanding of policy processes (Weiss 1979; Cairney 2016; Head 2016; Cairney and Oliver 2017; Parkhurst 2017). Public policymaking is often a complex and incremental struggle over political and epistemic authority (Strassheim and Kettunen 2014). In these muddied waters, where competing convictions, dogmas, and values clash and concessions are made on some issues in exchange for authority over others, evidence is unlikely to play the role sketched out by the simplistic template. Rather, critics worry that EBP routinely degenerates into its "evil twin," *policy-based evidence* (Ibid.), where policymakers might cherry-pick or commission the production of evidence that speaks in favor of preconceived agendas.

Second, even if no such attempts to unduly instrumentalize evidence take place, important worries about the entanglement of moral and political values in EBP remain. Specifically, some authors argue that the central methodological tenets of EBP can introduce (rather than mitigate) bias concerning what policy questions are considered salient and what policy options are implemented (Parkhurst 2017; Khosrowi and Reiss 2020). Let us take a closer look at this concern.

3.4 Value Entanglement: Precision Drills and Wooden Sculptures

In the promotion of the use of evidence for policy, one of the key promises of EBP is that evidence can figure as a neutral arbiter to adjudicate competing value-laden convictions pertaining to what should be done (Hertin et al. 2009; Teira and Reiss 2013; Reiss and Sprenger 2020; Reiss, Chapter 16). This picture has been challenged by authors arguing that several central methodological tenets of EBP are in tension with a variety of moral and political values that policymakers might be interested in pursuing (Khosrowi 2019b; Khosrowi and Reiss 2020). Specifically, subscription to EBP's tenets can make the pursuit of some kinds of questions and the promotion of some kinds of values substantially more difficult for policymakers.

An analogy can help us understand this concern. The crafting of policies on the basis of evidence is more like crafting an intricate sculpture than building a simple bench: there is no general recipe for how to do it right; it takes creativity and vision, a great deal of dedication, and lots of skill; and some good tools will be helpful, too. EBP's tools of choice are RCTs; they are methodologically vindicated precision drills. Yet, while they are excellent tools for getting some really difficult jobs done (drilling with precision), they are not the right tool for every job (carving) nor can they help us do any complex job from start to finish. Two important limitations of RCTs stand out: they are limited in the range of *questions* to which they can be applied and in the range of *answers* they can provide, both of which can hamper their ability to cater to the complex evidentiary needs that arise in policymaking.

First, RCTs are only usefully applicable to microquestions. Consider large-scale interventions such as tax reforms, infrastructure projects, or trade policies. Of course, observational studies also often find it difficult to estimate the effects of such interventions, but RCTs are at a distinct disadvantage: individuals or communities often cannot (realistically) be randomly subjected to the effects of expensive infrastructure projects, trade policies, or novel institutional designs that need to be implemented at scale.

Second, RCTs can only measure an *average treatment effect* (ATE), which, on its own, does not permit inferences about the individual-level effects that constitute it or the distribution of these effects (Heckman and Smith 1995). This is because any ATE can be realized in various ways, and it is impossible to distinguish between these alternatives through mere inspection of the ATE. For example, a small positive effect might be the result of all treated individuals benefiting by roughly the same amount or the result of a small group experiencing significant benefits while many others are made significantly worse off.

These two limitations give rise to two subsequent problems. First, an insistence on the superiority of RCTs can constrain the range of policy questions that can be clarified by evidence, for example, by privileging the pursuit of microquestions. This is problematic because it can distort what kinds of policy issues are targeted as relevant and what sorts of interventions are considered (see Barnes and Parkhurst 2014; Parkhurst and Abeysinghe 2016; Parkhurst 2017 on *issue bias*). Second, because RCTs and meta-analyses only supply ATEs, policymakers who are interested in distributive issues (say, prioritizing the worst-off individuals in a population) are put at a disadvantage because the information they need is not supplied (e.g. whether a policy benefits important subgroups) (Khosrowi 2019b). To make progress in clarifying whether a policy has desirable distributive effects, the evidence that conforms to existing quality standards is not informative enough. At the very least, it would need to be complemented by ancillary subgroup analyses that clarify the distribution of effects (Varadhan and Seeger 2013). Yet, even if such analyses were routinely available, which they are not, existing guidelines would not award them the same credibility as the primary RCT results that they are supposed to complement (Khosrowi 2019b).

This situation is undesirable for policymakers interested in distributive issues. First, it can lead them to pursue primarily those value schemes for which highly ranked evidence exists, for example, to focus on average outcomes instead of politically and morally salient subgroups. Second, to resist this pull might force policymakers to call on putatively inferior evidence, which makes it easier for opponents to challenge them. Either way, it seems that policies pursuing distributive aims could be crowded out of policy debates.

Together, these concerns suggest that EBP has a problem with values. Ideally, the evidence produced would be equally useful for the pursuit of a broad range of values and purposes (Khosrowi and Reiss 2020). However, because existing methodological tenets in EBP seem to render this unlikely, it remains doubtful whether evidence can really play the role of a neutral arbiter that promotes objectivity in policymaking processes. With these challenges in place, let us briefly consider some ameliorative proposals and draw some broader conclusions.

4. Conclusions and Outlook: Toward Better EBP

Despite pressing challenges, many critics of EBP agree that there is something sensible about the idea that evidence can, at least under some circumstances and in some ways, make valuable contributions toward improving the design and implementation of good public policy (see, e.g., Cartwright 2012: 975). Yet, while a minimalist commitment to using evidence, along the lines of broad EBP, seems sensible, the way in which narrow EBP has detailed how evidence is supposed to inform policy is doubly problematic: first, its strictures on evidence *production* seem too heavy-handed, inviting important value-related tensions. Second, evidence *use* (e.g. extrapolation) remains largely unregimented and little is said on how we can make evidence persuasively speak to questions about novel targets. There is, hence, a clear need for further refinements. Let us briefly consider some recent proposals addressing these problems.

Concerning value-related tensions, it seems clear that the limitations of gold-standard methods should not dictate which policy questions are considered relevant and which policy options appear salient. However, when we advocate for methods other than RCTs on the grounds of meeting important evidential needs, we must still remain accountable to genuine concerns about their credibility and departures from good scientific practice (Parkhurst 2017). Resolution of these tensions is far from trivial. Recent proposals taking issue with value entanglements emphasize that governing the production of evidence for policy must combine concerns about the quality and credibility of evidence with considerations of its *appropriateness* or *usefulness*, something upon which existing guidelines often remain silent (see Parkhurst 2017; Khosrowi and Reiss 2020).

For instance, Parkhurst (2017, chs. 7 and 8) makes detailed proposals for building a general framework that helps govern how evidence figures in policymaking. Retaining commitments to important ideals concerning the quality of evidence, he places particular emphasis on facilitating the *democratic legitimacy* of evidence advisory systems and on ensuring, through institutional design and procedural precautions, that stakeholder values play a central role in governing how evidence informs policy.

Khosrowi and Reiss (2020) call for an open methodological debate among methodologists, stakeholders, and producers and users of evidence about how to weigh different epistemic, value-related, and pragmatic criteria in refining the use of evidence for policy [see, e.g., Head (2010) and other articles in the same issue for an exemplary instance]. To use the metaphor once more: if our aim is to craft appealing sculptures, we need to consider the full array of tools available (files, sanders, saws, hammers, chisels, and drills, some fine, some coarse) and investigate how a *combination* of these tools can help us address the full range of sculptural needs. Without such attempts, we will be stuck with the oddly shaped sculptures that we can build when using only precision drills.

In contrast to value-related challenges, concerns about extrapolation are now more widely recognized (Bates and Glennerster 2017; Cowen et al. 2017; Duflo 2018; see Favereau and Nagatsu 2020 for a discussion). Yet, while abstract, general strategies for extrapolation are available, the arguments discussed previously suggest that more work is needed to devise concrete, practical recipes that work.

Promising proposals that address this need have been made in the realist evaluation literature (see e.g. Pawson and Tilley 1997, 2001; White 2009; Astbury and Leeuw 2010; Pawson 2013; Davey et al. 2019) and were recently reinforced by philosophers (Cartwright 2020). Rather than a focus on black-box estimates of policy effects, the aim in realist evaluation is to develop explicit *program theories* (also called "logic frames" or "theories of change") that elucidate (1) *how*, that is, by which mechanisms, interventions are effective, (2) what circumstances promote and hinder their success, (3) how interventions may work differently for different individuals, and (4) how their effects are experienced.

In addition to an emphasis on the important role of theory in facilitating extrapolation, there have also been calls to (re-)consider what kinds of *supplementary* evidence are needed for underwriting extrapolation and to provide recipes for how to produce and use such evidence (Khosrowi 2019a). RCTs, by themselves, cannot clarify whether there are important similarities and differences between populations. Additional evidence is, hence, required to support extrapolation, and this may include not only familiar kinds of evidence, such as quantitative observational data, but also evidence that is rarely considered in EBP, such as mechanistic evidence obtained from process tracing studies (Beach and Pedersen 2019), or evidence from qualitative studies, such as ethnographies.

Yet, while some of these proposals have recently been taken up by EBP institutions such as 3ie (Peters et al. 2019), they have yet to gain traction in other corners. The Campbell Collaboration's guidelines, for instance, mostly refer to the guidelines issued by its EBM relatives, the Cochrane Collaboration and Grade Working Group. While these guidelines alert authors and users of systematic reviews to some of the pitfalls involved in extrapolation (Guyatt et al. 2011) and recommend that evidence should be downgraded when differences between the study and target populations seem likely (Schünemann et al. 2019), they do not suggest strategies for how to overcome the problems encountered and leave it to evidence users to judge whether findings are applicable to their contexts. So, despite important theoretical progress, systematic proposals for how to manage extrapolation have yet to be accommodated in EBP's methodological guidelines.

In sum, the challenges outlined in this chapter and the ameliorative proposals to address them suggest that continued attention by methodologists, practitioners, EBP researchers, and others is needed to build a more compelling model of how evidence can bear on policy. In advancing this project, we must also recognize that a more compelling version of EBP is unlikely to work in the same way across different policy domains (cf. Head 2010). Instead, it seems that many different, domain-specific approaches are needed that each take into account (1) what types of policy issues arise in specific domains, (2) what values are pertinent to identifying and addressing them, (3) what kinds of questions require attention, (4) how (combinations of) existing and heretofore neglected methods can best cater to these questions, and (5) how evidence production and use can be best integrated into existing institutional and decision-making structures.

Some EBP areas, such as education, child safety, and policing have made good progress on this front, with domain-specific methodologies being developed that recognize the limits of narrow EBP (Cowen et al. 2017; Munro et al. 2017). There are also cases involving more principled obstacles to adapting a narrow EBP template to the concrete needs arising in a particular domain. For instance, in evidence-based environmental policy, it is widely recognized that RCTs cannot be feasibly implemented to assess the effects of environmental policies (Hayes et al. 2019) and that environmental management often requires information at a higher spatial and temporal resolution than typical effectiveness studies can provide (Ahmadia et al. 2015). Problems like these suggest that the simple adaptation of existing EBP templates to particular domains is not always possible and that new, local models for how evidence can inform decision-making might often be needed.

In refining EBP, adapting it to specific domains, and devising new models for how evidence informs policy, philosophers will have important opportunities to engage in methodological debates with EBP advocates, practitioners, and methodologists. Key to making these debates productive will be to ensure an up-to-date grasp of developments in the various areas in which EBP is gaining traction, as well as a commitment to making positive proposals that speak to ongoing practices.

The present chapter has provided a foundational overview of the philosophical and methodological debates surrounding EBP but, of course, makes no claim to be comprehensive. Nevertheless, it is hoped that by focusing on a selection of recent and largely unresolved issues, the overview provided here will help stimulate further critical and constructive contributions by philosophers toward improving EBP.

Related Chapters

Favereau, J., Chapter 25 "Field Experiments"
Henschen, T., Chapter 20 "Causality and Probability"
Northcott, R., Chapter 28 "Economic Theory and Empirical Science"
Reiss, J., Chapter 16 "Measurement and Value Judgments"

Notes

1 Although Cochrane, CONSORT, and GRADE are EBM institutions, their recommendations are frequently adopted in EBP contexts.
2 Extrapolation is also discussed under the rubric of external validity (Guala 2010; Marcellesi 2015; Reiss 2019), generalizability (Vivalt 2020), transferability (Cartwright 2013b), and transportability (Bareinboim and Pearl 2012).

Bibliography

Abraham, K., Haskings, R., Glied, S., Groves, R., Hahn, R., Hoynes, H., Liebman, J., Meyer, B., Ohm, P., Potok, N., Mosier, K.R., Shea, R., Sweeney, L., Troske, K., and Wallin, K. (2017) *The Promise of Evidence-Based Policymaking: Report of the Commission on Evidence-Based Policymaking*, Washington, DC, Commission on Evidence-Based Policymaking.

Addison, P.F.E, Collins, D.G., Trebilco, R., Howe, S., Bax, N., Hedge, P., Jones, G., Miloslavich, P., Roelfsema, C., Sams, M., Stuart-Smith, R.D., Sanes, P., von Baumgarten, P., and McQuatters-Gollop, A. (2018) "A New Wave of Marine Evidence-Based Management: Emerging Challenges and Solutions to Transform Monitoring, Evaluating, and Reporting," *ICES Journal of Marine Science* 75(3): 941–952.

Ahmadia, G., Glew, N., Provost, L., Gill, M., Hidayat, D., Mangubhai, N.I., Purwanto, S., and Fox, H.E. (2015) "Integrating Impact Evaluation in the Design and Implementation of Monitoring Marine Protected Areas," *Philosophical Transactions of the Royal Society B* 370: 20140275.

Angrist, J., and Pischke, J. (2010) "The Credibility Revolution in Empirical Economics: How Better Research Design Is Taking the Con out of Econometrics," *Journal of Economic Perspectives* 24(2): 3–30.

Astbury, B., and Leeuw, F. (2010) "Unpacking Black Boxes: Mechanisms and Theory Building in Evaluation," *American Journal of Evaluation* 31(3): 363–381.

Athey, S., and Imbens, G.W. (2017) "The State of Applied Econometrics: Causality and Policy Evaluation," *Journal of Economic Perspectives* 31(2): 3–32.

Banerjee, A., and Duflo, E. (2009) "The Experimental Approach to Development Economics," *Annual Review of Economics* 1: 151–178.

Bareinboim, E., and Pearl, J. (2012) "Transportability of Causal Effects: Completeness Results," in *Proceedings of the Twenty-Sixth Conference on Artificial Intelligence (AAAI-12)*, Menlo Park, CA.

Bareinboim, E., and Pearl, J. (2016) "Causal Inference and the Data-Fusion Problem," *Proceedings of the National Academy of Sciences* 113: 7345–7352.

Barnes, A., and Parkhurst, J. (2014) "Can Global Health Policy be Depoliticised? A Critique of Global Calls for Evidence-Based Policy," in G. Yamey and G. Brown (eds.) *Handbook of Global Health Policy*: 157–173, Chichester: Wiley-Blackwell.

Baron, R.M., and Kenny, D.A. (1986) "The Moderator-Mediator Variable Distinction in Social Psychological Research: Conceptual, Strategic and Statistical Considerations," *Journal of Personality and Social Psychology* 51: 1173–1182.

Bates, M.A., and Glennerster, R. (2017) "The Generalizability Puzzle," *Stanford Social Innovation Review*. Retrieved June 2020 from: https://ssir.org/articles/entry/the_generalizability_puzzle.

Beach, D., and Pedersen, R.B. (2019) *Process-Tracing Methods Foundations and Guidelines*, 2nd edition, Ann Arbor: University of Michigan Press.

Bruhn, M., and McKenzie, D. (2009) "In Pursuit of Balance: Randomization in Practice in Development Field Experiments," *American Economic Journal: Applied Economics* 1(4): 200–232.

Cabinet Office (2013) *What Works: Evidence Centres for Social Policy*, London: Cabinet Office.

Cairney, P. (2016) *The Politics of Evidence-Based Policymaking*, London: Palgrave Pivot.

Cairney, P., and Oliver, K. (2017) "Evidence-Based Policymaking is not Like Evidence-Based Medicine, so How Far Should You Go to Bridge the Divide Between Evidence and Policy?" *Health Research Policy and Systems* 15(1): 35.

Cartwright, N.D. (2007) "Are RCTs the Gold Standard?" *BioSocieties* 2(2): 11–20.

Cartwright, N.D. (2012) "Presidential Address: Will This Policy Work for You? Predicting Effectiveness Better: How Philosophy Helps," *Philosophy of Science* 79(5): 973–989.

Cartwright, N.D. (2013a) "Evidence, Argument and Prediction," in V. Karakostas and D. Dieks (eds.) *EPSA11 Perspectives and Foundational Problems in Philosophy of Science*, The European Philosophy of Science Association Proceedings, Cham: Springer International Publishing Switzerland.

Cartwright, N.D. (2013b) "Knowing What We Are Talking About: Why Evidence Doesn't Always Travel," *Evidence and Policy: A Journal of Research, Debate and Practice* 9(1): 97–112.

Cartwright, N.D. (2020) "Lullius Lectures 2018: Mid-Level Theory: Without it What Could Anyone Do?" in C. Martínez Vidal and C. Saborido (eds.) *Nancy Cartwright's Philosophy of Science*, Special Issue of *Theoria*.

Cartwright, N.D., Goldfinch, A., and Howick, J. (2009) "Evidence-Based Policy: Where is Our Theory of Evidence?" *Journal of Children's Services* 4(4): 6–14.

Cartwright, N.D., and Hardie, J. (2012) *Evidence-Based Policy: A Practical Guide to Doing it Better*, Oxford: Oxford University Press.

Cartwright, N.D., and Stegenga, J. (2011) "A Theory of Evidence for Evidence-Based Policy," *Proceedings of the British Academy* 171: 289–319.

Cowen, N., and Cartwright, N. D. (2019) "Street-level Theories of Change: Adapting the Medical Model of Evidence-based Practice for Policing," in N. Fielding, K. Bullock and S. Holdaway (eds.) *Critical Reflections on Evidence-Based Policing. Routledge Frontiers of Criminal Justice*: 52–71, London: Routledge.

Cowen, N., Virk, B., Mascarenhas-Keyes, S., and Cartwright, N.D. (2017) "Randomized Controlled Trials: How Can We Know 'What Works'?" *Critical Review* 29(3): 265–292.

Crump, R.K., Hotz, V.J., Imbens, G.W., and Mitnik, O.A. (2008) "Nonparametric Tests for Treatment Effect Heterogeneity," *The Review of Economics and Statistics* 90(3): 389–405.

Davey, C., Hassan, S., Cartwright, N.D., Humphreys, M., Masset, E., Prost, A., Gough, D., Oliver, S., Nonell, C., and Hargreaves, J. (2019) "Designing Evaluations to Provide Evidence to Inform Action in New Settings," CEDIL Inception Paper No 2: London.

Deaton, A. (2009) "Instruments of Development: Randomisation in the Tropics, and the Search for the Elusive Keys to Economic Development," *Proceedings of the British Academy* 162: 123–160.

Deaton, A. (2010) "Instruments, Randomization, and Learning About Development," *Journal of Economic Literature* 48(2): 424–455.

Deaton, A., and Cartwright, N.D. (2018a) "Understanding and Misunderstanding Randomized Controlled Trials," *Social Science & Medicine* 210: 2–21.

Deaton, A., and Cartwright, N.D. (2018b) "Reflections on Randomized Control Trials," *Social Science & Medicine* 210: 86–90.

Duflo, E. (2018) "*Machinistas Meet Randomistas: Useful ML Tools for Empirical Researchers*," Summer Institute Master Lectures, National Bureau of Economic Research.

Duflo, E., and Kremer, M. (2005) "Use of Randomization in the Evaluation of Development Effectiveness," in G. Pitman, O. Feinstein, and G. Ingram (eds.) *Evaluating Development Effectiveness*, New Brunswick, NJ: Transaction.

Evidence-Based Medicine Working Group (1992) "Evidence-Based Medicine. A New Approach to Teaching the Practice of Medicine," *JAMA* 268: 2420–2425.

Favereau, J., and Nagatsu, M. (2020) "Holding Back from Theory: Limits and Methodological Alternatives of Randomized Field Experiments in Development Economics," *Journal of Economic Methodology* 40(1): 1–21.

Fuller, J. (2019) "The Confounding Question of Confounding Causes in Randomized Trials," *The British Journal for the Philosophy of Science* 70(3): 901–926.

Guala, F. (2010) "Extrapolation, Analogy, and Comparative Process Tracing," *Philosophy of Science* 77(5): 1070–1082.

Guyatt, G.H., Oxman, A.D., Kunz, R., Woodcock, J., Brozek, J., Helfand, M., Alonso-Ciello, P., Falck-Yter, Y., Jaeschke, R., Vist, G., Akl, E.A., Post, P.N., Norris, S., Meerpohl, J., Shukla, V.K., Nasser, M., and Schünemann, H.J. (2011) "Grade Guidelines: 8. Rating the Quality of Evidence – Indirectness," *Journal of Clinical Epidemiology* 64(12): 1301–1310.

Hayes, K.R., Hosack, G.R., Lawrence, E., Hedge, P., Barrett, N.S., Przeslawski, R., Caley, J.M., and Foster, S.D. (2019) "Designing Monitoring Programs for Marine Protected Areas Within an Evidence Based Decision Making Paradigm," *Frontiers in Marine Science* 6: 746.

Haynes, L., Service, O., Goldacre, B., and Torgerson, D. (2012) *Test, Learn, Adapt: Developing Public Policy with Randomised Controlled Trials*, London: Cabinet Office Behavioural Insights Team.
Head, B.W. (2010) "Reconsidering Evidence-Based Policy: Key Issues and Challenges," *Policy and Society* 29(2): 77–94.
Head, B.W. (2016) "Toward More 'Evidence-Informed' Policy Making?" *Public Administration Review* 76: 472–484.
Heckman, J.J. (1992) "Randomization and Social Program Evaluation," in C. Manski and I. Garfinkel (eds.) *Evaluating Welfare and Training Programs:* 201–230, Cambridge, MA: Harvard University Press.
Heckman, J.J. (2010) "Building Bridges between Structural and Program Evaluation Approaches to Evaluating Policy," *Journal of Economic Literature* 48(2): 356–398.
Heckman, J.J., and Smith, J.A. (1995) "Assessing the Case for Social Experiments," *Journal of Economic Perspectives* 9(2): 85–110.
Hertin, J., Jacob, K., Pesch, U., and Pacchi, C. (2009) "The Production and Use of Knowledge in Regulatory Impact Assessment – An Empirical Analysis," *Forest Policy & Economics* 11(5–6): 413–421.
Holland, P. (1986) "Statistics and Causal Inference," *Journal of the American Statistical Association* 81(396): 945–960.
Hotz, V.J., Imbens, G.W., and Mortimer, J.H. (2005) "Predicting the Efficacy of Future Training Programs Using Past Experiences at Other Locations," *Journal of Econometrics* 125: 241–270.
Hyttinen, A., Eberhardt, F., and Järvisalo, M. (2015) "Do-Calculus When the True Graph is Unknown," UAI'15 Proceedings of the Thirty-First Conference on Uncertainty in Artificial Intelligence, 395–404.
Khosrowi, D. (2019a) "Extrapolation of Causal Effects – Hopes, Assumptions, and the Extrapolator's Circle," *Journal of Economic Methodology* 26(1): 45–58.
Khosrowi, D. (2019b) "Trade-Offs Between Epistemic and Moral Values in Evidence-Based Policy," *Economics and Philosophy* 35(1): 49–71.
Khosrowi, D. (2021) "What's (Successful) Extrapolation?" *Journal of Economic Methodology*, online first, DOI: 10.1080/1350178X.2021.1952290
Khosrowi, D., and Reiss, J. (2020) "Evidence-Based Policy: The Tension Between the Epistemic and the Normative," *Critical Review* 31(2): 179–197.
LaFollette, H., and Shanks, N. (1996) *Brute Science: Dilemmas of Animal Experimentation*, New York: Routledge.
Leamer, E. (1983) "Let's Take the Con Out of Econometrics," *The American Economic Review* 73(1): 31–43.
Leamer, E. (2010) "Tantalus on the Road to Asymptopia," *Journal of Economic Perspectives* 24(2): 31–46.
Lucas, R. (1976) "Econometric Policy Evaluation: A Critique," in K. Brunner and A. Meltzer (eds.) *The Phillips Curve and Labor Markets*, Amsterdam: North-Holland.
Marcellesi, A. (2015) "External Validity: Is There Still a Problem?" *Philosophy of Science* 82(5): 1308–1317.
Muller, S.M. (2013) "External Validity, Causal Interaction and Randomised Trials: The Case of Economics," unpublished manuscript.
Muller, S.M. (2014) "Randomised Trials for Policy: A Review of the External Validity of Treatment Effects," Southern Africa Labour and Development Research Unit Working Paper 127, University of Cape Town.
Muller, S.M. (2015) "Interaction and External Validity: Obstacles to the Policy Relevance of Randomized Evaluations," *World Bank Economic Review* 29(1): 217–225.
Munro, E., Cartwright, N.D., Hardie, J., and Montuschi, E. (2017) *Improving Child Safety: Deliberation, Judgement and Empirical Research*, Durham: Centre for Humanities Engaging Science and Society (CHESS).
Neyman, J. (1923) "On the Application of Probability Theory to Agricultural Experiments: Essay on Principles," (Section 9), translated in *Statistical Science* 5: 465–480 (1990).
Nutley, S. (2003) "Bridging the Policy/Research Divide: Reflections and Lessons from the UK," keynote paper: Facing the Future: Engaging Stakeholders and Citizens in Developing Public Policy, National Institute of Governance Conference, Canberrra, Australia.
Nutley, S., Powell, A., and Davies, H. (2013) "What Counts as Good Evidence?" discussion paper, London: Alliance for Useful Evidence.
Parkhurst, J. (2017) *The Politics of Evidence: From Evidence-Based Policy to the Good Governance of Evidence*, Abingdon, Oxon, UK: Routledge.
Parkhurst, J., and Abeysinghe, S. (2016) "What Constitutes 'Good' Evidence for Public Health and Social Policy-Making? From Hierarchies to Appropriateness," *Social Epistemology* 5: 665–679.
Pawson, R. (2006) *Evidence-Based Policy: A Realist Perspective*, London and Thousand Oaks, CA: SAGE Publications.
Pawson, R. (2013) *The Science of Evaluation: A Realist Manifesto*, London: SAGE Publications.
Pawson, R., and Tilley, N. (1997) *Realistic Evaluation*, London: SAGE Publications.
Pawson, R., and Tilley, N. (2001) "Realistic Evaluation Bloodlines," *American Journal of Evaluation* 22: 317–324.
Pearl, J. (2009) *Causality: Models, Reasoning, and Inference*, 2nd edition, New York: Cambridge University Press.
Peters, J., Jain, M., and Gaarder, M. (2019) "External Validity: Policy Demand is There But Research Needs to Boost Supply," 3ie blog post. Retrieved June 2020 from: www.3ieimpact.org/blogs/external-validity-policy-demand-there-research-needs-boost-supply.

Reiss, J. (2010) "Review: Across the Boundaries: Extrapolation in Biology and Social Science," *Economics and Philosophy* 26: 382–390.
Reiss, J. (2013) *The Philosophy of Economics: A Contemporary Introduction*, New York: Routledge.
Reiss, J. (2019) "Against External Validity," *Synthese* 196(8): 3103–3121.
Reiss, J., and Sprenger, J. (2020) "Scientific Objectivity," in *The Stanford Encyclopedia of Philosophy* (Winter 2020 Edition), Edward N. Zalta (ed.), https://plato.stanford.edu/archives/win2020/entries/scientific objectivity.
Rosenbaum, P.R., and Rubin, D.B. (1983) "The Central Role of the Propensity Score in Observational Studies for Causal Effects," *Biometrika* 70(1): 41–55.
Rubin, D.B. (1974) "Estimating Causal Effects of Treatments in Randomized and Nonrandomized Studies," *Journal of Educational Psychology* 66(5): 688–701.
Sackett, D., Rosenberg, W., Gray, M., Haynes, B., and Richardson, S. (1996) "Evidence Based Medicine: What it is and What it isn't," *BMJ* 312: 71.
Scheines, R. (1997) "An Introduction to Causal Inference," in McKim and Turner (eds.) *Causality in Crisis? Statistical Methods in the Search for Causal Knowledge in the Social Sciences*: 185–199, Notre Dame, IN: University of Notre Dame Press.
Schünemann, H.J., Higgins, J.P.T., Vist, G.E., Glasziou, P., Akl, E.A., Skoetz, N., and Guyatt, G.H. (2019) "Chapter 14: Completing 'Summary of Findings' Tables and Grading the Certainty of the Evidence," in J.P.T. Higgins, J. Thomas, J. Chandler, M. Cumpston, T. Li, M.J. Page, et al. (eds.) *Cochrande Handbook for Systematic Reviews of Interventions Version 6.0*. Retrieved June 2020 from: https://training.cochrane.org/handbook.
Scriven, M. (2008) "A Summative Evaluation of RCT Methodology & An Alternative Approach to Causal Research." *Journal of Multi-Disciplinary Evaluation* 5(9): 11–24.
Sidebottom, A., Tompson, L., Thornton, A., Bullock, K., Tilley, N., Bowers, K., and Johnson, S.D. (2018) "Gating Alleys to Reduce Crime: A Meta-Analysis and Realist Synthesis," *Justice Quarterly* 35(1): 55–86.
Steel, D. (2009) *Across the Boundaries: Extrapolation in Biology and Social Science*, Oxford: Oxford University Press.
Steel, D. (2010) "A New Approach to Argument by Analogy: Extrapolation and Chain Graphs," *Philosophy of Science* 77(5): 1058–1069.
Strassheim, H., and Kettunen, P. (2014) "When Does Evidence-Based Policy Turn into Policy-Based Evidence? Configurations, Contexts and Mechanisms," *Evidence & Policy* 10(2): 259–277.
Teira, D., and Reiss, J. (2013) "Causality, Impartiality and Evidence-Based Policy," in: Chao H.K., Chen S.T., and R. Millstein (eds.) *Mechanism and Causality in Biology and Economics*, History, Philosophy and Theory of the Life Sciences, vol. 3. Dordrecht: Springer.
van Eersel, G.G., Koppenol-Gonzalez, G.V., and Reiss, J. (2019) "Extrapolation of Experimental Results through Analogical Reasoning from Latent Classes," *Philosophy of Science* 86(2): 219–235.
Varadhan, R and Seeger, J.D. (2013) "Estimation and Reporting of Heterogeneity of Treatment Effects," in P. Velentgas, N.A. Dreyer, P. Nourjah, S.R. Smith, and M.M. Torchia (eds.) *Developing a Protocol for Observational Comparative Effectiveness Research: A User's Guide*: 35–44, Rockville, MD: Agency for Healthcare Research and Quality.
Vivalt, E. (2020) "How Much Can We Generalize from Impact Evaluations?" *Journal of the European Economics Association* (online first).
Weiss, C.H. (1979) "The Many Meanings of Research Utilization," *Public Administration Review* 39(5): 426–431.
White, H. (2009) "Theory – Based Impact Evaluation: Principles and Practice," *The Journal of Development Effectiveness* 1(3): 271–284
Worrall, J. (2002) "What Evidence in Evidence-Based Medicine?" *Philosophy of Science* 69: 316–330.
Worrall, J. (2007) "Why There's no Cause to Randomize," *The British Journal for the Philosophy of Science* 58(3): 451–488.

PART VII

Evidence

28

ECONOMIC THEORY AND EMPIRICAL SCIENCE

Robert Northcott

1. Introduction

I argue that economics, notwithstanding its recent "empirical turn," overinvests in orthodox theory. My reasons are not the familiar philosophical complaints about idealization (Jhun, Chapter 23), social ontology, or the foundations of rational choice theory (Elster 1988; Rosenberg 1992; Lawson 1997, Vredenburgh, Chapter 5).[1] Instead, they come from closely examining how economics achieves empirical success (when it does). To preview: in such cases, theory typically does not itself illuminate the world's causal structure and so does not directly explain. Rather, it is of benefit – when it is – only heuristically. Two further lessons follow, both of which, alas, run contrary to much contemporary practice: first, theory should be developed in close concert with empirical feedback, and second, theory has no special reason to be orthodox.[2]

A central goal of economics, like that of any science, must be empirical success. I understand the latter broadly, to include prediction, intervention, and retrospective accommodation and explanation. Other goals, such as understanding or insight (Verreault-Julien, Chapter 22), are also important, but, as will become apparent, they are dependent on empirical success, so such success must come first. Economics is a heterogeneous field. Nevertheless, there is enough uniformity of method, at least in the mainstream, that general analyses can be useful. How idealized theory can connect with messy reality is a philosophical issue that requires philosophical analysis – and there has been plenty. In the space available here, I bring some of that philosophical work to bear.

Obeying the editors' request, I state some lines of criticism bluntly. But I view these criticisms as friendly amendments concerning matters of balance and degree, and unlike some other philosophical critiques they allow for two *endorsements* of economics. First, the economist's outlook, in particular the theoretical machinery of incentives and opportunity cost and their consequences for decision-making, is useful very widely. This will be a familiar insight to any person with economic training listening to a person without such training. Second, there is, of course, much to economics besides theory: measurement (see Reiss, Chapter 16), commercial consultancy, applied studies, teaching, and more. These can all be of great value. Especially impressive is the sophisticated use of statistical techniques, covering research design, data analysis, and hypothesis testing (see Peden and Sprenger, Chapter 30, and Spanos, Chapter 29). These techniques are perhaps the aspects of contemporary economic work most exportable to social science more widely.

DOI: 10.4324/9781315739793-35

2. Idealization: A Red Herring

Economic theory is typically highly idealized. Often, perfectly rational agents with perfect information interact in perfectly competitive markets, simple elasticities and production functions are assumed, and so on. This immediately threatens such a theory's empirical prospects.

But economists have a ready reply. Many theories in other sciences too, such as physics, are highly idealized, and besides, given that any model must simplify reality, some idealization is inevitable. So, why worry?

Recent philosophy of science has studied idealization extensively.[3] There is broad agreement, but with a sting in the tail: roughly speaking, idealized theory can be endorsed, but only if it brings empirical success. For example, the most familiar form of idealization in physics is the so-called Galilean idealization. Particular factors are highlighted and others ignored, as when the effect of gravity on a projectile is modeled while assuming zero air resistance. In the best case, the idealized model accurately describes the projectile's actual trajectory. If it does not, factors that were idealized away may be reintroduced. The point is that at some stage the theoretical framework must deliver empirical success, otherwise it will be jettisoned, often pretty quickly. Similar remarks apply to other forms of idealization in physics, such as simulations or renormalizations in quantum theory. To survive, they must pay their way empirically. For this reason, by and large the history of modern physics shows a close co-evolution of theory with empirical feedback. Rare exceptions, such as string theory, are controversial precisely because they are exceptions.

The conclusion: idealization is not what matters. Rather, empirical success (or lack of it) is.

3. How Empirical Success Is Achieved

The empirical record of economics is notorious. Forecasts of real gross domestic product (GDP) 18 months ahead, for example, have proved unable to beat the naïve benchmark of simply extrapolating the current GDP growth rate. One study found that of 60 recessions, that is, instances of 1 year of negative growth, a recession was the consensus forecast beforehand on only three occasions. Moreover, there has been no improvement in 50 years.[4]

The fuller picture is more nuanced, though. Regarding prediction, even with GDP, forecasts for 6 or 9 months ahead do beat the naïve benchmark. Meanwhile, businesses use economic models every day to predict supply needs. Introductory textbook examples are instantiated all the time as well, as when, say, two popular teams reach a sports final and it is correctly predicted that black market ticket prices will be higher.

That said, empirical successes are often claimed rather casually. A model may accommodate retrospectively merely part of the variance of some data set. It can be easy to claim informally that economic theory "explains" some phenomenon or enables us to "understand" why something happened, but detailed and convincing case studies are rarer. It turns out to be much more instructive to look at one example in depth than to look at many superficially. This has been done precisely in a few cases. Here, I recount a well-known and representative one: the US government spectrum auctions of 1994–1996.[5] What exactly was theory's role there?

The radio spectrum is the portion of the electromagnetic spectrum between 9 kHz and 300 GHz. In the United States, spectrum not needed by the government is distributed to potential users – usually telecommunications companies – by the Federal Communications Commission (FCC). In the early 1990s, the FCC acquired the right to use competitive market mechanisms such as auctions. That left it the formidable task of designing such auctions. The importance of doing this well is best illustrated by the embarrassment of doing it badly. Examples include: an Otago university student winning the license for a small-town TV station by bidding just NZ$5 (New Zealand in 1990); an unknown outbidding everyone, but then turning out to have no money and so necessitating an expensive do-over (Australia in 1993); and collusion by four big companies to buy the four available licenses for prices only one-fifteenth of what the government had expected (Switzerland in 2000). In contrast, the FCC's series of seven auctions from 1994 to 1996 were remarkably successful. They attracted many bidders, allocated several thousand licenses, and raised an amount of money – US$20 billion – that surpassed all government and industry expectations. Even the first auctions passed off without a glitch, and there was reason to believe that licenses were allocated efficiently. How was this achieved?

The government set a wide range of goals besides maximizing revenue, such as using the spectrum efficiently and intensively, promoting new technologies, and ensuring that some licenses went to favored bidders such as minority- and women-owned companies. Exactly what design would reliably achieve these goals was a formidable puzzle for teams of economic theorists, experimentalists, lawyers, and software engineers. To give a flavor of the eventual solution's complexity, the country was subdivided geographically into 492 basic trading areas, each of which had four spectrum blocks up for license. The design put all of these licenses up for sale simultaneously as opposed to sequentially, in an open rather than a sealed-bid arrangement. Bidders placed bids on individual licenses as opposed to packages of licenses. When a round was over, they saw what other bids had been placed and were free to change their own combinations of bids. Bidders were also forced to maintain a certain level of activity, make up-front payments, increase the values of their bids from round to round by prescribed amounts, and obey caps on the amount of spectrum that could be owned in a single geographical area. The full rules ran to over 130 pages.

At the time, this gleaming success was hailed by the press as a triumph for game theory, which had revolutionized auction models in the 1980s. Many game theorists were hired as advisors by prospective bidders and by the FCC itself. However, the final design was not derived (or derivable) from game theory. No single model covered anywhere near all of the theoretical issues of the kind just mentioned. And in addition to the explicit and public instructions covering entry, bidding, and payment, much work also had to be put into perfecting other features such as the software, the venue and timing of the auction, and whatever aspects of the legal and economic environment the designers could control. Many experiments and ad hoc adjustments were crucial for the purpose of fine-tuning. These took the form of extensive testing in laboratory settings with human subjects, with the results often taking designers by surprise. For example, in some circumstances – and against theoretical predictions – "bubbles" emerged in the values of the bids. These bubbles, in turn, were unexpectedly sensitive to exactly what bidders knew about rival bidders' behavior. To solve the problem required the investigation of messy practical details.

What role did theory actually play? First, contrary to one philosophical view (Hausman 1992), the auction design was not achieved by satisfying, even approximately, theory's idealized assumptions, such as perfect rationality, no budget constraints on bidders, single units on sale (as opposed to hundreds of spectrum licenses simultaneously), and so on. And no model yielded the consequences of these assumptions not being satisfied.

Second, contrary to another philosophical view (Cartwright 1989; Mäki 1992), theory also did not identify *capacities* – causal relations that hold stably across many cases – that could be combined to design the auction.[6] Experiments demonstrated quite the opposite. The impact of any particular auction rule varied in a way not predicted by theory, depending both on the details of how it was implemented and also on which other rules were included. In other words, a rule's effect was unstable, not stable. As a result, testing had to be holistic: because individual rules did not have stable effects across different environments, the performance of any particular *set* of rules had to be tested as a *sui generis* package and, moreover, tested anew with every significant change in environment. The eventual result of a complex testing process was the perfection of one auction design as a whole. This design was not a case of component capacities being stitched together, because no relevant capacities were stable enough for that.

The role of auction theory was in fact a *heuristic* one (Alexandrova 2008; Alexandrova and Northcott 2009): it suggested some useful initial ideas and categories. This was no small contribution, but of course it then left the subsequent heavy lifting to experimentalists and others, namely, how to combine these and other factors into a workable design. The key to progress with that was clearly not theory. After all, much the same theoretical repertoire was available to the FCC as had been earlier to the New Zealand and Australia authorities, yet the FCC's auction fared much better, so it was not new theory that made the difference. The key instead was case-specific experiments and know-how, finely sensitive to local political and economic conditions. For this reason, spectrum auction designs do not transfer easily across cases, which is why the 2000 auction in Switzerland could fail even though it was held after the successful US one. The causes of the Swiss failure were specific to Swiss circumstances.

The same heuristic moral emerges from other case studies too, such as attempts to apply the prisoner's dilemma game (Northcott and Alexandrova 2015). The prisoner's dilemma itself rarely predicts accurately. Its value, when it has some, is instead indirect and heuristic, by guiding our attention to the strategic incentives that encourage cooperation and by alerting us to possible divergence between individual and social optimality.

Another moral that recurs across cases is the inadequacy of the capacities view. First, economic theory can usually derive a capacity only on the back of many idealized assumptions, so the capacity is established only in the idealized world of theory; supplementary empirical work is required to establish it in the actual world. But, second, experience shows that, by and large, this supplementary empirical work cannot successfully be done. If it could, then the capacities described by theory could be used as reliable guides for prediction and intervention in the actual world, but this is rarely the case, because causal relations established in the actual world are not stable. For example, one well-known study established a case in which an increase in the minimum wage increased employment (Card and Krueger 1994). But in other circumstances it no longer does – say, when the minimum wage is already high, when the increase in it is large, or when economic conditions are different. In response, crucially, rather than searching for countervailing capacities that might be outweighing the original one, researchers just assumed that that the original capacity no longer held, in other words, that an increase in the minimum wage no longer tended to increase employment (Reiss 2008: 173–176). This response is typical. Similar remarks apply to causal relations discovered by economic experiments (Reiss 2008: 92–96). *Economists' own practice indicates that the capacity view is not really believed.* The *form* of economic theory does suggest a world of stable causal relations, but this is misleading. In fact, causal relations are ubiquitously accepted to be fragile.

4. Methodological Lessons

What do these admirable cases of empirical success teach us? First, the need for *continuous empirical refinement* when developing theory, because without such refinement theory risks drifting into empirical irrelevance (Ylikoski 2019). Empirical refinement entered the spectrum auctions story only at the stage of the final design, via the experimental test beds. Its absence before then is why the game-theoretical models contributed only heuristically.

Next, and contrary to many casual claims, economic theory *typically does not explain* (Northcott and Alexandrova 2013). The main reason is simple: economic theory is false and therefore does not identify true causal relations (or at least approximately true ones), which is what it must do in order to causally explain.[7] The warrant for having truly identified causal relations must be empirical success, but empirical success is just what economic theory lacks. In the case of the spectrum auctions, for example, warrant from empirical success accrued only to the final auction design, not to the game-theoretical models.

Moreover, economic theory does not even "partially" explain in the sense of correctly identifying *some* of the relevant causes (Northcott 2013). To see why not, consider a textbook case from physics, such as Coulomb's law: even if this law's prediction that two positively charged bodies repel each other is not borne out, perhaps because of interference by other forces (such as gravity), we would have confidence that an electrostatic repulsion force was still influencing the bodies, so that Coulomb's law did explain the bodies' overall trajectory partially. Why this confidence? Because of the empirical success of Coulomb's law elsewhere, such as in laboratory experiments, combined with confidence that the electrostatic forces observed in a laboratory also operate in the relevant field environment too (Cartwright 1989). Alas, in economics the second confidence is not warranted because causal relations are typically not stable enough to be transportable. This is the instability problem for the capacities view again. The result: no warrant even for partial explanations.

The next important consequence of heuristicism is that *we lose motivation for orthodoxy*. Because economic theory typically is not causally explanatory, we cannot say that its internal structure picks out actual causes. Without that, a traditional motivation for orthodoxy, namely, that only in this way can we explain phenomena in terms of incentive structures and agent rationality, becomes moot. Meanwhile, if theory's value is heuristic, then any approach that is similarly heuristically useful will be similarly valuable, regardless of internal structure. We should therefore accept potential roles for heterodox approaches, such as Marxist or Austrian economics (Linsbichler, Chapter 12), behavioral economics (Lecouteux, Chapter 4), agent-based simulations (Kuorikoski and Lehtinen, Chapter 26), econophysics, or network analysis (Claveau et al., Chapter 11). (I neither endorse nor reject here the actual record of any of these.) For similar reasons, it is ill-motivated to insist on methodological individualism or to insist on orthodox "microfoundations" for macroeconomic theory.

This methodological liberalism runs counter not just to economists' expressed views but also to their widespread practice, which prizes orthodoxy above empirical accuracy. Here is one example of that (Reiss 2008: 106–122): Milton Friedman and Anna Schwartz proposed a mechanism for their famous finding that money is the main cause of changes in nominal income (Friedman and Schwartz 1963). The problem with this mechanism, in orthodox eyes, is that it assumes a money illusion and therefore contravenes agent rationality. Decades of effort followed to find a more acceptable alternative, culminating in a study by Benhabib and Farmer (2000). But although it satisfies orthodox criteria, Benhabib and Farmer's ingenious new mechanism is arguably less empirically adequate than Friedman and Schwartz's old one, featuring, as it does, not just a standard array of idealizing assumptions but also some unusual new ones, such as a downward-sloping labor supply curve. Yet, Benhabib and Farmer's paper was still seen as an important breakthrough. Why? Because orthodoxy is prized over empirical accuracy.

Heuristicism also renders illusory another often-cited advantage of theory, namely, that it is *generalizable*. A great motivation for developing causal models is that they can be applied to many cases. But if theory's value is only heuristic, this advantage melts away. Heuristic value carries over to new cases much less reliably, because each time new extratheoretical, local work is required (Alexandrova and Northcott 2009; Northcott 2015).

Heuristicism implies one further important thing: that *theoretical sophistication is no goal in itself*. Because economic theory typically has not been developed in close concert with empirical refinement, in practice greater sophistication often leaves theory more remote from empirical application, making it *less* valuable by rendering it less heuristically useful. Many empirical successes, such as the introductory textbook ones mentioned earlier, feature very simple models indeed, sometimes nothing more than a downward-sloping demand curve. Many empirical successes in other field sciences too are also very simple theoretically. Simpler theory, without the need for extensive idealizations to enable deductive derivation, is also more likely to predict or explain successfully. If so, then simpler theory should be endorsed, regardless of methodological orthodoxy. Examples include well-evidenced historical analyses and "theory-free" field experiments (Favereau, Chapter 25) carried out by developmental economists or by internet companies such as Google and Facebook.

All of this runs counter to a common motivation for orthodox theory, namely, that it enables us to understand phenomena in terms of the logic of incentives and rational choice. On some accounts, an economic analysis must *by definition* be couched in these terms, precisely because doing so guarantees (it is thought) such understanding. In its way, this commitment is noble and idealistic. But, alas, it is hard to defend. As noted, we have good reason to reject the claim that economic theory explains, and certainly the mere subjective feeling of understanding is no remedy for that because such a feeling is an unreliable indicator of explanation (Trout 2007; Northcott and Alexandrova 2013). We must, therefore, demonstrate some value for understanding independent of explanation. But a majority of the philosophical literature denies that this can be done (Khalifa 2012; Strevens 2013; de Regt 2017; for a discussion, see Verreault-Julien, Chapter 22).[8]

The leading contrary view is that understanding amounts to *how-possibly* explanations, which are distinct from actual ones. Gruene-Yanoff (2009), for example, holds that Schelling's famous checkerboard model of race and location serves to suggest a causal hypothesis about the actual world. It does this by establishing that such a hypothesis could *possibly* hold – in an idealized and, hence, non-actual world. Such hypotheses, as in the Schelling case, are often surprising and therefore potentially useful heuristically. But if so, then the value of understanding is just heuristic. No new third path appears separate from explanation and heuristics, and so understanding offers no salvation for orthodoxy.

5. Mill on Field Sciences

Perhaps the best available defense of economic theory's empirical shortcomings stretches back to John Stuart Mill. At its heart lies a distinction between experimental and field sciences. Roughly, a field science is one that studies uncontrolled phenomena outside the laboratory and therefore cannot run shielded experiments. Economics falls into this category. Mill (1843) argued that, unlike experimental sciences, field sciences should not adopt what he called the method of inductive generalizations, in other words, they should not insist that theory predict accurately. This is because the ever-changing mix of causes in field cases makes accurate prediction a naïve goal. Instead, we should follow a *deductivist* method, according to which theory states core causal tendencies such as human agents' tendency to maximize their wealth. These causal tendencies are (roughly) what we earlier called capacities. In any particular case, we compose relevant tendencies in a deductive way and then add in, as required, local "disturbing causes," in other words local factors not captured by theory. According to this view, deductivist theory delivers – even without empirical accuracy – explanation and understanding in terms of underlying causes.

Proposals similar to Mill's have recurred, with similar rationales. Examples include Weber's advocacy of ideal types and Popper's of situational analysis. By and large, deductivism has remained the dominant method in economics, periodic rebellions notwithstanding. Something like it was the winner of the *Methodenstreit* in late-19th-century Germany and over the institutionalists in the 20th century. The recent empirical turn (Section 6) is the latest chapter in the story.

According to Mill, although theory does not deliver empirical success directly, we can obtain it indirectly by adding in disturbing causes. In this way, deductivist theory is *more* empirically fruitful than inductivist alternatives, because it offers (indirectly) empirical success that generalizes to many cases by adding in different disturbing causes each time.

But does economic theory indeed play the role that Mill envisages, needing to be supplemented only by case-specific disturbing causes? We have seen, on the contrary, that this is *not* what happens. Theory does not identify Millian stable capacities but rather plays only a heuristic role. Empirical successes are built on local and empirically refined models, not by adding disturbing causes to general capacities. Mill-style theorizing therefore does not deliver explanations in terms of core tendencies. This methodological strategy does not work.

6. The Empirical Turn

Times are changing. In the five most prestigious journals in economics, the percentage of papers that were purely theoretical – in other words, free of any empirical data – fell from 57% in 1983 to 19% in 2011 (Hamermesh 2013).[9] Not only is there more empirical work, but this empirical work is also less often theory-based. Ever since the Cowles Commission at the end of the World War II, there has been a strong norm that econometrics should aim to test particular theoretical models rather than more fragmented or non-theory-derived causal relations. (In my view, this norm is motivated by a mistaken capacities interpretation of theory.) But Biddle and Hamermesh (2016) report that, whereas in the 1970s all microeconomic empirical papers in top-5 journals indeed exhibited a theoretical framework, in the 2000s there was some resurgence of nontheoretical studies. Citation numbers suggest that the nontheoretical work is at least as influential. Angrist and Pischke (2010) also report the rise of nontheoretical practice in several subfields. There are other, more anecdotal, indicators of an empirical turn too. One is that almost all recent Clark medalists have a strong empirical (albeit not nontheoretical) element to their work. Another is the rise of behavioral economics, often justified on the grounds of its greater fidelity to empirical psychology.

In my view, the empirical turn is a very positive development. I hope that it continues – for it needs to. After all, 19% of articles in the most prestigious journals are still purely theoretical, a large proportion of empirical work is still tied to testing a model derived from general theory, orthodox modeling is still considered the cornerstone of sound methodology (Rodrik 2015), and theorists still command a wage premium (Biddle and Hamermesh 2016). There is still a way to go.

7. The Efficiency Question

To recap: first, empirical success in economics is possible. Second, orthodox theory is not a good way to get it. Third, theory should instead be developed in close concert with empirical application and refinement, as is commonplace in other sciences. It might be that economics needs to become more of an idiographic than a nomothetic discipline. We will find out only by seeing what works, not by stipulation or wishful thinking.[10]

What is the alternative to the status quo? The answer is any mix of methods that leads more efficiently to empirical success. This is not just a matter of theory development being less abstract. In addition, once strict adherence to orthodoxy is dropped, economics may join other fields in taking advantage of a much wider range of empirical methods, generating results that in a virtuous circle then feed back into more theory development. These methods include ethnographic observation; small-N causal inference, such as qualitative comparative analysis; other qualitative methods such as questionnaires and interviews; causal process tracing; causal inference from observational statistics; machine learning from big data; historical studies; randomized controlled trials (Khosrowi, Chapter 27); laboratory experiments (Nagatsu, Chapter 24); and natural and quasi experiments (Favereau, Chapter 25).[11] Each of these methods has its own strengths and weaknesses, but each is already widely practiced and has a developed and rigorous methodological literature. To turn to them is in no way a return to the fuzzy verbal analysis that is the pejorative memory of much pre-World War II economics. To ignore them is parochial, not to mention self-damaging.

What is the optimal balance between, on one hand, building up a library of orthodox rational choice models and, on the other hand, pursuing more contextual work and utilizing a wider range of empirical methods? Current practice is already a mixture of the two, so the question becomes: is it the right mixture? Call this the *efficiency question* (Northcott 2018). To answer it requires, so to speak, an epistemic cost-benefit analysis. The costs are the resources invested into theory, such as the training of students, and perhaps more notably the opportunity costs, such as fieldwork methods not taught and fieldwork not done. The benefits are all the cases where theory explains and predicts successfully. Similar calculations can be made for alternatives.

Of course, such calculations can only be done imperfectly. It is hard to add up explanations and predictions in an objective way, hard to weigh those versus other goals of science, and also hard to evaluate the counterfactual of whether things would be better if resources were allocated differently.[12] But these calculations are *being done already* – implicitly, every time a researcher chooses, or a graduate school teaches, one method rather than another or journals or prizes or hirers choose one paper or candidate rather than another.[13] The recent empirical turn is a large-scale example, because it is in effect a claim that resources were not being optimally apportioned before. The status quo is not inevitable. This is shown not just by the empirical turn but also by different practices in other social sciences. It is surely better to assess the matter explicitly than to leave it to inertia and sociological winds.

Others might object that any choice here is illusory because orthodox theory and the various alternatives are too entangled to be separated. For example, a randomized trial might be testing a hypothesis derived from theory.[14] This objection is true up to a point – but not up to the point that the efficiency question can be wished away. The empirical turn itself, for example, shows that a substantive switch from theory to other methods is possible, entanglement notwithstanding.

8. Conclusion

The current emphasis on orthodox theory is inefficient. Common defenses are not persuasive: the generalizability offered by orthodox theory is illusory without empirical success, and so is the understanding in terms of agent rational choice. Empirical success comes first.

Acknowledgment

Many of the ideas in this article originated in past work with Anna Alexandrova.

Related Topics

Claveau, F., Truc, A., Santerre, O., and Mireles-Flores, L., Chapter 11 "Philosophy of Economics? Three Decades of Bibliometric History"
Favereau, J., Chapter 25 "Field Experiments"
Jhun, J., Chapter 23 "Modeling the Possible to Modeling the Actual"
Khosrowi, D., Chapter 27 "Evidence-Based Policy"
Kuorikoski, J., and Lehtinen, A., Chapter 26 "Computer Simulations in Economics"
Lecouteux, G., Chapter 4 "Behavioral Welfare Economics and Consumer Sovereignty"
Linsbichler, A., Chapter 12, "Philosophy of Austrian Economics"
Nagatsu, M., Chapter 24 "Experimentation in Economics"
Peden, W., and Sprenger, J., Chapter 30 "Statistical Significance Testing in Economics"
Reiss, J., Chapter 16 "Measurement and Value Judgments"
Spanos, A., Chapter 29 "Philosophy of Econometrics"
Verreault-Julien, P., Chapter 22 "Explanation in Economics"
Vredenburgh, K., Chapter 5 "The Economic Concept of a Preference"

Notes

1 I also do not criticize economic theory here on moral or political grounds. My concerns are purely methodological.
2 I use "orthodox" to label a commitment to formal rational choice models, which have been the dominant theoretical form since World War II. I will refer to such models generically as "theory."
3 See, for instance, work by Nancy Cartwright, Daniel M. Hausman, Uskali Mäki, Michael Strevens, and Michael Weisberg.
4 Betz (2006). Forecasting performance since then, such as the 2008 crisis, has arguably been even worse.
5 The following paragraphs draw on Guala (2005), Alexandrova (2008), and Alexandrova and Northcott (2009). See those works for references and detailed discussion.
6 Something like the capacities view of theory is held by many economists (Rodrik 2015).
7 Economic theory does not explain in noncausal ways either, such as via unification or via mathematical explanation (Northcott and Alexandrova 2013). Whether economic theory might still be explanatory in some nonstandard sense has been much debated in the philosophical literature – indeed perhaps too much so. But arguably what matters more is whether, however exactly we understand explanatory success, theory development is a good way to get it (Section 7). The literature has said little or nothing about this or, therefore, about, say, whether we should welcome the empirical turn (Section 6).
8 Two separate errors can occur here: first, thoughts that the feeling of understanding implies explanation when in fact it does not; second, when faced with good arguments that it does not, then insistence that there must be some *other* epistemic good, distinct from explanation, indicated by the feeling of understanding.
9 It is true that there always has been much empirical work in economics, in fields such as agricultural and labor economics, and in activities such as national accounting and cost-benefit analyses. Nevertheless, at a minimum, empirical work has become more prestigious (Cherrier 2016).
10 These lessons apply beyond economics: to some natural sciences, such as mathematical ecology (Sagoff 2016); to social sciences other than economics; and to heterodox economic approaches too. Thus, theory in, say, econophysics equally needs to earn its empirical keep.
11 Of course, the latter few of these have begun to be co-opted by economics already.
12 Two kinds of efficiency analysis are possible. The first is *global*: does the current overall allocation of resources serve economics well compared to a different allocation? This is the challenging one to assess. The second kind of efficiency analysis is *local*: what methods should be used to tackle a particular explanandum, and in what proportion? This is often much more tractable, and many case studies are in part just such analyses already (e.g. Northcott and Alexandrova 2015).
13 Of course, other factors enter these decisions too, such as what best serves one's own career. Nevertheless, an implicit efficiency analysis is certainly one important component.
14 It is a truism that all empirical work assumes *some* "theory" in the form of background assumptions. The issue here is whether these background assumptions must include those of economic orthodoxy.

Bibliography

Alexandrova, A. (2008) "Making Models Count," *Philosophy of Science* 75: 383–404.
Alexandrova, A., and Northcott, R. (2009) "Progress in Economics: Lessons from the Spectrum Auctions," in H. Kincaid and D. Ross (eds.) *The Oxford Handbook of Philosophy of Economics*, Oxford: Oxford University Press: 306–337.
Angrist, J., and Pischke, S. (2010) "The Credibility Revolution in Empirical Economics: How Better Research Design is Taking the Con out of Econometrics," *Journal of Economic Perspectives* 24: 3–30.
Benhabib, J., and Farmer, R. (2000) "The Monetary Transmission Mechanism," *Review of Economic Dynamics* 3: 523–550.
Betz, G. (2006) *Prediction or Prophecy?* Wiesbaden: Deutscher Universitaets Verlag.
Biddle, J., and Hamermesh, D. (2016) "Theory and Measurement: Emergence, Consolidation and Erosion of a Consensus," NBER Working Paper No. 22253.
Card, D., and Krueger, A. (1994) "Minimum Wages and Employment: A Case Study of the Fast Food Industry in New Jersey and Pennsylvania," *American Economic Review* 84: 772–793.
Cartwright, N. (1989) *Nature's Capacities and Their Measurement*, Oxford: Oxford University Press.
Cherrier, B. (2016) "Is There Really an Empirical Turn in Economics?" Institute for New Economic Thinking blog 29th September 2016. www.ineteconomics.org/perspectives/blog/is-there-really-an-empirical-turn-in-economics

de Regt, H. (2017) *Understanding Scientific Understanding*, New York: Oxford University Press.
Elster, J. (1988) "The Nature and Scope of Rational-Choice Explanation," in E. Ullmann-Margalit (ed.) *Science in Reflection*, Netherlands: Springer: 51–65.
Friedman, M., and Schwartz, A. (1963) "Money and Business Cycles," *Review of Economics and Statistics* 45: 32–64.
Gruene-Yanoff, T. (2009) "Learning from Minimal Economic Models," *Erkenntnis* 70: 81–99.
Guala, F. (2005) *Methodology of Experimental Economics*, Cambridge, England: Cambridge University Press.
Hamermesh, D. (2013) "Six Decades of Top Economics Publishing: Who and How?" *Journal of Economic Literature* 51: 162–172.
Hausman, D. (1992) *The Inexact and Separate Science of Economics*, Cambridge, England: Cambridge University Press.
Khalifa, K. (2012) "Inaugurating Understanding or Repackaging Explanation?" *Philosophy of Science* 79: 15–37.
Lawson, T. (1997) *Economics and Reality*, New York: Routledge.
Mäki, U. (1992) "On the Method of Isolation in Economics," *Poznan Studies in the Philosophy of the Sciences and the Humanities* 26: 319–354.
Mill, J.S. (1843) *A System of Logic*, London: Parker.
Northcott, R. (2013) "Degree of Explanation," *Synthese* 190: 3087–3105.
Northcott, R. (2015) "Opinion Polling and Election Predictions," *Philosophy of Science* 82: 1260–1271.
Northcott, R. (2018) "The Efficiency Question in Economics," *Philosophy of Science* 85: 1140–1151.
Northcott, R., and Alexandrova, A. (2013) "It's Just a Feeling: Why Economic Models do not Explain," *Journal of Economic Methodology* 20: 262–267.
Northcott, R., and Alexandrova, A. (2015) "Prisoner's Dilemma doesn't Explain Much," in M. Peterson (ed.) *The Prisoner's Dilemma*, Cambridge: Cambridge University Press: 64–84.
Reiss, J. (2008) *Error in Economics: Towards a More Evidence-Based Methodology*, New York: Routledge.
Rodrik, D. (2015) *Economics Rules: The Rights and Wrongs of the Dismal Science*, New York, NY: Norton.
Rosenberg, A. (1992) *Economics: Mathematical Politics or Science of Diminishing Returns?* Chicago: University of Chicago Press.
Sagoff, M. (2016) "Are There General Causal Forces in Ecology?" *Synthese* 193: 3003–3024.
Strevens, M. (2013) "No Understanding Without Explanation," *Studies in History and Philosophy of Science* 44: 510–515.
Trout, J. (2007) "The Psychology of Scientific Explanation," *Philosophy Compass* 2: 564–591.
Ylikoski, P. (2019) "Mechanism-Based Theorizing and Generalization from Case Studies," *Studies in the History and Philosophy of Science* 78: 14–22.

29
PHILOSOPHY OF ECONOMETRICS

Aris Spanos[1]

I fully agree with you about the significance and educational value of methodology as well as history and philosophy of science. So many people today – and even professional scientists – seem to me like somebody who has seen thousands of trees but has never seen a forest. Knowledge of the historic and philosophical background gives that kind of independence from prejudices of his generation from which most scientists are suffering. This independence created by philosophical insight is – in my opinion – the mark of distinction between a mere artisan or specialist and a real seeker after truth.
(Einstein to Thornton, 7 December 1944, Einstein Archives, 61–574).

1. Introduction

The preceding quotation from Einstein's reply to Robert Thornton, a young philosopher of science who began teaching physics at the university level in 1944, encapsulates succinctly the importance of examining the methodology, history, and philosophical foundations of different scientific fields to avoid missing the forest for the trees. The history of a scientific field gives researchers a glimpse of its roots and evolution, but, more importantly, it provides researchers with a balanced perspective on the current "paradigm" in which they find themselves engaged, as well as its potential growth and development. Broadly speaking, a paradigm is a conceptual framework that includes theories, beliefs, values, research methods, objectives, and the professional and educational structure of a scientific field, as well as standards for what constitutes legitimate contributions to a field. Philosophy of science emphasizes skills that are often absent from the training of scientists in most fields, including attentiveness to conceptual clarification and coherence, vigilance against equivocation, the accuracy of expression and weak links in arguments, the capacity to detect gaps in traditional arguments, and devise novel perspectives, and the ability to frame alternative conceptual perspectives. Successful scientific fields, such as physics, chemistry, astronomy, and biology, have repeatedly redefined their conceptual frameworks over time, along with their goals, methods, and tools. Such conceptual revisions are the result of long periods of reflection revolving around the incessant dialogue between theory and data and are guided by the systematic reexamination of the current methodology, and philosophical foundations.

The field of interest in the discussion that follows is modern econometrics, whose roots can be traced back to the early 20th century [see Morgan (1990), Qin (1993), and Spanos (2006a)]. Econometrics is primarily concerned with the systematic study of economic phenomena employing observed data in conjunction with statistical models and substantive subject matter information. The

DOI: 10.4324/9781315739793-36

philosophy of econometrics relates to *methodological* issues concerning the effectiveness of econometric methods and procedures used in empirical inquiry, as well as *ontological* issues concerned with the worldview of the econometrician (see Hoover, 2006). Hence, its success should be evaluated with respect to its effectiveness in enabling practitioners to "learn from data" about such phenomena, that is, the extent to which econometric modeling and inference give rise to trustworthy evidence that transforms tentative substantive conjectures into reliable knowledge about economic phenomena. One transforms tentative conjectures into real knowledge by testing the cogency of the substantive information using observable data given rise to by the phenomenon of interest. From this perspective, econometric modeling and inference provide a statistical framework with a twofold objective: to account for the chance regularity patterns in data and to construct "provisional" substantive models that shed adequate light (explain, describe, predict) on economic phenomena of interest.

When assessed on such grounds, current econometric methodology would be judged to be an inauspicious failure, or so it is argued in what follows. That makes the task of a meta-level appraisal of the methods, procedures, and strategies employed in studying economic phenomena using econometrics all the more urgent. It is often forgotten that scientific fields do not have a methodology written in stone with well-defined objectives and a fixed conceptual framework, even though it might look that way to newcomers in the field. The history of science teaches us that all of these components evolve toward (hopefully) better science, sometimes after long digressions.

2. Descriptive Statistics and Induction

The problem of induction, in the sense of justifying an inference from particular instances to realizations yet to be observed, has been bedeviling the philosophy of science since Hume's (1748) discourse on the problem. In its simplest form, *induction by enumeration* boils down to justifying the *straight-rule:* if the proportion of red marbles from a sample of size n is (m/n), we infer that approximately a proportion (m/n) of all marbles in the urn is red" (see Salmon 1967, p. 50). The key feature of inductive inference is that it is *ampliative* in the sense that it goes beyond the observed data (m/n) to the unknown $\theta=\mathbb{P}(R)$ – which reflects the proportion of red (R) marbles in the urn – enhancing our knowledge about the underlying setup that gave rise to the observed data. Numerous attempts to justify this inductive rule have failed, and the problem of induction is still unresolved in philosophy of science [see Henderson (2020), Reiss (2013, 2015) inter alia].

A case can be made that Karl Pearson's approach to descriptive statistics (Yule, 1916), can be viewed as a more sophisticated form of *induction by enumeration*. The approach is data driven in search of a model in the sense that one would begin with the raw data $\mathbf{x}_0:=(x_1,\ldots,x_n)$, and in step 1 one would summarize $\mathbf{x}_0$ using a histogram with $m\geq 10$ bins. In step 2, one would select a frequency curve $f(x;\theta)$, $x\in\mathbb{R}_X\subset\mathbb{R}$-real line, from *the Pearson family* whose members are generated by:

$$\left[d\ln f(x;\theta)/dx\right]=\left[(x-\theta_1)/\left(\theta_2+\theta_3 x+\theta_4 x^2\right)\right],\ x\in\mathbb{R},\qquad (29.1)$$

which aims to describe the data even more succinctly in terms of four unknown parameters $\boldsymbol{\theta}:=(\theta_1,\theta_2,\theta_3,\theta_4)$. Note that equation (29.1) includes several well-known distributions, such as the Normal, the Student's t, Beta, and Gamma, etc. This is achieved in step 3 by estimating θ using the first four data raw moments, $\hat{\mu}_k=\frac{1}{n}\sum_{t=1}^{n}x_t^k, k=1,2,3,4,$ and solving a system of four equations stemming from equation (29.1) for $\hat{\boldsymbol{\theta}}(\mathbf{x}_0)$ [see Spanos (2019, p. 551)]. In step 4, one would use the estimates $\hat{\boldsymbol{\theta}}(\mathbf{x}_0)$ to select a member of this family $f(x;\hat{\boldsymbol{\theta}})$ that "best" describes the data. In step 5, one would evaluate the "appropriateness" of $f(x;\hat{\boldsymbol{\theta}})$ using Pearson's goodness-of-fit chi-squared test based on the difference $\left(\hat{\boldsymbol{\theta}}(\mathbf{x}_0)-\boldsymbol{\theta}_0\right)$, where $\boldsymbol{\theta}_0$ denotes the selected $f(x;\boldsymbol{\theta}_0), x\in\mathbb{R}_X$, known parameters. Pearson's justification of his statistical analysis was based on the fact that the chosen frequency curve $f(x;\hat{\theta})$, $x \in \mathbb{R}_X$, is the "best on goodness-of-fit grounds," and that could justify going beyond the data in hand $\mathbf{x}_0$. Although his approach to statistical induction was Bayesian in spirit, his use of uniform priors routinely enhanced the role of $f(x;\hat{\theta})$, $x \in \mathbb{R}_X$.

Similarly, Pearson's approach to correlation and regression amounts to curve-fitting guided by goodness of fit with a view to describe succinctly the association between data series, say $\mathbf{z}_0 := \{(x_t, y_t), t = 1, 2, ..., n\}$. The conventional wisdom underlying Pearson-type statistics is summarized by Mills (1924), who distinguishes between "statistical description vs. statistical induction." In statistical description measures such as the "sample" mean $\bar{x} = \frac{1}{n}\sum_{t=1}^{n} x_t$, variance $s_x^2 = \frac{1}{n}\sum_{t=1}^{n}(x_t - \bar{x}_n)^2$, and correlation coefficient:

$$r = \left[\left(\sum_{t=1}^{n} (x_t - \bar{x}_n)(y_t - \bar{y}_n) \right) / \sqrt{\left[\sum_{t=1}^{n} (x_t - \bar{x}_n)^2 \right] \left[\sum_{t=1}^{n} (y_t - \bar{y}_n)^2 \right]} \right], \tag{29.2}$$

"provide just a summary for the data in hand" and "may be used to perfect confidence, as accurate descriptions of the given characteristics" (Ibid., p. 549). However, when the results are to be extended *beyond* the data in hand statistical induction, their validity depends on certain inherent *a priori* stipulations, such as (i) the "uniformity" for the *population* and (ii) the "representativeness" of the *sample* (Ibid., pp. 550–552). That is, statistical description does not invoke the validity of any assumptions, but if the same data are used to go beyond the data in hand (inductive inference), one needs to invoke (i) and (ii).

What Pearson and Mills did not appreciate sufficiently is that even for descriptive purposes, in going from the raw data $\mathbf{x}_0$ to the histogram, the assumptions of independence and identically distributed (IID) are invoked. When these assumptions are invalid, the histogram will provide an misinforming description of $\mathbf{x}_0$, and the frequency curve that is chosen on goodness-of-fit grounds will be highly misleading. Similarly, correlation and regression assume that the data $\mathbf{z}_t := (x_t, y_t)$, $t = 1, 2, ..., n$, are IID over the ordering t. When these assumptions are invalid, the summary statistics will be spurious (see Spanos, 2019).

3. Model-Based Statistical Modeling and Inference

3.1 Model-Based Statistical Induction

Fisher's (1922) recasting of statistics opens the door for the standpoint that data $\mathbf{x}_0 := (x_1, \ldots, x_n)$ can be viewed as a typical realization of stochastic processes $\{X_t, t \in \mathbb{N}\}$ to be integrated into modern statistics properly, although most of the statistical models introduced by Fisher were based on random samples (IID). The way he recast modern statistics was to turn Pearson's approach on its head. Instead of commencing with the raw data $\mathbf{x}_0 := (x_1, \ldots, x_n)$ in search of a statistical model, he would view data as a typical realization of a prespecified statistical model $\mathcal{M}_\theta(\mathbf{x})$ (which he called a "hypothetical infinite population") and answer the question: "Of what population is this a random sample" (Ibid., p. 313)? This is not just a reorganization of Pearson's approach but a complete reformulation of statistical induction, from generalizing observed "events" described by summary statistics to unobserved data events to modeling the underlying "process" in the form of a stochastic mechanism $\mathcal{M}_\theta(\mathbf{x})$ that gave rise to data $\mathbf{x}_0$, and not to summarize or describe $\mathbf{x}_0$.

Modern model-based frequentist inference revolves around a prespecified *parametric statistical model*, generically defined by

$$\mathcal{M}_\theta(\mathbf{x}) = \{f(\mathbf{x};\theta), \theta \in \Theta \subset \mathbb{R}^m\}, \ \mathbf{x} \in \mathbb{R}_X^n, \ n > m, \tag{29.3}$$

where $f(\mathbf{x};\theta), \mathbf{x} \in \mathbb{R}^n_X$ denotes the joint distribution of the sample $\mathbf{X} := (X_1,\ldots,X_n)$, $\mathbb{R}^n_X$ denotes the sample space, and Θ denotes the parameter space. This represents a statistical generating mechanism specified in terms of the observable stochastic process $\{X_t, t \in \mathbb{N} := (1,2,\ldots,n,\ldots)\}$ underlying data $\mathbf{x}_0 := (x_1,\ldots,x_n)$. The unknown parameters θ are viewed as *constants* and the interpretation of probability is frequentist, firmly anchored on the strong law of large numbers (SLLN). As argued in Spanos (2013), some of the criticisms of the frequentist interpretation of probability, including (i) the circularity of its definition, (ii) its reliance on "random samples," (iii) its inability to assign "single event" probabilities, and (iv) the "reference class" problem (Salmon, 1967; Hajek, 2007), stem from conflating the model-based frequentist interpretation anchored on the SLLN with the von Mises (1928) interpretation. In Bayesian statistics, by contrast, θ is viewed as a random variable (vector) and probability is interpreted as "degrees of belief."

The *primary objective* of frequentist inference is to use the sample information, as summarized by $f(\mathbf{x};\boldsymbol{\theta})$, $\mathbf{x} \in \mathbb{R}^n_X$, in conjunction with data $\mathbf{x}_0$, to *narrow down* Θ as much as possible, ideally to a single point:

$$\mathcal{M}^*(\mathbf{x}) = \{f(\mathbf{x};\boldsymbol{\theta}^*)\}, \ \mathbf{x} \in \mathbb{R}^n_X,$$

where θ^* denotes the "true" value of θ in Θ ; "the true value of a parameter θ , " in this context, is shorthand for saying that the generating mechanism specified by $\mathcal{M}^*(\mathbf{x})$ could have generated data $\mathbf{x}_0$. In practice, this ideal situation is unlikely to be reached, except by happenstance, but that does not preclude learning from $\mathbf{x}_0$. Learning from data about θ^* is often referred to as accurate "identification" of the generating mechanism $\mathcal{M}_\theta(\mathbf{x})$ that could have given rise to $\mathbf{x}_0$.

Example 1. The *simple normal model* is specified by:

$$X_t \sim \text{NIID}(\mu,\sigma^2), \ \boldsymbol{\theta} := (\mu,\sigma^2) \in \Theta := (\mathbb{R} \times \mathbb{R}_+), \ x_t \in \mathbb{R}, \ t \in \mathbb{N}\}, \tag{29.4}$$

where $\mu = E(X_t)$, $\sigma^2 = Var(X_t)$, and NIID are the assumptions comprising $\mathcal{M}_\theta(\mathbf{x})$.

Example 2: The simple Bernoulli model:

$$X_k \sim \text{BerIID}(\theta,\theta(1-\theta)), \ x_k = 0,1, \ E(X_k) = \theta \in [0,1], \ Var(X_k) = \theta(1-\theta), \ k \in \mathbb{N}. \tag{29.5}$$

The initial choice (specification) of a statistical model $\mathcal{M}_\theta(\mathbf{x})$ is based on rendering $\mathbf{x}_0$ a typical realization thereof, or equivalently, the probabilistic assumptions selected for the stochastic process $\{X_t, t \in \mathbb{N}\}$ underlying $\mathcal{M}_\theta(\mathbf{x})$ would reflect the chance regularity patterns exhibited by data $\mathbf{x}_0$. The search for patterns is not as unyielding as it might seen at first sight because that there are three broad categories of chance regularity patterns and corresponding probabilistic assumptions: distribution, dependence and heterogeneity (see Spanos, 2006b). It is worth noting that the simple normal model in equation (29.4) has one probabilistic assumption from each category, and the same applies to all statistical models in the model-based ($\mathcal{M}_\theta(\mathbf{x})$) approach.

What is particularly interesting from the philosophy of science perspective is that Fisher's specification process echoes Charles Sanders Peirce's process of *abduction*

> [T]here are but three elementary kinds of reasoning. The first, which I call abduction . . . consists in examining a mass of facts and in allowing these facts to suggest a theory. In this way we gain new ideas; but there is no force in the reasoning.
>
> [Peirce, collected in Burks (1958, 8.209)][2]

> Abduction is the process of forming an explanatory hypothesis. It is the only logical operation which introduces any new idea; for induction does nothing but determine a value, and deduction merely evolves the necessary consequences of a pure hypothesis.
>
> [Peirce, collected in Burks (1958, 5.172)]

One can make a strong case that the specification of $\mathcal{M}_\theta(\mathbf{x})$ relates directly to Peirce's abduction in the sense that "examining a mass of facts" comes in the form of detecting the chance regularity patterns exhibited by data $\mathbf{x}_0$, and abduction suggests an explanatory hypothesis in the form of $\mathcal{M}_\theta(\mathbf{x})$ that comprises the probabilistic assumption aiming to account for these regularities. Also, the next step of validating the initial choice is in sync with that of Fisher, when Peirce argues that "A hypothesis adopted by abduction could only be adopted on probation, and must be tested" [Peirce, collected in Burks (1958, 7.202)]. Hence, the crucial role of misspecification (M-S) testing: testing the validity of the probabilistic assumptions comprising $\mathcal{M}_\theta(\mathbf{x})$ vis-à-vis data $\mathbf{x}_0$. Related to that is another important insight about induction from Peirce: "[inductive] reasoning tends to correct itself, and the more so the more wisely its plan is laid. Nay, it not only corrects its conclusions, it even corrects its premises" [Peirce, collected in Burks (1958, 5.575); see Mayo (1996)]. That is, the key to model-based statistical induction consists of "selecting $\mathcal{M}_\theta(\mathbf{x})$ wisely" to account for all of the chance regularities in data $\mathbf{x}_0$, combined with validating its premises.

This insight has not been heeded by modern statisticians, even though the early pioneers were clear about the importance of validating $\mathcal{M}_\theta(\mathbf{x})$ [see Neyman (1952), p. 27].

Example 1 (continued). In the case of equation (29.4), the NIID assumptions need to be validate vis-à-vis data $\mathbf{x}_0$.

Figure 29.1 depicts the form of model-based induction described previously, with $\mathbb{Q}(\theta;\mathbf{x})$ denoting inferential propositions, such as optimal (i) estimators, (ii) confidence intervals and (iii) tests, that are derived *deductively* from $\mathcal{M}_\theta(\mathbf{x})$.

Example 1 (continued). $\mathbb{Q}(\theta;\mathbf{x}),\mathbf{x}\in\mathbb{R}^n_X$, could refer to the estimators $\bar{X}_n=\frac{1}{n}\sum_{i=1}^n X_i, s^2=\frac{1}{n-1}\sum_{i=1}^n(\bar{X}_n-X_i)^2$ being optimal because they satisfy certain properties, such as lack of bias, consistency, efficiency, and sufficiency; these properties stem from their sampling distributions (Lehmann and Romano, 2005):

$$\bar{X}_n\sim \mathrm{N}\left(\mu,\frac{\sigma^2}{n}\right),\ \left[\frac{(n-1)s^2}{\sigma^2}\right]\sim\chi^2(n-1), \tag{29.6}$$

where $\chi^2(m)$ denotes a chi-squared distribution with m degrees of freedom.

Fisher's enduring contributions to model-based induction include devising a general way to "operationalize" the reliability of inference by (i) *deductively* deriving error probabilities from $\mathcal{M}_\theta(\mathbf{z})$, and (ii) providing a measure of the procedure's "effectiveness" in learning from data about θ^*. The form of induction envisaged by Fisher and Peirce is one where the reliability of the inference stems from the "trustworthiness" of the inference procedure – how often it errs (see Mayo, 1996).

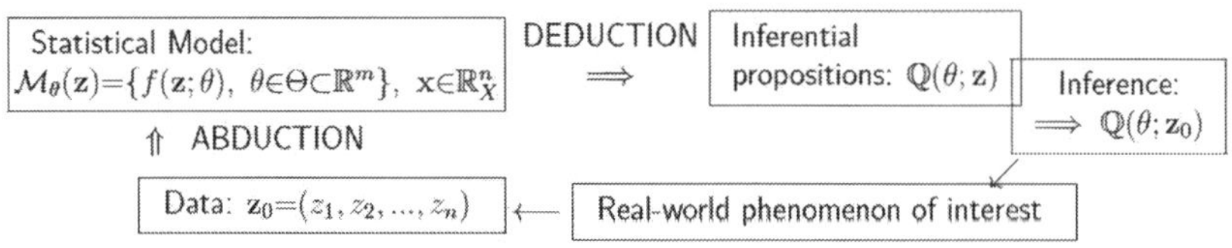

Figure 29.1 Model-based statistical induction

The inferential propositions in $\mathbb{Q}(\theta;\mathbf{z})$ are *deductively valid* when the truth of the premises ($\mathcal{M}_\theta(\mathbf{x})$) ensures the truth of the conclusions ($\mathbb{Q}(\theta;\mathbf{x})$), which is assured by valid mathematical derivations. $\mathbb{Q}(\theta;\mathbf{z})$ is rendered *sound* by securing the *statistical adequacy* of $\mathcal{M}_\theta(\mathbf{x})$ – the validity of its probabilistic assumptions vis-à-vis data $\mathbf{x}_0$ – which can be established by thorough misspecification testing. Statistical adequacy in turn guarantees the statistical reliability of the inference results $\mathbb{Q}(\theta;\mathbf{x}_0)$ based on $\mathbf{x}_0$ (see Spanos, 2019).

Example 1 (continued). $\mathbb{Q}(\theta;\mathbf{x}),\ \mathbf{x}\in\mathbb{R}^n_X$ represents sound inferential propositions only when the NIID assumptions are valid (see Spanos, 2019).

Fisher (1922) identified the "problems of statistics" to be: (i) **specification**, (ii) **estimation** and (iii) **distribution,** and emphasized that addressing (ii)–(iii) depends crucially on successfully dealing with (i) first. That is, the key to learning from data is an apropos specification: "how appropriate" (or wise per Peirce) the initial selection of $\mathcal{M}_\theta(\mathbf{x})$ is. Fisher (1922, 1925) laid the foundations of an optimal theory of (point) estimation, introducing most of the desirable properties. Under distribution, Fisher included all forms of inferential propositions based on sampling distributions of estimators and test statistics, including "statistics designed to test the validity of our specification" (p. 8).

In an attempt to address the statistical adequacy of $\mathcal{M}_\theta(\mathbf{x})$, error statistics (Mayo and Spanos, 2011) *refines* the Fisher's approach to frequentist inference by separating *the modeling facet* from the *inference facet*. The modeling facet includes *specification*, *estimation*, *M-S testing*, and *respecification* with a view to arrive at a statistically adequate model. This is because the *inference* facet presumes the validity of $\mathcal{M}_\theta(\mathbf{x})$ when posing substantive questions of interest to the data [see Mayo and Spanos (2004) and Spanos (2018)]. This ensures that the inference procedures enjoy the optimal properties invoking the validity of $\mathcal{M}_\theta(\mathbf{x})$ (see Spanos, 2019).

The effectiveness and reliability of inference procedures are evaluated using ascertainable *error probabilities* stemming from the sampling distribution $f(y_n;\theta)$, of statistics (estimator, test, predictor) of the form $Y_n = g(X_1, X_2, \ldots, X_n)$ derived via

$$F_n(Y_n \le y) = \underbrace{\int\int\cdots\int}_{\{\mathbf{x}:\, g(\mathbf{x})\le y\}} f(\mathbf{x};\theta)d\mathbf{x}, \forall y\in\mathbb{R}, \tag{29.7}$$

The value of θ in equation (29.7) is always prespecified, taking two different forms stemming from the underlying reasoning:

1. **Factual** (estimation and prediction): the true value of θ, say θ^*, whatever that happens to be in Θ. Confidence Intervals (CIs) are derived under $\theta=\theta^*$.
2. **Hypothetical** (hypothesis testing): various hypothetical scenarios based on θ taking different prespecified values under H_0: $\theta\in\Theta_0$ vs. H_1: $\theta\in\Theta_1$, where $\Theta_0\cup\Theta_1=\Theta, \Theta_0\cap\Theta_1=\varnothing$. The relevant error probabilities include the types I and II, the power, and the *p*-value (see Spanos, 2019).

The effectiveness of frequentist inference is defined in terms of the optimal properties of a statistic (estimator, test, predictor) $Y_n = g(\mathbf{X})$, and framed in terms of its sampling distribution $f(y_n;\theta), y_n \in \mathbb{R}$. These optimal properties, however, assume that $\mathcal{M}_\theta(\mathbf{x})$ is statistically adequate: its probabilistic assumptions are valid for $\mathbf{x}_0$.

Unreliability of inference. When any of these assumptions are invalid, $f(\mathbf{x};\theta)$ will be erroneous, and the *optimality* of the statistic $Y_n = g(\mathbf{X})$ and the *reliability* of any inference based on it –the approximate equality of the actual error probabilities with the nominal ones – will be undermined. The application of a .05 significance level test when the actual type I error [due to a misspecified $\mathcal{M}_\theta(\mathbf{z})$] is closer to .97 will lead that inference astray by inducing *inconsistency* in estimators and/or sizeable *discrepancies* between the actual and nominal (assumed) error probabilities (types I, II, *p*-values).

Simulation example (Spanos and McGuirk 2001). To get some idea of how misleading the inferences can be when $\mathcal{M}_\theta(\mathbf{z})$ is misspecified, consider the case of the linear regression (LR) model:

$$Y_t = \beta_0 + \beta_1 x_t + \varepsilon_t, \ (\varepsilon_t \mid X_t = x_t) \sim \text{NIID}\left(0, \sigma^2\right), \ t \in \mathbb{N}, \tag{29.8}$$

(see Table 29.4 for more details relating to the assumptions), where data $\mathbf{z}_0 := \{(x_t, y_t), t = 1,\ldots,100\}$ are replicated ($N = 10000$) by simulation under two scenarios. In scenario 1, all the LR probabilistic assumptions [1]–[5] are valid, and in scenario 2, assumption [5] is invalid ([1]–[4] are valid), stemming from the mean heterogeneity exhibited by $\mathbf{z}_0$ (e.g. the term $.14t$ is missing from equation (29.8)). The estimate of β_0 is $\hat{\beta}_0 = .228(.315)$ with its standard error in parentheses, indicating that β_0 is statistically insignificant because $\tau_{\beta_0}(\mathbf{z}_0) = .724$ and the *p*-value is $p(\mathbf{z}_0) = .470$, when the true value is $\beta_0^\star = 1.5$. Also, the nominal error type I probability is $\alpha = .05$, but the actual value is .968. On the other hand, $\hat{\beta}_1 = 1.989(.015), \tau_{\beta_0}(\mathbf{z}_0) = 298.4$, and $p(\mathbf{z}_0) = .0000$, when the true value is $\beta_1^\star = 0.5$, and the actual type I error probability is 1.0 – rejecting a true null hypothesis 100% of the time (see Spanos and McGuirk, 2001). It is important to note that most of the published results using the LR model are likely to have more than one invalid assumption among 1–5!

It is important to emphasize that when $\mathcal{M}_\theta(\mathbf{z})$ is statistically misspecified, it will undermine not just frequentist inference but also Bayesian because the posterior is defined by $\pi(\theta \mid \mathbf{x}_0) \propto \pi(\theta) \cdot f(\mathbf{x}_0;\theta), \theta \in \Theta$, where $\pi(\theta)$ is the prior. It will also undermine Akaike-type model selection procedures because they depend on the likelihood $L(\theta;\mathbf{x}_0), \theta \in \Theta$ (see Spanos, 2010a).

Modern statistical inference, as a form of induction, is based on data that exhibit inherent chance regularity patterns. They differ from deterministic regularities insofar as they cannot be accounted for (described) using mathematical equations. More specifically, chance regularities come from recurring patterns in numerical data that can be accounted for (modeled) using probabilistic assumptions from three broad categories: distribution, dependence and heterogeneity (see Spanos, 2019).

Model-based statistical induction differs from other forms of induction, such as induction by enumeration (Henderson, 2020), in three crucial respects. First, the inductive premise of inference, $\mathcal{M}_\theta(\mathbf{x})$, represents a stochastic generating mechanism that could have given rise to data $\mathbf{x}_0$ that and provides the cornerstone for the ampliative dimension of model-based induction (see Spanos, 2013). This should be contrasted with enumerative induction and Pearson's descriptive statistics which rely on the straight rule and summarizing the data $\mathbf{x}_0$. This relates to Hacking's (1965) questions concerning Salmon's claim about the straight rule

> Salmon and Reichenbach maintain that *if long-run frequencies exist, the straight rule for estimating long-run frequencies is to be preferred to any rival estimator.* Other propositions are needed to complete their vindication of induction, but only this one concerns us. Salmon claims to have

> proved it. This is more interesting than mere academic vindications of induction; practical statisticians need good criteria for choosing among estimators, and, if Salmon were right, he would have very largely solved their problems, which are much more pressing than Hume's.
>
> (Ibid., p. 261).

Example 2 (continued). If we view the straight rule in the context of model-based statistics, where $\mathcal{M}_\theta(\mathbf{x})$ is the simple Bernoulli model in equation (29.5), where with $\mathbb{P}(X_k=1)=\theta$ and $\mathbb{P}(X_k=0)=(1-\theta)$, the straight rule ratio $(m/n)=\frac{1}{n}\sum_{k=1}^{n}x_k$, and, thus, $\hat{\theta}(\mathbf{x}_0)=(m/n)$ constitutes an estimate of θ, the observed value of the estimator $\hat{\theta}(\mathbf{X})=\frac{1}{n}\sum_{k=1}^{n}X_k$ when evaluated at the data point $\mathbf{x}_0$. Hence, in the context of $\mathcal{M}_\theta(\mathbf{x})$ in equation (29.5), $\hat{\theta}(\mathbf{X})$ is the maximum likelihood estimator of θ and enjoys all optimal properties, including lack of bias, full efficiency, sufficiency, and consistency (see Spanos, 2019). Regrettably, the optimality of any estimator $\hat{\theta}(\mathbf{X})$ does not entail the claim $\hat{\theta}(\mathbf{x}_0)\simeq\theta^*$, for a large enough n. Therefore, the straight rule, when viewed in the context of model-based inference, is just a fallacious assertion. This unwarranted claim undermines the appropriateness of estimation-based effect sizes that are widely viewed as a replacement for *p*-values in the current discussions on the replicability and trustworthiness of evidence (see Spanos, 2020).

Second, in the context of model-based induction, Hacking's (1965) "Other propositions needed to complete their vindication of induction" include (i) the validity of the inductive premises (IID) for data $\mathbf{x}_0$, which ensures the trustworthiness of evidence and (ii) the optimality of the particular estimator $\hat{\theta}(\mathbf{X})$, which secures the effectiveness of the inference. Both issues lie at the core of *inductive (statistical) inference*: how we learn from data about phenomena of interest.

Third, the justification of model-based induction does not invoke *a priori* stipulations such as the "uniformity" of *nature* and the "representativeness" of the *sample*, as in the case of enumerative induction and Karl Pearson's curve-fitting, but relies on establishing the validity of model assumptions using comprehensive misspecification (M-S) testing. As Fisher (1922) argued:

> For empirical as the specification of the hypothetical population [statistical model] may be, this empiricism is cleared of its dangers if we can apply a rigorous and objective test of the adequacy with which the proposed population represents the whole of the available facts.
>
> (Ibid., p. 314).

3.2 Model-Based Frequentist Statistics: Foundational Issues

Model-based frequentist statistics, as cast by Fisher (1922, 1925) and extended by Neyman and Pearson (1933), and Neyman (1937), has been plagued by several foundational problems that have bedeviled its proper implementation since the 1930s, including the following two.

Foundational issue 1. How one can secure statistical adequacy: the validity of the probabilistic assumptions comprising the chosen $\mathcal{M}_\theta(\mathbf{x})$ vis-à-vis data $\mathbf{x}_0$.

The statistics and econometric literature paid little attention to the systematic testing of the validity of the model assumptions (M-S testing) or what one would do when any of the assumptions are found wanting [respecification; see Spanos (1986)].

Foundational issue 2. When data $\mathbf{x}_0$ provide good evidence for or against a hypothesis or an inferential claim? (Mayo, 1996): Fisher's *p*-value and Neyman-Pearson's accept/reject H_0 results did not provide a coherent evidential interpretation that could address this question.

Error statistics refines the Fisher recasting of frequentist inference by embracing the distinction between *the modeling facet* and the *inference facet* to address issue 1 (see Mayo and Spanos, 2004). In an attempt to address issue 2, error statistics *extends* the F-N-P approach by distinguishing between *predata* and *postdata* phases of frequentist testing to supplement the original framing with a post-data severity evaluation of testing results. This provides a sound *evidential account* that can be used to address several misconceptions and problems raised about F-N-P testing, including the large n problem (see Mayo and Spanos, 2006).

Foundational issue 3. What is the nature of the reasoning underlying frequentist inference? Spanos (2012) made a case for two types of reasoning: *factual reasoning* (used in estimation and prediction), under $\theta = \theta^*$, whatever the value θ^* happens to be in Θ, which underlines the evaluation of the sampling distributions of estimators, pivotal functions, and predictors; and *hypothetical reasoning* (used in testing), underlying the evaluation of sampling distributions of test statistics under the scenarios, (null) $H_0 : \theta \in \Theta_0$, and (alternative) $H_1 : \theta \in \Theta_1$. Parenthetically, these forms of reasoning underlying frequentist inference are at odds with the *universal* reasoning, for all $\theta \in \Theta$, underlying Bayesian inference (see Spanos, 2017).

Example 1 (continued). For the simple normal model in equation (29.4), assuming σ^2 is known for simplicity, equation (29.6) implies that:

$$\frac{\sqrt{n}\left(\bar{X}_n - \mu\right)}{\sigma} \sim \mathrm{N}(0,1). \tag{29.9}$$

What is not so obvious is how to interpret equation (29.9), because $d(\mathbf{X};\mu) = \frac{\sqrt{n}\left(\bar{X}_n - \mu\right)}{\sigma}$ involves the unknown parameter μ, and why $E\left(d(\mathbf{X};\mu)\right) = 0$ is not apparent. A simple answer is that because $\bar{X}_n$ is an unbiased estimator of μ, that is, $E\left(\bar{X}_n\right) = \mu^*$, and thus $E\left(\frac{\sqrt{n}\left(\bar{X}_n - \mu\right)}{\sigma}\right) = 0.$

For that to be the case, however, equation (29.9) must be evaluated under $\mu = \mu^*$, which is known as *factual reasoning*. Hence, a more informatory way to specify equation (29.9) is:

$$d(\mathbf{X};\mu^*) = \frac{\sqrt{n}\left(\bar{X}_n - \mu^*\right)}{\sigma} \overset{\mu=\mu^*}{\sim} \mathrm{N}(0,1). \tag{29.10}$$

For estimation and prediction the underlying reasoning is factual. For hypothesis testing, however, the reasoning is hypothetical and takes the form:

$$d(\mathbf{X};\mu_0) = \frac{\sqrt{n}\left(\bar{X}_n - \mu_0\right)}{\sigma} \overset{\mu=\mu_0}{\sim} \mathrm{N}(0,1), \quad d(\mathbf{X};\mu_1) = \frac{\sqrt{n}\left(\bar{X}_n - \mu_0\right)}{\sigma} \overset{\mu=\mu_1}{\sim} \mathrm{N}(0,\delta_1), \tag{29.11}$$

where $\delta_1 = \frac{\sqrt{n}\left(\mu_1 - \mu_0\right)}{\sigma}$, for $\mu_1 \neq \mu_0$, $\mu_i \in \mathbb{R}$, $i = 0,1$ (see Spanos, 2019).

3.2.1 Estimation (Point and Interval)

Example 1 (continued). For the simple normal model in equation (29.4) with σ^2 known, the maximum likelihood (ML) estimator of μ is $\hat{\theta}_{ML}(\mathbf{X}) = \frac{1}{n}\sum_{i=1}^{n} X_i$. Its optimality revolves around its sampling distribution, which is evaluated using *factual reasoning* $(\theta = \theta^*)$:

$$\hat{\theta}_{ML}(\mathbf{X}) = \frac{1}{n}\sum_{i=1}^{n} X_i \overset{\mu=\mu^*}{=} \mathrm{N}\left(\mu^*, \frac{\sigma^2}{n}\right). \tag{29.12}$$

It can be shown that equation (29.12) implies that $\hat{\theta}_{ML}(\mathbf{X})$ is unbiased, sufficient, fully efficient, and strongly consistent (see Lehmann and Romano, 2005).

Confidence intervals (CIs), $\left[L(\mathbf{X}),U(\mathbf{X})\right]$ are evaluated in terms of their capacity measured by the coverage probability $(1-\alpha)$ to overlay θ^{*} between the lower and upper bounds (Neyman, 1952):

$$\mathbb{P}(L(\mathbf{X})\leq\theta<U(\mathbf{X});\mu=\mu^{*})=1-\alpha.$$

Example 1 (continued). For equation (29.4) with σ^{2} known, the $(1-\alpha)$ CI takes the form:

$$\mathbb{P}(\bar{X}_{n}-c_{\frac{\alpha}{2}}\left(\frac{\sigma}{\sqrt{n}}\right)\leq\mu<\bar{X}_{n}+c_{\frac{\alpha}{2}}\left(\frac{\sigma}{\sqrt{n}}\right);\mu=\mu^{*})=1-\alpha, \tag{29.13}$$

stemming from the distribution of the pivot:

$$d(\mathbf{X};\mu)=\frac{\sqrt{n}\left(\bar{X}_{n}-\mu^{*}\right)}{\sigma}\overset{\mu=\mu^{*}}{\sim}\mathrm{N}(0,1). \tag{29.14}$$

3.2.2 Neyman-Pearson (N-P) Testing

Example 1 (continued). Consider testing the hypotheses:

$$H_{0}:\mu\leq\mu_{0}\text{ vs. }H_{1}:\mu>\mu_{0}, \tag{29.15}$$

in the context of the simple normal model in equation (29.4) with σ^{2} known. It is important to emphasize that the framing of H_{0} and H_{1} should constitute a partition of $\mathbb{R}$, because for N-P testing the whole range of values of μ is relevant for statistical inference purposes, irrespective of whether only a few values are of substantive interest.

A α -significance level uniformly most powerful (UMP) test is defined by (Lehmann and Romano, 2005):

$$T_{\alpha}:=\{d(\mathbf{X})=\frac{\sqrt{n}\left(\bar{X}_{n}-\mu_{0}\right)}{\sigma},\ C_{1}(\alpha)=\{\mathbf{x}:d(\mathbf{x})>c_{\alpha}\}\}, \tag{29.16}$$

where c_{α} is the α -significance level threshold based on:

$$d(\mathbf{X})=\frac{\sqrt{n}\left(\bar{X}_{n}-\mu_{0}\right)}{s}\overset{\mu=\mu_{0}}{\sim}\mathrm{N}(0,1). \tag{29.17}$$

The type I error probability and the p-value are evaluated by using equation (29.17):

$$\mathbb{P}(d(\mathbf{X})>c_{\alpha};\mu=\mu_{0})=\alpha,\quad\mathbb{P}(d(\mathbf{X})>d(\mathbf{x}_{0});\mu=\mu_{0})=p(\mathbf{x}_{0}).$$

The power of T_α, defined by:

$$\mathcal{P}(\mu_1) = \mathbb{P}(d(\mathbf{X}) > c_\alpha; \mu = \mu_1), \text{for all } \mu_1 > \mu_0, \tag{29.18}$$

is based on the distribution:

$$d(\mathbf{X}) = \frac{\sqrt{n}(\bar{X}_n - \mu_0)}{\sigma} \overset{\mu=\mu_1}{\sim} \mathrm{N}(\delta_1, 1),\ \delta_1 = \frac{\sqrt{n}(\mu_1 - \mu_0)}{\sigma}, \text{ for all } \mu_1 > \mu_0, \tag{29.19}$$

where δ_1 is the non-zero mean parameter. It is important to emphasize that the power of a test provides a measure of its *generic* (for any sample value $\mathbf{x} \in \mathbb{R}_X^n$) *capacity* to detect discrepancies from H_0. Also, none of the preceding error probabilities (types I and II and power) are conditional on values of μ because it is neither an event nor a random variable; $d(\mathbf{X})$ is evaluated under *hypothetical* values of θ (see Spanos, 2019).

Two crucial features of N-P testing are often flouted by statistical textbooks and practitioners alike, giving rise to much confusion and several misinterpretations. These features can be found in the classic paper by Neyman and Pearson (1933) who proposed two crucial preconditions for the effectiveness of N-P testing in learning from data that relate to the framing of hypotheses: (i) H_0 and H_1 should constitute a partition of Θ, in a way that renders (ii) the type I error probability as the most serious (see also Neyman, 1952). The partition of Θ is crucial in light of the primary objective of frequentist inference because the "true" value θ^* might lie outside the union of H_0 and H_1, turning an optimal N-P test into a wild goose chase.

Example 1 (continued). For the simple normal model in equation (29.4), Berger and Wolpert (1988) invoke the N-P lemma to frame the hypotheses as:

$$H_0 : \mu = 1 \text{ vs. } H_1 : \mu = -1, \tag{29.20}$$

Unfortunately, the N-P lemma assumes a partition $\Theta := \{\theta_0, \theta_1\}$ (see Spanos, 2011). Condition (ii) suggests that when no reliable information about the potential range of values of θ^* is available, the N-P test is likely to be more effective by using:

$$H_0 : \theta = \theta_0 \text{ vs. } H_1 : \theta \neq \theta_0. \tag{29.21}$$

When such reliable information is available, however, the N-P test will be more effective by using a directional framing for H_0 and H_1, as in equation (29.15), ensuring that H_1 includes the potential range of values of θ^* as departures from the null value, say θ_0. This is because the power of the test – its capacity to detect discrepancies from θ_0 – should be defined over the range most called for, the potential range of values of θ^*.

3.3 *Statistical Adequacy and Misspecification (M-S) Testing*

The current state of affairs on model validation is insightfully described by Freedman (2010, p. 16):

> Bayesians and frequentists disagree on the meaning of probability and other foundational issues, but both schools face the problem of model validation. Statistical models have been used successfully in the physical and life sciences. However, they have not advanced the

> study of social phenomena. How do models connect to reality? When are they likely to deepen understanding? When are they likely to be sterile and misleading? . . . I believe model validation to be a central issue. Of course many of my colleagues will be found to disagree. For them, fitting models to data, computing standard errors, and performing significance test is "informative," even though the basic statistical assumptions (linearity, independence of errors, etc.) cannot be validated. This position seems indefensible, nor are the consequences trivial. Perhaps it is time to reconsider.

Securing of the statistical adequacy of $\mathcal{M}_\theta(\mathbf{x})$ calls for testing the validity of its probabilistic assumptions vis-à-vis data $\mathbf{x}_0$, such as NIID in the case of equation (29.4). The most effective way to secure statistical adequacy is to separate the *modeling*, which includes (i) *specification*, the initial choice of $\mathcal{M}_\theta(\mathbf{x})$, (ii) *M-S testing*, and (iii) *respecification*, when any of its assumptions are found wanting, from the *inference* facet because the latter presumes the statistical adequacy of $\mathcal{M}_\theta(\mathbf{x})$, and they pose very different questions to the data (see Spanos, 2006a, 2018). The modeling facet aims to secure the validity of $\mathcal{M}_\theta(\mathbf{x})$, and the inference facet ensures the optimality of inference procedures with a view to secure the reliability and precision of inferential results. Treating the two as a single combined inference problem is akin to conflating the construction of a boat to given specifications (modeling) with sailing it in a competitive race (inference). The two are clearly related because the better the construction the more competitive the boat, but imagine trying to build a boat from a pile of plywood in the middle of the ocean while racing it.

Because inference presupposes the validity of $\mathcal{M}_\theta(\mathbf{x})$, statistical adequacy needs to be secured before optimal inference procedures can be reliably employed. Neyman-Pearson (N-P) constitutes *testing within* $\mathcal{M}_\theta(\mathbf{x})$ aiming to *narrow down* Θ to a much smaller subset, presupposing its validity. In contrast, M-S testing poses the question of whether the particular $\mathcal{M}_\theta(\mathbf{x})$ could have given rise to data $\mathbf{x}_0$, for any value of $\theta \in \Theta$, and constitutes *testing outside* $\mathcal{M}_\theta(\mathbf{x})$ because the default null is $\mathcal{M}_\theta(\mathbf{x})$ is valid vs. its negation $\neg\mathcal{M}_\theta(\mathbf{x}) := [\mathcal{P}(\mathbf{x}) - \mathcal{M}_\theta(\mathbf{x})]$, that is, some other statistical model in $[\mathcal{P}(\mathbf{x}) - \mathcal{M}_\theta(\mathbf{x})]$, where $\mathcal{P}(\mathbf{x})$ is the set of all possible statistical models that could have given rise to $\mathbf{x}_0$. The problem in practice is how to operationalize $[\mathcal{P}(\mathbf{x}) - \mathcal{M}_\theta(\mathbf{x})]$ to render possible comprehensive M-S testing (see Spanos, 2018).

4. Empirical Modeling in Econometrics

4.1 Traditional Curve-fitting and Respecification

Empirical modeling across different disciplines involves an intricate blend of *substantive* subject matter and *statistical information*. The substantive information stems from a theory or theories about the phenomenon of interest and could range from simple tentative conjectures to intricate *substantive* (structural) models, say $\mathcal{M}_\varphi(\mathbf{z})$, framed in terms of mathematical equations formulating the theory that are estimable in light of the available data $\mathbf{Z}_0 := (\mathbf{z}_1, \mathbf{z}_2, \ldots, \mathbf{z}_n)$. The substantive information has an important and multifaceted role to play by demarcating the crucial aspects of the phenomenon of interest (suggesting the relevant variables and data), as well as enhancing the learning from data when they do not belie the statistical information in $\mathbf{Z}_0$ that stems from the *chance regularity patterns* exhibited by data $\mathbf{Z}_0$. Scientific knowledge often begins with substantive conjectures based on subject matter information, but it becomes knowledge when its veracity is established by being tested thoroughly against actual data generated by the phenomenon of interest.

The Preeminence of Theory (PET) perspective, which has dominated empirical modeling in economics since the early 19th century, amounts to theory-driven curve-fitting guided by probabilistic assumptions assigned to the error term, and evaluated by goodness-of-fit measures (see Reiss, 2008; Spanos, 2009). The assignment of probabilistic assumptions to error term terms stems from the standpoint that relationships among the variables are mathematical (deterministic) in nature, but these are subject to stochastic disturbances due to simplification, approximation, and measurement errors. The theory-driven curve(s) is framed in terms of a structural model $\mathcal{M}_\varphi(\mathbf{z})$, and the aim is to use the data $\mathbf{Z}_0$ to quantify it by estimating $\varphi \in \Phi$. In this sense, the data $\mathbf{Z}_0$ play only a subordinate role in availing the quantification by attaching a random error term(s) to transform the curves into a stochastic model amenable to statistical analysis. The traditional textbook approach to empirical modeling in economics is summed up by Pagan (1984) as follows: "Four steps almost completely describe it: a model is postulated, data gathered, a regression run, some t-statistics or simulation performance provided and another empirical regularity was forged." (Ibid., p. 103)

Although his description is meant to be a witty caricature of textbook econometrics, like all perceptive parodies, it contains more than one home truth.

The first home truth is that the phenomenon of interest rarely is explicitly described so that one can evaluate the empirical findings in relation to what has been learned from data about that phenomenon.

The second home truth is that the modeling begins with a prespecified substantive model $\mathcal{M}_\varphi(\mathbf{z})$ – an estimable form of that theory in light of the available data – meant to provide a description/explanation of the phenomenon of interest.

The third home truth is that $\mathcal{M}_\varphi(\mathbf{z})$ is treated as established knowledge, and not as tentative conjectures to be tested against the data because the primary aim is to quantify $\mathcal{M}_\theta(\mathbf{z})$ by estimating the unknown structural parameters $\Theta \in \Phi \subset \mathbb{R}^p$.

The fourth truth is that the selection of data is often ad hoc, in the sense that the theory variables are assumed to coincide with the particular data $\mathbf{Z}_0$ chosen. No attempt is made to (i) compare the theoretical variables, often defined in terms of the intentions of individual economic agents stemming from an optimization problem, but the data refer to observed quantities and prices generated by the market, or (ii) provide a cogent bridging of the gap between them (see Spanos, 2015).

The fifth truth is that the estimation of φ amounts to foisting $\mathcal{M}_\varphi(\mathbf{z})$ onto the data by viewing it as curve-fitting guided by probabilistic assumptions assigned to the error term to be evaluated using goodness-of-fit measures.

The sixth truth is that the estimated φ of $\mathcal{M}_\varphi(\mathbf{z})$ and the associated statistics, such as t-ratios and goodness-of-fit measures, are usually taken at face value without any attempt to secure their reliability. Indeed, the validity of the probabilistic assumptions ascribed to the error term is treated as an afterthought that determines the estimation method for the curve-fitting, and if any departures from these assumptions are indicated by the computer program output, such as a Durbin-Watson (D-W) statistic close to zero, all one has to do is to modify the original estimation method to "account" for the departure designated by the alternative hypothesis of the D-W test. To be more specific, for the LR model in equation (29.8) the D-W test operationalizes $\left[\mathcal{P}(\mathbf{z})-\mathcal{M}_\theta(\mathbf{z})\right]$ by embedding equation (29.8) into:

$$Y_t=\beta_0+\beta_1 x_t+u_t,\ u_t=\rho u_{t-1}+\varepsilon_t,\ (\varepsilon_t \mid X_t=x_t)\sim \text{NIID}\left(0,\sigma_\varepsilon^2\right), t\in\mathbb{N}, \tag{29.22}$$

and testing the hypotheses: $H_0\ :\ \rho=0$ vs. $H_1\ :\ \rho\neq 0$. When H_0 is rejected, the traditional respecification is to accept H_1, that is, adopt equation (29.22) as the respecified model. This is fallacious because rejecting H_0 entitles one to infer that $E(u_t u_s \mid X_t=x_t)\neq 0$ for $t>s$, but not that $E(u_t u_s \mid X_t=x_t)=\left(\rho^{|t-s|}/\left(1-\rho^2\right)\right)\sigma_\varepsilon^2,\ t,s=1,2,\dots,n.$ Such a claim will require one to estimate equation (29.22) and test all its probabilistic assumptions to ensure statistical adequacy (see McGuirk and Spanos, 2009). Indeed, this traditional respecification strategy constitutes a quintessential example of the *fallacy of rejection*: (mis)interpreting rejected H_0 [evidence against H_0] as evidence *for* a particular H_1 (see Spanos, 2019).

A related fallacy is that *of acceptance*: (mis)interpreting a large p-value or accepting H_0 [no evidence against H_0] as evidence for H_0 – this can arise when a test has very low power (e.g. small n).

A case in point is the literature of unit root testing in the context of the AR(1) model traditionally specified as in Table 29.1 (see Choi, 2015, p. 21). As Phillips and Xiao (1998) show, the unit root test based on $H_0 : \alpha_1 = 1$ vs. $H_1 : \alpha_1 < 1$, has very low power ($<.33$) for $n \leq 100$, and thus, the null is often accepted erroneously. Worse still, none of the invoked probabilistic assumptions (i)–(iv) (Table 29.1) are testable with data $\mathbf{y}_0$, and thus the literature on unit root testing largely ignores the statistical misspecification problem (see Andreou and Spanos, 2003).

The specification in Table 29.2 reveals the inappropriateness of relying on nontestable probabilistic assumptions relating to "as $n \to \infty$, instead of the testable assumptions [1]-[5] in table 29.2. As argued by Le Cam (1986, p. xiv):

> [L]imit theorems "as n tends to infinity" are logically devoid of content about what happens at any particular n. All they can do is suggest certain approaches whose performance must then be checked on the case at hand. Unfortunately the approximation bounds we could get are too often too crude and cumbersome to be of any practical use.

In fact, the assumptions whose validity for $\mathbf{y}_0$ will secure the reliability of any test based on AR(1) are given in Table 29.2. It is worth noting that when the AR(1) model is properly specified (Table 29.2)

Table 29.1 AR(1) model: traditional specification

$$y_t = \alpha_0 + \alpha_1 y_{t-1} + u_t,\ t \in \mathbb{N}.$$

$$\text{(i) } E(u_t) = 0,\ \text{(ii)} \sup_t E|u_t|^{\delta+\varepsilon} < 0 \textit{ for } \delta > 2,\ \varepsilon > 0,\ \text{(iii)} \lim_{n\to\infty} E(\frac{1}{n}(\sum_{t=1}^{n} u_t)^2 = \sigma_\infty^2 > 0,$$

$$\text{(iv) } \{u_t,\ t \in \mathbb{N}\} \text{ is strongly mixing with } \alpha_m \underset{m\to\infty}{\to} 0 \text{ such that} \sum_{m=1}^{\infty} \alpha_m^{1-\delta/2} < \infty.$$

Table 29.2 Normal, autoregressive (AR(1)) model

Statistical GM : $y_t = \alpha_0 + \alpha_1 y_{t-1} + u_t,\ \ t \in \mathbb{N}$

$$\left.\begin{array}{l}
[1] \text{ Normality} : (y_t, y_{t-1}) \sim \text{N}(.,.), \\
[2] \text{ Linearity} : E(y_t \mid \sigma(y_{t-1})) = \alpha_0 + \alpha_1 y_{t-1}, \\
[3] \text{ Homoskedasticity} : Var(y_t \mid \sigma(y_{t-1})) = \sigma_0^2, \\
[4] \text{ Markov} : \{y_t,\ t \in \mathbb{N}\} \text{is a Markov process}, \\
[5]\ t-\text{invariance} : (\alpha_0, \alpha_1, \sigma_0^2) \text{are not changing with } t,
\end{array}\right\} t \in \mathbb{N}.$$

$$\alpha_0 = E(y_t) - \alpha_1 E(y_{t-1}) \in \mathbb{R}, \alpha_1 = \frac{Cov(y_t, y_{t-1})}{Var(y_{t-1})} \in (-1,1),\ \sigma_0^2 = Var(y_t) - \frac{Cov(y_t, y_{t-1})^2}{Var(y_{t-1})} \in \mathbb{R}_+$$

Note that $\sigma(y_{t-1})$ denotes the sigma – field generated by y_{t-1}.

using the probabilistic reduction $f(y_1, y_2, \ldots, y_n; \psi) = f_1(y_1; \psi_1) \prod_{t=2}^{n} f(y_t \mid y_{t-1}; \theta)$, stemming from the probabilistic assumptions normality, Markovness and stationarity, the coefficient $\alpha_1 \in (-1,1)$ and thus $\alpha_1 = Corr(y_t, y) = 1$ lies outside its parameter space. This is not unrelated to the low power mentioned previously (see Spanos, 2011).

The seventh home truth is that the "empirical regularity forged" is usually another set of statistically "spurious" numbers added to the ever-accumulating mountain of untrustworthy evidence gracing prestigious journals, which stems primarily from the inadequate criteria used to determine success in publishing in these journals:

1. **Statistical:** goodness-of-fit/prediction, statistical significance,
2. **Substantive:** theoretical meaningfulness, explanatory capacity,
3. **Pragmatic:** simplicity, generality, elegance.
   The problem is that the criteria 1–3 do not secure the reliability of inference or the trustworthiness of the ensuing evidence. As shown in Spanos (2007a), excellent fit is neither necessary nor sufficient for statistical adequacy, because the former seeks "small" residuals, but the latter relies on nonsystematic (white-noise) residuals. Criteria 1–3 are not even sufficient for the evaluation of the cogency of $\mathcal{M}_\varphi(\mathbf{z})$ in shedding adequate light on the phenomenon of interest. The combination of 1–3 neglects a fundamental criterion:
4. **Epistemic**: empirical adequacy, which relates to both *statistical adequacy* – validating the implicit statistical model $\mathcal{M}_\theta(\mathbf{x})$ vis-à-vis data $\mathbf{z}_0$, – and *substantive adequacy* – probing the cogency of $\mathcal{M}_\varphi(\mathbf{z})$ vis-à-vis the phenomenon of interest. Let us unpack this claim.

4.2 Traditional Econometric Techniques

The dominance of the Preeminence of Theory (PET) perspective in applied economics and econometrics seems to have largely ignored Fisher's (1922) paradigm shift of recasting Karl Pearson's descriptive statistic because it shares with the latter the curve-fitting perspective evaluated by goodness-of-fit measures. The difference between curve-fitting a frequency curve vs. a structural model, $\mathcal{M}_\varphi(\mathbf{z})$, is immaterial when the trustworthiness of evidence is a primary objective. A case in point is the anachronistic attribution of the Method of Moments to Pearson by the econometrics literature (Greene, 2018), oblivious to the fact that Pearson's method was designed for a very different paradigm, where one would begin with the data $\mathbf{z}_0$ in search of a descriptive model $f(z; \widehat{\psi}) \in \mathcal{F}_p(z; \psi)$, $z \in \mathbb{R}$, and not lead off with a prespecified model $\mathcal{M}_\varphi(\mathbf{z})$, assumed to have given rise to data $\mathbf{z}_0$ (see Spanos, 2019).

The emphasis in current applied econometrics is placed on the recipelike mechanical implementation of inference procedures, such as instrumental variables (IV), generalized method of moments (GMM), vector autoregresion (VAR), structural VAR, calibration, and matching moments. The probabilistic assumptions are assigned to error terms, treated as an afterthought when deriving consistent and asympotically normal (CAN) estimators, and then forgotten at the inference facet. Indeed, the notion that probabilistic assumptions imposed on one's data could be invalid is hardly mentioned in the recent textbooks on macroeconometrics (see Canova, 2007). As one would expect, Canova (2007) points out the major advancements in the mathematical, statistical, and computational tools in econometrics over the past 20 years. The problem is that "these improvements in tools" are inversely related to the trustworthiness of the empirical evidence. The empirical examples used in most recent textbooks in applied econometrics are *not* exemplars of how to do empirical modeling that gives rise to learning from data, but are illustrations on how to apply recipelike procedures, ignoring the problem of securing the *trustworthiness* of the empirical evidence when employing the proposed tools.

In an attempt to justify the neglect of statistical model validation, traditional textbooks often invoke misleading robustness results. Popular examples in textbook econometrics are the heteroskedasticity-consistent (HC) and autocorrelation-consistent (AC) standard errors (SEs), as well as HAC SEs (see Wooldridge, 2010). HAC SEs are used to justify ignoring any departures from homoskedasticity and non-autocorrelation assumptions such as [3] and [4] in Table 29.4. Unfortunately, the claim that such SEs based on asymptotic arguments can circumvent the unreliability of inference problem is unfounded (see Spanos and McGuirk, 2001). As shown in Spanos and Reade (2015), HC and HA SEs do nothing to ensure that the actual error probabilities closely approximate the nominal one. As argued previously, the idea that a consistent estimator of the SE of an estimator could save an inference from unreliability stems from another misapprehension of asymptotic properties.

A strong case can be made that the published literature in prestigious journals in econometrics pays little to no attention to statistical adequacy: validating the estimated models. There are several reasons for that, including the fact that the PET perspective dominates current practice (Spanos, 2018):

1. Views empirical modeling as theory-driven curve-fitting guided by error-term probabilistic assumptions and evaluated using goodness-of-fit measures.
2. Conflates the modeling facet with the inference facet, ignoring the fact that they pose very different questions to the data. It is similar to conflating the construction of a boat to given specifications with sailing it in a competitive race!
3. Blends the statistical with the substantive information model and neglects both statistical and substantive adequacy. Underappreciates the potentially devastating effects of statistical misspecification on the reliability of inference for both the substantive questions of interest and probing for substantive adequacy.
4. M-S testing [probing outside $\mathcal{M}_\theta(\mathbf{z})$] is often conflated with N-P testing [probing within $\mathcal{M}_\theta(\mathbf{z})$], and as a result, M-S testing is often criticized for being vulnerable to pretest bias, double use of data, data-mining, etc. (see Spanos, 2010b).
5. Statistical respecification is viewed as "error-fixing" on the basis of modifying the probabilistic assumptions assigned to the error term $\{\varepsilon_t, t \in \mathbb{N}\}$, so that one can get "good" estimators for the curve-fitting.
6. Current practice in econometrics unduly relies on asymptotics, in particular CAN estimators, and practitioners seem unaware that this does not suffice to secure the reliability of inferences. Because limit theorems, such as the LLN and CLT, only describe what happens at the limit (∞), asymptotic properties are useful for their value in excluding totally unreliable estimators and tests, but they do not guarantee the reliability of inference procedures for a given data $\mathbf{z}_0$ and n. For instance, an inconsistent estimator will give rise to unreliable inferences, but a consistent one does not guarantee their reliability.
7. There is a huge divide between a theoretical econometrician and a practitioner. An important contributor to the uninformed implementation of statistical procedures, such as IV, GMM, and VAR, that continues unabated to give rise to untrustworthy evidence is a subtle disconnect between the theoretician (theoretical econometrician), that leaves the practitioner hopelessly unable to assess the appropriateness of different methods for his or her particular data. The theoretician develops the statistical techniques associated with different statistical models for different types of data (time series, cross-section, panel), and the practitioner implements them using data, often observational. As observed by Rust (2016)

   > It is far easier to publish theoretical econometrics, an increasingly arid subject that meets the burden of mathematical proof. But the overabundance of econometric theory has not paid off in terms of empirical knowledge, and may paradoxically hinder empirical work

by obligating empirical researchers to employ the latest methods that are often difficult to understand and use and fail to address the problems that researchers actually confront.

Each will do a much better job at their respective tasks if only they understood sufficiently well the work of the other. The theoretician will be more cognizant of the difficulties for the proper implementation of these tools, and make a conscious effort to elucidate their scope, applicability, and limitations. Such knowledge will enable the practitioner to produce trustworthy evidence by applying such tools only when appropriate. For instance, in proving that an estimator is CAN, the theoretician could invoke *testable* assumptions comprising the relevant $\mathcal{M}_\theta(\mathbf{z})$. This will give the practitioner a chance to appraise the appropriateness of different methods and do a much better job in producing trustworthy evidence by testing the validity of the invoked assumptions (see Spanos, 2018).

Unfortunately, empirical modeling in economics is currently dominated by a serious disconnect between these two because the theoretician is practicing *mathematical deduction* and the practitioner uses recipe-like *statistical induction* by transforming formulae into numbers misusing the data. The theoretician has no real motivation to render the invoked $\mathcal{M}_\theta(\mathbf{z})$ testable. If anything, the motivation stemming from the perceived esteem level reflecting his/her technical dexterity is to make $\mathcal{M}_\theta(\mathbf{z})$ even less testable and obtuse by invoking the misleading claim that weaker assumptions are less vulnerable to misspecification. Also, the practitioner has no real motivation to do the hard work of establishing the statistical adequacy of $\mathcal{M}_\theta(\mathbf{z})$, given that no journal editor asks for that, and is happy to give credit/blame to the theoretician.

4.3 *Traditional Modeling and the Trustworthiness of Evidence*

Despite bold assertions in book titles, such as *Mostly Harmless Econometrics* by Angrist and Pischke (2008), to ignore the probabilistic assumptions one imposes on a particular data $\mathbf{W}_0$, is anything but "harmless," when trustworthy evidence and learning from data are important objectives in the empirical modeling (see also Peden and Sprenger, Chapter 30). Moreover, "better research designs, either by virtue of outright experimentation or through the well-founded and careful implementation of quasi-experimental methods" (Angrist and Pischke (2010, p. 26), as claimed by Angrist and Pischke (2010), will not take the "con" out of econometrics, because the untrustworthiness of evidence stemming from the imposition of (implicitly or explicitly) invalid probabilistic assumptions on one's data plagues modeling with experimental data as well (see Rust, 2016). A real-life example of statistical misspecification due to ignoring heterogeneity in cross-section experimental data is the case of the sleep aid Ambien. After the manufacturer went through the rigorous procedures and protocols required of a new medical treatment before approval, and after the medication was on the market for several years, as well as millions of prescriptions, it was discovered (retrospectively) that female patients are more susceptible to the risk of "next day impairment" because their bodies metabolize Ambien more slowly than male patients (see Spanos, 2020). If the rigorous process based on the "gold standard" for evidence, the randomized controlled trials (RCTs), for a new treatment could not safeguard the trustworthiness of evidence from statistical misspecification, one wonders how any impromptu "better research designs" and "quasi-experimental methods" would do better [see Deaton (2010), Heckman (1997), and Reiss (2015) for further discussion].

5. Recasting Curve-fitting Into Model-Based Inference

How does one secure the reliability of inference and the trustworthiness of evidence when the modeling begins with a substantive model $\mathcal{M}_\varphi(\mathbf{z})$? Answer: by a recasting the curve-fitting approach into a model-based induction with a view to accommodate the substantive information encapsulated by $\mathcal{M}_{\varphi}(\mathbf{z})$, but distinguishing between $\mathcal{M}_{\varphi}(\mathbf{z})$ and the statistical $\mathcal{M}_{\theta}(\mathbf{z})$, and ensure that its probabilistic assumptions are specified in terms of the observable process $\{\mathbf{Z}_t, t \in \mathbb{N}\}$ and not the error term. This is needed to establish the statistical adequacy of $\mathcal{M}_{\theta}(\mathbf{z})$, which, in turn, will ensure the reliability of the statistical procedures used to congruously coalesce the two models into an empirical model that is both statistically and substantively adequate.

5.1 Statistical vs. Substantive Models

A closer look at Fisher's (1922, 1925) recasting of statistics reveals that in his framing there is always a "material experiment," often specified in terms of alternative experimental designs – a simple $\mathcal{M}_{\varphi}(\mathbf{z})$ – that is embedded into a statistical model $\mathcal{M}_{\theta}(\mathbf{z})$. It turns out that behind every substantive model $\mathcal{M}_{\varphi}(\mathbf{z})$ there is an implicit statistical model $\mathcal{M}_{\theta}(\mathbf{z})$ that comprises the probabilistic assumptions imposed on data $\mathbf{Z}_0$, but one needs to bring it out explicitly and test the validity of these assumptions. This renders the current debate between structural vs. reduced-form models (Low and Meghir, 2017) a false dilemma, because the reduce form of any structural model $\mathcal{M}_{\varphi}(\mathbf{z})$ comprises the probabilistic assumptions (implicitly or explicitly) imposed on data $\mathbf{z}_0$, that is, the built-in statistical model $\mathcal{M}_{\theta}(\mathbf{z})$, whose statistical adequacy determines the reliability of inference of the estimated $\mathcal{M}_{\varphi}(\mathbf{z})$.

In direct analogy to $\mathcal{M}_{\theta}(\mathbf{z})$ the substantive model is generically specified by

$$\mathcal{M}_{\varphi}(\mathbf{z}) = \{f(\mathbf{z};\varphi), \varphi \in \Phi \subset \mathbb{R}^p\}, \mathbf{z} \in \mathbb{R}^n_Z, p \leq m. \tag{29.23}$$

A congruous blending of the two models is based on relating their parameterizations θ and φ by ensuring that $\mathcal{M}_{\varphi}(\mathbf{z})$ is parametrically nested in $\mathcal{M}_{\theta}(\mathbf{z})$.

The first step in that direction is to "transfer" the probabilistic assumptions from the error term to the observable process $\{\mathbf{Z}_t, t \in \mathbb{N}\}$ underlying $\mathcal{M}_{\varphi}(\mathbf{z})$, and separate the statistical from the substantive assumptions by distinguishing between statistical and substantive adequacy:

1. **Statistical adequacy**. $\mathcal{M}_{\theta}(\mathbf{z})$ adequately accounts for the chance regularities in $\mathbf{z}_0$, or equivalently, the probabilistic assumptions comprising $\mathcal{M}_{\theta}(\mathbf{z})$ are valid for data $\mathbf{z}_0$. It is "local" because it relates to the particular data and their chance regularities.
2. **Substantive adequacy**. The extent to which $\mathcal{M}_{\varphi}(\mathbf{z})$ sheds adequate light (describe, explain, predict) on the phenomenon of interest. Hence, any assumptions relating to ceteris paribus clauses, omitted variables, causality, etc., are substantive because they encode "tentative information" about "how the world really works." In this sense, substantive adequacy is phenomenon-oriented because it relates to the relationship between $\mathcal{M}_{\varphi}(\mathbf{z})$ and the phenomenon of interest. Indeed, the traditional criteria (2) substantive and (3) pragmatic relate to the substantive adequacy. The problem is that without securing the statistical adequacy first, none of these criteria can be properly implemented in practice.

It is important to emphasize at this point that the widely invoked slogan "*All models are wrong, but some are useful*" attributed to George Box (1979), is invariably misinterpreted as suggesting that statistical misspecification is inevitable. The "wrongness" to which Box refers, however, is not statistical but substantive: "Now it would be very remarkable if any system existing in the real world could be exactly represented by any simple model" (Ibid., p. 202). Box goes on to emphasize empirical modeling as an iterative process of selecting a model, testing its probabilistic assumptions by using the residuals, and respecifying it when any of them are invalid!

5.2 The Tale of Two Linear Regressions

To illustrate the difference between a statistical and a substantive perspective let us compare and contrast the traditional textbook specification of the linear regression (LR) model (Table 29.3) with the model-based specification (Table 29.4).

In terms of their assumptions, the two specifications differ in several respects.

First, Table 29.3 is usually supplemented by additional assumptions that include the following:

{5} $\mathbf{X}_t$ is fixed at $\mathbf{x}_t$ in repeated samples,
{6} All relevant variables have been included in $\mathbf{X}_t$,
{7} No collinearity: $\text{rank}(\mathbf{X}) = m+1, \mathbf{X} = (\mathbf{1}, \mathbf{x}_1, \mathbf{x}_2, \ldots, \mathbf{x}_m)$.

Second, the generating mechanism (GM) in Table 29.3 is (implicitly) *substantive*: how the phenomenon of interest generated data $\mathbf{Z}_0 := (\mathbf{y}_0, \mathbf{X}_0)$, but the GM in Table 29.4 is *statistical*: how the stochastic mechanism underlying $\mathcal{M}_\theta(\mathbf{z})$ could have generated data $\mathbf{Z}_0$. Equivalently, this could represent how one could generate data Y_t given $X_t = x_t$ on a computer using pseudorandom numbers for u_t.

Third, the error terms ε_t and u_t, associated with the two specifications in Tables 29.3 and 29.4, are interpreted very differently because they represent different types of errors. For a statistical model, such as 3 in Table 29.4, the error term u_t is assumed to represent the *nonsystematic* statistical information in data $\mathbf{Z}_0 := (\mathbf{y}_0, \mathbf{X}_0)$, neglected by the systematic component $m(t) = E(Y_t \mid X_t = x_t)$;

Table 29.3 Linear regression model: traditional specification

$$Y_t = \beta_0 + \beta_1^\top \mathbf{x}_t + \varepsilon_t, \quad t \in \mathbb{N},$$

$$\{1\}\ (\varepsilon_t \mid \mathbf{X}_t = \mathbf{x}_t) \sim \text{N}(.,.),\ \{2\}\ E(\varepsilon_t \mid \mathbf{X}_t = \mathbf{x}_t) = 0,$$

$$\{3\}\ Var(\varepsilon_t \mid \mathbf{X}_t = \mathbf{x}_t) = \sigma_\varepsilon^2,\ \{4\}\ Cov(\varepsilon_t \varepsilon_s \mid \mathbf{X}_t = \mathbf{x}_t) = 0,\ t > s,\ t, s \in \mathbb{N}.$$

Table 29.4 Normal, linear regression model

Statistical GM: $Y_t = \beta_0 + \beta_1 x_t + u_t, \quad t \in \mathbb{N}$

[1] Normality: $(Y_t \mid X_t = x_t) \sim \text{N}(.,.)$,

[2] Linearity: $E(Y_t \mid X_t = x_t) = \beta_0 + \beta_1 x_t$,

[3] Homoskedasticity: $Var(Y_t \mid X_t = x_t) = \sigma^2$,

[4] Independence: $\{(Y_t \mid X_t = x_t),\ t \in \mathbb{N}\}$ *is an independent process*,

[5] t-invariance: $\theta := (\beta_0, \beta_1, \sigma^2)$ are not changing with t,

(Assumptions [1]–[5] hold for $t \in \mathbb{N}$.)

$$\beta_0 = E(y_t) - \beta_1 E(X_t),\ \beta_1 = \left(\frac{Cov(X_t, y_t)}{Var(X_t)}\right),\ \sigma^2 = Var(y_t) - \beta_1 Cov(X_t, y_t).$$

more formally, $\{(u_t \mid \mathcal{D}_t), t \in \mathbb{N}\}$ is a Martingale difference process relative to the information $\mathcal{D}_t \subset \Im$ of the probability space $(S, \Im, \mathbb{P}(.))$ underlying $\mathcal{M}_\theta(\mathbf{x})$. Hence, the statistical error term u_t is (i) *derived* in the sense that $u_t = Y_t - E(Y_t \mid X_t = x_t)$ represents the nonsystematic component of the orthogonal decomposition of Y_t defining the statistical GM:

$$Y_t = E(Y_t \mid X_t = x_t) + u_t,$$

where by "design" $E(u_t \mid X_t = x_t) = 0$ and $E(m(t) \cdot u_t \mid X_t = x_t) = 0$. Hence, the probabilistic structure of $\{(u_t \mid X_t = x_t), t \in \mathbb{N}\}$ is completely determined by that of $\{(Y_t \mid X_t = x_t), t \in \mathbb{N}\}$ ([1]–[5], Table 29.4). This implies that when any of the assumptions [1]–[5] are invalid, u_t will include the systematic statistical information in $\mathbf{Z}_0$ unaccounted for by $m(t)$. The statistical error term u_t is also (ii) *data-oriented,* in the sense that its validity or invalidity (departures from assumptions [1]–[5]) revolves solely around the statistical, systematic information in $\mathbf{Z}_0$.

When Table 29.3 is viewed in the context of curve-fitting, ε_t is a *structural error* term assumed to represent the *nonsystematic* substantive information unaccounted for by $Y_t = \beta_0 + \beta_1 x_t$. In this sense, ε_t is (i)★ *autonomous* in the sense that its probabilistic structure also depends on other relevant substantive information that $Y_t = \beta_0 + \beta_1 x_t$ might have overlooked, including omitted variables, unobserved confounding factors, external shocks, and systematic errors of measurement or approximation. ε_t is also (ii)★ *phenomenon-oriented,* in the sense that the validity of the probabilistic structure of ε_t revolves around how adequately $Y_t = \beta_0 + \beta_1 x_t$ accounts for the phenomenon of interest. Hence, when probing for substantive adequacy one needs to consider the different ways $Y_t = \beta_0 + \beta_1 x_t$ might depart from the actual data-generating mechanism giving rise to the phenomenon of interest, not just the part that generated $\mathbf{Z}_0$.

Fourth, when the assumptions {1}–{4} from Table 29.3 are viewed from a purely *probabilistic* perspective, one can see that they relate directly to assumptions [1]–[4] from Table 29.4 (see Spanos, 2019). In particular:

$$\{2\} E(\varepsilon_t \mid X_t = x_t) = 0 \Leftrightarrow [2] E(Y_t \mid X_t = x_t) = \beta_0 + \beta_1 x_t. \tag{29.24}$$

On the other hand, assumption {2} (Table 29.3) in textbook econometrics is referred to as an *exogeneity* assumption (Greene, 2018, p. 55), which reveals that {2} is viewed from a *substantive* (curve-fitting) perspective, where a potential departure can arise when ε_t includes an omitted but relevant variable, say W_t, such that $Cov(X_t, W_t) \neq 0$, implying that $\neg$ {2}: $E(\varepsilon_t \mid \mathbf{X}_t = \mathbf{x}_t) \neq 0$. This argument makes no sense when ε_t is viewed as a statistical error term (see equation (29.24)) because it has nothing to do with data $\mathbf{Z}_0$, but it does make sense when ε_t is viewed as an autonomous substantive error term $\varepsilon_t = Y_t - \beta_0 - \beta_1 x_t$, which includes any systematic substantive information neglected by $Y_t = \beta_0 + \beta_1 x_t$. This issue is particularly important in econometrics because $E(\varepsilon_t \mid \mathbf{X}_t = \mathbf{x}_t) \neq 0$ is used to motivate one of the most widely used (and abused; Spanos, 2007b) methods of estimation, known as the instrumental variables (IVs) method (see Wooldridge, 2010). Another variation on the substantive departure ($\neg$ {2}) gives rise to the so-called omitted variable bias, which is erroneously viewed as a form of statistical misspecification in the econometric literature (see Spanos, 2006c).

Fifth, assumptions 5–7 are not probabilistic assumptions that make sense in the context of a statistical model, because 5 is superfluous when X_t is viewed as a conditioning variable, 6 is a substantive assumption (Spanos, 2010c), and 7 is a condition that relates to the particular data $\mathbf{Z}_0$, and not the generating mechanism (see Spanos, 2019).

Sixth, when viewed from a purely probabilistic perspective, there are two clear differences between Tables 29.3 and 29.4. The first is that all assumptions [1]–[5] relate to the observable process

$\{(Y_t \mid X_t = x_t), t \in \mathbb{N}\}$ and are directly testable vis-à-vis data $\mathbf{Z}_0$, with [5] missing from Table 29.3. The second difference is the implicit statistical parameterization in Table 29.4, indicating what "statistical" (as opposed to substantive) parameters the unknown θ represents. This is crucial because the statistical GM in conjunction with this parameterization separates the statistical from the substantive perspective, indicating that one does not need to invoke a substantive model to estimate the statistical model in Table 29.4. This clear separation of the statistical and substantive models, ab initio, stems from viewing the former as a particular parameterization of the stochastic process $\{\mathbf{Z}_t, t \in \mathbb{N}\}$ underlying the data $\mathbf{Z}_0$. To derive the particular parameterization one can invoke the Kolmogorov extension theorem that enables one to fully describe the stochastic process $\{\mathbf{Z}_t, t \in \mathbb{N}\}$ using its joint distribution $D(\mathbf{Z}_1, \mathbf{Z}_2, \ldots, \mathbf{Z}_n; \phi)$ (see Billingsley, 1995). Note that the probabilistic reduction that relates $D(\mathbf{Z}_1, \mathbf{Z}_2, \ldots, \mathbf{Z}_n; \phi) \overset{\text{IID}}{=} \prod_{t=1}^{n} D(Y_t \mid \mathbf{x}_t; \varphi_1) D(\mathbf{X}_t; \varphi_2), \forall \mathbf{z}_t \in \mathbb{R}^{nm}$ to the distribution $D(Y_t \mid \mathbf{x}_t; \varphi_1)$, underlying the LR model in Table 29.4, also ensures the internal consistency of assumptions [1]–[5] (see Spanos, 2019).

The parameterization of θ provides the first link between the statistical and substantive models because θ is chosen in such a way as to parametrically nest the substantive model parameters φ. This relationship can be expressed in the generic form:

$$\mathbf{G}(\theta, \varphi) = 0, \ \varphi \in \mathbb{R}^p, \ \theta \in \mathbb{R}^m, p \leq m. \tag{29.25}$$

Figure 29.1 can be easily extended to accommodate a substantive $\mathcal{M}_\varphi(\mathbf{z})$ model in addition to the statistical model $\mathcal{M}_\theta(\mathbf{z})$, as articulated earlier (see Spanos, 2020).

5.3 From Statistical and Substantive to Empirical Models

As emphasized previously, what renders the estimated LR model (Table 29.4) and the associated statistical inference a statistical regularity is the validity of [1]–[5] and nothing else. It becomes an empirical regularity when a worthy substantive model explains the phenomenon of interest without belying the statistically adequate $\mathcal{M}_\theta(\mathbf{z})$.

Kepler's first law. Spanos (2007a) illustrates this by using Kepler's 1609 statistical regularity for the motion of the planets ($\mathcal{M}_\theta(\mathbf{z})$) and the substantive model ($\mathcal{M}_\varphi(\mathbf{z})$) provided by Newton almost 80 years later. In particular, Kepler's first law states that, "a planet moves around the sun in an elliptical motion with one focus at the sun." The loci of the elliptical motion are based on r distance of the planet from the sun, and ϑ - angle between the line joining the sun and the planet and the principal axis of the ellipse. If one uses the polar coordinate transformations $y := (1/r)$ and $x := \cos\vartheta$, Kepler's first law becomes $y_t = \alpha_0 + \alpha_1 x_t$, which can be estimated as a LR model in (??). Estimating (??) using the original Brahe data for Mars ($n = 28$) yields

$$y_t = \underset{(.000002)}{.662062} + \underset{(.000003)}{.061333} x_t + u_t, \ n = 28, \ R^2 = .9999, \ s = .00001115, \tag{29.26}$$

which can be shown to be statistically adequate (see Spanos, 2007a).

The substantive interpretation of Kepler's first law had to wait for Newton's (1687) *Law of Universal Gravitation* (LUG): $F = [G(m \cdot M)]/r^2$, where F is the force of attraction between two bodies of *mass* m (planet) and M (sun), G is a constant of gravitational attraction, and r is the *distance* between the two bodies. LUG attributed a clear structural interpretation to β_0 and β_1 : $\beta_0 = [MG/4\kappa^2]$, where κ denotes the Kepler constant and $\beta_1 = ([(1/d) - \beta_0]$, where d is the shortest distance between the planet and the sun (see Hahn, 1998). Also, the error term ε_t enjoys a substantive interpretation in the form of "departures" from the elliptical motion due to potential *measurement errors* and *unmodeled effects*. Hence, the assumptions i–iv in Table 29.1 could be inappropriate in cases where (i) the data suffer from "systematic" observation errors, (ii) the third body problem effect is significant, and (iii) the general relativity terms (Lawden, 2002) are significant.

Duhem's thesis. The distinction between the statistical $\mathcal{M}_\theta(\mathbf{z})$ and substantive $\mathcal{M}_\varphi(\mathbf{z})$ models can be used to address *Duhem's* (1914) thesis that "no hypothesis can be tested separately from the set of auxiliary hypotheses" needed for such empirical tests. The statistical assumptions of $\mathcal{M}_\theta(\mathbf{z})$ are the only "auxiliary hypotheses" needed, and their validity can be established independently of the substantive hypotheses in equation (29.25). Indeed, the adequacy of $\mathcal{M}_\theta(\mathbf{z})$ is needed for testing the validity of such substantive hypotheses. For instance, the statistically adequate model in equation (29.26), can provide the basis for testing the Copernicus hypothesis that the motion of a planet around the sun is circular ($y_t = \alpha_0$) using the hypotheses: $H_0 : \beta_1 = 0$ vs. $H_1 : \beta_1 \neq 0$, yielding $\tau(\mathbf{z}_0;\beta_1) = \frac{.061333}{.000003} = 20444[.000000]$, which strongly rejects H_0.

5.4 The Propensity Interpretation of Probability

The distinction between $\mathcal{M}_\theta(\mathbf{z})$ and $\mathcal{M}_\varphi(\mathbf{z})$ models can also be used to address a conundrum associated with the propensity interpretation of probability, attributed to Popper and Peirce, as it relates to Humphrey's (1985) paradox: the propensity interpretation has a built-in *causal connection* between different events, say A and B, which renders the reverse of conditional probabilities, such as $\mathbb{P}(A \mid B)$ to $\mathbb{P}(B \mid A)$ meaningless when A is the effect and B is the cause. The paradox goes away by noting that the propensity interpretation is associated with real-world stochastic mechanisms, such as a radioactive atom has a "propensity to decay" that gives rise to stable relative frequencies. This suggests that the mechanism is viewed as a substantive model $\mathcal{M}_\varphi(\mathbf{z})$ that carries with it substantive information, including causal. Thus, even though the statistical information encapsulated in $\mathcal{M}_\theta(\mathbf{x})$ satisfies all the rules of conditional probability, in the context of $\mathcal{M}_\varphi(\mathbf{z})$ the substantive causal information imposes additional restrictions (including causal) on $\mathcal{M}_\varphi(\mathbf{x})$ which are often testable via equation (29.25) (see Spanos, 2019). Hence, there is no conflict between the frequentist and propensity interpretations of probability, as the former is germane to the statistical $\mathcal{M}_\theta(\mathbf{x})$, and the latter to the substantive model $\mathcal{M}_\varphi(\mathbf{x})$.

5.5 Revisiting the Koopmans vs. Vining Debate

Koopmans (1949), in his exchange with Vining (1949), used the historical episode of Kepler's statistical regularities concerning planetary motion to criticize the primitive state of development of empirical business cycle modeling represented by Burns and Mitchell (1946) compared to that of the theory-driven curve-fitting modeling of the Cowles Commission (see Morgan, 1990). He called the former the "Kepler stage" of empirical modeling, in contrast to the "Newton stage," where these statistical regularities were given a substantive interpretation by Newton's LUG.

Arguably, Koopmans did not draw the right lessons from this episode, in the sense that the inductive process best describing it is that of *data-to-theory,* because the statistical regularity of the elliptical motion of Mars around the sun was established based on the basis of (i) meager substantive information, but (ii) reliable statistical information using Brahe's data, and (iii) it was instrumental in inspiring Newton to devise the LUG; Newton called the elliptical motion Kepler's *first law*.

The right lesson to be learned from this episode is that a statistically adequate $\mathcal{M}_\theta(\mathbf{z})$ provides the starting point for the statistical regularities in data $\mathbf{z}_0$ that a worthy theory aiming to explain the particular phenomenon of interest needs to account for. Newton understood Kepler's statistical regularity as a launching pad for his substantive explanation in the form of the LUG.

6. Summary and Conclusions

By using a philosophy of science perspective, the preceding discussion provides a critical view of current econometric modeling and inference with a view to provide a deeper understanding of what econometricians are engaged in and what they are trying to accomplish in empirical modeling.

The primary aim of the discussion is to place econometrics in the broader statistical context of model-based statistical induction and to focus on issues that call for conceptual clarification and coherence, detect gaps in traditional econometric arguments and frame alternative conceptual perspectives. The success of current econometric methodology has been evaluated with respect to its effectiveness in giving rise to "learning from data" about economic phenomena of interest.

The overall assessment is that current econometric methodology has so far failed to shed sufficient light on economic phenomena, for several reasons. The most important is that the view of empirical modeling as curve-fitting guided by impromptu stochastic error terms and evaluated by goodness of fit will not give rise to learning from data. In hard sciences (physics, chemistry, geology, astronomy), curve-fitting is more successful due to several special features: (i) laws of nature are usually *invariant* with respect to the time and location. Their experimental investigation is (ii) guided by *reliable substantive knowledge* pertaining to the phenomenon of interest and (iii) framed in terms of tried and trusted *procedural protocols*, and (iv) empirical knowledge has a high degree of *cumulativeness*. In contrast, empirical modeling in *social sciences* pertains to (i) fickle human behavior that is not invariant to time or location. The empirical modeling in the soft sciences (including economics) is (ii) guided by tentative conjectures that are often misconstrued as *established knowledge*, (iii) by foisting a substantive model $\mathcal{M}_{\varphi}(\mathbf{z})$ on the data without validating the implicit $\mathcal{M}_{\theta}(\mathbf{z})$. (iv) The end result is invariably an estimated $\mathcal{M}_{\varphi}(\mathbf{z})$ that is *statistically and substantively misspecified*; Spanos (2007a).

To ameliorate the untrustworthiness of the evidence problem arising from curve-fitting, the traditional approach needs to be modified in ways that allow the systematic statistical information in data (chance regularities) to play a more crucial role than the subordinate one of "quantifying substantive models presumed true." Hence, the need for a much broader and more coherent modeling framework based on several nuanced distinctions, including (i) statistical vs. substantive information, model, and adequacy, (ii) statistical modeling vs. inference, (iii) factual vs. hypothetical reasoning in frequentist inference, (iv) Neyman-Pearson testing (within $\mathcal{M}_{\theta}(\mathbf{z})$) vs. M-S testing (outside $\mathcal{M}_{\theta}(\mathbf{z})$), (v) predata vs. postdata error probabilities, and (vi) untestable vs. testable probabilistic assumptions comprising $\mathcal{M}_{\theta}(\mathbf{z})$. The cornerstone of this framework is the concept of a statistical model $\mathcal{M}_{\theta}(\mathbf{z})$ and its adequacy. This is crucial because the combination of observational data and the absence of reliable substantive knowledge pertaining to the phenomenon of interest, a statistically adequate model $\mathcal{M}_{\theta}(\mathbf{z})$ can provide the basic benchmark for what a worthy substantive model $\mathcal{M}_{\varphi}(\mathbf{z})$ needs to explain to begin with.

The preceding discussion calls for certain changes in the current paradigm of econometric modeling and inference, including the overall conceptual framework, the research methods, the objectives, the professional and educational subject system, as well as the standards for what constitutes a real contribution to trustworthy evidence in applied economics. The proposed framework offers suggestions for journal editors and referees on several ways to ameliorate the untrustworthiness of published empirical evidence. First, decline forthwith papers that ignore the establishment of the adequacy of the invoked statistical model(s) by their inferences. Second, call out authors for uninformed implementation of inference procedures and unwarranted interpretations of their results. Third, demand that authors probe adequately for any potential substantive misspecifications, after the adequacy of the underlying statistical model has been secured. Fourth, demand that theoreticians ensure that the probabilistic assumptions underlying their proposed tools are testable. As argued by Rust (2016): "journals should increase the burden on econometric theory by requiring more of them to show how the new methods they propose are likely to be used and be useful for generating new empirical knowledge."

That is, the current stalemate in econometrics will improve only when an unremitting dialogue between economic theory and observed data begins to guide a systematic reexamination of the current economic and econometric methodologies, and their philosophical foundations.

Related Chapter

Peden, W., and Sprenger, J., Chapter 30 "Statistical Significance Testing in Economics"

Notes

1 Thanks are due to Julian Reiss for several comments and suggestions that improved the discussion substantially.
2 All references to Peirce are to his Collected Papers, and are cited by volume and paragraph number (see Burks, 1958).

Bibliography

Andreou, E. and A. Spanos (2003) "Statistical adequacy and the testing of trend versus difference stationarity", *Econometric Reviews*, **3**: 217–237.

Angrist, J.D. and J.S. Pischke (2008) *Mostly Harmless Econometrics: An Empiricist's Companion*, Princeton University Press, Princeton, NJ.

Angrist, J.D. and J.S. Pischke (2010) "The credibility revolution in empirical economics: How better research design is taking the con out of econometrics", *Journal of Economic Perspectives*, **24**(2): 3–30.

Berger, J.O. and R.W. Wolpert (1988) *The Likelihood Principle*, Institute of Mathematical Statistics, Lecture Notes - Monograph series, 2nd ed., vol. 6, Hayward, CA.

Billingsley, P. (1995) *Probability and Measure*, 4th ed., Wiley, New York.

Box, G.E.P. (1979) "Robustness in the strategy of scientific model building", in *Robustness in Statistics*, ed. by Launer, R.L. and G.N. Wilkinson, Academic Press, New York.

Burks, A.W., editor. (1958) *Collected Papers of Charles Sanders Peirce*, volumes I–VIII, Harvard University Press, Cambridge, MA.

Burns, A.F. and W.C. Mitchell (1946) *Measuring Business Cycles*, NBER, New York.

Canova, F. (2007) *Methods of Macroeconometric Research*, Princeton University Press, Princeton, NJ.

Choi, I. (2015) *Almost all about Unit Roots: Foundations, Developments, and Applications*, Cambridge University Press, Cambridge.

Deaton, A. (2010) "Instruments, randomization, and learning about development", *Journal of Economic Literature*, **48**(2): 424–455.

Dickhaus, T. (2018) *Theory of Nonparametric Tests*, Springer, New York.

Doob, J.L. (1953) *Stochastic Processes*, Wiley, New York.

Duhem, P. (1914) *The Aim and Structure of Physical Theory*, English translation published by Princeton University Press, Princeton, NJ.

Fisher, R.A. (1922) "On the mathematical foundations of theoretical statistics", *Philosophical Transactions of the Royal Society A*, **222**: 309–368.

Fisher, R.A. (1925) "Theory of statistical estimation", *Proceedings of the Cambridge Philosophical Society*, **22**: 700–725.

Freedman, D.A. (2010) *Statistical Models and Causal Inference,* Cambridge University Press, Cambridge.

Greene, W.H. (2018) *Econometric Analysis*, 8th ed., Prentice Hall, NJ.

Hacking, I. (1965) "Salmon's vindication of induction", *The Journal of Philosophy*, **62**(10): 260–266.

Hacking, I. (1980) "The theory of probable inference: Neyman, Peirce and Braithwaite", pp. 141–60 in *Science, Belief and Behavior: Essays in Honour of Richard B. Braithwaite*, ed. by D. Mellor, Cambridge University Press, Cambridge.

Hahn, A.J. (1998) *Basic Calculus: From Archimedes to Newton to its Role in Science*, Springer, New York.

Hajek, A. (2007) "Interpretations of probability", in *The Stanford Encyclopedia of Philosophy*, http://plato.stanford.edu/entries/probability-interpret/.

Heckman, J.J. (1997) "Instrumental variables: A study of implicit behavioral assumptions used in making program evaluations", *Journal of Human Resources*, **32**(3): 441–462.

Henderson, L. (2020) "The problem of induction", in *The Stanford Encyclopedia of Philosophy*, ed. by Edward N. Zalta, https://plato.stanford.edu/archives/spr2020/entries/induction-problem/.
Hoover, K.D. (2006) "The methodology of econometrics", pp. 61–87 in *New Palgrave Handbook of Econometrics,* vol. 1, ed. by T.C. Mills and K. Patterson, Macmillan, London.
Hume, D. (1748) *An Enquiry Concerning Human Understanding*, Oxford University Press, Oxford.
Humphreys, P. (1985) "Why propensities cannot be probabilities", *The Philosophical Review*, **94**: 557–570.
Kolmogorov, A.N. (1933) *Foundations of the Theory of Probability*, 2nd English ed., Chelsea Publishing Co., New York.
Koopmans, T.C. (1947) "Measurement without theory", *Review of Economics and Statistics*, **17**: 161–172.
Lawden, D.F. (2002) *Introduction to Tensor Calculus, Relativity and Cosmology*, Dover, New York.
Le Cam, L. (1986) *Asymptotic Methods in Statistical Decision Theory*, Springer, New York.
Lehmann, E.L. and J.P. Romano (2005) *Testing Statistical Hypotheses*, Springer, New York.
Low, H. and C. Meghir (2017) "The use of structural models in econometrics", *Journal of Economic Perspectives*, **31**(2): 33–58.
Mayo, D.G. (1996) *Error and the Growth of Experimental Knowledge*, The University of Chicago Press, Chicago.
Mayo, D.G. and A. Spanos (2004) "Methodology in practice: Statistical misspecification testing", *Philosophy of Science*, **71**: 1007–1025.
Mayo, D.G. and A. Spanos (2006) "Severe testing as a basic concept in a Neyman-Pearson philosophy of induction", *The British Journal for the Philosophy of Science,* **57**: 323–357.
Mayo, D.G. and A. Spanos (eds.) (2010) *Error and Inference: Recent Exchanges on Experimental Reasoning, Reliability and the Objectivity and Rationality of Science*, Cambridge University Press, Cambridge.
Mayo, D.G. and A. Spanos (2011), "Error Statistics", pp. 151–196 in the *Handbook of Philosophy of Science*, vol. 7: Philosophy of Statistics, D. Gabbay, P. Thagard, and J. Woods (editors), Elsevier.
McGuirk, A. and A. Spanos (2009) "Revisiting error autocorrelation correction: Common factor restrictions and granger non-causality", *Oxford Bulletin of Economics and Statistics,* **71**: 273–294.
Mills, F.C. (1924) *Statistical Methods*, Henry Holt and Co., New York.
Morgan, M.S. (1990) *The History of Econometric Ideas*, Cambridge University Press, Cambridge.
Neyman, J. (1937) "Outline of a theory of statistical estimation based on the classical theory of probability", *Philosophical Transactions of the Royal Statistical Society of London*, A, **236**: 333–380.
Neyman, J. (1952) *Lectures and Conferences on Mathematical Statistics and Probability*, 2nd ed., U.S. Department of Agriculture, Washington, DC.
Neyman, J. and E.S. Pearson (1933) "On the problem of the most efficient tests of statistical hypotheses", *Phil. Trans. of the Royal Society, A,* **231**: 289–337.
Pagan, A.R. (1987) "Three econometric methodologies: A critical appraisal", *Journal of Economic Surveys,* **1**: 3–24. Reprinted in C.W.J. Granger (1990).
Phillips, P.C.B. and Z. Xiao (1998) "A primer on unit root testing", *Journal of Economic Surveys*, **12**: 423–470.
Qin, D. (1993) *The Formation of Econometrics: A Historical Perspective*, Clarendon Press, Oxford.
Reiss, J. (2008) *Error in Economics: Towards a More Evidence–Based Methodology*, Routledge, New York.
Reiss, J. (2013) *Philosophy of Economics: A Contemporary Introduction*, Routledge, New York.
Reiss, J. (2015) *Causation, Evidence, and Inference,* Routledge, New York.
Rust, J. (2016) "Mostly useless econometrics? Assessing the causal effect of econometric theory", pp. 23–34 in *Causal Inferences in Capital Markets Research*, edited by Iván Marinovic, NOW, Hanover, MA.
Salmon, W. (1967) *The Foundations of Scientific Inference*, University of Pittsburgh Press, Pittsburgh, PA.
Spanos, A. (1986) *Statistical Foundations of Econometric Modelling*, Cambridge University Press, Cambridge.
Spanos, A. (2006a) "Econometrics in retrospect and prospect", pp. 3–58 in *New Palgrave Handbook of Econometrics*, vol. 1, ed. by T.C. Mills and K. Patterson, Macmillan, London.
Spanos, A. (2006b) "Where do statistical models come from? Revisiting the problem of specification", pp. 98–119 in *Optimality: The Second Erich L. Lehmann Symposium*, edited by J. Rojo, Lecture Notes-Monograph Series, vol. 49, Institute of Mathematical Statistics.
Spanos, A. (2006c) "Revisiting the omitted variables argument: Substantive vs. statistical adequacy", *Journal of Economic Methodology*, **13**: 179–218.
Spanos, A. (2007a) "Curve-fitting, the reliability of inductive inference and the error-statistical approach", *Philosophy of Science*, **74**: 1046–1066.
Spanos, A. (2007b) "The instrumental variables method revisited: On the nature and choice of optimal instruments", pp. 34–59 in *Refinement of Econometric Estimation and Test Procedures*, ed. by G.D.A. Phillips and E. Tzavalis, Cambridge University Press, Cambridge.
Spanos, A. (2009) "The pre-eminence of theory versus the European CVAR perspective in macroeconometric modeling", *Economics: The Open-Access, Open-Assessment E-Journal,* **3**, 2009–10, http://www.economics-ejournal.org/economics/journalarticles/2009-10.

Spanos, A. (2010a) "Statistical adequacy and the trustworthiness of empirical evidence: Statistical vs. substantive information", *Economic Modelling*, **27**: 1436–1452.
Spanos, A. (2010b) "Akaike-type criteria and the reliability of inference: Model selection vs. statistical model specification", *Journal of Econometrics*, **158**: 204–220.
Spanos, A. (2010c) "Theory testing in economics and the error statistical perspective", pp. 202–246 in *Error and Inference*, edited by D.G. Mayo and A. Spanos (2010).
Spanos, A. (2011) "Revisiting unit root testing in the context of an AR(1) model with variance heterogeneity", Virginia Tech working paper.
Spanos, A. (2012) "Philosophy of econometrics", pp. 329–393 in *Philosophy of Economics*, ed. by U. Maki, in the series *Handbook of Philosophy of Science*, Elsevier (eds.) D. Gabbay, P. Thagard, and J. Woods.
Spanos, A. (2013) "A frequentist interpretation of probability for model-based inductive inference", *Synthese*, **190**: 1555–1585.
Spanos, A. (2015) "Revisiting Haavelmo's structural econometrics: Bridging the gap between theory and data", *Journal of Economic Methodology*, **22**: 171–196.
Spanos, A. (2017) "Why the decision-theoretic perspective misrepresents frequentist inference", chapter 1, pp. 3–28 in *Advances in Statistical Methodologies and Their Applications to Real Problems*, ISBN 978-953-51-4962-0.
Spanos, A. (2018) "Mis-specification testing in retrospect", *Journal of Economic Surveys*, **32**(2): 541–577.
Spanos, A. (2019) *Introduction to Probability Theory and Statistical Inference: Empirical Modeling with Observational Data*, 2nd ed., Cambridge University Press, Cambridge.
Spanos, A. (2020) "Yule–Simpson's paradox: The probabilistic versus the empirical conundrum", *Statistical Methods & Applications*, https://doi.org/10.1007/s10260-020-00536-4.
Spanos, A. and A. McGuirk (2001) "The model specification problem from a probabilistic reduction perspective", *Journal of the American Agricultural Association*, **83**: 1168–1176.
Spanos, A. and J.J. Reade (2015) "Heteroskedasticity/autocorrelation consistent standard errors and the reliability of inference", VT working paper.
Vining, R. and T.C. Koopmans (1949) "Methodological issues in quantitative economics", *Review of Economics and Statistics*, **31**: 77–94.
Von Mises, R. (1928/1957) *Probability, Statistics and Truth*, Dover, New York.
Wasserman, L. (2006) *All of Nonparametric Statistics*, Springer, New York.
Wooldridge, J.M. (2010) *Econometric Analysis of Cross Section and Panel Data*, 2nd ed., MIT Press, Cambridge, MA.
Yule, G.U. (1916) *An Introduction to the Theory of Statistics*, 3rd ed., Griffin, London.

30

STATISTICAL SIGNIFICANCE TESTING IN ECONOMICS

William Peden and Jan Sprenger

1. Introduction

The origins of testing scientific models with statistical techniques go back to 18th-century mathematics. However, the modern theory of statistical testing was primarily developed through the work of Sir R.A. Fisher, Jerzy Neyman, and Egon Pearson in the interwar period. Some of Fisher's papers on testing were published in economics journals (Fisher, 1923, 1935) and exerted a notable influence on the discipline. The development of econometrics and the rise of quantitative economic models in the mid-20th century made statistical significance testing a commonplace, albeit controversial, tool within economics.

In the debate about significance testing, methodological controversies intertwine with epistemological issues and sociological developments. Our aim in this chapter is to explain these connections and to show how the use of, and the debate about, significance testing in economics differs from other social sciences, such as psychology.

Section 2 explains the basic principles of statistical significance testing with particular attention to its use in economics. In Section 3, we sketch how significance testing became entrenched in economics, and we highlight some early criticisms. Section 4 deals with Ziliak and McCloskey's criticism that significance tests, and the economists who apply them, confuse statistical and proper economic significance (i.e., effect size). Section 5 relates significance testing to the problem of publication bias in science and compares the debates about significance testing in economics and in psychology. Section 6 wraps up and briefly discusses some suggestions for methodological improvement.

2. Statistical Significance Testing

There are two grand traditions of interpreting statistical testing procedures. Jerzy Neyman and Egon Pearson's behavioral *decision-theoretic approach* contrasts two competing hypotheses, the "null" hypothesis H and the "alternative" H, and conceptualizes statistical tests as an instrument for controlling the rate of erroneous decisions in rejecting or accepting one of them. Although such decision-theoretic formalisms have a natural affinity to rational choice theory and economic reasoning, econometric testing generally follows R.A. Fisher's *evidential approach* (Fisher, 1935/74, 1956) based on an interpretation of low p-values as evidence against the tested hypothesis.

We shall start by explaining Fisher's approach. For Fisher, the purpose of statistical analysis consists of assessing the relation of a null hypothesis H to a body of observed data. That hypothesis usually

DOI: 10.4324/9781315739793-37

stands for there being no effect of interest, no causal relationship between two variables, or simply as a scientific default assumption. For example, suppose we run a simple linear regression model $y = \alpha + \beta x + E$ (with IID[1] error term E), where the data points x and y are paired realizations of the quantities of interest X and Y. A possible null hypothesis would be H: $\beta = 0$, claiming that there is no systematic relationship between the variables X and Y. McCloskey and Ziliak (1996, 98) give the example of a regression analysis for purchasing power, comparing prices of goods abroad to those at home: $\beta = 1$ (and $\alpha = 0$) would then express a perfect match between home prices (X) and abroad prices (Y), modulo random error.

Testing of such null hypotheses for compatibility with the data is called a **null hypothesis significance test (NHST)**. The alternative hypothesis H is typically unspecific and expresses the presence of an effect that differs from the hypothesized null effect (e.g., H: $\beta = 0$ if the null is H: $\beta = 0$). Now, the basic rationale of significance tests is that results that fall into the extreme tails of the probability distribution postulated by the null hypothesis H compromise its tenability: "either an exceptionally rare chance has occurred, or the theory [=the null hypothesis] is not true" (Fisher, 1956, 39). The occurrence of such an exceptionally rare event has both epistemological and practical consequences: first, the null hypothesis is rendered "objectively incredible" (Spielman, 1974, 214); second, the null should be treated as if it were false.

Fisher's ideas are close to Popper's falsificationism (Popper, 2002). They agree that the only purpose of an experiment is to "give the facts a chance of disproving the null hypothesis" (Fisher, 1935/74, 16). They also agree that failure to reject a hypothesis does not conclude positive evidence for the tested (null) hypothesis. However, while Popper gives a negative characterization of scientific knowledge, Fisher uses statistical tests to give a positive account of experimental knowledge: the existence of causal effects can be *demonstrated* experimentally by means of (statistically) rejecting the hypothesis that the observed effect occurred due to chance.

The central concept of modern significance tests – the p-value – is now illustrated in a two-sided testing problem. Suppose we want to infer whether the mean θ of an unknown distribution is significantly different from the null value H: $\theta = \theta$. We observe data x: = $(x, \ldots, x)$, corresponding to N IID realizations of an experiment with (unknown) population mean θ and (known) variance σ^2. Then, one measures the discrepancy in the data x with respect to the postulated mean value θ using

$$\text{standardized statistic } z(x) := \frac{\frac{1}{N}\Sigma_{i=1}^{N} x_i - \theta_0}{\sqrt{N\ \sigma^2}} \tag{30.1}$$

We may reinterpret equation (1) as

$$z = \frac{\text{observed effect - hypothesized effect}}{\text{standard error}} \tag{30.2}$$

The p-value then depends on the probability distribution of z given the null hypothesis:

$$p := p_{H_0}\left(\left|z(X)\right| \geq \left|z(x)\right|\right) \tag{30.3}$$

or in other words, the p-value describes the probability of observing a more extreme discrepancy under the null than that actually observed. The lower the p-value, that is, the more the observed effect diverges from the effect postulated by the null hypothesis, the less the null hypothesis explains the data.

Such *p*-values or "observed significance levels" play a large role in econometrics: they serve as an indicator of whether a finding is noteworthy, interesting, and ultimately publishable. Moreover, the conventional classification into various levels of significance is used for annotating correlation tables and for making them more readable: one asterisk behind an entry corresponds to $p <. 05$ ("significant"), two asterisks correspond to $p <. 01$ ("highly significant"), and three asterisks correspond to $p <. 001$ ("very highly significant"). It is primarily this suggestive annotation practice that has attracted trenchant criticism in the past decades, because it obliterates the differences between statistical and genuine scientific significance. Before entering this debate, however, we first review the history of significance testing in econometrics and some early debates. Specifically, we illustrate how the methodological controversies raised by significance testing are philosophically interesting, and we show that issues in the philosophy of statistics are consequential for important issues in economics.

3. Early Debates About Significance Testing in Econometrics

3.1 Econometrics and the Tinbergen Debates

We start with an important distinction between *economic statistics* and *econometrics*. Economic statistics consists of gathering and formulating descriptive statistical information about economic facts. By contrast, econometrics is the use of inferential statistics to formulate answers to theoretical questions, such as "Are interest rates procyclical?" or "Is the fiscal multiplier greater than unity?" (see Spanos, Chapter 29).

The Tinbergen debates occurred quite early in the history of econometrics. Jan Tinbergen was a Dutch economist who in 1936 had already constructed the first econometric model of the business cycle. In a study for the League of Nations, Tinbergen sought to popularize his approach to econometric research, to apply it to modeling actual economies, and to test a theory of the business cycle with these data. His approach to statistics was typical of the spirit of the day: econometrics cannot not prove economic theories right, but it could prove that a theory is incorrect (Tinbergen, 1939, 12). Tinbergen applied a large number of goodness-of-fit tests of statistical significance to the equations of his models (Morgan, 1990, 108–120). His approach was sophisticated, and he might easily have expected a positive reaction from his contemporary business cycle theorists.

He would have been wrong. John Maynard Keynes (1939) scathingly criticized Tinbergen's research and stated that the results of Tinbergen's statistical work "probably have no value" (Keynes, 1939, 559). Keynes's principal objections were that Tinbergen's work failed to meet some requirements that Keynes considered to be vital: (1) full knowledge of the causally relevant factors; (2) these causal factors must be measurable and mutually independent; (3) the relationships must be linear; and (4) one must know the relevant time lags and trends. Keynes thought that these conditions were more or less never met in economics, so he saw practically no role for significance testing by econometricians. This criticism led to a brief series of exchanges between Tinbergen (1940a, 1940b)[2] and Keynes (1940), with other economists joining in. Mary S. Morgan (1990, 123–124) argues that an underlying epistemological issue in the Tinbergen debates was a disagreement between Tinbergen and Keynes on the potential function of statistical testing: for Keynes, its only possible role was to identify the strength of factors within a causal framework that had already been developed by theoretical analysis; for Tinbergen, statistical testing could also inform – though not determine – the theoretical analysis. This antagonism resurfaces in later critiques of significance testing by Ziliak and McCloskey.

There were other methodological debates that arose out of Tinbergen's work in the late 1930s (e.g., Haavelmo, 1940). For instance, in a 1940 letter, Oskar Lange argued that Tinbergen's results lacked "statistical significance" because he had failed to take serial correlation (i.e., autocorrelation, a positive or negative association between a variable and its future or past values) into account, and serial correlation is exactly one of the reasons why we want a business cycle model in the first place. Hence, Lange thought that Tinbergen's methods were either flawed or redundant (Louçã, 2007; Orcutt and Irwin, 1948). This criticism illustrates how some economists in the 1940s used "statistical significance" to refer to an *epistemic achievement*, rather than its contemporary sense of controlling error rates or p-values below a certain level (typically 0.05).

Another example was the reaction of a young Milton Friedman:

> Tinbergen's results cannot be judged by ordinary tests of statistical significance. The reason is that the variables with which he winds up, the particular series measuring these variables, the leads and lags, and various other aspects of the equations besides the particular values of the parameters (which alone can be tested by the usual statistical technique) have been selected after an extensive process of trial and error *because* they yield high coefficients of correlation [with that sample data].
>
> (Friedman, 1940, 659)

Here, Friedman is contending that statistical significance tests of an economic model are only appropriate if they are out-of-sample tests.[3] Unlike Keynes, Friedman thought that significance testing had a potential function within theory choice. However, he regarded work like Tinbergen's as useful only for identifying whether models are worth testing further with more data (Friedman, 1940, 660). In Hans Reichenbach's terminology, Friedman saw in-sample testing as limited to the "context of discovery," where we *develop* economic theories, and not the "context of justification," where we *evaluate* theories on the basis on their theoretical and empirical merits (Reichenbach, 1938). The methodological value of out-of-sample testing continues to be debated in economics (Gelfond and Murphy, 2016).

3.2. The "Con" in Econometrics

Economists were always somewhat skeptical of post-World War II econometrics. However, the end of postwar economic stability in the 1970s and poor performance of econometric models during that decade encouraged intense methodological reflections (Hayek, 1989; Hendry, 1980; Lucas, 1976; Sims, 1980). One of the most important was Edward Leamer's "Let's Take the Con Out of Econometrics" (Leamer, 1983). Leamer covers many methodological issues, but his general critique is that significance testing in econometrics normally involves a large number of often unrealistic assumptions, for example, that the model's error terms are uncorrelated. Due to the influential instrumentalist manifesto of Milton Friedman (1953), economists are generally comfortable with unrealistic assumptions. However, if the data are relevant to the model *only in conjunction with unrealistic assumptions*, then these assumptions can no longer be regarded as useful idealizations or be used as such in statistical testing. Leamer grants that the assumptions may be *approximately true*, but the results of the test then depend on their exact details. Therefore, Leamer recommends (and helped develop) sensitivity analysis: given that economic theory or background knowledge cannot uniquely specify the statistical assumptions to make in our tests, we should report the consequences of adopting various assumptions. This will help identify test results that are very sensitive to particular assumptions and increase the robustness of our statistical practices. Although Leamer's paper has been cited thousands of times, he is unimpressed by subsequent efforts toward more robust significance testing in econometrics (Leamer, 2010).

Leamer also advocates a subjective Bayesian methodology over the (alleged) objectivity of classical significance testing. One of his reasons is that even sophisticated econometric models can easily be tested using modern computers. This makes some types of statistical malpractice much easier

(Leamer, 1983, 36–37). Before the 1970s, the testing of complex econometric models was extraordinarily difficult or even impossible. This changed in the early 1970s, transforming econometric practice. While this transformation was useful in many ways, it also created methodological hazards, as Leamer (1983) noted: computational limitations had been a partial shield against *p-hacking*, that is, the use of questionable research practices (e.g., selective reporting of studies, removing outliers, adding further covariates) in order to obtain a statistically significant result (i.e., $p < .05$). In a context where a test could take weeks or months, even with the aid of computers, statistically significant results were genuinely surprising and systematic *p*-hacking was not feasible. Modern computers can carry out analogous tests in seconds, so statistically significant results are less surprising for economists. There is also some empirical evidence of *p*-hacking in economics (Brodeur et al., 2016). We discuss strategies to counteract this danger in Section 5.

4. The Cult of Statistical Significance? Effect Size vs. *p*-Values

Another forceful criticism of significance tests concerns their relation to effect size and the confusion between *p*-values and proper effect size measures. The economists Deirdre McCloskey and Stephen Ziliak (henceforth, ZMC) have made this point in a series of papers and books (McCloskey and Ziliak, 1996; Ziliak and McCloskey, 2004, 2008). We illustrate the difference with one of their favorite examples (Ziliak and McCloskey, 2008, ch. 1). Assume that we have to choose between diet pills A and B. Pill A makes us lose 10 pounds on average, with an average variation of 5 pounds.[4] Pill B makes us lose 3 pounds on average, with an average variation of 1 pound. Which one leads to a more significant loss? Naturally, we opt for pill A because the effect of the cure is so much larger.

However, if we translate the example back into significance testing, the order is reversed. Assume the standard deviations are known for both pills. Compared to the null hypothesis of no effect at all, a 3-pound weight loss after taking pill B is a more significant result, as evidence for the efficacy of that cure, than a 10-pound weight loss after taking pill A:

$$z_A(10) = \frac{10-0}{5} = 2 \qquad z_B(3) = \frac{3-0}{1} = 3$$

Thus, there is a notable discrepancy between our intuitive judgment and that suggested by the *p*-values. This occurs because statistical significance is supposed to be "a measure of the strength of the signal relative to background noise" (Hoover and Siegler, 2008, 58). On this score, pill B indeed performs better than pill A. According to ZMC, however, economists and policymakers are primarily interested in the effect size, not the signal/noise ratio: they do not want to ascertain the presence of *some* effect but to demonstrate a *substantial* effect. Due to the importance of the latter for practical decisions and economic policy – ZMC call this "policy oomph" – we should actually focus on *practically meaningful effect sizes* rather than significance levels. The former can be measured by standardized regression coefficients or specific statistics such as Cohen's d or Pearson's r^2 (for the strength of correlations), but not by *p*-values. An effect need not be statistically significant to be big and remarkable (like pill A), and a statistically significant effect can be quite small and uninteresting (like pill B).

This fundamental difference is, however, frequently neglected: in practice, the level of significance often acts as a cue to scientific importance [compare Cohen (1994) for a similar diagnosis in psychology]. By scrutinizing the statistical practice in the top journal, *American Economic Review*, as well as by surveying the opinions of economists on the meaning of statistical significance, McCloskey and Ziliak (1996) derive the conclu sion that statistical concepts and tools are frequently abused. For example, researchers tend to confound economic with statistical significance (70% of the papers do not make an explicit distinction), relate effect sizes to the scientific context (72%), or engage in "sign econometrics," where the sign, but not the size, of a coefficient is commented on (53%).

Worse still, there has been no visible improvement over time. According to ZMC, the discussion in statistics and methodology journals has done little to nothing to alleviate the problems, because the proportion of articles with questionable use of significance tests has not decreased over time (Ziliak and McCloskey, 2004, 2008).

ZMC's critique of significance testing can be summarized as follows: (1) significance tests encourage reasoning fallacies (e.g., statistical significance = null hypothesis refuted or effect economically meaningful); (2) they are not a suitable tool for economic analysis (because they do not aim at effect size or "policy oomph"); and (3) they give rise to a culture of mindless use of statistical inference without proper considerations of economic and policy implications (see also Gigerenzer, 2004). Few statistics or econometric textbooks highlight this difference, thus preventing the proper appreciation of the limits of significance tests in upcoming generations.

The echo of ZMC's work in the economic community and beyond was mainly positive, but not exclusively so. For eminent statisticians like Arnold Zellner or methodologists like Nathan Berg (2004), Edward Leamer (2004), and Bruce Thompson (2004), the critique of (the mindless use of) NHSTs fits into a broader project of changing and improving scientific method. Even if they do not all agree about the right direction for the future, they agree that NHSTs are flawed and need to be replaced. A second group agrees with ZMC on their central points, but nuance their criticism. For example, Joel Horowitz (2004) observes that significance testing, with all its problems, may well be inevitable when we want to test whether an economic model is well specified or when we are interested in the *existence* of an effect rather than its magnitude. Finally, a third group (e.g., Elliott and Granger, 2004; Hoover and Siegler, 2008) defends NHSTs and argues that (1) testing theories is inevitable; (2) there is a need for a nonsubjective method of theory testing and NHSTs provide it; (3) ZMC's focus on effect size is not without problems (e.g., it does not adequately quantify the uncertainty of the estimate); and (4) misuse of procedures is not unique to NHSTs but occurs in all parts of statistical reasoning. The view expressed in the last point is also shared by Gigerenzer (2004), who warns that the shift to another framework (e.g., Bayesian reasoning) may just lead to a reiteration of mindless statistical inferences with different tools.[5]

5. New Challenges: Publication Bias, the Replication Crisis, and Comparison with Psychology

The last years have seen increasing distrust in scientific findings due to concerns about publication bias and lack of replicability. Publication bias means bias in what is published with respect to what is researched, and it is related to significance tests because they often act as gatekeeper for whether a finding is "interesting" or "publishable." The standard approach to significance tests makes it hard to interpret nonsignificant results or to draw any substantive inference from them. By contrast, as shown by ZMC, it is easy to lure oneself into identifying a statistically significant result with an important scientific finding. While this mechanism of suppressing nonsignificant results, called the *file drawer effect*, and its impact on the published literature, was identified long ago in theoretical models (e.g., Ioannidis, 2005; Rosenthal, 1979; Rozeboom, 1960; Sterling, 1959), it has been ignored by many economists for a long time, especially by those not involved in methodological debates. Recently, the severity of the problem has been demonstrated by systematic replication projects for experimental findings in psychology, medicine, and economics, revealing a disappointingly low replication rate in all featured disciplines [e.g., Open Science Collaboration (2015) for psychology and Camerer et al. (2016) for experimental economics].

The problem is not only that significance tests lead to a depreciation of nonsignificant findings (even if they are methodologically sound) but that researchers often use questionable research methods, such as selective reporting of results, adding covariates, or eliminating outliers, in order to obtain a significant (and therefore publishable) finding. Such p-hacking is easy to achieve with modern computational tools.

Meta-analytic techniques such as funnel plots and p-curves have provided evidence of publication bias in various research areas (Simonsohn et al., 2014; Weiß and Wagner, 2011); the file drawer effect and p-hacking are plausible causes of these findings. Specifically in economics, Brodeur et al. (2016) have found a two-humped distribution of p-values, suggesting not only an excess of just-significant results but also that researchers try to "work away" ambiguous significant p-values either toward significance or toward clear nonsignificance. Crucially, one need not assume mischievous or badly trained researchers for explaining such findings – complex data analysis problems require many judgment calls, and researchers may be unconsciously influenced by their own biases and incentives when making such decisions.

Olken (2015) discusses compulsory preregistration of the data analysis plan (i.e., before data are collected or analyzed) as an antidote to p-hacking and *HARKing* – that is, hypothesizing after the results are known and relabeling exploratory as confirmatory research. Researchers complying with such a plan would decide in advance on primary and secondary outcome variables, measurement scales, statistical tests, covariates, and so on, to minimize the potential for p-hacking. However, Olken's judgment is mixed: while such plans may be both efficient and feasible for controlled trials in psychology or medicine, econometric data analysis typically deals with complex data sets and a high number of secondary outcome variables and aims at unraveling hidden theoretical mechanisms. The trade-off between lack of bias, efficiency, and nuance implied by compulsory preregistration may be nontrivial in economics. Finally, the registered reports model, where the publication of an article is decided on the basis of the research question (e.g., Chambers, 2013), the experimental design, and the data analysis plan, may help to counter the file drawer effect and publication bias for disciplines where simply structured, controlled trials are the norm (e.g., medicine, psychology). However, it is not easily transferable to the type of (observational) data analysis that economists typically undertake.

Compared to economists, psychologists worry more about flawed incentives in their discipline and the shortcomings of significance tests (e.g., Bakker et al., 2012; Cumming, 2012; Schmidt, 1996). They have a tradition of critically reflecting on NHST and relating it to philosophical questions that is almost absent in economics (e.g., Cohen, 1994; Meehl, 1967). However, in psychology, the scathing criticisms of significance tests also have *not* led to an abolition of that practice, even if significance levels are now routinely accompanied by standard errors and effect size estimates. Where does this inertia come from? Why does the persuasive force of pro-reform arguments not result in real change? Martin Altman (2004) and Bruce Thompson (2004) identify various sources, which may also play a role in economics. The problem is not a lack of awareness or knowledge distribution but a lack of willingness to implement them at anything faster than an excruciatingly slow pace, if at all. Barriers to change may be the time delay caused by the bureaucratic constraints on procedures within large professional associations such as the American Economic Association (AEA) and the American Psychological Association (APA), fear of the cognitive dissonance that would result from giving up a practice that one has followed for ages, and lack of commitment on behalf of key figures such as senior practitioners and editors-in-chief of major journals, who could "force" authors to abide by more sophisticated procedures. We are curious whether the sense of urgency created by the replication crisis and the evidence of p-hacking and the publication crisis leads to genuine methodological reform and to more sustainable statistical practice.

6. Conclusion

Significance testing in economics has been hotly contested from its very beginnings. However, the focal points of the criticism have shifted. Early criticisms, like those found in the Tinbergen-Keynes-Friedman debate, sustained that the assumptions of significance tests are seldom, if ever, met for economic data. While unrealistic assumptions are common in economic modeling, they invalidate significance tests, according to critics, when they are the crucial nexus between the tested theoretical model and the data.

These criticisms did not prevent significance testing from becoming a highly influential and widespread tool in economics, and in econometrics in particular. And widespread use came with frequent misuse, especially when *p*-values became standard measures of statistical evidence. Critics like ZMC object that statistical significance levels are not good indicators of actual relevance for economic policy decisions (because the *p*-value by itself is not an indicator of effect size). According to ZMC, this confusion has created a lot of damage to economic science and to society as a whole. Recently, the debate about significance testing has developed a new twist due to increasing evidence of *p*-hacking and questionable research practices and doubts about the replicability and trustworthiness of research findings. These phenomena were first identified in other sciences, such as psychology and medicine, but they are a problem for economics, too.

Responses to these challenges can be grouped into three categories (e.g., Romero, 2019): (1) *statistical reform*, such as the use of confidence intervals and Bayesian models; (2) *methodological reform*, such as preregistration of experiments and data analysis plans; and (3) *social reform*, such as changing institutions to reward scientists who produce confirmatory research and nonsignificant findings. Which combination of these three approaches is the best reply to save the reliability of significance testing in economics is an exciting question for future research.

Related Chapter

Spanos, A., Chapter 29 "Philosophy of Econometrics"

Notes

1 For convenience, "independent and identically distributed" will be abbreviated as "IID."
2 Anticipating some later comments about statistical significance and economic significance, Tinbergen (1940b, 143–145) distinguishes between "statistical independence" – the absence of a correlation between variables – and "economic independence" – a type of *causal* independence.
3 That is, the models are not tested with the same data used to estimate their parameters.
4 The concept of "average variation" is intuitively explicated as the statistical concept of standard deviation, which is, for a random variable X, defined as $\sqrt{E\left[(X-E(X))^2\right]}$.
5 However, surveys of statistical research practice suggest that fallacious interpretations of inference procedures are particularly frequent for NHSTs as compared to confidence intervals or Bayesian inference (e.g., Cumming, 2012; Fidler, 2005).

Bibliography

Altman, M. (2004). Statistical significance, path dependency, and the culture of journal publication. *The Journal of Socio-Economics*, 33(5):651–663.

Bakker, M., Wicherts, J., and van Dijk, A. (2012). The rules of the game called psychological science. *Perspectives on Psychological Science*, 7:543–554.

Berg, N. (2004). No-decision classification: An alternative to testing for statistical significance. *The Journal of Socio-Economics*, 33(5):631–650.

Brodeur, A., Lé, M., Sangnier, M., and Zylberberg, Y. (2016). Star wars: The empirics strike back. *American Economic Journal: Applied Economics*, 8(1):1–32.

Camerer, C. F., Dreber, A., Forsell, E., Ho, T.-H., Huber, J., Johannesson, M., Kirchler, M., Almenberg, J., Altmejd, A., Chan, T., Heikensten, E., Holzmeister, F., Imai, T., Isaksson, S., Nave, G., Pfeiffer, T., Razen, M., and Wu, H. (2016). Evaluating replicability of laboratory experiments in economics. *Science*, 351(6280):1433–1436.

Chambers, C. D. (2013). Registered reports: A new publishing initiative at Cortex. *Cortex*, 49:609–610.

Cohen, J. (1994). The earth is round (*p* <. 05). *Psychological Review*, 49:997–1003.

Cumming, G. (2012). *Understanding the New Statistics*. Routledge, New York.

Elliott, G. and Granger, C. W. (2004). Evaluating significance: Comments on "size matters". *The Journal of Socio-Economics*, 33(5):547–550.

Fidler, F. (2005). *From Statistical Significance to Effect Estimation: Statistical Reform in Psychology, Medicine and Ecology*. PhD Thesis, Department of History and Philosophy of Science, The University of Melbourne.

Fisher, R. (1923). Statistical tests of agreement between observation and hypothesis. *Economica*, (8):139–147.

Fisher, R. (1935). The mathematical distributions used in the common tests of significance. *Econometrica*, 3(4):353–365.

Fisher, R. A. (1935/74). *The Design of Experiments*. Hafner Press, New York. Reprint of the ninth edition from 1971. Originally published in 1935 (Edinburgh: Oliver & Boyd).

Fisher, R. A. (1956). *Statistical Methods and Scientific Inference*. Hafner, New York.

Friedman, M. (1940). Review of "business cycles in the United States of America, 1919–1932" by J. Tinbergen. *American Economic Review*, 30(3):657–660.

Friedman, M. (1953). *Essays in Positive Economics*. University of Chicago Press., Chicago.

Gelfond, R. and Murphy, R. H. (2016). A call for out-of-sample testing in macroeconomics. *Libertas: Segunda Epoca*, 1(1):1–1.

Gigerenzer, G. (2004). Mindless statistics. *The Journal of Socio-Economics*, 33(5):587–606.

Haavelmo, T. (1940). The inadequacy of testing dynamic theory by comparing theoretical solutions and observed cycle. *Econometrica*, 8(4):312–321.

Hayek, F. v. (1989). The pretence of knowledge (Nobel lecture). *American Economic Review*, 79(6):3–7.

Hendry, D. F. (1980). Econometrics – alchemy or science? *Economica*, 47(188):387–406.

Hoover, K. D. and Siegler, M. V. (2008). Sound and fury: McCloskey and significance testing in economics. *Journal of Economic Methodology*, 15(1):1–37.

Horowitz, J. L. (2004). Comments on "size matters". *The Journal of Socio-Economics*, 33(5):551–554.

Ioannidis, J. P. A. (2005). Why most published research findings are false. *PLoS Medicine*, 2.

Keynes, J. M. (1939). Professor Tinbergen's method. *The Economic Journal*, 49(195):558–577.

Keynes, J. M. (1940). On a method of statistical business-cycle research. A comment. *The Economic Journal*, 50(197):154–156.

Leamer, E. E. (1983). Let's take the con out of econometrics. *American Economic Review*, 73(1):31–43.

Leamer, E. E. (2004). Are the roads red? comments on "size matters". *The Journal of SocioEconomics*, 33(5):555–557.

Leamer, E. E. (2010). Tantalus on the road to asymptopia. *Journal of Economic Perspectives*, 24(2):31–46.

Louçã, F. (2007). *The years of high econometrics: A short history of the generation that reinvented economics*. Routledge, London and New York.

Lucas, R. E. (1976). Econometric policy evaluation: A critique. In *Carnegie-Rochester conference series on public policy*, volume 1. Elsevier Science Publishers B. V., North Holland, pages 19–46.

McCloskey, D. and Ziliak, S. (1996). The standard error of regressions. *Journal of Economic Literature*, 34(1):97–114.

Meehl, P. E. (1967). Theory-testing in psychology and physics: A methodological paradox. *Philosophy of Science*, 34:103–115.

Morgan, M. (1990). *The History of Econometric Ideas*. Cambridge University Press, Cambridge.

Olken, B. A. (2015). Promises and perils of pre-analysis plans. *Journal of Economic Perspectives*, 29(3):61–80.

Open Science Collaboration (2015). Estimating the reproducibility of psychological science. *Science*, 349. Retrieved from http://science.sciencemag.org/content/349/6251/aac4716.full.pdf.

Orcutt, G. and Irwin, J. (1948). A study of the autoregressive nature of the time series used for Tinbergen's model of the economic system of the united states, 1919–1932. *Journal of the Royal Statistical Society. Series B*, 10(1):1–53.

Popper, K. R. (1959/2002). *The Logic of Scientific Discovery*. Routledge, London. Reprint of the revised English 1959 edition. Originally published in German in 1934 as "Logik der Forschung".

Reichenbach, H. (1938). *Experience and Prediction. An Analysis of the Foundations and the Structure of Knowledge*. The University of Chicago Press, Chicago.

Romero, F. (2019). Philosophy of science and the replicability crisis. *Philosophy Compass*, 14:e12633.

Rosenthal, R. (1979). The file drawer problem and tolerance for null results. *Psychological Bulletin*, 86(3):638–641.

Rozeboom, W. W. (1960). The fallacy of the null-hypothesis significance test. *Psychological Bulletin*, 57:416–442.

Schmidt, F. (1996). Statistical significance testing and cumulative knowledge in psychology: Implications for training of researchers. *Psychological Methods*, 1:115–129.

Simonsohn, U., Nelson, L. D., and Simmons, J. P. (2014). *P* curve: A key to the file drawer. *Journal of Experimental Psychology: General*, 143:534–547.

Sims, C. A. (1980). Macroeconomics and reality. *Econometrica: Journal of the Econometric Society*, 1–48.

Spielman, S. (1974). The logic of tests of significance. *Philosophy of Science*, 41(3):211–226.

Sterling, T. D. (1959). Publication decisions and their possible effects on inferences drawn from tests of significance – or vice versa. *Journal of the American Statistical Association*, 54:30–34.

Thompson, B. (2004). The "significance" crisis in psychology and education. *The Journal of Socio-Economics*, 33(5):607–613.

Tinbergen, J. (1939). Statistical testing of business – cycle theories. Technical report, League of Nations Economic Intelligence Service., Geneva.

Tinbergen, J. (1940a). Econometric business cycle research. *Review of Economic Studies*, 7(2):73–90.

Tinbergen, J. (1940b). On a method of statistical business-cycle research. A reply. *The Economic Journal*, 50(197):141–154.

Weiß, B. and Wagner, M. (2011). The identification and prevention of publication bias in the social sciences and economics. *Jahrbücher für Nationalokonomie und Statistik*, 231:661–684.

Ziliak, S. T. and McCloskey, D. N. (2004). Size matters: The standard error of regressions in the American economic review. *The Journal of Socio-Economics*, 33(5):527–546.

Ziliak, S. T. and McCloskey, D. N. (2008). *The Cult of Statistical Significance: How the Standard Error Costs Us Jobs, Justice, and Lives*. University of Michigan Press, Ann Arbor, MI.

31
QUANTIFYING HEALTH

Daniel M. Hausman

1. Introduction

Suppose that the Department of Health in some country must determine how to allocate a fixed budget among various uses, including health care. Roughly utilitarian thinking has permeated the government, and it has accordingly assigned the Department of Health the objective of using its budget to maximize population health. This charge may be shortsighted, given how important health-care policies are to other aspects of society such as education, financial security, and economic growth, but for the purposes of this chapter, let us suppose that the objective of health policy is to allocate resources to maximize population health (see also Voorhoeve, Chapter 34).

The health department has a difficult task. It must, for example, decide how much of the health budget to set aside for research, health education, and public health policies, such as sanitation. Let us narrow its task even further by supposing that it has a fixed budget to be used exclusively for health care. Huge difficulties remain, however. The health department needs to distinguish diseases and their medical treatments from other undesirable conditions. The suffering of those who are in the middle of a divorce is usually not a disease, and medical treatment is typically inappropriate. On the other hand, though fertility is not a disease, millions make use of what we call health care to control it.

For the purposes of this chapter, let us sidestep these problems and take it for granted that the health department knows what is a disease, when medical treatment or prevention is called for, and what outcomes can be expected from the treatments of various conditions. We can then zero in on the remaining problem, which is to evaluate or measure the health improvements resulting from medical interventions. If the health department is to maximize health with a fixed budget, it must compare, add, and subtract the benefits of different health-care interventions. For example, to know whether more frequent blood-pressure screening enhances population health more than the greater availability of dialysis, the health authority needs quantitative measures of the costs and benefits of these policies.

The problem this chapter addresses concerns how to render health improvements commensurable so that one can compare the health improvements resulting from different investments in health care. The most obvious way to measure an improvement in health due to some treatment is to subtract the value of the untreated health state from the value of the health state expected after treatment. This chapter asks how health economists assign values to health states.

DOI: 10.4324/9781315739793-38

What makes the measurement of health difficult is the heterogeneity of health states. If health affected only one thing that people value, such as longevity or mobility, then health measurement would pose only practical problems. But health states differ in a great many different ways. Some involve physical disabilities. Others involve pain or cognitive limitations. Still others show themselves in our emotions. How can a scalar (a single number) be assigned to each health state that is interpersonally comparable and that can be added and subtracted so as to permit claims concerning changes to overall population health? How is it possible to define what is called "a generic health measure"?

Section 2 discusses what is required to measure health and argues that health cannot be literally measured. However, as Section 3 explains, health can, nevertheless, be valued. Section 4 defines health states – that is, the health-related states of affairs to which "quality weights" (which are discussed in Section 5) are assigned. Section 6 describes one of the main methods by which quantitative quality weights are assigned to health states, which Section 7 criticizes. Section 8 concludes that the quantification of health is a precarious endeavor.

2. Measuring Health

I maintain that there is no useful way to quantify health other than to assign values to states of health. This assertion may appear unjustified. Why is it not possible for physiologists and pathologists to define a complete relation, "A person in health state H_1 is at least as healthy as one in H_2," as "H_1 makes at least as large a contribution to the probability of survival (and reproduction) as H_2," given a particular distribution of traits, a reference class, and a specific environment?

A standard notion of measurement begins by specifying a set of axioms concerning a relational predicate such as, "is at least as healthy as," which is defined over some set of objects or states. If this relation over the set of states is reflexive, complete, and transitive, and if the set is finite or satisfies a continuity condition, then the relation can be represented by numbers (see Chao, Chapter 13), such that healthier states receive higher numbers and the same number is assigned to states of equal health. In addition, what is described as the "is at least as healthy as" relation must conform at least approximately to our pretheoretic health comparisons.

To make sense of maximizing health, economists need a great deal more than a mere ordering of health states in terms of the relation, "is at least as healthy as." But they cannot even take the first step toward such a measure, because the relation "is at least as healthy as" is massively incomplete: not only are we unable to specify how to find out whether someone with a limp is healthier than someone with a mild cognitive deficiency but the comparison is not well defined. Units of health cannot be counted. Masses of health impact cannot be weighed. The numbers that economists have assigned to health states do not measure any quantity or magnitude of health itself. What are called "measures of health" are measures of the *value* of health, not of the quantity or magnitude of health. Except in cases of "dominance" (where one health state is in every regard at least as good as another), there are no nonevaluative truth conditions for the claim that a person in one health state is healthier than a person in another.[1]

Furthermore, whether or not a measure of the quantity or magnitude of health could be defined, it is not the relation people have in mind when they compare different health deficiencies. The study of population health and the application of cost-effectiveness analysis to rationing problems aim to ameliorate suffering and disability, to expand opportunities and capabilities, to express respect and solidarity, and to promote well-being. What is wanted of a generic health measure to guide the allocation of health-related resources is a measure of health impact and, hence, a measure of the harm of diminished health. The numbers that most systems of generic health measurement assign to health states are supposed to reflect the bearing of health on well-being and capabilities, rather than to provide a nonnormative measure of the overall functioning of parts and processes within people's bodies and minds. What is wanted of generic health measures is, accordingly, a quantification of the *value* of health.[2]

3. Valuing Health

Just as there is no way to say that A is, in the relevant sense, healthier than B, unless A dominates B, so also there is no way to say that one bundle of commodities is "larger" than another, unless it contains at least as much of every commodity as another bundle. However, the fact that bundles of commodities cannot be ranked *by size* does not rule out a quantitative comparison of commodity bundles in other ways. Economists typically measure commodity bundles by their monetary value. Although Donald Trump's holdings of commodities is not *larger* than that of most Americans, because by all accounts it contains fewer books, his holdings have an exceptionally large market value. In much the same way, health economists can compare health states in terms of their value. However, in the case of health, the value in question is not market price.

The efforts by staff at the World Health Organization and at the Institute for Health Metrics and Evaluation, about which I shall have little to say, are an exception to the typical substitution of valuation for measurement. Their explicit goal has been to measure health itself – how much or little there is of it – rather than to quantify the value of health. The Global Burden of Disease study in 2010 (GBD 2010; see Murray *et al.* 2002) surveyed people about their views concerning which of two people in different health states "is healthier overall, *in terms of having fewer physical or mental limitations on what they can do in life*" (Salomon *et al.* 2012b, emphasis added). If one reads this phrase literally, it calls on respondents to compare the number of physical and mental limitations the two people have, but it is unclear how to individuate and count physical and mental limitations, and the interviewers did not expect the respondents to do so. Instead, they expected respondents to compare the *severity* or *importance* of the limitations. GBD 2010 appears to seek a measure of health "impact" that is neither a measure of the value of health nor a measure of the overall functional efficiency of parts and processes within people's bodies and minds. I deny that a measure of health in this sense is possible. Despite the intentions of those responsible for GBD 2010, it measures the value rather than the quantity or magnitude of health.

4. Defining Health States

To assign a value to health states, one must be able to distinguish them. Aspects of health can be described in many ways: Mary has diabetes; Joseph broke his leg. Consequently, they both have trouble walking. Identification of their conditions as diabetes or as a broken leg describes their problems walking by their causes, and it also provides some basis for expectations concerning the evolution of their health states over time. However, the description of health states in this way makes it difficult to generate any compact or systematic categorization. Accordingly, health economists categorize health states by their phenomenological properties, without reference to cause or prognosis. Because the description of health states omits cause and prognosis, most health economists distinguish a person's *health* over some extended period of time from their *health state* at a particular moment. Health economists have conceived of health over some period as the time integral of instantaneous "health states." In this way, the problem of classifying people's health reduces to the problem of classifying their instantaneous health states. Notice that someone's health state at time *t* may be just fine, even though their health expectations and their health as ordinarily understood are poor.

The units in which health is measured reflect this conceptualization of health as a matter of time spent in health states. The value of a health state is the individual's "health-related quality of life," and hence the unit used to quantify the quality of someone's health is the quality-adjusted life year or QALY.[3] A crucial advantage of classifying health states in terms of instantaneous quality multiplied by time is that it permits a unified treatment of morbidity, which lowers quality, and mortality, which reduces time. A person's *health* depends on both the sequence of their health states and the length of time the person is in each of them.

The adoption of this approach simplifies a more complicated reality. Because the measure of people's health is the product of the quality of a health state multiplied by how long they are in that health state, this approach implies that the quality of a health state is independent of how long an individual is in it and independent of what health states come before or after it. These assumptions are false, but convenient. Without this simplification, it would be necessary to separately categorize the countless different sequences of health states that people pass through (Mehrez and Gafni 1989, 1993).

For practical purposes, a coarse classification of health states is needed. Most systems of health valuation define health states in terms of a small number of easily observable levels along some small number of dimensions. The dimensions have been functional capacities, such as vision or cognition, consequences of multiple physical and mental capacities, such as "self-care," and subjective states such as pain or anxiety. For example, the Health Utilities Index, Mark 3 (HUI(3)), has eight dimensions: vision, hearing, speech, ambulation, dexterity, emotion, cognition, and pain (see Feeny *et al.* 1996 and www.healthutilities.com/hui3.htm). If one distinguishes several gradations along each dimension, the number of health states becomes very large. With five or six levels along each dimension, the HUI(3) defines 972,000 health states. The EQ-5D, a health classification system that is common in Europe, has five rather than eight dimensions – mobility, self-care, usual activities, pain/discomfort, and anxiety/depression – and only three levels along each dimension – no problem, moderate problems, and severe problems. With five dimensions and three levels along each, the EQ-5D distinguishes 243 (3^5) health states, in addition to dead and unconsciousness, for a total of 245.[4] As the EQ-5D illustrates, health states can be classified in terms of their effects on capabilities such as "self-care" or "usual activity," as well as in terms of biological functioning.[5]

5. Health-Related Quality of Life

Once health economists have a classification system for health states, such as the EQ-5D or the HUI(3), they need to assign numbers to health states that specify the value of the health state and, once one takes into account time, health. Health economists call these numbers "quality weights." They are supposed to measure the value or "quality" of each health state. It is not easy to assign values to health states. How can one locate the values of different health states along a single dimension? Some evaluative criterion is needed in terms of which to compare (for example) the impact of Jack's limited eyesight to Jane's limited mobility or Jessica's difficulty with persistent migraine headaches.

The HUI(3) and the EQ-5D assign the value 1 to full health and 0 to death. Health states have "quality weights" between 0 and 1, except for those worse than death, which have negative values in the EQ-5D. The severity of ill health and the effects of disease or treatment depend on the distribution of health states at moments in time and on how long those health states last. The unit of health is, accordingly, the quality-adjusted life year or QALY. For example, if a treatment allows someone 10 additional years of life in a health state whose value is .9, the health benefit (ignoring for the moment any discounting of future benefits and costs) is 9 QALYs. Health economists can also quantify expected health benefits in units of "QALEs" (quality-adjusted life expectancies).

What is the value of health states that the weights attached to them are supposed to measure? There are many possibilities and conflicting views about which evaluative criterion is most appropriate (Broome 2002; Brock 2002; Daniels 1985; Dolan 2011; Sen 1993; Prah Ruger 2010; Venkatapuram 2011). Most health economists have settled on "health-related quality of life" (HRQoL; see Kind 1996) as the criterion against which to value health states, but this agreement is not very enlightening because health economists have said little about what HRQoL might be. Philosophical commentators such as Bognar and Hirose describe HRQoL as "that fraction of overall well-being that is determined by health" (2014: 31). Health economists such as Gold *et al.* (1996: 83) write, "We will use 'health-related quality of life' (HRQL) to connote the values assigned to different health states."[6] When EQ-5D surveys ask people to report their health on a visual analogue scale running from 0 to 100, they ask respondents to locate their health between good health and the worst imaginable health state, without any mention of HRQoL.

6. Valuing Health States by Eliciting Preferences

In practice, health economists usually assign values to health states by eliciting people's preferences among health states.[7] However, by eliciting preferences, they have only shifted the question of how to value health states. If health economists or epidemiologists do not know how to judge which person is in better health, how are those whom they survey supposed to know? What does it *mean* to claim that someone with vision deficits is in better health than someone who has lost a foot? What facts make this claim true? What *evidence* bears on the question?

Because people make comparisons of health states that do not dominate one another, it must somehow be possible to make these comparisons. How do survey respondents do it? I suggest that they rely in large part on platitudes concerning when one health deficiency x is worse than another y: for example, that health states are worse if they impose greater limits on what one can do or impose greater burdens on others. However, it is hard to see how to derive a quantitative scale measuring the value of health from these modest generalizations.

The crucial step health economists take is to outsource the task of assigning values to health states to a sample of the population. In the case of the EQ-5D, economists have elicited quantitative measures of the value of health by asking survey respondents to make "time trade-offs" among health states. These consist of questions such as, "Would you prefer to live for 7 years from now in full health to 10 years with moderate problems with mobility and self-care?" If a respondent reports indifference between the two alternatives, then 7 years in full health – that is, 7 QALYs, is equal to 10 times the HRQoL of moderate problems with mobility and self-care. So the quality weight of moderate problems with mobility and self-care would be 0.7.

It is important to distinguish surveys designed to *determine* the quality weights to assign to health states from surveys designed to assign values to people's health by applying already determined quality weights. Once one has the quality weights for health states, one can use them to calculate the value of population health, the burden of disease, and the benefit of treatments. Surveys that use the values of health states to quantify the health of individuals, unlike those that aim to determine the quality weights of health states, are straightforward. For example, to ask people whether they are in severe pain makes only weak cognitive demands on them. In contrast, the surveys that are used to assign quality weights are cognitively demanding.

An additional complication derives from the practical impossibility of directly eliciting quality weights for hundreds, or in the case of the HUI(3) tens of thousands, of health states. To make the assignment of quality weights feasible, health economists have supposed that people possess an implicit "multi-attribute utility function" that relates the values they place on deficits with respect to specific dimensions in the health state classification to the values they place on overall health states (Richardson *et al.* 2014). If health economists can estimate the parameters of this function from direct preference measurements, then they can calculate the utilities of all the health states in the classification. To do this requires an a priori specification of the functional form that this mapping will have. There are some empirical controls on this specification, because health economists can compare the values they derive from such a multi-attribute utility function to some direct measurements of the values respondents assign to health states. Reliance on an estimated multi-attribute utility function to assign numbers to health states nevertheless creates further room for error.

To infer HRQoL from preferences, health economists assume that there is some connection between the two. Perhaps preferences among health states *determine* which has a better health-related quality of life, or perhaps individuals are good judges of HRQoL and their preferences can serve as *evidence* concerning HRQoL. In fact, health economists do not generally worry about such philosophical niceties. Because most economists associate welfare and preference satisfaction, perhaps one should not find this fact surprising. If, like many economists, one assumes that welfare is preference satisfaction, then it might seem unproblematic to take preferences as measuring HRQoL.

7. Problems With Valuing Health by Eliciting Preferences

But there are many objections to valuing health by means of preference surveys. I shall discuss eight. First, people's preferences among health states do not depend only on their judgments of quality of life in those health states. For an extreme example, suppose that Jill prefers 10 years in some diminished health state to 7 years in full health because she wants to be able to complete her study of 17-year cicadas, not because of any judgments about her quality of life (beyond the belief that her diminished health will still permit her to complete her study).

Second, the values individuals assign to health states depend on individual objectives and the technological, geographical, and cultural environment. Restricted mobility is much worse in an environment in which the only feasible way of getting from one place to another is on foot. A broken ankle is much worse for a dancer than for a dentist. Health states have no single value. The numbers gleaned from preference surveys are, at best, averages over the differing values of health states in different circumstances.

Third, such averaging is problematic, however, because there is no reason to suppose that averaging picks out some central value that is endorsed (with errors) by the survey responses. It thus could be the case that the average quality weight assigned to a health state does not conform to anybody's preferences.

Fourth, the preference surveys that health state valuation relies on ask people questions that are too difficult to expect reliable answers. If individuals are asked to make a time trade-off between 10 years of incontinence and x years in full health, they need to know what it is like to be incontinent. What sorts of pads and other equipment would they need? Would they smell of urine? How would incontinence affect their sex lives? Without knowing the answers to questions such as these, how could one possibly judge the time trade-off?

Fifth, the questions in the surveys are not well defined. When asked to make a time trade-off between 10 years with "moderate anxiety and depression" and x years in full health, what constitutes "moderate anxiety and depression"? Until the question is clarified, there is no way for individuals to specify a trade-off that reflects any stable preference or judgment. Moreover, clarification of the time trade-off question reveals that health states, as individuated by classifications such as the EQ-5D, should be assigned a range of values rather than a single value, because within each health state in the EQ-5D there is a range of severity.

The fourth and fifth problems with relying on preference surveys lead immediately to the sixth. Because individuals who are surveyed do not ask for more information and instead answer time trade-off questions readily, they must be answering some other question than the difficult one that the surveys are posing. If, in reality, individuals were to face a time trade-off question, it would be one of the most momentous choices that they ever faced. Sensible people would want to think over their answer and consult with friends and family. No sane survey respondent would ever work so hard to answer a mere survey question. Why should anyone – including the survey respondents themselves – suppose that snap answers to survey questions will coincide with the preferences they would have if they actually faced such a choice and had time to gather information and reflect on the alternatives?

Another way to think about this difficulty is to recognize that the surveys do not confront individuals with a choice between a longer life with diminished health versus a shorter life in full health. Respondents are instead being asked to predict how they *would* choose if they were to face such a choice. This prediction is not the same task as actually making the choice, and there is little reason to take the ready predictions of respondents as good evidence concerning the values of health states.

A seventh problem, which aggravates the fifth, is that surveys frequently discourage individuals from thinking seriously about the values of health states. What is required is a *judgment* from a respondent concerning which of two different time periods in different health states would be better or worse. Although a difficult question, whose answer may differ across people, it is a real question whose answers may be correct or incorrect. Unfortunately, questionnaires asking people to evaluate health states commonly contain wording such as, "There are no right or wrong answers."[8] Such a phrase would not be problematic in instructions for a survey of consumer preferences among barbeque sauces. In the context of health-state evaluation, it is troubling. Although the phrase has benign interpretations, those filling out the questionnaires might also reasonably interpret this claim as, "Don't worry about whether your answers are correct or incorrect. There's no way to be mistaken. It's just a matter of how you feel." But health economists seeking to assign values to health states hope to rely on the good judgment of respondents, not on their off-the-cuff remarks.[9]

Finally, because preferences among health states vary systematically among individuals with different experiences, health economists face a choice of whose preferences to measure.[10] Erik Nord (1999: 82–89) argues that to measure health-related quality of life, health economists should rely on the attitudes of those who have actually experienced the health state in question, while Paul Dolan (1999) argues for placing greater weight on the preferences of those who have more knowledge of what a health state is like, regardless of whether they are currently experiencing it. On the other hand, Gold *et al.* (1996) argue that the attitudes of the entire target population should determine the values of health states, because members of the public at large are more impartial and because it is their health system that they are paying for. But whether individuals are paying for a health system has little bearing on the accuracy of their judgment of the values of health states.[11]

The question of whom to survey is important because there are large and systematic differences in the values assigned to many impairments, depending on whether respondents have had experience of them.[12] For example, according to the HUI(3), two years of life for someone who is deaf produces fewer QALYs than one year of life for someone in full health. In contrast, many in the deaf community deny that deafness is a disability at all (Lane 2002).

These discrepancies should make one skeptical about relying on preferences to assign quality weights. It is hard to justify relying either on the attitudes of those who experience the health issues in question or on the attitudes of the community. The use of averaging, which is implicit in deriving quality weights for the population at large, does not solve the problem. If neither the (average) values of the population at large nor the (average) values of those who are especially knowledgeable concerning the disability are satisfactory, why should their average be informative?

Rather than attempting to adjudicate this dispute and determine whose preferences are the better guide to the values of health states, I am drawn to the conclusion that the disagreements provide good reason not to rely on the attitudes of either those experiencing the condition or those in the community. Now that we have identified so many factors that distort assessments, why place any confidence in attitude surveys? Would it not be better to avoid relying on preferences altogether?

In the light of these eight objections, can it make sense to rely on preference surveys? In defense of doing so, economists can argue that much of the critique of relying on informants is based on a misconception. In measuring preferences, economists are not piggybacking on the judgments of survey respondents. They are instead eliciting preferences in order to measure the subjective welfare consequences of health states, which determine the value of health states. But if the value of health states consists of the subjective experience of them, there are more direct ways to measure that experience.[13]

A second line of defense is to maintain that economists ask others instead of answering the hard questions themselves, because it would presumptuous or inappropriate for them to answer. In this view, the valuation of health states is a social decision that should be responsive to everyone's views. The social ranking of alternatives depends on individual rankings – as one might naively suppose democratic sovereignty says it should – and the economist's job is to clarify that dependence so that social policies will be responsive to individual preferences. However, it is questionable whether the assignment of values of health states should be regarded as a social choice. On the contrary, it aims to provide the public with reliable information concerning the values of health states. Unless the elicitation of preferences is a good way to get that information, why elicit preferences?

A third and more practical defense of the reliance on a random sample from the population is that it helps to allay popular skepticism and resistance to the values assigned to health states. Asked to justify the assignment, the health economist can say, "These are *your* values." However, the fact that values derived from surveys are easier to "sell" is not evidence that they are correct.

Perhaps the best argument in defense of eliciting preferences is to point to the absence of any practical alternative.

8. Conclusion

The health economist, who faces extremely difficult questions in assigning values to health states, answers them by asking the same questions of members of the population, who have less relevant knowledge and whose answers reflect little serious reflection. *If* health were entirely a matter of public opinion or individual feelings, then questions about how good or bad health is could be answered by polling, just as one answers questions about which movie stars are the most popular by asking people which movie stars they like most. But the assignment of an index by averaging the opinions of poorly informed respondents is hard to justify. The investigation of people's preferences among health states has replaced the substantive evaluative task of determining the values of health states. Why should this be the case? When health economists want to measure the prevalence of the flu or its cost in workdays lost, they do not ask people's opinions. They count flu cases and (albeit via the use of surveys) workdays lost.

When those who are surveyed are asked to evaluate health states, they do so somehow without in turn polling their neighbors. If survey respondents can make time trade-offs, health economists should be able to do so too.

One is left, I believe, with health state values of dubious precision whose accuracy is not well defined. What remains unanswered in this chapter is the practical question of whether the values assigned to health states, as these are individuated in a scheme such as the EQ5D or the HUI(3), are good guides to how best to improve population health.

Related Chapters

Chao, Chapter 13 "Representation"

Voorhoeve, Chapter 34 "Policy Evaluation Under Severe Uncertainty: A Cautious, Egalitarian Approach"

Notes

1 Brazier *et al.* (2007) is the best text addressing issues in generic health measurement. See also Drummond *et al.* (1997, ch. 6), Torrance (1985), and Salomon (2014).

2 As discussed in the following section, this claim is controversial: those responsible for the recent global burden of disease studies maintain that they are ascertaining nonevaluative measures of health.

3 An alternative approach, which I shall not discuss, is to focus on health deficiencies and to value health in terms of disability-adjusted life years or DALYs.

4 There is currently an effort (Rabin *et al.* 2011) to revise the EQ-5D to allow five levels along each dimension for a total of 3,125 (or with unconsciousness and death, 3,127) distinguishable health states.

5 Staff members at the World Health Organization (WHO) and at the Institute for Health Metrics and Evaluation (IHME) have taken a different path, defining a set of abnormal conditions resulting from disease – "disease sequelae" – rather than formulating a general classification of health states. The contrast to their approach, which they regard as a shortcut rather than as a competitor to a general classification of health states, is not germane to the issues this chapter discusses.

6 Similarly, in distinguishing the assessment of health in terms of quality of life from a traditional "biomedical" assessment, Kaplan 2003 never says what constitutes quality of life. Lenert and Kaplan (2000) regard preference elicitation as one way to measure health-related quality of life. For a literature review that reveals how ill-defined the general notion of "quality of life" is, see Taillefer *et al.* (2003).

7 GBD 2010 claims that the results of its surveys define a measure of the quantity of health rather than a measure of preferences among health states. As Salomon *et al.* (2003) point out, people are able to compare many health states. They write,

> if we say that somebody with a mild sore throat is, all else being equal, healthier than somebody with two broken arms, perhaps not everybody would agree, but most people could at least interpret this statement in reference to some common-sense understanding of health.

They do not explain how their surveys establish whether one condition contains "more health" than another.

8 Quoted from the GBD 2010 surveys.

9 Evidence that elicited preferences conform to actual choices is reassuring – at least to the extent that one believes that actual choices are thoughtful. For some evidence see Carter *et al.* (1986) and Heckerling *et al.* (1997).

10 See, for example, Gold *et al.* (1996), Nord (1999), Dolan (1999), Murray (1996), and Menzel (1999).

11 There is empirical evidence that survey respondents do not want surveys of their preferences to guide policies. See Richardson *et al.* (2005).

12 For some of the evidence, see Revicki *et al.* (1996), Bennett *et al.* (1997), Boyd *et al.* (1990), Dolan (1999), Nord (1999, 84–88), Wu (2001), Ubel *et al.* (2003), Smith *et al.* (2006), and Sackett and Torrance (1978).

13 See, for example, Kahneman and Dolan (2008) and Dolan (2011).

Bibliography

Bennett, C., Chapman, G., Elstein, A., *et al.* (1997) "A Comparison of Perspectives on Prostate Cancer: Analysis of Utility Assessments of Patients and Physicians," *European Urology* 32 (S3): 86–88.

Bognar, G. and Hirose, I. (2014) *The Ethics of Health Care Rationing: An Introduction*, London: Routledge.

Boyd, N., H. Sutherland, H., Heasman, K., Tritchler, D. and Cummings, B. (1990) "Whose Utilities for Decision Analysis?" *Medical Decision Making* 10: 58–67.

Brazier, J., Ratcliffe, J., Tsuchiya, A. and Salomon, J. (2007) *Measuring and Valuing Health Benefits for Economic Evaluation*, New York: Oxford University Press.

Brock, D. (2002) "The Separability of Health and Well-being," in Murray *et al.* (eds.): 115–120.

Broome, J. (2002) "Measuring the Burden of Disease by Aggregating Well-Being," in Murray *et al.* (eds.): 91–113.

Carter, W., Beach, L., Inui, T.S., Kirscht, J.P. and Prodzinski, J.C. (1986) "Developing and Testing a Decision Model for Predicting Influenza Vaccination Compliance," *Health Services Research* 206: 897–932.

Daniels, N. (1985) *Just Health Care*, Cambridge: Cambridge University Press.

Dolan, P. (1999) "Whose Preferences Count?" *Medical Decision Making* 19: 482–486.

Dolan, P. (2011) *Using Happiness to Value Health*, London: Office of Health Economics, www.ohe.org.

Drummond, M., O'Brien, B., Stoddart, G. and Torrance, G. (1997) *Methods for the Economics Evaluation of Health Care Programmes*, 2nd ed., Oxford: Oxford University Press.

Feeny, D., Torrance, G. and Furlong, W. (1996) "Health Utilities Index," in B. Spilker (ed.) *Quality of Life and Pharmaoeconomics in Clinical Trials*, 2nd. ed., Philadelphia: Lippincott-Raven.

Gold, M., Patrick, D., Torrance, G., Fryback, D., Hadorn, D., Kamlet, M., Daniels, N. and Weinstein, M. (1996) "Identifying and Valuing Outcomes," in *Cost-Effectiveness in Health and Medicine: Report to the U.S. Public Health Service, Panel on Cost-Effectiveness in Health and Medicine,* New York: Oxford University Press: 82–134.

Hausman, D. (2015) *Valuing Health: Well-Being, Freedom, and Suffering*, New York: Oxford University Press.

Heckerling, P., Verp, M.S. and Albert, N. (1997) "Prenatal Testing for Limb Reduction Defects. How Patients' Views Affect their Choice of CVERSUS," *Journal of Reproductive Medicine* 42: 14–129.

Kahneman, D. & Dolan, P. (2008) "Interpretations of Utility and their Implications for the Valuation of Health," *Economic Journal* 118: 215–234.

Kaplan, R. (2003) "The Significance of Quality of Life in Health Care," *Quality of Life Research* 12: 2–16.

Kind, P. (1996) "The EuroQoL Instrument: An Index of Health-Related Quality of Life," in B. Spiker (ed.) *Quality of Life and Pharmacoeconomics in Clinical Trials*, 2nd ed., Philadelphia: Lippincott-Raven: 191–201.

Lane, H. (2002) "Do Deaf People Have a Disability?" *Sign Language Studies* 2: 356–379.

Lenert, L. and Kaplan, R. (2000) "Validity and Interpretation of Preference-Basic Measures of Health-Related Quality of Life," *Medical Care* 38 Supplement II: II-138 – II-150.

Mehrez, A. and Gafni, A. (1989) "Quality-Adjusted Life Years, Utility Theory, and Healthy-Years Equivalents," *Medical Decision Making* 9: 142–149.

Mehrez, A. and Gafni, A. (1993) "Healthy-Years Equivalents versus Quality-Adjusted Life Years: In Pursuit of Progress," *Medical Decision Making* 13: 287–292.

Menzel, P. (1999) "How Should What Economists Call 'Social Values' Be Measured?" *The Journal of Ethics* 3: 249–273.

Murray, C. (1996) "Rethinking DALYs," in C. Murray and A. Lopez (eds.) *The Global Burden of Disease: A Comprehensive Assessment of Mortality and Disability from Diseases, Injuries, and Risk Factors in 1990 and Projected to 2020*, Boston: Harvard School of Public Health: 1–98.

Murray, C., Murray, J.L., Ezzati, M., Flaxman, A.D., Lim, S., Lozano, R., Michaud, C., Naghavi, M., Salomon, J.A., Shibuya, K., Vos, T., Lopez, A.D. *et al.* (2012) "The Global Burden of Disease Study 2010," *The Lancet* 380, No. 9859: 2053–2260.

Murray, C., Salomon, J., Mathers, C. and Lopez, A. (eds.) (2002) *Summary Measures of Population Health: Concepts, Ethics, Measurement and Applications*, Geneva: World Health Organization.

Nord, E. (1999) *Cost-Value Analysis in Health Care: Making Sense Out of QALYs*, Cambridge: Cambridge University Press.

Prah Ruger, J. (2010) *Health and Social Justice*, Oxford: Oxford University Press.

Rabin, R., Oemar, M., Oppe, M., Janssen, B. and Herdman, M. (2011) *EQ-5D-5L User Guide: Basic Information on How to Use the EQ-5D-5L Instrument*, Rotterdam: EuroQol Group.

Revicki, D.A., Shakespeare, A. and Kind, P. (1996) "Preferences for Schizophrenia-related Health States: A Comparison of Patients, Caregivers, and Psychiatrists," *International Clinical Psychopharmacology* 11: 101–108.

Richardson, J., McKie, J. and Bariola, E. (2014) "Multiattribute Utility Instruments and their Use," in A. Culyer (ed.) *Encyclopedia of Health Economics*, Amsterdam: Elsevier: 341–357.

Richardson, J., McKie, J. and Olsen, J. (2005) "Welfarism or Non-Welfarism? Public Preferences for Willingness to Pay Versus Health Maximisation," Monash University, Centre for Health Economics Research Paper 10. www.buseco.monash.edu.au/centres/che/publications.php.

Sackett, D.L. and Torrance, G.W. (1978) "The Utility of Different Health States as Perceived by the General Public," *Journal of Chronic Diseases* 31: 697–704.

Salomon, J. (2014) "Techniques for Valuing Health States," in A. Culyer (ed.) *Encyclopedia of Health Economics*, Amsterdam: Elsevier: 454–458.

Salomon, J., Murray, C., Bedirhan Üstün, T. and Chatterji, S. (2003) "Health State Valuations in Summary Measures of Population Health," in C. Murray and D. Evans (eds.) *Health Systems Performance Assessment Debates, Methods and Empiricism*, Geneva: World Health Organization: 409–436.

Salomon, J., Vos, T., Hogan, D. *et al.* (2012b) "Common Values in Assessing Health Outcomes from Disease and Injury: Disability Weights Measurement Study for the Global Burden of Disease Study 2010," Appendix. *The Lancet* 380, www.thelancet.com

Sen, A. (1993) "Capability and Well-Being," in M. Nussbaum and A. Sen (eds.) *The Quality of Life*, Oxford: Clarendon Press: 30–53.

Smith, D., Sherriff, R., Damschroder, L., Lowewenstein, G. and Ubel, P. (2006) "Misremembering Colostomies? Former Patients Give Lower Utility Ratings Than Do Current Patients," *Health Psychology* 25: 688–695.

Taillefer, M., Dupuis, G., Roberge, M. and LeMay, S. (2003) "Health-related Quality of Life Models: Systematic Review of the Literature," *Social Indicators Research* 64(2): 293–323.

Torrance, G. (1985) "Measurement of Health State Utilities for Economic Appraisal: A Review," *Journal of Health Economics* 5: 1–30.

Ubel, P., Loewenstein, G. and Christopher, J. (2003) "Whose Quality of Life? A Commentary Exploring Discrepancies between Health State Evaluations of Patients and the General Public," *Quality of Life Research* 12: 599–607.

Venkatapuram, S. (2011) *Health Justice: An Argument from the Capabilities Approach*, London: Polity Press.

Wu, S. (2001) "Adapting to Heart Conditions: A Test of the Hedonic Treadmill," *Journal of Health Economics* 20: 495–508.

PART VIII

Policy

32
FREEDOMS, POLITICAL ECONOMY, AND LIBERALISM

Sebastiano Bavetta

1. Introduction

Political economy is a positive, interdisciplinary intellectual project that rests on a frugal understanding of liberalism. Although it contains many accounts of liberalism (e.g., North 1990; Acemoglu *et al.* 2005; Mukand and Rodrik 2020; Besley and Perssons 2011), it is uninterested in its specific normative attributes, and it is often content with no more than a generic, credible commitment on the part of rulers to respect property rights as a workable definition of a liberal political order (North 1990). A similar attitude extends to freedoms. Analytical descriptions and measurements of freedom in political economy follow, by and large, the narrative introduced by Isaiah Berlin (1969) that distinguishes *negative* and *positive freedoms*. These notions are loosely embodied in a society's institutional arrangements – taxation, the regulatory web, the de jure political institutions, the exercise of civil or political prerogatives – to describe the individual's space of unimpeded action and her set of opportunities, with the aim to study the consequences that the incentives created by institutions have on societal outcomes.

Frugality has hindered neither political economy's huge success nor its ability to provide arguments for and explanations of the expansion of liberalism beyond the confines of the Western world – witness the third democratization wave (Teorell 2010) or the increase in economic and political freedoms (Gwartney *et al.* 2019 and Marshall 2014). However, the historical process of expansion of a liberal order that prevailed at the end of the twentieth century (Shleifer 2009) is nowadays under threat from many quarters, and new analytical and political strategies must be imagined for preserving its desirable features. One wonders, therefore, if it would not be useful to complement, from an analytical perspective, political economy's minimal requirement – that is, the ruler's commitment to respect property rights – with an intellectual effort better suited to confront (at least some of) the challenges that liberalism faces these days.

There are reasons that militate in favor of such an analytical strategy and suggest where to base this effort. Economic prosperity in the West has led to an empirically documented change in values (Welzel 2013; Inglehart and Welzel 2005) that shifts the weight of a defense of liberalism from institutions and the realm of negative freedoms to the domain of personal values and "psychological freedoms," to borrow a Schmidtz and Brennan (2010) label. At the same time, the role of cultural traits and informal institutions has gained importance in the analysis of the emergence of prosperity and the affirmation of liberal political orders (e.g., Guiso *et al.* 2006; Passarelli and Tabellini 2017; Tabellini 2010; Acemoglu and Robinson 2019; Phelps 2013). It would be odd if political

DOI: 10.4324/9781315739793-40

economy – which decisively contributed to the accumulation of this body of knowledge – would not put it to the service of a defense of liberalism. More importantly, the nature of the threats that liberalism is facing depends less on institutional failures than on a shift in personal attitudes. Technological and social change is likely to have generated anxieties (Mokyr *et al.* 2015), whose effects have reduced individuals' readiness to take risks and inflated their perception of increasing inequalities and fear of diversity. Political economy has shed much light on the dynamics of institutional change (Acemoglu *et al.* 2005) and suggested reasons for skepticism that institutions may maintain, let alone improve, their liberal features under the prevailing political sentiments.

In fact, what all of these reasons suggest is that the defense of a liberal order gains as much from bottom-up shifts in attitudes as it does from institutional change (Acemoglu and Robinson 2019; Bavetta and Navarra 2012). Knowledge of what individuals think and how to interpret their perceptions, anxieties, and beliefs is therefore instrumental to set in motion policies and institutional changes that are respectful of liberal institutions and to maintain the material and immaterial benefits secured by a liberal political order, because individual and institutional freedoms complement each other in the affirmation and evolution of a liberal order. This is the suggestion that I advance in this chapter. The expansion of antipluralist sentiments, the increasing perception of unfairness, and the fears spawned by systemic risks such as pandemics are problematic challenges to the prosperity granted by a political system based on the tenets of liberalism. To fight them and their political consequences, we must take advantage of the spread of self-realization values, and we must know better the vast array of individual motivations that govern how a person is likely to act in the social arena. It is this knowledge that the chapter suggests to embody within a description of liberalism in political economy.

In the next section, I introduce the idea of a credible commitment that ties rulers' hands in the arbitrary seizure of their citizens' rights of property and that is central in the political economy's treatment of liberalism. In Section 3, I present the evidence for a motivational perspective on the relation between economics, freedoms, and liberalism. Because the credible commitment is not specified in detail and political preferences may vary, the degree of institutional encroachment on individual freedoms may vary substantially and still be compatible with liberalism because it is balanced by the manifestation of individuality. In Section 4, I sketch a strategy for an analysis of freedoms that matches the challenges. The aim is to identify measurable variables related to the manifestation of individuality that capture what motivates individuals to change their institutional environment. In Section 5, I connect my argument to the affirmation of liberalism in contemporary societies. In particular, I suggest that the preservation of personal freedoms would be an effective strategy to tackle two forces that are compressing liberalism: antipluralism and perception of inequality.

2. Liberalism and Political Economy

Liberalism is embedded in political economy as a set of nonintrusive institutions that grant extensive property rights that protect (and are protected by) individual freedoms (Gaus *et al.* 2018). If effective, low transaction cost mechanisms for transferring rights – such as competitive markets – operate in society, the relevant attributes of property rights fall in the hands of those who value them the most, leading to Pareto efficiency and material prosperity (North 1990). The precise extent of transaction costs matters for efficiency but, within limits, many historically contingent arrangements of property rights consent the achievement of decent degrees of efficiency, insofar as they offered adequate protection to returns on investment. What really matters from the perspective of political economy is rather the government's (or the ruler's) credible commitment to the protection of a relevant set of property rights so as to make returns on private investments secure (Acemoglu *et al.* 2005; Mokyr 2009; North and Weingast 1989; North *et al.* 2009; Rajan and Zingales 2003; Cox 2017). The government's (or the ruler's) credibility is crucial because it creates the conditions for economic actors to invest with reasonable confidence and gives them political maneuverability to modify the structure of de jure power, if it is in their interest to do so (Acemoglu *et al.* 2005). Liberalism (or liberalisms, as I ought to say) is therefore nested in political economy by appealing to commitment, a meta-institution that focuses on the game-theoretic meta-conditions that permit the affirmation of a liberal order (Rajan and Zingales 2003). In turn, commitment guarantees the pervasiveness of the rule of law and the decentralization of decision mechanisms, in terms of hierarchies of governments and, more importantly, of individual voluntariness.

The approach pursued by political economy carries its own benefits. By appealing to commitment, political economy sets liberalism as a nonideal political theory and deliberately chooses not to focus on creating a normative vision of a political order for society, but to provide, through its rich armamentarium of empirical tools and statistical strategies, a methodology to disentangle the pervasive economic and moral trade-offs with which liberal societies present us (Zwolinski 2015). The setting of liberalism within the realm of nonideal theories has two components. First, it separates the characterization of liberalism from the historically contingent institutions that shape it. Second, it casts the debate on its merit in terms of how favorable the contingent institutions are to some desirable economic or political outcomes.

Consider separation, to start with. It implies that many historically contingent arrangements of property rights are compatible with a liberal political order. Early nineteenth-century Britain should likely be considered a liberal political order by political economy's standard, even if it failed in certain essential domains, even more so viewed with contemporary lenses. For example, the ruling oligarchy was composed of a few thousand families that exploited their position for rent-seeking, political competition was nonexistent in many constituencies, the tight liaison between the Church of England and the political power limited the participation of many, and enfranchisement was far from universal (Cannadine 2017). And yet, the British political order of those days was built on the idea of commitment, in the interest of quite limited groups at first, but of larger, multiform, and diversified elites as time progressed (Mokyr 2009).

Moreover, once the attributes of a liberal order are independent of its historically contingent characteristics, its merit is assessed in consequentialist terms and tied to the performance that economic and political institutions achieve. In principle, the more affirmed the rule of law and voluntariness are, the higher the economic prosperity, the enjoyment of political and civil liberties, and, ultimately, the pursuit of the affirmation of the self, as empirical evidence confirms (Scully 1992). The consequentialist requirement should not be underestimated. In a nonideal approach, it is the effect that the rule of law and decentralization have on political and economic outcomes that legitimates liberalisms (Zwolinski 2015). Again, at the dawn of the nineteenth century, Britain's political order granted better standards of living than its European counterparts, legitimizing, in relative terms, the label of liberalism for the institutions in which that political order was embedded, despite its imperfections in the realization of the commitment principle.

Another important benefit delivered by reliance on commitment is the "dematerialization" of the relationship between government (or the ruler), on the one hand, and citizens (or subjects), on the other. Credibility does not need to be stated in a formal constitution: it may be the outcome of a virtuous, self-enforcing game played by rulers and economic actors that emerged under favorable historical circumstances. For example, in Cox (2017), the fundamental historical circumstance that has prevailed since 600 CE is Western Europe's political fragmentation, which granted merchants an extensive degree of economic liberty. To fend off competition from neighbors and foes, European sovereigns kept regulations at bay and made trading easier. The virtuous game between rulers and individuals was not codified in legal documents, but sovereigns' commitment was de facto enforced by political competition. This is not to say that formal institutions are not important; rather, dematerialization shows that they are not the sole relevant construct of a liberal order that relies, no less firmly, upon informal rules, perceptions, individual motivations, and civil society.

A recent and prominent example that shows how far the interaction between formal institutions and civil society is determinant for commitment and a liberal order is given by Acemoglu and Robinson (2019). Taking a page from Philip Pettit's idea of *freedom as nondominance* (Pettit 1997, 2001),[1] they investigate the co-evolution of institutions and societies in many historical circumstances and imagine a set of dynamic interactions that may establish (or maintain) what they call a *corridor* where individual freedoms flourish and a liberal political order materializes. Credible commitment, Acemoglu and Robinson (2019) argue, depends on a fragile balance between elites with their favorable, formal institutions, on the one hand, and how firmly citizens can keep at bay intrusiveness and infringements of their economic liberties and political prerogatives, on the other. If either side prevails, the conditions for the affirmation of individual freedoms weaken, leading to an unrestrained Leviathan where society is no firewall against predatory attitudes or to forms of a Hobbesian state of nature where no legitimate, central authority is capable of enforcing its rule.

The general – and necessarily incomplete – description of how political economy embeds a liberal order that I have pursued so far leaves the question of how liberalism evolves underexplored. Acemoglu and Robinson (2019) devote many pages to the formal and informal forces that govern the corridor mentioned in the previous paragraph and dwell at length on the paths that may restore (or create) desirable equilibria. They are motivated, like this chapter, by the challenges posed by our times that they see as "wrenching destabilization," an expression that refers to the threats to which the narrow corridor, our liberties, and our prosperity are currently exposed. Yet, they leave open an issue that finds increasing support from recent and consistent empirical evidence. It is a behavioral issue with a Hayekian flavor, nicely captured by Deirdre McCloskey (2017), that emphasizes, at the same time, our ignorance of the motivations that drive human action and their importance for an enlargement of the corridor from below.

Here is McCloskey:

> [G]overning sensibly the trillions of shifting plans daily by the 324 million individuals in the American economy, much less nation-building abroad, is impossible – because, as Smith. . .] put it, "in the great chess-board of human society, every single piece has a principle of motion of its own." The principles of motion are idiosyncratic, because people are motivated in varying proportions by prudence and temperance and courage and justice and faith and hope and love. By way of such virtues, and less happily their corresponding vices, you and I pursue our endlessly varied projects.
>
> (McCloskey, 2017)

By way of such motivations, I would add, we set in motion a dynamic that, combined with the mechanics of formal institutions, generates a most disparate set of outcomes, some unfavorable and others conducive to lower entropy (Pinker 2018), to better coordination (North 1990), or to enlarging the corridor (Acemoglu and Robinson 2019). As I have argued elsewhere (Bavetta and Navarra 2012), these motivations are an important component in a defense of a liberal order. Some of them favor the engagement of individuals in the affirmation of self-realization and the defense of personal liberties, leading, in turn, institutional evolution along paths compatible with the containment of state intervention and the reinforcement of civil society. Take the case of material enrichment – or better coordination in North's neoclassical framework. As Phelps (2013) observes, "prosperity . . . comes from broad involvement of people in the processes of innovation: the conception, development, and spread of new methods and products – indigenous innovation down to the grassroots" (p. vi). And later on, he describes grassroots innovation in terms of personal motivations: "the drive to change things, the talent for it, and the receptivity to new things, . . . the willingness and capacity to innovate, leaving aside current conditions and obstacles" (Ibid.: 20). In the economic, as in the political, dimension of life the involvement of individuals in the processes of innovation depends on the dynamic ignited by personal motivations.[2]

It is knowledge of this set of motivations that is most helpful in these days of wrenching destabilization. The headwinds that liberalisms face blow mainly from individuals' fears, anxieties, feelings, or motivations. There are reasons, reputable or not, for these headwinds. And there are analytical benefits that political economy may produce from studying these headwinds. If we want to establish an effective firewall against the destabilization, we must accommodate information about those sentiments in the policy toolkit of a social scientist. We must include, in other words, the personal motivations that fuel the headwinds for both the expansion of the Leviathan or the contraction of the civil society in the components of any analysis of liberalisms. To argue why this set of motivations is so crucial, I review the empirical evidence recently accumulated by political economists on the role of perceptions and motivations in shaping institutions and institutional outcomes and then connect it to the characteristics of a nonideal liberal order.

3. Empirical Evidence

The relevance of motivations, cultural traits, and preferences has recently emerged with pressing insistence and consistency in the social sciences. It is impossible to summarize such evidence in the limited space that I have been assigned. I will therefore briefly touch upon some empirical findings in the literature of political economy that confirm the role of perceptions and preferences in shaping institutions and the chances to maintain a liberal order.

The first set of findings concerns a thorny yet central issue for a commitment-based political construction: how much to redistribute. Empirical evidence supports the view that behavioral, cultural, and demographic variables, on the one hand, and individual preferences for redistribution, on the other, affect the institutional structure of taxes and transfers. In their comprehensive review of the literature, Alesina and Giuliano (2011) single out a number of nonexclusive, empirically measured variables that are associated with individual preferences for redistribution.[3] For example, personal experiences affect optimism and risk aversion, predisposing individuals to income equalization if, on balance, they go through unfavorable historical events (depressions, pandemics, revolutions, etc.). Personal cultural backgrounds, formed either through ethnic or religious group identity or through indoctrination, are also important as they shape the informal norms that govern individual views about redistribution. Also important is the organization of the family as it transmits values on personal autonomy and independence. The pursuit of a high social standing is also associated with preferences for redistributive policies. This social rivalry effect – as it is labeled in the literature – depends on the effect that redistribution may have on the quality of the individuals' social environment. If transfers fuel the fear of a lower quality environment, redistribution is opposed, even if it does not carry any monetary disadvantage.

Gimpelson and Treisman (2018) highlight another motivational dimension for individual preference or action that is far more important for my purpose: the perception of inequality. They observe, on the basis of substantial statistical support, that individuals are rarely aware of the actual distribution of income:

> [r]esults from nine large, cross-national surveys suggest that in recent years ordinary people have known little about the extent of income inequality in their societies, its rate and direction of change, and where they fit into the distribution. What they think they know is often wrong. This finding is robust to data sources, definitions, and measurement instruments.
>
> (Ibid.: 28)

The inference of, as political economy does, economic and political change from objective statistical indicators that individuals systematically misperceive, Gimpelson and Treisman (2018) say, is problematic, and the implications of using perceived information are far-reaching: to be convincing, theories of redistribution, revolution, and democratization (theories of economic, social, and political change, for all intents and purposes),

> must be reformulated as theories about not actual inequality but perceptions of it, with no presumption the two coincide. Although actual inequality – as captured by the best current estimates – is not related to preferences for redistribution, we show that perceived inequality is. Actual poverty correlates only weakly with reported tension between rich and poor, but the perceived poverty rate strongly predicts such inter-class conflict.
>
> (Gimpelson and Treisman 2018: 28)

What Gimpelson and Treisman suggest, together with the literature that explores the role of values in political preferences, is that perceived inequality stands out as a motivation that individuals display in their preferences for institutional structures and for social action. Causality is hard to determine, and the empirical evidence that I am reporting supports no more than associations among the relevant variables. Yet, the reasoning is compelling: perceived inequality embodies the view of fairness that each of us possesses (Bavetta *et al.* 2019, 2020), and such a view is politically relevant in the sense that where individuals observe that fairness is violated (society is perceived as unequal), they express a preference for redressing it (for example, a preference for redistribution) or a readiness to modify the relevant social circumstances (for example, through some form of protest).

The political relevance of the perception of inequality is further refined in Bavetta *et al.* (2020). With US data only, they observe that perceptions of inequality can be inconsistent, namely, they do not always reflect the general view of inequality that a respondent has. Imagine that I perceive the society where I live as generally unequal. Does it necessarily follow that I favor redistributive policies or institutions? Well, it does not, because the reasons that determine inequality are important in my view. If I regard these reasons as largely a responsibility of my fellow citizens, I hold them accountable and, even if society is unfair, I may backpedal on supporting redistribution. Besides shedding light on the motivational structure of individual preference or action, the perception of inequality is also a valuable tool to elicit the prevailing views on what should be equalized (see also Voorhoeve, Chapter 34, and Vromen, Chapter 9).

The perception of inequality that individuals display can also be viewed from a different perspective. Fairness is an indicator of the perceived opportunities that an individual has of advancing herself, materially and immaterially, in society. In other words, if a person regards the society where she lives as just, she is likely to believe that there are open opportunities and that her economic success and personal realization depend, to a large extent, on her own effort rather than on luck or circumstances outside her control. Verme (2009) and Bavetta and Navarra (2012) support this statement with empirical evidence. More interestingly, they show that individuals who perceive society as fair – who think, in other words, that they have control over their outcomes in life because it is the effort they deploy that matters – appreciate freedom of choice more than those who believe that the social playing field is uneven. Therefore, they are more likely to defend freedoms and to rely, if needed, upon themselves rather than on government intervention.

Overall, the empirical evidence on the perception of inequality offers a lot of valuable information that may improve upon the nonideal approach to liberalisms pursued by political economy. First, it confirms that there is more than mere commitment at a stake. As individual motivations and informal norms matter, a more satisfactory nonideal approach to liberalisms would benefit from embodying the perception of inequality in political economy. For example, protesters in Tahrir

Square in Cairo, Egypt, in January 2011 were motivated by rampant income inequality. Yet, statistical indicators show that income inequality in Egypt was probably in decline in the years that preceded the protest (Ianchovichina *et al.* 2015). Perhaps, the protesters' pursuit of some degree of freedoms in Egypt were motivated by a different perception of their society. As a lower income inequality opened up some opportunities to individuals, it probably made the general perception of inequality less bearable, increasing the benefits of protest. The pursuit of commitment could then be based on grassroots political innovation ignited by individual perceptions.

Second – and more to the point in this chapter – the empirical evidence on the perception of inequality confirms that the views of freedom that matter for a nonideal approach to liberalisms are manifold. Berlin's negative freedoms are an obvious candidate to support commitment but, by no means, the only one. Consistent with the historical account of freedoms given by Schmidtz and Brennan (2010), another candidate comes from the realm of politically relevant psychological freedoms, and it is a good fit to articulate the role of perceptions in a general view of liberalisms within political economy. This view of freedom is the focus of the next section.

4. Freedoms Reloaded: A Proposal

Reliance on the perception of inequality is intimately connected with a view of freedom centered on the idea of leading an autonomous life, whose origin is quintessentially Millian (Mill 1859; Bavetta and Navarra 2012). In *On Liberty*, John Stuart Mill refers to *individuality* (or autonomy freedom, in this chapter) as the condition of an individual whereby she has autonomously formed her preferences over the different courses of action open to her. To build up her own autonomy freedom, a person must be exposed to "experiments in lifestyle" to promote the discovery of new avenues she would otherwise be unaware of had society discouraged the emergence of alternative and eccentric individual perspectives. Moreover, even if exposed to a range of experiments in lifestyle, to fortify her own autonomy freedom a person must explore for herself, directly or indirectly, their relative fitness to her view of the good that would not be autonomously shaped lacking such an exposition and exploration. The Millian conception of autonomy freedom that I am advancing here is therefore composed of both a sufficiently wide range of available courses of action or opportunities and an ample spectrum of alternative preferences to use in the decision process that permit the achievement of a feeling of control over the outcomes of one's life.

From the liberal perspective, the main attraction of this view of freedom is its procedural character:

> autonomy provides a certain value to one's action by linking in a coherent fashion one's achievements with one's preferences, as part of a process of self-conscious creation. In the ideal autonomous life, what is achieved must have been chosen, what is chosen must have been preferred and preferences must be "of one's own" (not borrowed, for example, or not hetero-directed).
>
> (Bavetta and Guala 2003: 428)

This perspective fits nicely into the political economy's framework because it requires that freedom be independent of any particular conception of the good and makes it consistent with a nonideal, commitment-based approach to liberalism. More importantly, this view of freedom is embedded in the liberal tradition and is relevant for policy purposes.

In his fundamental contribution to a contractarian theory of the state, James Buchanan writes that, "the free market offers maximal scope for private, personal eccentricity, for individual freedom in its most elementary meaning" (Buchanan 1975: 18). Similarly, Milton Friedman highlights in

Capitalism and Freedom and *Free to Choose* the intimate relationship that ties economic freedom to diversity.[4] Consider the following, enlightening passage.

> The characteristic feature of action through political channels is that it tends to require or enforce substantial conformity. The great advantage of the market, on the other hand, is that it permits wide diversity. It is, in political terms, a system of proportional representation. Each man can vote, as it were, for the color of the tie he wants and get it; he does not have to see what color the majority wants and then, if he is in the minority, submit.
>
> It is this feature of the market we refer to when we say that the market provides economic freedom.
>
> (Friedman 1962: 15)

The interesting point in both Buchanan and Friedman is that they identify the possibility of shaping one's own life in a unique fashion offered by decentralized (market) exchanges as the essential feature of freedom (see also Binder, Chapter 33). Undeniably, a crucial presupposition of the affirmation of eccentricity and diversity must be the juridical protection of contractual liberty and the rights to private property or, what Robert Sugden (2003) labels, "the reasons of rules," as upheld by the commitment principle. However, by separating individual choice from a collective view of the good, Buchanan and Friedman highlight another essential dimension of liberalisms in political economy: the pursuit of one's own, unique or eccentric, view of the good. A pursuit that requires "the critical and self-critical man whose allegiance to his society's norms is informed by the best exercise of his rational powers" (Gray 1995: 59). Such a man and, more importantly, such a conception of autonomous behavior, "which avoids the rationalist metaphysics of the self of the sort criticized by Berlin and which has an insight into the role of conventions and traditions as conditions of freedom. . ., seems entirely congenial to liberalism" (Gray 1995: 59).

The reloading of freedoms in political economy to defend liberalisms would be of limited interest if autonomy freedom is not relevant for policy purposes. Its importance for policy is surely validated by the empirical findings on the role of perceived inequality in shaping how individuals form their preferences over institutions, as well as in undertaking socially relevant actions or risks. However, its policy relevance extends further, for example, to personal satisfaction (Bavetta *et al.* 2014; Verme 2009). It would be surprising that the proliferation of opportunities has no impact on individual well-being because, by permitting the affirmation of a self-constructed view of the good, it expands the feeling of control that individuals perceive over their lives.

In Bavetta *et al.* (2017, 2019), I use the reported level of happiness in the World Value Survey to measure well-being, the responses to a question on freedom of choice and control, in the same database, to assess personal freedom, and the KOF Globalisation Index to gauge the extent of globalization and estimate the marginal effect of an increase in personal freedom on individual happiness, given a set of sociodemographic controls. Data from 77 countries, from 1989 to 2011, establish that autonomy freedom and happiness stand in a positive relation no matter the degree of globalization, and that globalization has a multiplicative effect on the reported happiness. This latter point should not be underestimated. It unveils the existence of a "cross-effect" between globalization and happiness, mediated by experiments in living. The cross-effect amplifies the impact of autonomy freedom on the reported level of happiness as experiments in living become more abundant.

Experiments in living are therefore a powerful "manufacturer" of satisfaction because they trigger an emotional process driven by choice. They give free scope to the variety of characters and expand the possibility to experience, directly or indirectly, different modes of living. They favor comparisons across lifestyles, sharpen evaluations, allow the creation of new niches, speak to the peculiar values or views of the good to which an individual subscribes, and, by facilitating the matching of each person's lifestyle to her values and views, they increase happiness. There is evidence in psychology that satisfaction with life depends on the feeling of control over outcomes that an individual experiences – "locus of control" theory (Rotter 1966, 1990) – and, in turn, that the feeling of control depends on the extent of experiments in living – "attribution theory" (Deci and Ryan 1985) and the opportunity for trial-and-error processes.

The positive relation between personal freedom and happiness sides with a procedural view of the good also advanced by Phelps (2013). Attitudes such as searching, exploring, and experimenting are fulfilling and they contribute to personal flourishing. They engage the individual, challenge her perceived wisdom, call her to try the new, and provoke her excitement to venture into unknown directions. Of course, there is another side to this coin: they present the prospect of failure, the discomfort of missing the outcomes strived for, and the precariousness of adventuring. However, empirical evidence on what determines happiness scores a point for procedures over achievements and opens a perspective on the assessment of globalization otherwise missed in the literature. Irrespective of the distributional consequences of globalization that rightly concern scholars and the public opinion, the increase in experiments in living is a welcome outcome for individual well-being.

5. Fitting the Current Political Landscape

Autonomy freedom and the perception of inequality allow us to detect and measure some salient forces that lead individuals to shape liberalism from below by acting in ways that change institutions. As autonomy freedom and the perception of inequality vary, so do the direction of these forces and the chances that they are respectful of freedoms and pluralism. Empirical and historical evidence suggest that the respect for the values of liberalism is associated with the process that shapes these forces. Again, causality cannot be established; however, cultural variables and individual perceptions are linked to each other (Alesina and Fuchs-Schündeln 2007; Bavetta *et al.* 2017). More interestingly, the role played by experiments in lifestyles emerges as prominent. Through a process of trial and error, they contribute to the exercise of autonomous behavior, allow pluralism, and limit preferences for state intervention. Where individuals are not "educated" to experimenting in life, their autonomous behavior is limited and so is their readiness to rely upon themselves, if required by their circumstances. It follows that how much favor the environment would grant to experimentation and innovation depends on whether a community may "keep the soil fertile" for such experiments and favor grassroots innovation. If the soil is fertile, autonomy freedom and the perception of inequality are likely to push for liberalism. Of course, how far and how exactly cannot be predicted, but a steadier firewall is a plausible bet.

Recent developments in politics and society are depleting the soil's fertility, reducing opportunities for innovation and experimentation. First, antipluralist attitudes have emerged and consolidated worldwide in politics (Galston 2018). The combination of dislocation of productive activities, demographic changes, challenges to traditional values, and technological progress has altered both autonomy freedom and the perception of inequality for far too many who feel that their lives are no longer under their control (Case and Deaton 2020). As confidence in a better future is shaken and community life is in disarray, a sense of generational despair has emerged, fueled by insurgent politicians who have promised to use the power of the nation-state to restore an imagined past irremediably canceled by history. As Galston (2018) writes, demand for strong, anti-establishment leaders has grown while questioning key liberal principles, such as the rule of law, the freedom of the press, and minority rights. The door seems to be opening for a return to some forms of anticapitalism, cultural nationalism, and authoritarianism.

Second, a diffuse perception is gaining ground that equality of opportunity is receding. The issue is not the objective level of inequality but the evidence of its perception as reported by respondents through surveys. As the belief that inequality is expanding takes a firmer hold, the motivation to make an effort in the pursuit of original experiments in living contracts because opportunities appear to decision-makers to be no longer available or harder to realize. As for antipluralist attitudes, the consequence is a preference for both the involvement of the state in the economy to redress unfair inequalities and the expansion of collective processes of decision-making. In both cases, one should expect fewer experiments in living, the curtailment of the culture for refinement and improvement that is necessary for liberalism and prosperity (Friedman and Friedman 1980), and lower degrees of personal satisfaction (Bavetta *et al.* 2014, 2017; Phelps 2013).

With headwinds from the perception of unfairness or antipluralist sentiments, it would be naive to imagine that the direction institutional change could take is to embrace a freer society. Populist success is there to confirm it, as is the inability of legislatures or executive powers to conceive, let alone approve, full-fledged freedom-enhancing reforms. Speak out, debate, educate, foster the conditions for a shift in sentiments through conversation and nonviolent persuasion, and apply political economy's toolkit to offer evidence for nonintrusive policies in the fight against social exclusion and in the establishment of equal dignity: these are the arms liberals are left with in these times.

To a perfunctory observer they may appear to be firing blanks. They are not. A closer look reveals that conversation, education, debate, and enlarging the intellectual perspectives of the members of a community present them with new experiments in living that, in turn, trigger personal awareness, self-realization, and, ultimately, autonomy freedom. If I should lend credibility to the empirical evidence reviewed in this chapter, this is the component that commitment is looking to erect a firm firewall around liberalism.

And here is this chapter's modest analytical suggestion: political economy needs to grasp a quantitative idea of the individual motivations that compose, albeit incompletely, a fundamental aspect of liberalism, equal dignity, through the assessment of autonomous behavior. My suggestion stands on the traditions of John Stuart Mill – when he talks about the importance of choice – of Jim Buchanan – when he talks about the importance of eccentricity and its intimate relation with the dignity offered by the enjoyment of freedoms – and of Milton Friedman – when he praises private choices over collective decisions. The role of freedoms in political economy would then be reloaded to a fuller dimension, and our understanding of liberalism and how it may continue to offer material and immaterial prosperity to the present and future generations of human beings would be reinforced.

Acknowledgments

I wish to thank Pietro Navarra, Eleonora Montuschi, and Paolo Li Donni for their insightful suggestions to an earlier version of this chapter. All mistakes remain my own.

Related Chapters

Binder, Chapter 33 "Freedom and Markets"

Voorhoeve, this volume, "Policy Evaluation Under Severe Uncertainty: A Cautious, Egalitarian Approach"

Vromen, Chapter 9 "*As If* Social Preference Models"

Notes

1 Nondominance requires the absence of an arbitrary – even if merely potential – interference that makes an individual subject to another's will. This is, by and large, what commitment endeavors to prevent, even potentially, in the realm of institutions. However, nondominance transcends the relationships between institutions and individuals to include social interactions characterized by circumstances in which a person lives at the mercy of another – as dependent, slave, or debtor – because of imbalances of power that do not permit the enjoyment of the psychological status of an equal.

2 Many historical accounts exist that illustrate how the motivations underlying prosperity also apply to the political and social dimensions (see, for example, Mokyr 2017, 2019; Griffin 2013).
3 In fact, Alesina and Giuliano (2015) show that the two-way causal relation between culture and institutions goes beyond taxes and transfers.
4 Friedman, M. (1962) and Friedman and Friedman (1980).

Bibliography

Acemoglu, D., Johnson, S. and Robinson, J. (2005) "Institutions as a Fundamental Cause of Long-run Growth," in P. Aghion and S. Durlauf (eds.) *Handbook of Economic Growth*, Volume IA, Amsterdam: Elsevier.

Acemoglu, D. and Robinson, J. (2012) *Why Nations Fail: The Origins of Power, Prosperity, and Poverty*, London: Crown Publisher.

Acemoglu, D. and Robinson, J. (2019) *The Narrow Corridor: States, Societies, and the Fate of Liberty*, New York: Penguin Press.

Alesina, A. and Fuchs-Schündeln, N. (2007) "Goodbye Lenin (or Not?): The Effect of Communism on People," *American Economic Review* 97(4): 1507–1528.

Alesina, A. and Giuliano, P. (2011) "Preferences for Redistribution," in J. Benhabib, A. Bisin and M. Jackson (eds.), *Handbook of Social Economics*, Volume 1, Amsterdam: North-Holland.

Alesina, A. and Giuliano, P. (2015) "Culture and Institutions," *Journal of Economic Literature* 53(4): 898–944.

Bavetta, S. and Guala, F. (2003) "Autonomy Freedom and Deliberation," *Journal of Theoretical Politics* 15(4): 423–443.

Bavetta, S., Li Donni, P. and Marino, M. (2019) "An Empirical Analysis of the Determinants of Perceived Inequality," *Review of Income and Wealth* 65(2): 264–292.

Bavetta, S., Li Donni, P. and Marino, M. (2020) "How Consistent Are Perceptions of Inequality?" *Journal of Economic Psychology*, in press, https://doi.org/10.1016/j.joep.2020.102267.

Bavetta, S., Maimone, D., Miller, M. and Navarra, P. (2017) "More Choice for Better Choosers: Political Freedom, Autonomy, and Happiness," *Political Studies* 65(2): 316–338.

Bavetta, S. and Navarra, P. (2012) *The Economics of Freedom: Theory, Measurement and Policy Implications*, Cambridge: Cambridge University Press.

Bavetta, S., Navarra, P. and Maimone, D. (2014) *Freedom and the Pursuit of Happiness*, Cambridge: Cambridge University Press.

Berlin, I. (1969) "Two Concepts of Liberty," in I. Berlin (ed.) *Four Essays on Liberty*, London: Oxford University Press.

Besley, T. and Persson, T. (2011) *Pillars of Prosperity: The Political Economics of Development Clusters*, Princeton: Princeton University Press.

Buchanan, J. (1975) *The Limits of Liberty: Between Anarchy and Leviathan*, Chicago: University of Chicago Press.

Cannadine, D. (2017) *Victorious Century: The United Kingdom, 1800–1906*, New York: Viking.

Case, A. and Deaton, A. (2020) *Deaths of Despair and the Future of Capitalism*, Princeton, NJ: Princeton University Press.

Cox, G. (2017) "Political Institutions, Economic Liberty, and the Great Divergence," *The Journal of Economic History* 77(3): 724–755.

Deci, E. and Ryan, R. (1985) *Intrinsic Motivation and Self-Determination in Human Behavior*, New York: Plenum Press.

Friedman, M. (1962) *Capitalism and Freedom*, Chicago: University of Chicago Press.

Friedman, M. and Friedman, R. (1980) *Free to Choose: A Personal Statement*, New York: Harcourt Brace Jovanovich.

Galston, W. (2018) *Anti-Pluralism. The Populist Threat to Liberal Democracy*, New Haven: Yale University Press.

Gaus, G., Courtland, S. and Schmidtz, D. (2018) "Liberalism," *The Stanford Encyclopedia of Philosophy*, E. Zalta (ed.). Available online at: https://plato.stanford.edu/archives/spr2018/entries/liberalism/.

Gimpelson, V. and Treisman, D. (2018) "Misperceiving Inequality," *Economics & Politics* 30(1): 27–54.

Gray, J. (1993) *Post-Liberalism: Studies in Political Thought*, New York: Routledge.

Gray, J. (1995) *Liberalism (Second Edition)*, Buckingham: Open University Press.

Griffin, E. (2013) *Liberty's Dawn: A People's History of the Industrial Revolution*, New Haven: Yale University Press.

Guiso, L., Sapienza, P. and Zingales, L. (2006) "Does Culture Affect Economic Outcomes?" *Journal of Economic Perspectives* 20(2): 23–48, https://doi:10.1257/jep.20.2.23.

Gwartney, J., Lawson, R., Hall, J. and Murphy, R. (2019) *Economic Freedom of the World: 2019 Annual Report*, Vancouver: Fraser Institute.

Hayek, F.A. (1960) *The Constitution of Liberty*, Chicago: University of Chicago Press.
Hayek, F.A. (1978) "Liberalism," in F.A. Hayek (ed.) *New Studies in Philosophy, Politics, Economics and the History of Ideas*, London: Routledge and Kegan Paul.
Ianchovichina, E., Mottaghi, L. and Devarajan, S. (2015) *Inequality, Uprisings, and Conflict in the Arab World*, Washington, DC: The World Bank.
Inglehart, R. and Welzel, C. (2005) *Modernization, Cultural Change, and Democracy: The Human Development Sequence*, Cambridge: Cambridge University Press, https://doi:10.1017/CBO9780511790881.
Marshall, M. (2014) *Polity IV Project: Political Regime Characteristics and Transitions, 1800–2013*, Vienna, VA: Center for Systemic Peace.
McCloskey, D. (2017) "Manifesto for a New American Liberalism, or How to Be a Humane Libertarian." Available online at: https://capx.co/a-manifesto-for-a-new-american-liberalism/.
Mill, J.S. (1859) *On Liberty*, London: John W. Parker and Son.
Mokyr, J. (2009) *The Enlightened Economy: An Economic History of Britain, 1700–1850*, New Haven: Yale University Press.
Mokyr, J. (2017) *A Culture of Growth: The Origins of the Modern Economy*, Princeton: Princeton University Press.
Mokyr, J., Vickers, C. and Ziebarth, N. (2015) "The History of Technological Anxiety and the Future of Economic Growth: Is This Time Different?" *Journal of Economic Perspectives* 29(3): 31–50.
Mukand, S. and Rodrik, D. (2020) "The Political Economy of Liberal Democracy," *The Economic Journal* 130(627): 765–792, https://doi.org/10.1093/ej/ueaa004
North, D. (1990) *Institutions, Institutional Change and Economic Performance*, Cambridge: Cambridge University Press.
North, D., Wallis, J. and Weingast, B. (2009) *Violence and Social Orders: A Conceptual Framework for Interpreting Recorded Human History*, Cambridge: Cambridge University Press.
North, D. and Weingast, B. (1989) "Constitutions and Commitment: The Evolution of Institutions Governing Public Choice in Seventeenth-Century England," *The Journal of Economic History* 49(4): 803–832.
Passarelli, F. and Tabellini, G. (2017) "Emotions and Political Unrest," *Journal of Political Economy* 125(3): 903–946.
Persson, T. and Tabellini, G. (2000) *Political Economics: Explaining Economic Policy*, Cambridge, MA: MIT University Press.
Pettit, P. (1997) *Republicanism: A Theory of Freedom and Government*, Oxford: Oxford University Press.
Pettit, P. (2001) *A Theory of Freedom: From the Psychology to the Politics of Agency*, Oxford: Oxford University Press.
Phelps, E. (2013) *Mass Flourishing: How Grassroots Innovation Created Jobs, Challenge, and Change*, Princeton: Princeton University Press.
Pinker, S. (2018) *Enlightenment Now: The Case for Reason, Science, Humanism, and Progress*, New York: Viking.
Rajan, R. and Zingales, L. (2003) *Saving Capitalism from the Capitalists*, London: Random House.
Rotter, J. (1966) "Generalized Expectancies for Internal Versus External Control of Reinforcement," *Psychological Monographs*, 8 Whole No. 609.
Rotter, J. (1990) "Internal Versus External Locus of Control of Reinforcement: A Case History of a Variable," *American Psychologist* 45: 489–493.
Schmidtz, D. and Brennan, J. (2010) *A Brief History of Liberty*, London: Wiley Blackwell.
Scully, G. (1992) *Constitutional Environments and Economic Growth*, Princeton: Princeton University Press.
Shleifer, A. (2009) "The Age of Milton Friedman," *Journal of Economic Literature* 47(1): 123–135.
Sugden, R. (2003) "Opportunity as A Space for Individuality: Its Value and the Impossibility of Measuring It," *Ethics* 113: 783–809.
Tabellini, G. (2010) "Culture and Institutions: Economic Development in the Regions of Europe," *Journal of the European Economic Association* 8(4): 677–716.
Teorell, J. (2010) *Determinants of Democratization: Explaining Regime Change in the World, 1972–2006*, Cambridge: Cambridge University Press.
Verme, P. (2009) "Happiness, Freedom and Control," *Journal of Economic Behavior & Organization* 71: 146–161.
Welzel, C. (2013) *Freedom Rising: Human Empowerment and the Quest for Emancipation*, Cambridge: Cambridge University Press, https://doi:10.1017/CBO9781139540919.
Zwolinski, M. (2015) "A Libertarian Case for the Moral Limits of Markets," *The Georgetown Journal of Law & Public Policy* 30: 275–290.

33
FREEDOM AND MARKETS

Constanze Binder

1. Introduction

Freedom is omnipresent in public and theoretical debates about markets. People in Greece demonstrate against European Union (EU) austerity policies with reference to the freedom of their nation to choose its own path out of the economic crisis. The very same European policies are justified in the name of economic freedom in Brussels. Textile workers in Cambodia demonstrate for better working conditions in the name of freedom, while the global market for which they produce is justified by an increase in freedom of choice for consumers.

Indeed freedom is one of the values most prominently invoked throughout history to both defend and criticize markets. What is striking though is that these arguments are based on very different conceptions of freedom. Market proponents, for instance, often invoke so-called negative conceptions of freedom, where freedom can (only) be curtailed by (intentional) interference (by the state). Market skeptics usually invoke conceptions of freedom where a lack of resources or power asymmetries due to material inequalities can lead to a decrease in freedom as well. A drawback of this practice is that regulatory state interference, say, redistribution policies, might by definition infringe upon freedom along the conception employed by proponents of the markets, whereas they often are taken to lead to an increase in freedom along conceptions invoked by market skeptics.

A risk is thus that one's assessment of markets in terms of freedom ultimately depends on one's choice of the conception of freedom, making a more nuanced assessment of markets in different contexts difficult. The objective of this chapter is to shed new light on the arguments voiced to defend and criticize markets in the name of freedom in order to provide the grounds for a more nuanced debate on how markets can possibly both promote and limit freedom in different circumstances.

For this purpose, we provide an overview of some of the most prominent arguments put forward by market proponents and critics in Section 2. Section 3 discusses the differences in the conceptions of freedom in the different arguments by drawing on the more general concept of freedom pioneered by MacCallum [1]. This will allow us to identify more nuanced differences in the respective conceptions of freedom employed in the various arguments, such as the constraints that are deemed relevant, and thus set the stage for a more fine-grained assessment of markets in terms of freedom. We will then use this more general perspective to discuss the role of freedom in contemporary welfare economics in Section 4. In Section 5 we then move on to explore how our discussion of the use of a more general concept of freedom allows us to assess specific (regulatory) policies, namely, policies of redistribution, in terms of their effect on freedom. We will see that the more general

DOI: 10.4324/9781315739793-41

concept of freedom introduced in Section 3 allows one to develop more nuanced insights regarding the conditions under which redistributive policies can increase or decrease freedom.

2. Defending and Criticizing Markets in the Name of Freedom

Markets refer to a range of different societal institutions. In this chapter, we will understand markets as institutions that allocate scarce resources by means of price signals that are determined by supply and demand of a commodity. The two most common values employed to justify and defend markets theoretically are efficiency and freedom.[1] Freedom especially features prominently in arguments both defending and opposing markets. Libertarians like Nozick [2], for instance, usually employ a notion of freedom as non–state interference and defend the market as the most freedom-promoting societal system. Friedman [3] adopts a notion of freedom as choice and defends markets for their positive effect on it. Socialists like Cohen [4], on the other hand, often criticize markets for the unfreedom they create for the proletariat. Yet others argue for specific limitations of markets on the basis of a republican notion of freedom [5] or to safeguard the socioeconomic preconditions for freedom and autonomy [6].

How can it be that markets are both defended and opposed in the name of freedom? One reason for such opposing views are the many different conceptions of freedom used in debates about markets. Greek protesters might associate freedom with a nation choosing its own destiny. An austerity policy is justified by a notion of economic freedom requiring minimal state interference. Western consumers might be concerned about the freedom of choice afforded by free markets, and textile workers in Cambodia might think of minimum wages as a precondition for their freedom.

Philosophical arguments defending or opposing free markets usually start out from very different definitions of freedom. Libertarians drawing on Nozick [2], for instance, belong to the most prominent defenders of a minimal state and proponents of the market. Nozick adopts a moralized notion of freedom: freedom as the absence of illegitimate interference or illegitimately imposed constraints. What counts as illegitimate interference is derived from Nozick's principles of just acquisition and just transfer. If these principles are met, interference with a person's possessions violates his property rights and constitutes an illegitimate interference, which is thus an infringement upon his freedom. Some negative conceptions of freedom [7] yield a similar conclusion based on a different definition of freedom: negative freedom is curtailed by government intervention. Thus, most, if not all, government policies, ranging from laws that oblige people to use seat belts to redistributive taxation schemes, diminish freedom in its negative conception.

What is striking in these two examples is that government regulation of markets, such as in welfare states or redistributive government policies, decreases freedom by definition. In Nozick's conception of freedom [2], for instance, any intervention with a person's rightfully obtained property leads to an infringement of freedom. The tasks of government are reduced to safeguarding property rights and providing the (legal) basis of voluntary transaction, by securing public safety and the enforceability of contracts. Similarly, because most negative conceptions of freedom view that it is only curtailed by government intervention, most regulatory policies infringe upon freedom, by definition. In both of these cases, the argument in defense of markets from freedom seems to be begging the question: redistribution implemented by the government leads to a decrease in freedom by the very definition of freedom employed. Although less directly, other arguments for and against markets are equally dependent on the notion of freedom they adopt.

Those who criticize markets in the name of freedom usually employ very different conceptions of freedom. Cohen [4] for instance, relies upon a notion of group freedom when criticizing market structures due to the unfreedom they create for the proletariat as a collective to move up the social hierarchy. Even though individuals enjoy the freedom to become part of the capital-owning class, this freedom is structurally prevented for the proletariat as a collective in capitalist systems. Anderson

[6], on the other hand, argues for moral limits on markets to preserve the social preconditions of freedom. In her account, a person's freedom consists of the availability of a range of significant options through which she can express her various valuations. To develop and exercise such a plurality of valuations requires putting limitations to markets in order to create a plurality of different spheres subject to different norms and valuations. Sen [8, 9] is concerned with developing a notion of freedom that allows one to account for information about freedom in welfare economic assessments. The objective is to assess markets not only in terms of individual welfare achievements but also in terms of the life paths effectively open to people. For this purpose, he employs a notion of effective freedom that allows for (a lack of) resources to constrain the life paths open to people and thereby the freedom they enjoy. The neo-republican notion of freedom employed by Pettit in his criticism of markets [5] goes beyond Sen's conception insofar as it also accounts for constraints on people's freedom due to potential interference in a person's freedom (even if not actually exercised) due to, say, power imbalances created in markets. Thus, we can see that, in this great variety of conceptions employed by critics of markets, the argument about their freedom-limiting effects crucially relies upon the conception of freedom invoked, as well, whether one accounts for the preconditions to exercise it, as Anderson does, or allows for a lack of resources or power asymmetries to constrain it, as in case of Sen's and Pettit's arguments.

The drawback of this practice of starting out from one specific conception of freedom is that one's assessment of markets will be limited: it makes it impossible to scrutinize under which conditions markets can promote or limit freedom, and it does not allow for a more nuanced assessment of markets and their possible different impacts on freedom in different contexts. It risks inhibiting one's understanding of how markets can possibly both promote and limit the freedom of different actors in different circumstances [10]. However, precisely such nuanced insights are necessary for policy assessment and for a constructive debate about the merits and possible limitations of markets in general to gain a clear understanding of how inequality and redistributive policies affect freedom.

How should one proceed? Does the defense of or opposition to markets in the name of freedom ultimately depend on one's acceptance of the conception of freedom employed? Does the disagreement about markets ultimately come down to a disagreement about the right conception of freedom? Does one have to settle first on the conception of freedom (for the purpose of the assessment of markets) before one can proceed to assess markets in terms of their impact on human freedom? In this chapter, an alternative method is proposed. Instead of first settling on a conception of freedom – which itself might be a mission impossible if freedom is, as has been argued, ultimately a contested concept [11] – we shall draw on a more general concept of freedom proposed by MacCallum [1].

3. A Framework To Assess Markets in Terms of Freedom

MacCallum [1] prominently argued that different conceptions of freedom put forward in the literature ultimately come down to different interpretations of one of the same "formula of freedom." All conceptions refer to a person or group of persons *X* who is free from a set of relevant constraints *Y*, in order to do or not do, be or not be *Z*. Different conceptions differ with regard to the interpretation of these three parameters, that is, who can be free (*X*), what are the constraints relevant to freedom (*Y*), and whether freedom is ultimately concerned with actions or states of being (*Z*). To illustrate, let us consider the conceptions of freedom employed by Nozick and Sen.

In cases of Nozick and Sen, the main focus is on individual persons *X*. Similarly, in the case of *Z*, both authors consider mainly actions or states of being. When it comes to the constraints *Y*, however, the conceptions of freedom the two authors use differ considerably. Sen [12] considers a very wide set of constraints to be relevant, ranging from natural or environmental constraints, to social or legal constraints, such as the norms prevailing in a society, to a lack of resources. Nozick [2], on the other hand, focuses on a very specific sort of moral constraint: only actions that interfere with a person's rightfully acquired personal sphere and possessions are limiting her freedom. To illustrate, consider a redistributive policy. For Sen, the focus is on the constraints relieved from (or imposed on) the agent to whom resources are given (or from whom resources are taken). In Nozick's case, however, the focus is on the question of whether the interference with a person's possessions is legitimate. This led him to the by now famous exclamation that redistributive taxation can be considered as forced labor.

If one accepts MacCallum's triadic formula as encompassing most if not all conceptions of freedom, then the question is how it can be used to assess markets in terms of freedom. The advantage of MacCallum's formula is that we can discuss separately (a) the impact of markets on different actors involved in or affected by market transactions, (b) the constraints markets impose or relieve, and (c) the (sort of) options markets open up or restrict. Given the general way we have discussed markets so far and their manifold effects on different aspects of society in different contexts, we shall constrain ourselves here to a discussion of the preceding three aspects in general terms. In the following, we shall discuss each of these three aspects in turn before we apply the general framework to a more specific question, namely, whether, and if so under which conditions, redistribution can be justified in terms of freedom. Starting with the relevant agents (*X*): who are the relevant (groups of) actors whose freedom can be interfered with by market forces? At first these are the individuals engaging in market transactions. However, besides the people actually engaging in the respective transaction, as pointed out by Cohen [13] in his criticism of Nozick, there can be other persons or groups who are affected by side effects. These might be the people who have increasing difficulty affording basic nutrition if the respective world market prices rise due to speculative transactions, for instance. Other actors that might undertake market transactions and/or are affected by them are groups of persons such as companies, governments, or labor unions, for instance.

Concerning the relevant constraints (*Y*), if markets are taken in very general terms to be institutions that allocate scarce resource by means of price signals, then the two main relevant constraints seem to be resource constraints and legal constraints. Resources obviously determine what is within reach of a person in the marketplace. Similarly, legal constraints determine which transactions are legally allowed. Satz [14] argues, for instance, that certain areas of life should not be subject to market transactions due to moral reasons, such as trade in organs. Another set of constraints might become relevant in some cases of externalities, say, if environmental costs are not properly accounted for in markets and, as a result, the activities of some actors lead to the pollution of water and air, imposing severe constraints upon others. Note that this last case would not count as a limitation of a person's freedom in most of the notions of freedom discussed in the literature for two main reasons: first, some might argue that it counts as a natural constraint because the causal chain leading back to the actions of the polluting company is not strong enough. Second, they assume a constraint only counts as relevant if it was imposed intentionally, a requirement that many (negative) conceptions of freedom impose. In this case, the reason that can be invoked is that the relevant action was not intended to bring about the side effects in question.

What are the relevant actions or states of being (*Z*) that markets affect? Most conceptions of freedom focus on actions people can perform in the assessment of people's freedom. Some [15, 16] also include states of being, such as living in a malaria-free country. One question that has received much attention in the formal literature on the conceptualization and measurement of freedom is whether the relevant diversity of the available options affects a person's freedom. The question is, for instance, whether a person's freedom is indeed increasing if he has five marginally different brands of washing powders available than if he only has two to choose between. Similarly, a crucial question is whether the value a person attributes to the available actions affects her freedom. Is a person who can choose on which of three different park benches to spend the night freer than a person who can choose between two different hotels?

This preliminary discussion of the three parts of MacCallum's general concept of freedom is meant as a first illustration of how his framework could be employed to move beyond a particular conception of freedom in the assessment of markets. In the next section, we will draw on MacCallum's framework to discuss recent attempts to account for freedom in welfare economic assessments.

4. Freedom in Contemporary Welfare Economics

Recent decades have witnessed a revival of debates about freedom in contemporary welfare economics. Traditional welfare economics rested for a long time purely on utilitarian or welfarist pillars (for further discussions related to welfarism, see Baujard, Chapter 15). The maximization of social welfare, understood as an aggregate of individual welfare or utility, formed the main guiding principle of the discipline [17]. Increased skepticism about, among others, the possibility of making interpersonal utility comparisons led to a search regarding how welfare judgments can be made without relying on interpersonal comparisons. The Pareto principle became one prominent minimal condition used to assess allocations resulting from market outcomes. Allocations are Pareto optimal if it is not possible to make anybody better off (in terms of utility) without making somebody else worse off by reallocation.

One drawback of the Pareto principle, though, is that it leads to an incomplete ranking of allocations. It leaves Pareto-optimal allocations, which might differ greatly with regard to other values such as equality or the freedom people enjoy, unranked. One way to appreciate the contribution of the Arrovian impossibility result [18] is to address precisely this question of how incomplete Pareto rankings can be completed in a democratic way, that is, by a procedure that aggregates all preference orderings of members in a society into a social ranking that can steer theoretical and practical welfare assessments. One pathbreaking insight of Arrow's impossibility result was that there is no procedure that satisfies a weak version of the Pareto-optimality requirement, as well as some minimally plausible conditions of democratic procedure. The literature of social choice theory, following Arrow's result, explores a number of different escape routes from this impossibility [19, 20].

One of these avenues, pioneered by Sen [21], is to overcome the informational parsimony underlying Arrow's welfarist framework by including information about rights and freedom people enjoy in the respective societal states. As a result, a literature developed on how information about freedom could be incorporated in welfare economic assessments. Some focused on the formalization of rights [22, 23], while others [24] pioneered a literature aiming to conceptualize freedom and axiomatize so-called freedom rankings with the aim to assess individual choice situations in terms of the freedom they offer to a person [25]. In the following, we discuss some of the main questions currently being debated within this field of inquiry.

The freedom-ranking literature employs an axiomatic approach to explore the conditions for ranking choice situations in terms of the freedom they offer to people. Choice situations are depicted by (opportunity) sets of alternatives from which the person whose freedom is under assessment can choose precisely one. These alternatives can be interpreted in various ways. They can depict actions, bundles of commodities, or bundles of "doings and beings," such as capabilities. An axiomatic approach is employed to address the question of how these sets can be ranked in terms of the freedom (of choice) they offer to a person. One advantage of the formal framework is it allows one to explore in general terms the plausibility and mutual compatibility of conditions a freedom ranking is supposed to fulfill and the implications these yield.

One of the first rankings, the Simple Cardinality Ranking [24], is based solely on information about the number of alternatives available in a set: the more options a set contains, the more freedom of choice it offers. No information about the alternatives other than their number is taken to influence the freedom a person enjoys in a certain situation. Many, including the authors themselves, consider this ranking that equates a person's freedom with the quantity of alternatives open to her to be counterintuitive.

In response, most contributions within the freedom-ranking literature strive to account for additional information that is relevant to a person's freedom. One can roughly distinguish two main areas. The first explores how information about the differences between the options open for choice can be integrated in freedom rankings. For instance, does a set allowing one to choose from five different brands of water in a supermarket that only differ with regard to the shape of the bottles offer more freedom than a set allowing one to choose between the use of the public water supply and two brands in the supermarket? The second area focuses on ways in which information about the values of alternatives can be taken into account in the assessment of a person's freedom (for a survey, see [25, 26]). For instance, does having the additional option to accept a job in a garment-making plant without labor protection increase one's freedom to the same extent as a job with social security and labor protection?

An important issue in these debates about the role of the diversity of options and their value is which conception of freedom underlies the respective ranking and whether we interpret freedom rankings as ranking sets in terms of the extent or the value of freedom [27]. The generality of the axiomatic framework employed is often taken to be a crucial advantage in this respect, as it can accommodate a wide range of different conceptions of freedom relevant in welfare economic assessment. This advantage comes with a risk though, namely, that one refrains from exploring the possible limitations of the general framework as to the conceptions of freedom it can accommodate and thereby risks excluding conceptions that are highly relevant in debates about markets and freedom. It is useful to draw again on MacCallum's general concept of freedom to explore this point and identify possible limits to the conceptions of freedom that the axiomatic framework can accommodate.

In MacCallum's formula, *X* refers to a person whose freedom is under assessment. In the freedom-ranking literature, freedom rankings usually refer to the ranking of opportunity sets in terms of the freedom they offer to an individual agent.[2] The interpretation of alternatives (*Z*) can range from commodity bundles to actions or states of being and can accommodate the range of conceptions of freedom relevant for market assessments [28].

To move on to the set of relevant constraints *Y*: the question of which constraints have to be absent for an option to form part of an opportunity set is not addressed in the freedom-ranking literature. The general framework allows for a wide range of relevant constraints, ranging from legal norms to a lack of resources. However, it is not clear how the framework based on subset rankings can accommodate constraints crucial to neo-republican notions of freedom and with them the possibility to assess a possible freedom-decreasing effect that markets can have due to asymmetries of power. More specifically, a characteristic feature of (neo)republican notions of freedom is that potential interference, even if not actually undertaken, can also limit a person's freedom. Say, for example, one can be fired at any time due to the arbitrary will of one's employer. Conceptualization of freedom in terms of set rankings cannot account for the interpersonal dependency of the options available in a person's opportunity set [29] or thus for constraints that account for potentially arbitrary interference by others that are crucial to neo-republican notions of freedom. This seems particularly troublesome as a considerable share of the literature in political philosophy on the freedom-constraining effects of markets draws on the republican notion of freedom [30].

So what is the upshot of this first rather crude attempt to employ MacCallum's general concept of freedom to explore potential limits to the conceptions of freedom that the subset ranking literature on freedom in welfare economics can accommodate? The generality of the formal framework employed in the freedom-ranking literature allows one to account for a wide range of conceptions of freedom. In light of the motivation that sparked the freedom-ranking literature, that is, to overcome the informational parsimony of welfarism by accounting for information about freedom, the relevant conceptions of freedom, such as the one of effective freedom employed by Sen in the capability approach [16], can be taken into account [31].[3] However, there are limits to the conceptions of freedom that the formal framework in the freedom-ranking literature based on subset rankings can accommodate. As it cannot account for the interpersonal dependency of opportunity sets, it does not serve to formalize neo-republican notions of freedom. Game-theoretic frameworks to analyze freedom [32] and power hold much promise to fill this lacuna in the freedom-ranking literature though.

5. Redistribution, Inequality, and Freedom

The question addressed in this section is under which conditions redistribution of income can increase freedom in a society. To address this question requires us to move from the question of how individual freedom should be conceptualized, addressed in the previous sections, to the question of how freedom should be assessed in a society as a whole (as it is relevant when it comes to questions of redistribution). Questions of how to assess the overall impact of inequality and measures of redistribution upon society require not only an understanding how to fill in the three parts of MacCallum's formula but also some understanding of how different possible impacts of a policy upon the freedom of different people should be assessed as a whole. One can distinguish between three different classes of approaches to do this: to aggregate individual freedom into overall freedom, to focus on those cases in which one can increase the freedom of some members of society without decreasing the freedom of others, or to focus on certain specific freedoms and the question of whether these freedoms are open to all members of society. In the following, we shall discuss each of these approaches in turn.

Overall freedom refers to some aggregate of freedom across all people in a society. If it takes money and wealth to lift constraints on freedom [33], then redistribution will increase the freedom of the poor and decrease the freedom of the rich. The question, however, is whether it does so to the same extent. If one assumes wealth to contribute positively to freedom but to do so with decreasing marginal returns, that is, the increase in freedom decreases with every extra euro, then redistribution would be justified until the marginal rate of return in terms of freedom is equal among all members of society. If the freedom gained with every extra euro were the same for every member in society, this would demand the equal distribution of wealth for the maximization of overall freedom in society.

This aggregation approach, even though variants of it are defended in the literature [33], faces a number of problems. The main question is whether freedom can and should be traded off across people in society. Can a sufficiently large increase in the freedom of some indeed justify a reduction in the freedom of others? In the extreme case, this could justify the enslavement of some members of society as long as the increase in the freedom of others is large enough to outweigh the loss of freedom of the new slaves. Arguments against redistribution often proceed along these veins, that the decrease in freedom of the rich cannot be traded off against the increase in freedom of the poor due to redistributive measures.

A Pareto criterion of freedom avoids trade-offs being made across people by demanding that a social state is only better in terms of overall freedom if the freedom of any member cannot be increased further without decreasing the freedom of anybody else in society. So, the question now is (under which conditions) can redistribution increase the freedom of some without diminishing the freedom of others? First, this can be the case if above a certain level of wealth freedom does not increase with an extra euro. Put differently, if the marginal return of freedom becomes zero at some point, to tax away income above this level will not decrease the freedom of the respective person anymore. Second, it can be the case if inequality diminishes the freedom of "the rich" to a greater extent than the money given up in the course of redistribution reduces it. Indeed, there is a growing literature on the adverse effects inequality in wealth can have on freedom [30, 34].

One of the main problems with the application of the Pareto criterion to freedom should be emphasized here, namely, that it can allow for great inequalities in the distribution of freedom. Indeed it could justify a totalitarian state in which one group enjoys all the freedom and most citizens hardly enjoy any freedom. If the first group would "suffer" even the slightest decrease in freedom by extending the freedom of the majority of its citizens, then the Pareto principle of freedom would justify this state of affairs.

Given these severe problems of overall freedom and the Pareto principle of freedom, it is not surprising that the main focus in the literature shifted toward a set of basic liberties that should be guaranteed to all citizens equally and that cannot be traded off against each other or across different persons. Rawls [35], for instance, takes these liberties to consist of the basic democratic liberties and liberty of bodily integrity, among others. The question now is, again (under which conditions), can redistribution be justified in terms of such basic liberties? First, this is the case if some basic liberties require a basic subsistence level of material resources in order to be able to exercise them. In the case where "the poor become too poor" and fall below this subsistence level, redistribution would thus be justified in the name of freedom up to the point that it guarantees equal basic liberties for all. Second, inequality can itself undermine certain basic liberties of both the rich and the poor in a society. One instance is if inequality leads to inequalities in power and undermines democratic liberties. Another instance is if inequality leads to a decrease in social cohesion and an increase in the criminality rate, which undermines the liberty of bodily integrity. In this case, redistribution would be justified in the name of freedom until inequality is reduced to a level at which it no longer undermines the basic liberties in the previously described ways.

The last case is an especially interesting one, because it refers to cases in which redistribution does not lead to a decrease in freedom on the side of the rich and sometimes even increases it along with increasing the freedom of the poor. One objection that might be raised at this point is that the preceding analysis relies to a large extent on the fact that a lack of resources is considered to be a relevant constraint to freedom. What if one were to adopt one of the conceptions of freedom that are commonly used by opponents of redistributive policies, such as the Nozickean one discussed in Section 2? Could redistribution be justified using such a conception as well?

In case of the Nozickean conception of freedom, a lack of resources does not constrain a person's freedom. Only interference with her rightfully acquired property or intervention in voluntary transactions between consenting parties does. Interestingly enough, if wealth is not considered a relevant constraint of freedom, a decrease in it will also not per se diminish it. The reason why redistributive transactions are opposed by libertarians following Nozick is that they are taken to interfere with the allocation of property that is the result of voluntary transactions and thus interfere with voluntary decisions. The only role Nozick assigns to the state is to provide the basis for background conditions to make such voluntary agreements possible. This includes matters of security, such as police or national defense, as well as institutions necessary to enforce contract law and property rights. However, it has been argued [36] that a lack of resources can undermine the voluntariness of transactions themselves. Similarly, Fleurbaey [37] argues that inequality in wealth can undermine the voluntariness of trade. A related, but different, argument has been voiced by Cohen [13], namely, that inequality can be the result of unintended side effects of voluntary transactions among consenting adults. In this case, existing inequality in a society could not be justified by the value of free and voluntary choices along Nozickean lines, because these free choices are undermined by inequality.

In these cases, redistribution can be justified in terms of providing the basis for voluntary transactions themselves. If (a) poverty leads to a lack of choice options that undermines the voluntariness of decisions, and/or if (b) inequality in wealth leads to a strong imbalance of power undermining the voluntariness of the decisions of the parties engaging in a transaction or of third parties due to unintended side effects, then redistribution can be justified in terms of the very same ideal underlying the Nozickean conception of freedom, namely, voluntariness of choice.

6. Conclusion

The objective of this chapter was to survey arguments defending and opposing markets in terms of freedom. For this purpose, conceptions of freedom employed in different arguments in the literature were scrutinized (for further discussions related to freedom, see Bavetta, Chapter 32). It turns out that the conceptions of freedom employed in the various arguments for and against free markets are very different, making a more nuanced assessment and analysis of the conditions under which markets promote or curtail freedom difficult. To overcome this problem, we introduced a more general concept of freedom [1] that encompasses the different conceptions of freedom of the various arguments as special cases and put it to use in theory and practice. On a theoretical level, we discussed the literature on freedom rankings in contemporary welfare economics and found that, even though the general axiomatic analysis does not restrict one to a specific conception of freedom, it excludes some neo-republican notions of freedom and with them the potential to analyze markets and their effect on freedom in terms of the possible power imbalances they create. On a practical level, we turned to the assessment of specific policies, namely, redistributive policies, and the question of under which conditions redistribution can be justified in the name of freedom. It was shown that especially in cases in which inequality risks undermining democratic liberties or the voluntariness of transactions due to an imbalance of power, redistribution can be justified even using the conceptions of freedom usually employed to defend markets.

Related Chapters

Bavetta, Chapter 32 "Freedoms, Political Economy, and Liberalism"
Baujard, Chapter 15 "Values in Welfare Economics"

Notes

1 In welfare economics, efficiency became the more prominent criterion in the last century. It is usually defined as Pareto efficiency, showing that markets can lead, under a number of idealized conditions, to Pareto-optimal allocations in which it is not possible to make any member of society better off without making anybody else worse off (in terms of utility). Freedom, on the other hand, featured more in earlier defenses of markets and is prominently invoked by free marketeers from the libertarian tradition.

2 Even though the framework allows for an interpretation of the set rankings in terms of group freedom as well, the plausibility of the axioms might differ considerably, depending on whether one is concerned with individual or group freedom.

3 It has been questioned though whether this necessarily entails a departure from a welfarist framework in welfare economics [38].

Bibliography

1. MacCallum, Gerald G. Jr. (1967). 'Negative and Positive Freedom', *The Philosophical Review* 76: 312–334.
2. Nozick, Robert (1974). *Anarchy, State and Utopia,* New York: Basic Books.
3. Friedman, Milton (1992). *Capitalism and Freedom,* Chicago: University of Chicago Press.
4. Cohen, G. A. (1983). 'The Structure of Proletarian Unfreedom', *Philosophy and Public Affairs* 12: 3–33.
5. Pettit, P. (2006). 'Freedom in the Market', *Politics, Philosophy & Economics* 5: 131–149.
6. Anderson, Elizabeth (1993). *Value in Ethics and Economics*, Cambridge: Harvard University Press.
7. Berlin, Isaiah (1969). *Four Essays on Liberty*, Oxford: Oxford University Press.
8. Sen, Amartya K. (1993). 'Markets and Freedoms: Achievements and Limitations of the Market Mechanism in Promoting Individual Freedoms', *Oxford Economic Papers* 45: 519–541.
9. Sen, Amartya K. (2002). *Rationality and Freedom*, Cambridge: Harvard University Press.
10. Herzog, Lisa (2013). 'Markets', *The Stanford Encyclopedia of Philosophy* (Winter 2013 Edition), Edward N. Zalta (ed.), http://plato.stanford.edu/archives/fall2013/entries/markets/
11. Gallie, Walter B. (1956). 'Essentially Contested Concepts', *Proceedings of the Aristotelian Society* 56: 167–198.

12. Sen, Amartya K. (1985). *Commodities and Capabilities*, Amsterdam: North-Holland.
13. Cohen, G. A. (1995). *Self-Ownership, Freedom, and Equality*, Cambridge: Cambridge University Press.
14. Satz, Debra (2007). 'Liberalism, Economic Freedom, and the Limits of Markets', *Social Philosophy and Policy* 24: 120–140.
15. Carter, Ian (1999). *A Measure of Freedom*, Oxford: Oxford University Press.
16. Sen, Amartya K. (1999). *Development as Freedom*, Oxford: Oxford University Press.
17. Backhouse, Roger, Antoinette Baujard and Tamotsu Nishizawa (2021). *Welfare Theory, Public Action, and Ethical Values Revisiting the History of Welfare Economics*, Cambridge: Cambridge University Press.
18. Arrow, Kenneth J. (1951/1963). *Social Choice and Individual Values*, New Haven: Yale University Press.
19. Gaertner, Wulf (2006). *A Primer in Social Choice Theory*, Oxford: Oxford University Press.
20. Sen, Amartya K. (1986). 'Social Choice Theory', in: *Handbook of Mathematical Economics*, Volume 3, Kenneth J. Arrow and Michael D. Intriligator (eds.), pp. 1073–1181, Amsterdam: North-Holland.
21. Sen, Amartya K. (1970/2018). *Collective Choice and Social Welfare*, Cambridge: Holden Day.
22. Gaertner, Wulf, Prassanta Pattanaik and Kotaro Suzumura (1992). 'Individual Rights Revisited', *Economica* 59: 161–177.
23. Stiglitz, Joseph (2000). *Legal Reductionsim and Freedom*, Dordrecht: Kluwer.
24. Pattanaik Prasanta K. and Yongsheng Xu (1990). 'On Ranking Opportunity Sets in Terms of Freedom of Choice', *Recherches Economiques de Louvain* 56: 383–390.
25. Dowding, Keith and Martin van Hees (2009). 'Freedom of Choice', in: *The Handbook of Rational and Social Choice*, Paul Anand, Prasanta K. Pattanaik and Clemens Puppe (eds.), Oxford: Oxford University Press, 374–392.
26. Baujard, Antoinette (2007). 'Conceptions of Freedom and Ranking Opportunity Sets. A Typology', *Homo Oeconomicus* 24: 231–254.
27. Stiglitz, Joseph (2010). 'The Specific Value of Freedom', *Social Choice and Freedom* 35: 687–703.
28. Binder, Constanze (2019). *Agency, Freedom and Choice*, Springer Series: Theory and Decision Library A: Philosophy and Methodology of the Social Sciences, Dordrecht: Kluwer.
29. Pattanaik, Prasanta K. and Yongsheng Xu (2019). 'On Capability and its Measurement', in: *The Cambridge Handbook of the Capability Approach*, E. Chiappero Martinetti S. Osmani, and M. Qizilbash (eds.), chapter 14, pp. 271–292, Cambridge: Cambridge University Press.
30. Vrousalis, Nicholas (2020). 'Structural Domination and Collective Agency in the Market?', *Journal of Applied Philosophy* 37: 1–19.
31. Binder, Constanze and Ingrid Robeyns (2019). 'Economic Ethics and the Capability Approach?' in: *The Oxford Handbook of Ethics and Economics*, Mark D. White (ed.), Oxford: Oxford University Press.
32. Bervoets, Sebastian (2007). 'Freedom in a Social Context: Comparing Game Forms', *Social Choice and Welfare* 29: 295–315.
33. Loevinsohn, Ernest (1977). 'Liberty and the Redistribution of Property', *Philosophy and Public Affairs* 6: 226–239.
34. Claassen, Rutger and Lisa Herzog (2019). 'Why Economic Agency Matters: An Account of Structural Domination in the Economic Realm', *European Journal of Political Theory*.
35. Rawls, John (1971/1999). *A Theory of Justice*, Cambridge: Harvard University Press.
36. Olsaretti, Serena (2009). *Liberty, Desert and the Market: A Philosophical Study*, Cambridge: Cambridge University Press.
37. Fleurbaey, Marc (2015). 'Forced Trades in a Free Market', in: *Individual and Collective Choice and Social Welfare*, Constanze Binder, Giulio Codognato, Miriam Teschl and Yongsheng Xu (eds.), Heidelberg/ Dordrecht/ London: Springer: 217–252.
38. Binder, Constanze (2021). 'Welfare Economics and the Capability Approach?' in: *Welfare Theory, Public Action, and Ethical Values Revisiting the History of Welfare Economics*, Tamotsu Nishizawa, Roger Backhouse and Antoinette Baujard (eds.), Cambridge: Cambridge University Press.
39. Atkinson, Tony B. (2015). *Inequality What Can Be Done?* Cambridge: Harvard University Press.
40. Browning, Edgar K. (2002). 'The Case Against Income Redistribution', *Public Finance Review November* 30: 509–530.
41. Keeley, B. (2015). 'Income Inequality: The Gap between Rich and Poor', *OECD Insights*, Paris: OECD Publishing, http://dx.doi.org/10.1787/9789264246010-en
42. Piketty, Thomas (2014). *Capital in the Twenty-First Century*, Cambridge: Harvard University Press.
43. Robeyns, Ingrid (forthcoming). 'Having Too Much', in: *NOMOS LVI: Wealth. Yearbook of the American Society for Political and Legal Philosophy*, J. Knight and M. Schwartzberg (eds.), New York University Press.
44. Stiglitz, Joseph (2012). *The Price of Inequality: How Today's Divided Society Endangers Our Future*, New York: W.W. Norton & Company.

34

POLICY EVALUATION UNDER SEVERE UNCERTAINTY

A Cautious, Egalitarian Approach

Alex Voorhoeve

1. Introduction

When policymakers evaluate a policy, they are typically unsure what will result from choosing it. In welfare economics, such a lack of knowledge is commonly dealt with by (i) assigning precise probabilities to the possible outcomes of every policy under evaluation; (ii) assigning a value to each of these possible outcomes, for example, by using a social welfare function that evaluates the distribution of well-being in each possible outcome; and finally (iii) recommending the policy with the highest expected value (the probability-weighted sum of the values of its possible outcomes) (Fleurbaey 2010; Adler 2019). Here, I will follow the common practice in decision theory and call situations in which a decision-maker is in a position to make such expected value calculations "decision-problems under risk."

Sometimes, however, those who decide on a policy are not able to compute these expected values for it because they are unable to nonarbitrarily assign precise probabilities to every one of its possible outcomes. Here, I shall follow Knight (1921) and Keynes (1937) and refer to such situations as "uncertain." [Following Ellsberg (1961), such situations are also commonly referred to as "ambiguous".] Throughout, I use both "risk" and "uncertainty" in their subjective senses – as pertaining to the beliefs about the chances of possible outcomes of their decisions that a rational decision-maker can form on the basis of their prior beliefs and the evidence available to them. (For further discussion of the contrast between risk and uncertainty, see Stefánsson, Chapter 3.)

In welfare economics and political philosophy, there has been far more discussion of how to complete the expected value evaluation of policies than of how to make public decisions under uncertainty. In this chapter, I take a step toward remedying this comparative neglect. This project is worth pursuing because severely uncertain situations are common and important. One example is climate change (Heal and Millner 2018). In judging climate policies, policymakers face both climate-scientific uncertainty – about how the climate system works and would react to various emissions scenarios – and socioeconomic uncertainty – about how individuals and societies will respond to changes in climate. Climate-scientific uncertainty arises because our main source of predictions about what might happen in various emissions scenarios are climate models. These are sensitive to changes in specified initial conditions, which are only imperfectly known. They are also highly sensitive to the choice of functional forms by which key relationships are represented and the choice of key parameter values, both of which are also imperfectly known (Frigg et al. 2014). There is also scientific disagreement about some key causal mechanisms, how important they are, and how they

DOI: 10.4324/9781315739793-42

interact with widely accepted mechanisms. Because of the diversity of these sources of uncertainty, some of which cannot be captured by probability distributions over different potential initial values, functional forms, parameter values, and causal mechanisms, and because these different sources interact in the context of extremely sensitive models, it is commonly thought that it is not possible to nonarbitrarily capture current climate-scientific knowledge by assigning a precise probability to key propositions, such as that, for example, in a "medium emissions scenario," the Earth will warm by more than 2.0 degrees centigrade (Dietz 2014; Heal and Millner 2018). For this reason, the most authoritative report available, that produced by the Intergovernmental Panel on Climate Change (IPCC), assigns only ranges of probabilities to such propositions. For example, it reports that in one medium emissions scenario, "warming is *likely* to exceed 2.0 degrees centigrade," where "likely" means "has a probability of between 66% and 100%" (IPCC 2014, p. 10).

Social-scientific uncertainty about the impact on societies and people's lives of various degrees of warming is arguably greater still (Heal and Millner 2018), for there is very little evidence about how changes in climate might affect such things as political stability, migration flows, or economic growth. Consequently, experts regard socioeconomic impact assessments as highly speculative (Dietz 2014; Heal and Millner 2018). It follows that it would represent a leap beyond the information available to assign precise probabilities to outcomes of interest, such as "there is 3.0 degrees warming, a permanent loss of economic output of 5% of GDP, and there are large forced migration flows."

A second example of decision-making under severe uncertainty is presented by novel pandemics. Again, the sources of uncertainty are multifarious. In the early months of the COVID-19 pandemic, for example, there was lack of information and there were grave differences in expert opinions about such key variables as the transmissibility of the virus that causes COVID-19, its infection fatality rate, and the potential effectiveness of novel treatments and vaccines. There was also a notable lack of information and consensus about how various social and movement measures (e.g., mask wearing and lockdowns) might be expected to impact the virus' spread and, more broadly, health and other components of well-being. A significant source of information for policy decisions in the early months was non-peer-reviewed models of disease spread. These models are nonlinear, and their outcomes are highly dependent on assumed initial conditions and parameter values. Because of this sensitivity, small differences in these assumptions readily generated outcomes of interest (e.g., "deaths from disease with a given policy") that differed by several orders of magnitude (Avery et al. 2020, pp. 10–11, 20). Moreover, these assumptions were highly uncertain: initial conditions were unknown, functional forms were disputed, and parameter values were often ad hoc. These diverse sources of uncertainty meant that there was no clear basis to assign precise probabilities to even one aspect of interest in evaluating policies, namely, their impact on the spread of disease and associated deaths. Indeed, among five models of possible numbers of deaths in the United Kingdom and the United States that achieved prominence in policy discussions early in the pandemic, only one provided probabilities for its estimates, and those were dubious (Avery et al. 2020, p. 26). The quality of information on the possible wider health, social, and economic impacts of social and movement measures such as lockdowns was, at the time, equally poor, in part because of the lack of precedent for such measures in contemporary economies. The assignment of precise probabilities to the possible outcomes of key policies would therefore have represented a leap beyond the available evidence.

In this chapter, I outline an approach to policy evaluation for such uncertain situations. There is political-philosophical work to be done in using the tools of decision theory for this purpose, for the bulk of the literature has been devoted to the question of how, under uncertainty, people actually do and rationally may make decisions *on their own behalf*. There is less work on how to make *public* decisions in the absence of precise probabilities.[1]

I proceed as follows. In Section 2, I outline a pluralist egalitarian theory of distributive justice for situations of risk that I will take as my point of departure. In Section 3, I make the case for the permissibility of using a cautious decision criterion under uncertainty. In Section 4, I explore some implications of incorporating this form of caution into the outlined egalitarian view. I show that caution strengthens one element of egalitarian solidarity by reinforcing its concern for those who may end up worse off than others. But I also show that it may counteract another element of such solidarity, namely, the tendency to ensure that everyone "sinks or swims" jointly. In Section 5, I conclude.

2. Egalitarianism Under Risk

In the pluralist egalitarian view that I shall draw on here, people's interests should be considered from two perspectives. The first is in terms of the value of their prospects. A person's prospects are important because they capture the extent to which a policymaker's actions promote this person's interests as they are rationally viewed with the information at hand when deciding on a policy. The second is in terms of each person's final well-being. This is relevant because it represents the interests that a policymaker should aim to see advanced equally, if they were fully informed about how each person would end up faring.

In the proposed egalitarian view, it is unfair when people's interests in having good prospects and in faring well are advanced unequally. Besides the goal of limiting these two forms of inequality, the view in question is also concerned with promoting people's interests, both in prospects and in terms of their final well-being. In sum, in this view, a policymaker should adopt the following aims: (i) to reduce inequalities in the value of people's prospects; (ii) to reduce inequality in final well-being; (iii) to improve people's prospects; and (iv) to improve final well-being.[2]

Throughout, I assume an interpersonally comparable, cardinal measure of well-being derived from idealized preferences under risk. By this measure, a first policy yields higher expected well-being for a person than a second policy just in case it would be preferred for this person's sake after rational deliberation with relevant knowledge while taking into account only this person's self-interest. A first policy yields the same expected well-being as a second policy for a person if and only if such a deliberator would be indifferent between the two policies on this person's behalf. [For a defense of this measure, which is common in some areas of welfare economics, see Adler (2019), Appendix D.] I shall also assume that, even though individuals' actual preferences of risk may diverge from this idealization because of reasoning errors and biases, individuals accept the idea that their good should be measured by the preferences they would have after deliberation that corrected these errors and biases, so that in measuring their well-being by these idealized preferences, we are aligning ourselves with their judgments (Arneson 1990). Finally, I assume that in situations of risk it is permissible for a policymaker to maximize expected moral value. In sum, I adopt an orthodox approach under risk. This allows me to focus on the departure I make from orthodoxy in cases of severe uncertainty.

To illustrate the outlined egalitarian view under risk, picture a resource allocation manager in a government-run health system. Two 20-year-old citizens, Ayan and Bashir, face a debilitating illness which, if untreated, will leave them unable to walk and so limited in dexterity that they will require the help of another person for most tasks. Consequently, they will have a lifetime well-being value of 30 (a merely tolerable quality of life). If fully cured, each would have a lifetime well-being value of 80 (a very good quality of life). The manager does not have enough resources to fully cure them both for sure. Instead, they can allocate resources toward one of the alternatives outlined in the top section of Table 34.1. To use Ellsberg's (1961) paradigmatic contrasting presentations of risky and uncertain alternatives, risk will be represented by a random draw from an urn that is known to contain only 50 red balls and 50 black balls. The numbers in parentheses in the table are the probabilities associated with each draw.

In what follows, for simplicity, I shall evaluate such alternatives while setting aside all considerations besides the well-being of the individuals in question. In a choice between *inequality under*

Table 34.1 Final well-being for all alternatives

Risky alternatives	*Draw from a risky urn*	
	Red (0.5)	*Black (0.5)*
Inequality under certainty		
Ayan	80	80
Bashir	30	30
Equal risk, unequal final well-being		
Ayan	80	30
Bashir	30	80
Equality under certainty		
Ayan	55	55
Bashir	55	55
Equality under risk		
Ayan	80	30
Bashir	80	30
Uncertain alternatives	*Draw from an uncertain urn*	
	Red (0.2–0.8)	*Black (0.2–0.8)*
Equality under uncertainty		
Ayan	80	30
Bashir	80	30
Equal uncertainty, unequal final well-being		
Ayan	80	30
Bashir	30	80

certainty, which cures Ayan and leaves Bashir severely debilitated, and *equal risk, unequal final well-being*, which will cure precisely one of them but gives each an equal chance at being cured, the outlined egalitarian view chooses the latter. There is, the view holds, less unfairness when each is given an equal chance at a cure than when one is given a cure outright and the other has no chance of receiving it. *Equality under certainty* is, naturally, better still because, by giving both a partially effective treatment that leaves them with a moderately good life with a level of well-being precisely midway between grave disability and a full cure, it eliminates inequality in final well-being at no cost in total expected well-being. Finally, the view regards *equality under certainty* to be just as good as *equality under risk*, because the latter also involves no inequality and offers each person the same expected well-being as the former.

This series of judgments is the upshot of combining a concern for eliminating unfair disadvantage in the value of prospects and in how people end up with a decision theory that is risk neutral in personal good and moral value. It also has a grounding in a central idea of much of the post-WWII egalitarian literature on distributive justice, namely, that an individual's life has a unity that a bare mass of people does not and that, consequently, moral precepts for pure intrapersonal trade-offs without inequality differ from precepts for trade-offs between distinct individuals' interests (Gauthier 1963, pp. 121–127; Nagel 1970, p. 138; Rawls 1999, pp. 23–24). The integrality of a person's life gives us reason to make pure intrapersonal trade-offs with the aim of maximizing this person's expected well-being, as prudence dictates (given the assumed measure of well-being). The distinctions between persons, meanwhile, demand that when people's interests conflict, we have greater concern for those who are less well-off. This idea motivates choosing *equal risk, unequal final well-being* over *inequality under certainty*. This choice involves an opposition of interests in having valuable prospects between Ayan and Bashir, which – given the fact that total expected well-being is constant – it resolves by maximizing the prospects of the least well off. It also motivates choosing *equality under certainty* over *equal risk, unequal final well-being*, because this choice involves a conflict of final well-being interests, with it being in the final well-being interest of whoever would end up worse off under *equal risk, unequal final well-being* that *equality under certainty* had been chosen instead, while the opposite would be in the final well-being interest of whoever would end up better off under *equal risk, unequal final well-being*. Given that these alternatives yield the same total well-being, the separateness of persons requires that this conflict be resolved in favor of the least well off. Finally, respect for the unity of the individual supports regarding *equality under certainty* and *equality under risk* as equally choice worthy, because the choice between them involves no conflicts of interest in terms of prospects or final well-being (and no inequality), so that we may choose any policy that maximizes each person's prospects.

3. Caution Under Uncertainty

Let us now consider cases of uncertainty. Suppose again that Ayan and Bashir will suffer the aforementioned grave disability unless they are treated. The resource allocation manager must either allocate resources toward the treatment described by *equality under risk* from Table 34.1, which, due to its extensive track record, they rationally believe offers a 0.5 chance of fully curing both and a 0.5 chance of being wholly ineffective for both, or instead allocate resources toward a new treatment, *equality under uncertainty*, which will also either fully cure both or be wholly ineffective for both and for which the limited evidence available suggests that its chance of yielding a full cure ranges somewhere from 0.2 to 0.8. It is depicted in the lower part of Table 34.1. In line with Ellsberg's (1961) presentation, uncertainty here is represented by a random draw from an urn known to contain precisely 100 balls, all of which are either red or black, with the only information available being that at least 20 and at most 80 of these balls are red (i.e., no information is available about the process by which the urn has been filled). Which treatment(s) is it permissible for the manager to provide?

In this choice, I submit that it is permissible for the manager to provide the treatment to which they can assign precise probabilities. Moreover, it would be permissible for them to have a strict preference for this treatment and to provide it even if it carried some small cost, in the sense of slightly worsening the final well-being outcomes for Ayan and Bashir. To be precise, suppose that the choice of *equality under risk* would result in cost c for each person in every event, so that if red were drawn, Ayan and Bashir would each end up with a well-being of $80 - c$, and if black were drawn, they would each end up with $30 - c$. My claim is that there is a $c > 0$ for which it would be permissible to choose *equality under risk*.

The argument for this judgment proceeds in three steps (Joyce 2005, pp. 168–171; Gilboa, Postlethwaite, and Schmeidler 2009). First, rationality does not require us to go beyond the evidence and assign, arbitrarily, precise probabilities to the outcomes of each alternative that we might choose. Instead, it permits us simply to represent our beliefs in terms of ranges of probabilities assigned to each possible outcome as, say, the IPCC does for the medium emissions policy mentioned in the Introduction when they judge that there is between a 66% and 100% chance that this policy would lead to warming of more than 2.0 degrees. In our novel treatment example, this means we need not move beyond the assumption that the chance of this treatment fully curing Ayan and Bashir ranges from 20% to 80%.

Second, when we have only such imprecise probabilities, we cannot compute a single expected value for a prospect. But we can compute a range of such expected values. In the IPCC example, if we assume that more warming is worse, the worst expected value of the medium emissions policy will be one in which there is a 100% chance that it leads to more than 2.0 degrees of warming, and the best expected value of this policy is that there is only a 66% chance that it leads to such warming. All the IPCC's information allows us to say is that the expected value of this medium emissions prospect is in the range given by these values. In our novel treatment example, this means that for each person, *equality under uncertainty* has an expected value in the range of 40 (the possible outcomes weighted by the least favorable probability distribution consistent with our evidence, that is, $0.8 \times 30 + 0.2 \times 80$) to 70 (the possible outcomes weighted by the most favorable probability distribution consistent with our evidence, that is, $0.2 \times 30 + 0.8 \times 80$).

Third, in the face of this range of expected values, it is permissible to be cautious, in the sense that, in making an overall assessment of the uncertain prospect's value, we may permissibly give more decision weight to the less good expected values than the better expected values. To apply it to our examples: when assessing the prospect associated with a policy of medium emissions, we are permitted to give more decision weight to the possibility that this would certainly lead to more than 2.0 degrees of warming than to the possibility that this would only have a 66% chance of leading to such warming. And in the novel treatment case, we can permissibly take the prospective value of the novel medicine for Ayan and Bashir to be less than the midpoint between 40 and 70. (So less than 55, the expected value of the well-known medicine.)

The basic ideas in this argument are simple and attractive: there is no requirement to go beyond the evidence and permission to be cautious in the face of lack of evidence. The upshot is that what is known as *uncertainty aversion* (a strict preference for prospects with precise probabilities over otherwise analogous prospects without such probabilities) is permissible. There is a further dimension to the issue that arises for policymakers, namely, the attitudes toward uncertainty of the people whose prospects and fates hang in the balance. In general, respect for citizens' reasonable judgments of their own good makes it fitting for a policymaker to, as far as possible, track the rationally permissible attitudes of their citizens toward their own interests (Arneson 1990). Here, I include people's rationally permissible attitudes toward uncertainty in these judgments that policymakers have reason to respect. I also assume what I take to be a common situation for policymakers, which is that they do not know the uncertainty attitudes of every member of their population, but they do know the general social-scientific findings about these attitudes. Empirical studies suggest that, in self-interested choices, both uncertainty aversion and uncertainty neutrality (which involves indifference between uncertain and analogous risky alternatives) are common, and uncertainty-loving behavior (which involves a strict preference for uncertain over comparable risky alternatives) is rare (Trautmann and van de Kuilen 2015, Table 34.1; Voorhoeve et al. 2016; Chew et al. 2018). It is therefore reasonable to hold that the assumption of a modest degree of uncertainty aversion on behalf of citizens would be the upshot of a procedure that minimized a reasonable measure of "aggregate distance" between citizens' diverse attitudes toward uncertainty. (For example, the mean attitude toward uncertainty suggested by the aforementioned studies would be one of modest uncertainty aversion.) If, for the reasons just outlined, uncertainty aversion is rationally permissible (possibly alongside uncertainty-neutral and uncertainty-loving behaviors), this would therefore make it reasonable for the decision-maker to employ a degree of uncertainty aversion as a good approximation of (or a reasonable compromise between) the differing reasonable attitudes of the individuals on whose behalf they are deciding.

It is important to note that, despite its appeal, the rationality of uncertainty aversion is disputed. The reason is that the assumption of uncertainty aversion is in tension with a core axiom of decision theory, the Sure Thing Principle. This means that uncertainty aversion has some unappealing implications.[3]

I cannot review here the extensive debate on the rational permissibility of uncertainty aversion. I will, therefore, briefly report my perspective on it, which is that the arguments show that not all independently attractive principles of rationality can be reconciled. In particular, there is at least an apparent tension between (i) the ideas that rationality does not require a decision-maker to posit precise probabilities for which they lack adequate ground and that a decision-maker is allowed a degree of caution in the face of such imprecision, and (ii) the idea that a decision-maker should respect other attractive principles of rational choice, such as the Sure Thing Principle. There are different reasonable ways of navigating this inconsistency, among which are uncertainty-averse decision principles (Gilboa et al. 2009; Siniscalchi 2009; Heal and Millner 2018).

There are several leading uncertainty-averse decision criteria. For concreteness, here I shall use a well-known, simple criterion that is often traced back to Leonard Hurwicz' work on decision-making under ignorance (Hurwicz 1951). My conclusions also hold for other leading criteria, for example, those advanced in Gilboa and Schmeidler (1989) and Klibanoff et al. (2005).

In what is known as α-maxmin expected utility, the decision-maker values a prospect by taking α × the worst expected value that is consistent with their information and prior probability distribution and adding $(1 - \alpha)$ × the best expected value that is so consistent, where $0 \leq \alpha \leq 1$ is the decision weight given to the worst expected value (Binmore 2009; Wakker 2010, sec. 11.5.) A cautious evaluator will give more decision weight to the worst expected value – that is, they will have $\alpha >$ 0.5 – and this will lead them to be uncertainty averse. An uncertainty-neutral evaluator will give equal weight to both – that is, they will have $\alpha = 0.5$. An uncertainty-loving evaluator will give greater weight to the best expected value, that is, they will have $\alpha < 0.5$. I shall, in the rest of this chapter, explore what follows if we assume a fixed, moderate degree of uncertainty aversion for all objects of evaluation – that is, for the evaluation of individual and social prospects. This implies an invariant α somewhat larger than 0.5.

To illustrate, consider again the novel treatment represented by *equality under uncertainty*, and suppose for concreteness that $\alpha = 0.6$. The α-maxmin expected utility criterion then evaluates Ayan's uncertain prospect as follows: $0.6 \times (0.8 \times 30 + 0.2 \times 80)$ (the worst expected value) $+ 0.4 \times (0.2 \times 30 + 0.8 \times 80)$ (the best expected value) $= 52$. This is 3 units of well-being less than the corresponding risky treatment. In what follows, I shall refer to this diminution of the value of an individual's prospects due to uncertainty as the "individual-level burden" of uncertainty. Naturally, the value of Bashir's prospects under *equality under uncertainty* is similarly depressed. But besides these individual-level burdens, this case involves what I shall call "social-level uncertainty" about the distribution of final well-being, for the facts that either both will end up fully cured or both will end up with a severe disability and that there are no precise probabilities for these outcomes may depress the prospective value of the social distribution of final well-being as compared to a counterpart policy under risk.

4. Cautious Egalitarianism

I shall now review a few key implications of incorporating this form of uncertainty aversion in the form of pluralist egalitarianism outlined in Section 2. In each instance, I shall connect the findings from simple cases to general considerations of justice and policymaking.

First, uncertainty-averse egalitarianism posits a novel object of egalitarian concern: the degree to which individual-level uncertainty depresses the value of individuals' prospects (Rowe and Voorhoeve 2018, pp. 255–256). An illustrative case of unequal burdens of uncertainty arises in the comparison of the uncertainty faced by people who live in regions and work in professions that are unlikely to be gravely disrupted by temperature rises (e.g., office workers in temperate zones) and those whose locations and jobs are such that their lives and livelihoods would be severely affected by changes in the climate (e.g., farmers in marginal lands in the Sahel) (Denning et al. 2015). Another illustration concerns the differential burden of uncertainty around the negative impact on well-being of lockdowns to deal with COVID-19 in many countries. When first implemented, the range of potential impacts on well-being (and therefore the depressing effect of uncertainty on individuals' prospects at the moment of implementation) was arguably less for those in rich nations who could work remotely and who had access to government support if they should need it than it was for those in poorer nations who rely on the informal economy, whose work might be most disrupted by these measures, and who often have difficulty accessing social safety nets (Ray and Subramanian 2020). An uncertainty-averse, egalitarian view sees strong reasons to improve the prospects of those who face greater uncertainty, for example, by insuring them against the downside of their imprecisely estimated risks or by gaining additional information and thereby narrowing the imprecision in these estimates.

Second, the proposed cautious, egalitarian approach will favor policies for which a better basis is available for assigning probabilities to outcomes. This was already clear in the comparison made (at the end of Section 3) of *equality under risk* with its uncertain counterpart, *equality under uncertainty*. The same is true in a choice between *equal risk, unequal final well-being* and its uncertain counterpart, *equal uncertainty, unequal final well-being*, which is depicted in the lower part of Table 34.1. After all, the individual-level uncertainty created by the latter policy depresses the value of both individuals' prospects compared to its risky counterpart. One practical implication is that it is permissible for governments to go to greater expense to mitigate severely uncertain threats to life (e.g., posed by a novel pandemic) than to mitigate threats to which they can readily attach probabilities (e.g., posed by traffic accidents).[4]

A third key implication is that when, under uncertainty, some will gain and others will lose, uncertainty aversion reinforces the egalitarian tendency to allocate resources to those who will end up less well off (Rowe and Voorhoeve 2018, pp. 257–259). To see why, suppose that a policymaker must choose between *equal uncertainty, unequal final well-being* and *equality under certainty* in Table 34.1, but with the latter modified so that it comes at a cost c to each person's final (and prospective) well-being, so that it would yield only $55 - c$ for each person for sure, with $0 \leq c \leq 25$. In the proposed egalitarian view, in choosing between these options, we should consider both the value of individual prospects and the prospective value of the distribution of final well-being. Under *equal uncertainty, unequal final well-being*, the value of individuals' prospects is depressed by the limited information available about their likelihood of ending up badly off. An uncertainty-averse policymaker should therefore be willing to incur at least some small cost to eliminate this uncertainty. In considering the distribution of final well-being, a downside of *equal uncertainty, unequal final well-being* is inequality in how people will end up faring. Inequality aversion will therefore prompt a policymaker to incur a cost to eliminate this inequality.

It follows that both uncertainty aversion and inequality aversion will direct us to incur a cost to remove inequality in this kind of case. What is more, together, they will direct us to incur a higher cost to achieve equality than either one of these considerations alone would countenance (Rowe and Voorhoeve 2018, pp. 258–259). To understand why, assume for a moment that our inequality-averse policymaker was uncertainty neutral (that is, their $\alpha = 0.5$). They would then evaluate *equal uncertainty, unequal final well-being* as equivalent to *equal risk, unequal final well-being*. Suppose that in a choice between *equal risk, unequal final well-being* and *equality under certainty*, with a cost c to each person, the correct degree of inequality aversion will direct us to incur a cost of up to, but no greater than, c^* units of prospective well-being for each person, so that both *equal uncertainty, unequal final well-being* and *equal risk, unequal final well-being* would be equivalent to giving Ayan and Bashir each $55 - c^*$ for sure. Next, assume that our policymaker becomes uncertainty averse (that is, their $\alpha > 0.5$). They will then find *equal uncertainty, unequal final well-being* strictly worse than *equal risk, unequal final well-being*. By transitivity, they will then regard the uncertain alternative as strictly worse than giving Ayan and Bashir each $55 - c^*$. In other words, they will find *equal uncertainty, unequal final well-being* to be as good as *equality under certainty* only for a cost larger than c^*. We can conclude that, in cases in which individual-level uncertainty will lead to some faring better than others, uncertainty-averse egalitarianism justifies incurring a larger cost in order to achieve both equality and certainty than an uncertainty-neutral egalitarian view would countenance. After all, under these circumstances, the direction of benefits from the lucky to the unlucky reduces the stakes for each and thereby reduces the burden of uncertainty; naturally, it also diminishes inequality. A policy issue to which this may be relevant is levying "windfall taxes" on firms and people who gain due to severely uncertain economic developments and spending these taxes on improving the situation of the losers. [This is a policy that has been considered in the United Kingdom, for example, in response to the COVID-19 crisis; see Cowburn (2021)]. Such policies that reduce the variability of incomes under uncertainty will be valuable both because they reduce the burden of uncertainty and because they reduce inequality.

A fourth key conclusion starts from the observation that individual-level uncertainty need not imply social-level uncertainty about the distribution of final well-being. To see why, consider again *equal uncertainty, unequal final well-being* in Table 34.1. The individual-level uncertainty depresses the value of everyone's prospects. However, it has no social-level uncertainty about the value of the possible distributions of final well-being. The anonymized distribution of final well-being is known: one person will be fully cured, while another will remain severely disabled.

This has an important implication for how the ranking of policies under risk compares to the ranking of their counterpart policies under uncertainty. *Equality under risk* is, in the proposed egalitarian view, strictly preferred to *equal risk, unequal final well-being*, because the former eliminates all inequality without any loss in terms of the value of individual prospects or in the value of the prospective distribution of final well-being. However, the ranking of these policies' uncertain counterparts is less straightforward. In terms of the value of individual prospects, *equality under uncertainty* and *equal uncertainty, unequal final well-being* are identical. However, in terms of the prospective value of the possible distributions of final well-being, a concern for equality and a concern to reduce uncertainty may pull in opposite directions. On the one hand, it counts in favor of *equality under uncertainty* that it eliminates all inequality. On the other hand, because under this policy everyone sinks or swims together, it generates problematic uncertainty at the collective level. In contrast, *equal uncertainty, unequal final well-being* does not generate such collective-level uncertainty. This is one respect in which *equal uncertainty, unequal final well-being* may be better.[5]

The view I put forward here does not pronounce which of these two policies is superior overall. The key conclusion is just that uncertainty aversion may oppose the solidaristic, egalitarian impulse to bind everyone's fates together. In doing so, it changes egalitarianism in one important way (Rowe and Voorhoeve 2018, pp. 261–262). Under risk, the outlined egalitarian view has a tendency to allocate benefits away from the lucky and toward the unlucky, *if and only if the lucky are (or would be without an egalitarian allocation) better off than others and the unlucky are (or would be) less well off than others.* By way of illustration, as we have seen, the proposed form of egalitarianism is indifferent between *equality under risk* and *equality under certainty* in Table 34.1. Moreover, if *equality under certainty* could be purchased at only a small cost c to each person's well-being (so that it would yield only $55 - c$ for each person for sure, with c positive and small), the proposed egalitarian view would be unwilling to pay any cost in order to redistribute from the better off potential futures of Ayan and Bashir to their less well off potential futures. By contrast, under uncertainty, a cautious egalitarian will see reason to direct benefits from the lucky toward the unlucky *even when these are merely two potential futures of the same person and there is no inequality*. To see this, compare *equality under uncertainty* with *equality under certainty*. Due to uncertainty aversion, the latter is clearly preferable. Moreover, if *equality under certainty* could be purchased at only a cost c to each person's final (and prospective) well-being (so that it would yield only $55 - c$ for each person for sure), the proposed view would strictly prefer *equality under certainty* over *equality under uncertainty* for some small, positive c. Under uncertainty, cautious egalitarianism is therefore keen to direct benefits away from Ayan and Bashir's better possible futures toward their worse possible futures, even when their rosier futures would not involve them being better off than others.

As a practical matter, it follows from the proposed view that governments have a special reason to make provisions for collective setbacks to which they are not able to assign a precise probability. As a concrete illustration, if natural resource revenues are of this kind, then for governments that are highly dependent on revenues from these resources, this favors instruments such as hedges against price falls [used, for example, by Mexico to cover its oil revenues; see Reuters (2015)] or the creation of fiscal space to support the economy in the face of a price collapse [as has been practiced in Chile; see Céspedes et al. (2014)].

5. Conclusion

I have argued that, in uncertain situations, it is permissible for a policymaker to consider a range of expected values for each policy, rather than a single expected value. I have also argued that, in response to this range, it is permissible for a policymaker to assign greater decision weight to the lower expected values within this range. One reason I have offered for this approach is that a substantial share of the population whose fates are at stake in these decisions are likely to be uncertainty averse, and very few are likely to be uncertainty loving, so that a modest degree of uncertainty aversion in public decision-making is a reasonable compromise.

I have also explored some key implications of incorporating such uncertainty aversion into a pluralistic egalitarian theory of justice and of using such a theory for policy evaluation. I have argued that uncertainty aversion reinforces egalitarian reasons to reduce unfair inequalities and to resolve *inter*personal conflicts of interest in favor of the less well off. Moreover, it gives us new reasons to make *intra*personal trade-offs under uncertainty in a way that favors the person's less fortunate potential future. The upshot is a theory of justice that offers stronger reasons for safety-net policies, such as universal health coverage, unemployment insurance, and disability pay, that guard against individual and collective misfortune. Such policies are commonly defended as valuable because they improve people's prospects by reducing risks in relation to income and health in an efficient manner and because they reduce inequalities (Barr 2012; WHO 2014). But a consideration of severely uncertain situations reveals further functions of such a safety net. By aiding the unfortunate, it both reduces the depressing impact of uncertainty on the value of individuals' prospects and reduces policymakers' uncertainty about social outcomes. This finding is relevant for our two opening examples. In the context of climate change, higher emissions pathways are associated with greater variability in the moral value of possible outcomes and, therefore, with a larger disvalue of uncertainty (Millner et al. 2013); they are also projected to generate greater inequality (Denning et al. 2015). A cautious, inequality-averse approach will therefore hold that we have strong reasons to lower emissions (and more reasons than a common, expected-value-maximizing, utilitarian approach would register). In the context of the COVID-19 pandemic, this approach reinforces reasons to develop treatments and vaccines (because these will tend to improve worse possible futures) and to introduce social and movement measures to contain the spread of disease, so long as these are accompanied by income support for the worst off (Adler et al. 2020; Ray and Subramanian 2020). In short, uncertainty adds to policymakers' reasons to make provisions for the least fortunate.

Acknowledgments

I am grateful to Richard Bradley, Roman Frigg, Conrad Heilmann, Kaname Miyagishima, Paloma Morales, Joe Roussos, and Thomas Rowe for comments. Work on this chapter was supported through the Bergen Centre for Ethics and Priority Setting's project "Decision Support for Universal Health Coverage," funded by NORAD grant RAF-18/0009.

Related Chapter

Stefánsson, Chapter 3 "The Economics and Philosophy of Risk"

Notes

1 In moral and political philosophy, an exception to the neglect of severe uncertainty has been the discussion of how to make decisions behind John Rawls' veil of ignorance, which creates a severely uncertain situation by denying people knowledge of the probability of ending up in any particular social position (Rawls 1999, p. 134). In welfare economics, contributions that take account of this aspect of severe uncertainty in policy evaluation focus on environmental policy and pandemics. See, e.g., Liu et al. (2005), Treich (2010), Heal and Millner (2018), Berger et al. (2020), and Inoue and Miyagishima (2021).

2 This formulation leaves open the precise way these different aims of reducing inequality and promoting well-being are defined. For concreteness, I shall assume that the degrees to which prospects and final well-being are promoted are given by their total value. See Fleurbaey (2010), Voorhoeve and Fleurbaey (2016), and Voorhoeve (2021, appendix) for a proposed, more precise formulation of pluralist egalitarianism. The proposed form of egalitarianism builds on an extensive literature that emphasizes the importance of both people's prospects and final well-being, including Ulph (1982), Cohen (1989), Broome (1990), and Temkin (2001).

3 For a discussion on the Sure Thing Principle and uncertainty aversion, see Stefánsson, Chapter 3. For discussion of the problems to which this violation gives rise, see Al-Najjar and Weinstein (2009).

4 Such greater expense to prevent imprecise risks aligns with surveys on the value of reductions in fatality risks, in which individuals tend to place a premium on reductions in imprecisely over precisely specified chances of death (see Hammitt 2020, pp. 140–8).

5 This is true, at least, for some policymakers with a modest degree of inequality aversion. An extremely inequality-averse policymaker may well hold that there is no respect in which *equal uncertainty, unequal final well-being* is more valuable. For example, take a policymaker who uses the maximin rule to evaluate distributions of final well-being. They will hold that *equality under uncertainty* has a better distribution of final well-being than *equal uncertainty, unequal final well-being* in one state of the world and an equivalent distribution of final well-being in another, so that the former dominates the latter, despite uncertainty.

Bibliography

Adler, M. (2019) *Measuring Social Welfare: An Introduction.* Oxford: Oxford University Press.

Adler, M., R. Bradley, M. Ferranna, M. Fleurbaey, J. Hammitt, and A. Voorhoeve. (2020) *How to Assess the Well-Being Impacts the COVID-19 Pandemic and Three Policy Types: Suppression, Control and Uncontrolled Spread.* Policy brief published as part of the final communique of the T20 (Thinktank 20) accompanying the G20 in Saudi Arabia. https://t20saudiarabia.org.sa/en/briefs/Pages/Policy-Brief.aspx?pb=TF4_PB8.

Al-Najjar, N., and J. Weinstein. (2009) "The Ambiguity Aversion Literature: A Critical Assessment," *Economics and Philosophy* 25: 249–284.

Arneson, R. (1990) "Liberalism, Distributive Subjectivism, and Equal Opportunity for Welfare." *Philosophy & Public Affairs* 19(2): 158–194.

Arneson, R. (1997) "Postscript to 'Equality and Equal Opportunity for Welfare'," in L. Pojman and R. Westmoreland (eds.) *Equality: Selected Readings.* Oxford: Oxford University Press, pp. 238–241.

Avery, C., W. Bossert, A. Clark, G. Ellison, and S. Fisher Ellison. (2020) "Policy Implications of Models of the Spread of Coronavirus: Perspectives and Opportunities for Economists." NBER Working Paper 27007, version of April. www.nber.org/papers/w27007.

Barr, N. (2012) *The Economics of the Welfare State*, 5th ed. Oxford: Oxford University Press.

Berger, L., N. Berger, V. Bosetti, I. Gilboa, L. P. Hansen, C. Jarvis, M. Marinacci, and R. D. Smith. (2020) "Uncertainty and Decision Making During a Crisis: How to Make Policy Decisions in the COVID-19 Context?" Innocenzo Gasparini Institute for Economic Research Working Paper n. 666, July.

Binmore, K. (2009) *Rational Decisions.* Princeton: Princeton University Press.

Bognar, G., and I. Hirose. (2014) *The Ethics of Health Care Rationing: An Introduction.* Abingdon: Routledge.

Bradley, R. (2017) *Decision Theory with a Human Face.* Cambridge: Cambridge University Press.

Broome, J. (1990) "Fairness," *Proceedings of the Aristotelian Society* 91: 87–101.

Céspedes, L. F., E. Parrado, and A. Velasco. (2014) "Fiscal Rules and the Management of Natural Resource Revenues: The Case of Chile," *Annual Review of Resource Economics* 6: 105–132.

Chew, S. H., M. Ratchford, and J. S. Sagi. (2018) "You Need to Recognise Ambiguity to Avoid It," *The Economic Journal* 128(614): 2480–2506.

Cohen, G. A. (1989) "On the Currency of Egalitarian Justice," *Ethics* 99: 906–44.

Cowburn, A. (2021) "Covid: Government 'Considering Excess Profits Tax' on Companies Cashing in During Pandemic," *The Independent*. www.independent.co.uk/news/uk/politics/covid-profits-amazon-rishi-sunak-budget-b1798839.html [accessed 28 February 2021].

Denning, F., M. B. Budolfson, M. Fleurbaey, A. Siebert, and R. H. Socolow. (2015) "Inequality, Climate Impacts on the Future Poor, and Carbon Prices," *Proceedings of the National Academy of Sciences* 120(52): 15827–15832. www.pnas.org/cgi/doi/10.1073/pnas.1513967112.

Dietz, S. (2014) "Climate Change Mitigation as Catastrophic Risk Management," *Environment: Science and Policy for Sustainable Development* 56(6): 28–36. DOI:10.1080/00139157.2014.964096.

Ellsberg, D. (1961) "Risk, Ambiguity, and the Savage Axioms," *The Quarterly Journal of Economics* 75: 643–669.

Fleurbaey, M. (2010) "Assessing Risky Social Situations," *Journal of Political Economy*, 118: 649–680.

Frigg, R. S. Bradley, H. Du, and L. A. Smith. (2014) "Laplace's Demon and the Adventures of His Apprentices," *Philosophy of Science* 81(1): 31–59.

Gauthier, D. (1963) *Practical Reasoning*. Oxford: Clarendon Press.

Gilboa, I., A. Postlethwaite, and D. Schmeidler. (2009) "Is It Always Rational to Satisfy Savage's Axioms?" *Economics and Philosophy* 25: 285–296.

Gilboa, I., and D. Schmeidler. (1989) "Maximin Expected Utility with Non-Unique Prior," *Journal of Mathematical Economics* 18: 141–153.

Hammitt, J. (2020) "Valuing Mortality Risk in the Time of COVID-19," *Journal of Risk and Uncertainty* 61: 129–154.

Heal, G., and A. Millner. (2018) "Uncertainty and Decision Making in Environmental Economics: Conceptual Issues," in P. Dasgputa, S. Pattanayak, and V.K. Smith (eds.), *Handbook of Environmental Economics*, vol. 4. North-Holland: Elsevier, chap. 10.

Hurwicz, L. (1951). "Optimality Criteria for Decision Making under Ignorance," *Cowles Commission Discussion Paper, Statistics* 370.

Inoue, A., and K. Miyagishima. (2021) "A Defense of Pluralist Egalitarianism Under Severe Uncertainty: Axiomatic Characterization," manuscript, version of March 9, 2021.

IPCC. (2014) *Climate Change 2014: Synthesis Report. Contribution of Working Groups I, II and III to the Fifth Assessment Report of the Intergovernmental Panel on Climate Change*. Geneva: IPCC.

Joyce, J. M. (2005) "How Probabilities Reflect Evidence," *Philosophical Perspectives: Epistemology* 19: 153–178.

Keynes, J. M. (1937) "The General Theory of Employment," *The Quarterly Journal of Economics* 51(2): 209–223.

Klibanoff, P., M. Marinacci, and S. Mukerji. (2005) "A Smooth Model of Decision Making Under Ambiguity," *Econometrica* 73: 1849–1892.

Knight, F. (1921) *Risk, Uncertainty and Profit*. Boston, MA: Hart, Schaffner and Marx.

Liu, J. T., J. K. Hammitt, J. D. Wang, and M. W. Tsou. (2005) "Valuation of the Risk of SARS in Taiwan," *Health Economics* 14: 83–91.

Millner, A., S. Dietz, and A. Heal. (2013) "Scientific Ambiguity and Climate Policy," *Environmental and Resource Economics* 55: 21–46. DOI:10.1007/s10640-012-9612-0.

Nagel, T. (1970) *The Possibility of Altruism*. Princeton: Princeton University Press.

Ray, D. S., and S. Subramanian. (2020) "India's Lockdown: An Interim Report," *Indian Economic Review*, online first. DOI:10.1007/s41775-020-00094-2.

Rawls, J. (1999) *A Theory of Justice*, rev. ed. Cambridge, MA: Harvard University Press.

Reuters. (2015) "Mexico Wraps $1.1 Billion Oil Options Hedge to Lock in $49 Floor," 20 August. www.reuters.com/article/us-mexico-oil-idUSKCN0QP0X020150820 [accessed 22 February 2021].

Rowe, T., and A. Voorhoeve. (2018) "Egalitarianism Under Severe Uncertainty," *Philosophy & Public Affairs* 46(3): 239–268.

Siniscalchi, M. (2009) "Two Out of Three Ain't Bad: A Comment on 'The Ambiguity Aversion Literature: A Critical Assessment'," *Economics and Philosophy* 25: 335–356.

Temkin, L. (2001) "Inequality: A Complex, Individualistic, and Comparative Notion," *Philosophical Issues* 11: 327–353.

Trautmann, S., and G. van de Kuilen (2015) "Ambiguity Attitudes," in G. Keren and G. Wu (eds.) *The Wiley Blackwell Handbook of Judgment and Decision Making*. Chichester: Wiley, pp. 89–116.

Treich, N. (2010) "The Value of a Statistical Life under Ambiguity Aversion," *Journal of Environmental Economics and Management* 59: 15–26.

Ulph, A. (1982) "The Role of Ex Ante and Ex Post Decisions in the Valuation of a Life," *Journal of Public Economics* 18: 265–276.

Voorhoeve, A. (2021) "Equality for Prospective People: A Novel Statement and Defence." *Utilitas*, 1–17. DOI: 10.1017/S0953820821000017

Voorhoeve, A., K. Binmore, A. Stefansson, and L. Stewart. (2016) "Ambiguity Attitudes, Framing and Consistency," *Theory and Decision* 81: 313–337.

Voorhoeve, A., and M. Fleurbaey. (2016). "Priority or Equality for Possible People?," *Ethics* 126: 929–954.

Wakker, P. (2010) *Prospect Theory for Risk and Uncertainty*. Cambridge: Cambridge University Press.

World Health Organization. (2014) *Making Fair Choices on the Path to Universal Health Coverage: Final Report of the WHO Consultative Group on Equity and Universal Health Coverage*. Geneva: WHO.

35
BEHAVIORAL PUBLIC POLICY
One Name, Many Types. A Mechanistic Perspective

Till Grüne-Yanoff

1. Introduction

Behavioral public policy (BPP) is often treated as a single type, as witnessed, for example, in the popular use of the "nudge" label to encompass all BPP and also in the academic discussion of the pros and cons of BPP *generally*. This has led, first, to an unwarranted polarization in the debate; second, to a neglect of the context sensitivity of these pro and con arguments; and third, to a disregard of multiple stable kinds of policies within the BPP category that could capture these context sensitivities.

Against this *uniformity assumption*, we have argued that the BPP category contains multiple types of policies, distinguished by mechanisms (Grüne-Yanoff and Hertwig 2016; Hertwig and Grüne-Yanoff 2017). Our main argument for this distinction is that there are systematic differences in the context sensitivity of both the effectiveness and the ethical evaluation of these mechanism-based types. Specifically, we claim that there are at least two kinds of behavioral policies, *nudges* and *boosts*, operating through different kinds of mechanisms. We do not claim, however, that these are the only kinds of BPP.

The main purpose of distinguishing the types of BPP by mechanism is to provide a systematic base for the context-sensitive evaluations of their effectiveness and ethical acceptability, thus overcoming the current polarization. The argument therefore is not directed against nudge-type interventions. Instead, it criticizes those who treat BPPs as of one kind, either to universally praise or to universally condemn them. Instead, it is argued that nudge and boost mechanisms have different *moderators*, thus explaining why the respective policy types exhibit different degrees of effectiveness in different contexts and different populations and that they have different potential *side effects*, thus explaining why the respective policy types exhibit different degrees of ethical permissibility in different contexts and different populations. To overcome the polarization and to provide a more powerful tool to analyze which policy type might fare better (either effectively or morally) in which environment is what motivates our categorization proposal.

I start this chapter by sketching the diversity of BPPs (Section 2) and arguing why this diversity matters (Section 3). Section 4 outlines the notion of mechanism used in the analysis. Section 5 develops the distinction between nudges and boosts on the basis of mechanisms and illustrates some of the uses of this categorization. Section 6 concludes.

DOI: 10.4324/9781315739793-43

2. The Diversity of BPPs

In both economics and psychology, investigations of nonincentivizing and noncoercive determinants of individual human behavior have enjoyed increasing popularity in recent decades. Research of this kind has often been summarized under the label "behavioral" (Heukelom 2014). When these academically driven efforts turned their attention to devising policy recommendations (Jolls et al. 1998; Camerer et al. 2003; Sunstein and Thaler 2003), and policymakers began paying attention (Lunn 2014; Chetty 2015; Geiger 2016), the moniker followed, and "behavioral policy" or "behavioral public policy" became the widely adopted collective term for these recommendations and their implementation. At the same time, due to the popularity of Thaler and Sunstein's (2008) book, "nudges" became a near-synonym for "behavioral policy," and various policy institutions, most prominently the British Behavioural Insights Team (BIT), became known unofficially as "Nudge Units."

Unsurprisingly, perhaps, such attempts at shaping policy have attracted a fair amount of criticism, both from an ethical perspective (for reviews, see Barton and Grüne-Yanoff 2015; Schmidt and Engelen 2020) and from those worried about the effectiveness of the proposed intervention (e.g. House of Lords 2011). At least in the early days, that literature often treated BPP (or the synonymously used nudges) as a single kind, to be either uniformly praised or uniformly condemned. This implicit *uniformity assumption* quite strongly polarized the debate into those rejecting nudges and those endorsing them.

Upon closer inspection, however, one finds a lot of diversity contained within the terms BPP or nudge. Here, I want to emphasize this variety in terms of three dimensions: theory background, various definition attempts, and heterogeneous mechanisms.

First, the theoretical background of behavioral policy recommendations has been quite diverse. For example, although Thaler and Sunstein, in their book *Nudge*, stress their commitment to the heuristics and biases (H&B) tradition initiated by the research of Tversky and Kahneman, many of the policy interventions they describe in fact do not fit well with that tradition. To name but just two examples presented in *Nudge*: one, the famous Amsterdam airport fly in the urinal was developed long before behavioral scientists turned to policy (Kulich 2009), and it is unclear what H&B model would explain its success. The other, the arrangement of stovetop knobs in such a way that they more obviously relate to the burners they control, arose from ergonomics experiments in the 1950s (Chapanis and Lindenbaum 1959). Again, the relation to any H&B model is unclear.

Second, attempts to define nudges broadly as encompassing all behavioral policies have run into various difficulties. Thaler and Sunstein (2008: 6) defined nudges as

> any aspect of the choice architecture that alters people's behavior in a predictable way without forbidding any options or significantly changing their economic incentives. To count as a mere nudge, the intervention must be easy and cheap to avoid.

This definition largely characterizes nudges by what they are *not*: not coercive and not incentivizing. It probably gave rise to the idea that all BPPs are of one kind, contrasted with only coercive and incentivizing interventions. However, some of the interventions discussed in *Nudge* do not fit well even within this very broad definition. For example, the placement of mandatory fuel consumption stickers on the back of cars "for other drivers to see" (Thaler and Sunstein 2008: 194), which produce public shaming effects, although probably an effective intervention, does not square well with incentive neutrality and noncoerciveness. Furthermore, Thaler and Sunstein proceed to qualify this definition by arguing that nudges affect only the behavior of those who are not fully rational, while leaving fully rational agents unaffected (Thaler and Sunstein 2008: 8), implying that nudges operate by harnessing these irrationalities somehow. This is a considerably narrower characterization than the one cited earlier, leaving room for other, nonnudge interventions in the BPP category. Many authors have struggled to draft more specific definitions of nudges (Bovens 2009; Hausman and Welch 2010; Rebonato 2012; Heilmann 2014; Hansen 2016; Mongin and Cozic 2018), but there is currently no agreement between them.

Third, where authors have investigated the causal pathways through which BPPs operate, this yielded quite diverse results. Some policies operate by removing environmental factors that allegedly influence people to make bad decisions, for example, by banning the sale of supersized soft drink portions or by avoiding the presentation of saving decisions as between "now" and "much later." Other policies operate by encouraging people to rely on their intuitive rules of thumb ("gut instincts") in appropriate circumstances (Gigerenzer 2015). Yet others operate by training people in new heuristics more suitable for the relevant tasks than the ones they are currently using, for example, by representing uncertainty as natural frequencies instead of probabilities when dealing with base-rate-sensitive problems (Hoffrage et al. 2000).

To conclude, BPPs are diverse in a number of dimensions. This is a prima facie reason against treating them as one kind. However, useful kinds often contain a fair amount of diversity as long as it does not defeat the purpose for which the kind is used. In the next section, I will argue that treating BPPs as one kind has such defeating consequences.

3. Consequences of BPP Diversity: Context Dependence

In the previous section, I showed that BPPs are diverse. In this section, I argue that this diversity is problematic because it makes BPPs' effectiveness and ethical evaluation context sensitive. That is, the same intervention is effective and ethically acceptable in one context, but not in another. Such context sensitivity is undesirable, as long as it is not systematically analyzed, because it makes it difficult to anticipate the performance of a policy in a new context.

Consider this example. A municipality might offer consumers a choice of energy providers, setting a slightly more expensive but more sustainable provider as the default. For many consumers, comparing the alternative providers and determining which one is best is an effortful undertaking: they are likely to stick to the default, because they sense that the effort of performing the comparison is higher than the potential gains. In such environments, the municipality's intervention might well be effective in getting these people to choose the green provider. Now imagine instead that, at an earlier point in time, a nongovernmental organization (NGO) had developed a web-based tool that allows a simple but trustworthy comparison of the providers suited for individual consumers' needs. The comparison might become so much less effortful that more consumers will actually perform the comparison and choose accordingly. In such an environment, it is less likely that the municipality's default-setting intervention is effective: people who want green energy at the given price are likely to choose the green provider, and those who do not are likely to choose an alternative, irrespective of how the default was set.

A lot of evidence for such context sensitivities can be found in experimental studies of BPP. Most experiments investigate the *effect size* of an intervention on subjects' behavior, either in a laboratory or in some specific field context. Recorded effect sizes for many behavioral interventions vary widely. Take, for example, information interventions aiming to reduce household energy consumption. The most recent meta-analysis in this domain, covering 156 studies, found a weighted average treatment effect of −7.40%, that is, on average, information interventions produced more than 7% in potential savings (Delmas et al. 2013). However, the range of individual effect sizes varied from −55% to +18.5%! Possible explanations for this wide range of results include study quality (high-quality studies, according to the meta-analysis, found lower effect sizes than low-quality studies) and differences in what information the intervention provided (e.g. consequences of high energy consumption, suggestions for how to lower consumption, the consumer's own past consumption, others' consumption), as well as contextual variations: who the subjects were and in what context they received the information. For example, in a highly politicized context, information about the consequences of behavior is often discounted along partisan lines (Tannenbaum et al. 2017); procedural information about energy savings will have little impact if a subject does not have access to the necessary technology; and information about others' consumption tends to have a higher impact if they are part of the subject's peer network (Gächter et al. 2013). Context sensitivity means that the effect size of the intervention depends on the presence or absence of such contextual factors as politicization, access to technology, and peer networks.

Information policies are not equally sensitive to all of these factors, though. Information about consequences is not likely to be sensitive to technological access, nor is procedural information to peer network. This is because the information provided by these interventions affects behavior through different *causal pathways*: one affects evaluations, another instrumental beliefs, and a third social norm conformity. All of these policies employ the same *intervention lever*: they provide relevant information to subjects. Nevertheless, these policies need to be further differentiated by the mechanism through which they operate. Only by distinguishing them by mechanism does it become clear why different information policies are sensitive to some contextual factors but not to others. To make unambiguous claims about a policy's effectiveness in certain contexts, one needs to determine whether the contextual factors impact the intervention's effect size. This requires the identification of the mechanism through which it operates (see also Clarke, Chapter 21).

Knowledge about a policy's mechanism is also important for assessing its ethical acceptability (Smith et al. 2013; Grüne-Yanoff 2016). For example, it might be important to know, for such an assessment, whether an intervention like the preceding green default setting is transparent to the subject. This requires insight into how it operates on subjects, for example, subconsciously or by signaling some relevant information. But this again requires knowledge about the intervention mechanism, which is not available from the mere categorization by intervention lever.

Thus, BPPs' effectiveness and ethical acceptability often depend on the context in which they are implemented. Simply accepting such context sensitivity is not a viable option. Policymakers need to make ex ante judgments about the effectiveness and ethical acceptability of intervention alternatives in target environments and for target audiences. If the specific policy has already been tested in that environment, judgment can be passed with some confidence. But most policies have not been tested in their target environment, and the performance of a serious test would be prohibitively expensive or cause significant delay (also note the difficulty of selecting what to test). The policymaker thus faces the problem of *extrapolation* (Steel 2008; Cartwright 2012): an intervention *I* is found to be effective and ethically acceptable in context *C*, but it is unclear whether it will be in context *D*. If one cannot examine *I* in *D* directly, then one must link *I* to *D* in other ways, which requires some form of generalization and categorization (e.g. "Interventions of type ***T*** tend to perform like this in *D*. *I* is a ***T***. Therefore, expect *I* to perform like this in *D*"). For this reason, ex ante judgments require categorization. A naive plea for policy assessment on a "case-by-case" basis (e.g. Sims and Müller 2019) founders on this observation.

But not just any categorization works. Current practices seem to sometimes use intervention levers as relevant subcategories for different BPPs.[1] This is an entirely plausible strategy in the early stages of a research field. However, for the purposes of evaluating interventions, such a categorization is not sufficiently stable, for at least two reasons. First, as I already indicated, interventions with the same lever might operate through different mechanisms. Second, one often cannot even properly determine the intervention lever without knowing through which mechanism the policy operates. The answers to questions like, "Does the intervention provide information or set a frame?" or "Does it offer incentives or change the choice architecture?" require reference to at least some features of the causal pathways through which the intervention operates.

Categorization by levers does not help with context sensitivity. Because the same lever might trigger different mechanisms, each of these mechanisms might be affected differently by contextual variables, both in terms of preventing or amplifying the intervention's effect and also in terms of preventing or producing various side effects. Thus, attempts to categorize policies characterized merely by their intervention levers as more or less ethically acceptable (Oliver 2013; Baldwin 2014) are hopeless, as it is the population and the environment that at least partially determine ethical evaluation, which thus undermines such simple classification attempts.

Instead, we have suggested the categorization of BPPs according to the mechanisms through which they operate and then, on the basis of this categorization, infer the transferability of an intervention's effectiveness and ethical acceptability from one context to another (Hertwig and Grüne-Yanoff 2017; Grüne-Yanoff et al. 2018). The examples we discussed in this section make this an intuitive solution: the context sensitivities exemplified here depend on the causal pathways through which the default-setting interventions operate. In order to give a more general analysis that justifies our proposal, I need to discuss the notion of mechanism in more detail.

4. Systematizing Diversity: A Mechanistic Account

The current philosophy of science characterizes *mechanisms* broadly as systems of causally interacting parts and processes, which under certain conditions predictably produce one or more effects (e.g. Craver and Tabery 2019; Glennan 2017). For BPPs, the relevant mechanisms link intervention levers to agents' behavior. The link between these components is mediated by the agents' decisions and the environment in which these decisions are taken.

Many authors understand talk of mechanisms as talk about elements of the real world. A grandfather clock's mechanism consists of the actual pendulum, spring, and gears. But models that represent such components either fully or partially (e.g. different number of teeth, but same ratio in the gear train) are not considered mechanisms in this *ontic* sense. In contrast, I consider mechanisms to comprise abstracting models, for three reasons. First, in the behavioral sciences, there is little agreement about the correct level of description. Decision mechanisms can often be described on both the social and the individual-mental levels, and sometimes the neurological level. While these levels typically supervene each other, multiple realizabilities complicate attempts at reduction and thus leave open the question of whether any level is ontologically prior to the others. Second, even if one fixes the level of description, there is uncertainty how fine grained the individuation of mediators should be. For example, should one describe the cognitive-cost-based default intervention as operating though one mediator ("cost-benefit-assessing module"), or should this be unpacked into a sequence of observations, belief formations, comparisons, and evaluations? Because the behavioral sciences lack an atomistic framework for their ontology (contrast this, for example, with the molecular level that biochemists can refer to), any "more fine grained is better" strategy runs into the issue of dividing ad infinitum without any clear benefit. Finally, besides these ontological worries, there also are epistemic considerations that speak against relying on an ontic conception of mechanism for the purpose of categorizing BPP. It is difficult to obtain evidence for behavioral mechanisms, and the more fine grained the description of the mechanism, the more pressing the problem of underdetermination by the evidence. Therefore, also for epistemic reasons, it is often advisable to rely on abstract mechanistic models instead of an ontic conception of mechanisms.

But what is the right level of abstraction, then? This depends on the model user's epistemic and pragmatic interests. For behavioral policymaking, mechanisms are chiefly of interest because they hold important information about what factors further or inhibit the policy's effectiveness and what side effects a policy might have in certain environments (Grüne-Yanoff 2016; Marchionni and Reijula 2019).

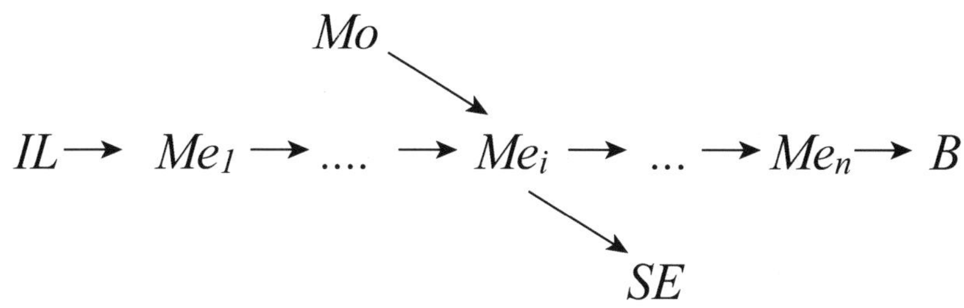

Figure 35.1 Mechanisms in behavioral policy making

Figure 35.1 describes the schematic form of such mechanisms, using the following terminology. A *behavioral policy* consists of an *intervention lever* (*IL*) that the policymaker cranks with the intention of effecting some change in individual *behavior* (*B*). The causal chain from intervention level to behavior can be represented as consisting of a sequence of *mediators* (Me_i). A mediator can either pass on a causal signal or block it. This depends on *modulators* (*Mo*): factors that affect mediators. Besides passing on causal signals to their successor in the causal chain, mediators also might have *side effects* (*SE*).

To illustrate, the provision of procedural information is an *IL* that might change an instrumental belief about thermostat settings, leading to the intention to set the thermostat 2 degrees lower when absent (Me_1). But if there is no thermostat in the apartment (*Mo*), this intention cannot be implemented. The modulator *Mo* thus prevents the effect of the intervention on consumption behavior *B*.

To give another illustration, the default setting of a green energy provider is an *IL* that might make the subject feel that a comparison is too costly given the potential gains (Me_i) and thus lead her to stick to the default option (*B*). The provision of a simple and trustworthy comparison tool might reduce costs to such an extent that the effect of *IL* on *B* is blocked. If it is not blocked (*Mo* absent), the elicitation of such a feeling might contribute to a general sense that bureaucratic communications are not worth serious consideration (*SE*), and such a side effect might be important when assessing the effectiveness and ethical dimensions of such interventions.

This mechanistic account helps to make precise the analysis of context sensitivity from the previous section. To evaluate the effectiveness of an *IL*, in a given context *C*, the mechanism through which *IL* affects *B* determines which modulators Mo_i must be either present or absent. By checking whether *C* contains these Mo_i we will be able to draw justified conclusions about the effectiveness of *IL* in *C*. To assess the ethical acceptability of an *IL*, knowledge of the mechanism allows us to check whether its operation, through specific Me_i or having particular *SE*, is ethically problematic.

Admittedly, policymakers often do not know the exact mechanisms through which their BPP options might operate. But if full knowledge is not attainable, a second-best option of knowing through which mechanism *kind* a BPP operates still serves the same purpose of assessing effectiveness and ethical acceptability. But how could one meaningfully distinguish between different kinds of BPP mechanisms? To this question I now turn.

I will start with an abstract and highly simplified mechanism scheme of decision-making, depicted in Figure 35.2. Individual decision-makers distinguish a number of *alternatives*, identify their relevant *properties* (e.g. their possible consequences and the uncertainty with which they come about), and choose one of the alternatives according to some *selection rule*. This rule might involve the *evaluation* of consequences and their uncertainty, but it might also be a rule as simple as "choose the alternative highest up on the list."

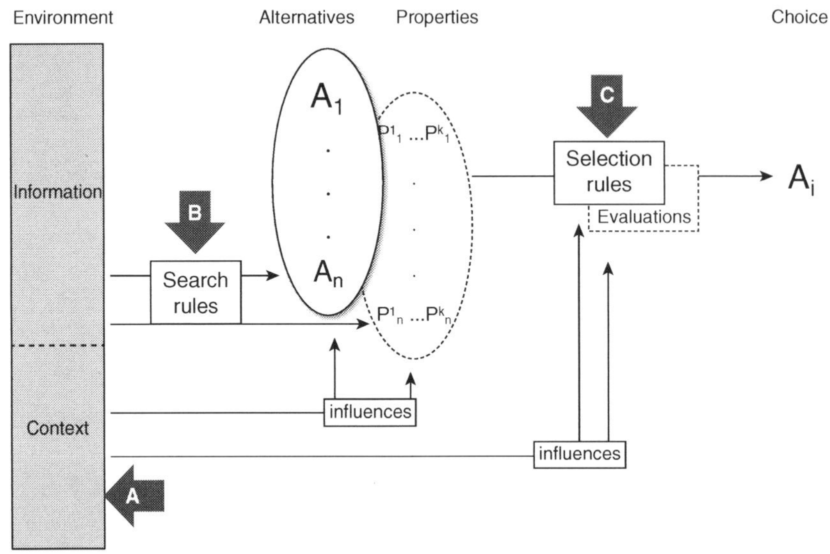

Figure 35.2 A simplified mechanism scheme of decision making

But how do individuals arrive at a list of alternatives and their relevant properties? They search the environment according to some *search rules* that tell them what information to focus on, how to mark distinctions, and when to stop searching. This also means that individuals consider only some features of the environment as relevant, while ignoring others. The search rule therefore divides the decision environment into relevant *information* and irrelevant *context*. What behavioral research has shown, however, is that context considered irrelevant by individuals might nevertheless have causal impact on their decision. Some such contextual factors as, for example, "anchors" or "frames," purportedly influence the representation of alternatives and their properties; other factors like "default effects" or "reference points purportedly influence the evaluation and selection of alternatives, although the individual considers them irrelevant.

This scheme describes ways in which individuals make decisions (albeit, as mentioned, in a simplified way). Now we can identify various points at which a BPP intervention might attack.

The large dark gray arrows in Figure 35.2 indicate different possible interventions on these decision mechanisms.[2] Intervention A intervenes in the contextual factors, removing, rearranging, or adding some, with the intention of exerting influence through them on the individuation and characterization of alternatives and on the search rule and the underlying evaluation. For example, the "Save More Tomorrow" intervention offers deliberators the choice between more consumption *in a year's time* and higher pension payouts *later*, thus avoiding the "present bias" impact of a choice of more consumption *now* on the evaluation of the alternatives (Thaler and Benartzi 2004).

Interventions B and C, in contrast, intervene in the search and selection rules directly, by teaching people new skills or training existing ones. For example, Finkel et al.'s (2013) intervention to reduce marital strife trains people a new selection rule ("assume the perspective of a third-party spectator"). Drexler et al.'s (2014) physical accounting intervention, in contrast, teaches people with little formal education a better search rule for their business purposes ("physically separate private and business receipts"). The first difference between these policy mechanisms thus consists of the location of the *entry point* for the intervention lever.

The second difference consists of the different mediators that connect the intervention lever with the behavior. "Save More Tomorrow," for example, operates through the mechanism that underlies the present bias, while Drexler et al.'s physical accounting intervention operates through changing the search rule. Sometimes the same intervention lever can operate though different mechanisms. Default-setting policy interventions, for example, have been speculated to operate though either cognition-cost avoidance, status-quo bias, or receiving recommendation signals (Grüne-Yanoff 2016; Jachimowicz et al. 2019). But in those cases, in order to determine *where* the intervention lever comes in, one must refer to the mechanism: a loss-aversion-driven, default-setting policy, for example, comes in through an intervention on context factors, while a recommendation-driven, default-setting policy operates through enlarging the searchable information set and, thus, comes in through an intervention on relevant information.

Third, policies also differ in the moderators that might inhibit their operation. Default setting driven by cognition costs, as I argued in Section 2, is sensitive to changes in cognition costs, while default setting driven by status-quo bias is not. "Save More Tomorrow" operates through the mechanism that shapes the intertemporal discounting curve hyperbolically and thus produces present bias. If that curve were to change under the intervention, then the policy would not be effective. Finkel et al.'s marital strife intervention would be blocked if people did not want to end an altercation, even though the policy had now taught them how to do it. And Drexler et al.'s physical accounting intervention likely would not be effective if the lacking business discipline was not caused by the inability to extract relevant information but by, for example, rampant corruption. All of these factors are examples of modulators that reduce the effectiveness of those behavioral policies, whose mediators they block. Policies that operate through other kinds of mediators, in contrast, will not be affected by those factors.

Fourth, policies that differ in mediators also might differ in their side effects. For example, a default-setting intervention operating through a cognitive-cost mechanism might leave the people thus affected with the general impression that bureaucracy communications are hard to comprehend and not worth the effort (after all, the intervention must elicit this impression for its specific communication to be effective). In contrast, default-setting interventions operating through recommendation or loss-aversion mechanisms are less likely to have such a side effect. Similarly, a normative feedback intervention operating through a social pressure mechanism might induce people thus affected to hide their behavior from public view (and thus from potential sanctions), while a normative feedback intervention operating through a reference point mechanism is unlikely to cause such side effects.

BPP mechanisms thus can be systematically distinguished with respect to at least these four criteria. With this, I now turn to the proposed distinction between boosts and nudges.

5. Boost vs. Nudge

Nudges and boosts have been characterized in multiple dimensions, some of which explicitly distinguish the causal pathways through which these two types of interventions operate (Hertwig and Grüne-Yanoff 2017: 974). Nudges "harness cognitive and motivational deficiencies in tandem with changes in the external choice architecture"(Ibid.). Boosts, in contrast, "foster competences through changes in skills, knowledge, decision tools, or external environment" (Ibid.). The distinction thus rests on two criteria. First, *where* the intervention lever is applied: nudges intervene in the choice architecture, while boosts intervene in skills, knowledge, decision tools, or external environment. Nudge intervention entry points thus largely correspond to intervention A in Figure 35.2, while boosts largely correspond to intervention entry points B and C, but they sometimes also attack through A.

The second criterion is *how* the intervention affects behavior: nudges harness cognitive and motivational deficiencies, while boosts foster competences. Nudge interventions typically operate by harnessing factors that the decision-maker herself regards as irrelevant but that have been shown to have an influence nevertheless, This corresponds to the pathways in the lower part of Figure 35.2. Boost interventions, in contrast, typically operate by affecting competences that the decision-maker considers relevant, for example, by providing new competences or by better matching existing competences with the task at hand, This corresponds to the pathways in the upper part of Figure 35.2. This also helps to distinguish those boosts that intervene on the external environment and thus have A as their entry point. In contrast to nudges, which attack at A in order to harness factors that are effective but disregarded by the decision-maker, boosts intervening at A seek to turn a disregarded factor into one that the decision-maker takes into account and thus increases her competence. For example, an intervention that translates statistical information from a relative probability format into a natural frequency format helps decision-makers become aware of the framing effects these formats have on their decisions and, through that, improve their competences. A nudge, in contrast, would choose to present the information in that format which is expected to yield the desired framing effect, without necessarily teaching the decision-maker any competence.

The mechanisms supporting this categorization are highly abstract models. Why this level of abstraction? The preceding epistemic considerations give at least a partial answer: to distinguish mechanisms (and hence BPP categories) only to the degree to which such distinction is supported by evidence, either directly from experiments or other empirical studies or indirectly through empirically supported background theory. But this is only a partial answer. The BPP categorization is determined not only by available evidence but also by the purposes that such a categorization may have. The recent literature gives clear indications of what pragmatic considerations make researchers and policymakers turn to mechanisms (Hertwig 2017; Grüne-Yanoff et al. 2018; Strassheim 2019; Löfgren and Nordblom 2020): to provide resources for ex ante evaluations of interventions' effectiveness and ethical acceptability. Reference to mechanisms facilitates such ex ante evaluations because it helps to identify which factors in the intended context of implementation make a difference to the effectiveness and the side effects of the intervention. What matters, therefore, is that the mechanisms by which BPPs are categorized are sufficiently fine grained to flag such difference-making contextual factors.

Different BPP interventions are sensitive to some contextual factors but not to others. Categorization of BPPs into nudges and boosts collects BPPs sensitive to some factors in one category and all those not sensitive to those factors in another. This is because the mechanisms on which these categories are built either have that factor as a modulator or they do not. Such a categorization is helpful for the policymaker in at least two ways. First, she only needs to worry about the contextual factors to which her policy category of interest is sensitive. Second, she now knows to which factors her policy category of interest is sensitive, so she can go and check whether these factors are active in the target environment. Let us consider a few such factors now (Table 35.1).[3]

Nudges operate by harnessing cognitive and motivational heuristics. The cognitive-cost version of default setting, for example, relies on the subject's feeling that the choice alternatives are not worth looking at, thus making her stick to the default. This reliance makes the intervention sensitive to any factor that destabilizes such a feeling, be it a simple app that allows a cheap and reliable comparison or a prod from a trusted friend. Such modulators undermine the *heuristic stability* of nudge

Table 35.1 Context conditions of Nudges and Boosts

Context conditions	*Nudges*	*Boosts*
Heuristic stability	☑	–
Agent motivation	–	☑
Teachability of heuristics	–	☑
Homogeneity of heuristic repertoire	☑	–

mechanisms, thus rendering them less effective. Boosts, in contrast, because they do not harness deficiencies in this way, are not sensitive to this kind of modulator. Thus, policymakers intending to implement a nudge in a specific context are well advised to check whether it contains such modulators; policymakers intending to implement a boost do not need to worry.

Boosts operate by fostering competences, which might, for example, consist of search or decision rules more suitable for a given task. But such interventions will only have an effect on behavior if the subject, when addressing the task, is actually motivated to choose these newly acquired or newly identified rules. Factors that reduce or eliminate *agent motivation* thus are modulators of boost mechanisms. A boost, even if it succeeds in teaching a new competence, will not be effective if the agent is not motivated to use what the boost taught her. Nudges, in contrast, because they do not operate through the motivation of agents, are not sensitive to this kind of modulator. Thus, policymakers intending to implement a boost in a specific context are well advised to check whether it contains such modulators; policymakers intending to implement a nudge do not need to worry.

The way boosts foster competences is by teaching skills, knowledge, decision tools, etc. But what if these cannot be taught? Some modes of human cognition or perception are not very malleable. One cannot teach humans to "see" that the two lines in the Müller-Lyer illusion are of equal length (Fodor 1983); even if people have convinced themselves otherwise, they will still see them as unequal in length. Furthermore, the policymaker might fail to teach people even about malleable features, if contextual factors causing distraction, inattention, or inability are present. Such factors undermine the *teachability of heuristics* and, thus, constitute modulators of any boost mechanism that seeks to teach them. Nudges, in contrast, because they do not operate through teaching agents, are not sensitive to this kind of modulator. Thus, policymakers intending to implement a boost in a specific context are well advised to check whether it contains such modulators; policymakers intending to implement a nudge do not need to worry.

Nudges and boosts are interventions that target individuals. But realistically, both are most often applied to large populations where, for example, individual therapeutic approaches are not feasible. Thus, nudges intervene in the choice architecture of all agents in the population, and boosts intervene in the skills, knowledge, decision tools, etc. of all of them. This poses more of a problem for nudges than for boosts. Imagine a nudger "reframing" the description of an unhealthy product, expecting that the new frame would signal its riskiness and thus deter those susceptible to this signal. The nudger thus implicitly assumes that individuals either pick up the signal and react in the desired way (i.e. consume less of the product) or are not susceptible to the signal. Yet, what if some in the population are susceptible to the signal but react to it by consuming more? In such a heterogeneous population, it becomes unclear what effect the nudge has; it might have no effect, or the effect might be the opposite of what was expected. Factors that undermine the *homogeneity of the heuristic repertoire* are modulators of nudge mechanisms. Boosts, in contrast, do not require this homogeneity of the population. To the extent that agents already know what the boost intervention teaches them, they can safely ignore it. To the extent that it teaches something new, it is the agents' choice to make use of it, and thus little homogeneity (beyond basic learning abilities) is required. Thus, boosts are not sensitive to this kind of factor. Policymakers intending to implement a nudge in a specific context are well advised to check whether it contains such modulators; policymakers intending to implement a boost do not need to worry.

My discussion so far has focused on how mechanism-based categorization can help to deal systematically with the context sensitivity of BPP interventions' effectiveness. Now, I briefly discuss some ways in which mechanism-based categorization can also help to deal systematically with the context sensitivity of BPP interventions' ethical acceptability.

I will start with *transparency*, which is widely regarded as an ethically relevant feature of behavioral policy (Bovens 2009). Policy is transparent only if people affected by the intervention can easily learn about the factors influencing them. Boosts guarantee such transparency. A boost seeks to impart a competence by teaching skills, knowledge, decision tools, etc. But such teaching requires the cooperation of the subject to be influenced: she must pay attention when taught, she must grasp the content she is taught, she must be aware of what these skills and tools can be used for, and she must elect to use them at some point for the boost to have had any effect on her behavior. This might sound more involved than it is. To teach the simple third-party perspective of the marital strife intervention (Finkel et al. 2013), for example, will not require more than a few minutes of attention, comprehension, and awareness, nor does it require huge cognitive effort from the subjects. But it is hard to imagine how an individual could cooperate in these ways without learning about the factors influencing them. Transparency is, in this sense, built into the boost such that people affected by it are aware of it its inevitable side effect. That is not the case with nudges. Although nontransparency might not be necessary for a nudge to be effective (Loewenstein et al. 2015), transparency certainly is not necessary for its effectiveness and is not its inevitable side effect. A change in the choice architecture is often effective even if the influenced agents are not aware of it. Thus, nudges require more ethical scrutiny than boosts because they can circumvent transparency, while boosts cannot.

A second ethical issue is to what extent BPPs affect the *autonomy* of decision-making (Hausman and Welch 2010). The philosophical debate about what constitutes autonomous decisions is, of course, enormous, so I will simply pick one prominent account, coherentism, to illustrate how mechanism-based categorization facilitates a systematic discussion. According to coherentist views, an individual has control over her own action, if and only if she is motivated to act in this way because this motivation coheres with some mental state that represents her point of view on the action (Buss and Westlund 2018). There is little agreement on what these relevant mental states are. However, even without specifying that, a consideration of BPP mechanisms can help clarify the debate. The agent's motivation is what causes her to act. She can endorse these causes (in that case the mental states representing her point of view cohere with them) or she can repudiate them. To have reasonable grounds for repudiation, the agent must experience some disconnect between her motives and her point of view. Someone or something might force her to act in this way, for example, or she must consider some of her own motivations are "not really her own." It would not be reasonable for her to repudiate motivations that she formed without external pressure and absent any internal conflict (see also Lecouteux, Chapter 4).

Boosts operate through imparting skills, knowledge, decision tools, etc. These interventions are not effective without the individual's cooperation. She must elect to make use of the thus imparted competences; the fact that she learned a new skill, for example, has no effect on her behavior unless she is capable and motivated to apply it. Unless the agent repudiates this motivation, the application of the boost constitutes an autonomous decision. Such repudiation is not likely, for at least two reasons. First, genuine boosts do not impose pressure on agents to use the competences they impart, so the individual has little reason to repudiate her motivation for that reason. Second, motivations for applying a boosted competence arise from reflections of what might be best for the agent in this situation, and typically they are neither impulsive or subtly seductive. Therefore, the individual has little reason to repudiate her motivation for those reasons either. Consequently, *due to the boost mechanisms*, it is very unlikely that the application of boosted competences would constitute heteronomous decisions (Grüne-Yanoff 2018).

This stands in marked contrast to nudge mechanisms. Nudges operate through causal pathways that might circumvent agential reflection or that might overrule existing motivation. They often proceed through mechanisms parallel to and independent of the deliberative processes that facilitate reflection about one's motivations. For these reasons, it is likely (but of course not necessary) that that nudges produce motivation that the agent repudiates as not her own and that therefore constitute heteronomous decisions. Nudges thus require more ethical scrutiny than boosts, because their mechanisms are more likely to produce heteronomous decisions (according to coherentist views) than boosts.

6. Conclusion

Although BPP interventions are often treated as if they form one category, members of this category are actually rather diverse. A consequence of this diversity is not only that BPPs differ in their effectiveness and ethical evaluations but that their effectiveness and ethical evaluations are context dependent. For a systematic treatment of their context-dependent performance, BPPs should be categorized according to the mechanisms through which they operate. In particular, BPPs should be distinguished into two categories, nudges and boosts. Relevant conclusions about effectiveness and ethical acceptability of a BPP in novel contexts can be derived from this mechanistic distinction between nudges and boosts, thus offering the policymaker a strategy to deal with the problem of extrapolation.

Acknowledgments

I thank Julian Reiss and Ralph Hertwig for very helpful comments on an earlier draft of this chapter.

Related Chapters

Clarke, Chapter 21 "Causal Contributions in Economics"
Lecouteux, Chapter 4 "Behavioral Welfare Economics and Consumer Sovereignty"

Notes

1 That the literature categorizes BPPs according to such levers is not surprising. A lot of effort in behavioral research has gone into establishing standardized experimental designs, through which stable phenomena or stable intervention effects can be established (Guala 2005). Consequently, the different intervention proposals have often been categorized according to these standardized experimental manipulations (e.g. "default-setting," "framing," or "feedback" designs).

2 There are other possible interventions not illustrated here, for example, information campaigns enlarge searchable information and coercion eliminates some alternatives, while incentives change some of the alternatives' properties.

3 For a more comprehensive treatment of such factors, see Hertwig and Grüne-Yanoff (2017), Hertwig (2017), Grüne-Yanoff et al. (2018), Grüne-Yanoff (2018).

Bibliography

Baldwin, R. (2014) "From Regulation to Behaviour Change: Giving Nudge the Third Degree," *The Modern Law Review* 77(6): 831–857.

Barton, A., and Grüne-Yanoff, T. (2015) "From Libertarian Paternalism to Nudging – and Beyond," *Review of Philosophy and Psychology 6*(3): 341–359.

Bovens, L. (2009) "The Ethics of Nudge," in T. Grüne-Yanoff and S.O. Hansson (eds.) *Preference Change* (pp. 207–219), Dordrecht: Springer.

Buss, S., and Westlund, A. (2018) "Personal Autonomy," in Edward N. Zalta (ed.) *The Stanford Encyclopedia of Philosophy* (Spring 2018 Edition), https://plato.stanford.edu/archives/spr2018/entries/personal-autonomy/.

Camerer, C., Issacharoff, S., Loewenstein, G., O'Donoghue, T., and Rabin, M. (2003) "Regulation for Conservatives: Behavioral Economics and the Case for 'Asymmetric Paternalism'," *University of Pennsylvania Law Review 151*(3): 1211–1254.

Cartwright, N. D. (2012) "Presidential Address: Will This Policy Work for You? Predicting Effectiveness Better: How Philosophy Helps," *Philosophy of Science 79*(5): 973–989.

Chapanis, A., and Lindenbaum, L.E. (1959) "A Reaction Time Study of Four Control-Display Linkages," *Human Factors 1*(4): 1–7.

Chetty, R. (2015) "Behavioral Economics and Public Policy: A Pragmatic Perspective," *American Economic Review 105*(5): 1–33.

Craver, C., and Tabery, J. (2019) "Mechanisms in Science," in Edward N. Zalta (ed.) *The Stanford Encyclopedia of Philosophy* (Summer 2019 Edition), https://plato.stanford.edu/archives/sum2019/entries/science-mechanisms/.
Delmas, M. A., Fischlein, M., and Asensio, O. I. (2013) "Information Strategies and Energy Conservation Behavior: A Meta-Analysis of Experimental Studies from 1975 to 2012," *Energy Policy 61*: 729–739.
Drexler, A., Fischer, G., and Schoar, A. (2014) "Keeping It Simple: Financial Literacy and Rules of Thumb," *American Economic Journal: Applied Economics 6*(2): 1–31.
Finkel, E. J., Slotter, E. B., Luchies, L. B., Walton, G. M., and Gross, J. J. (2013) "A Brief Intervention to Promote Conflict Reappraisal Preserves Marital Quality Over Time," *Psychological Science 24*: 1595–1601.
Fodor, J. A. (1983) *The Modularity of Mind*, Cambridge, MA: MIT Press.
Gächter, S., Nosenzo, D., and Sefton, M. (2013) "Peer Effects in Pro-Social Behavior: Social Norms or Social Preferences?" *Journal of the European Economic Association 11*(3): 548–573.
Geiger, N. (2016) "Behavioural Economics and Economic Policy: A Comparative Study of Recent Trends," *Œconomia. History, Methodology, Philosophy* (6–1): 81–113.
Gigerenzer, G. (2015) *Bauchentscheidungen: Die Intelligenz des Unbewussten und die Macht der Intuition*, München: C. Bertelsmann Verlag.
Glennan, S. (2017) *The New Mechanical Philosophy*, Oxford: Oxford University Press.
Grüne-Yanoff, T. (2016) "Why Behavioural Policy Needs Mechanistic Evidence," *Economics and Philosophy* 32(3): 463–483.
Grüne-Yanoff, T. (2018) "Boosts vs. Nudges from a Welfarist Perspective," *Revue d'Économie politique* 128(2): 209–224.
Grüne-Yanoff, T., and Hertwig, R. (2016) "Nudge Versus Boost: How Coherent Are Policy and Theory?" *Minds and Machines* 26: 149–183.
Grüne-Yanoff, T., Marchionni, C., and Feufel, M. (2018) "Toward a Framework for Selecting Behavioural Policies: How to Choose Between Boosts and Nudges," *Economics and Philosophy* 34(2): 243–266.
Guala, F. (2005) *The Methodology of Experimental Economics*, Cambridge: Cambridge University Press.
Hansen, P. G. (2016) "The Definition of Nudge and Libertarian Paternalism: Does the Hand Fit the Glove?" *European Journal of Risk Regulation* 7(1): 155–174.
Hausman, D. M., and Welch, B. (2010) "Debate: To Nudge or Not to Nudge," *Journal of Political Philosophy 18*(1): 123–136.
Heilmann, C. (2014) "Success Conditions for Nudges: A Methodological Critique of Libertarian Paternalism," *European Journal for Philosophy of Science 4*(1): 75–94.
Hertwig, R. (2017) "When to Consider Boosting: Some Rules for Policy-Makers," *Behavioural Public Policy 1*(2): 143–161.
Hertwig, R., and Grüne-Yanoff, T. (2017) "Nudging and Boosting: Steering or Empowering Good Decisions," *Perspectives on Psychological Science 12*(6): 973–986.
Heukelom, F. (2014) *Behavioral Economics: A History*, Cambridge: Cambridge University Press.
Hoffrage, U., Lindsey, S., Hertwig, R., and Gigerenzer, G. (2000) "Communicating Statistical Information," *Science 290*: 2261–2262. doi:10.1126/science.290.5500.2261
House of Lords, Science and Technology Select Committee (2011) *Behaviour Change* (Second report), London: House of Lords.
Jachimowicz, J. M., Duncan, S., Weber, E. U., and Johnson, E. J. (2019) "When and Why Defaults Influence Decisions: A Meta-Analysis of Default Effects," *Behavioural Public Policy 3*(2): 159–186.
Jolls, C., Sunstein, C.R., and Thaler, R. H. (1998) "A Behavioral Approach to Law and Economics," *Stanford Law Review* 50(5): 1471–1550.
Krulwich, R. (2009) "There's a Fly in My Urinal," *NPR*, December 19. www.npr.org/templates/story/story.php?storyId=121310977. Last accessed June 12, 2020.
Loewenstein, G., Bryce, C., Hagmann, D., and Rajpal, S. (2015) "Warning: You Are About to Be Nudged," *Behavioral Science & Policy 1*(1): 35–42.
Löfgren, Å., and Nordblom, K. (2020) "A Theoretical Framework of Decision Making Explaining the Mechanisms of Nudging," *Journal of Economic Behavior & Organization 174*: 1–12.
Lunn, P. (2014) *Regulatory Policy and Behavioural Economics*, Paris: OECD. doi:10.1787/9789264207851-en
Marchionni, C., and Reijula, S. (2019) "What Is Mechanistic Evidence, and Why Do We Need It for Evidence-Based Policy?" *Studies in History and Philosophy of Science Part A 73*: 54–63.
Mongin, P., and Cozic, M. (2018) "Rethinking Nudge: Not One but Three Concepts," *Behavioural Public Policy 2*(1): 107–124.
Oliver, A. (2013) "From Nudging to Budging: Using Behavioural Economics to Inform Public Sector Policy," *Journal of Social Policy 42*(4): 685–700.

Rebonato, R. (2012) *Taking Liberties: A Critical Examination of Libertarian Paternalism*, London: Palgrave Macmillan.

Schmidt, A. T., and Engelen, B. (2020) "The Ethics of Nudging: An Overview," *Philosophy Compass 15*(4): e12658.

Sims, A., and Müller, T. M. (2019) "Nudge Versus Boost: A Distinction Without a Normative Difference," *Economics & Philosophy 35*(2): 195–222.

Smith, N. C., Goldstein, D. G. and Johnson, E. J. (2013) "Choice Without Awareness: Ethical and Policy Implications of Defaults," *Journal of Public Policy & Marketing 32*(2): 159–172.

Steel, D. (2008) *Across the Boundaries: Extrapolation in Biology and Social Science*, Oxford: Oxford University Press.

Strassheim, H. (2019) "Behavioural Mechanisms and Public Policy Design: Preventing Failures in Behavioural Public Policy," *Public Policy and Administration*. doi:10.1177/0952076719827062.

Sunstein, C. R., and Thaler, R. H. (2003) "Libertarian Paternalism Is not an Oxymoron," *The University of Chicago Law Review*: 1159–1202.

Tannenbaum, D., Fox, C. R., and Rogers, T. (2017) "On the Misplaced Politics of Behavioural Policy Interventions," *Nature Human Behaviour 1*(7): 1–7.

Thaler, R. H., and Benartzi, S. (2004) "Save More Tomorrow™: Using Behavioral Economics to Increase Employee Saving," *Journal of Political Economy 112*(S1): S164–S187.

Thaler, R. H., and Sunstein, C. R. (2008) *Nudge: Improving Decisions About Health, Wealth, and Happiness*, New York: Penguin.

36

THE CASE FOR REGULATING TAX COMPETITION

Peter Dietsch

1. Introduction

According to conservative estimates, 8% of global wealth or around $5.9 trillion is held in tax havens (Zucman 2013). Few of the owners of this capital declare their capital gains to the tax authorities of their country of residence as they should; these individuals evade taxes. A similar phenomenon occurs in the corporate world. It is standard procedure for multinational enterprises (MNEs) today to shift their profits to low-tax jurisdictions, thus avoiding taxes in the country where their economic activity actually takes place. While these maneuvers are often legal, they violate the spirit of tax law. The OECD (2015) estimates revenue losses from profit-shifting at $100–240 billion annually, with developing countries being the hardest hit.

To merely blame individuals and MNEs for their lack of fiscal compliance would be too simple. They respond to the fiscal incentives created and maintained by states. Tax evasion would not be possible without the complicity of states that pass bank secrecy laws or other pieces of regulation making it hard or even impossible to track capital ownership. Similarly, tax avoidance exploits differences in the fiscal codes of states and relies on some states actively cultivating these differences to attract capital. Even when there is no avoidance involved, states often use low tax rates on corporate income to attract foreign direct investment (FDI). All of these phenomena are instances of tax competition between states.

This chapter argues that the case for regulating tax competition is overwhelming. On the triple grounds of democratic self-determination, distributive justice, and economic efficiency, tax competition produces undesirable outcomes. Regulation would plausibly take the form of some form of tax cooperation between states. They would pledge not to compete on fiscal policy in ways to be specified, thus modifying the incentive structure of both individuals and MNEs when it comes to tax evasion and avoidance.

A comprehensive normative evaluation of tax competition of the sort presented here combines several analytic tools of philosophy of economics. First, an understanding of the dynamics of tax competition allows us to refine our theories of distributive justice in an important way.[1] Whereas standard theories of distributive justice would take inequalities in income and wealth as given and call for their adjustment through tax and transfer mechanisms, the regulation of tax competition opens up the more effective alternative of preventing some of these inequalities from arising in the first place (Dietsch & Rixen 2014b). Second, even though I will only treat this aspect in passing, a game-theoretic analysis of the incentives of states provides a nuanced understanding of what it takes

 DOI: 10.4324/9781315739793-44

to break the vicious circle of tax competition. Third, and finally, a probe of the use of the concept of efficiency in economic models and theories allows us to see why regulating tax competition is in fact preferable from this perspective, too.

The chapter is structured as follows. Section 2 provides a taxonomy of three different kinds of tax competition. This is crucial because an appropriate normative response to tax competition will be sensitive to these differences. Subsequent sections will present the case for regulating tax competition on three normative grounds. Section 3 will show that tax competition undermines the fiscal autonomy of political communities; section 4 will argue that tax competition tends to exacerbate inequalities in income and wealth; and finally, section 5 will demonstrate that, on a plausible understanding of the concept of economic efficiency, tax competition promotes inefficient fiscal policy. All of these considerations represent *pro tanto* arguments to regulate tax competition. Taken together, they constitute an overwhelming case for regulation.

2. The Dynamics of Tax Competition

Tax competition is the interactive tax setting by independent governments in a non-cooperative, strategic way (Dietsch & Rixen 2014a: 153). Some parts of the tax base are mobile, and tax setting is sensitive to the reaction of the tax base. Capital, in particular, has become very mobile since the abolition of capital controls as well as of withholding taxes in most countries (Avi-Yonah 2000), and it is therefore the prime target of tax competition. Small countries have a structural advantage in the game of attracting capital from abroad (Bucovetsky 1991). In contrast to larger states, they can often lower their tax rate and still increase their tax revenue.[2] The resulting payoff structure under asymmetric tax competition is represented in Table 36.1 (Dietsch 2015: 56).[3] However, as we shall see, larger countries have also become very adept at competing for tax base.

We can distinguish three types of capital that states vie for and that give rise to three types of tax competition. The differences between these are relevant for the specifics of regulating tax competition, and I will therefore give a brief description of each.[4]

First, states compete for the *portfolio capital* of individuals. Low rates of taxation combined with regulatory measures that obscure the ownership of the capital such as bank secrecy or trusts allow rich individuals to illegally hide their wealth and the capital gains it produces from the eye of tax authorities in their country of residence. Traditionally, the image we have of these classical tax havens is one of a small state either surrounded by the sea or in a secluded location in the mountains, but this perception is skewed.

Since the financial crisis of 2008, cash-strapped governments have clamped down on tax evasion and, through the OECD and the G20, taken several steps toward the automatic information exchange that is required to stamp out tax evasion of this kind.[5] While these initiatives certainly represent a step in the right direction and prove that tax cooperation is politically feasible in principle, important challenges remain. To mention just one, while the United States, by passing its Foreign Account Tax Compliance Act (FATCA) in 2010, effectively forced transparency with respect to American bank accounts abroad, the US has not signaled that it will sign the OECD's automatic

Table 36.1 Payoffs under asymmetric tax competition

Big country \ *Small country*	*Tax*	*Undertax*
Tax	0;0	−10;5
Undertax	3;−8	−5;3 (Nash equilibrium)

information exchange agreement. Thus, its geopolitical weight has allowed the US to turn the dynamics of tax competition for portfolio capital in its favor (see Hakelberg 2016) and cement its position as a tax haven in its own right (Drucker 2016). According to a ranking of secrecy jurisdictions produced by the nongovernmental organization (NGO) Tax Justice Network, several other large states are also important tax havens.[6]

Second, states compete for the *paper profits* of MNEs. Using a variety of techniques, MNEs shift profits generated by activities in high-tax jurisdictions to lower tax ones. For instance, they use overinvoicing in transactions between subsidiaries; they engage in corporate inversions by acquiring a foreign company and then shifting their headquarters to its jurisdiction; they practice what is called thin capitalization where subsidiaries in high-tax jurisdictions take out loans from their counterparts in low-tax jurisdictions to then deduct the interest from their tax bill; or they transfer intellectual property rights to low-tax jurisdictions, which then receive royalty payments from the other subsidiaries. The latter arrangement was, for example, employed in the infamous "Double Irish" structure (Darby III 2007) used by Google and other MNEs. All these maneuvers explain the frequent discrepancies between actual economic activity[7] and the profits generated – a corporate presence of a letterbox, two employees, and a fax machine can account for millions or even billions in profit. Empirical studies show that the transfer of taxable profits is highly sensitive to nominal tax rates (de Mooij & Ederveen 2008). The OECD's base-erosion and profit-shifting (BEPS) initiative attempts to curtail tax competition for paper profits, but there are concerns about the effectiveness of the strategy employed by the OECD (e.g. Woodward 2016). The latest OECD initiative, still being negotiated at the time of this writing, goes further than BEPS, notably by proposing what is effectively a global minimum corporate tax.[8]

Competition for paper profits is similar to competition for portfolio investments in that, in both cases, there is no real change in economic behavior. The tax evader keeps his residence, and the tax-avoiding company does not relocate any real economic activity. The state that is attracting their capital is *poaching* (OECD 1998: 16) on the fiscal territory of the states of residence or economic activity.

Third, and finally, states compete for FDI. The economic success of Ireland in recent decades, for example, is in part due to its low corporate tax rate of 12.5%, which has attracted investments that would not have occurred otherwise. Of course, FDI depends on a range of other factors too, such as human capital, infrastructure, an efficient bureaucracy, and so on. MNEs will often select a number of potential destinations for their investment that satisfy these other criteria and then negotiate for the best possible tax deal (Palan 2002).

Note two things concerning this third type of tax competition. First, if the first two types constitute *poaching*, this third one is better described as *luring* (Dietsch & Rixen 2014a: 161). After all, whereas the tax-evading resident or the tax-avoiding MNE should be paying taxes in the resident or source country, respectively, but are not, no such discrepancy exists in the present case. The MNE actually relocates its economic activity in question and thus *changes* source jurisdiction. As we shall see, the difference between poaching and luring matters for the normative analysis of tax competition. Second, there is a substitutive relationship between poaching and luring. To see why, let us put ourselves in the shoes of the CFO of any MNE. Under the current regime with its many loopholes, we can produce in high-tax jurisdictions without actually paying the nominal tax rate. If these loopholes were closed, that is, if poaching were prohibited, our effective tax rate as well as our incentive to actually relocate to a lower tax jurisdiction would increase dramatically. This substitutive relationship between poaching and luring is an important constraint on the feasibility of any regulation of tax competition.

3. Why Tax Competition Is Undemocratic

Political self-determination is an attractive ideal because it gives people a say over the decisions that affect them. According to the principle of subsidiarity, the particular group that makes these decisions should, ideally, include all beneficiaries and cost bearers. Plausibly, therefore, some decisions – concerning environmental policy issues for instance – will include more individuals than others – such as garbage collection. Historically, states have developed into a particularly salient level of decision-making. Even though the size of states varies, giving states a certain level of autonomy in decision-making can be justified by the preceding considerations.

Someone might object that there are situations in which other values trump self-determination. I agree. If people are starving in a neighboring country, one cannot appeal to the importance of self-determination to justify building a new motorway instead of helping them (see Caney 2006: 732). However, within the constraints of a minimal level of global justice, self-determination retains its appeal (Dietsch 2018).

> In the public finance literature, a stylized definition of fiscal self-determination covers two basic choices regarding the size of the public budget (the level of revenues and expenditures relative to GDP) and the question of relative benefits and burdens (the level of redistribution).
>
> (Dietsch 2015: 35; see also Avi-Yonah 2000)

Letting polities make fiscal decisions that reflect their preferences regarding these two variables is what it means to respect their fiscal autonomy.

If one accepts that fiscal autonomy so defined represents a value to be respected,[9] then one should deem tax competition to be problematic. Why? Because tax competition undermines fiscal autonomy in important ways (Dietsch & Rixen 2014a: 155–156, 2019). First, by putting pressure on tax rates on capital, tax competition pushes countries toward more regressive tax structures. Developed countries have been able to compensate for the revenue loss from lower tax rates on capital by shifting the tax burden to less mobile factors such as labor and consumption. However, this move toward a more regressive tax system has meant a sacrifice of the second element of their fiscal self-determination (the level of redistribution) to protect the first (the size of the public budget relative to GDP). Second, developing countries, who usually lack the administrative capacity to adapt in the aforementioned way, have seen a loss in revenue in addition to a more regressive system. In their case, both aspects of fiscal autonomy are undermined.

The corrosive impact of tax competition goes even deeper than this threat to fiscal autonomy. By opening up possibilities for some members of society to evade or avoid taxes, it threatens the very foundations of the social contract. It allows some members to benefit from the public goods provided by a political community without paying their fair share toward the cost of these goods, and it allows them to partially opt out of the redistributive policies of the community. They are free riders. Seen in this light, tax competition poses a fundamental threat to political economic life as we have come to know it over the last century.

Combination of the analysis of how tax competition works in the previous section with its impact on fiscal autonomy gives a first indication of the form that a regulation of tax competition should take. It is the first two kinds of tax competition – for portfolio capital and for paper profits of MNEs – that are emblematic for the free riding described in the previous paragraph. Both of these forms of *poaching* tax base should be prohibited. One way to do so is by enforcing the *membership principle* (Dietsch & Rixen 2014a: 157ff.), which calls for natural and legal persons to pay their taxes where they are a resident or where they conduct their economic activity. In principle, international tax law today is already in line with this idea, but the institutional structure of bilateral double-taxation agreements (Rixen 2010) opens up loopholes and makes enforcement of the membership principle very difficult.

The question of luring – the third type of tax competition – is trickier. As we saw earlier, there is no free riding involved in this case, because the individual or MNE actually relocates to a different jurisdiction. Does this mean that luring FDI is unproblematic from the viewpoint of fiscal autonomy? Dietsch and Rixen (2014a: 161ff.) argue that luring, to the extent that it is strategic and successful,[10] should also be prohibited in order to protect the fiscal autonomy of other states. Ireland's low corporate tax rate of 12.5%, for instance, would most likely be ruled out by this criterion. Others have argued that Dietsch and Rixen's notion of fiscal autonomy is too inclusive (van Apeldoorn 2016), that it underestimates the demands of global justice and thus suffers from a status quo bias (Risse & Meyer 2019), or that their proposed regulation of luring is insufficient (Ronzoni 2016). An alternative from the latter perspective is a form of tax cooperation that includes elements of tax harmonization, such a minimum tax rate as proposed under the latest reform initiative by the OECD (see World Economic Forum 2019).

4. Why Tax Competition Creates Unjust Inequalities

The argument in this section proceeds in two steps. First, what is the impact of tax competition on inequalities in income and wealth? Second, are these inequalities unjust and, if so, why?

The answer to the first question is already implicit in the analysis of the previous section. The shift toward more regressive tax structures in the wake of tax competition, with a heavier burden on immobile factors such as work and consumption and a lighter burden on capital, tends to increase inequalities in income and wealth within states (Dietsch 2011; Rixen 2011). Moreover, given the difficulties developing countries face to tax work or consumption effectively, they face lower revenue and thus have less money available to spend on education, health, or direct transfers to the poorest members of their societies. This asymmetry between developed versus developing countries arguably increases intercountry inequalities as well.

Finally, the effects of tax competition on inequalities are not limited to its direct impact on income and wealth. Where tax competition dents revenues, it reduces the capacity of the state to promote equality of opportunity among its citizens. And, independent of the effects on tax revenue or expenditure, tax competition affects the distribution of jobs. For instance, when MNEs can engage in profit-shifting, this allows high-tax jurisdictions to hold on to economic activities and the jobs attached to them, some of which would shift to jurisdictions with lower tax rates were profit-shifting not an option. Take a concrete example. Volkswagen does not have a large share of its productive facilities left in Germany. But if antipoaching regulations forced them to actually pay the nominal corporate tax rate, they would most likely shift even the remaining facilities abroad. Incidentally, this example illustrates nicely why the motivation of the governments of developed countries to put an end to poaching is likely to be feeble indeed. The existence of poaching offers them a way to retain many jobs they would otherwise lose. Thus, poaching acts as a brake on the economic convergence between rich, high-tax countries and poor, low-tax ones.

In sum, the preceding considerations warrant the conclusion that tax competition tends to exacerbate inequalities. How we assess the resulting inequalities from the perspective of distributive justice depends on the criterion or theory of justice on which we rely. Here, I will present three such criteria, in ascending order of demandingness.

First, even if one abstains from endorsing any particular theory of distributive justice, one can interpret the democratic preferences of a polity about redistribution – see the second component of fiscal autonomy in section 2 – as preferences about distributive justice. Then, to the extent that tax competition exacerbates inequalities and undermines the satisfaction of these preferences, it can be called unjust.

Second, even though there is no theoretical consensus about any particular criterion of justice, political discourse suggests a consensus about the fact that current inequalities are excessive. In other words, even though we do not know what would be a just world, we do know that ours is an unjust one. To the extent that tax competition contributes to this injustice, it is itself unjust.

The third criterion differs from the first two in that it does posit a theory of global justice in order to evaluate the distributive impact of tax competition. While I will not go into the substance of such a criterion here, it is worth identifying some of the normative questions it will add to the debate. It introduces a sensitivity to the distributive background against which tax competition occurs (van Apeldoorn 2018; Risse & Meyer 2019). In particular, a theory of justice adds an important element to the evaluation of luring FDI compared to its assessment on the basis of fiscal autonomy alone. It will likely lead to a more permissive stance toward certain forms of luring by poorer countries (Dietsch 2015, chapter 5). For instance, we might tolerate some forms of tax competition by poor countries as a form of redistribution, as retribution for past or current injustices (colonialism, structural injustices of the global economy) or as a way to promote a level playing field in the global economy.[11] These cases show that in some, albeit relatively rare, circumstances, the inequalities created by tax competition might compensate for other preexisting forms of inequality and injustice.

In sum, this leads to us the following conclusion. When tax competition exacerbates inequalities – and the previous paragraph shows that there might be some circumstances in which contextual factors mean that, all things considered, it does not – these inequalities are unjust. That said, the extent of this injustice depends on the specific criterion or theory of distributive justice one chooses to adopt.

5. Why Tax Competition Is Inefficient

The concept of efficiency is used in several different ways in economic analysis. Due to space constraints, I will set aside a discussion of tax competition from the perspective of Pareto optimality[12] and concentrate instead on efficiency as an instrumental value to balance other social objectives (LeGrand 1990).[13] In particular, my focus will be on optimal tax theory (OTT), which proposes to find an efficient balance between economic growth and equity. As we shall see, tax competition has a profound impact on the recommendations put forward by OTT.

In the early 1970s, the ideas of James Mirrlees (1971) brought about a paradigm shift in tax theory and policy. The innovation of OTT was to take into account the incentive effects of taxation (Stiglitz 1987: 4) and thereby to recognize that pursuing redistributive goals through fiscal policy will entail costs due to the behavioral response of economic agents to this policy.

In its early formulations, OTT concentrated on the response in terms of labor supply – if I get taxed more, will I work less and, if so, how much less? – but later the analysis was widened to include all behavioral responses to taxation, notably including tax evasion and tax avoidance (Slemrod 2006: 73). In sum, from the perspective of OTT, the higher the elasticity of taxable income, the lower and the less progressive the efficient level of taxation.

Now, think about the impact of tax competition on the elasticity of taxable income. The first two kinds of tax competition discussed in Section 2 clearly have the effect of *increasing* the elasticity of taxable income. When individuals can hide wealth from tax authorities with little chance of getting caught, and when MNEs can legally shift profits to low-tax jurisdictions, it is obvious that pursuing redistributive policies is more "costly" in terms of the behavioral response it triggers. Thus, the efficient level of taxation will be lower.

However, it would be premature to take this as a sufficient reason to in fact lower taxes. After all, in contrast to the elasticity of the labor supply, the elasticity of taxable income due to tax evasion and avoidance is, in principle, under the control of the government (Slemrod 2006: 81). Thus, rather than treating it as a parameter of OTT analysis, it should be considered a policy variable instead. The optimal response to a high elasticity of taxable income due to evasion and avoidance is, at least up to a point, better enforcement of tax policy rather than the lowering of rates (Slemrod 1994; Piketty et al. 2013).

In a nutshell, the impact of tax competition on fiscal policy design is to drive a wedge between a *locally* optimal level of taxation given current enforcement levels and a *globally* optimal, higher level of taxation when enforcement is treated as an endogenous variable. This distinction invites two observations.

First, analyses that ignore this distinction under conditions of tax competition will recommend inefficiently low rates. This might seem obvious, but even seasoned economists fall into this trap (e.g. Feldstein 1999). Second, it is part and parcel of the pernicious nature of tax competition that it blocks unilateral efforts to reach the global optimum. Any attempt to unilaterally raise tax rates on capital to globally optimal levels will be punished by capital outflows. In other words, under tax competition it is in fact individually rational for states to pursue fiscal policies that are less progressive than under the globally optimal tax structure (Slemrod & Kopczuk 2002).

In sum, there is a vicious circle between the existence of loopholes for individual tax evasion and corporate tax avoidance on the one hand, and the incentives for governments to lower tax rates on capital on the other. This inefficiency of tax competition – which, it should be noted, only applies to the two forms of poaching and *not* to luring – can only be overcome through a multilateral regulation of tax competition along the lines sketched in previous sections. An international tax organization (ITO) would be an effective tool to design and enforce such regulation (Dietsch & Rixen 2014a, section III).

6. Conclusion

Some of the thorniest questions in normative political economy arise when there are trade-offs between different social objectives such as equity, efficiency, or autonomy. It is rare to come across policy questions that are "no-brainers" in the sense that all relevant social objectives at play point in the same direction.

This chapter has worked to show that the regulation of tax competition is one of these rare cases. Tax competition is undemocratic because it undermines the fiscal autonomy of polities; it is unjust because it exacerbates inequalities in income and wealth; and it is inefficient because it makes countries pursue fiscal policies that are less progressive than socially optimal. In this unambiguous form, these assessments only apply to the two types of tax competition characterized as poaching, but I have shown that there are reasons to push for certain kinds of regulation of luring, too.

While the multilateral coordination that is necessary for an effective regulation of tax competition faces formidable feasibility constraints, an understanding of the corrosive impact of tax competition on important social values is a first step in mobilizing support for this reform.[14]

Related Chapter

Bavetta, Chapter 32 "Freedoms, Political Economy, and Liberalism"

Notes

1 Even though most theories of justice directly or indirectly appeal to fiscal policy as the principal tool for implementing their ideal of justice, normative scrutiny of fiscal policy itself has been the exception. Murphy and Nagel (2002) as well as O'Neill and Orr (2018) are notable exceptions. For an overview of discussions of tax in political philosophy, see Halliday (2013). Explicit references by political philosophers to the phenomenon of tax competition are relatively recent (Cappelen 2001; Brock 2008; Ronzoni 2009; Dietsch & Rixen 2014a, 2014b, 2016, 2019; Dietsch 2015, 2018; Gaisbauer et al. 2015; Risse & Meyer 2019; Kern 2020).

2 For small countries, the tax base effect – that is, the capital inflow in response to the lower rate – outweighs the tax rate effect – that is, the loss of domestic revenue due to the lower rate (see Dehejia & Genschel 1999: 43).

3 The Nash equilibrium of this game is the general undertaxation scenario (−5;3). However, note that it is *not* the case that all countries would prefer the collectively optimal taxation scenario (0;0). In other words, tax competition is not a prisoner's dilemma. The structural advantage of small countries under tax competition introduces the complication that they in fact prefer tax competition to tax cooperation. Any regulation of tax competition thus requires some kind of compensation to bring the winners of tax competition on board.

4 For a more detailed account, see Dietsch and Rixen (2014a) as well as Dietsch (2015). Other comprehensive analyses of tax competition include Avi-Yonah (2000), Tax Justice Network (2005), Rixen (2008), Palan et al. (2010), Clausing (2016), Dietsch and Rixen (2016), Risse and Meyer (2019), and Dietsch and Rixen (2019).

5 In particular, the OECD has passed a new Global Reporting Standard for the automatic exchange of information between tax authorities (see OECD 2014).

6 See www.financialsecrecyindex.com/.

7 The issue of what counts as real economic activity represents a highly political question in its own right (see Christians & van Apeldoorn 2018).

8 See World Economic Forum (2019) for a good overview of the two pillars of the OECD's latest initiative.

9 As I show in Dietsch (2018), even cosmopolitans who have a critical disposition toward the state as a force for justice have reason to accept this.

10 That is, it actually leads to a net capital inflow into the country that is pursuing the luring strategy.

11 In principle, arguments of this kind could also apply in the case of poaching (e.g. Risse & Meyer 2019). However, because the *pro tanto* arguments against poaching and the free riding it involves are more robust, they are less likely to be overturned by other considerations.

12 Elsewhere, I show that the Pareto criterion is too weak to arbitrate between tax competition and tax cooperation (see Dietsch 2015: 136–156).

13 Note that, in this case, efficiency itself is not a primary social objective on a par with these other objectives, but merely a second-order, instrumental value.

14 See also Bavetta, Chapter 32.

Bibliography

Avi-Yonah, R.S. (2000) "Globalization, Tax Competition, and the Fiscal Crisis of the Welfare State," *Harvard Law Review* 113(7): 1573–1676.

Brock, G. (2008) "Taxation and Global Justice: Closing the Gap Between Theory and Practice," *Journal of Social Philosophy* 39(2): 161–184.

Bucovetsky, S. (1991) "Asymmetric Tax Competition," *Journal of Urban Economics* 30(2): 167–181.

Caney, S. (2006) "Cosmopolitan Justice and Institutional Design: An Egalitarian Liberal Conception of Global Governance," *Social Theory and Practice* 32(4): 725–756.

Cappelen, A. (2001) "The Moral Rationale for International Fiscal Law," *Ethics & International Affairs* 15(1): 97–110.

Christians, A. and van Apeldoorn, L. (2018) "Taxing Income Where Value Is Created," *Florida Tax Review* 22(1): 1–39.

Clausing, K. (2016) "The Nature and Practice of Tax Competition," in P. Dietsch and T. Rixen (eds.), *Global Tax Governance – What Is Wrong with It and How to Fix It*, Colchester: ECPR Press: 27–53.

Darby III, J.B. (2007) "Double Irish More than Doubles the Tax Saving: Hybrid Structures Reduces Irish, U.S. and Worldwide Taxation," *Practical US/International Tax Strategies* 11(9): 2–16.

Dehejia, V.H. and Genschel, P. (1999) "Tax Competition in the European Union," *Politics & Society* 27: 403–430.

de Mooij, R.A. and Ederveen, S. (2008) "Corporate Tax Elasticities: A Reader's Guide to Empirical Findings," *Oxford Review of Economic Policy* 24(4): 680–697.

Dietsch, P. (2011) "Tax Competition and Its Effects on Domestic and Global Justice," in A. Banai, M. Ronzoni, and C. Schemmel (eds.), *Social Justice, Global Dynamics: Theoretical and Empirical Perspectives*, London: Routledge: 95–114.

Dietsch. P. (2015) *Catching Capital – The Ethics of Tax Competition*, Oxford: Oxford University Press.

Dietsch, P. (2018) "The State and Tax Competition – A Normative Perspective," in M. O'Neill and S. Orr (eds.), *Taxation – Philosophical Perspectives*, Oxford: Oxford University Press: 203–223.

Dietsch, P. and Rixen, T. (2014a) "Tax Competition and Global Background Justice," *Journal of Political Philosophy* 22(2): 150–177.
Dietsch, P. and Rixen, T. (2014b) "Redistribution, Globalisation, and Multi-Level Governance," *Moral Philosophy and Politics* 1(1): 61–81.
Dietsch, P. and Rixen, T. (eds.) (2016) *Global Tax Governance – What Is Wrong With It and How to Fix It*, Colchester: ECPR Press.
Dietsch, P. and Rixen, T. (2019) "Debate: In Defence of Fiscal Autonomy: A Reply to Risse and Meyer," *Journal of Political Philosophy* 27(4): 499–511.
Drucker, J. (2016) "The World's Favorite New Tax Haven Is the United States," 27 January. www.bloomberg.com/news/articles/2016-01-27/the-world-s-favorite-new-tax-haven-is-the-united-states, accessed 19 August 2020.
Feldstein, M. (1999) "Tax Avoidance and the Deadweight Loss of the Income Tax," *The Review of Economics and Statistics* 81(4): 674–680.
Financial Secrecy Index, www.financialsecrecyindex.com/, accessed 19 August 2020.
Gaisbauer, H., Schweiger, G. and Sedmak, C. (eds.) (2015) *Philosophical Explorations of Justice and Taxation – National and Global Issues*, Dordrecht: Springer.
Hakelberg, L. (2016) "Redistributive Tax Co-Operation: Automatic Exchange of Information, US Power and the Absence of Joint Gains," in P. Dietsch and T. Rixen (eds.), *Global Tax Governance – What Is Wrong With It and How to Fix It*, Colchester: ECPR Press: 123–155.
Halliday, D. (2013) "Justice and Taxation," *Philosophical Compass* 8(12): 1111–1122.
Kern, A. (2020) "Illusions of Justice in International Taxation," *Philosophy & Public Affairs* 48(2): 151–184.
LeGrand, J. (1990) "Equity Versus Efficiency: The Elusive Trade-Off," *Ethics* 100(3): 554–568.
Mirrlees, J.A. (1971) "An Exploration in the Theory of Optimum Income Taxation," *Review of Economic Studies* 38(2): 175–208.
Murphy, L. and Nagel, T. (2002) *The Myth of Ownership*, Oxford: Oxford University Press.
O'Neill, M. and Orr, S. (eds.) (2018) *Taxation – Philosophical Perspectives*, Oxford: Oxford University Press.
Organization for Economic Co-operation and Development (1998) *Harmful Tax Competition – An Emerging Global Issue*, Paris: OECD Publishing.
Organization for Economic Co-operation and Development (2014) *Standard for Automatic Exchange of Financial Account Information in Tax Matters*, Paris: OECD Publishing, http://dx.doi.org/10.1787/9789264216525-en, accessed 19 August 2020.
Organization for Economic Co-operation and Development (2015) "OECD Presents Outputs of OECD/G20 BEPS Project for Discussion at G20 Finance Ministers Meeting," www.oecd.org/ctp/oecd-presents-outputs-of-oecd-g20-ps-project-for-discussion-at-g20-finance-ministers-meeting.htm, accessed 19 August 2020.
Palan, R. (2002) "Tax Havens and the Commercialization of State Sovereignty," *International Organization* 56(1): 151–176.
Palan, R., Murphy, R. and Chavagneux, C. (2010) *Tax Havens: How Globalization Really Works*, Ithaca, NY: Cornell University Press.
Piketty, T., Saez, E. and Stantcheva, S. (2011) "Optimal Taxation of Top Labour Incomes: A Tale of Three Elasticities," NBER Working Paper No. 17616, revised 2013.
Risse, M. and Meyer, M. (2019) "Tax Competition and Global Interdependence," *Journal of Political Philosophy* 27(4): 480–498.
Rixen, T. (2008) *The Political Economy of International Tax Governance*, Basingstoke: Palgrave Macmillan.
Rixen, T. (2010) "From Double Tax Avoidance to Tax Competition: Explaining the Institutional Trajectory of International Tax Governance," *Review of International Political Economy* 18(2): 197–227.
Rixen, T. (2011) "Tax Competition and Inequality: The Case for Global Tax Governance," *Global Governance: A Review of Multilateralism and International Organizations* 17(4): 447–467.
Ronzoni, M. (2009) "The Global Order: A Case of Background Injustice? A Practice-Dependent Account," *Philosophy & Public Affairs* 37(3): 229–256.
Ronzoni, M. (2016) "Tax Competition: A Problem of Global or Domestic Justice," in P. Dietsch and T. Rixen (eds.), *Global Tax Governance – What Is Wrong with It and How to Fix It*, Colchester: ECPR Press: 201–214.
Slemrod, J. (1994) "Fixing the Leak in Okun's Bucket – Optimal Tax Progressivity When Avoidance Can Be Controlled," *Journal of Public Economics* 55(1): 41–51.
Slemrod, J. (2006) "The Consequences of Taxation," *Social Philosophy and Policy* 23(2): 73–87.
Slemrod, J. and Kopczuk, W. (2002) "The Optimal Elasticity of Taxable Income," *Journal of Public Economics* 84(1): 91–112.
Stiglitz, J.E. (1987) "Pareto Efficient and Optimal Taxation and the New Welfare Economics," NBER Working Paper No. 2189, http://hassler-j.iies.su.se/COURSES/DynPubFin/Papers/Stigliz1987w2189.pdf.

Tax Justice Network (2005) "Tax Us if You Can. The True Story of a Global Failure." London: Tax Justice Network. https://www.taxjustice.net/cms/upload/pdf/tuiyc_-_eng_-_web_file.pdf, accessed 30 July 2021.

van Apeldoorn, L. (2016) "International Taxation and the Erosion of Sovereignty," in P. Dietsch and T. Rixen (eds.), *Global Tax Governance – What Is Wrong with It and How to Fix It*, Colchester: ECPR Press: 215–230.

van Apeldoorn, L. (2018) "BEPS, Tax Sovereignty, and Global Justice," *Critical Review of International Social and Political Philosophy* 21(4): 478–499.

Woodward, R. (2016) "A Strange Revolution: Mock Compliance and the Failure of the OECD's International Tax Transparency Regime," in P. Dietsch and T. Rixen (eds.), *Global Tax Governance – What Is Wrong with It and How to Fix It*, Colchester: ECPR Press: 103–121.

World Economic Forum (2019) "Corporate Tax, Digitalization and Globalization," White Paper, December, www.weforum.org/whitepapers/corporate-tax-digitalization-and-globalization, accessed 19 August 2020.

Zucman, G. (2013) "The Missing Wealth of Nations: Are Europe and the U.S. Net Debtors or Net Creditors?" *Quarterly Journal of Economics* 128(3): 1321–1364.

INDEX

Note: Page numbers in *italics* indicate figures; page numbers in **bold** indicate tables.

Made in the USA
Monee, IL
13 September 2026

62977690R10293